FAITH AND FEMINISM IN NINETEENTH-CENTURY RELIGIOUS COMMUNITIES

THE BIBLE AND WOMEN

An Encyclopaedia of Exegesis and Cultural History

Edited by Christiana de Groot, Irmtraud Fischer,
Mercedes Navarro Puerto, and Adriana Valerio

Volume 8.2: Faith and Feminism in
Nineteenth-Century Religious Communities

FAITH AND FEMINISM IN NINETEENTH-CENTURY RELIGIOUS COMMUNITIES

Edited by
Michaela Sohn-Kronthaler and Ruth Albrecht

Atlanta

Copyright © 2019 by SBL Press

All rights reserved. No part of this work may be reproduced or transmitted in any form or by any means, electronic or mechanical, including photocopying and recording, or by means of any information storage or retrieval system, except as may be expressly permitted by the 1976 Copyright Act or in writing from the publisher. Requests for permission should be addressed in writing to the Rights and Permissions Office, SBL Press, 825 Houston Mill Road, Atlanta, GA 30329 USA.

Library of Congress Cataloging-in-Publication Data

Names: Sohn-Kronthaler, Michaela, 1969– editor. | Albrecht, Ruth, editor.
Title: Faith and feminism in nineteenth-century religious communities / edited by Michaela Sohn-Kronthaler and Ruth Albrecht.
Description: SBL Press, [2018] | Series: Bible and women ; Number 8.2 | Includes bibliographical references and index.
Identifiers: LCCN 2018020291 (print) | LCCN 2018034863 (ebook) | ISBN 9780884142744 (ebk.) | ISBN 9781589835825 (pbk. : alk. paper) | ISBN 9780884142751 (hbk. : alk. paper)
Subjects: LCSH: Women in Christianity—Europe—History—19th century. | Bible—Feminist criticism. | Women theologians—Europe.
Classification: LCC BV639.W7 (ebook) | LCC BV639.W7 F325 2018 (print) | DDC 274/.081082—dc23
LC record available at https://lccn.loc.gov/2018020291

Printed on acid-free paper.

Contents

Preface
    Ruth Albrecht and Michaela Sohn-Kronthaler ix

Abbreviations xi

Introduction
    Ruth Albrecht and Michaela Sohn-Kronthaler 1

Methodist Women and the Bible: Early Nineteenth-Century
    Engagement with Scripture
    Paul W. Chilcote 13

Women and Biblical Criticism in Nineteenth-Century England
    Marion Ann Taylor 29

Deborah: A Lightning Rod for Nineteenth-Century
    Women's Issues
    Christiana de Groot 63

"The Lord Has Given Me a Learned Tongue" (Isa 50:4):
    Catherine McAuley Interprets Scripture with Authority
    and Intention
    Elizabeth M. Davis 99

American Jewish Women Reading the Bible in the Year 1893
    Pamela S. Nadell 113

The Bible in the Evangelizing Activity of the Biblewomen
    Marina Cacchi 135

Biblical Inspiration in the Transformation of Women's Religious
    Communities in Nineteenth-Century Italy
    Adriana Valerio 163

Conservative Feminism in Catholic Spain in the Nineteenth
    Century: Gimeno de Flaquer's "Evangelios de la Mujer"
    Inmaculada Blasco Herranz..183

Orthodox Women and the Bible in Nineteenth-Century Russia
    Alexej Klutschewsky and Eva Maria Synek 203

The Bible in Liturgy and Spirituality: The Example of the
    Kreuzeskränzchen in Bonn
    Angela Berlis 225

Let the Woman Keep Silent? Protestant Controversies about
    Female Preachers and Evangelists
    Ruth Albrecht..255

A Swiss Champion of Women's Rights: The Reception of the
    Bible by Helene von Mülinen
    Doris Brodbeck..287

In the Discipleship of Jesus: Deaconesses and Biblical Explanation;
    The Example of Eva von Tiele-Winckler
    Ute Gause 303

Bible Reading as Motivation for Diaconal-Social Initiatives:
    The Example of Countess Elvine de La Tour (1841–1916)
    Michaela Sohn-Kronthaler 317

Reading among German-Speaking Catholic Women and the
    Significance of the Bible between 1850 and 1914
    Bernhard Schneider 341

Between Service and Rebellion: German-Speaking Women
    Authors and Their Relationship to the Bible
    Magda Motté...385

Portraits of Mary and of Biblical Scenes in the Work of
    Marie Ellenrieder (1791–1863): The Construction of
    Feminine Religious Spheres of Communication
    Katharina Büttner-Kirschner 407

Old Testament Women in Bible Illustrations of the Nineteenth
    Century in the Works of Julius Schnorr von Carolsfeld
    and Gustave Doré
    Elfriede Wiltschnigg 425

Contributors...457
Ancient Sources Index...459
Modern Authors Index..467

Preface

The present volume is the result of an initial inquiry, which occurred from 2008 to 2014, into Bible reading or Bible interpretation by women during the long nineteenth century. The women studied represent very different approaches to the Bible and come from Europe and North America. In addition, the contributors also stem from several countries and language contexts. This publication presents some previously unpublished source material from representatives of different Christian confessions as well as Judaism. New perspectives shed light on people and traditions hitherto not noticed in the field of biblical reception studies.

The international research colloquium featured scholars from four continents who explored this subject. It occurred at the University of Graz and at the Cultural Center at the Minorites from December 4 to 6, 2008, in Graz. The title of this colloquium was "Departing for Modernity versus Clinging to the Outdated: Women's Biblical Hermeneutics in the Context of Modern Times."

Our thanks go to all those who made this volume financially possible, especially to the vice-rectorate for research and continuing education (University of Graz) and to Renate Dworczak, vice rector for human resources, personnel development, NAWI Graz and gender equality (University of Graz), as well as Abbot Bernard Lorent von Maredsous (Belgium). To all of them our warmest thanks, including Irmtraud Fischer, who always was willing to answer any questions and provided support in many areas, especially in financing. We also thank above all Markus Zimmermann and Stephanie Glück for their editorial cooperation as well as Christine Schönhuber for her support in layout. A special thank you goes to Andrea Taschl-Erber and Herbert Meßner who helped us meticulously in proofreading the articles. We also thank warmly Nina Kogler and Christian Blinzer for their assistance in organizing the research colloquium. Antonia Schmidinger incorporated the illustrations into the art history article.

Preface

The German edition of this volume was published in 2014, and we now present the English version. We would like to thank the translators who faithfully conveyed the meaning of the original languages into English. These include Dennis Lee Slabaugh, Gabriele Stein, Dana Sophie Brüller, and Annemarie del Cueto Lopez-Mörth. The Calvin Center for Christian Scholarship contributed to the cost of translating, as well as to the support of a student assistant, Erin Tanis. In addition, the Gender Studies program at Calvin College underwrote the assistance of Alyssa Gagnon. The general editor, Christiana de Groot, is very grateful to Calvin College and to these undergraduate students for their careful attention to detail and commitment to this project.

We hope these publications will inspire international researchers to do further studies in these subject areas. We could include here only their first endeavors. In our opinion, however, it has become obvious that there are many further aspects that have not yet been sufficiently studied.

Michaela Sohn-Kronthaler and Ruth Albrecht
Graz and Hamburg

Abbreviations

Add MSS	British Library Additional Manuscripts
ADK	Archiv der Diakonie Kärnten
AF	*Altkatholisches Frauenblatt*
AFP	*Archivum Fratrum Praedicatorum*
AGAJU	Arbeiten zur Geschichte des antiken Judentums und des Urchristentums
AGP	Arbeiten zur Geschichte des Pietismus
AHSI	*Archivum Historicum Societatis Iesu*
AIA	*Album Ibero-americano*
AISP	*Archivio Italiano per la Storia della Pietà*
AM	*Arminian Magazine* (later *Bible Christian Magazine*)
AngSS	Anglican Studies Series
AR	Ancien Régime: Aufklärung und Revolution
ASMSA	Archivio Storico della Congregazione delle Suore di Mara SS. Addolorata
ATL	Ästhetik–Theologie–Liturgik
ATLAMS	American Theological Library Association Monograph Series
Ath	*Athenaeum*
ATV	Archive of the Tavola Valdese
AV	Akademie-Vorträge
AW	America in the World
b.	Babylonian Talmud
Bail	*Bailamme*
BBB	Burgerbibliothek Bern
BBCom	Blackwell Bible Commentaries
BBKL	*Biographisch-bibliographisches Kirchenlexikon*
BCR	Blackwell Companions to Religion
Ber.	Berakot
BET	Beiträge zur Evangelischen Theologie

BGAMB	Beiträge zur Geschichte des alten Mönchtums und des Benediktinerordens
BKK	Beiträge zur Kirchen- und Kulturgeschichte
BLT	Broadview Literary Texts
B. Metz.	Bava Metzi'a
BNGO	Beiträge zur Neueren Geschichte Österreichs
BonB	Bonifatius-Broschüren
BR	Beck'sche Reihe
BSF	Bund Schweizerischer Frauenvereine
BSJW	Brandeis Series on Jewish Women
BT	Die bibliophilen Taschenbücher
CBS	Collana La Bibbia nella storia
CCR	Cambridge Companions to Religion
CFTL	Clark's Foreign Theological Library
CJSLH	*The Canadian Journal of Science, Literature and History*
COT	Commentary on the Old Testament
CQS	Chapman's Quarterly Series
CSSV	Collana della Società di Studi Valdesi
DM	*Deutscher Merkur*
DPJA	Archive of the German Province of the Jesuits, Munich
Dracma	Dracma: Collana di Testi su Donne e Cristianesimo
DRV	Douay-Rheims Version
EB	*Extrablatt der Berna*
EBT	Elberfeld Bible Translation
EDB	Encyclopedic Dictionary of the Bible
EK	Europäische Kulturgeschichte
ELThG	*Evangelisches Lexikon für Theologie und Gemeinde*
ENPJ	*The Edinburgh New Philosophical Journal*
ET-S	*ET-Studies*
EW	Europäische Wallfahrtsstudien
Fem	Feminae
Femin	Feminismos
GAC	Gender & American Culture
GG	Geschichte und Geschlechter
GH	Gender in History
GKL	Geschichte des kirchlichen Lebens
GP	Geschichte des Pietismus
GRLH	Garland Reference Library of the Humanities
GT	Gesellschaft und Theologie

GW	Gender Wissen
HBGHS	Historische Bibliothek der Gerda Henkel Stiftung
HC	*Historia Contemporánea*
HE	Historische Einführungen
HS	L'Homme Schriften: Reihe zur feministischen Geschichtswissenschaft
HTG	Historisch-theologische Genderforschung
HWP	*Historisches Wörterbuch der Philosophie*
HZFG	*L'Homme: Zeitschrift für feministische Geschichtswissenschaft*
IKZ	*Internationale Kirchliche Zeitschrift*
IS	Italia Sacra
ITL	International Theological Library
IW	Industrielle Welt
JE	*Jewish Encyclopedia*
JHMT	*Journal for the History of Modern Theology*
JPRS	*Journal of Pre-Raphaelite Studies*
JSL NS	*Journal of Sacred Literature* New Series
KADOC	KADOC Studies on Religion, Culture and Society
KG	Konfession und Gesellschaft
KIG	Die Kirche in ihrer Geschichte
KJV	King James Version
KK	Klassiker der Karikatur
KKF	*Kvinder, Kønog Forskning*
KLA	Kärntner Landesarchiv
KM	Kirchengeschichtliche Monographien
KSGW	Kritische Studien zur Geschichtswissenschaft
LB	Lutherbibel
LBS	T&T Clark Library of Biblical Studies
LCI	*Lexikon der christlichen Ikonographie*
Leu	*Leuchtfeuer*
LHB/OTS	Library of Hebrew Bible/Old Testament Studies
LQR	*London Quarterly Review*
LSVB	Literature and Society in Victorian Britain
LThK	*Lexikon für Theologie und Kirche*
LV	I Libri di Viella
MCSR	*Monatsschrift für christliche Sozialreform*
MHS	Mainzer Hymnologische Studien
MSt	Mariologische Studien
NASB	New American Standard Bible

NBEC	Nueva Biblioteca de Erudición y Crítica
NRSV	New Revised Standard Version
NZZ	Neue Zürcher Zeitung
ODNB	*Oxford Dictionary of National Biography*
Paed	Paedagogica: Testi e Studi Storici
Par	*Paradigm*
PBG	Paderborner Beiträge zur Geschichte
PCI	Post-Contemporary Interventions
PKV	Politik- und kommunikationswissenschaftliche Veröffentlichungen der Görres-Gesellschaft
PL	Pietas Liturgica
Pro	*Protestantesimo*
PTHe	Praktische Theologie Heute
PuN	*Pietismus und Neuzeit: Ein Jahrbuch zur Geschichte des neueren Protestantismus*
QAMK	Quellen und Abhandlungen zur mittelrheinischen Kirchengeschichte
QFESH	Quellen und Forschungen zum evangelischen sozialen Handeln
QR	Quaderni della Rassegna
RF	Reihe Frauenforum
RGG	*Religion in Geschichte und Gegenwart*
RHE	*Revue d'histoire ecclésiastique*
RKM	Religiöse Kulturen der Moderne
RomQ	*Romance Quarterly*
RQ	*Römische Quartalschrift für christliche Altertumskunde und Kirchengeschichte*
Sag	Sagardiana: Estudios Feministas
SBWS	*Schweizerische Blätter für Wirtschafts- und Socialpolitik*
SCH	Studies in Church History
SD	Soggetto Donna
SKK	Staatliche Kunsthalle Karlsruhe
SPCK	Society for Promoting Christian Knowledge
SPR	Archives of San Paolo fuori le Mura, Rome
SQWFG	Studien und Quellen zur westfälischen Geschichte
SRS	Studi e Ricerche Storiche
S/S	Sacro/Santo
SStor	Studi Storici
SGKG	Sankt Galler Kultur und Geschichte

Stor	Storia
STPS	Studien zur Theologie und Praxis der Seelsorge
SymS	Symposium Series
TA	Theologische Akzente
TEM	Textos y Estudios de Mujeres
ThkD	Theologie im kulturellen Dialog
Tra	*Trajecta*
TRE	*Theologische Realenzyklopädie*
TSR	Text and Studies in Religion
TTZ	*Trierer Theologische Zeitschrift*
UTB	Uni-Taschenbücher
UTR	Utrechtse Theologische Reeks
VGMK	Veröffentlichungen zur Geschichte der Mitteldeutschen Kirchenprovinz
VHKT	Veröffentlichungen der Historischen Kommission für Thüringen
VKZG	Veröffentlichungen der Kommission für Zeitgeschichte
VP	*Victorian Poetry*
Vulg.	Vulgate
WCA	Women and the Church in America
WestF	*Westfälische Forschungen*
WF	Wolfenbüttler Forschungen
WMM	*Wesleyan Methodist Magazine*
WR	Women's Rights
WWLOU	*Worte der Wahrheit und Liebe für Österreich und Ungarn*
YESWTR	Yearbook of the European Society of Women in Theological Research
ZGG	Zeugen des gegenwärtigen Gottes
ZSR	*Zeitschrift für schweizerisches Recht*

Introduction

Ruth Albrecht and Michaela Sohn-Kronthaler

The Transformation of the World was the title given by Jürgen Osterhammel, historian from Constance, to his voluminous history of the nineteenth century, which reached five editions within a short period.[1] In spite of all the changes that characterize the epoch between 1789 and 1914/1918, the permanent elements should not be overlooked. Among the characteristics of the so-called long nineteenth century is the fact that the Christian confessions and milieus became, to a considerable extent, more and more diversified. This internal differentiation was accompanied at the same time by tendencies toward secularization, which, however, did not lead, as was assumed for a long time by research, to a decrease in the significance of religious interpretive systems as a whole.[2]

All the Christian churches and also the denominations that originated during the course of this century, whether through separations or new beginnings, attributed a decisive significance to the biblical texts, yet careful examination reveals great differences. Bible reading and the interpretation of biblical texts were influenced by disparate currents. The simple reading and hearing of Holy Scripture in worship services and private devotions continued to have their place. Along with this, however, critical exegetical consideration of the biblical tradition increasingly gained ground during the course of the long nineteenth century. The diverse approaches to the Bible are reflected, among other ways, in the many different Bible editions and Bible translations, a small portion of which are reflected in the essays gathered here. The established Bible editions—especially the Vulgate used

---

1. Jürgen Osterhammel, *Die Verwandlung der Welt: Eine Geschichte des 19. Jahrhunderts*, HBGHS (Munich: Beck, 2010). A further special edition was published in 2011.
2. Osterhammel, *Verwandlung*, 1239–78.

by the Catholic Church and the translation by Martin Luther used by the Lutheran churches—retained their significance, of course, but new editions and translations heralded the replacement of authoritative exegetical traditions through a broad range of different approaches to Scripture. Not every group or current in the nineteenth century availed itself of its own Bible edition; however, new ways of approaching biblical tradition also were connected with some new beginnings.

The transformations that took place in the long nineteenth century were felt in all areas of life and thought. Men as well as women stood before new challenges, though as a rule they were different for the two sexes. Women acquired areas of freedom greater than ever before; thus the following statement applies to the female gender as a whole but not to each individual woman.

> It was only the modern age at all that opened up the possibility that women could claim a place as subject, as an independent individual, as a political actor and citizen of the state. In spite of the extreme normative codification of their daily lives, the area of what was possible for women expanded in this period, and new, bold prospects became a distinct possibility.[3]

These sentences from the introduction to the volume titled *19. Jahrhundert* in the five-part *Geschichte der Frauen* stand under the leitmotif "Orders and Freedoms." With these two concepts, the editors of the book attempt to describe the contradictory tendencies of the century from the perspective of women. The treatment of the nineteenth century belongs among the principal areas of women's historical research, which in the 1970s began to apply feminist theories to the past. Religious aspects found little consideration at first, but since then a reconstruction of this century is no longer possible without regard for the religious orientations, which in many respects determined the life plans of many women.[4] The *Geschichte*

---

3. Geneviève Fraisse and Michelle Perrot, "Einleitung," in *19. Jahrhundert*, vol. 4 of *Geschichte der Frauen*, ed. Geneviève Fraisse and Michelle Perrot (Frankfurt: Campus, 1994), 11–17. The original edition of this work appeared in 1991 in Italian.

4. The series *Women and Religion in America*, which was published in three volumes from 1981 to 1986, begins with the nineteenth century. See Rosemary Radford Ruether and Rosemary Skinner Keller, eds., *The Nineteenth Century*, vol. 1 of *Women and Religion in America* (New York: Harper & Row, 1981).

der Frauen devotes three of its twenty analytical chapters to this aspect and analyzes in turn Catholicism, Protestantism, and Judaism.[5]

The Bible as the fundamental written document of Christianity unites all Christian confessions, but different approaches to the Holy Scriptures at times create disjunctions between the members of this confessional family. However, differences in regard to the reception and interpretation of the biblical tradition also divide the opposing currents in the major Christian branches from each other. In the nineteenth century, these contrasts clashed sharply with each other and gave rise to vehement confrontations.

Apart from individual investigations, there appeared in 2006 and 2007 two volumes of essays devoted to the relationship of women to the biblical tradition: Marion Ann Taylor and Heather E. Weir edited a volume that presented women and their reception of the book of Genesis; Christiana de Groot and Taylor (both authors in the present volume) edited another volume that makes female interpreters of the Bible from the nineteenth century better known; further works have been added since then.[6]

The Handbook of Women Biblical Interpreters, published in 2012 in the United States and edited by Taylor with Agnes Choi, presents for the first time a compilation of works by women from all centuries as interpreters of biblical texts. This volume comprises altogether 180 essays, more than a third of which are devoted to female writers from the nineteenth century.[7] While this handbook presents, above all, major representatives

---

5. Michela De Giorgio, "Das katholische Modell," in Fraisse and Perrot, *19. Jahrhundert*, 187–220; Jean Baubérot, "Die protestantische Frau," in Fraisse and Perrot, *19. Jahrhundert*, 221–36; Nancy Green, "Die jüdische Frau: Variationen und Transformationen," in Fraisse and Perrot, *19. Jahrhundert*, 237–52.

6. Marion Ann Taylor and Heather E. Weir, eds., *Let Her Speak for Herself: Nineteenth Century Women Writing on Women in Genesis* (Waco, TX: Baylor University Press, 2006); Christiana de Groot and Taylor, eds., *Recovering Nineteenth Century Women Interpreters of the Bible*, SymS 38 (Atlanta: Society of Biblical Literature, 2007). See, in addition, Nancy Calvert-Koyzis and Weir, eds., *Strangely Familiar: Protofeminist Interpretations of Patriarchal Biblical Texts* (Atlanta: Society of Biblical Literature, 2009); and Calvert-Koyzis and Weir, eds., *Breaking Boundaries: Female Biblical Interpreters Who Challenged the Status Quo*, LHB/OTS 524, LBS (Edinburgh: T&T Clark, 2010). For the individual studies, see, for example, Anne Loads, "Elizabeth Cady Stanton's The Woman's Bible," in *The Oxford Handbook of the Reception History of the Bible*, ed. Michael Lieb et al. (Oxford: Oxford University Press, 2011), 307–22.

7. Marion Ann Taylor, ed., with Agnes Choi, *Handbook of Women Biblical Interpreters: A Historical and Biographical Guide* (Grand Rapids: Academic, 2012).

of the various currents of Bible reading, the focus of the present volume is on the diversity of women's understanding of the Bible and their biblical interpretations. The different Christian confessions thus show different opportunities for action for women. Protestant females had a different type of freedom than, for example, Catholic females, whose autonomous exegesis of Scripture was fundamentally limited or regulated through the church hierarchy, apart from special exceptions, as Adriana Valerio's essay in the present volume shows.

In the individual studies of this volume, our concern is to document, in word and image, both well-known and largely unknown women and their relationships to the Bible. Women authors from the late eighteenth century up to the beginning of the twentieth century are presented along with their explanations and interpretations. Even the relatively few exemplary investigations gathered here demonstrate the diversity of feminine reading of the Bible. In spite of the necessary limitations to a few detailed analyses, one can recognize that a broad range of the treatment of the Holy Scriptures can be documented. This range extends from the application of biblical figures as models for the structuring of one's own life to participation in academic exegesis. The literary genres in which women's occupation with the Bible finds expression extend from letters, diaries, and autobiographical records to stories, novels, songs, and poems and to specialized exegetical treatises and commentaries on individual books of the Bible. Women spoke and wrote about their understanding of the Bible in distinctively varied contexts, from the smallest private circle to mass public meetings. A few were concerned through their own exegesis only to confirm and to testify to the interpretation of biblical texts found in their own ecclesiastical tradition; for others, the express intention to change the prevailing interpretations of the Bible through their own contributions stood in the foreground. Scripture remained an important frame of reference, even if women distanced themselves from its claim to validity. The diversity of biblical receptions by women is astounding, but until now that diversity has not been so portrayed. Confessional paradigms are broken apart, as Jewish women, Christian women, and women at the edge of the Christian tradition read biblical texts in part from comparable impulses. They are thereby encouraged to speak out for equality and educational opportunities for women because they find models in the biblical tradition for their action. However, confessional characteristics also distinguish the female authors: a Russian Orthodox recluse or abbess of a cloister reads the Bible with a perspective different from that of an American Methodist woman or a German female evangelist of Lutheran background whose impulses stem from the Anglo-Saxon Holiness Movement.

Most of the essays in this volume can be assigned to large regions. The analyses by Paul W. Chilcote, Taylor, de Groot, Elizabeth M. Davis, and Pamela S. Nadell contain perspectives on the Anglo-American sphere.

Chilcote devotes himself to the Methodism of the late eighteenth and early nineteenth centuries, a period of the unwritten history of Methodist women and their relationship to the Bible. He discusses how Methodist women in this phase dealt with Holy Scripture, which stood at the center of their lives, and shows how these women interpreted the Bible in innovative ways and used it for the transmission of their own experiences of faith in order to justify the Wesleyan vision of Christian life.

Taylor's essay illuminates a forgotten chapter of the history of critical biblical exegesis in England in the nineteenth century. She investigates women's reactions to the ideas and results of historical-critical exegesis, as well as their role in the dissemination of those results. Did the biblical interpretations by these women reflect the general tendencies of biblical studies? What role did privileged, well-educated women, only a few of whom dedicated themselves explicitly to academic research, play in the transformation leading up to the triumph of historical-critical exegesis? Taylor devotes herself especially to women who took an exemplary part in this movement, such as Sarah Trimmer, Florence Nightingale, Constance and Henrietta de Rothschild, Elizabeth Rundle Charles, and Christina Rossetti.

The varied history of the reception of the Deborah narrative is analyzed by de Groot in extracts from six female writers of the nineteenth century. She explains how these women read the Bible in the light of their own experiences and how they found echoes of the themes of their own times in the book of Judges. De Groot investigates in what ways these female authors interpreted the Deborah narrative and Deborah's song insofar as their positions in the women's question or in the relationship of the sexes in the private as well as the social realm are concerned.

Roman Catholic nun Davis deals with Catherine McAuley, the founder of Davis's own community of sisters. This Irish woman started a religious congregation of women in the nineteenth century that today is found around the world and thus contributed to social change. Davis shows the influence of McAuley's biblical exegesis upon the community she founded. Although McAuley interpreted Holy Scripture intuitively and without critical self-reflection, she nevertheless used the Bible selectively and with authority in order to have a part in effecting social change. In so doing, she anticipated currents in biblical hermeneutics. McAuley was primarily a Bible reader whose texts on Holy Scripture were disseminated far and wide and were read for decades by religious communities around the world. With her study, Davis aims to debunk the assumption that the Bible was completely alien to Catholic women in the early nineteenth century.

Nadell's essay directs our attention to a group of American Jewish women who in 1893 at the World's Columbian Exposition in Chicago publicly claimed the right to interpret the Bible and postbiblical Jewish texts. They read these sources against the backdrop of their own biographies and their own epoch; later they even published their results. At the World Parliament of Religions, which took place in temporal proximity to the Exposition, Josephine Lazarus and Henrietta Szold not only made clear how broad Judaism was in the nineteenth century; they also presented their own interpretations of Jewish tradition and contemporary existence. Women demanded for themselves the right to help shape Judaism as well as to reinterpret its past. With their own biblical exegeses, they underscored their demand to read rabbinical texts and to apply their understanding of this holy literature to the great questions of their time. Nadell draws a direct line of connection from the women speakers at the congress of Jewish women and the World Parliament of Religions to those women who eventually used the Bible and the holy texts of Judaism to demand further rights for women, such as education, admission to university study, and the right to become rabbis and thereby set in motion a process of change within Judaism.

The areas of southern and eastern Europe are illuminated by Marina Cacchi, Adriana Valerio, and Inmaculada Blasco Herranz, as well as by Alexei Klutschewski and Eva Maria Synek.

The essay by Cacchi presents a specific characteristic of Waldensian evangelization in Italy in the nineteenth century. It analyzes the role of Holy Scripture in the official reports of the Biblewomen (*Bibelfrauen*, *Signore della bibbia*), the female employees of the Waldensian Church who sent their reports regularly to the Committee for Evangelization (*Comitato di Evangelizzazione*) to which they were responsible. These women, for several years or throughout a large portion of their lives, carried out systematic preaching activity within the framework of their home visits. The value that these female Waldensian preachers attached to the biblical text during their evangelization work is shown in concrete ways. In addition, the position and significance the Bible assumed in the formation of their identities as women, believers, and teachers, as well as the Bible's use by the Biblewomen, is highlighted in these reports.

Valerio, one of the editors of the Bible and Women series to which this volume belongs, investigates the dissemination of the Bible in Italy and the relationship of women to it as reflected in the works of different female founders of Italian religious congregations. What role did Holy Scripture play in the origin of these nineteenth-century women's religious associations? Valerio presents in this context the example of congregational founder Sister Maria Luisa Ascione, who between 1837 and 1865, in a practice of independent biblical exegesis, committed to paper forty-five Bible commentaries in her *Illustrazioni*.

Blasco Herranz provides a Spanish perspective on the reception of the Bible. She looks at the work of writer and journalist María de la Concepción Gimeno de Flaquer, who characterized herself as a conservative feminist. The essay "Evangelios de la Mujer" ("Women's Gospels") is one of Gimeno de Flaquer's most representative works, and Blasco Herranz is able to use it to demonstrate clearly how Catholicism served the writer in substantiating the validity and legitimacy of her feminist demands. This is true not only for the biblical texts but also for the voices of ecclesiastical authority that she put forward. Gimeno de Flaquer used her writings to demonstrate the intellectual equality of women and men as well as the special role played by women in human history and in church history. At the same time, she advocated for better educational opportunities for females with arguments she derived from her historical material.

Klutschewski and Synek concern themselves with access to the Bible for Orthodox women and with the significance of Holy Scripture for the spirituality of nuns and other Russian women who, in various forms, led spiritual and ascetic lives. Just as seen in the essays in this volume on the Catholic Church, the fact that women interacted intensively with the Bible also applies to the Orthodox churches, which until now have been examined under this aspect much less intensively. The results of Klutschewski's and Synek's work will encourage others, we hope, to inquire about Orthodox women in other countries who likewise engaged the Bible in a lively manner within the context of their tradition.

The essays by Angela Berlis, Ruth Albrecht, Doris Brodbeck, Ute Gause, and Michaela Sohn-Kronthaler have women and texts from the German-speaking world as their objects.

Berlis deals with the relationship between women and the Bible in the nineteenth century with respect to liturgy. She directs her view primarily toward the way in which a group of women who came from the nobility and the bourgeoisie read the Bible in the nineteenth century, interpreted it for their lives, and shaped it into religious practice. Her essay focuses on women who belonged to a spiritual circle in Bonn, who were, as a rule, unmarried (*Bonner Kreuzeskränzchen*); and who can be assigned to early Old Catholicism. Berlis draws upon unpublished letters to celibate male spiritual members of this circle as well as a litany written by the women investigated. The female members of this Bonn circle dealt with the biblical texts in the contexts of catechesis, liturgy, and the (common) reading of the church fathers, but also in reflection and conversation, thereby establishing a connection to their own lives.

Albrecht investigates controversies in the milieu of the Protestant renewal movements. In some of these groups, women established themselves as preachers and evangelists on the basis of new interpretations of biblical texts. Albrecht presents protagonists for whom the Bible was of central significance. They justified their activities by appeal to biblical texts but proceeded in quite different ways. Their varied ways of reading the Bible show many commonalities that rest upon the condition that the texts of the Old and New Testaments contain the revelation of God that speaks directly to individual readers. So, for example, Adeline Duchess von Schimmelmann was among the few women in the period around 1900 who took an active part within the framework of the new piety movements and openly advocated that both sexes were called to proclaim the gospel.

Brodbeck directs her view toward Helene von Mülinen, who belonged to the Reformed Church in Switzerland. The Bible was important to this patrician daughter from Berne in two ways: it lent her a language for lamenting against ecclesiastical and social traditions and for formulating new visions. Using biblical texts, she expressed her doubts about interpretations of the Bible that, for her, had become hostile to life. But in its texts, too, she found the first beginnings of a strengthening of women's emancipation and of social policy, which she pursued as president of the Alliance of Swiss Women's Associations. In her letters, lectures, and articles, Mülinen often took up biblical images and expressions without making these explicit. Brodbeck's essay also shows how she came to this way of reading the Bible.

Gause deals with Eva von Tiele-Winckler from Silesia, who published numerous biblical interpretations. Her devotional writings, which were widely distributed, were intended above all for the sisterhoods of deaconesses that Tiele-Winckler called into being. This Silesian noblewoman used an individual interpretation of the biblical texts typical in the revival movements, which assumes the literal inspiration of the Bible: every verse speaks directly to reader, whether male or female, since God reveals himself in his word. The investigation in this essay focuses upon Tiele-Winckler's interpretations of texts from the prophet Isaiah and from the Sermon on the Mount.

Like Tiele-Winckler, Countess Elvine de La Tour is one of the typical representatives of female social welfare work. Sohn-Kronthaler shows in her essay the significance of Bible reading for de La Tour, who on the basis of her revivalist piety created a substantial network of social welfare institutions in Friaul and in Carinthia that still exist in Austria today. De La Tour's existential appropriation of Holy Scripture made active love of neighbor indispensable for the Christian life. She interpreted the growth of her charitable institutions in the light of Holy Scripture; her concern for popular missionary evangelization also played an important role. For this she recruited, on the basis of her international network, female and male evangelists from Switzerland and various German centers of the revival movement for the purpose of proclaiming the message of salvation in her home country.

The subject of (religious) literature and art is treated by Bernhard Schneider, Magda Motté, Katharina Büttner-Kirschner, and Elfriede Wiltschnigg.

Schneider pursues a rather innovative question insofar as he concerns himself in detail with more popular spiritual literature that was explicitly intended for a Catholic female reading public. The authors of this literature were primarily men, especially the clergy. The following aspects guide Schneider's analyses: Can gender-specific differences be determined? What images of women did the authors develop from the Bible? Did they verify their already-existing images of women through the Bible, or did they project the desired conduct of women back upon biblical figures? Upon the basis of his extensive research, Schneider concludes that the Bible represented only one point of reference next to others in the devotional and edificatory literature for women.

Motté analyzes the adaptation of biblical material in the literature of the long nineteenth century. As she explicitly emphasizes, she offers only a summary of the abundant material to a specific complex of questions; the results can be characterized in her view as only meager, since other material stood in the foreground of the chosen literary subjects. Using selected texts from German-speaking female writers, Motté traces out how these writers shaped literarily the biblical traditions regarding Mary of Magdala, Lilith, and Judith, thus providing the opportunity to discuss unusual gender options.

Büttner-Kirschner presents selected Marian portraits and other biblical pictures by the painter from Constance, Marie Ellenrieder, who, as one of the few female artists of this epoch, took up themes from Holy Scripture. Büttner-Kirschner's analysis deals with unity and difference in the representation of the sexes in Ellenrieder's work. The pictures printed along with the text of the article show how the artist located herself between tradition and innovation when she, for example, portrays Mary as the author of the Magnificat. It is striking that, in Ellenrieder's rendering of women, she emphasizes the aspect of communication.

Wiltschnigg examines the Bible illustrations by two famous artists: Julius Schnorr von Carolsfeld and Gustave Doré. She deals first of all with the profiles of the two painters and provides an introduction to the techniques that each used in shaping his artistic interpretation of the Bible. This comparison of the two reveals similarity as well as great differences in regard to conception of biblical themes. Old Testament women in individual and mass scenes, in many instances documented through the reproduction of the woodcuts and wood engravings, are then examined. The tension between traditional gender concepts and individual, unusual interpretations of the conduct of men and women is one of the aspects that Wiltschnigg emphasizes.

Bibliography

Baubérot, Jean. "Die protestantische Frau." Pages 221–36 in *19. Jahrhundert*. Vol. 4 of *Geschichte der Frauen*. Edited by Geneviève Fraisse and Michelle Perrot. Frankfurt: Campus, 1994.

Calvert-Koyzis, Nancy, and Heather E. Weir, eds. *Breaking Boundaries: Female Biblical Interpreters Who Challenged the Status Quo*. LHB/OTS 524. LBS. Edinburgh: T&T Clark, 2010.

———. *Strangely Familiar: Protofeminist Interpretations of Patriarchal Biblical Texts*. Atlanta: Society of Biblical Literature, 2009.

De Giorgio, Michela. "Das katholische Modell." Pages 187–220 in *19. Jahrhundert*. Vol. 4 of *Geschichte der Frauen*. Edited by Geneviève Fraisse and Michelle Perrot. Frankfurt: Campus, 1994.

Fraisse, Geneviève, and Michelle Perrot. "Einleitung." Pages 11–17 in *19. Jahrhundert*. Vol. 4 of *Geschichte der Frauen*. Edited by Geneviève Fraisse and Michelle Perrot. Frankfurt: Campus, 1994.

Green, Nancy. "Die jüdische Frau: Variationen und Transformationen." Pages 237–52 in *19. Jahrhundert*. Vol. 4 of *Geschichte der Frauen*. Edited by Geneviève Fraisse and Michelle Perrot. Frankfurt: Campus, 1994.

Groot, Christiana de, and Marion Ann Taylor, eds. *Recovering Nineteenth-Century Women Interpreters of the Bible*. SymS 38. Atlanta: Society of Biblical Literature, 2007.

Loads, Anne. "Elizabeth Cady Stanton's *The Woman's Bible*." Pages 307–22 in *The Oxford Handbook of the Reception History of the Bible*. Edited by Michael Lieb, Emma Mason, and Jonathan Roberts, with consultation by Christopher Rowland. Oxford: Oxford University Press, 2011.

Osterhammel, Jürgen. *Die Verwandlung der Welt: Eine Geschichte des 19. Jahrhunderts*. HBGHS. Munich: Beck, 2010.

Ruether, Rosemary Radford, and Rosemary Skinner Keller, eds. *The Nineteenth Century*. Vol. 1 of *Women and Religion in America*. New York: Harper & Row, 1981.

Taylor, Marion Ann, ed. with Agnes Choi. *Handbook of Women Biblical Interpreters: A Historical and Biographical Guide*. Grand Rapids: Baker Academic, 2012.

Taylor, Marion Ann, and Heather E. Weir, eds. *Let Her Speak for Herself: Nineteenth-Century Women Writing on Women in Genesis*. Waco, TX: Baylor University Press, 2006.

Methodist Women and the Bible:
Early Nineteenth-Century Engagement with Scripture

Paul W. Chilcote

The Wesleyan revival, like other movements of Christian renewal, was at its heart a rediscovery of the Bible. The early Methodist people believed that [the Bible] was not simply a compilation of letters and histories, of prayers and biographies, of wise sayings and encouraging words. They realized that these ancient words could become the "Living Word" for them as they encountered scripture anew through the inspiration of the Holy Spirit. They understood the Bible to be the supreme authority in matters of faith and practice. In both preaching and personal study, the scriptural text sprang to new life, forming, informing, and transforming their lives with immediate effect and lasting influence.[1]

John Wesley (1703–1791), the eighteenth-century founder of Methodism, considered himself to be "a man of one book."[2] His immersion in Scripture not only shaped his own spiritual life and that of his cofounder and brother, the great hymn-writer Charles Wesley (1707–1788), but also formed those who committed themselves to the religious awakening that they led. This movement liberated those who stood on the periphery of society through the rediscovery of the gospel message of free grace and love for all. Given the nature of these rediscoveries within the Church of England, it is not surprising that early Methodism was, for all intents and purposes, a movement of women. Despite the fact that the most visible leaders were men, like the Wesleys, women functioned as pioneers, lead-

---

1. Paul W. Chilcote, ed., *Early Methodist Spirituality: Selected Women's Writings* (Nashville: Abingdon, 2007), 28.
2. John Wesley, *Sermons 1:1–33*, vol. 1 of *The Works of John Wesley*, ed. Albert C. Outler (Nashville: Abingdon, 1984), 105.

ers, and even preachers in this movement of renewal, and the Bible played a central role in all of these activities.

After the death of the Wesley brothers in the late eighteenth century, women continued to exert a profound influence upon the Methodist Societies. The early decades of the nineteenth century were particularly important because it was during this period that Methodists gained functional autonomy from the Church of England. The story of Methodist women and the Bible during this era of consolidation remains, essentially, an untold story. In order to understand how Methodist women engaged Scripture during this period, some background on Wesleyan hermeneutics will be helpful. Following an examination of this foundational material, we will explore how women understood and used the Bible to frame narratives concerning their journeys of faith and to defend their Wesleyan vision of the Christian life. In closing, we will look briefly at the contributions of three women in this arena: in particular, Mary Hanson, Mary Tatham, and Mary Fletcher.

1. Wesleyan Hermeneutics

The Wesleys taught a very dynamic conception of Scripture. They confessed, with all members of the Church of England, that "Holy Scripture containeth all things necessary to salvation" (article 6 of the Articles of Religion). They believed that God inspired all of the material contained in the Bible, but they also affirmed that the Spirit inspires the communities that seek to appropriate God's truth in them. Scripture is doubly inspired, as it were, both in its composition and in its appropriation. Because of this continuing work of the Spirit in the community of faith, the Bible actually comes to life in new historical settings, cultural contexts, and communities as its narratives are illuminated by tradition, vivified in personal religious experience, and confirmed by reason. The dynamic interrelation of these four elements—Scripture, tradition, experience, and reason—is generally knows as the "Wesleyan quadrilateral." The Wesleys approached Scripture, therefore, in an open, receptive, and humble manner. They especially attended to the application of God's word as it relates to the personal and communal practices related to the faith.

John Wesley made frequent reference to "reading, marking, and inwardly digesting" the word of God. As Steve Harper has noted, "The higher critical study of scripture was not foreign to Wesley, but the ancient practice of *lectio divina* ("divine reading") was still his favored way of approaching the Bible."³ Wesley inculcated a great love of the Bible in his followers. "Searching the Scriptures" defined their piety. Their deep contemplation of the texts engaged all their faculties and senses. They read the Bible daily, generally in the morning and evening in conjunction with their devotional use of the *Book of Common Prayer*. Their singular purpose was to know God's will and to follow it. They were taught to practice what they had learned as a consequence of their reflection on and contemplation of the Bible. In addition to this general, biblical foundation for life, the Wesleys also emphasized an approach to the Scriptures through the use of the analogy of faith and correlation.

The first of these two hermeneutical principles is complicated only because of the language that Wesley used, a terminology less well-known today. He drew his concept of the "analogy of faith" from Rom 12:6, in which *analogian tes pisteos* can also be rendered "in proportion to faith," "in agreement with faith," or "by the measure of faith." He believed that all Scripture ought to be read over against the measuring rod of the Christ who is known in the community of faith. Whenever he engaged the Bible, he attempted to understand it in relation to the Jesus he knew by faith. Scripture itself forms a Christ-shaped lens, as it were, through which one looks when interpreting the text. To articulate this principle on its most basic level, one could simply say: "a Christian understands the Bible on the basis of the spirit or mind of Christ." In this way, the New Testament (particularly the gospels) provides the framework for understanding all texts in the Bible. The Christian reads the Bible with Jesus's eyes.

While Wesley did not use this precise terminology, today a second important hermeneutical principle might well be called the principle of correlation. Scripture interprets Scripture. This basic approach to the Bible has two interrelated parts. First, difficult texts that are hard to understand should be read in relation to other texts that relate to the same issue. Parallel passages provide the key that unlocks meaning. Secondly, isolated parts of Scripture need to be understood within the context of the whole of the biblical narrative. Obviously, this requires a breadth of knowledge concerning the biblical witness, and this is one of the reasons why Methodists devoted themselves to the serious study of Scripture. They correlated any given text, therefore, with the general tenor of Scripture as a whole. An operative ques-

---

3. Steve Harper, "Works of Piety as Spiritual Formation," in *The Wesleyan Tradition: A Paradigm for Renewal*, ed. Paul W. Chilcote (Nashville: Abingdon, 2002), 91–92.

tion governs both dimensions of this biblical principle: is this passage of Scripture consistent with the rest of the Bible? When a student of Scripture interfaces the principles of correlation and analogy of faith, a potent hermeneutical tool emerges that potentially enriches her understanding.

2. An Illustration of Women's Biblical Exegesis

A letter of Mary Bosanquet (1739–1815) (a noted woman preacher discussed more fully below) to John Wesley illustrates the potency of this Wesleyan approach to Scripture. It could not be more appropriate in this study of Methodist women and the Bible since it relates to the issue of women in ministry and the so-called prohibitive passages in the writings of Paul. In the 1760s and 1770s the issue of women preachers loomed large in the Wesleyan Revival. Up to that point, Wesley had given only tacit approval to these practices, but a number of distinguished women, Bosanquet among them, pressed the issue of God's call upon women with great urgency. For the women, Scripture was liberating, but the freedom they discovered in Christ through the Word often demanded their prophetic witness to the truth in the face of opposition. Bosanquet's defense of the ministry of women ran counter to the accepted social and ecclesial norms of her day and required great courage. The Bible was for her not only the source of women's strength, it was a book of promise that held the key to a faithful, abundant life.

While this letter dates from June 1771, the approach outlined by Bosanquet with regard to these difficult texts governed her actions until her death in 1815. This very letter set the stage for the ministry of many other women in the early nineteenth century and was referenced perennially by women in their quest to retain their newfound status within Methodism. Here, then, is an example of a woman's use of the Bible to defend her right to proclaim the good news of the gospel. Two extracts from the letter illustrate the hermeneutical principles most relevant here. Bosanquet first addresses objections based upon texts from 1 Cor 11 and 14:

> Objection. But the Apostle says, "I suffer not a woman to speak in the Church, but learn at home."
> I answer, was not that spoke[n] in reference to a time of dispute and contention, when many were striving to be heads and leaders, so that his saying, "She is not to speak," here seems to me to imply no more than the other, she is not to meddle with Church government.

> Objection. Nay, but it meant literally, not to speak by way of edification while in the Church or company of promiscuous worshippers.
> Answer. Then why is it said, "Let the woman prophesy with her head covered," or can she prophesy without speaking? Or ought she to speak, but not to edification?[4]

Not only does Bosanquet properly describe the unique context in which these directives were given, but she correlates the seemingly prohibitive language of chapter 14 with the apparently permissive language of chapter 11. In other words, she demonstrates the tension between two texts related to the same issue in the very same letter. That correlation opens the door to her defense of the practice of women on the basis of the general tenor of Scripture.

Her response to the criticism of women on the basis of purportedly immodest behavior elicits a response that points to other women in Scripture who did speak on the basis of God's command and simultaneously reflects her interpretation of these texts on the basis of the analogy of Christ:

> Objection. Well, but is [preaching] consistent with that modesty the Christian religion requires in a woman professing godliness?
> Answer. It may be, and is, painful to it, but I do not see it inconsistent with it, and that for this reason. Does not Christian modesty stand in these two particulars, purity and humility? First, I apprehend it consists in cutting off every act, word and thought that in the least infringes on the purity God delights in. Secondly, in cutting off every act, word and thought which in the least infringes on *humility*, knowing thoroughly our own place, and rendering to everyone their due. Endeavouring to be little, and unknown, as far as the order of God will permit, and simply following that order, leaving the event to God. Now I do not apprehend Mary sinned against either of these heads, or could in the least be accused of immodesty, when she carried the joyful news of her Lord's Resurrection and in that sense taught the Teachers of Mankind. Neither was the woman of Samaria to be accused of immodesty when she invited the whole city to come to Christ.[5]

---

4. Sarah Crosby, Manuscript Letterbook, 1760–1774, Perkins Library, Duke University, Durham, NC.

5. Crosby, Manuscript Letterbook, emphasis original.

3. Early Nineteenth Century Women's Use of Scripture

After the death of the Wesleys, Methodist women continued to engage Scripture in this dynamic way. Their writings reflect other hermeneutical rules, however, that had governed the earlier Methodists' conception and use of Scripture as well. The women believed that Scripture, for example, was self-authenticating; their tendency was simply to let Scripture speak for itself. They took the context of statements seriously and sought to interpret literary devices in the most appropriate ways. They viewed commands as covert promises. Examining closely this panoply of issues related to the Bible reveals a complex hermeneutical nexus, much too large for full exploration here. A survey of the writings of the early nineteenth century Methodist women, however, reveals two critical areas, in particular, in which Scripture played a vital role. First, the biblical narrative provided the language and images for the women's own stories of faith. Secondly, the women used Scripture to guide their sisters and brothers in the life of faith and to defend the Wesleyan vision of the Christian life.

3.1. Spiritual Narratives

The Wesleys encouraged all of their followers to share their stories of faith with one another and to record their experiences of God. Because of this, the Methodists left behind an amazing legacy of stories of conversion, liberation, and growth in grace. The Bible figures prominently in the spiritual narratives of the women's lives. In many cases, their engagement with Scripture actually provided the catalyst for transformation and growth. The experience of Hester Ann Rogers (1756–1794), one of the most highly esteemed women of early Methodism, illustrates this biblical focus: "Reading the word of God in private this day was an unspeakable blessing. O! how precious are the promises. What a depth in these words: 'For all the promises of God in him are yea, and in him, amen, unto the glory of God' [2 Cor 1:20]. Yes, my soul, they are so to you!"[6] Excerpts from the spiritual narratives of several women, in which the scriptural allusions are identified, demonstrate the pervasive use of biblical imagery in the narration of their religious experience.

---

6. Hester Ann Rogers, *An Account of the Experience of Hester Ann Rogers* (New York: Hunt & Eaton, 1893), 132.

Rogers narrates the liberating effect of God's grace at one of the most critical turning points of her life:

> His power alone can change my rebel heart. My disease is too deep for any other. I can only perish. Nothing can be worse. So there is no hazard. If he is God, he is able and he will save me according to his promise, "Come unto me, all ye that labor and are heavy laden, and I will give you rest" [Matt 11:28].
>
> Then did he appear to my salvation. In that moment my fetters were broken, my bands were loosed, and my soul set at liberty. The love of God was shed abroad in my heart [cf. Rom 5:5] and I rejoiced with joy unspeakable.[7]

In the early nineteenth century, nothing tested the faith and courage of women more than the experience of childbirth. Mary Entwisle (1770–1804), noted diarist and indefatigable wife of a distinguished Methodist itinerant preacher, prays to God as she confronts this life-threatening situation:

> Several symptoms assure me the hour of trial is very near. I feel no painful anxiety. I feel power to cast my burden upon the Lord. He has promised he will not leave or forsake me. He has said I will strengthen you. I will help you, yes, I will uphold you with the right hand of my righteousness [cf. Isa 41:10]. O my God, I rely upon your word. You will be a very present help in the time of trouble [cf. Ps 46:1]. How great and precious are your promises and they all are yea and amen in Christ Jesus to them that believe [cf. 2 Cor 1:20]. O increase my faith, confirm my hope, and may I trust in you and not be confounded. Amen. Even so, Lord Jesus.[8]

Sarah Crosby (1729–1804), the first woman preacher of Methodism, recounts God's confirmation of her special calling, inferring a close connection between her vocation and that of Peter's through her biblical allusions:

> Not long after this, as I was praying, my soul was overwhelmed with the power of God. I seemed to see the Lord Jesus before me and said, "Lord, I am ready to follow thee, not only to prison, but to death [cf. Luke 22:33], if thou wilt give me strength." And he spoke these words to my heart,

---

7. Rogers, *An Account of the Experience of Hester Ann Rogers*, 24.
8. Mary Entwisle, Manuscript Diary, The Methodist Archives and Research Centre, John Rylands University Library of Manchester.

"Feed my sheep" [John 21:17]. I answered, "Lord, I will do as thou hast done; I will carry the lambs in my bosom, and gently lead those that are with young" [Isa 40:11].[9]

The biblical witness enabled these women to interpret the events of their lives in such a way as to incorporate their own experiences into the grand narrative of God's care and provision. Scripture provided the language by which they narrated their lives. Their use of the Bible also validated their legitimate place in the community of faith.

3.2. Apologetics and Spiritual Guidance

Several excerpts illustrate the women's use of Scripture in apologetics and spiritual guidance. Mary Hanson's Methodist apologia is extracted here from a letter of 1810, dated about one year from the time of her first introduction to the Methodists. Responding to the questions of a friend, Hanson defends a holistic understanding of the gospel in which justification by grace through faith provides a firm foundation for a life devoted to love. In her vision of biblical Christianity, faith and works must be held together in a dynamic tension. Note the masterful weaving of gospel and Pauline material in her defense:

> That the doctrines of the Wesleyans are those of the Bible, I am more and more convinced.... You ask me, "If I place any dependence on my own performances, as being at all able to recommend me to the favour of God?" Not in the least. Justified freely by his grace [cf. Rom 3:24], I must come just as I am, poor, blind, and naked, or he will never receive me. But, observe, I believe that sanctification follows; the tree is known by its fruits. "If a man love me He will keep my commandments" [John 14:15]. Faith works by love [cf. Gal 5:6]; this is the wedding garment [cf. Matt 22:12]. By the fruits of faith I believe you and I shall be judged at the last day. Read Matthew chapter 25....
>
> While we continue in the grace of God freely imparted, watching and praying, loving God with all our hearts, none shall pluck us out of the Redeemer's hands [cf. John 10:28–29]; nothing shall separate us from his love [cf. Rom 8:39]....
>
> I do believe that if you and I have once received the grace of God, it is our own fault, and chargeable alone upon ourselves, that we ever lose

---

9. "An Account of Mrs. Crosby, of Leeds," *WMM* 29 (1806): 471–72.

it. God deals with us as with reasonable creatures, and certain conditions are prescribed to us. We are to ask, seek, and knock for the Holy Spirit [cf. Matt 7:7]; having received it, we are to watch and pray [cf. Matt 26:41], deny ourselves [cf. Luke 9:23], abstain from all appearance of evil [cf. 1 Thess 5:22]. The power is from above, and through Christ we can do all these things [cf. Phil 4:13].[10]

The women often expressed their feelings openly with regard to the repression they experienced as women, both outside and inside the life of the church. They found consolation in the support they provided to one another. Often that support was couched in the language of Scripture. They used the words and concepts of the Bible as reminders of God's presence and provision. Crosby wrote the following letter of encouragement to an aspiring preacher and potential colleague, describing the central conviction that had sustained her own life and ministry:

> Where we know we have the Lord's approbation, we should stand like the beaten anvil to the stroke, or lie in his hands as clay in the hands of the potter [Jer 18:6]. Through evil report and good we pass, but all things work together for good to them that love God [Rom 8:28].
> Speak and act as the spirit gives liberty and utterance. Fear not the face of man, but with humble confidence trust in the Lord, looking unto him who is able and willing to save to the uttermost all that come unto God by him [cf. Heb 7:25]. In waiting upon the Lord, we renew our strength [cf. Isa 40:31].[11]

In similar fashion, in 1807, Fletcher attempts to console, encourage, and support a fellow preacher during a time of trial. Note how she draws upon the image of the potter and the clay as well, one of the women's favorite biblical metaphors to describe the nature of their relationship with God:

> Remember we are now "heirs of God, and joint heirs with Jesus Christ, if so be that we suffer with Him, that we may be glorified together" [Rom 8:17].
> The one thing our Lord aims at in all our many trials is to bring us perfectly to lose our wills in his. Therefore if you strive by acts of resig-

---

10. Adam Clarke, ed., *Memoirs of the Late Eminent Mrs. Mary Cooper, of London* (New York: Waugh & Mason, 1833), 122–24, language updated.

11. Zechariah Taft, ed., *Original Letters, Never before Published on Doctrinal, Experimental and Practical Religion* (Whitby: George Clark, 1821), 66–67.

nation to lie as clay before the potter [cf. Jer 18:6], your soul shall grow as the lily, and cast out its root like Lebanon [cf. Hos 14:5] … hang on the word of the Lord, with a continual cry in your heart, "Thy will be done" [Matt 26:42]. Let it comfort you to remember that our bodies are, as St. Paul says, members of Jesus Christ [cf. 1 Cor 6:15], and the body is for the Lord, and the Lord for the body [cf. 1 Cor 6:13]. Will he not then take care of his own?[12]

4. Three Exemplary Women

By the closing decades of the eighteenth century, a number of women had risen through the ranks of the Methodist Societies and functioned as role models—saintly women who demonstrated the Wesleyan vision of faith working by love leading to holiness of heart and life. In the early decades of the nineteenth century, three Marys stood out in terms of their knowledge of and wisdom concerning the Word of God: Hanson, theologically astute and spiritually perspicacious; Tatham, renowned biblical exegete; and Fletcher, perhaps the most famous woman preacher of the time. Each of these women engaged Scripture in unique ways, but all pointed to the dynamic use of Scripture in the Wesleyan spirit.

4.1. Mary Hanson (1786–1812)

Little is known about Hanson. Born in London in 1786 and introduced to Methodism in 1809, she became an avid member of the Methodist Society in 1810. She married John Cooper in 1811 and the following year gave birth to a son who died in less than a week due to complications related to the delivery. The same year she came into contact with the Methodists, she began to write personal meditations that reflect a depth of spirituality beyond her years. The titles of these reflections resonate in significant ways with the Methodist themes she embraced. She articulates a vision of the Christian life that is transformational and liberationist at its core. The biblical portrait of redeemed humanity that she paints is an image of nobility, joy, dignity, and value. True happiness or blessedness is the ultimate goal toward which the child of God is compelled to move, not out of self-interest but for the glory of God.

---

12. Mary Fletcher, "Letter of Mary Fletcher to Elizabeth Collet," *AM* 2.8 (1823): 286–287.

Excerpts from two of her meditations, one on "Trust in the Lord" and the other on "Experimental Religion," provide an interesting glimpse into the way in which she draws on Scripture and integrates the biblical narrative into her understanding of faith:

> Blessed is the man that trusts in the Lord [cf. Jer 17:7], that makes the Lord his portion, who, with eyes filled with tears of gratitude can say, "The Lord is my Shepherd" [Ps 23:1]. Blessings beyond mortal calculation are included in this personal appropriation.
>
> My soul, diligently seek to be included in the number of that blessed flock. He who said, "Let there be light, and there was light" [Gen 1:3], who, by an act of his will, created man and, but for infinite love, might have destroyed him when he broke the only command imposed on him. He who takes up the isles as a very little thing, who counts the nations as a drop of a bucket [cf. Isa 40:15]—even this God proposes himself for your portion, O my soul![13]

While Mary draws most of her allusions in this excerpt from the Old Testament, her reflections on religion as an experienced relationship demonstrate the centrality of the gospels in her vision of the Christian life. She writes,

> O for simplicity of heart to receive the kingdom of God as a little child [cf. Mark 10:15]! Away with cavilings and skeptical reasonings. When did these ever produce joy and peace in believing [Rom 15:13]? ... O may the religion I profess be a well of water springing up within me [cf. John 4:14]! A holy principle producing joy and peace. A principle which shall make me soar above the world, feel the divine origin of my soul, and be constantly tending toward the source of all true felicity.[14]

This poetic, somewhat mystical, language characterized the writings of many Methodist women of her time.

4.2. Mary Tatham (1764–1837)

Mary Strickland was born into a family of strict Calvinist Dissenters in 1764. When she was five or six years old, while reading the Bible, she was powerfully struck by the description of the new heaven and the new earth

---

13. Clarke, *Memoirs of the Late Eminent Mrs. Mary Cooper*, 23–24.
14. Clarke, *Memoirs of the Late Eminent Mrs. Mary Cooper*, 108.

in the Revelation of John, her first religious impression. She was greatly influenced by her study of these texts and received her first Methodist class ticket in 1784.[15] Three years later she married John Tatham at the Old Church in Leeds, a historic center of Methodist women's activities. Over the course of more than forty years, she had the charge of at least three classes—small groups within Methodism that functioned as the heartbeat of every society. To prepare herself properly for the spiritual direction of those under her care, she provided commentary on biblical texts, thirteen of which were published in her *Memoirs*.[16] Some of these statements were tightly argued expositions of critical doctrines such as justification by grace through faith and sanctification.

Tatham's exposition of Rom 3:10 demonstrates her amazing ability to navigate the nuances of Pauline soteriology. She gives particular attention to the effect of justifying faith on the heart of the true believer:

> It fills him with love and with astonishment at the greatness of God's mercy. It works an utter abhorrence of all sin and casts out slavish fear [cf. 1 John 4:18]. It opens a way of access between God and the believing soul and imparts unto him the spirit of adoption, whereby he cries, "Abba, Father" [Rom 8:15]. Thus delivered, the language of his heart is no longer, "O wretched man that I am, who shall deliver me from the body of this death" [Rom 7:24]? but, "Thou art my God [Ps 118:28], and my Deliverer [cf. Ps 40:17], the Holy One of Israel! whom have I in heaven but thee? and there is none upon earth that I desire in comparison of thee" [cf. Ps 73:25]. Being thus freed from the guilt and dominion of sin and initiated into the family and favour of God, he becomes a servant of righteousness, has his fruit unto holiness, and his end everlasting life [cf. Rom 6:22].[17]

Having described justification as the foundation of the life of faith, she turns her attention to the goal. She roots her exposition of sanctification

---

15. Members of Methodist Societies received a ticket that verified their faithful participation in class meetings. The leadership of the society reviewed the status of each member regularly, and tickets were renewed quarterly. This reflects the high value placed on accountable discipleship.

16. Her commentaries include expositions of Luke 10:41; Matt 15:16; 1 John 2:15; Ps 37:16; Mal 2:7; Lev 22:2; Matt 3:11; 1 Pet 1:5, Gen 49:19; Rom 12:14; Ps 11:6; Isa 33:14; and Luke 13:5.

17. Joseph Beaumont, ed., *Memoirs of Mrs. Mary Tatham* (London: Simpkin & Marshall, 1838), 66–67.

in the two great Pauline texts, Gal 5:6 and Eph 3:19, that figured so prominently in the preaching of the Wesleys:

> Until the love of God becomes the ruling principle of the soul, no work is acceptable unto him. For whatsoever is not of faith working by love [cf. Gal 5:6] has in it of the nature of sin, not flowing from a pure principle within. But saving faith purifies the heart, converts the soul, sanctifies the affections, and enlarges the desires towards God and man so that, if it were possible, it would embrace the whole world and bring every soul to taste and enjoy the sweetness of that love of which he so freely partakes. O that I may no longer rest satisfied without a full salvation, but seek to be saved even to the uttermost, that I may be filled with all the fullness of God [cf. Eph 3:19].[18]

4.3. Mary Bosanquet (1739–1815)

Mary Bosanquet Fletcher stands without a rival in the annals of early Methodism. In addition to her multifarious roles as advisor, counselor, small group leader, minister's wife, patron, and prolific writer, she was the most beloved woman preacher of the Methodist movement. She continued this work diligently until her death in 1815. While her preaching, in terms of themes and goals, closely resonated with that of Wesley and his male itinerant preachers, her approach and homiletical style deviated in some ways from her "father in God." Whereas Wesley tended to advocate a minimalist hermeneutic, Fletcher did not fear following the lead of the Spirit in her attempt to communicate the truth of the biblical narrative. Put simply, Wesley implied that the best interpretation of the Bible was no interpretation at all; Fletcher enjoyed the adventure of allegorical interpretation. One could even say that she reveled in imaginative explorations of the text as long as her exposition remained deeply rooted in the general tenor of Scripture. Two examples demonstrate her abilities in this regard.

The first example is drawn from her exposition of the prayer of Jabez in 1 Chr 4:10. She imaginatively expands the central concept of the prayer encapsulated in the phrase "enlarge my coast." "May you not ask," she inquires, "'Lord, enlarge my coast of *prayer*.' Drive out those spirits of unbelief or distraction which so interrupt my approaches to the throne of grace." She asks the Lord, second, to "enlarge my coast of *understanding*."

---

18. Beaumont, *Memoirs of Mrs. Mary Tatham*, 73–74.

She encourages all to apprehend the dimensions of God's incomprehensible love. The quest to "know God" exceeds all other pursuits. Third, Mary pleads for an enlargement of spiritual affections. "Give us, O Lord," she prays, "the ardent flaming love.... Grant us love to you with our whole hearts. For whatever we have besides, or without this love, we are but as sounding brass or a tinkling cymbal [cf. 1 Cor 13:1]." Fourth, she cautions that all these enlargements are misplaced if they have any goal other than the glory of God and the realization of God's reign. Finally, "enlarge my coast of *faith*," pleads Mary, "since God has chosen this grace to be the measure of all the rest."[19]

In Fletcher's sermon on Acts 27:29, the only extant sermon of a woman from the early nineteenth century, she exhibits this same allegorical method. The text itself—"They cast four anchors out of the stern, and wished for the day" (KJV)—begs for her kind of exposition. "Well, let us try to cast out one anchor now," she admonishes. "I am sensible your cable is short. Therefore we must seek for some ground as *near* you as we can. We will try, if we can, to find it in the 'Creating Love of God,' surrounding us on every side" (emphasis original). She drops her second anchor on "Redeeming love." Those who fail to find sure ground in the sacred sacrifice of Christ may try to secure it in God's "Promises." Fletcher then enumerates the amazing promises offered to all on the basis of God's grace and demonstrates how "God delights to do great things by little means." Finally, she sets her final anchor in "Resignation." "Now cast your whole soul, your everlasting concerns," she pleads, "on the free unmerited love of the Saviour, and live upon, 'Thy will be done'.... For the very end of our creation is, that we may become 'the habitation of God through the Spirit.'"[20]

5. Methodist Women's Witness to the Living Word

Methodist women in the early nineteenth century rooted their lives in the Bible. Like their Wesleyan foremothers, they developed a dynamic conception of Scripture and mitigated a narrow or reductionistic hermeneutical vision. They shaped their spiritual narratives with the language and imag-

---

19. Mary Fletcher, "Letters from Mrs. Fletcher to Mrs. Dalby," *WMM* 41 (1818): 688–90, all emphasis original.

20. See the entirety of the sermon in Paul W. Chilcote, *John Wesley and the Women Preachers of Early Methodism*, ATLAMS 25 (Metuchen, NJ: Scarecrow, 1991), 321–27.

ery of the Bible and employed Scripture in their defense of the Wesleyan way and in spiritual counsel and guidance. The writings of these women impress the reader simply in terms of the pervasiveness of the biblical witness. The women devoted themselves to a serious study of Scripture and encountered the Living Word in the narratives of God's grace and love. They inwardly digested the words, ideas, and vision of the sacred text. Then they sought to live biblical Christianity with authenticity so as to be transparent to the love and grace they encountered in the narrative of God's mighty acts of salvation. The confession drawn from the manuscript journal of a little-known Methodist woman by the name of Anna Reynalds (1775–1840) bears witness to the experience of her sisters in the faith: "The word of God became my delight and was truly spirit and life to my soul."[21]

Bibliography

"An Account of Mrs. Crosby, of Leeds." *WMM* 29 (1806): 465–73.
Beaumont, Joseph, ed. *Memoirs of Mrs. Mary Tatham*. London: Simpkin & Marshall, 1838.
Chilcote, Paul W., ed. *Early Methodist Spirituality: Selected Women's Writings*. Nashville: Abingdon, 2007.
———, ed. *Her Own Story: Autobiographical Portraits of Early Methodist Women*. Nashville: Abingdon, 2001.
———. *John Wesley and the Women Preachers of Early Methodism*. ATLAMS 25. Metuchen, NJ: Scarecrow, 1991.
Clarke, Adam, ed. *Memoirs of the Late Eminent Mrs. Mary Cooper, of London*. New York: Waugh & Mason, 1833.
Crosby, Sarah. Manuscript Letterbook, 1760–1774. Perkins Library, Duke University, Durham, NC.
Entwisle, Mary. Manuscript Diary. The Methodist Archives and Research Centre, John Rylands University Library of Manchester.
Fletcher, Mary. "Letters from Mrs. Fletcher to Mrs. Dalby." *WMM* 41 (1818): 687–90.
———. "Letter of Mary Fletcher to Elizabeth Collet." *AM* 2.8 (1823): 286–88.

---

21. Cited in Paul W. Chilcote, ed., *Her Own Story: Autobiographical Portraits of Early Methodist Women* (Nashville: Abingdon, 2001), 116. Her manuscript journal was transcribed by Thomas Shaw in 1961. This modernized excerpt of the text is based on the manuscript material collated with the Shaw transcription.

Harper, Steve. "Works of Piety as Spiritual Formation." Pages 87–97 in *The Wesleyan Tradition: A Paradigm for Renewal*. Edited by Paul W. Chilcote. Nashville: Abingdon, 2002.

Rogers, Hester Ann. *An Account of the Experience of Hester Ann Rogers*. New York: Hunt & Eaton, 1893.

Taft, Zechariah. *Original Letters Never before Published, on Doctrinal, Experimental, and Practical Religion*. Whitby: George Clark, 1821.

Wesley, John. *Sermons 1:1–33*. Vol. 1 of *The Works of John Wesley*. Edited by Albert C. Outler. Nashville: Abingdon, 1984.

Women and Biblical Criticism in Nineteenth-Century England

Marion Ann Taylor

The history of the development of biblical criticism in England has been rehearsed many times. John Rogerson discerns three phases of development of criticism in nineteenth-century England. In the first phase, 1800-1857, critical ideas and methods were known and were sometimes applied but more often refuted in England. During the second phase, 1858-1879, critical ideas and methods became much more widely known through a number of highly publicized and controversial works by scholars and church leaders. Then, during the third phase, 1880-1900, Rogerson suggests biblical criticism took hold in England in a form that was compatible with Evangelical and Catholic versions of progressive revelation.[1]

Scholars such as Rogerson have focused their histories of biblical criticism on the lives and publications of key academics and religious leaders. Missing from standard histories are the noncredentialed interpreters of Scripture, the *vox populi*, whose writings show how those who had neither official voice nor position in the academy or church received biblical criticism. This article examines the female responses to biblical criticism in England chronologically using Rogerson's three phases of development to divide the century. It shows that women's interpretations of the Bible

---

1. John Rogerson, *Old Testament Criticism in the Nineteenth Century: England and Germany* (London: SPCK, 1984); See also Hans-Joachim Kraus, *Geschichte der historisch-kritischen Erforschung des Alten Testaments* (Neukirchen-Vluyn: Neukirchener, 1988); Rudolf Smend, *Epochen der Bibelkritik*, vol. 3 of *Gesammelte Werke*, BET 109 (Munich: Kaiser, 1991); Marie-Theres Wacker, "Geschichtliche, Hermeneutische, und Methodologische Grundlagen," in *Feministische Exegese: Forschungserträge zur Bibel aus der Perspektive von Frauen*, ed. Luise Schottroff, Silvia Schroer, and Marie-Theres Wacker (Darmstadt: Wissenschaftliche Buchgesellschaft, 1995), 3-79.

reflect wider trends in biblical scholarship. It demonstrates that women played an important part in the move toward the triumph of criticism in England; women were consumers, critics, popularizers, and practitioners of biblical criticism. Further, it recovers a forgotten chapter in the history of the development of criticism in England.

1. Women Interpreters in "The Woman's Century" in England

The century that witnessed a paradigmatic shift toward the acceptance of biblical criticism in England also witnessed great changes in society's perceptions of the nature and role of women in the home and society.[2] Anne Mercier captured the sentiments of many living in the closing decades of the century when the leading character in her book declared, "This has been called the woman's century ... and it is certain that women are a great power, and are doing an immense amount of work, mostly good."[3] Women and men debated the "Woman Question" and deliberated about such fundamental issues as women's education and suffrage and such specific theological concerns as women's right to preach, to engage in theological reflection, to teach, and to interpret Scripture.[4]

The obstacles nineteenth-century women interpreters of the Bible faced were many. They had to battle cultural assumptions that women were by nature unfit for serious learning. The renowned author, Elizabeth Barrett Browning, for example, believed "there is a natural inferiority of mind in women ... [women have] minds of quicker movement, but less power and depth ... and that we are under your [men's] feet, because we can't stand upon our own."[5] Theology and biblical interpretation in

---

2. For a discussion of the world of women in the nineteenth century, women and biblical interpretation in the nineteenth century, and women's approaches to interpretation, see Marion Ann Taylor and Heather E. Weir, eds., *Let Her Speak for Herself: Nineteenth Century Women Writing on Women in Genesis* (Waco, TX: Baylor University Press, 2006), 2–17.

3. Anne Mercier, *The Story of Salvation: Thoughts on the Historic Study of Scripture* (London: Rivington, 1887), 10.

4. On the question of women and theology, see Julie Melnyk, ed., *Women's Theology in Nineteenth-Century Britain: Transfiguring the Faith of their Fathers*, GRLH 2055, LSVB 3 (New York: Garland, 1998).

5. Barrett to Browning, 4 July 1845, in *Letters of Robert Browning and Elizabeth Barrett* (New York: Harper & Brothers, 1899), 116–17 as cited in Joan N. Burstyn, *Victorian Education and the Ideal of Womanhood* (London: Croom Helm, 1980), 71.

particular were viewed as objectionable and "unladylike" intellectual activities for women. Those who did trespass into the world of erudition and scholarship often veiled their learning by writing for select audiences (the poor, the unlearned, women, or children) and claiming that their work was derivative. The renowned high churchman, John Keble, for example, thought his young protégé Charlotte Yonge revealed too much of her own expertise in Greek and theology in her book *Conversations on the Catechism* when she depicted ladies as being conversant with Greek.[6] Instead, rather tongue-in-cheek, he advised Yonge to mask her own learning and that of her female characters: "It occurred to me whether, when the ladies quote Greek, they had not better say they have heard their fathers and brothers say things."[7]

In spite of such obstacles, women in England produced hundreds of books on the Bible. Many adopted a topos of humility in their prefaces and minimized the importance of their own scholarship, claiming their work was a simplification or compilation of the work of male scholars or theologians. To add more credence to their work, they often included endorsements written by notable clergy or academics. For example, as a sign of her gratitude, Anglican clergy wife Mercier dedicated her book on the historical study of the Bible to "The Right Reverend Lord Bishop of Gloucester and Bristol," Charles Ellicott (1819–1905), claiming it did not pretend to be learning. Similarly, Julia Greswell's scholarly publication, *Grammatical Analysis of the Hebrew Psalter* began with two letters of endorsement from male scholars addressed to her father, the Rev. Richard Greswell, commending the use of the grammar by students preparing for divinity studies at Oxford.[8]

English women published books on the Bible for a wide variety of audiences, young and old, male and female, educated and uneducated. They interpreted the Bible using both the traditional genres of commentary,

---

6. Charlotte Yonge, *Conversations on the Catechism* (London: Mozley, 1859).

7. Elizabeth Jay, citing *Rev. John Keble's Musings Over the "Christian Year,"* 36, in "Charlotte Mary Yonge and Tractarian Aesthetics," *VP* 44 (2006): 51.

8. Julia Greswell, *Grammatical Analysis of the Hebrew Psalter* (Oxford: Parker, 1873). See J. Glen Taylor, "Miss Greswell Honed Our Hebrew at Oxford: Reflections on Joana J. Greswell and Her Book, *A Grammatical Analysis of the Hebrew Psalter* (1873)," in *Breaking Boundaries: Female Biblical Interpreters Who Challenged the Status Quo*, ed. Nancy Calvert-Koyzis and Heather E. Weir (Edinburgh: T&T Clark, 2010), 85–106.

sermon, catechism, and Bible storybooks, and nontraditional genres such as novels and letters.[9] Their books often went through multiple editions, and some were internationally published and translated. While most women's books on the Bible featured devotional, popular, and noncritical approaches, a surprising number of women's writings specifically engaged the methods and conclusions of biblical criticism.[10] Generally speaking, the authors of these books had ready access to scholarly and theological resources, came from middle- or upper-class families, and were well-educated—most having benefited from private education, including training in French, German, Greek, and/or Hebrew. Not surprisingly, their responses to biblical criticism were similar to those of men writing for similar audiences using similar resources.[11] Differences in interpretation arose, however, when women engaging criticism also used their distinctive experiences as daughters, wives, and mothers as an additional interpretive lens.[12]

2. Phase 1 (1800–1857): Ideas Known, Applied, and Refuted

During Rogerson's first phase of criticism in England, few scholars and theologians and still fewer popular writers directly engaged European critical scholarship. Women with direct access to scholars or to the published resources of the academy and church were aware of new developments;

---

9. For examples of the wide variety of genres used by women writing on the Bible see Taylor and Weir, *Let Her Speak for Herself*.

10. For examples of nineteenth-century women's "ordinary" interpretations of the Psalms see Marion Ann Taylor, "The Psalms outside the Pulpit: Applications of the Psalms by Women of the Nineteenth Century," in *Interpreting the Psalms for Teaching and Preaching*, eds. Herbert W. Bateman IV and D. Brent Sandy (Saint Louis: Chalice, 2010), 219–32.

11. See Linda Wilson's important comparative study of male and female spirituality: *Constrained by Zeal: Female Spirituality amongst Nonconformists, 1825–1875* (Carlisle: Paternoster, 2000).

12. Examples of nineteenth-century women's "ordinary" interpretations of Genesis that were shaped by their distinctive experiences as women are found in Taylor and Weir, *Let Her Speak for Herself*. See also Marion Ann Taylor, "'Cold Dead Hands upon Our Threshold': Josephine Butler's Reading of the Story of the Levite's Concubine, Judges 19–21," in *The Bible as a Human Witness to Divine Revelation: Hearing the Word of God through Historically Dissimilar Traditions*, ed. Randall Heskett and Brian P. Irwin, LHB/OTS 469, LBS (London: T&T Clark, 2010), 259–73.

they engaged some of the debated issues and incorporated new insights into their writing.

2.1. Sarah Trimmer (1741–1810)

The educational writer Sarah Trimmer is an example of a well-educated English woman who popularized contemporary British biblical scholarship. She read widely on the subject of education and Scripture and educated her twelve children. Trimmer's first educational book, *An Easy Introduction to the Knowledge of Nature and the Reading of the Holy Scriptures*, drew on her experience of teaching her own children.[13] Her experiences teaching Sunday school to poor children in the Brentford Sunday school prompted her to write for wider audiences than her peers and their children. The last of her more than thirty publications was a commentary on the entire Bible. In this opus, she "adapted" the "opinions of approved commentators" to the "common apprehensions" of the "unlearned who could not afford to buy expensive aids to interpreting the Bible."[14] She explained what she thought was difficult to understand and focused on passages that she thought were especially important "to produce a rational faith and right practice."[15] Occasionally she introduced readers to interpretive issues related to chronology or the meaning of the Hebrew or Greek original. In her commentary on Gen 20, for example, Trimmer introduces the idea that the incident with Abimelech may have happened at an earlier period in Abraham's life. In her comments on chapter 21, Trimmer notes that the Hebrew word translated as "laugh" in the Authorized Version (KJV) could also be translated as "rejoice." In this way, she redeemed Sarah by suggesting she rejoiced instead of laughed at the news that they would have a child.[16] Trimmer did not always follow the lead of experts. At times she avoided theological controversy by sidestepping passages, and in the

---

13. Sarah Trimmer, *An Easy Introduction to the Knowledge of Nature and the Reading of the Holy Scriptures* (London: Printed for the Author, 1780).

14. Sarah Trimmer, *A Help to the Unlearned in the Study of the Holy Scriptures: Being an Attempt to Explain the Bible in a Familiar Way* (London: Printed by T. Bensley, 1805). See Heather E. Weir, "Helping the Unlearned: Sarah Trimmer's Commentary on the Bible," in *Recovering Nineteenth-Century Women Interpreters of the Bible*, ed. Christiana de Groot and Marion Ann Taylor, SymS 38 (Atlanta: Society of Biblical Literature, 2007), 19–30.

15. Trimmer, *A Help to the Unlearned*, i.

16. Trimmer, *A Help to the Unlearned*, 25.

case of the Song of Songs, she failed to comment on the sexually explicit book, except to say that readers could glean its theological meaning from other biblical texts. Trimmer's approach to interpretation was consonant with the mainstream English biblical scholarship of the late eighteenth and early nineteenth century, which was just beginning to engage with biblical criticism. Trimmer popularized biblical scholarship, stressing the importance of the literal historical sense, adapting an organic view of history, and harmonizing the gospels.

2.2. Mary Cornwallis (1758–1836)

Mary Cornwallis engaged biblical scholarship more directly.[17] Cornwallis (née Harris) was well educated and knew French and Hebrew and likely Greek and Latin. In 1778 she married William Cornwallis, an Oxford fellow and Anglican priest who served the parish of Elham and Wittersham, Kent, for over fifty years. As part of her spiritual discipline, Mary Cornwallis studied Scripture assiduously. She made careful notes using the books found in the family's extensive library and buying any other books she needed. She used her study notes when teaching her children and later reworked them into a Scripture commentary for her grandson. His untimely death at age twelve inspired Cornwallis to publish her four-volume, two-thousand-page work, *Observations, Critical, Explanatory, and Practical, on the Canonical Scriptures*, as the means of endowing a free primary school in her husband's parish in memory of her grandson.

Cornwallis's opus resembles a standard multivolume commentary that addresses textual, interpretive, and practical issues. It references commentaries, sermons, and collections of essays on such subjects as travel, oriental customs, and theology. In her comments on the book of Daniel, for example, Cornwallis called attention to critical issues relating to the dating of the book, noting that "modern Jews deny Daniel to have been a prophet; and infidel Christians have asserted that his predictions, relative to the kings of Syria and Egypt, were written after the times of Antiochus Epiphanes, consequently after the events had taken place, which he affects

---

17. Mary Cornwallis, *Observations, Critical, Explanatory, and Practical, on the Canonical Scriptures*, 2nd ed., 4 vols. (London: Baldwin, Cradock & Joy, 1820). For a fuller treatment of Cornwallis's work as a biblical interpreter, see Taylor, "Mary Cornwallis: Voice of a Mother," in de Groot and Taylor, *Recovering Nineteenth-Century Women Interpreters of the Bible*, 31–44.

to foretell."[18] Cornwallis valued scholarship that shed light on the Bible's geography, history, and customs. Her commentary on Prov 31 shows that she was aware of differences between the culture of ancient Israel and that of England, that "necessarily produce diversity in the proper occupations of women, as well as in their duties," citing in a footnote Samuel Burder's comments on the spinning and embroidery practices of ancient women. At the same time, she read Prov 31 through her own cultural lens, proposing such lines of continuity between ancient and modern women as "fidelity, economy, active industry … careful education of children, and a constant concern for the temporal and eternal interests of all with whom she is connected, [that] will ever render a woman dear to her husband."[19] Like Trimmer, Cornwallis depended on the British scholarship of the late eighteenth and early nineteenth centuries. Both commentators were consumers of scholarship that reflected the influence of the new historiography and nascent critical ideas and methods. Cornwallis was a popularizer as well as a critic of rational criticism.

2.3. Fanny Corbaux (1812–1883)

During this early period in the development of critical scholarship in England, Marie Francoise Catherine (Fanny) Corbaux distinguished herself as a biblical scholar. History remembers her as a brilliant, self-taught artist and biblical scholar. Fascinated by biblical history and languages, she mastered Hebrew and Greek and entered into scholarly discussions about the early history of Israel. She lectured to the Syro-Egyptian Society on the subject of the identity of the Rephaim in early Israel, proposing that the Egyptian An, On, or Onnos be identified with the Chaldean Oannes. Part of this lecture was published as "The Rephaim, and Their Connection with Egyptian History," in the *Journal of Sacred Literature* in 1851. Corbaux also published a series of academic articles on the route the Israelites followed leaving Egypt.[20] Her scholarship was respected by those in the

---

18. Cornwallis, *Observations*, 3:358.
19. Cornwallis, *Observations*, 3:48–49. Samuel Burder, *Oriental Customs; or, An Illustration of the Sacred Scriptures, by an Explanatory Application of the Customs and Manners of the Eastern Nations, and Especially the Jews, Therein Alluded To* (London: Whittingham, 1802). This book was republished many times.
20. Fanny Corbaux, "On the Comparative Physical Geography of the Arabian Frontier of Egypt, at the Earliest Epoch of Egyptian History and at the Present Time,"

academy and is referenced in many academic books and articles.[21] She was an exceptional critical scholar during this early period of English engagement with criticism.

2.4. Mary Anne Evans (1819–1880) and Sophia Taylor (1817–ca. 1901–1911)

Mary Anne Evans, better known by her pseudonym, George Eliot, spent her early life in rural England where she received a good education and adopted evangelical piety.[22] At twenty-two, after reading a number of scholarly books, including Charles Christian Hennell's *Inquiry Concerning the Origin of Christianity*,[23] she revised her views about the faith and refused to attend church. Like Corbaux, Eliot associated herself with scholars directly involved with continental biblical criticism. Her translation of Strauss's groundbreaking work, *Life of Jesus*, helped to disseminate German higher criticism in Britain. Eliot also translated Feuerbach's *Essence of Christianity*.[24]

Sophia Taylor was another of the many woman involved in translating continental scholarly works, although little else is known about her. For almost forty years, Taylor translated the works of such German confessional scholars as Carl Friedrich Keil, Franz Delitzsch, and Gustav Oehler,

---

ENPJ 44 (1848): 13–42. See also Corbaux, "Geography of the Exodus," *Ath* (October 21, 1850): 1048, 1053–54; (March 23, 1850): 311–12; (April 27, 1850): 449–50; and Corbaux, "The Rephaim, and Their Connection with Egyptian History," *JSL* 2/1 (1851): 151–72.

21. Corbaux's identification of the Egyptian An, On, or Onnos with the Chaldean Oannes and the Philistine god Dagon spawned debate. Joseph Bonomi excerpted her article in his book, *Nineveh and Its Palaces: The Discoveries of Botta and Lanyard* (London: Bohn, 1857), 330. Quoting Bonomi, John Campbell wrote, "she has some ingenious speculations to prove that the Chaldean Oannes, the Philistine Dagon, and the Mizramite On are identical." See Campbell, "The Primitive History of the Ionians," *CJSLH* 14 (1875): 403.

22. Evans changed her name frequently. She was born Mary Anne Evans, dropped the "e" from Anne in 1837, became Marian Evans in 1851, Marian Evans Lewes in 1854, and Mary Ann Cross in 1880.

23. Charles Christian Henell, *An Inquiry Concerning the Origin of Christianity* (London: Smallfield, 1838).

24. David Friedrich Strauss, *The Life of Jesus*, trans. George Eliot, 3 vols. (London: Chapman, 1846); Ludwig Feuerbach, *The Essence of Christianity*, trans. Marian Evans, CQS 6 (London: Chapman, 1854).

who argued against the rationalism they believed stood behind German biblical criticism.[25] By translating primary works of higher criticism's proponents and critics, women like Eliot and Taylor played an important role in popularizing criticism in England.

3. Phase 2 (1858–1879): Critical Ideas and Methods Disseminated

While criticism quietly spread during Rogerson's first phase of development, it took on a much more public and controversial face during the second phase, when a number of prominent English scholars appropriated the methods and results of German criticism. *Essays and Reviews*, a collection of seven essays on religion—covering such topics as German biblical criticism, the evidences of Christianity, and the cosmology of Genesis—provoked great controversy over criticism and the naturalistic approach to Christianity assumed by the essayists.[26] It was followed by such influential publications as Bishop Colenso's seven-part work, *The Pentateuch and the Book of Joshua Critically Examined*, which called into question the historical credibility of large parts of the Old Testament, and Arthur P. Stanley's moderately critical work, *History of the Jewish Church*.[27] Such publications prompted responses in both popular and academic presses, enabling those outside of the academy to gain access to the world of biblical criticism.

3.1. Florence Nightingale (1820–1910)

Florence Nightingale spent much of her life surrounded by books, scholars, and church leaders involved in biblical criticism. Born into a wealthy family, she received the equivalent of a Cambridge education at home and travelled extensively. She felt called to a vocation of service in 1837, but

---

25. Taylor, for example translated Franz Delitzsch, *A New Commentary on Genesis*, trans. Sophia Taylor, 5th ed., CFTL 2/36–37 (Edinburgh: T&T Clark, 1888–1894); Carl Friedrich Keil, *Ezra, Nehemiah*, trans. Sophia Taylor, COT (Grand Rapids: Eerdmans, 1982); and Gustav Friedrich Oehler, *Theology of the Old Testament*, trans. Ellen D. Smith and Sophia Taylor, 2 vols., CFTL 4/48 (Edinburgh: T&T Clark, 1880).

26. Frederick Temple, Rowland Williams, Baden Powell, Henry Bristow Wilson, C. W. Goodwin, Mark Pattison, and Benjamin Jowett, *Essays and Reviews* (London: Parker, 1860).

27. John William Colenso, *The Pentateuch and the Book of Joshua Critically Examined*, 7 vols. (London: Longman, Green, 1862–1879); Arthur P. Stanley, *Lectures on the History of the Jewish Church*, 3 vols. (London: Murray, 1863–1876).

her family had other plans for her life. At thirty, her father gave her a small living allowance, and she became the superintendent of an Institute for the Care of Sick Gentlewomen in London. Her interests in health care continued, and in 1854 she led a group of volunteer nurses to the Crimea, where she worked tirelessly to improve hospital conditions and medical care. When she returned to England, she worked to reform many areas of public life. She also continued her study of classics, medieval mysticism, philosophy, theology, and the Bible. Her private study notes on Scripture, her correspondence, and her unpublished manuscripts reveal her profound engagement with nineteenth-century theology and biblical scholarship.

Nightingale's interests in Scripture and theology were wide-ranging and included the question of theodicy, universal salvation, and biblical interpretation. Her facility with languages gave her direct access to the publications of German critical scholars. Especially important were her friendships with such leading thinkers as Orientalist, Julius Mohl, German critical scholar and Egyptologist, Baron Christian von Bunsen, and Benjamin Jowett, Regius Professor of Greek at Oxford University, renowned for his essay, "On the Interpretation of Scripture," in *Essays and Reviews*.[28] Nightingale's annotated Bible attests to her knowledge of contemporary theories of the compositional history of biblical books. For example, her note on Gen 7:2 indicates that she used the criteria established by higher critics to distinguish sources: she designated Gen 7:2 as "Jehovistic because clean and unclean [animals] not known till Leviticus 11."[29] Nightingale was also familiar with the dating issues surrounding the book of Daniel. In her annotations, she commented on the second-century setting for parts of Daniel, stating, "it bears the marks of the time of Antiochus Epiphanes."[30]

Nightingale was not simply a consumer of criticism, however; she was herself a critic. Her collaborative work with Jowett and William Rogers on *The School and Children's Bible* shows her reputation as an informed reader of the Bible, her commitment to an organic view of history, and

---

28. For more on these relationships, see Lynn McDonald, ed., *Florence Nightingale's Spiritual Journey: Biblical Annotations, Sermons, and Journal Notes*, vol. 2 of *Collected Works of Florence Nightingale* (Waterloo, ON: Wilfred Laurier University Press, 2001), 34, 94.

29. McDonald, *Spiritual Journey*, 104.

30. McDonald, *Spiritual Journey*, 223.

her critical attitude toward the Scriptures themselves.[31] In this *Children's Bible*, she reordered the prophets chronologically, harmonized the Synoptic Gospels, and omitted stories that she felt were offensive.[32] In a letter to Jowett, Nightingale complained:

> The story of Achilles and his horses is far more fit for children than that of Balaam and his ass, which is only fit to be told to asses. The stories of Samson and of Jephthah are only fit to be told to bulldogs and the story of Bathsheba to be told to Bathshebas. Yet we give all these stories to children as "Holy Writ." There are some things in Homer we might better call "holy" writ, many in Sophocles and Aeschylus. The stories about Andromache and Antigone are worth all the women in the Old Testament put together, nay, almost all the women in the Bible.[33]

The School and Children's Bible was one of many children's Bibles that promoted criticism. As Barbara MacHaffie has argued, "the edited Bible for children and young people" was "the genre most favoured for teaching the generally accepted results of biblical scholarship."[34]

While Nightingale appropriated criticism into her reading of Scripture, she also recognized its limitations. In an unpublished essay, she questioned the value of the insights of critics like Strauss. She wondered if "any of the critics, with all that patient, daring and laborious investigation, brought us one shadow of a shade nearer ... to a true thodicy?"[35]

Nightingale also judged that criticism was having a negative effect on preaching. In a letter to Jowett, she comments on how sermons at Oxford had changed: "You never hear now a sermon on miracles, or on atonement or on everlasting damnation, deathbeds." Then she comments tongue-in-cheek, "(you don't take your disciples to the deathbed)" and asks "(Then what *are* they [the sermons] on?)" Nightingale then answers her own

---

31. William Rogers, *The School and Children's Bible* (London: Longmans, Green, 1873).

32. McDonald, *Spiritual Journey*, 35–36.

33. Lynn McDonald, ed., *Florence Nightingale's Theology: Essays, Letters, and Journal Notes*, vol. 3 of *Collected Works of Florence Nightingale* (Waterloo, ON: Wilfred Laurier University Press, 2002), 550.

34. Barbara MacHaffie, "Old Testament Criticism and the Education of Victorian Children" in *Scottish Christianity in the Modern World*, ed. Stewart J. Brown and George Newlands (Edinburgh: T&T Clark, 2000), 108.

35. An unpublished essay ADD MSS 4584 f281 cited in McDonald, *Spiritual Journey*, 35.

question, "Chiefly on reconciling science with religion or philosophy with religions, or on good works."[36]

Like most English biblical critics, Nightingale did not simply read the Bible "like any other book." Like her mentor Jowett, she recognized the many ways that the Bible was "not like any other book."[37] She wed faith and criticism. She not only sensed her divine call to servant ministry as she read about the suffering servant in Isaiah, but she also read Heinrich Ewald's critical commentary on the prophets to enrich her understanding of Isaiah. Nightingale's comments on Isa 49:3–4, for example, show how she read the prophetic text devotionally and also included a quotation from Ewald's *Die Propheten des Alten Bundes*: "5 November 1871: these seventeen years since the landing at Scutari. 'Allein mein Recht ist bei Jahve' ['yet my cause is with Yahweh']."[38] Nightingale stands as an example of a well-educated, privileged, and wealthy woman who lived much of her life close to the center of the intellectual debates around criticism. She embraced biblical criticism, popularized it through *The School and Children's Bible*, experienced criticism's limitations, and adopted a revisionist view of biblical inspiration.

3.2. Constance de Rothschild (1843–1931) and Annie Henrietta de Rothschild (1844–1926)

Baroness Constance de Rothschild and her sister, Baroness Annie Henrietta de Rothschild, were born into a wealthy Jewish family in London. They were educated at home by private tutors in mathematics, philosophy, English literature, French, Hebrew, and art. Their mother provided their religious instruction, which unusually included the New Testament. She also encouraged her daughters to visit and teach the poor. The sisters' two-volume work for teenagers, *The History and Literature of the Israelites*, grew out of their teaching experiences and their reading of contempo-

---

36. McDonald, *Spiritual Journey*, 360. Citing an exchange with Jowett on sermons, ADD MSS 45785 ff 90–91.

37. Reginald H. Fuller, "Historical Criticism and the Bible," in *Anglicanism and the Bible*, ed. Frederick H. Borsch, AngSS (Wilton, CT: Morehouse Barlow, 1984), 147.

38. "Und sagte zu mir, ‚mein Diener bist du,' Wohl dachte ich: ‚zum Eiteln hab' ich mich gemühet, vergeblich und nichtig meine Kraft verschwendet.'" McDonald notes that Nightingale is quoting Heinrich Ewald, *Die Propheten des Alten Bundes*, 2nd ed., 3 vols. (Stuttgart: Krabbe, 1867–1868), 3:76. In McDonald, *Spiritual Journey*, 201.

rary biblical scholarship.[39] In their retelling of the biblical narratives, the Rothschilds followed the biblical account closely, interpreting the texts in similar ways to their contemporaries.[40] In the second volume of their work, the sisters felt their readers were ready to be introduced to the idea of the dual authorship of Isaiah, an idea that was not widely accepted in England until the last decade of the nineteenth century.[41] They carefully set out the scholarly arguments for distinguishing a first and second Isaiah dated to the eighth and sixth centuries, respectively:

> There are indeed many similarities between the earlier and the later work.... They are both characterised by the same lofty patriotism, the same earnest desire to promote the moral and material well-being of the people, and the same unobtrusiveness of personal identity; they are, in fact, effusions of kindred minds; yet they cannot be the creations of the same author. The later prophet, whose name is unknown to us, proves his individuality by salient differences both in the subject and style of his orations.[42]

The Rothschilds were early proponents of the idea that the results of criticism should be taught to older children.[43] They popularized an approach to the study of the Old Testament as history that also embraced the results of biblical criticism. Their work gives witness to the spread of criticism among those outside of the academy.

3.3. Christina Rossetti (1830–1894)

Christina Rossetti, one of the most important nineteenth-century female poets in England, was born into a family of talented poets, artists, and critics. She was educated at home by her Italian mother, a devout evangelical

---

39. Constance de Rothschild and Annie Henrietta de Rothschild, *The History and Literature of the Israelites According to the Old Testament and the Apocrypha*, 2nd ed., 2 vols. (London: Longmans, Green, 1871).

40. See the discussion of the de Rothschilds' treatment of the Jacob story in Taylor and Weir, *Let Her Speak for Herself*, 369–76.

41. See Samuel R. Driver, *An Introduction to the Literature of the Old Testament*, ITL (New York: Scribner's Sons, 1891).

42. Rothschild and Rothschild, *The History and Literature of the Israelites*, 2:49.

43. See Barbara MacHaffie's excellent study of how Old Testament criticism was taught to Victorian children in MacHaffie, "Old Testament Criticism and the Education of Victorian Children," 91–118.

Anglican, and later, together with her mother and sister, became Anglo-Catholic. Best known for her poetry, Rossetti also published a number of devotional prose works, including two commentaries: *Letter and Spirit* is a commentary on the Ten Commandments and *The Face of the Deep* a commentary on the book of Revelation.[44] Rossetti's works of biblical interpretation offer an alternative theological and almost poetic approach to reading Scripture that is critical of contemporary "scientific and objective" critical approaches.

Rossetti was aware of contemporary developments in biblical studies. In fact, she used critical tools and scholarly resources in her own exegetical work (examples include archaeological finds, data on comparative ancient Near Eastern religions, and grammatical analysis).[45] Rossetti's published "Notes on Genesis and Exodus" attest to her grappling with commonplace questions.[46] Her commitment to the Bible's infallibility "in matters of piety and faith, but not to all aspects of history" meant that she was open to reconciling the findings of geologists, evolutionary biologists, and astronomers with the Bible and wrestling with difficult passages and apparent inconsistencies or contradictions.[47] Her "Notes on Genesis and Exodus," for example, show that she wondered about how to understand the "days" of creation: "Is it necessary, however, (suppose there be any truth in the vast-periods theory) to estimate the Seventh Day according to the same standard as the preceding Six?" She rationalized that the seventh day did not have to be interpreted in the same way, stating: "That Seventh alone fell within the cognizance of man and might therefore be subjected to his scale: 'The Sabbath was made for man, & not man for the Sabbath.'"[48]

Commenting on Exod 7:22, Rossetti asked where the Egyptian magicians found water for their enchantments, if all the water had been really changed into blood. She then reasoned: "Possibly any [water] stored in

---

44. Christina Rossetti, *Letter and Spirit: Notes on the Commandments* (London: SPCK, 1883); Rossetti, *The Face of the Deep: A Devotional Commentary on the Apocalypse* (London: SPCK, 1892).

45. Amanda W. Benckhuysen, "The Prophetic Voice of Christina Rossetti," in De Groot and Taylor, *Recovering Nineteenth-Century Women Interpreters of the Bible*, 173.

46. For a discussion of the possible dates of Rossetti's notes, see Diane D'Amico and David A. Kent, "Christina Rossetti's Notes on Genesis and Exodus," *JPRS* 13 (2004): 49–98.

47. See Benckhuysen, "Prophetic Voice," 167.

48. D'Amico and Kent, "Notes on Genesis and Exodus," 88.

vessels of *metal* (not named in v. 19) or equally of glass or earthenware, was exempt. Or possibly God's mercy spared the *springs* (not specified) so that when the Egyptians dug they found."[49] Comments like these that show Rossetti's inquiring mind are not found in her later prose writings on Scripture. Instead, she questions the value of asking questions that lead to answers that do not open up the spiritual, theological, or moral meaning of a text.

In her commentary on the Decalogue, *Letter and Spirit*, Rossetti questions the value of an approach to Scripture that focuses primarily or even exclusively on details that have nothing to do with the spiritual, theological, or moral meaning of the text:

> It is, I suppose, a genuine though not a glaring breach of the Second Commandment, when instead of learning the lesson plainly set down for us in Holy Writ we protrude mental feelers in all directions above, beneath, around it, grasping, clinging to every imaginable particular except the main point.
>
> Take the history of the Fall. The question of mortal sin shrinks into the background while we moot such points as the primitive status of the serpent: did he stand somehow upright? did he fly? what did he originally eat? how did he articulate?... At every turn such questions arise. What was the precise architecture of Noah's ark?... Clear up the astronomy of Joshua's miracle. Fix the botany of Jonah's gourd.... In the same vein we reach at last the conjecture which I have heard quoted: In which version was the Ethiopian Eunuch studying Isaiah's prophecy when Philip the Deacon met him? "By these, my son, be admonished: of making many books there is no end" [Eccl 7:12].[50]

Rossetti does not criticize the asking of questions; rather, she questions the value of the answers. She opines: "our light may be intellectual luminosity but spiritual darkness, how great darkness!"[51] Rossetti's approach to reading the text stands consciously apart from a highly rational historical approach that separated itself from Christian tradition and theological reflection. Instead Rossetti read Scripture theologically in continuity with precritical exegetes and contemporary Anglo-Catholic exegetes like Edward Pusey. However, Rossetti's faithful, theological reading of Scrip-

---

49. D'Amico and Kent, "Notes on Genesis and Exodus," 84.
50. Rossetti, *Letter and Spirit*, 85–87.
51. Rossetti, *Letter and Spirit*, 150.

ture was different than her male contemporaries; she challenged cultural norms, creating a space for a female voice to be heard.[52]

4. Phase 3 (1880–1900): The Triumph of Criticism

During the closing decades of the nineteenth century, higher criticism gained a more secure foothold in England as it was embraced by such respected Anglican clerics as Samuel R. Driver. In his 1901 publication, *Modern Criticism and the Preaching of the Old Testament*, Old Testament scholar George Adam Smith asserted: "Modern criticism has won its war against the traditional theories. It only remains to fix the amount of the indemnity."[53] Discussions about modern criticism and faith were commonplace in publications on the Bible during this period. Nigel M. de San Cameron writes:

> During the last decades of the nineteenth century, the presses deluged the reading public with literature *pro* and *con* "criticism." To the Critics, the failure of Conservative scholars to be moved by their literary and historical arguments was inexcusable, and could be explained only as obscurantism. To the Conservative, the Critical method and conclusions were so shot through with "rationalism" and so destructive of Biblical authority as to be patently out of harmony with the Christian faith.[54]

Women wrote a number of the books that "deluged" the presses. Given new educational and vocational opportunities during this period and the increased public awareness of biblical criticism, more women engaged biblical scholarship, and some did so in new ways.

4.1. Anne Mercier (1843–1917)

Mercier was married to Jerome Mercier, the Anglican rector of Kemerton, near Gloucester in England. She was teacher and author of more than twenty-five works, including the *Last Wolf: A Story of England in the*

---

52. Timothy Larsen, "Christina Rossetti, the Decalogue, and Biblical Interpretation," *JHMT* 16 (2009): 21–36; Benckhuysen, "The Prophetic Voice," 166, 176ff.
53. George Adam Smith, *Modern Criticism and the Preaching of the Old Testament* (London: Hodder & Stoughton, 1901), 72.
54. Nigel M. de San Cameron, *Biblical Higher Criticism and the Defense of Infallibilism in the Nineteenth Century Britain*, TSR 33 (Lewiston, NY: Mellen, 1987), 2.

Fourteenth Century and *Our Mother Church: Being Simple Talks on High Topics*, a very popular book for girls on English church history, doctrine, and ritual that went through many editions, as well as many works of religious fiction. Mercier's 1887 publication, *The Story of Salvation: Thoughts on the Historic Study of Scripture*, is one of the many books written for young readers during this period that set out to correct "the old ways" of teaching the Bible by introducing critical methods and ideas and a revised understanding of inspiration and revelation. Mercier presented her overview of the Bible as a series of conversations between an aunt and her two nieces. The aunt, a well-read Anglican named Mrs. Askell, introduced her nieces/readers to various Bible study methods and provided them with an overview of the entire Bible, including such resources as chronological charts, a harmonization of the gospels, an appendix on the versions of the Bible, and a list of reference books. The aunt engaged the work of scholars throughout. She popularized revisionist views about the Bible's inspiration, critical ideas about its compositional history, and alternative ways of determining its moral or spiritual meaning.

In her discussion of Genesis, Mercier's character Mrs. Askell introduced the idea of Genesis being a compilation from earlier documents, pointing out the evidence for "at least two writers of the book, one of whom they [Hebrew scholars] call the *Elohist*, the other the *Jehovist*, from the holy name used by each."[55] She even thought it important to mention it was a "French physician, named Astruc, court physician to Louis XIV" and not "a divine" that first called attention to the source-critical significance of the alteration of divine names in Genesis.[56] Mercier also introduced numerous examples of biblical anachronisms, suggesting, for example, that Gen 1 is not "a handbook of science" but is nevertheless true, "the facts being so ordered by God as to bear a higher spiritual meaning, which later ages should perceive."[57] Mercier's rationalist bent is also seen in Mrs. Askell's response to her niece's incredulity that "God should cause Saul to be plagued and tempted by an evil spirit":

> Yes, dear Joan; in the plain, literal sense it is quite incredible. But remember what I have said more than once. By inspiration God did not destroy the natural disposition of the sacred writers, nor take from them their

---

55. Mercier, *Story of Salvation*, 47.
56. Mercier, *Story of Salvation*, 47.
57. Mercier, *Story of Salvation*, 52–53.

> ordinary style of expression. The belief in evil spirits, in witches, and sorcery, was, and still is, strong in the East.... The fact, no doubt, was that the mental balance of Saul was always somewhat uncertain; he was subject to moods and sudden impulses. And when he once allowed jealousy to obtain possession of him, his moods became so weird that men fancied them the attacks of an evil spirit, instead of those of a wayward heart and uncertain mind.[58]

Mercier wanted her readers to be comfortable with the idea that the Bible was both a human and a divine book. She pointed out evidence for its humanity at every turn, noting, for example, the chronological problem in 1 Sam 17 where David appears "before Saul as a stranger … when it has been said in the sixteenth that David became Saul's armour-bearer, and Saul loved him (v. 21)." Mrs. Askell's reasoned suggestion was that the confusion originated with the editor, who was working with historical documents and transposed the chapters, "having taken chap. xvii exactly as it stood in a record of the time, and inserted it in his history."[59]

Although Mercier dedicated her book to a conservative scholar Ellicott, her position is not conservative. Like many believing English critics, she thought that modern criticism was a gift to the church. She defended German criticism, appreciating the details of its scholarship. To bolster her own position, Mercier gives an account of a conversation with "a venerable bishop" who, in admitting "the merits of modern German criticism," recounted: "I am old enough to remember the time when we were taught that the Bible tumbled straight down from heaven, bound in calf."[60] Mercier believed that modern criticism's assured results should be part of a Christian education curriculum. She held a view of inspiration that accommodated human error. She thought that the new approach to the Bible aided readers in understanding the Bible, especially as they struggled with issues related to chronology, morality, science, and history.

4.2. Mary (née Arnold) Ward (1851–1920)

Mary Ward was born to English parents in Tasmania and attended a series of boarding schools in Britain before her father, Thomas Arnold

---

58. Mercier, *Story of Salvation*, 128.
59. Mercier, *Story of Salvation*, 128–29.
60. Mercier, *Story of Salvation*, 38.

(1823–1900) took up a university teaching post at Oxford. In 1872, she married Humphry Ward, a fellow and tutor at Brasenose College Oxford, and she soon established herself as a best-selling novelist. Ward kept company with many leading intellectuals and was very interested in questions related to faith and the interpretation of the Bible.

A year after Mercier published her defense of the new approach to Scripture study, Ward published her best-selling novel that similarly argued for the legitimacy of biblical criticism and modern developments in theology.[61] In *Robert Elsmere*, Ward explored the colliding worlds of faith and doubt, reason and the supernatural, and traditional piety and critically informed faith. The novel's protagonist, Robert Elsmere, was a student of theology at Oxford who married a devout evangelical and became a priest. The reader follows Robert on his journey from belief to unbelief, a journey that causes him great personal, vocational, and marital anguish. Readers hear his haunting cry: "Oh God! My wife—my work!"[62] Ultimately, Robert adopts a rational and scientific-critical approach to the Scriptures and resigns his priestly vocation. As readers walk with Robert on his pilgrimage from faith to doubt, they encounter the philosophical underpinnings of higher criticism. They read detailed arguments about such issues as the nature of the resurrection and the second-century dating of the book of Daniel. Readers understand clearly criticism's appeal to the mind and challenge to the soul. Ward opened the side of criticism that was rarely discussed as she explored the effects of ideological change on individuals and families. Although the novel was not the traditional genre used for biblical interpretation, Ward found it a useful forum for discussing contemporary biblical scholarship and the spiritual, personal, and psychological implications of its changing paradigms. Through her best seller, Ward effectively disseminated critical ideas.

4.3. Julia Wedgwood (1833–1913)

Julia Wedgwood—a privileged, self-educated woman who lived life surrounded by intellectuals engaged in vigorous debates about science,

---

61. See Robert Lee Wolff, *Gains and Losses: Novels of Faith and Doubt in Victorian England* (New York: Garland, 1977), for a discussion of how the English novel provided an effective venue for women to explore issues related to higher criticism and theology.

62. Mary Augusta [Mrs. Humphry] Ward, *Robert Elsmere*, vol. 2 (London: Smith, Elder, 1888), 292–93.

history, and religion—was born in Langham Place, London. Wedgwood became a renowned conversationalist, debater, and author of both fiction and nonfiction. Her article featuring the theological significance of her cousin Charles Darwin's *Origin of Species* was appreciated by him. Like Mercier, Wedgwood thought that the old ways of interpreting the Bible needed to be overturned. In 1894, Wedgwood published *The Message of Israel in the Light of Modern Criticism*, which popularized the modern critical approach to the study of the Bible. Like Driver, who had published his *Introduction to the Literature of the Old Testament* three years earlier, Wedgwood presented a case for a reconstructed history of Israel based on the literary sources behind the text. She was particularly interested in reading the sources independently and determining their distinctive ideologies. As a feminist, Wedgwood called attention to how the various sources portrayed women. She contrasted the depiction of the creation of woman in the Priestly Code (P) in Gen 1 and in the earlier and more anthropomorphic "Jehovist source" (J) in Gen 2–3. She observed that in P, "Mankind is male and female from its first existence, the sexes are coeval," whereas in J, the creation of woman was "an afterthought."[63] Wedgwood argued further that these differences in the ideologies of women were rooted in different understandings of sex: "'Be fruitful, and multiply and replenish the earth,' says Elohim to the newly created pair. 'In sorrow shalt thou bring forth children,' says Jahveh to Eve."[64] Wedgwood also stressed the differences between the creation accounts, arguing that their purposes in writing were "totally heterogeneous" and "incomparable." The author of Gen 1 was "consciously starting a history of the world, and must lay some foundation for whatever is of importance in all subsequent history" whereas the writer of Gen 2–3 was only interested in the relationship of man with God.[65]

Wedgwood's commitment to the higher critical enterprise was unconditional. She popularized the work of English scholars like Driver, whose goal was to make German criticism palatable to English readers. Wedgwood is also an early example of a woman who used biblical criticism as a tool to promote feminist ideology.

---

63. Julia Wedgwood, *The Message of Israel in the Light of Modern Criticism* (London: Isbister, 1894), 261.
64. Wedgwood, *Message of Israel*, 261.
65. Wedgwood, *Message of Israel*, 262.

4.4. Mary (Petrie) Carus-Wilson (1861–1935)

Mary (Petrie) Carus-Wilson graduated from the University of London with a Bachelor of Arts degree, taught at a number of small colleges, and lectured and published on a variety of subjects, including the Bible. Carus-Wilson's book, *Clews to Holy Writ*, was designed as a textbook for a correspondence school for women called The College by Post. It set out a scheme for reading and studying the Scriptures "in the chronological order of the events it relates and the books it contains, so far as that can be ascertained."[66] It also introduced students to a modern, though theologically conservative, approach to Scripture study. Students learned about the questions raised by source critics, scientists, geologists, ethnologists, and historians about Genesis; they read about the controversy over whether Deuteronomy was written, not merely discovered, in the reign of Josiah; they had to grapple with the issue of the exilic dating of the so-called Second Isaiah. Although Carus-Wilson was more conservative theologically than Mercier, Ward, or Wedgwood, her attitude to new developments in scholarship was one of openness and caution. She advised: "We must avoid on the one hand rash assumption that traditional views are wrong; and on the other hand equally rash assumption that all traditional views can hold their own."[67]

Like Mercier, Carus-Wilson was interested in teaching students effective methods for Bible study and in addressing problems in interpretation that make Scripture inaccessible to readers. *Unseal the Book: Practical Words for Plain Readers of Holy Scripture* demonstrates Carus-Wilson's impressive knowledge of text criticism, exegesis, contemporary biblical scholarship, and hermeneutics. Her goal in writing the book was to "unseal" the Bible so that the average or "plain" reader knew how to read, understand, and then live out its message.[68] The seven seals that Carus-Wilson suggested made the Bible inaccessible to readers are related to problems with the text, translation, and arrangement, on the one hand,

---

66. Mary Carus-Wilson, *Clews to Holy Writ; or, The Chronological Scripture Cycle: A Scheme for Studying the Whole Bible in Its Historical Order during Three Years* (London: Hodder & Stoughton, 1893), ix.

67. Carus-Wilson, *Clews to Holy Writ*, 7.

68. Carus-Wilson, *Unseal the Book: Practical Words for Plain Readers of Holy Scripture* (London: Religious Tract Society, 1899), 3.

and with the reader, on the other.[69] She introduced her readers to text criticism and stressed the importance of using accurate translations.

Carus-Wilson was committed to reading the Bible as history. She was aware of the difficulties involved in reconstructing biblical history, noting an "examination of Scripture chronology proves that there is not a single event in Biblical history, not even the Nativity or the Crucifixion, with which an undisputed date of a given year can be associated."[70] She made the case for relative rather than absolute dates for events and texts. She saw development within Scripture history, citing Mark 10:5 and Heb 7:18–19 as examples of how later teaching transcends earlier teaching.[71] She was excited by the new possibilities that historical study of the Bible offered:

> There is a spurious reverence for the Bible, which shrinks from the plainest and most natural meaning of its narratives and thus misses in its history altogether the lessons for our lives with which even uninspired history, thoughtfully studied abounds. This reduces its matchless portraits of men and women, saints and sinners, heroes and caitiffs, men of God and worldlings, to church-window effigies in strained attitudes and impossible guise.... Historical study of the Bible has made it a new book of surpassing interest for many; and though it involves some trouble, there is no better example of the fact that when we have fairly breasted the Hill Difficulty, the House Beautiful lies before us.[72]

Carus-Wilson also commended specialized methods and tools for interpreting Scripture. She provided examples of how knowledge of geography, comparative literature, and archaeology shed light on misunderstood words or passages. For example, she drew on anecdotal information from a traveler to Palestine to unravel the puzzle of Absalom's adventure of being caught up by his long hair in the woods. She reasoned that "what actually happened, as a traveller through the Wood of Ephraim can perceive to-day, was that his head was caught in the low forked branches of the trees, a catastrophe which the rider there is warned against now."[73]

Like Mercier and Wedgwood, Carus-Wilson wrote to educate readers on the new ways of reading and interpreting the Bible. Although she

---

69. Carus-Wilson, *Unseal the Book*, 15.
70. Carus-Wilson, *Unseal the Book*, 80–81.
71. Carus-Wilson, *Unseal the Book*, 104.
72. Carus-Wilson, *Unseal the Book*, 86–88.
73. Carus-Wilson, *Unseal the Book*, 107.

would not have endorsed Wedgwood's full-blown reconstruction of the history of Israel, Carus-Wilson was an advocate of biblical criticism that was consonant with an evangelical version of progressive revelation. She cautiously embraced literary and textual criticism and fully endorsed an organic view of biblical history. She was very confident in the Bible and at the same time confident in scientific research, historicism, evolution, human development, and the human mind.

4.5. Elizabeth Rundle Charles (1828–1896)

Elizabeth Rundle Charles was born in Tavistock, Devonshire, England, the only child of John Rundle, a banker and Member of Parliament, and his wife Barbara Gill. Her parents valued education, the arts, and a Christian faith that expressed itself in love of God and love of all persons. While Charles was a member of the Church of England throughout her life, she experienced and embraced the breadth of the Christian tradition. She was an influential and successful author of over fifty volumes, which include novels, poetry, hymns, essays, a travel journal, scriptural reflections on various themes or biblical books, and teaching resources intended for use by those involved in the catechesis of children or adult converts. Charles spoke out as a learned voice of moderation and caution during this third phase of the triumph of criticism.[74]

Charles's approach to interpreting the Bible was multifaceted. Her experiences of traveling in the Holy Land enabled her to make the history and geography of the Bible live for her readers. Unlike many of her contemporaries, Charles believed that a historical approach to the study of Scripture was inadequate. Like Rossetti, she relativized the importance of such questions as: "Did Deuteronomy, or Job or Daniel belong to this century or that? Were those tender fiery words written by the first Isaiah or the second, or not by Isaiah at all?"[75] Instead, Charles focused on the divine author of Scripture and the Holy Spirit to transform "the husks of

---

74. For a fuller treatment of Charles as an interpreter of Scripture, see Marion Ann Taylor, "Elizabeth Rundle Charles: Translating the Letter of Scripture in Life," in De Groot and Taylor, *Recovering Nineteenth-Century Women Interpreters of the Bible*, 149–64.

75. Elizabeth Rundle Charles, *By the Coming of the Holy Ghost: Thoughts for Whitsuntide* (London: SPCK, 1889), 81.

antiquarianism into living history," the letter of Scripture into life.[76] For Charles the Bible was more than "a dead letter, or mere phonograph of stored-up past utterances, that dreadful mockery of a voice." The voice of the living God, "a living responsive voice," speaks through Scripture.[77] Like Rossetti, Charles was critical of an approach to the study of the Bible that did not recognize its spiritual nature. She recognized the Scriptures' depths and called readers to "come again and again to draw out His meaning, for the well is deep."[78]

At the same time, Charles was open to new ideas and found many of the insights of critical scholars helpful. In a discussion of the post-resurrection narratives, for example, Charles entered into the debate about the authorship of John 21. She maintained that whether John or his disciples wrote chapter 21 did not change its "beauty," since "it was from St. John's heart and from his telling, if not from his pen."[79] For Charles, the meaning of a text did not rest on the identity of a human author. Unlike most nineteenth-century interpreters, Charles refused to be drawn into schemes of harmonizing the gospels, a task she likened to "trying to make a perfect picture out of the fragments of an ancient mosaic of which some pieces are lost." She averred, "if we insist on joining the remaining pieces together without gaps, the pieces must be shattered, and the picture must lose its proportions and be distorted."[80] Instead Charles listened to the distinctive voice of each gospel.

Charles was open to new ideas that deepened her understanding of Scripture. She refused to be boxed into traditional interpretations or approaches to interpreting Scripture. She believed that Scripture was the voice of God, and she used all available knowledge for the interpretive task.

Charles's linguistic expertise allowed her to study the biblical texts in depth. In her exposition of the beatitudes, she provided readers with insights into the meaning of key words, often citing the Greek text. She presented readers with various interpretive options but also offered her own views. Commenting on the meaning of "Blessed are they that mourn" (Matt 5:4 KJV), Charles wrote:

---

76. Charles, *By the Coming of the Holy Ghost*, 81.
77. Charles, *By the Coming of the Holy Ghost*, 81.
78. Charles, *By Thy Glorious Resurrection and Ascension: Easter Thoughts* (London: SPCK, 1888), 81.
79. Charles, *By Thy Glorious Resurrection*, 103.
80. Charles, *Ecce Ancilla Domini, Mary the Mother of Our Lord: Studies in the Christian Ideal of Womanhood* (London: SPCK, 1894), 53.

Amongst all meanings, in a sense, before all others, this Beatitude may therefore well seem to belong to those who mourn for their own sins, negligences, ignorances, transgressions, short-comings, failures; sin intertwined with our best actions, dragging us back again and again from our highest purposes, dimming and marring our truest ideals, hindering our being what we would be, doing what we would do for those we love best. Whatever other mourning for the sorrow at the root of all sorrows cannot be excluded. And it is through *this* mourning that we most naturally approach the meaning of the Beatitude on those that mourn.[81]

Charles advocated a close reading of texts, an approach she likened to drinking deeply from the well. Thus, she concluded her study of the word "comforted" (Matt 5:4): "But when we drink deep enough into this quiet word we find it indeed all we want."[82]

As a writer, Charles was aware of the relationship between literary genre and hermeneutics. On occasion, she spoke candidly about the challenges of interpretation. She raised the issue of the literary genre of the story of the fall with the women in India for whom she wrote *Sketches of the Women of Christendom*. Anticipating their questions about interpretation, Charles asked if the story of the garden was "fact, or poem? parable, or history?" Her answer that it was both fact and poem, parable and history and "true, with the deepest truth," revealed that she understood that the literal/historical sense of a text did not always lead one to its "truest" sense. She advocated multivalent readings: "To get at truth in all histories we must read them also as parables and poems; that is, as a sacred story which does not merely gossip about the external facts, but penetrates to the divine and human meanings enfolded in these."[83] Charles believed that the sacred story of the creation of Eve had contemporary relevance for readers who, like Eve, struggled with temptation. Like many nineteenth-century female interpreters, Charles redeemed Eve. She reasoned that just as Eve looked at the forbidden tree and saw that "it was beautiful and seemed good," so we are all tempted by things "which seem, and probably are, beautiful and good in themselves, only not just *then* or not *for*

---

81. Charles, *The Beatitudes: Thoughts for All Saint's Day* (London: SPCK, 1889), 47, emphasis original.

82. Charles, *Beatitudes*, 49.

83. Charles, *Sketches of the Women of Christendom* (New York: Dodd, Mead, 1880), 5.

us [emphasis original]."[84] She argued that Eve sinned by not trusting God rather than by taking the fruit; whereas Adam fell deeper into sin than Eve when he accused her of offering him the fruit.[85] Charles highlighted Eve's role as the mother of all the living, suggesting that Adam and all the world would be delivered through her seed, Jesus.[86] In this way, Charles redeemed Eve from the burden of guilt the history of interpretation had placed upon her for the fall.

Like Rossetti, Charles was a complex reader of texts. She appropriated ideas set out by critics if she thought the ideas opened the Scripture in helpful ways. Unlike many who saw weaknesses in biblical criticism, she was not defensive about issues of authorship or historical accuracy. At the same time, she felt that a scientific, objective historical approach to the Bible was rather empty. She used all the traditional and contemporary tools that allowed her to fully probe the Scriptures and so transform the letter of Scripture into life.

4.6. Agnes Smith Lewis (1843–1926) and Margaret Dunlop Gibson (1843–1920)

During the closing decade of the nineteenth century, privately-educated, wealthy twin sisters in their fifties from Scotland, Agnes Smith Lewis and Margaret Dunlop [née Smith] Gibson, began their scholarly careers when they made the first of six journeys to Egypt and Palestine (1892, 1893, 1895, 1897, 1901, and 1906), where they discovered, photographed, copied, purchased, and later published important manuscripts related to the Bible and its reception history. Agnes Lewis's discovery of a second-century palimpsest of the Syriac Gospels in 1892 not only brought the sisters instant fame but also compelled them to acquire the scholarly knowledge necessary to become Oriental and paleographic scholars of international repute. The sisters' fluency in modern Greek and Arabic, ancient Hebrew, Syriac, and several Aramaic dialects, their extensive travel experience, their money, and their sense of vocation enabled them to travel and recover ancient manuscripts that might shed light on issues related to the dating and authenticity of the New Testament and the history of the transmission of biblical and extrabiblical texts. Of the many impressive discoveries of

---

84. Charles, *Sketches of the Women of Christendom*, 9.
85. Charles, *Sketches of the Women of Christendom*, 10.
86. Charles, *Sketches of the Women of Christendom*, 13.

the sisters was a fragment in Hebrew of Jesus Ben Sira (Ecclesiasticus), from the Cairo *genizah* in 1896. This second-century BCE text had until then only been known in Greek. For their very impressive work as Arabic and Syriac scholars, Lewis and Gibson received honorary doctorates from Saint Andrews (honorary DD, 1901), Heidelberg (honorary DD, 1904), and Dublin (LittD, 1911) and the triennial gold medal of the Royal Asiatic Society in 1915.[87] Lewis also received an honorary doctorate from Halle an der Saale (PhD, 1899). The scholarly community in Cambridge, where the sisters resided, did not formally recognize their scholarship, prompting the columnist of the women's column of the Cambridge Independent to ask:

> Is there anything in the Statues of our University to prevent Mrs Lewis and Mrs Gibson from having Honorary Degrees conferred upon them? These highly prized titles are reserved for distinguished persons who have contributed to the sum of human knowledge to a conspicuous extent. Many men who have received them are far less distinguished than these ladies.... It is not a question of sex but of scholarship, and many men as well as many women here are loudly pleading for Honour to whom Honour is due.[88]

Although the "question of sex" was an issue for some scholars at Cambridge, such renowned scholars as William Robertson Smith, James Rendel Harris, Robert Kennett, and Solomon Schechter supported the endeavors of the sisters.

Lewis and Gibson entered into the male world of scholarship as mature women. Their work stood in the Cambridge tradition of J. B. Lightfoot, one of the most influential biblical scholars of the nineteenth century, who had written in 1855, that "the timidity, which shrinks from the application of modern science or criticism to the interpretation of the Holy Scriptures evinces a very unworthy view of its character.... From the full light of science and criticism we have nothing to fear."[89] Unlike the many well-educated, privileged women of the nineteenth century who consumed,

---

87. Christa Müller-Kessler, "Lewis, Agnes Smith (1843–1926)," *ODNB* 33:579–80; Müller-Kessler, "Gibson, Margaret Dunlop (1843–1920)," *ODNB* 22:89–91.

88. "Pertilote" in the *Cambridge Independent*, April 1897, as cited in Janet Soskice, *Sisters of Sinai: How Two Lady Adventurers Found the Hidden Gospels* (London: Chatto & Windus, 2009), 261.

89. Soskice, *Sisters of Sinai*, 322 n. 10.

popularized, and criticized biblical criticism, Lewis and Gibson were themselves scholars whose textual work advanced the efforts of biblical scholarship in the nineteenth and twentieth centuries.

5. Women Internationally Acclaimed as Veritable Biblical Scholars

Listening to the voices of women who interacted with biblical criticism in nineteenth-century England opens a new chapter in the history of the reception and popularization of criticism. It shows that biblical criticism was not simply the preserve of scholars and clerics: it had a considerable impact on the lives of many outside the academy. It demonstrates that privileged, well-educated women were more involved in higher criticism in the nineteenth century than has been previously recognized. Women were consumers, popularizers, practitioners, and critics of criticism. Their engagement with criticism follows the broad lines of the development sketched out by Rogerson. In the early phase of the development of scholarship, women interacted with and then popularized the ideas of contemporary scholarship, as Cornwallis prepared her commentary on Scripture and women such as Corbaux engaged even more directly with biblical criticism and the academy. As the debates over criticism became more public and as English scholars and theologians increasingly appropriated critical methods and ideas into their own work during the second phase of the development of criticism, more women engaged with criticism as consumers, popularizers, practitioners, and critics. Then, during the final decades of the century, women became even more involved in the movement aimed at popularizing the methods and results of biblical criticism. Women were important voices calling for change in how the Bible had traditionally been interpreted. Even theologically conservative women such as Charles, Carus-Wilson, Lewis, and Gibson cautiously adapted some critical insights and used some critical tools in their own interpretive work. As the century progressed, the obstacles women interpreters faced began to break down, and Lewis and Gibson were acclaimed internationally as veritable biblical scholars. Biblical criticism enabled women to be critical of traditional, dogmatic, theological, or even literal readings of Scripture that affected how they viewed themselves in relation to the world or that they found to be irrational, problematic, or antiquated. Critical methods also gave women such as Wedgwood new freedom to read the texts in fresh ways as women. As early feminists became more adept practitioners of criticism, they began to see how biblical criticism could be helpful in confronting issues of patriarchy in the biblical texts and in society in general. Finally, women's voices were also important voices of resistance and caution in the movement aimed at popularizing the methods and results of criticism in England. As honored purveyors of the faith, some women regarded the philosophical underpinnings of biblical criticism as a threat to the faith they embraced. Some women questioned its value. Rossetti and Charles in particular felt that critical methods failed to open up the meaning of the biblical texts for the edification of the community of faith. In their writings, they offered what they thought were viable alternatives that would bring spiritual life and hope to their readers. History suggests that some of their misgivings regarding the ability of criticism to open the meaning of the Scriptures for the church were well founded.

Bibliography

Benckhuysen, Amanda W. "The Prophetic Voice of Christina Rossetti." Pages 165–80 in *Recovering Nineteenth-Century Women Interpreters of the Bible*. Edited by Christiana de Groot and Marion Ann Taylor. SymS 38. Atlanta: Society of Biblical Literature, 2007.

Bonomi, Joseph. *Nineveh and Its Palaces: The Discoveries of Botta and Lanyard*. London: Bohn, 1857.

Burder, Samuel. *Oriental Customs; or, An Illustration of the Sacred Scriptures, by an Explanatory Application of the Customs and Manners of the Eastern Nations, and Especially the Jews, Therein Alluded To*. London: Whittingham, 1802.

Burstyn, Joan N. *Victorian Education and the Ideal of Womanhood*. London: Croom Helm, 1980.

Campbell, John. "The Primitive History of the Ionians." *CJSLH* 14 (1875): 395–431, 559–79.

Carus-Wilson, Mary. *Clews to Holy Writ; or, The Chronological Scripture Cycle: A Scheme for Studying the Whole Bible in Its Historical Order during Three Years*. London: Hodder & Stoughton, 1893.

———. *Unseal the Book: Practical Words for Plain Readers of Holy Scripture*. London: Religious Tract Society, 1899.

Charles, Elizabeth Rundle. *By the Coming of the Holy Ghost: Thoughts for Whitsuntide*. London: SPCK, 1889.

———. *By Thy Glorious Resurrection and Ascension: Easter Thoughts*. London: SPCK, 1888.

———. *Ecce Ancilla Domini, Mary the Mother of Our Lord: Studies in the Christian Ideal of Womanhood*. London: SPCK, 1894.

———. *Sketches of the Women of Christendom*. New York: Dodd, Mead, 1880.

———. *The Beatitudes: Thoughts for All Saint's Day*. London: SPCK, 1889.

Colenso, John William. *The Pentateuch and Book of Joshua Critically Examined*. 7 vols. London: Longman, Green, 1862–1879.

Corbaux, Fanny. "Geography of the Exodus." *Ath* (October 21, 1850): 1048, 1053–54; (March 23, 1850): 311–12; (April 27, 1850): 449–50.

———. "On the Comparative Physical Geography of the Arabian Frontier of Egypt, at the Earliest Epoch of Egyptian History and at the Present Time." *ENPJ* 44 (1848): 13–42.

———. "The Rephaim, and Their Connection with Egyptian History." *JSL* 2/1 (1851): 151–72.

Cornwallis, Mary. *Observations, Critical, Explanatory, and Practical, on the Canonical Scriptures*. 2nd ed. 4 vols. London: Baldwin, Cradock & Joy, 1820.

D'Amico, Diane, and David A. Kent. "Christina Rossetti's Notes on Genesis and Exodus." *JPRS* 13 (2004): 49–98.

Delitzsch, Franz. *A New Commentary on Genesis*. Translated by Sophia Taylor. 5th ed. CFTL 2/36–37. Edinburgh: T&T Clark, 1888–1894.

Driver, Samuel R. *An Introduction to the Literature of the Old Testament*. ITL. New York: Scribner's Sons, 1891.

Ewald, Heinrich. *Die Propheten des Alten Bundes*. 2nd ed. 3 vols. Stuttgart: Krabbe, 1867–1868.

Feuerbach, Ludwig. *The Essence of Christianity*. Translated by Marian Evans. CQS 6. London: Chapman, 1854.

Fuller, Reginald H. "Historical Criticism and the Bible." Pages 143–68 in *Anglicanism and the Bible*. Edited by Frederick H. Borsch. AngSS. Wilton, CT: Morehouse Barlow, 1984.

Greswell, Julia. *Grammatical Analysis of the Hebrew Psalter*. Oxford: Parker, 1873.

Henell, Charles Christian. *An Inquiry Concerning the Origin of Christianity*. London: Smallfield, 1838.

Jay, Elizabeth. "Charlotte Mary Yonge and Tractarian Aesthetics." *VP* 44 (2006): 43–59.

Keil, Carl Friedrich. *Ezra, Nehemiah*. Translated by Sophia Taylor. COT. Grand Rapids: Eerdmans, 1982.

Kraus, Hans-Joachim. *Geschichte der historisch-kritischen Erforschung des Alten Testaments*. Neukirchen-Vluyn: Neukirchener, 1988.

Larsen, Timothy. "Christina Rossetti, the Decalogue, and Biblical Interpretation." *JHMT* 16 (2009): 21–36.

MacHaffie, Barbara J. "Old Testament Criticism and the Education of Victorian Children." Pages 91–118 in *Scottish Christianity in the Modern World*. Edited by Stewart J. Brown and George Newlands. Edinburgh: T&T Clark, 2000.

McDonald, Lynn, ed. *Florence Nightingale's Spiritual Journey: Biblical Annotations, Sermons, and Journal Notes*. Vol. 2 of *Collected Works of Florence Nightingale*. Waterloo, ON: Wilfred Laurier University Press, 2001.

———, ed. *Florence Nightingale's Theology: Essays, Letters, and Journal Notes*. Vol. 3 of *Collected Works of Florence Nightingale*. Waterloo, ON: Wilfred Laurier University Press, 2002.

Melnyk, Julie, ed. *Women's Theology in Nineteenth-Century Britain: Transfiguring the Faith of Their Fathers*. GRLH 2055. LSVB 3. New York: Garland, 1998.

Mercier, Anne. *The Story of Salvation: Thoughts on the Historic Study of Scripture*. London: Rivington, 1887.

Müller-Kessler, Christa. "Gibson, Margaret Dunlop (1843–1920)." *ODNB* 22 (2004): 89–91.

———. "Lewis, Agnes Smith (1843–1926)." *ODNB* 22 (2004): 579–80.

Oehler, Gustav Friedrich. *Theology of the Old Testament*. Translated by Ellen D. Smith and Sophia Taylor. 2 vols. CFTL 4/48. Edinburgh: T&T Clark, 1880.

Rogers, William. *The School and Children's Bible*. London: Longmans, Green, 1873.

Rogerson, John. *Old Testament Criticism in the Nineteenth Century: England and Germany*. London: SPCK, 1984.

Rossetti, Christina. *The Face of the Deep: A Devotional Commentary on the Apocalypse*. London: SPCK, 1892.

———. *Letter and Spirit: Notes on the Commandments*. London: SPCK, 1883.

Rothschild, Constance de, and Annie Henrietta de Rothschild. *The History and Literature of the Israelites According to the Old Testament and the Apocrypha*. 2 vols. London: Longmans, Green, 1871.

San Cameron, Nigel M. de. *Biblical Higher Criticism and the Defense of Infallibilism in Nineteenth Century Britain*. TSR 33. Lewiston, NY: Mellen, 1987.

Smend, Rudolf. *Epochen der Bibelkritik*. Vol. 3 of *Gesammelte Werke*. BET 109. Munich: Kaiser, 1991.

Smith, George Adam. *Modern Criticism and the Preaching of the Old Testament*. London: Hodder & Stoughton, 1901.

Soskice, Janet. *Sisters of Sinai: How Two Lady Adventurers Found the Hidden Gospels*. London: Chatto & Windus, 2009.

Stanley, Arthur P. *Lectures on the History of the Jewish Church*. 3 vols. London: Murray, 1863–1876.

Strauss, David Friedrich. *The Life of Jesus*. Translated by George Eliot. 3 vols. London: Chapman, 1846.

Taylor, Marion Ann. "'Cold Dead Hands upon Our Threshold': Josephine Butler's Reading of the Story of the Levite's Concubine, Judges 19–21." Pages 259–73 in *The Bible as a Human Witness to Divine Revelation: Hearing the Word of God through Historically Dissimilar Traditions*. Edited by Randall Heskett and Brian Irwin. LHB/OTS 469. LBS. London: T&T Clark, 2010.

———. "Elizabeth Rundle Charles: Translating the Letter of Scripture into Life." Pages 149–64 in *Recovering Nineteenth-Century Women Interpreters of the Bible*. Edited by Christiana de Groot and Marion Ann Taylor. SymS 38. Atlanta: Society of Biblical Literature, 2007.

———. "Mary Cornwallis: Voice of a Mother." Pages 31–44 in *Recovering Nineteenth-Century Women Interpreters of the Bible*. Edited by Christiana de Groot and Marion Ann Taylor. SymS 38. Atlanta: Society of Biblical Literature, 2007.

———. "The Psalms outside the Pulpit: Applications of the Psalms by Women of the Nineteenth Century." Pages 219–32 in *Interpreting the Psalms for Teaching and Preaching*. Edited by Herbert W. Bateman IV and D. Brent Sandy. Saint Louis: Chalice, 2010.

Taylor, J. Glen. "Miss Greswell Honed Our Hebrew at Oxford: Reflections on Joana J. Greswell and Her Book, *A Grammatical Analysis of the Hebrew Psalter* (1873)." Pages 85–106 in *Breaking Boundaries: Female Biblical Interpreters Who Challenged the Status Quo*. Edited by Nancy Calvert-Koyzis and Heather E. Weir. Edinburgh: T&T Clark, 2010.

Taylor, Marion Ann, and Heather E. Weir, eds. *Let Her Speak for Herself: Nineteenth-Century Women Writing on Women in Genesis*. Waco, TX: Baylor University Press, 2006.

Temple, Frederick, Rowland Williams, Baden Powell, Henry Bristow Wilson, C. W. Goodwin, Mark Pattison, and Benjamin Jowett. *Essays and Reviews*. London: Parker, 1860.

Trimmer, Sarah. *An Easy Introduction to the Knowledge of Nature and the Reading of the Holy Scriptures.* London: Printed for the Author, 1780.

———. *A Help to the Unlearned in the Study of the Holy Scriptures: Being an Attempt to Explain the Bible in a Familiar Way.* London: Printed by T. Bensley, 1805.

Wacker, Marie-Theres. "Geschichtliche, Hermeneutische, und Methodologische Grundlagen." Pages 3–79 in *Feministische Exegese: Forschungserträge zur Bibel aus der Perspektive von Frauen.* Edited by Luise Schottroff, Silvia Schroer, and Marie-Theres Wacker. Darmstadt: Wissenschaftliche Buchgesellschaft, 1995.

Ward, Mary Augusta [Mrs. Humphry]. *Robert Elsmere.* Vol. 2. London: Smith, Elder, 1888.

Wedgwood, Julia. *The Message of Israel in the Light of Modern Criticism.* London: Isbister, 1894.

Weir, Heather E. "Helping the Unlearned: Sarah Trimmer's Commentary on the Bible." Pages 19–30 in *Recovering Nineteenth-Century Women Interpreters of the Bible.* Edited by Christiana de Groot and Marion Ann Taylor. SymS 38. Atlanta: Society of Biblical Literature, 2007.

Wilson, Linda. *Constrained by Zeal: Female Spirituality amongst Nonconformists, 1825–1875.* Carlisle: Paternoster, 2000.

Wolff, Robert Lee. *Gains and Losses: Novels of Faith and Doubt in Victorian England.* New York: Garland, 1977.

Yonge, Charlotte. *Conversations on the Catechism.* London: Mozley, 1859.

Deborah:
A Lightning Rod for Nineteenth-Century Women's Issues

Christiana de Groot

1. Introduction

The nineteenth century witnessed many changes in the status and role of women in the United States and England. Laws changed the rights of women within marriage, for example, allowing them to keep some of their income and property. Divorce laws expanded the grounds for divorce, laws regulating prostitution were contested and finally struck down in England, and toward the end of the century, women were admitted to some universities. Although the right of women to vote was not granted in the nineteenth century, the suffragette movement continued to gain momentum. In many and diverse ways, women were gaining more rights, and the restrictions on them were being loosened.[1]

These changes in society occurred in tandem with many essays, plays, poems, commentaries, and devotional literature which addressed what Christianity, Judaism, and the Bible taught about women's rightful place in the home, place of worship, and public sphere. As will be evident in this study of six women's writings, women held a variety of opinions and based those opinions on their interpretations of Scripture. Because the narrative of Deborah in Judges portrays her as a prophet, a judge who heard cases, a military leader who led Israel into battle, and a poet who composed a victory song, it was a *locus classicus* for discussions on the relationship

---

1. See the introductory essay by Christiana de Groot and Marion Ann Taylor, "Recovering Women's Voices in the History of Biblical Interpretation," in *Recovering Nineteenth-Century Women Interpreters of the Bible*, ed. Christiana de Groot and Marion Ann Taylor, SymS 38 (Atlanta: Society of Biblical Literature, 2007), 3–7 for an in-depth discussion of the social context for women in the English-speaking world.

between women and men and the rightful sphere of women's activity. Since Judg 4 and 5 functioned as a lightning rod, women's interpretations of these chapters will be the focus of this essay.

Out of many nineteenth-century women who wrote on Deborah,[2] this essay will explore writings by Elizabeth Baxter (1837-1926), Clara Lucas Balfour (1808-1878), Grace Aguilar (1816-1847), Harriet Beecher Stowe (1811-1896), Julia McNair Wright (1840-1903), and Clara Neyman (1840-1931) because they represent six different, substantial responses to the issues raised in the narrative, especially "the Woman Question." Their writings will be presented according to the positions they advocated, rather than in chronological order. As will become evident, it is not possible to assume that women writers throughout the century were advocating for more and more opportunities for women. Baxter, the most traditional of the six, published the second edition of *The Women in the Word* in 1897.[3] Balfour, somewhat less traditional, published *The Women of Scripture* in 1847.[4] Aguilar, who holds the middle position in the spectrum, published *The Women of Israel* in 1845, and Stowe, who also straddles the middle, published *Woman in Sacred History* in 1873.[5] On the more progressive side is Wright's *Saints and Sinners* in 1873.[6] Neyman, the most progressive,

---

2. Some of the lengthier essays that will not be examined here include Sarah Hale, "Deborah," in *Woman's Record; or, Sketches of all Distinguished Women from Creation to 1854*, WR 89 (New York: Harper & Brothers, 1855), 34-36; Sarah Towne Martyn, "Deborah: The Wife of Lapidoth," in *Women of the Bible* (New York: American Tract Society, 1868), 29-38; Lady Morgan, "Women of the Hebrews under the Judges: Deborah," in *Women and Her Master* (Philadelphia: Carey & Hart, 1840), 1:66-73; Leigh Norval, "Women in the Book of Judges," in *Women of the Bible: Sketches of All the Prominent Female Characters in the Old and the New Testament* (Nashville: M. E. Church, South, 1899), 83-90; and Elizabeth Cady Stanton, "The Book of Judges," in *Comments on the Old and New Testaments from Joshua to Revelation*, part 2 of *The Woman's Bible*, ed. Elizabeth Cady Stanton (New York: European, 1898), 18-20.

3. Elizabeth Baxter, *The Women in the Word*, 2nd ed. (London: Christian Herald, 1897), 72-82.

4. Clara Lucas Balfour, *The Women of Scripture* (London: Houlston & Stoneman, 1847), 88-104.

5. Grace Aguilar, *The Women of Israel; or, Characters and Sketches from the Holy Scripture and Jewish History* (London: Groombridge & Sons, 1845), 202-11; Harriet Beecher Stowe, *Woman in Sacred History: A Series of Sketches*, WCA 41 (New York: Ford, 1873), 99-106.

6. Julia McNair Wright, *Saints and Sinners of the Bible* (Philadelphia: Ziegler & McCurdy, 1873), 189-99.

was a contributor to the second volume of *The Woman's Bible*, published in 1898.[7]

Nor was either side of the Atlantic more traditional or progressive on the Woman Question. Within England and the United States, the full spectrum of positions was promoted. This survey includes three interpreters from England: Aguilar, Balfour, and Baxter; and three from the United States: Stowe, Wright, and Neyman. In addition, the women included in this essay are representative of various faith traditions that engaged the discussion. Four write out of their Christian convictions, Aguilar writes as a Jew, and Neyman writes as a Freethinker.

What were the issues that this diverse group of women responded to in their interpretation of Scripture? Briefly, they include whether women and men were essentially the same or different, and whether women and men were to be treated as equals, or if men were to be superior and women subordinate. Overlapping those issues was the discussion concerning what masculinity and femininity entails and what rightful roles men and women should play in public and private life. Typically, the nineteenth century held that women were to remain in the private sphere and concern themselves with domestic tasks. They were to nurture their family and were idealized as the "angel of the home." Men were to compete in the public sphere, a place where they earned income to provide for their dependent family members. To equip them for these tasks, men required a rigorous education in science, math, and theology, while women learned the domestic arts of embroidery, music, and drawing. According to this ideal, men were dominant and women subordinate in both the public and private realms. Scientific evidence was also part of the debate, as phrenology and evolutionary theory were cited to support a traditional division of labor. Men were to produce and women to reproduce. Finally, the nineteenth century debated whether Christianity and the Bible had benefitted women. Some women claimed that Christianity enhanced the position of women and hence advocated for foreign missions and the conversion of Jews, and some concluded that Christianity was an obstacle to women's liberation and advocated an exodus from the faith and its oppressive practices.[8]

---

7. Clara Neyman, "Judges," in Stanton, *Joshua to Revelation*, 21–23.

8. Volume 2 of Stanton, *Woman's Bible Commentary*, included an appendix, 185–214, in which responses to two questions posed by the editors were published. The questions were: Have the teachings of the Bible advanced or retarded the emancipa-

The narrative of Deborah in Judg 4 and 5 required the nineteenth-century interpreter to evaluate her actions. Writers considered whether Deborah should be a model of what women are capable of or an exception who should not be emulated. They investigated whether she and Barak related to each other as partners and whether they were properly "masculine" and "feminine" in their endeavors. Further, they wondered what kind of education Deborah's leadership required and whether women in the nineteenth century should be likewise educated. Our six interpreters will answer the questions raised by this narrative in quite different ways, and each will find support for her position in these two chapters in Judges.

2. Elizabeth Baxter (1837–1926)

Baxter was a member of the Anglican Church and very involved in the evangelical wing of Protestantism. For a time, she and her husband were itinerant preachers with Dwight Moody, an American evangelist who led a revival movement in England. She initiated a variety of ministries and was involved in a world mission tour in 1894. She published over forty books in her life, as well as booklets, tracts, and Sunday school material.[9] *The Women in the Word*, published in 1897, focused on the women in Scripture, using their lives to instruct women on how to live Christian lives. The chapter on Deborah is one of many, including Eve, Miriam, and Hannah.

Baxter immediately tips her hand about her assessment of Deborah. Her essay begins: "It is not the usual order of God to put woman in the place of authority: 'Adam was first formed, then Eve.' (I Tim. ii.13). Deborah was an exception."[10] It was because the Israelites were so sinful that the usual hierarchy between men and women was overturned. The effective leadership of Deborah in the political realm does not indicate that women

---

tion of women? Have they dignified or degraded the Mothers of the Race? The twenty responses by women from both sides of the Atlantic are very diverse.

9. See the brief biographical sketch in Marion Ann Taylor and Heather E. Weir, eds., *Let Her Speak for Herself: Nineteenth-Century Women Writing on Women in Genesis* (Waco, TX: Baylor University Press, 2006), 98–100. Nathaniel Wiseman's biography, *Elizabeth Baxter (Wife of Michael Paget Baxter): Saint, Evangelist, Preacher, Teacher and Expositor* (London: Christian Herald, 1928) includes lengthy excerpts from her journals and letters.

10. Baxter, *Women in the Word*, 72.

should seek to be equal partners with men. Rather, as Baxter states later in the essay:

> When it so happens that, in politics, in the affairs of nations, in Church matters, and in Christian work, women are found to dare things which men are not courageous enough to undertake, it is not intended to institute a new order of things, but rather to provoke men to jealousy, that they may take the first place, which God had given them.[11]

As the reader might anticipate, Baxter is critical of Barak's dependence on Deborah. She writes:

> A true man of God is not dependent upon any man; and when Barak refused to go except Deborah go with him, there was an evident want of manliness in his character, which gives one easily to understand why a woman should have been used in such an exceptional way to be over him in Israel.[12]

Baxter's conclusions indicate that men are to be autonomous and superior, while women are to be dependent and inferior. Their essential differences should play out in the hierarchy of roles in the public realm. The relationship between Deborah and Barak reversed the ideal of patriarchy.

Not only was Barak unmanly, but Deborah was unfeminine. Baxter notes how the events leading up to the war with Sisera are described in the Song of Deborah. She cites the passage:

> In the days of Shamgar the son of Anath, in the days of Jael, the highways were unoccupied, and the travelers walked through by-ways. The inhabitants of the villages ceased, they ceased in Israel, until I Deborah arose, that I arose a mother in Israel. (Judg 5:6–7 KJV)

She concludes that Deborah thinks too highly of herself: "Here we see the danger of her position. O how much more blessed would it be if she had said, 'Until the Lord arose.' Deborah was no small person in her own eyes."[13] Later in the song, Baxter notes that Deborah sings "My heart is toward the governors of Israel" (Judg 5:9a KJV) and again reprimands Deborah for being somebody great in her own eyes rather than being

---

11. Baxter, *Women in the Word*, 76–77.
12. Baxter, *Women in the Word*, 74.
13. Baxter, *Women in the Word*, 79.

simply an instrument of the Lord. By speaking of "my heart," Deborah was not self-effacing but drew attention to her own agency. Baxter summarizes her negative assessment at the end of the essay—"Deborah was an imperfect, but a useful woman."[14]

As the flip side of castigating Deborah for her involvement in the political realm, Baxter promotes the home as women's rightful sphere of activity. In concluding her essay, Baxter notes that we know nothing of Deborah's private life: "Yet how many there are who would like to know how such a woman dealt with the details of home life. No prophetic gift, no calling of the Spirit of God into active and public service can excuse a woman for unfaithfulness in family and domestic matters."[15] At the same time that Baxter espouses these traditional views, she also applauds the many women who have made significant contributions to the work of Christian ministry. Apparently, the time that Baxter lived in was similar to the time of the judges—men were not stepping forward to assume their rightful place, and hence God called women to do what was needed. She applauds the work of Elizabeth Fry, a leader in prison work, and Sarah Foster in the rescue of the fallen. She notes that women led the temperance movement, that a woman, Mrs. Daniells, initiated the Soldier's Homes, and that another woman, Miss Marsh, began the work among policemen, railway men, and sailors.[16] These figures are held up as examples of women who inspired men in the same way that Deborah inspired Barak. Baxter's stance here is consistent with her view that women's work in the public sphere is to provoke the men to jealousy, with the intended goal that men take over the task which rightfully is theirs. These women are not usurpers but called by God, and they successfully managed their domestic affairs as well as their public calling. Baxter claims: "The being a worker together with God can never excuse her from being a helpmeet to her husband: but the two things can go blessedly together where the public call is really from God."[17] Baxter does not in this essay reflect on her own work as a speaker, organizer, and writer, but we can suppose that in her mind she has been called because there was a shortage of willing men and that she has managed to be faithful in carrying out her domestic duties as well as her public career. According to Baxter, with God's help, women can do it all.

---

14. Baxter, *Women in the Word*, 82.
15. Baxter, *Women in the Word*, 82.
16. Baxter, *Women in the Word*, 75.
17. Baxter, *Women in the Word*, 82.

3. Clara Lucas Balfour (1808–1878)

Another British writer, Balfour, agreed with Baxter in many ways, and yet the tone and agenda of her essay on Deborah was very different. Deborah was a positive role model for Balfour. She read nothing in the text to suggest that Deborah was unwomanly or that God only used her because there were no men available. Her higher view of women is apparent in the introductory chapter of her book, *The Women of Scripture*, when she briefly commented on the creation of woman as the "helpmeet" of man (Gen 2:18, 20). She writes, commenting on the woman:

> She is emphatically called the 'help-meet' of man. Not help-less, not inadequate, and therefore not inferior; but suited, by moral qualities, and mental capacities, to be the tender guardian of infancy, the teacher of childhood, the companion of youth, the partner of maturity, the friend of every age.[18]

Perhaps her different life experience explains why, although she was quite traditional in her understanding that women and men were essentially different, Balfour still applauded Deborah.

Balfour's life did not follow a smooth trajectory.[19] She was born to middle-class parents, but then they separated. Clara lived with her father. She was nine when he died, and she went to live with her mother. They were poor and earned a living by doing needlework. Still, they managed to support her attending a boarding school for three years, from 1819 to 1822. She married James Balfour when she was not quite sixteen and often lived in poverty for the first twenty years of their married life because of his drinking. They had seven children, four of whom survived into adulthood, and in the midst of these difficult circumstances, she managed to continue reading and also began to write. A turning point in their lives occurred in 1837 when both she and her husband signed "the pledge" after hearing a temperance address. Balfour became a prolific writer in the cause of temperance and in 1840 joined a Baptist church, and she remained an active member throughout her life. Her work in the temperance movement propelled her on to a career as a lecturer and writer on many subjects and

---

18. Balfour, *Women of Scripture*, 12.
19. See the essay on her by Kristin G. Doern, "Balfour, Clara Lucas (1808–1878)," *ODNB* 3 (2004): 514–15.

in many genres: poetry, novels, literary criticism, and works advocating reform. Her fame on both sides of the Atlantic is illustrated in that an early temperance novel, *Morning Dew Drops*, was prefaced by Stowe.[20] In her later years, she became a key player in the British Women's Temperance Association, which advocated for "social purity" and women's suffrage.

As mentioned, Balfour is insistent that Deborah is essentially feminine. Time and again she describes Deborah's actions, writings, and self-identification as womanly or feminine. For example, she introduces Deborah in this way: "Deborah, notwithstanding her office, being a peculiarly feminine character."[21] Balfour concludes this because Deborah chose to be known as a wife—she is introduced in Judg 4:4 as the wife of Lapidoth. In this instance, being feminine means that women identify themselves by their relationship to their husbands—a traditional understanding. In the next sentence, Balfour indicates the context against which she is making the claims that Deborah, a judge, military leader, poet, and prophet was feminine. She writes: "The common opinion that when a woman is called in the arrangements of Providence to fulfill any great public office, if she fill it well, it is by the sacrifice of womanly qualities, is a mere vulgar error."[22] Here she is engaging the debate about the split between the public and private sphere, that men are suited to the public sphere and women to the private. The argument she is opposing claims that when women enter the public sphere, they become masculine. Balfour's position, to the contrary, is that women retain their feminine qualities when they engage in public life. In fact, members of the temperance movement advocated for women's suffrage because they believed that women's character as nurturing, compassionate, and other-focused was needed in public life. Society, they claimed, would benefit when women could vote and hold positions of leadership.

Although Balfour advocates an essentialist position that understands that women and men are different, she also tends to expand and redefine what feminine means. She reflects on Deborah's dwelling under a palm tree in this way: "Here is no human pomp, none of the parade and circumstance that excite the admiration and awe of vulgar minds. It is manifest that Deborah's was an authority based alone on intellectual superiority."[23]

---

20. Balfour, *Morning Dew Drops* (London: Starie, 1853).
21. Balfour, *Women of Scripture*, 91.
22. Balfour, *Women of Scripture*, 91.
23. Balfour, *Women of Scripture*, 92.

Deborah displayed traditional feminine qualities in that she was modest, but she also is intellectual—a quality not traditionally considered feminine. Several times in the course of the essay, Balfour lists the characteristics that define Deborah as womanly and feminine, and they include the more traditional qualities, such as benevolent and spiritual, as well as qualities associated with masculinity: namely, strong, thoughtful, and intellectual.

When describing Deborah's role as a military leader, Balfour is especially adamant that Deborah was feminine. She claims that it was precisely because she was feminine that Barak wanted her to lead. She writes:

> Had Deborah been a fierce, stern, masculine woman, she would have aroused no enthusiasm, her character would have approximated too closely to their own—she would have been a sort of second-rate man, instead of being who she was, "A perfect woman, nobly planned to warn, to comfort, to command."[24]

Balfour nowhere names who she is debating, as she insists on Deborah's femininity, but there was an ongoing discussion on what "woman" entailed. Her claims seem to be engaging this debate. The scientific debate over what masculinity and femininity involve seems the most likely dialogue partner. In the first part of the nineteenth century, the proponents of phrenology claimed to be objective and drew conclusions about character and abilities on the basis of skull measurements and brain size.[25] Although most of its findings were later refuted, and the science itself lost credibility, during the time when Balfour was writing its findings were accepted. In sum, it claimed that there was less vigor in the female intellect; women were dominated by their feelings, they were more cautious, vainer, more tied to place, and more nurturing. This was not due to their different educational opportunities or social situation, but to their biology. Phrenology supported the conventional division of labor by claiming "physiological determinism."[26] As the century progressed, phrenology became discredited as bad science, but its assertions about the nature of men and women

---

24. Balfour, *Women of Scripture*, 94. The quote is from the poem "She Was a Phantom of Delight" by William Wordsworth (1770–1850) and describes the ideal woman. She is angelic and possesses the qualities which this excerpt praises: the ability to plan and command.

25. See the discussion in Cynthia Eagle Russett, *Sexual Science: The Victorian Construction of Womanhood* (Cambridge: Harvard University Press, 1989), 16–47.

26. Russett, *Sexual Science*, 19.

continued. Balfour's description of Deborah as feminine and womanly at the same time that she showed superior intellect and strength criticizes these conclusions. In this way, she moves away from traditional notions of women's limited abilities and vocations.

In her own life, Balfour mirrored the abilities and moral qualities of Deborah. She was often the breadwinner in the family due to her husband's alcoholism. She participated in organizations engaged in public issues, wrote books, conferred with publishers, gave lectures, and did not experience a diminishment of her femininity in pursuing these vocations. Her interpretation of the Deborah narrative can be seen as a validation of her choices to remain fully committed to her family and at the same time to engage actively in intellectual work and public life.

Although pushing the envelope on the Woman Question, Balfour upheld a typically evangelical Christian contrast between the dispensations of the Old Testament and the New. She does not characterize ancient Israel as more sinful than contemporary England, but she does contrast the laws of the Old with those of the New Testament. She writes: "We break a code of laws far more perfect and spiritual than those of Moses, with as little compunction as ever the Israelites did."[27] At several points in her essay, she contrasts the Old and New Testaments in some facet of its teaching, and in each case, the New is elevated at the expense of the Old. For example, when writing of the Song of Deborah, which praises Jael even though she killed Sisera, Balfour writes: "Little wonder is it then that the Mosaic dispensation, with its retributive policy and morals, this mother in Israel should praise the treacherous and cruel act of Jael."[28] By contrast, she exalts her own faith as superior: "Happy are we that our pure and holy Christianity appeals to our nobler feelings, and recognizes pardon, love, and peace, as the divine attributes of our faith and practice."[29] It is this understanding of the relationship between Christianity and Judaism that fueled the movement to convert Jews in England in the nineteenth century. The writings of Aguilar, our next interpreter, are written in response to this characterization of Judaism. She sought to make Jews proud of their heritage in the face of the dominant Christian culture which tended to disparage it.

---

27. Balfour, *Women of Scripture*, 89.
28. Balfour, *Women of Scripture*, 100.
29. Balfour, *Women of Scripture*, 103.

4. Grace Aguilar (1816–1847)

Aguilar's chapter on Deborah is part of her three-volume work *The Women of Israel*. This female-centered history of the women of Israel begins with Eve and continues through the Hebrew Bible, the time of dispersion, and the Talmud. These volumes are part of a remarkable body of work that Aguilar produced in her short life. She wrote fiction, poetry, apologetics, and theology from an explicitly Jewish standpoint. She wrote as a Jew promoting Jewish emancipation in England in a time when Jews had limited rights. For example, they were not allowed to vote or hold seats in Parliament, and they were prohibited from operating businesses in the city of London. Aguilar also worked as a reformer within the Jewish community: she promoted religious education for girls, advocated for women participating in worship by delivering prayers and sermons, and opposed separate seating for women and men in the synagogue.

Aguilar strove to make Jewish women proud of their identity, and the essays in *The Women of Israel* were part of this endeavor.[30] In particular, she wrote to refute the claims made by some Christians, among them, Sarah Stickney Ellis, author of *The Women of England: Their Social Duties and Domestic Habits*, in 1839.[31] In addition to describing the home as women's sphere of activity and the selfless work of serving family and friends as the true vocation of women, Ellis claimed that Christianity was the cause for women's high status in English society, and this claim became a key "talking point" in the attempts of Christians to convert Jews. The evangelical Christian subculture especially targeted Jewish women because Christianity was portrayed as "feminine," engaging the emotions and worshipping a God of love in contrast to Judaism, which was portrayed as a legalistic religion whose laws degraded women and which worshipped a distant God.[32]

Aguilar's interpretation of the Deborah narrative and song reflects many of her convictions. For example, she notes that Deborah's calling indicates the high status of women in ancient Israelite society:

---

30. The introduction in *Grace Aguilar: Selected Writings*, ed. Michael Galchinsky, BLT (Peterborough, ON: Broadview, 2003), 11–47, is an excellent account of her life, her literary and social context, and the reception history of her work.

31. Sarah Stickney Ellis, *The Women of England: Their Social Duties and Domestic Habits*, 15th ed. (London: Fischer, 1839).

32. Michael Ragussis, *Figures of Conversion: "The Jewish Question" and English National Identity*, PCI (Durham, NC: Duke University Press, 1995), 146.

> Had there been the very least foundation for the supposition of the degrading and heathenizing the Hebrew female, we should not find the offices of prophet, judge, military instructor, poet and sacred singer, all combined and all perfected in the person of a woman; a fact clearly and almost startlingly illustrative of what must have been their high and intellectual training, as well as natural aptitude for guiding and enforcing the statutes of their God, to which at that time woman could attain.[33]

Aguilar especially notes women's high level of education. Deborah becomes a model for those within the Jewish community who advocate for religious instruction for girls, as well as an example to refute the claims made of the superior treatment of women in the Christian religion.

Aguilar continues reflecting on Deborah's call and claims that God's choice of Deborah is not extraordinary but reveals that God holds women in the same high regard as men. She writes:

> The Eternal had inspired her, a WOMAN and a WIFE, in Israel, with His spirit expressly to do His will, and make manifest to her countrymen how little is He the respecter of persons; judging only by hearts perfect in His service, and spirits willing for the work: heeding neither the weakness nor apparent inability of one sex, compared with the greater natural powers of the other.[34]

This statement describes the complex view Aguilar held concerning women's status and role. Women and men are different, yet those differences are insignificant in God's eyes when a leader of the Israelites is needed. In terms of what matters—the heart—women and men are equal. They are essentially the same.

Aguilar continues her exposition on the status of women that is reflected in the call of Deborah. She makes the case that women should not be classed with slaves, lepers, or heathens. She notes that God never entrusted such persons with a prophetic spirit since "the social conditions of such persons would and must prevent their obtaining the respect, obedience or even attention of the people. For the same reason, had woman really been on a par with these, as she is by some declared to be, she never would have been entrusted with gifts spiritual and mental."[35] Here, Aguilar

---

33. Aguilar, *Women of Israel*, 203–4.
34. Aguilar, *Women of Israel*, 204, emphasis original.
35. Aguilar, *Women of Israel*, 204–5.

makes explicit that she is writing to combat the classification of women with slaves, the ill, and the heathen, a classification she claims was prevalent in the nineteenth century and which is contrary to the position held by Deborah.

Aguilar continues her discussion of Deborah by noting that she was faithful to her domestic duties. Similar to Baxter, Aguilar understands that women typically are most suited to caring for the home and family: she, too, assumes the split between the public and the private and situates women's typical duties in the private realm. However, unlike Baxter, Aguilar finds no fault with Deborah for her activity in the political and public realm. For example, when Aguilar considers the Song of Deborah, she notes firstly what a beautiful composition it is, rivaling the psalms of David. Then she notes the modesty that is evident:

> We find her taking no glory whatever to herself, but calling upon the princes, and governors, and people of Israel, to join her in "blessing the Lord for the avenging of Israel.… The simplicity and lowliness of the prophetess's natural position is beautifully illustrated by the term she applies to herself—neither princess, nor governor, nor judge, nor prophetess, though both the last offices she fulfilled—'until that I, Deborah, arose, until I arose a MOTHER in Israel.'"[36]

Whereas Baxter noted the use of the first-person, Aguilar focuses on the humility displayed in choosing the title of mother. Aguilar further supports her assessment of Deborah's self-effacement in the text's notice that the land had rest for forty years following this military victory. The silence of the text regarding Deborah's role during this time "is a simple confirmation of the meekness and humility with which we found her judging Israel under her own palm-tree. Deborah resumes her personally humble station, evidently without an ambitious wish, or attempt to elevate her rank or prospects."[37] According to Aguilar's portrayal, traits such as modesty that women were valued for in the private realm remain even when they enter the public sphere. In this scenario, Deborah does not develop masculine characteristics, such as being self-promoting. Aguilar's description reveals that she understands women's submissive traits to be essential rather than resulting from women's context in a patriarchal society.

---

36. Aguilar, *Women of Israel*, 206–7.
37. Aguilar, *Women of Israel*, 208.

Aguilar's claim that Deborah is not an exception and that she successfully held both her public and private positions makes her a role model for Jewish women in the nineteenth century. Although women cannot "*practically*" follow her example, "*theoretically*" they can take the history of Deborah to heart, "both *nationally* and individually."[38] First, she notes that Deborah was endowed with many gifts but that it was not only aptitude that equipped her to carry out her tasks. The gifts God had entrusted to her needed to be cultivated and improved. In the same way, Aguilar insists, Jewish girls need to be educated in the Bible and their religious traditions:

> His Word is open to her, as to man. In Moses' command to read and explain the law to all people, woman was included by name.... Shame, shame on those who would thus cramp the power of the Lord, in denying to any one of His creatures the power of addressing and comprehending Him, through the inexhaustible treasure of His gracious Word![39]

Second, Deborah is a model demonstrating that family responsibilities and a feminine character are compatible with fulfilling public office. She writes: "To a really great mind, domestic and public duties are so perfectly compatible, that the first need never be sacrificed for the last."[40] To support this claim, Aguilar infers that Lapidoth supported Deborah's military leadership on the basis of the silence of the text. This indicates that he never interfered with Deborah's public responsibilities because he had a "noble confidence" in her.

Aguilar then applies the lessons learned to married women and single women separately. Married women are called to lead in the home, and through their leadership there to influence society at large, "secretly and unsuspectedly indeed, but more powerfully than she herself can in the least degree suppose."[41] Although in principle more open than Baxter to women's leadership, in practice Aguilar supports the ideal of Victorian England that married women should lead indirectly by influence. To single women, Aguilar counsels that they need to give up frivolous pursuits and to make good use of the talents which God has given them. "Have we not all some precious talent lent us by our God, and for the use of which He

---

38. Aguilar, *Women of Israel*, 208–9, emphasis original.
39. Aguilar, *Women of Israel*, 210.
40. Aguilar, *Women of Israel*, 209.
41. Aguilar, *Women of Israel*, 210.

will demand an account?… Were there but one object on whom we have lavished kindness, and taught to look up to God and heaven … we shall not have lived in vain."[42] In picturing the fulfilling life for single women, Aguilar also conforms to the picture of a virtuous single woman in Victorian England. There were very few opportunities available for respectable women, and working among the poor and downtrodden was one of these. These vocations are consistent with the view of women's nature as nurturing and fulfilled in living a life of service to others. Hence, although opposing the claim that Christianity was the source of women's high value in English society by showing that Judaism revered and exalted women long before Jesus of Nazareth walked the earth, she is in agreement with the depiction of women and their vocation promoted in the work of Ellis mentioned above.

Aguilar concludes her essay with this sentence: "Deborahs in truth we cannot be, but each and all have talents given, and a sphere assigned them, and like her, all have it in their power, in the good performed toward man, to use the one, and consecrate the other to the service of their God."[43] When Aguilar's life is compared with these sentiments, there is much coherence; Deborah functioned as a role model for her. Aguilar was a single woman endowed with remarkable abilities which she used for the benefit of her own marginalized Jewish people, as well as for the benefit of girls and women who were oppressed within the Jewish community. In her writing and teaching, Aguilar was a Deborah to her generation. In fact, shortly before her untimely death, the Jewish women of England presented her with a tribute which alluded to the Deborah narrative. It declared: "Until you arose, it has, in modern times, never been the case, that a woman in Israel should stand for the public advocate of the faith of Israel."[44]

5. Harriet Beecher Stowe (1811–1896)

On the other side of the Atlantic, Stowe published an essay on Deborah that contains many claims similar to Aguilar's, yet does so from a Christian standpoint.[45] Of all the non-Jewish women interpreters surveyed, Stowe

---

42. Aguilar, *Women of Israel*, 211.
43. Aguilar, *Women of Israel*, 211.
44. Cited in Galchinsky, *Grace Aguilar*, 355.
45. Stowe, *Woman in Sacred History*, 99–106.

has the highest regard for Judaism; however, she also presents Deborah as a step on the way to God's fuller revelation in the New Testament. In Stowe's assessment, Deborah is in a line of women prophetesses and poets which culminated in Mary. For example, reflecting on Deborah as an inspired poet, Stowe writes: "To this class belonged Hannah, the mother of Samuel, and Huldah, the prophetess, and in the fullness of time, Mary, the mother of Jesus, whose *Magnificat* was the earliest flower of the Christian era."[46]

Stowe is a remarkable interpreter in many ways. Of the women included in this survey, she is the most educated. She was born into an illustrious family.[47] Her father was Lyman Beecher (1775–1863), a Congregational minister, a theologian, and a seminary president. Harriet Beecher was the seventh of nine children born to his first wife, Roxanne (1775–1816). Seven of her brothers went on to become ministers, and her elder sister, Catherine, founded several schools for girls—including the one that Stowe attended, Hartford Female Seminary—as well as writing on education, abolition, household management, and women's issues. Harriet's mother Roxanne died when Harriet was five, and her father quickly remarried. Isabella, daughter of this marriage, became a leader in the women's suffrage movement. She was especially capable in organizing conventions and was in close contact with Stanton and Susan B. Anthony. Stowe became a supporter of women's suffrage, although she did not campaign publicly.[48] She married Calvin Ellis Stowe (1802–1886), who at that time was a theologian at Lane Theological Seminary. Throughout their lives, they collaborated in their work, relying on each other both for encouragement, resources, and critical engagement with the material they were reading and writing. Through her father, brothers, and husband, Stowe had access

---

46. Stowe, *Woman in Sacred History*, 105.

47. There is a large body of literature on this family. Two helpful studies that focus on the women in the family include Barbara A. White, *The Beecher Sisters* (New Haven: Yale University Press, 2003); and Jeanne Boydston, Mary Kelley, and Anne Margolis, *The Limits of Sisterhood: The Beecher Sisters on Women's Rights and Woman's Sphere*, GAC (Chapel Hill: University of North Carolina Press, 1988).

48. White discusses Harriet's thinking on suffrage in *Beecher Sisters*, 141–46. Isabella introduced Harriet to the work of John Stuart Mill, "The Subjection of Women," in *Essays on Sex Equality: John Stuart Mill and Harriet Taylor Mill*, ed. Alice S. Rossi (Chicago: University of Chicago Press, 1970), 123–242; and Harriet Taylor Mill, "Enfranchisement of Women," in *Essays on Sex Equality: John Stuart Mill and Harriet Taylor Mill*, ed. Alice S. Rossi (Chicago: University of Chicago Press, 1970), 89–121. Influenced by Mill's position, Harriet came to espouse an equal rights point of view.

to a vast library and the latest in theological discussions and incorporated the new insights yielded by the critical study of Scripture.[49] For example, she cites Johann Gottfried Herder's *The Spirit of Hebrew Poetry* and uses his "charming" translation when commenting on the Song of Deborah in Judg 5.[50]

In the introduction to *Woman in Sacred History*, Stowe elaborates on her basic interpretive principles when reading the Old Testament, and in the essay on Deborah, they are consistently applied. She operates with a notion of progressive revelation and employs this notion to explain features of the Old Testament which nineteenth-century readers would find offensive. For example, she notes that the laws dealing with concubines (Exod 21:7) and women taken during warfare (Deut 21:10–14) allow for and regulate polygamy.[51] Stowe makes two claims when interpreting these laws. Firstly, she argues that the laws show great consideration for women, for example, limiting the rights of the man over the woman, and secondly, she contrasts that care with the degraded status held by women in the surrounding nations. For example, she compares the role of the wife as given in the Ten Commandments with her role in ancient Greece and Rome. She writes:

> Among the Greeks, the wife was a nonentity, living in the seclusion of the women's apartments, and never associated publicly with her husband as an equal. In Rome, the father was all in all in the family, and held the sole power of life and death over his wife and children. Among the Jews, the

---

49. The essay by Marion Ann Taylor, "Harriet Beecher Stowe and the Mingling of Two Worlds: The Kitchen and the Study," in De Groot and Taylor, *Recovering Nineteenth-Century Women Interpreters of the Bible*, 99–115, describes Stowe's social context and her interpretation of Scripture.

50. Stowe, *Woman in Sacred History*, 102. She is quoting from Johann Gottfried Herder, *The Spirit of Hebrew Poetry*, trans. James Marsh, vol. 2 (Burlington: Smith, 1833), 186–91.

51. See my discussion of Aguilar's interpretation of the laws dealing with the concubine in Exod 21:7 in the essay, Christiana de Groot, "Nineteenth-Century Feminist Responses to the Laws in the Pentateuch," in *Strangely Familiar: Protofeminist Interpretations of Patriarchal Biblical Texts*, ed. Nancy Calvert-Koyzis and Heather Weir (Atlanta: Society of Biblical Literature, 2009), 106–19. Aguilar differs from Stowe in that she interprets the clause, "she shall not go out as men-servants do" (KJV) to mean that the maid servants did not do the rougher and harder field work.

wife was the co-equal queen of the home, and was equally honored and obeyed with her husband.[52]

She concludes her study by claiming that: "By thus hedging in polygamy with restraints of serious obligations and duties, and making every concubine a wife, entitled to claim all the privileges of a wife, Moses prepared the way for its gradual extinction."[53] By New Testament times, she notes, the practice of polygamy has all but disappeared.

Stowe devotes a surprising amount of attention to the laws dealing with women in the Pentateuch, and here, too, she echoes many themes found in Aguilar. She assumes that the laws predate Israel's life in the land of Israel, that they present the norm for Israelite society, and that as a result they can be used to sketch the setting for the lives of individual women. Because, according to Stowe, the laws contain such a high view of women's status, she concludes, again in agreement with Aguilar, that Deborah's role as judge is not exceptional. She characterizes the era of the Judges as the "Dark Ages of the Jewish Church,"[54] in which the Jewish people were disobedient, were oppressed, and were delivered by a divinely inspired leader. She continues:

> It is entirely in keeping with the whole character of Mosaic institutions, and the customs of the Jewish people, that one of these inspired deliverers should be a woman. We are not surprised at the familiar manner in which it is announced as a thing quite in the natural order, that the chief magistrate of the Jewish nation, for the time being, was a woman divinely ordained and gifted.[55]

The laws in the Pentateuch are not only valued because of their high regard for women but also, according to Stowe, lay the groundwork for a democratic society. The opening paragraph in her sketch on Deborah claims that "the ideal policy of Moses was that of an ultra-democratic community, so arranged that perforce there must be liberty, fraternity and equality."[56] These three values were the impetus for the French and American revolutions, as well as justifying the abolition of slavery, a cause which Stowe

---

52. Stowe, *Woman in Sacred History*, 23, 24.
53. Stowe, *Woman in Sacred History*, 25.
54. Stowe, *Woman in Sacred History*, 99.
55. Stowe, *Woman in Sacred History*, 100.
56. Stowe, *Woman in Sacred History*, 99.

had championed in her novel *Uncle Tom's Cabin*.[57] For Stowe, there is no tension between the ideal presented in the Mosaic laws and the ideals of the United States. It is interesting to consider how her notion of progressive revelation plays out here. It seems that in this aspect, the laws had reached their zenith. In fact, she concludes this paragraph in terms that echo Jesus's response to the lawyer's question, "What must I do to inherit eternal life?" (Luke 10:25 NRSV) Stowe writes: "The supreme law of the land was love. Love, first, to the God and father, the invisible head of all; and secondly, towards the neighbor, whether a Jewish brother or a foreigner or a stranger."[58] The laws not only set up the ideal state, but they also teach how to live daily life on the practical level. By following the laws, Jews would learn: "Refinement of feeling, personal cleanliness, self-restraint, order and purity ... so that the Jew who lived up to his law must of necessity rise to a noble manhood."[59] We might expect that Stowe would continue by reflecting on the role played by Barak in this narrative and perhaps elevate him as an example of enlightened Jewish manhood, but she does not. Deborah's husband, Lapidoth, is also not a role model. Stowe only notes that he is remembered through his wife, Deborah.

Although Deborah clearly participated in public life in addition to her domestic roles, her roles as mother and poetess are the only ones that Stowe engages. In her remarks on the high status of women in the law, she notes: "The person of the woman was hedged about by restraints and ordinances which raised her above the degradation of sensuality to the honored position of wife and mother. Motherhood was exalted into special honor, and named as equal with fatherhood in the eye of God."[60] For Stowe herself, it was her experience as a mother that gave her moral authority. It was as a mother that she wrote *Uncle Tom's Cabin*. According to Stowe: "I wrote what I did because as a woman, as a mother, I was oppressed and heartbroken, with the sorrows and injustice I saw."[61] For her, the task of mother and writer are interdependent. She wrote out of her place in the

---

57. Stowe published *Uncle Tom's Cabin* serially in the antislavery magazine *National Era* in 1851, and a two-volume set appeared in 1852. A modern critical edition that includes background information is edited by Elizabeth Ammons (New York: Norton, 1994).

58. Stowe, *Woman in Sacred History*, 99.

59. Stowe, *Woman in Sacred History*, 99, 100.

60. Stowe, *Woman in Sacred History*, 99.

61. Cited in Boydston, Kelley, and Margolis, *Limits of Sisterhood*, 48.

domestic setting, so it is perhaps not surprising that she notes that Deborah is a writer and praises her first and foremost as a poet. Although Stowe supported many reforms for women in the nineteenth century, she did not connect the Deborah narrative with calls for women's education or for suffrage for women. Rather, Stowe presents the laws and interprets the narrative of Deborah as upholding a traditional view of women as "queens of the interior."[62]

Stowe's position here is another variation of the response to the Woman Question. Although, as noted previously, she was convinced by Mill's arguments that women and men are essentially the same and that both bear moral responsibility—and hence should both be permitted to vote—Stowe also argued that women's roles as mothers give them a unique platform from which to address issues of public morality, such as the institution of slavery. In her Introduction, Stowe contrasts the poetesses in Scripture with women writers in the surrounding nations. Elsewhere, in Greece and Rome, women who wrote were courtesans or vestal virgins. Judaism is unique, she claims, in combining the tasks of mother, wife, and prophetess. She writes, using Deborah as her paradigmatic example: "So far as we know, there is not a Jewish prophetess who is not also a wife, and the motherly character is put forward as constituting a claim to fitness in public life. 'I, Deborah arose a mother in Israel.'"[63] In this way, Stowe also espouses the ideology of separate spheres and on that basis creates the argument for women's participation in politics.[64] She ends her Introduction by describing the ideal woman, one on which Stowe seemed to model her own life: "That pure ideal of a sacred woman springing from the bosom of the family, at once wife, mother, poetess, leader, inspirer, prophetess, is peculiar to sacred history."[65]

The second half of Stowe's essay on Deborah focuses on the Song of Deborah, and here Stowe draws heavily on the work of Herder. She cites the entire poem, interrupting it every few verses for some comments. For

---

62. This phrase is used by Stowe to describe women's position in the premonarchical period. See Stowe, *Woman in Sacred History*, 20.

63. Stowe, *Woman in Sacred History*, 28.

64. See the more detailed discussion on domesticity and natural rights theory in the Introduction to Margolis, *Limits of Sisterhood*, 4–6. White, *Beecher Sisters*, 146 also comments that it was not unusual for the Beecher sisters, Harriet and Isabella, to veer back and forth between the two positions of equal rights and separate spheres.

65. Stowe, *Woman in Sacred History*, 28.

example, after Judg 5:12, she interrupts to draw attention to a transition. Speaking of Deborah, Stowe writes: "She reviews, with all a woman's fiery eloquence, the course which the tribes have taken in contest, giving praise to the few courageous, self-sacrificing patriots, and casting arrows of satire and scorn on the cowardly and selfish."[66] Here again we see her emphasis on the special merits of women as writers. She continues in this paragraph to speak of battles in her own time, presumably referring to the Civil War, and of how they were similar to the battles fought by ancient Israel. In both cases "there were all sorts of men. There were those of the brave, imprudent, generous, 'do-or-die' stamp, and there were the selfish conservatives, who only waited and talked."[67]

In this remarkable essay, Stowe has brought together her commitments to abolition, the ideals of the American revolution, the moral weight of being a mother, the calling of a poet and prophet as well as a very appreciative rendition of ancient Judaism. At the same time, she has altogether omitted from consideration Deborah's role in leading military campaigns and the relationship between Deborah and Barak. Stowe's agenda equipped her to see some features of the narrative and ignore others, making clear that the study of interpretation needs to consider not only what is said but what is neglected.

6. Julia McNair Wright (1840–1903)

Wright published *Sinners and Saints* in 1872, one year before Stowe's *Woman in Sacred History*. Both are American, Protestant, white, and middle-class and were prolific writers.[68] Their ideas on slavery and the Woman Question were quite similar yet expressed very differently. For example, Wright is a much more typically Protestant in that she nowhere mentions Judaism or considers the laws in the Pentateuch when explaining the customs of ancient Israel. Unlike Stowe, Wright makes much more explicit connections between the Deborah narrative and women's rights, focusing especially on education.

---

66. Stowe, *Woman in Sacred History*, 103.
67. Stowe, *Woman in Sacred History*, 103.
68. William A. Newman Dorland, *The Sum of Feminine Achievement* (Boston: Stratford, 1917), 226, includes her in his chart in the Novelist section and lists *The Heir of Athole* (1887) as her Magnum Opus.

Much less is written about Wright's life, but the main outlines are clear. She was born in Oswego, New York, into an upper-middle-class family and received her education at private schools. She married William J. Wright, a minister in the Presbyterian Church, had two children, and eventually settled in Fulton, Missouri where her husband was vice-president of Westminster College. She was an accomplished author, writing novels, short stories, poems, religious essays, and lessons for children on temperance, as well as cookbooks and works on botany.[69] The essay on Deborah is part of her biblical study on *Saints and Sinners*. It explores women and men in Scripture, including Miriam, Deborah, and Jezebel as well as Samson and David. In the preface, she provides her rationale for studying these figures. She claims that unlike other literature in which heroes are perfect, and villains are notorious criminals, the Bible presents us with saints and sinners who are true to human experience.[70] Because the people in Scripture are "bone of our bone, and flesh of our flesh,"[71] the reader will learn much about the godly and ungodly life by reflecting on them.

Wright's chapter on Miriam and Deborah, subtitled "The Theocratic Status of Woman," makes explicit why she has brought these two women together in one chapter. She writes: "Scripture sets before us as glorious types of womanhood both in domestic and public life; two who teach us the status of woman before her God; and in these times when the questions of woman's rights and position occupy so much attention, it is well to go back to the fountain of all truth and draw our lesson thence."[72] Both women, she claims, were appointed by God to participate in public life. They did not do so out of their own ambition but because God called them. She notes that women generally stay in the domestic sphere, but occasionally, as the need arises and as women show themselves capable, they participate in politics or education.

Wright's position mediates between the natural rights position and the separate spheres position. She writes: "In general terms, God has assigned men one line of work in the world, and women another; in physical conformation, he has fitted them for their grand and customary departments

---

69. See the entry, Lois Fowler, "Julia McNair Wright," in vol. 4 of *American Women Writers: A Critical Reference Guide from Colonial Times to the Present*, ed. Lina Mainiero and Langdon L. Faust (New York: Ungar, 1982), 466–69.
70. Wright, *Saints and Sinners*, 6.
71. Wright, *Saints and Sinners*, 7.
72. Wright, *Saints and Sinners*, 182.

of labor; but he has made it no sin to go out of one sphere into the other, *if there is necessity for it*."[73] In terms that resonate with modern scholarship on the differences between the sexes, she notes sometimes there are small muscled men and large muscled women and later points to the example of Elena Carnaro (1646–1684), an exceptional woman whose mastery of languages, philosophy, theology, and mathematics resulted in her having no women or men who could compete with her.[74]

Echoing the position of Balfour, Wright further claims that women entering public life do not change their essential identity; they remain women. Speaking of Deborah, she claims: "Her high position and mighty deeds did not unsex her; she was not a king, but a *mother in Israel*" (emphasis original).[75] Wright is supportive of women who respond to need and who are called by God to perform their duty in unusual ways but is critical of women "who have been loudly vaunting their fitness and demanding opportunity."[76] Perhaps she is alluding to the work of suffragettes who at this time were travelling around the country lecturing on women's rights.

Although critical of some women, Wright herself was an advocate for women's education and makes a strong case against those men who would legislate against women's entry into certain schools and professions. There are several facets of her argument. Firstly, she claims that most women are suited to the domestic sphere, so men do not need to worry that women will want to take over their domain. In colorful language she writes: "Therefore, there need be no more masculine trepidation lest women usurp the pulpit and the gubernatorial chair, the general's star, and the sea captains floating kingdom, because wifedom and motherhood will interpose their mysterious ban."[77] We do not know whether or not Wright read Mill's treatise, "The Subjection of Women," but several of her arguments, including this one, are found in Mill's essay. Mill also argues that although men and women should hold the same status under the law, be given educational and economic opportunities, and be allowed to vote, married women will still mostly remain in the domestic sphere. He explains:

---

73. Wright, *Saints and Sinners*, 188, emphasis original.
74. Wright, *Saints and Sinners*, 188; Wright, *Saints and Sinners*, 196.
75. Wright, *Saints and Sinners*, 195.
76. Wright, *Saints and Sinners*, 195.
77. Wright, *Saints and Sinners*, 197.

> Like a man when he chooses a profession, so, when a woman marries, it may in general be understood that she makes a choice of the management of a household, and the bringing up of a family, as the first call upon her exertions, during as many years of her life as may be required for the purpose; and that she renounces, not all other objects and occupations, but all which are not consistent with the requirements of this.[78]

Also, for both Mill and Wright, because there is this inclination against women's entry into public life, there needs to be no legal prohibition against it.[79] In addition, Wright claims that prohibiting those few women who are called is going against God's will.

So far, Wright's position coheres most with those who see women and men as essentially different and on that basis limit women's involvement. Her difference with this view seems to be that she allows for exceptions and strives to change the laws so that exceptional women are accommodated. However, when she goes on to write about women's education and understanding, she claims that men and women are essentially the same. She espouses education for women as being in accord with God's intentions. She writes: "We work in the line of Divine intent when women are educated, as men are educated, in the ratio of their capacity. The capacity of women for learning is, on the whole, the same as that of men. More than half of each sex is unequal to a liberal education."[80] Later, Wright disputes the claim that women's and men's ways of thinking are different, as well as the claim that women's intuitive way of knowing is superior. She writes: "There has been much prating about woman's *intuition* and *instinct*, and her weakness being her strength. Woman's weakness is *not* her strength; for her as for man knowledge is power. Intuition is no more the peer of education than the dog's instinct is the equal of his master's power."[81] Here she makes very explicit that she sees only one kind of knowledge that is valuable, and it is the knowing that is typically attributed to men and is the result of education.

Yet another facet of Wright's argument, which has affinities with the position of Mill, is that women will seek work outside the home only if they have time and energy left over. Involvement by women in the public

---

78. Mill, "Subjection of Women," 179.
79. Mill writes, "What women by nature cannot do, it is quite superfluous to forbid them from doing." See Mill, "Subjection of Women," 154.
80. Wright, *Saints and Sinners*, 196.
81. Wright, *Saints and Sinners*, 196, emphasis original.

sphere will occur only when they have met all their obligations at home, and there is surplus. This need for women to expend surplus energy is connected to God's call that people exercise their talents to the best of their ability. These two arguments again appeal to the men's concern that the home and family will be neglected if women enter the public sphere, coupled with men and women's commitment to be faithful to God.[82] In summary Wright claims: "The status of woman under the Divine Government is a mental and spiritual equality with man."[83] She then adds in her conclusion that "to claim equality is not to deny a difference."[84] A brief look at the circumstances of many women writers in the nineteenth century illustrates that Wright's position presents an ideal that was unattainable for most. Writers such as Susan Warner (1819–1885), Christina Rosetti (1830–1894), Aguilar, Balfour, and Stowe wrote out of economic necessity. Their earnings from publishing were needed in order to support themselves and their families. Nor was it the case that they wrote out of the surplus of their energy.[85] Stowe describes the circumstances of her writing in a letter that captures the busyness of many married women's lives:

> Since I began this note, I have been called off at least a dozen times; once for the fish-man, to buy a codfish; once to see a man who had brought me some barrels of apples; once to see a book agent; then to Mrs. Uphams to see about a drawing I promised to make for her; then to nurse the baby; then into the kitchen to make a chowder for dinner; and now I am at it again, for nothing but deadly determination enables me ever to write; it is rowing against wind and tide.[86]

Wright's notion of women working outside of their homes only if their responsibilities there have been met and there is yet a surplus reveals her upper-class status. She seems oblivious to the realities experienced by many lower- and middle-class women.

More than previous interpreters, Wright fleshed out the ramifications of claiming that women, like Deborah, can be used by God in the public sphere. In each case, the interpreters note that Deborah remains a woman, even while leading. This indicates to them that women, as well as men, are

---

82. Wright, *Saints and Sinners*, 197.
83. Wright, *Saints and Sinners*, 196.
84. Wright, *Saints and Sinners*, 199.
85. This list is taken from Taylor and Weir, *Let Her Speak for Herself*, 4.
86. Cited in Taylor and Weir, *Let Her Speak for Herself*, 4.

useful to God and that both are equal in the eyes of God. Yet, each of these also claim that the domestic sphere is the most likely arena where women will fulfill their calling. They differ in how much they are willing to advocate for women being allowed to enter the public sphere and to have equal access to education. Aguilar and Wright make the strongest cases that women and men ought to be educated. Aguilar limits her case to learning about religion, while Wright extends it to include a liberal education. Stowe is unusual in that she does not make explicit connections between Deborah's role and the opportunities for women in the nineteenth century.

7. Clara Neyman (1840–1931)

The final interpreter, Neyman, defines the progressive end of this spectrum. Very little is known about her life apart from her work for women's suffrage in the state of New York. Stanton states that Neyman was a member of the Freethinkers, and she is listed as a member of the Revising Committee in the second volume of *The Woman's Bible* and contributed four entries on Judges.[87] She is in fundamental agreement with the volume's critique of Christianity as a religion which supports patriarchy and is more oppressive to women than other religions, including Judaism. For example, as Neyman considers the many roles of Deborah as priestess, prophetess, poetess, and judge, she concludes that the position of women in Judaism was very high. She suggests: "The writer who compiled the story of her gifts and deeds must have had women before him who inspired him with such a wonderful personality."[88] Deborah's high status and authority in Israelite society was not an exception. According to Neyman's historical reconstruction: "It is now an assured fact that not only among the Hebrews, but also among the Greeks and the Germans, women formerly maintained greater freedom and power."[89]

---

87. Neyman is mentioned in Stanton, Susan B. Anthony, and Matilda J. Gage, eds., *History of Woman's Suffrage* (Rochester: Mann, 1887), 3:68, 241, 251–52, 258, 260, 405, 422, 424–25, 433, 481, 690. She spoke at the first meeting of the German suffragette organization formed in New York in 1872. The *History of Woman's Suffrage* notes, "Clara Neyman became afterwards a popular speaker in many suffrage and free religious associations."

88. Neyman, "Judges," 21.

89. Neyman, "Judges," 22.

Her view on the existence of matriarchal societies that predated patriarchal societies was popular in the nineteenth century. For example, a speech given by Stanton in 1891 is entitled, "The Matriarchate, or Mother State."[90] She reviews the research which supports this view, drawing especially on the anthropological study by Lewis Henry Morgan, *Ancient Society*, which was published in 1877.[91] The view shared by Stanton and Neyman is that long ago, society flourished under matriarchy and that over time women slowly lost their authority. Neyman asks why this is so. She writes: "If Deborah, way back in ancient Judaism, was considered wise enough to advise her people in time of need and distress, why is it that at the end of the nineteenth century, woman has to contend for equal rights and fight to regain every inch of ground she has lost since then?"[92] The villain is Christianity. It is Christians who have taught, for example, that women must be silent in churches. Neyman continues: "The truth is that Christianity has in many instances circumscribed woman's sphere of action, and has been guilty of great injustice to her whole sex."[93] Not surprisingly, Neyman, writing as a Freethinker, and Aguilar, writing as a Jew, are in agreement against those, such as Balfour and Baxter, who believe that women in Christian lands are better off than those in "heathen" lands. Balfour writes the strongest statements of any of the interpreters championing Christianity over other religions, and the Bible over other ancient writings. In her introductory chapter she writes:

> The Bible, in remarkable contrast to all other ancient writings, distinctly recognises woman's moral responsibility, her high mental capacity, the important personal and relative duties resulting therefrom; and her perfect equality with man of spiritual privileges and eternal destiny. The more polished nations of antiquity, on the contrary, seem invariably to have formed a low estimate of the female character.[94]

---

90. The speech is included in the anthology Ellen Carol DuBois and Richard Candida Smith, eds., *Elizabeth Cady Stanton: Feminist as Thinker* (New York: New York University Press, 2007), 264–75.

91. Lewis Henry Morgan, *Ancient Society; or, Researches in the Lines of Human Progress from Savagery, through Barbarism to Civilization* (London: Macmillan, 1877).

92. Neyman, "Judges," 22.

93. Neyman, "Judges," 21.

94. Balfour, *Women of Scripture*, 2.

Balfour continues by comparing women in Christian lands with those in Hindu lands and Muslim lands and makes the claim that "civilization follows constantly in the train of Christianity."[95] She couples this with the further claim that "wherever woman is treated with injustice, national advancement is retarded, and the literature of the country is deteriorated."[96] Bringing together Christianity, civilization, and the treatment of women leads Balfour to conclude that women are better off in England due to Christianity. Although she does not explicitly mention Judaism in this introductory section, later, in her essay on Deborah, she does make the claim that the New Testament's morality is more enlightened than the Old Testament's. It would be contra views such as Balfour's that both Aguilar and Neyman claim that women in Judaism fared better than women in Christianity.

Although not endorsing either Judaism or Christianity as her religion, Neyman yet uses Deborah and Barak as role models for what is possible for women and men. Her position is in agreement with the views of other contributors to *The Woman's Bible* who explored the new religious movements that emerged in the nineteenth century. For example, the Revising Committee included three Universalist ministers: Olympia Brown, Phebe Hanaford, and Augusta Chapin; adherents to New Thought: Clara Colby, Matilda Joslyn Gage, and Ursula Gesterfeld; and Spiritualists: Lucinda Chandler, Catherine Stebbins, and Charlotte Wilbour.[97] Followers of New Thought and Spiritualists tended to read the Bible for its spiritual, esoteric meaning. Rather than focusing on the plain, material meaning of the text, they claimed that the Bible taught a spiritual androgyny: men and women have a sexless soul. As a result, they did not ground arguments for women's equality in "natural rights" but presented a gender-neutral foundation.[98] Neyman's interpretation of the Deborah narrative coheres with these convictions. She concludes that the narrative of Deborah teaches: "Genius knows no sex; and woman must again usurp her Divine prerogative as a leader in thought, song and action. The religion of the future will honor

---

95. Balfour, *Women of Scripture*, 8.
96. Balfour, *Women of Scripture*, 6.
97. See Kathi Kern's discussion of the composition of the Revising Committee in *Mrs. Stanton's Bible* (Ithaca, NY: Cornell University Press, 2001), 138–44. See also the excellent exposition of the history of New Thought ideas in Beryl Satter, *Each Mind a Kingdom: American Woman, Sexual Purity, and the New Thought Movement, 1875–1920* (Berkeley: University of California Press, 1999).
98. Kern, *Mrs. Stanton's Bible*, 163–69.

and revere motherhood, wifehood and maidenhood."[99] Because women and men have sexless souls, genius also knows no sex. Spiritual androgyny becomes the basis for recognizing the abilities of both women and men to be leaders. Consistent with the vision of New Thought, Neyman claims that women can be leaders in thought and action, areas that typically included only men. At the same time, the religion of the future will also honor the traditional roles that women occupy, namely, motherhood, wifehood, and maidenhood. Neyman argues for more opportunities for women to be active in public life, and at the same time, reveres the typical roles of women in the domestic sphere. In seeing both as arenas for women's and men's equal involvement, she goes the furthest in breaking down the separation and unequal value placed on the private and public realms.

From Neyman's claim that women and men are equal, she continues to call for women and men to work together and again accuses the church for creating the animosity which currently exists between men and women. She writes: "The antagonism which the Christian church has built up between the male and the female must entirely vanish. Together they will slay the enemies—ignorance, superstition and cruelty. United in every enterprise they will win; like Deborah and Barak, they will clear the highways and restore peace and prosperity to their people."[100] Unlike Baxter, who reprimanded Barak for being dependent on Deborah and Deborah for usurping Barak's role, Neyman sees an effective partnership between Deborah and Barak and holds it up as a model. Neyman is also the only interpreter who considers who the enemies are for residents in the nineteenth century, and her list of enemies is not gender specific. Neither men nor women are the enemy. As partners, they have the same enemies: ignorance, superstition, and cruelty.

Neyman's vision of partnership and equality between men and women is not solely based on Scripture. She differs from both Baxter and Aguilar, who consider the Bible—whether that be the Hebrew Bible or the Old and New Testaments—the word of God. When Aguilar and Baxter read the text, they may arrive at different interpretations of the meaning of a passage, but both agree that the Bible is an inspired book by which believers are to regulate their lives. Neyman, by contrast, agrees with Stanton that the Bible is an uneven book. She writes in her comments on Judg 1: "The

---

99. Neyman, "Judges," 22.
100. Neyman, "Judges," 22.

Bible has been of service in some respects; but the time has come for us to point out the evil of many of its teachings. It now behooves us to throw the light of a new civilization upon the women who figure in the Book of Judges."[101] This view that the Bible is not inspired and authoritative explains her conclusion that:

> God never discriminates; it is man who has made the laws and compelled woman to obey him. The Old Testament and the New are books written by men; the coming Bible will be the result of the efforts of both, and contain the wisdom of both sexes, their combined spiritual experience. Together they will unfold the mysteries of life, and heaven will be here on earth when love and justice reign supreme.[102]

This vision of what might be is derived not only from Scripture but also has roots in nonscriptural texts. Like New Thought advocates, Neyman did not restrict herself to the Old and New Testaments but also drew inspiration from mystical texts, such as the Kabbalah. These texts taught the spiritual, esoteric insight that clarified the true meaning of the biblical text.[103]

Neyman's vision of the intended equality in status and role of men and women is also consistent with the task she carved out for herself as a proponent of women's suffrage. Her claim, and that of the movement, was that the voices of women in the public sphere will make it a better place. The virtues of women—their compassion, fidelity and modesty—will transform the competitive, harsh reality of the present society. The partnership of men and women in political life will result in the entire country becoming a paradise where love and justice reign supreme.

8. The Deborah Narrative: A Blueprint for Women's and Men's Lives

Lest this paper give the impression that these six women exhaust all the issues that interpreters noted in the narrative, let me briefly indicate some of the themes noted by other women interpreters. Emily Dibdin, writing *Lessons on Women of the Bible* in 1893, titles her lesson on Deborah "Simplicity."[104] She writes that Deborah did not rule from a mansion or

---

101. Neyman, "Judges," 17.
102. Neyman, "Judges," 23.
103. Kern, *Mrs. Stanton's Bible*, 163–65.
104. Emily Dibdin, "Deborah," in *Lessons on Women of the Bible*, ed. Emily Dibdin (London: Church of England Sunday School Society, 1893), 8–10.

palace but from under a tree. She was a great leader who was an example of the virtue of simplicity. Lady Morgan, who wrote *Woman and Her Master*, treats the song of Deborah in chapter 6 of the first volume, noting:

> This canticle was sung 2285 years before the birth of Christ. A fine immortality! a grand celebrity! There are among the learned some who believe that Homer took it as his model, and found in it the germ of his own immortal poem. In an article in the British Quarterly Review, in which the intellectual nature of Woman is treated with contempt, their supporters (few in number) are called upon to produce anything that can compare to the poetry produced by men. The first ode on record was the joint effusion of a brother and sister, Moses and Miriam; and Deborah's canticle, which succeeded it, besides its higher poetic inspiration, has the distinction of preceding Homer's epic by thirteen centuries.[105]

Susanna Rowson, who wrote *Biblical Dialogue between a Father and His Family* in 1822, makes the case that Deborah was qualified to hold the office of judge. In the words of the grandfather she writes: "In the midst of this distress, appeared Deborah a woman of eminent holiness, prudence, and knowledge of the Holy Scriptures."[106]

More recently, the commentary by David M. Gunn on Judges has also included the reception history of Judges.[107] In his presentation on Judg 4 and 5, he draws from rabbinic writings, ancient and medieval commentaries, and writings from the early modern and modern period. The first woman interpreter he cites is Christine de Pisan.[108] Then he includes, when discussing nineteenth-century interpretation, the commentary by Mrs. Trimmer, the contribution of Aguilar and Balfour, and briefly mentions Stanton's selections.[109] In addition, Gunn includes drawings and paintings as part of the history of the Bible's reception, resulting in an especially rich presentation. This commentary series marks the movement from margin to center for the field of women's interpretation of Scripture. Their writings

---

105. Morgan, *Women and Her Master*, 1:70.
106. Susanna Rowson, *Biblical Dialogue between a Father and his Family: Comprising Sacred History, from the Creation to the Death of Our Saviour Christ* (Boston: Richardson & Lord, 1822), 269.
107. It is part of the Blackwell Bible Commentaries, whose intention is to include the reception of the text as a valuable component of the commentary's agenda. See David M. Gunn, *Judges*, BBCom (Oxford: Blackwell, 2005).
108. Gunn, *Judges*, 59.
109. Gunn, *Judges*, 63–66.

are considered alongside many well-known commentators on Scripture through the ages, and their insights are brought into the wider conversation. Women's readings of Scripture are not treated as a niche interest of a few, mostly women scholars, but as sources worthy of consideration by all biblical scholars. This series occasions the hope that many neglected women's voices will be given the hearing that they deserve.

This essay has briefly explored the rich reception of the Deborah narrative in women's writings in the nineteenth century and discovered that women read Scripture in light of their own experience and saw reflected in these chapters in Judges the issues relevant in their own time. Interestingly, none of them understood the Deborah narrative to teach a message contrary to the positions that they held on the Woman Question. In part, that can be explained by the authority granted to the biblical text by most interpreters—given that the Hebrew Bible or Old Testament is the word of God, it would be difficult for women to be openly critical of its message. However, even Neyman, who held the view that this book was written by men and was not always inspired, did not find fault with the message she understood this passage to teach. All six interpreters agreed that women and men needed to reflect on these important chapters in the book of Judges, for they illuminated the ideal relationship between men and women and what sphere of activity God intended each to operate within. The Deborah narrative and poem provided for them, by means of positive or negative role models, a blueprint of how to achieve God's goal that men and women flourish in the home and in the wider society.

Bibliography

Aguilar, Grace. *The Women of Israel; or, Characters and Sketches from the Holy Scripture and Jewish History*. London: Groombridge & Sons, 1845.

Balfour, Clara Lucas. *Morning Dew Drops*. London: Starie, 1853.

———. *The Women of Scripture*. London: Houlston & Stoneman, 1847.

Baxter, Elizabeth. *The Women in the Word*. 2nd ed. London: Christian Herald, 1897.

Boydston, Jeanne, Mary Kelley, and Anne Margolis. *The Limits of Sisterhood: The Beecher Sisters on Women's Rights and Woman's Sphere*. GAC. Chapel Hill: University of North Carolina Press, 1988.

Dibdin, Emily. "Deborah." Pages 8–10 in *Lessons on Women of the Bible*. Edited by Emily Dibdin. London: Church of England Sunday School Society, 1893.

Doern, Kristin G. "Balfour, Clara Lucas (1808–1878)." *ODNB* 3 (2004): 514–15.

Dorland, William A. Newman. *The Sum of Feminine Achievement*. Boston: Strafford, 1917.

Ellis, Sarah Stickney. *The Women of England: Their Social Duties and Domestic Habits*. 15th ed. London: Fischer, 1839.

Fowler, Lois. "Julia McNair Wright." Pages 466–69 in vol. 4 *American Women Writers: A Critical Reference Guide from Colonial Times to the Present*. Edited by Lina Mainiero and Langdon L. Faust. New York: Ungar, 1982.

Galchinsky, Michael, ed. *Grace Aguilar: Selected Writings*. BLT. Peterborough, ON: Broadview, 2003.

Groot, Christiana de. "Nineteenth-Century Feminist Responses to the Laws in the Pentateuch." Pages 106–19 in *Strangely Familiar: Protofeminist Interpretations of Patriarchal Biblical Texts*. Edited by Nancy Calvert-Koyzis and Heather E. Weir. Atlanta: Society of Biblical Literature, 2009.

Groot, Christiana de, and Marion Ann Taylor. "Recovering Women's Voices in the History of Biblical Interpretation." Pages 1–17 in *Recovering Nineteenth-Century Women Interpreters of the Bible*. Edited by Christiana de Groot and Marion Ann Taylor. SymS 38. Atlanta: Society of Biblical Literature, 2007.

Gunn, David M. *Judges*. BBCom. Oxford: Blackwell, 2005.

Hale, Sarah. "Deborah." Pages 34–36 in *Woman's Record; or, Sketches of all Distinguished Women from Creation to 1854*. WR 89. New York: Harper & Brothers, 1855.

Herder, Johann Gottfried. *The Spirit of Hebrew Poetry*. Translated by James Marsh. Vol. 2. Burlington: Smith, 1833.

Kern, Kathi. *Mrs. Stanton's Bible*. Ithaca, NY: Cornell University Press, 2001.

Martyn, Sarah Towne. "Deborah: The Wife of Lapidoth." Pages 29–38 in *Women of the Bible*. New York: American Tract Society, 1868.

Mill, Harriet Taylor. "Enfranchisement of Women." Pages 89–121 in *Essays on Sex Equality: John Stuart Mill and Harriet Taylor Mill*. Edited by Alice S. Rossi. Chicago: University of Chicago Press, 1970.

Mill, John Stuart. "The Subjection of Women." Pages 123–242 in *Essays on Sex Equality: John Stuart Mill and Harriet Taylor Mill*. Edited by Alice S. Rossi. Chicago: University of Chicago Press, 1970.

Morgan, Lady. "Women of the Hebrews under the Judges: Deborah." Pages 66–73 in vol. 1 of *Woman and Her Master*. Philadelphia: Carey & Hart, 1840.

Morgan, Lewis Henry. *Ancient Society; or, Researches in the Lines of Human Progress from Savagery, through Barbarism to Civilization*. London: Macmillan, 1877.

Neyman, Clara. "Judges." Pages 21–23 in *Joshua to Revelation*. Vol. 2 of *The Woman's Bible*. Edited by Elizabeth Cady Stanton. New York: European, 1898.

Norval, Leigh. "Women in the Book of Judges." Pages 83–90 in *Women of the Bible: Sketches of All the Prominent Female Characters in the Old and the New Testament*. Nashville: M. E. Church, South, 1899.

Ragussis, Michael. *Figures of Conversion: "The Jewish Question" and English National Identity*. PCI. Durham, NC: Duke University Press, 1995.

Rowson, Susanna. *Biblical Dialogues between a Father and His Family: Comprising Sacred History, from the Creation to the Death of Our Saviour Christ*. Boston: Richardson & Lord, 1822.

Russett, Cynthia Eagle. *Sexual Science: The Victorian Construction of Womanhood*. Cambridge: Harvard University Press, 1989.

Satter, Beryl. *Each Mind a Kingdom: American Women, Sexual Purity, and the New Thought Movement, 1875–1920*. Berkeley: University of California Press, 1999.

Stanton, Elizabeth Cady. "The Book of Judges, Chapter II." Pages 18–20 in *Joshua to Revelation*. Vol. 2 of *The Woman's Bible*. Edited by Elizabeth Cady Stanton. New York: European, 1898.

———. "The Matriarchate, or Mother-Age." Pages 264–75 in *Elizabeth Cady Stanton: Feminist as Thinker; A Reader in Documents and Essays*. Edited by Ellen Carol DuBois and Richard Candida Smith. New York: New York University Press, 2007.

Stanton, Elizabeth Cady, Susan B. Anthony, and Matilda J. Gage, eds. *History of Woman Suffrage*. 6 vols. Rochester: Mann, 1887.

Stowe, Harriet Beecher. *Uncle Tom's Cabin*. Edited by Elizabeth Ammons. New York: Norton, 1994.

———. *Woman in Sacred History: A Series of Sketches*. WCA 41. New York: Ford, 1973.

Taylor, Marion Ann. "Harriet Beecher Stowe and the Mingling of Two Worlds: The Kitchen and the Study." Pages 99–105 in *Recovering Nineteenth-Century Women Interpreters of the Bible*. Edited by Christiana de Groot and Marion Ann Taylor. SymS 38. Atlanta: Society of Biblical Literature, 2007.

Taylor, Marion Ann, and Heather E. Weir, eds. *Let Her Speak for Herself: Nineteenth-Century Women Writing on Women in Genesis*. Waco, TX: Baylor University Press, 2006.

White, Barbara A. *The Beecher Sisters*. New Haven: Yale University Press, 2003.

Wiseman, Nathaniel. *Elizabeth Baxter (Wife of Michael Paget Baxter): Saint, Evangelist, Preacher, Teacher, and Expositor*. London: Christian Herald, 1928.

Wright, Julia McNair. *Saints and Sinners of the Bible*. Philadelphia: Ziegler & McCurdy, 1872.

"The Lord Has Given Me a Learned Tongue" (Isa 50:4): Catherine McAuley Interprets Scripture with Authority and Intention

Elizabeth M. Davis

> She seemed to inherit the great gift bestowed by God on the Prophet Isaias who said, "The Lord hath given me a learned tongue, whereby to support with a word him that is weary" (Isa 50:4).
> — Mary Ann Doyle, "The Annals of the Sisters of Mercy, St. Joseph's, Tullamore"

This biblical image ascribed to a Roman Catholic woman by one of her first religious sisters[1] places her in the line of prophets and teachers of the Old Testament and reflects the impact her biblical interpretation made on her community.

Catherine McAuley (1778–1841) was active publicly in Irish society and was involved in social action oriented to social change. Although she seems to have interpreted Scripture intuitively, without critical self-awareness, she intentionally and authoritatively used the Bible to effect that social change. Her engagement with the text anticipates emerging directions in biblical hermeneutics today. McAuley was a nontraditional interpreter, a woman who was not in the academy or in the church hierarchy, an ordinary reader whose biblical works in nontraditional genres were widely disseminated and read over time and across the world by commu-

---

1. Mary Ann Doyle, "The Annals of the Sisters of Mercy, St. Joseph's, Tullamore," in Mary C. Sullivan, *Catherine McAuley and the Tradition of Mercy* (Notre Dame, IN: University of Notre Dame Press, 1995), 67. Doyle was a member of Catherine McAuley's first religious community. All biblical citations in this paper come from the Douay-Rheims Version (DRV), sometimes with deliberate modifications by McAuley, as noted in section 2.

nities for whom they were and are instruments for social change. A study of her writings dispels the myth that the Bible was completely foreign to Catholic women in the early 1800s.

1. Social Location

John Barton writes, "Knowledge is socially situated, insisting that we should not just ask what the text meant or means, but who is reading the text and with what interests."[2] Social location for Catherine McAuley's interpretation is identified in three dimensions: societal, ecclesial/scriptural, and personal.

McAuley lived in Ireland during the pivotal years of the late eighteenth and early nineteenth centuries. This was a time of social ferment flowing from the impact of the Enlightenment as well as the Industrial, American, and French Revolutions. In this time period in the United Kingdom, laws were passed ensuring the emancipation of Catholics (1829) and Dissenters and Jews (1846, 1858) and ending first the slave trade (1807) and then slavery (1833). Ireland had been subject to penal laws which restricted the social, political, and economic rights of Roman Catholics. The subsequent poverty was intensified by successive crop failures and growing slums resulting from increasing industrialization and urbanization. As the repeal of the penal laws appeared imminent, the church hierarchy had begun to focus on revitalizing the faith primarily through services to poor people and education of children.

In this time period, the Bible was losing its absolute authority, and the roots of historical criticism were taking hold in Britain and Europe.[3] Forerunners of historical criticism—Friedrich Schleiermacher, Johann Eichhorn, Johann Gabler, and Wilhelm de Wette—were McAuley's contemporaries. However, the Bible was not central to the religious lives of Catholics. Avery Robert Dulles concludes: "In the Middle Ages, and, even more since the Reformation, Catholicism tended to become the church of

---

2. John Barton, *The Cambridge Companion to Biblical Interpretation*, CCR (Cambridge: Cambridge University Press, 1998), 3.

3. See the introductions in Gerald Bray, *Biblical Interpretation: Past and Present* (Downers Grove, IL: InterVarsity Press, 1996); John Sandys-Wunsch, *What Have They Done to the Bible? A History of Modern Biblical Interpretation* (Collegeville, MN: Liturgical Press, 2005); and William Yarchin, *History of Biblical Interpretation: A Reader* (Peabody, MA: Hendrickson, 2004).

law and sacraments rather than the church of the gospel and the word."[4] There was a popular misconception that Catholics were forbidden to read the Bible and that indeed the Bible was a Protestant book.

McAuley was born into a prosperous middle-class Catholic family in 1778 in Dublin, Ireland.[5] From her father, she learned to respond personally to the needs of those around her; from her mother, she learned to function graciously in society. For part of her adolescence, after the death of her father and the loss of the family income, she lived with relatives who were members of the Church of Ireland. As a young adult, she became a companion for a Quaker woman, Catherine Callaghan, with whom she lived for almost twenty years. After Callaghan and her husband William died, McAuley used her considerable inheritance from them to build a house in a fashionable section of Dublin for poor servant girls and homeless women.

In 1831, with the direction of church leaders, she founded the Congregation of the Sisters of Mercy whose purpose was described in this way:

> The sisters admitted into this religious congregation besides the principal and general end of all religious orders … must also have in view what is peculiarly characteristic of this Institute of the Sisters of Mercy, that is, a most serious application to the Instruction of poor Girls, Visitation of the Sick and protection of distressed women of good character.[6]

Like all women of her time, McAuley was not allowed to study or teach at a university, nor could she have been a member of her Church hierarchy. There is no evidence that she had her own Bible, although there are existing Bibles that had belonged to two members of her first religious

---

4. Avery Robert Dulles, *The Reshaping of Catholicism: Current Challenges in the Theology of Church* (San Francisco: Harper & Row, 1988), 23.

5. See books on the life of McAuley, including Mary Bertrand Degnan, *Mercy unto Thousands: Life of Mother Mary Catherine McAuley, Foundress of the Sisters of Mercy* (Westminster, MD: Newman, 1957); Mary Austin Carroll, *Life of Catherine McAuley* (New York: Sadlier, 1890); and Mary C. Sullivan, *The Path of Mercy: The Life of Catherine McAuley* (Washington, DC: Catholic University of America Press, 2012).

6. Catherine McAuley, "Rule and Constitutions," in *Catherine McAuley and the Tradition of Mercy*, ed. Mary C. Sullivan (Notre Dame, IN: University of Notre Dame Press, 1995), 295. The Rule is the foundational document of a religious institute in which members pronounce public vows and live a life in common as brothers or sisters. Constitutions embody the charism and theology of a religious community and set down norms to govern its life and activities.

community. She did not use traditional literary genres for interpretation (e.g., sermon, commentary, and treatise) but used letters, poetry, a religious tract, and retreat instructions. Her works were faithful to her religious tradition of Roman Catholicism but showed the influence of her association with Quakers and followers of the Church of Ireland. These works were not published in her lifetime, although they were circulated extensively through the communities of the Sisters of Mercy which she had founded in Ireland and England. After her death, several critical editions of her two-hundred-seventy extant letters, two collections of her sayings, and the tract, *Cottage Controversy*, were published.

2. Methodology Used to Reinforce Authority in Interpretation

McAuley's authoritative and confident interpretation permeated her biblically based instructions as she directed and motivated her first community members. In letters to her community, she used direct citations: "Oh, death, where is thy sting?" (1 Cor 15:55),[7] but she also modified citations to accommodate the statement she was making. For example: "His ways are not like our ways, nor His thoughts like our thoughts" (Isa 55:8).[8] She alluded to verses in Scripture: "Since to the obedient victory is given, may God continue his blessings to you" (cf. Prov 21:28).[9] She echoed scriptural themes: "May God bless and animate you with His own divine Spirit" (cf. Rom 8:14; Gal 4:6).[10] She mimicked biblical literary structure by using the endings of Paul's letters as her way of ending her own letters: "May God preserve and bless you," or "God bless you and send you every comfort and restore you to health."[11]

Scriptural references legitimated McAuley's directions to her trusted companions. In acknowledging the early deaths of the first sisters, she said: "Without the Cross the real Crown cannot come" (cf. Rev 2:10).[12] Despite

---

7. McAuley to Mary Frances Ward, August 1837, in *The Correspondence of Catherine McAuley, 1818–1841*, ed. Mary C. Sullivan (Dublin: Four Courts, 2004), 91.

8. McAuley to Mary Catherine Leahy, November 13, 1840, 321.

9. McAuley to Ward, early 1839, in *The Correspondence of Catherine McAuley, 1827–1841*, ed. Mary Angela Bolster (Cork: Congregation of the Sisters of Mercy, 1989), 79.

10. McAuley to Ward, October 23, 1837, 101.

11. McAuley to Ward, December 23, 1837, 116; McAuley to Ward, April 25, 1838, 134.

12. McAuley to Mary Elizabeth Moore, March 21, 1840, 259.

the crosses, she emphasized joy in doing God's work: "If He looks on us with approbation for one instant each day, it will be sufficient to bring us joyfully on to the end of our journey" (cf. Ps 94:1).[13] She directly quoted the words of Jesus to encourage the sisters: "By practice it will not only become easy but delightful, for Jesus Christ has said, 'My yoke is sweet and My burden light'" (Matt 11:30).[14] She used a maternal image of God as a source of comfort for her sisters: "God says He will comfort and console us as the loving mother cherishes her child, the greatest example of affection he could give" (cf. Isa 49:15).[15] She constantly relied on trust in God's providence: "Put your whole confidence in God [cf. 1 John 3:21]. He will never let you want necessities for yourself or children."[16] She used Scripture to lead the sisters to personally identify with the first followers of Jesus: "With the Apostle a religious must consider herself a stranger and pilgrim on earth, having her conversation in heaven" (cf. Phil 3:20),[17] or again: "God has never bestowed all his blessings on one person. He did not give to St. Peter what he gave to St. Paul, nor to either what He gave to St. John."[18]

McAuley often presented Scripture texts in ways that determined how they should be interpreted. She modified a reference from 2 Kings by substituting "I who have called you" for "I that command you" and by deleting the word "men." Her revision reads: "Let us imagine that God says to us, as we read in Holy Scripture 'Fear nothing, it is I who have called you, take courage, and be of resolution'" (cf. 2 Kgs 13:28), thus highlighting free choice and inclusivity. She quoted directly a verse and then gave an application for a religious woman:

> "If I wash thee not," He said, "you shall have no part with Me," [John 13:8] as if He would say: "If the instructions I have given you do not correct your erroneous worldly notions and ideas, do not change your proud spirit and root up and destroy whatever in manner or otherwise is unbecoming the dignity you aspire to, you shall not be My Spouse."[19]

---

13. McAuley to Mary de Sales White, 20 December 20, 1840, 332.
14. McAuley to White, December 20, 1840, 51, 144.
15. McAuley to White, December 20, 1840, 51.
16. McAuley to Mary Angela Dunne, December 20, 1837, 115.
17. Mary Teresa Purcell, *Retreat Instructions of Mother Mary Catherine McAuley*, ed. Mary Bertrand Degnan (Westminster, MD: Newman, 1952), 32.
18. Mary Clare Moore, *A Little Book of Practical Sayings, Advices, and Prayers of Our Revered Foundress, Mother Catherine McAuley* (London: Burns, Oates, 1868), 3.
19. Purcell, *Retreat Instructions*, 116–17.

She deliberately reinterpreted the story of Martha and Mary found in Luke by using images from Matthew: "The functions of Martha should be done for Him as well as the choir duties of Mary.... He requires that we should be shining lamps giving light to all around us. How are we to do this if not by the manner we discharge the duties of Martha?" (cf. Luke 10:38–42; Matt 5:16).[20] She rhetorically contrasted what Jesus did not say with what he did say: "Jesus Christ did not say, 'Come to me, you that are free from faults' but 'Come to Me, all you that labor and are burdened and I will refresh you'" (Matt 11:28).[21]

A tract that highlights both the social and religious reality of nineteenth century Ireland and the misconceptions about Catholics and the Bible has been attributed to McAuley.[22] *Cottage Controversy*, surprisingly avoiding language of prejudice and self-righteousness, presents a series of conversations between Margaret Lewis, a humble Catholic cottager, and Lady P., the Protestant Lady of the manor.[23] In a discussion on the Catholic practice of confession, the following conversation takes place:

> *Lady P.*: We should depend on the holy Bible, and not on the voice of men or tradition, as you Roman Catholics term it.
> *Margaret*: Sure it is in the Protestant Bible that Thomas[24] has—nothing can be plainer—how, when our blessed Saviour rose from the dead and came into the room where the disciples were, though the doors and the windows were shut, standing in the midst of them; that when he had

---

20. Purcell, *Retreat Instructions*, 155.
21. Purcell, *Retreat Instructions*, 91.
22. Although the term *tract* has several meanings ranging from a lengthy theological discourse to a short, written work of either political or religious nature, in the nineteenth century tracts generally were religious works written in small pamphlets and used by both Catholics and Protestants to defend their religious positions.
23. Catherine McAuley, *Cottage Controversy* (New York: O'Shea, 1883; repr., Baltimore: Lowry & Lubman, 1964). In a letter to Mary Josephine Warde, dated October 18, 1839, McAuley wrote: "Tell dear Sr. M. Vincent that I am quite disappointed that she never writes me one little note. I fear she will not patronize my next work, I dare not venture to dedicate it to her, if she does not give me more encouragement." To date, most published copies of McAuley's life or writings infer that this is a reference to *Cottage Controversy*. However, an original copy of the tract has not yet been found. Sullivan, *Correspondence*, 123, concludes that the work may have been a transcription of an earlier document not written by McAuley, although no such document has been found.
24. Thomas, Margaret's husband, had become a Catholic when he married Margaret.

saluted them and said, "My peace be with you," he breathed on them, saying "Receive ye the Holy Ghost; whose sins ye forgive, they are forgiven" [John 20:22–23].[25]

In another conversation in the tract, this reflection on Luke 1:48–49 occurs:

Lady P.: Speak truly, are you not taught to believe that she (Mary) has the same power as Christ himself?
Margaret: Sure, the Blessed Virgin never thought it, for when she said, "All generations shall call me blessed," she added; "Because he that is mighty has done great things for me." She did not say she was to be called "blessed" on her own account.[26]

The tract illustrates the depth of theology understood by the two women, the respect they show each other, and their knowledge of the words of the Bible as well as doctrines regarding its authority. Biblical interpretation is subtly presented as a legitimate work for women.

3. Interpretation with Intention: "To Support with a Word"

McAuley interpreted Scripture with intention but not with the intention of historical criticism or proof for doctrine. Although she would not have used or known these terms, for her, scriptural interpretation was primarily about praxis and embodied or lived theology. The modern theological concept of "praxis" is understood as "the critical relationship between theory and practice whereby each is dialectically influenced and transformed by the other."[27] McAuley's purpose in quoting or alluding to Scripture was clear. She wanted her community to "consecrate themselves to the service of the poor for Christ's sake."[28] This emphasis is evident in her paraphrase of a Scripture passage in her adaptation of the Rule of the Presentation Sisters[29] for use by her own newly formed community:

---

25. McAuley, *Cottage Controversy*, 33.
26. McAuley, *Cottage Controversy*, 43–44.
27. David Tracy, *Blessed Rage for Order: The New Pluralism in Theology* (New York: Seabury, 1975), 243.
28. McAuley to Moore, July 28, 1840, 282.
29. Each religious institute adopts a Rule as its foundation document subject to approval from Rome and developed on the basis of a previous Rule from a religious institute that shares a similar ministry or way of life. McAuley, the founder of a new

> In undertaking the arduous, but very meritorious duty of instructing the poor, the Sisters whom God has graciously pleased to call to this state of perfection, shall animate their zeal and fervor by the example of their Divine Master Jesus Christ, who testified on all occasions a tender love for the poor and declared that He would consider as done to Himself whatever should be done unto them [cf. Matt 25:40].[30]

The original Presentation Rule had spoken about Jesus's "tender love for little children" supported by the gospel reference "whosoever receiveth these little ones in his name, receiveth himself" (Matt 18:5).[31] This narrow emphasis on education of children McAuley had broadened to service to poor people by substituting the reference to Matt 25:40.

In both her *Sayings* and her *Retreat Instructions*, this theme continues:

> We find those who can enumerate very particularly all that Jesus Christ said and did, but what does He care for that? He said and did so, not that we should recount it in words, but shew Him in our lives, in our daily practice [cf. Matt 23:1–12].[32]

> It is not sufficient that Jesus Christ be formed in us; he must be recognized in our conduct ... "let us love not in word nor in tongue but in deed and in truth" [1 John 3:18].[33]

McAuley's most dramatic statement of praxis is expressed in her description of five young English women entering her community. She did this by amending Luke 12:49: "Consecrate themselves to the service of the poor for Christ's sake ... this is some of the fire He cast on the earth—kindling."[34] For McAuley, praying and studying Scripture were intentionally intertwined with service to poor people.

A second dimension of McAuley's intention in interpretation is related to her belief that her sisters, in order to be effective in praxis, must "labour to impress humility and meekness by example more than precept—the

---

institute, completed her initial formation with the Presentation Sisters and adapted their Rule for her community.

30. "Rule and Constitutions," 295.
31. Sullivan, *Tradition of Mercy*, 262.
32. Moore, *Little Book of Practical Sayings*, 25.
33. Purcell, *Retreat Instructions*, 71.
34. McAuley to Moore, July 30, 1840, 226. She is speaking about five English postulants who were entering the community.

virtues recommended most by our Saviour and chiefly by example."[35] She was intuitively ascribing to what is understood today as embodied or lived theology. She was seeking to shape a community that had "the same mind that was in Christ Jesus" (Phil 2:5). Referring to Exod 25:40, she said: "The words of Scripture are decisive, 'Look, and make it according to the pattern that was shown thee in the mount.'" In *Retreat Instructions*, her chosen words were: "As little infants, you must be born anew until Jesus Christ is formed in you [cf. John 3:5]. To have Jesus Christ formed in us is to think as He did, to speak as he spoke, and to will as He willed."[36] In *A Little Book of Practical Sayings*, we read: "Be always striving to make yourselves like our Blessed Lord; endeavour to resemble Him in some one thing at least, so that any person who sees you or speaks with you may be reminded of His sacred life on earth."[37] Mary Clare Moore, in her memories of McAuley, said: "Catherine, when instructing the Sisters, loved to dwell on those words of our Divine Lord: 'Learn of me because I am meek and humble of heart' [Matt 11:29]."[38]

4. Sources for McAuley's Interpretation

Although McAuley's Bible has not been found, there is substantial evidence that she had access to and regularly used texts that were biblically based. Her Sisters were obliged to read three times daily the short *Office of our Blessed Lady*, a shorter version of the *Divine Office*, which contained psalms, hymns, New Testament canticles (*Benedictus* [Luke 1:68–79], *Magnificat* [Luke 1:46–55], and *Nunc Dimittis* [Luke 2:29–32]), and lessons and chapters taken from the Bible.[39] They recited this *Office* in English, not Latin.[40] In *Cottage Controversy*, Margaret and Lady P. discussed the *Office* in this way:

> *Lady P.*: Is this a prayer book?
> *Margaret*: Yes, my lady, the Primer with the office of our blessed lady.
> *Lady P.*: Oh, Margaret, all the prayers in this great book to the Virgin! You cannot but offend her Creator.

---

35. McAuley to Moore, July 28, 1840, 283.
36. Purcell, *Retreat Instructions*, 71.
37. Moore, *Little Book of Practical Sayings*, 16.
38. Sullivan, *Tradition of Mercy*, 111.
39. "Rule and Constitutions," 306.
40. Sullivan, *Tradition of Mercy*, 60.

Margaret: It is odd that you should say that, my lady, for almost the whole office is taken from the Bible.[41]

The daily meditations of the sisters usually involved readings from *A Journal of Meditations for Every Day in the Year*,[42] a series of biblically based meditations collected from ascetical writers. For example, the fourth Sunday of Advent has the theme of invitation and welcome: Jesus invites Zaccheus to come down (Luke 19:5), Christ desires to become the guest of our souls (Rev 3:20), Abraham welcomes the three angels (Gen 18), the Shunamite woman welcomes Elisha (2 Kgs 4:8), Martha welcomes Jesus (Luke 10:38), and Prov 23:26 pleads, "My son, give me your heart."[43] In an interesting intertextual approach to Scripture, the New Testament references use Jesus's words to speak about his presence in the life of a person, while the Old Testament references are not used typologically or allegorically but give concrete examples of hosts (men and women) who show respect for their guests.

Another biblically based devotional text favored by McAuley was *The Following of Christ* written about 1530 by Thomas à Kempis.[44] On Scripture, Thomas wrote: "Charity and not eloquence is to be sought in Holy Scripture, and it should be read in the same spirit with which it was first made ... if you will profit by reading Scripture, read humbly, simply and faithfully."[45] This way of approaching Scripture was a model for McAuley about whom Moore relates: "She did not like the Sisters to use long words in speaking or writing, remarking that in the Psalms and other parts of Holy Scripture inspired by divine wisdom, there was scarcely a word more than three syllables."[46]

5. McAuley's Influence on Her Community

The centrality of Scripture in McAuley's teaching is reflected in the written and artistic works of the first members of her community. After McAuley's

---

41. McAuley, *Cottage Controversy*, 96.
42. Nathaniel Bacon, *A Journal of Meditations for Every Day in the Year Gathered out of Divers Authors*, trans. Edward Mico, 1669 (repr., Ann Arbor: University Microfilms International, 1984), A3.
43. Bacon, *Journal of Meditations*, 66–67.
44. Sullivan, *Tradition of Mercy*, 116; Moore, *Little Book of Practical Sayings*, 34.
45. Thomas à Kempis, *The Imitation of Christ*, ed. Harold C. Gardiner (1530, repr., New York: Hanover House, 1955), 37.
46. Moore, *A Little Book of Practical Sayings*, 28.

death, Moore and Mary Vincent Harnett wrote their memories of her, often associating moments of her life with Scripture. Moore noted that, on an occasion when the sisters were deeply saddened by illness, McAuley "repeated aloud the verse of the *Benedicite* said in the Refectory at Easter: 'This is the day the Lord hath made; let us rejoice and be glad therein' [Ps 117:24], reminding them that the trial came from Him Whose will we ought not only to obey but love with our whole hearts."[47] Moore said McAuley could die saying: "Now Thou dost dismiss Thy servant, O Lord, according to Thy word in peace. Because mine eyes have seen Thy salvation" (Luke 2:29).[48] Harnett, in describing the pressure placed on McAuley to establish a religious institute, recalled McAuley's words: "Blessed are ye when they shall revile you, and persecute you, and speak all that is evil against you untruly for my sake, be glad and rejoice for your reward is very great in heaven" (Matt 5:11).[49] Harnett also authored the *Catechism of Scripture History*, a "penny catechism" intended for use in the schools of the Sisters of Mercy.[50] Given the presumed attitude to the Bible by Catholics in this time, it is remarkable that this *Catechism* was ever written, and, even more, that it was extensively used and published both in Dublin in 1852 and in the United States in 1854.[51] McAuley's interpretation of Scripture is also reflected in the visual art of the early sisters. Moore used scriptural scenes and allusions in her illustrations deemed to be among the best of nineteenth century illumined works. Mary Clare Agnew was inspired by the work of the Sisters of Mercy in the poorest parts of Dublin to illustrate the spiritual and corporal works of mercy in a book published with commentary in four languages.[52]

---

47. Sullivan, *Tradition of Mercy*, 110.
48. Sullivan, *Tradition of Mercy*, 124.
49. Sullivan, *Tradition of Mercy*, 166.
50. Mary Vincent Harnett, *A Catechism of Scripture History Compiled by the Sisters of Mercy for the Use of Children Attending Their Schools*, rev. Edmund O'Reilly (London: Charles Dolman, 1852); John P. Marmion, "The Penny Catechism: A Long Lasting Text," *Par* 26 (1998): 19–24, https://tinyurl.com/SBLPress60071.
51. *Catechism of Scripture History* was revised by M. J. Kerney and published by Murphy in Baltimore in 1854.
52. Corporal and spiritual works of mercy are a Catholic tradition of charitable practices based in Scripture and dated to the early Middle Ages. The spiritual works are to admonish the sinners (Luke 15:7), instruct the ignorant (Mark 16:15), counsel the doubtful (John 14:27), comfort the sorrowful (Matt 11:28), bear wrongs patiently (Luke 6:27–28), forgive all injuries (Matt 6:12), and pray for the living and the dead

6. Interpretation with Authority, Intention, and Influence

McAuley used scriptural citations and allusions and intentionally interpreted them in letters to and works of guidance for the members of her community. Immediately after her death, her letters and other writings continued to guide and motivate the Sisters as they established missions, today carried out in forty-four countries. Her influence has extended over almost two hundred years, over the lives of approximately thirty thousand women who have been Sisters of Mercy during those years, and over the millions of people whose lives the Sisters of Mercy have touched in their ministries in health care, education, parish work, social services, justice, ecology, housing, administration, catechetics, and communications. Among the Sisters of Mercy today are a number of well-known Scripture scholars, including Carmel McCarthy, an Old Testament scholar from Ireland, and Elaine Wainwright, a New Testament scholar from Australia.

In the scriptural references woven into her written communications with her sisters living throughout Ireland and the British Isles, in her biblically based descriptions of the purpose and nature of the Sisters of Mercy, and in her assumption of authoritative leadership in interpreting Scripture for her community, this nineteenth-century Irish woman intentionally used the Bible to shape a community of women motivated by the life and teachings of Jesus and dedicated to the service of "the poor, the sick, and the ignorant."[53] In so doing, she anticipated a number of emerging directions in biblical hermeneutics today: attention to social location (in its multiple dimensions) in influencing interpretation, inclusion of women's experiences and voices (past and present) in biblical interpretation, plurality of interpretation as the norm, the expansion of hermeneutics to include praxis, attention to the source of the interpreter's authority to interpret credibly and legitimately, and the legitimacy of nontraditional biblical interpreters (outside academy and religious leadership) as a positive and transformative force in society.

There is little wonder why the members of McAuley's first religious community would conclude that she was a prophet speaking with author-

---

(John 17:24). The corporal works, based in Matt 25:31–46, are to feed the hungry, give drink to the thirsty, clothe the naked, shelter the homeless, visit the sick, visit the imprisoned, and bury the dead.

53. Traditional phrase used by the Sisters of Mercy to describe their focus in ministry.

ity and a teacher speaking with intention: "She seemed to inherit the great gift bestowed by God on the Prophet Isaias who said, 'The Lord hath given me a learned tongue, whereby to support with a word him that is weary'" (Isa 50:4).[54]

Bibliography

Bacon, Nathaniel. *A Journal of Meditations for Every Day in the Year Gathered out of Divers Authors*. Translated by Edward Mico. 1669. Repr., Ann Arbor: University Microfilms International, 1984.

Barton, John. *The Cambridge Companion to Biblical Interpretation*. CCR. Cambridge: Cambridge University Press, 1998.

Bolster, Mary Angela, ed. *The Correspondence of Catherine McAuley, 1827–1841*. Cork: Congregation of the Sisters of Mercy, 1989.

Bray, Gerald. *Biblical Interpretation: Past and Present*. Downers Grove, IL: InterVarsity Press, 1996.

Carroll, Mary Austin. *Life of Catherine McAuley*. New York: Sadlier, 1890.

Degnan, Mary Bertrand. *Mercy unto Thousands: Life of Mother Mary Catherine McAuley, Foundress of the Sisters of Mercy*. Westminster, MD: Newman, 1957.

Doyle, Mary Ann. "The Annals of the Sisters of Mercy, St. Joseph's, Tullamore." Page 67 in *Catherine McAuley and the Tradition of Mercy*. Edited by Mary C. Sullivan. Notre Dame: University of Notre Dame Press, 1995.

Dulles, Avery Robert. *The Reshaping of Catholicism: Current Challenges in the Theology of Church*. San Francisco: Harper & Row, 1988.

Harnett, Mary Vincent. *A Catechism of Scripture History Compiled by the Sisters of Mercy for the Use of Children Attending Their Schools*. Revised by Edmund O'Reilly. London: Dolman, 1852. Revised by M. J. Kerney. Baltimore: Murphy, 1854.

Kempis, Thomas à. *The Imitation of Christ*. Edited by Harold C. Gardiner. 1530. Repr., New York: Hanover House, 1955.

Marmion, John P. "The Penny Catechism: A Long Lasting Text." *Par* 26 (1998): 19–24. https://tinyurl.com/SBLPress6007l.

McAuley, Catherine. *Cottage Controversy*. New York: O'Shea, 1883. Repr., Baltimore: Lowry & Lubman, 1964.

---

54. Doyle, "Annals of the Sisters of Mercy," 67.

---. "Rule and Constitutions." Pages 295–328 in *Catherine McAuley and the Tradition of Mercy*. Edited by Mary C. Sullivan. Notre Dame, IN: University of Notre Dame Press, 1995.

Moore, Mary Clare. *A Little Book of Practical Sayings, Advices, and Prayers of Our Revered Foundress, Mother Catherine McAuley*. London: Burns, Oates, 1868.

Purcell, Mary Teresa. *Retreat Instructions of Mother Mary Catherine McAuley*. Edited by Mary Bertrand Degnan. Westminster, MD: Newman, 1952.

Sandys-Wunsch, John. *What Have They Done to the Bible? A History of Modern Biblical Interpretation*. Collegeville, MN: Liturgical Press, 2005.

Sullivan, Mary C. ed. *Catherine McAuley and the Tradition of Mercy*. Notre Dame, IN: University of Notre Dame Press, 1995.

---, ed. *The Correspondence of Catherine McAuley: 1818–1841*. Dublin: Four Courts, 2004.

---. *The Path of Mercy: The Life of Catherine McAuley*. Washington, DC: Catholic University of America Press, 2012.

---. *The Practical Sayings of Catherine McAuley: With a New Preface, Introduction, and Appendix*. New York: Sisters of Mercy of the Americas, New York, Pennsylvania, Pacific West Community, 2010.

---. *A Shining Lamp: The Oral Instructions of Catherine McAuley*. Washington, DC: Catholic University of America Press, 2017.

Tracy, David. *Blessed Rage for Order: The New Pluralism in Theology*. New York: Seabury, 1975.

Yarchin, William. *History of Biblical Interpretation: A Reader*. Peabody, MA: Hendrickson, 2004.

American Jewish Women Reading the Bible in the Year 1893

Pamela S. Nadell

An outpouring of biblical interpretation by Jewish women in the latter decades of the twentieth and the early twenty-first centuries has given us sermons from the first women ever ordained rabbis; feminist midrashim, stories reimagining the Torah from women's perspectives; and even novels, like Anita Diament's wildly popular *The Red Tent*, a modern midrash in which Jacob's only surviving daughter Dinah whispers tales of the lives of her four mothers Rachel, Leah, Zilpah, and Bilhah and of her own seduction and betrayal.[1]

Our intentional preoccupation suggests that American Jewish women's biblical interpretation is new, a happy by-product of the modern feminist movement. But such presentism obscures the historical precedent that these modern Jewish women, with their woman-focused biblical readings, stand on the shoulders of an earlier group of American Jewish women. In 1893, at the World's Columbian Exposition in Chicago, another cohort of American Jewish women asserted in public their right to explicate the Bible and postbiblical Jewish texts. As they read these sources through the prism of their lives and times, raising their voices for others to hear and later publishing their remarks, they boldly staked out a new claim for American Jewish women, that of the expert on Judaism.

This was, in its day and age, a revolutionary departure from the historic Jewish experience. In the enormous corpus of literature the Jewish people created in the more than two millennia since the close of the canon of the Hebrew Bible, only rarely are women's voices heard. The

---

I thank Dr. Rebecca DeWolf for her assistance.
1. Anita Diamant, *The Red Tent* (New York: St. Martin's, 1997).

major postbiblical Jewish texts, the Mishnah—a body of Jewish law codified circa 200 CE—and the Talmud—a wide-ranging discussion of the Mishnah: the Jerusalem Talmud was completed in Palestine at the end of the fourth century CE; the Babylonian Talmud redacted in Sura, then in the Sassanian Empire, by the end of the fifth century CE—have much to say about women's lives but record relatively few women's voices. For example, the Mishnah is deeply interested in women's status as daughters, as wives, as divorcees, as widows. Another genre of postbiblical rabbinic literature, midrash haggadah—that is, nonlegal texts that include commentaries on the Hebrew Bible—valorized women as nurturing mothers and dutiful spouses. Scholar Judith Baskin argues that when women's voices surface in these texts, what they say, how they say it, and what behaviors they describe have all been mediated by the men who constructed these texts.[2] Given that the entire corpus of rabbinic literature was constructed by men for men, its literary conventions, which scholar Tal Ilan has decoded, make its historical narratives about women's behaviors and their statements highly suspect.[3]

Medieval Jewish sages continued the Jewish tradition of exegesis of the Hebrew Bible. Down to this day, Jews studying the Hebrew Bible turn first to the great commentaries of the medieval French scholar Rashi (1040–1105). But few Jewish women in the medieval, early modern, and modern eras had access to the prerequisite learning—fluency in Hebrew and Aramaic languages, mastery of the great corpus of rabbinic literature—necessary to join in this tradition of writing biblical commentaries. Occasionally female voices do surface in the seventeenth and eighteenth centuries as authors of women's devotional literature, as in the prayers called *tkhines*, written in Yiddish, then the vernacular of much of European Jewry. But, as religion scholar Chava Weissler notes, even when these prayers—which often drew upon biblical traditions—were attributed to women, most of this literature, although not all, was written by men for women.[4]

Hence, the appearance of a number of American Jewish women in the late nineteenth century commenting publicly upon Jewish texts and

---

2. Judith R. Baskin, *Midrashic Women: Formations of the Feminine in Rabbinic Literature*, BSJW (Hanover, NH: University Press of New England, 2002), 3.

3. Tal Ilan, *Mine and Yours Are Hers: Retrieving Women's History from Rabbinic Literature*, AGAJU 41 (Leiden: Brill, 1997).

4. Chava Weissler, *Voices of the Matriarchs: Listening to the Prayers of Early Modern Jewish Women* (Boston: Beacon, 1998), 9–10.

traditions signifies a historic break with Jewish custom. Demonstrating their ability to explicate the Bible and to read the texts of Jewish tradition, and presenting these interpretations to a wide audience, Jewish women asserted religious authority. That assertion became another of the unanticipated byproducts and revolutions wrought as a result of Judaism's encounter with modernity. In appropriating for American Jewish women the right to explicate Jewish texts, these late nineteenth-century women set in motion a process that would eventually pave the way for Jewish women's mastery of the texts of Jewish tradition. In time, some would become students, scholars, and teachers of Judaism's sacred literature, and some would crash the male bastion of the rabbinate claiming for Jewish women, as well as Jewish men, the right to lead their people as religious leaders.

1. The 1893 World's Columbian Exposition and America's Jewish Women

The grand setting in which American Jewish women first staked out their claim to interpret Jewish texts and traditions in public was at the 1893 World's Columbian Exposition. Held in Chicago, Illinois, to commemorate the four-hundredth anniversary of Christopher Columbus's voyage to America, this grand world's fair drew over twenty-five million people in the six months it was open to the public and included more than two hundred auxiliary conferences, called congresses, and parliaments. The largest of these was the World's Parliament of Religions, held from September 11 to 27, 1893, an extraordinary meeting of representatives of diverse Western and Eastern religions.

Chicago Woman's Club member Ellen Henrotin was charged with finding women from the major religious denominations to organize women's committees for the Parliament of Religions and its auxiliary congresses. When it came to find someone to head the Jewish women's committee, Henrotin could find no nationally known female Jewish leader and no Jewish female clergy, for Judaism did not then ordain women. Hence, she turned to her friend, Chicago Woman's Club member Hannah Solomon (1858–1942) to orchestrate the participation of Jewish women. Solomon recognized "that it was a new departure for the Jewish woman to occupy herself with matters pertaining to religion."[5] But, after much searching

---

5. Hannah G. Solomon, "Address," in *Papers of the Jewish Women's Congress (1893)* (Philadelphia: Jewish Publication Society of America, 1894), 10.

across the United States, she found twenty-eight whom she invited to speak at the Congress.

After her plans were well underway, Solomon encountered an unanticipated obstacle. She had expected the female speakers to be part of the Parliament's auxiliary Jewish Denominational Congress. But, when she met with the rabbis organizing that program, she was stunned to see that not a single woman's name appeared on their roster of invited speakers. Hence, thanks to Solomon's efforts, the Jewish women held their own independent gathering, the Congress of Jewish Women.

Solomon's determination to prevent the rabbis from co-opting her plans for Jewish women to bring their thoughts to bear on the great task of solving contemporary problems and bridging the divide among men resulted in an unprecedented assembly of women displaying their knowledge of Judaism, their scholarship, their erudition, and their piety. As Sadie American (1862–1944), a member of the organizing committee of the Jewish Women's Congress, observed in her address there: "Never before in the history of Judaism has a body of Jewish women come together for the purpose of presenting their views, nor for any purpose but that of charity and mutual aid; never before have Jewish women been called upon to take any place in the representation of Judaism."[6] There was also a significant lasting outcome of this Congress: the founding of the first major nationwide US Jewish women's organization, the Council of Jewish Women, later renamed the National Council of Jewish Women.

2. The Congress of Jewish Women

Jewish women's participation in the World's Parliament of Religions denotes a historic break with Jewish tradition. In 1893 in Chicago, for the first time in history, Jewish women collectively asserted their authority to interpret the sacred texts of Judaism. The published papers of the Congress of Jewish Women disclose a group of late nineteenth-century American Jewish women explicating Jewish texts.

This public demonstration of women's Judaic erudition must be set against the backdrop of nineteenth-century Jews' adaptations of Judaism to the modern world. Over the course of the nineteenth century in

---

6. Sadie American, "Organization," in *Papers of the Jewish Women's Congress (1893)*, 245.

Europe, revolutions separating church and state had propelled Jews out of the ghetto and into the mainstream of western civilization. Jews crafted a host of responses to this radical change in their status: some even converted to Christianity. Others divided Jewish identity into its component parts, radically revisioning the concept of a Jew. For many, the most salient remaining component of Jewish identity was religion. The extent of the religious accommodations which modernizing Jews were willing to make—hearing a sermon in the vernacular, dispensing with Jewish religious garb, abandoning separatist Jewish dietary laws—led to the evolution of the various streams of modern Judaism. Immigrant Jews and their rabbis in the United States had similarly engaged in this process of religious modernization.

Adapting Judaism to the modern world concomitantly opened up new opportunities for Jewish women. Jewish girls and women began attending public worship in far greater numbers than heretofore. New religious ceremonies (e.g., confirmation) included women. In Philadelphia in 1838, Rebecca Gratz invented the Hebrew Sunday school, and it became a venue for women to become religious teachers for children. Over the course of the nineteenth century, Jewish women in every community in the United States had founded benevolent societies to care for the poor, ladies' aid societies to sustain their synagogues, and foster homes and orphanages to care for abandoned Jewish children. Now their expanding public activities moved to a new direction—a public presentation of women as Jewish experts. This unparalleled public demonstration not only owed its impetus to the modernization of Judaism but also to that of the nineteenth-century American woman's movement, which had demanded with increasing urgency and stridency an expansion of women's roles in American life.

For four days, from September 4 to 7, 1893, the presenters in the Congress of Jewish Women shared their understanding of Jewish history, culture, religion, and philanthropy to overflowing audiences. As American explained, their papers illuminated "what some Jewish women have been, have done, have thought, and what a few are thinking and planning."[7] The Congress began with historical overviews. Louise Mannheimer (1844–1920) presented "Jewish Women of Biblical and Medieval Times,"[8] followed

---

7. American, "Organization," 218.
8. Louise Mannheimer, "Jewish Women of Biblical and Medieval Times," in *Papers of the Jewish Women's Congress (1893)*, 15–25.

by Helen Kahn Weil, who surveyed "Jewish Women of Modern Days."[9] Weil's paper was then discussed by Solomon's sister, Henrietta G. Frank, and two of the most prominent rabbis of the day, Kaufman Kohler and Emil G. Hirsch, both leading exemplars of Reform Judaism. The next day, speakers considered specific aspects of Jewish women's historic and contemporary roles. Ray Frank (1861?–1948), then hailed for her preaching as the "girl rabbi of the golden west," discussed "Woman in the Synagogue."[10] Pauline Rosenberg considered the "Influence of the Discovery of America on the Jews."[11] Mary M. Cohen (1854–1911) contemplated the "Influence of the Jewish Religion in the Home."[12] Julia Richman examined "Women as Wage-Workers."[13] On the third day, Minnie D. Louis and others reflected upon Jewish women as mission workers, philanthropists, and combatants of anti-Semitism. At the conclusion of the Congress, American issued her call for "Organization," and those assembled agreed to found the Council of Jewish Women.

2.1. Biblical Women at the Congress of Jewish Women

The women presenting papers at the Congress of Jewish Women deliberately looked behind, turning to the past, seeking out Jewish women who had come before them—those who were wives and mothers, prophetesses and actors in the national narrative of the Jewish past. The Congress speakers sought out role models among the women of the past, looking for those whose roles and behaviors could affirm these later women's actions and conduct.

Mannheimer, educated at the University of Cincinnati, a rabbi's wife, a composer, a poet, and translator of Nahida Remy's *The Jewish Woman*,[14]

---

9. Helen Kahn Weil, "Jewish Women of Modern Days," in *Papers of the Jewish Women's Congress (1893)*, 26–42.

10. Ray Frank, "Woman in the Synagogue," in *Papers of the Jewish Women's Congress (1893)*, 52–65.

11. Pauline Rosenberg, "Influence of the Discovery of America on the Jews," in *Papers of the Jewish Women's Congress (1893)*, 66–73.

12. Mary M. Cohen, "The Influence of the Jewish Religion in the Home," in *Papers of the Jewish Women's Congress (1893)*, 115–21.

13. Julia Richman, "Women as Wage-Workers," in *Papers of the Jewish Women's Congress (1893)*, 91–114.

14. Nahida Remy, *Nahida Remy's The Jewish Woman*, trans. Louise Mannheimer (Cincinnati: Krehbiel & Co., 1895).

opened her paper on Jewish women in the biblical and medieval eras by voicing her trepidation by referring to the story of the spies Moses sent out to the promised land. Most returned terrified of the giants they glimpsed there. "But Caleb and Joshua were not afraid, for they trusted in the Lord" (cf. Num 32:12).[15] So, too, would she trust in the Lord, refusing to fear the giants, that is, the men whose authority as the sole custodians of Jewish tradition her voice challenged.

Mannheimer did not underestimate the difficulty of her task to explicate the history of women in the Bible by "enlarg[ing] the scant but suggestive material which the Scriptures supply."[16] She divided biblical women into three categories: "Mothers in Israel, the Prophetesses in Israel, and the women who solved the problem of the proper sphere of woman's activity in Israel at this early historical time."[17]

2.1.1. Mothers in Israel

Mannheimer and many of the women speaking at the Congress of Jewish Women saw a Jewish woman's central role as that of the mother in Israel. She wrote: "There is no title of honor which through all the generations of the adherents of Mosaic law was more revered than this sweet, blessed name of 'mother.'"[18] Scholar Dianne Lichtenstein has identified the mother in Israel as a leading trope in the writing of nineteenth-century American Jewish women, a stereotyped version of Jewish womanhood fully consonant with the then prevailing glorification of well-to-do American women as wives and mothers.[19] The mother in Israel signified the ideal Jewess, a woman whose primary roles—that of daughter, wife, and mother—kept her within the bosom of her family. Her "watchful care ... tender devotion ... self-sacrificing love," qualities which Mannheimer saw evident in the lives of the matriarchs Sarah, Rebecca, Rachel, and Leah, sustained her

---

15. Mannheimer, "Jewish Women," 15. Note: When the speakers at the Jewish Woman's Congress cited the Bible, they relied upon the King's James Version. Hence, I have used that for biblical quotations throughout this essay.
16. Mannheimer, "Jewish Women," 16.
17. Mannheimer, "Jewish Women," 17.
18. Mannheimer, "Jewish Women," 17.
19. Diane Lichtenstein, *Writing Their Nations: The Tradition of Nineteenth-Century American Jewish Women Writers* (Bloomington: Indiana University Press, 1992), 23–24.

family.[20] From within the bastion of her family and home, the contemporary mother in Israel upheld her people in America.

For nineteenth-century American Jewish women, Sarah "of womanly dignity" was the paradigmatic mother in Israel. As Mannheimer and others at the Congress read her, Sarah was deeply devoted to her home, "the faithful friend and companion of her husband" concerned with the welfare of others, the one who opened her home "to the poor and the needy," the one rewarded in her old age for her just actions with the birth of a son upon whom she doted.[21] Cohen offered that from the time of Sarah, the Jewish wife and mother has shown herself, "as a rule … faithful to her husband and children … as generous a hospitality as her means will permit."[22] Cohen understood Sarah as fulfilling the commandment: "And thou shalt rejoice in every good thing which the Lord thy God hath given unto thee, and unto thine house, thou and the Levite, and the stranger that is among you" (Deut 26:11).[23] Of course, Sarah was not the only mother in Israel to appear in these addresses. The women speaking at the Congress of Jewish Women lauded the Bible's many exemplary mothers in Israel: Hannah, whose "work in and for the synagogue lies in bringing to the Temple the Samuels to fulfil the Law,"[24] "brought him [Samuel] unto the house of the LORD in Shiloh" (1 Sam 1:24); Ruth, the faithful daughter-in-law; Abigail, a model of self-possession and dignity, who used her homemaker skills to feed the army of David and calm his wrath; and, of course, the anonymous model wife of Prov 31:10–31, versed in the arts and industries necessary to run a household, to buy a field. "She seeketh wool, and flax, and worketh willingly with her hands.… She considereth a field, and buyeth it" (Prov 31:13, 16). As Frank, who was then unmarried and who never did bear a child, urged: "The ancient Jewish woman was, above all, wife and mother, and as such she was a religious teacher.… As mothers in Israel I appeal to you to first make of our homes temples, to rear each child a priest by teaching him to be true to himself."[25]

---

20. Mannheimer, "Jewish Women," 17.
21. Mannheimer, "Jewish Women," 17.
22. Cohen, "Influence," 120.
23. Cohen, "Influence," 120.
24. Frank, "Women in the Synagogue," 65.
25. Frank, "Women in the Synagogue," 56, 65.

2.1.2. Prophetesses in Israel

The next category of biblical women delineated by Mannheimer was the prophetesses. She saw these women as blessed with "responsive souls." Others might "hear nothing, feel nothing," but these women had souls "moved by the breath of the Lord."[26]

Those who referred to the prophetesses invariably mentioned that most of them were first and foremost wives and mothers. Frank called Hannah "an inspired prophetess, a wise mother," and Mannheimer said the only title Deborah ever claimed was "Deborah, a Mother in Israel."[27] "That I Deborah arose, that I arose a mother in Israel" (Judg 5:7). Even after the king's officers had come to Huldah, she still retained "the true womanly modesty of a Mother in Israel."[28]

The speakers at the Jewish Woman's Congress thus carefully couched their remarks about this remarkable group of biblical women to stay within the constructions accepted of their time and place for women of the leisured classes. For these writers, prophetesses were naturally not only prophetic but also exemplary mothers in Israel. Nevertheless, the speakers lauded the prophetesses for their leadership, concluding that, when the Jewish woman of the Bible led, "she led successfully."[29]

Miriam was the first among the prophetesses in ancient Israel "whose responsive soul was moved by the breath of the Lord." Mannheimer saw her intelligence made manifest as she patiently watched over Moses in the Nile until "she saw her little brother safe in the arms of Pharaoh's daughter."[30] Then, drawing upon "the gifts of her womanhood" nurtured in the act of saving her little brother," Miriam "took a timbrel in her hand" (Exod 15:20) to lead the women of Israel by the shores of the sea and sing a song of triumph. "Sing ye to the Lord, for He hath triumphed gloriously; the horse and his rider hath He thrown into the sea" (Exod 15:21).[31] Even when Miriam was punished for speaking against "Moses because of the Ethiopian woman" (Num 12:1) and stricken with leprosy, all of Israel had to wait for her until the time of her punishment had passed. "And Miriam

---

26. Mannheimer, "Jewish Women," 20.
27. Frank, "Women in the Synagogue," 55; Mannheimer, "Jewish Women," 21.
28. Mannheimer, "Jewish Women," 22.
29. Frank, "Women in the Synagogue," 56.
30. Mannheimer, "Jewish Women," 20.
31. Mannheimer, "Jewish Women," 20.

was shut out from the camp seven days: and the people journeyed not till Miriam was brought in again" (Num 12:15). Frank made an even larger claim for Miriam's influential role, concluding that she "must have been one of the leaders in Israel before the journey across the sea was made."[32] It is not clear whether or not Frank was thinking of the prophet Micah, who located Miriam within the triumvirate of the Exodus's leaders: "For I brought thee up out of the land of Egypt, and redeemed thee out of the house of servants; and I sent before thee Moses, Aaron, and Miriam" (Mic 6:4). Frank instead found other prooftexts for her claim, concluding from the emphasis given to the word prophetess before Miriam sang her song— "And Miriam the prophetess, the sister of Aaron, took a timbrel in her hand" (Exod 15:20)—and from Moses's words to Miriam and Aaron as he journeyed to the mount that she too was a leader in the exodus.

As for the prophetess Deborah, Mannheimer saw in her "a glorious culmination" of the "growing intellectual and spiritual development of the women of Israel." She was "prophet, judge, leader in battle, poet, and sacred singer," gifted with "natural talents" which she had carefully cultivated and perfected in her service to God (cf. Judg 5:1).[33] Frank, in fact, likened this "ruler, warrior, poet … prophet" to Moses, claiming both great leaders of ancient Israel shared the important quality of modesty, recognizing not what they accomplished themselves, but rather what God did through them for Israel.[34]

Mannheimer also admired the prophetess Huldah, concluding that it was her "reputation for superior wisdom and profound knowledge of the Law" that compelled the king's officers to seek her out. When they did, where did they find her, but *"in the College"* (cf. 2 Kgs 22:14). From this, Mannheimer, surely thinking of women's growing access to higher education in her own time, concluded that "there were, then, no restrictive regulations … exclud[ing] women from colleges among the Israelites … even married women."[35]

By highlighting the prophetesses as leaders in ancient Israel, speakers at the Jewish Women's Congress affirmed their own sense that, when the Lord said to Moses: "And ye shall be unto Me a nation of priests and

---

32. Frank, "Women in the Synagogue," 54.
33. Mannheimer, "Jewish Women," 21.
34. Frank, "Women in the Synagogue," 55.
35. Mannheimer, "Jewish Women," 22, emphasis original.

an holy nation" (Exod 19:6), the message was not directed at one sex.[36] By drawing attention to the prophetesses speaking and leading in their own right in the ancient past, the speakers at the Jewish Women's Congress were, by inference, asserting their own right to stand and to speak for American Judaism within the World's Parliament of Religions.

2.1.3. Women Solving the Problem of Their Sphere

The third category delineated by Mannheimer focused on the biblical "women who solved the problem of the proper sphere of woman's activity in Israel at this early historic time."[37] Just the phrasing of this question indicated how much Mannheimer was influenced by late nineteenth-century rhetoric about woman's proper sphere. In this group of "energetic" women, whose quiet dignity in solving problems she deliberately emphasized, she pointed to the five daughters of Zelophehad, who pleaded for their inheritance rights before Moses and the whole congregation of Israel and who won for themselves a share in their father's property. They asserted: "Why should the name of our father be taken away from among his family, because he had no son? Give unto us a possession among the brethren of our father" (Num 27:4). They were answered: "The daughters of Zelophehad speak right: thou shalt surely give them a possession of an inheritance among their father's brethren; and thou shalt cause the inheritance of their father to pass unto them" (Num 27:7).

Mannheimer wrote of Abigail's independence from her husband, of how when he refused to give David and his warriors food, she set forth to feed them and to calm David's wrath. She admired the Shunammite who, returning from Philistine lands to find her house and land confiscated, refused to ask a man, the prophet Elisha, to intercede for her with the king. Instead, she herself sought redress and obtained it. From these examples Mannheimer concluded: "So we find woman in the full enjoyment of equality of rights in Israel."[38]

Mannheimer then ranged over postbiblical Jewish women, for traditionally Jewish exegesis moves across the millennia of the Jewish experience with ease. She found powerful postbiblical examples for Jewish women's equality: Alexandra Salome, who reigned over Judea for nine

---

36. Frank, "Women in the Synagogue," 53–54.
37. Mannheimer, "Jewish Women," 17.
38. Mannheimer, "Jewish Women," 24.

years after the death of her husband, the Hasmonean king Alexander Jannaeus; and "many a woman whose authority in the expounding of the Law was acknowledged even by the rabbis," among them Beruriah, the wife of the second-century sage Rabbi Meir.[39]

2.2. Congress of Jewish Women: Significance

Even as the women speaking at the Congress of Jewish Women exalted the mother in Israel, professing nothing could replace her, these women's performances belied their rhetoric. For rather than remaining secluded in the sanctuaries of their homes, they had come to stand in the hallowed halls of this auxiliary congress of the World's Parliament of Religions, daring to represent Judaism to the world, albeit primarily addressing the subject of women and Judaism. Thus, at the same time that they glorified Jewish women as wives and mothers, they mined Jewish tradition to affirm woman's right to go outside her proper sphere. These women deliberately reread biblical and rabbinic texts much the way modernizing rabbis did, so that the weight of the past would sanction the privileges they now took for themselves in the present. Hannah Solomon explained: "In the pages of history in the lives of the heroes and heroines, the destinies and possibilities of a people are written. In them, we have been trying to discover ideals for ourselves, our daughters and our granddaughters."[40] These speakers maintained that, even as Jewish tradition exalted the mothers in Israel, it also honored women who stepped outside traditional female and feminine roles, the prophetesses and those women who sought at their moment in time to solve the problem of a woman's proper sphere. Speaking at the Jewish Women's Congress, Mannheimer, Frank, Cohen, Solomon, and others identified with all three groups of biblical women. Even as they called themselves mothers in Israel, they also took direction from the prophetesses and the other biblical women who had expanded women's roles. Presenting their voices and views alongside those of the Jewish Denominational Congress rabbis who had not managed to find a place for women on their program, these women were, in fact, expanding women's roles and proper sphere at their moment in time. When, at the end of the Congress of Jewish Women, they founded the Council of Jewish

---

39. Mannheimer, "Jewish Women," 24.
40. Solomon, "Address," 166.

Women, they created a new and lasting mechanism to allow them to continue to stake out a claim to play a role in solving the problems of their day and expanding women's proper sphere.

3. Two Views of Judaism: The World's Parliament of Religions

The Congress of Jewish Women was not the only setting where women represented Judaism at the World's Parliament of Religions. Solomon's organizing committee had selected two notable American women to stand alongside the rabbis representing Judaism in the unique interfaith setting of the World's Parliament of Religions itself. Scholars rightly consider the World's Parliament of Religions—with addresses by those from the Protestant mainstream, Roman Catholicism, Eastern Orthodoxy, Islam, Buddhism, Hinduism, other Asian religions, and Judaism—a progenitor of the modern interfaith movement. Here, participation of American Catholics and American Jews revealed the incipient broadening of American religious life. The Parliament was also hailed as a breakthrough for women in religion. Protestantism was represented by Julia Ward Howe, author of the "Battle Hymn of the Republic," and Frances E. Willard, president of the Woman's Christian Temperance Union, the largest American women's organization of its time. Judaism was represented by a number of rabbis and scholars and by Josephine Lazarus (1846–1910) and Henrietta Szold (1860–1945).

Lazarus and Szold represented opposing views within an evolving American Judaism. Lazarus, influenced by contemporary biblical scholarship and those shaping the modernizing religious movement of Reform Judaism, preached Judaism as a universal religion. Szold, from a family closely associated with those American Jews who opposed many, although by no means all, of the reformist thrusts, preached a far more traditional view of Judaism. Yet, even she allowed for certain accommodations to speak to her contemporaries' sensibilities.

3.1. Josephine Lazarus, "The Outlook of Judaism"

Josephine Lazarus was the second of the children born in New York to a well-to-do family that could trace its roots back to colonial America. She began publishing her own writing only after the death, at age thirty-eight, of her younger sister Emma, who was renowned in her short lifetime as a poet, essayist, and champion of the persecuted Jews of the Russian Empire.

After Emma Lazarus died in 1887, she became known forevermore as the author of "The New Colossus." Its famous lines inscribed on a plaque in the base of the Statue of Liberty—"Give me your tired, your poor / Your huddled masses yearning to breathe free"—welcomed millions of immigrants to America.[41]

Josephine Lazarus had already published a collection of her sister's verse when she was invited to address the World's Parliament of Religions. Her paper "The Outlook of Judaism" asked "what is the content and significance of modern Judaism in the world to-day?"[42] Her answer reveals Lazarus standing squarely at the far end of one spectrum of late nineteenth-century Jewish thought, among those who believed it imperative to revise Judaism as a universal religion. She charged that across the millennia, the Jew had "drifted away from his spiritual bearings, and lost sight of spiritual horizons."[43] She demanded that Judaism reclaim "its broad ethical and social basis, its seeming universality."[44] The time had come, so she argued, for Jews and Judaism to join with others in a "unity of spirit."[45]

Lazarus came to revision Judaism by reading the Bible through the prism of late nineteenth-century higher biblical criticism. As it dismissed the historicity of many persons and events in the Hebrew Bible and departed from the traditional Jewish view that God had given the five books to Moses on Mount Sinai, so, too, did she. Writing of the ancient Hebrews' "mythical beginnings," of a "tribe of wanderers in eastern lands, roaming beside the water-ways, feeding their flocks on the hill-sides," Lazarus depicted its "patriarchal leaders" as "large, tribal composite figures, rather than actual persons."[46] Similarly, Moses also stands "upon a background of myth"; he is, for her, a "semi-historic or a purely symbolic figure." Not until the formation of David's kingdom did Lazarus concede "the dawn of history," signifying that at last the Bible began to speak of historical actors.[47]

---

41. Emma Lazarus, "The New Colossus," 1883, Jewish Women's Archive, http://jwa.org/media/new-colossus-from-emma-lazarus-copy-book.
42. Josephine Lazarus, "The Outlook of Judaism," in *Judaism at the World's Parliament of Religions* (Cincinnati: Union of American Hebrew Congregations, 1893), 296.
43. Lazarus, "The Outlook of Judaism," 302.
44. Lazarus, "Outlook of Judaism," 299.
45. Lazarus, "Outlook of Judaism," 303.
46. Lazarus, "Outlook of Judaism," 297.
47. Lazarus, "Outlook of Judaism," 297.

But the true merit of the nation she styled as this "'God-intoxicated' race" lay not in the "outward greatness" of the kingdom of David and Solomon, nor even in the sacred sanctuary in Jerusalem, but rather "wholly in the inner impulse and activity, the spiritual impetus which was now shaping itself into Prophetism." Lazarus believed that the "prophets owned the clearer vision." They led the ancient Israelites to transcend their "petty, tribal god, cruel and partisan," prophesying of the "universal and eternal God." That is "the core of the Hebrew conception."[48]

For Lazarus, Israel's "true grandeur and originality" lay exclusively "in the moral sphere" as preached by the prophets. Unfortunately, however, the light of the prophets, with its "broad ethical and social basis," never became "the religion of the masses." The people needed something "more congenial to their actual development at the time." Consequently, the people Israel lived circumscribed by the punctilious minutiae of Jewish law, "in which the spirit was incased [sic] as in a mummy shroud … covering the most insignificant acts of life."[49] Even though "the kingdom perished, the Temple fell, the people scattered," the law made them "more intensely national, more exclusive and sectarian … than they had ever been before." In the next eras of Jewish history, when the Talmud and the rabbis held sway, Judaism "lost its power to expand, its claim to become a universal religion, and remained the prerogative of a peculiar people."[50]

That was, according to Lazarus, the state of Judaism and the Jewish people until the modern era. But the French Revolution had "sounded a note of freedom so loud, so clamorous that it pierced the Ghetto walls, and found its way to the imprisoned souls."[51] In its wake Judaism reverted "to its original type, the pure and simple monotheism of the early days."[52]

But what of today? Looking about her, Lazarus saw that she lived in an age and land which celebrated the "liberal, progressive, humanitarian." Yet, gazing across the ocean, she found Jews persecuted "in barbarous Russia, liberal France, philosophic Germany."[53] How to end this persecution of the Jews? Her solution: "Away then with all the Ghettos and with spiritual isolation in every form.… The Jew must change his attitude before the

---

48. Lazarus, "Outlook of Judaism," 298.
49. Lazarus, "Outlook of Judaism," 299–300.
50. Lazarus, "Outlook of Judaism," 300.
51. Lazarus, "Outlook of Judaism," 300.
52. Lazarus, "Outlook of Judaism," 301.
53. Lazarus, "Outlook of Judaism," 302.

world and come into spiritual fellowship with those around him."⁵⁴ But what, then, of the future of Judaism? It must return to its historic, truest vision, to its "higher calling and destiny.... It must be a spiritual force."⁵⁵ Climbing over the wall between Judaism and Christianity, she dared to claim "for our own ... John, Paul, Jesus himself." While she did not expect Jews to become "Presbyterians, Episcopalians, members of any dividing sect," she demanded that "Christians as well as Jews ... embrace ... the unity of spirit" and recognize that Judaism could lead the way. She concluded: "Mankind at large may not be ready for a universal religion, but let the Jews with their prophetic instinct, their deep, spiritual insight, set the example and give the ideal."⁵⁶

3.2. Henrietta Szold, "What Has Judaism Done for Woman?"

If Lazarus's understanding of the Jewish past led her to revision Judaism as a universal religion, Szold, the only other woman to speak alongside the many rabbis addressing the World's Parliament of Religions, asked an entirely different question. Szold is, of course, widely known as the founder of Hadassah, the Women's Zionist Organization of America, which she established in 1912. Yet in 1893, when she addressed the World's Parliament of Religions, she was already the best known American Jewish woman of her day. The eldest of the five surviving daughters born to a Baltimore rabbi and his wife, she had earned a well-deserved reputation as a writer, educator, and community organizer for her founding of one of the first night schools in the United States dedicated to teaching adult immigrants English and the principles of American citizenship. She had also recently become the secretary, in truth the editor-in-chief, of the Jewish Publication Society, the first successful such venture in the US for the publishing of Jewish books.

Unknowingly anticipating that much of her life's future work would revolve around shaping new avenues for Jewish women's activism and leadership in both the United States and British-Mandate Palestine, Szold asked "What Has Judaism Done for Woman?" Szold's question, of course, must also be set against the expanding opportunities for women of the late nineteenth century. Szold herself had wanted to go to college. However,

---

54. Lazarus, "Outlook of Judaism," 303.
55. Lazarus, "Outlook of Judaism," 295, 303.
56. Lazarus, "Outlook of Judaism," 303.

there were no colleges for women in Baltimore, and she was unable to leave home. She was fully cognizant of the contemporary woman suffrage movement and also of its implications for women's roles within Judaism. She read biblical and postbiblical texts to argue not for "the sameness in function ... of man and woman" but for their "equality in position."[57] Late twentieth-century feminist theorists would call this "difference feminism." Later, as the founder and leader of Hadassah, she would preach that American women working for Hadassah took their places in a chain of tradition which linked them to biblical women who had also devoted their lives to their people.

Szold opened by recognizing the inherent equality between the sexes fixed by Judaism back to the moment of creation. "Whatever incipient Judaism did for man, that precisely it did for woman: it made man, created male and female."[58] "So God created man in his own image, in the image of God created he him; male and female created he them" (Gen 1:27). Szold then peered inside the "tent of Abraham" where "the woman ... presided" and where "the humanity of civilization" had its origins. Viewing Abraham as "the typical father" commanding his children to "keep the way of the Lord, to do righteousness and justice," she wondered "What was Sarah's share in this paramount work of education?" Sarah knew that Ishmael had "to be removed" so that Isaac "might not, by bad example, be lured away from 'the way of the Lord.'" Szold, the teacher, understood "this plan" as "wholly educational in its aims" and indicative of Abraham and Sarah's equal share in raising their son, which compelled Abraham to "hearken unto [Sarah's] voice" (Gen 21:12).[59]

Szold then turned to the next couple in Genesis, Rebekah and Isaac, finding that, like Abraham and Sarah, while they were "not sharing in the sameness of function," they, too, enjoyed "the equality of position, of man and woman."[60] Together they stood "at one" before their children. Szold believed that Isaac "completely adopted the tactics of Rebekah" in conveying to Esau his disapproval of the daughters of the Canaanites.[61]

---

57. Henrietta Szold, "What Has Judaism Done for Woman?," in *Judaism at the World's Parliament of Religions* (Cincinnati: Union of American Hebrew Congregations, 1893), 305.
58. Szold, "What Has Judaism Done for Woman?," 305.
59. Szold, "What Has Judaism Done for Woman?," 305.
60. Szold, "What Has Judaism Done for Woman?," 305.
61. Szold, "What Has Judaism Done for Woman?," 306.

"Thou shalt not take a wife of the daughters of Canaan" (Gen 28:1). As for Rebecca, Szold called her the "first social innovator, the first being to act contrary to tradition, and the iron-bound customs of society" for subverting the traditional custom of primogeniture. Szold thus read Genesis as establishing "the ideals of equality between man and woman that have come down to us from the days of the Patriarchs" and which remain "the ideal toward which the Jewish woman was to aspire."[62] There were, of course, other examples of women in the Bible affirming this ideal. She considered the honored mothers of great men—Jochebed, the mother of Moses; Hannah, the mother of Samuel, "the sole director of his career."[63]

Szold also found Jewish law emphasizing a woman's equality of position with her husband. Fathers and mothers exert equal authority over their children, for the law decrees that a son who refuses to hearken to the voice of his father or to the voice of his mother shall be chastised by both. "If a man have a stubborn and rebellious son: which will not obey the voice of his father, or the voice of his mother, and that, when they have chastened him, will not hearken unto them, then shall his father and his mother lay hold on him" (Deut 21:18–19).[64] Szold continued her discussion of Mosaic legislation—the same legislation Lazarus had repudiated—by evaluating its laws governing the relations of the sexes. Knowing of the lesser status accorded women in the surrounding nations, she explained that Jewish law had sought, as far as possible, to safeguard the position of Jewish women, especially with respect to rights of inheritance and protections in marriage and divorce.

But when the Jewish people forgot its original purposes, including straying from the fundamental equality between woman and man fixed at creation and evident in the lives of the patriarchs and matriarchs, then the nation stumbled. Szold brought forward the prophet Malachi who "set forth the whole misery" of the "later days," showing how they had culminated "in the disregard of woman ... and the collapse" of the "ideal of woman's co-equality with man."[65] Szold took as her prooftext Malachi's words: "the Lord hath been witness between thee and the wife of thy youth, against whom thou hast dealt treacherously; yet is she thy

---

62. Szold, "What Has Judaism Done for Woman?," 306.
63. Szold, "What Has Judaism Done for Woman?," 306.
64. Quoted in Szold, "What Has Judaism Done for Woman?," 306.
65. Szold, "What Has Judaism Done for Woman?," 307.

companion, and the wife of thy *covenant*" (Mal 2:14).[66] For Szold, the result was a disequilibrium that "intrenched the Jewess' position even unto this day."[67]

This disequilibrium becomes key to understanding Szold's position. An observant Jewish woman, she lived within a circle of others who shared her regard for Jewish tradition, even as she was willing to reread the texts of that tradition to bring them into consonance with her age's rhetorical claim for women's equality.

In concluding remarks, Szold returned again, not to the sameness of function of Jewish men and women, but to assert once more her original argument for the sameness of position. For Szold, a Jewish woman's commandment to kindle the Sabbath lights was symbolic of her influence in the home and from there, upon larger circles of society. The Jewish woman was the inspirer of a pure, chaste family life, whose hallowing influences were incalculable; she stood at the center of all spiritual endeavors, the confidante and fosterer of every undertaking. To her the Talmudic sentence applied:

> It is woman alone through whom God's blessings are vouchsafed to a house. She teaches the children, speeds the husband to the place of worship and instruction, welcomes him when he returns, keeps the house godly and pure, and God's blessings rest upon all these things.[68]

---

66. Quoted in Szold, "What Has Judaism Done for Woman?," 307, emphasis original.

67. Szold, "What Has Judaism Done for Woman?," 307, 309.

68. Quoted in Szold, "What Has Judaism Done for Woman?," 310. I am deeply grateful to University of Oregon Professor Judith Baskin, who affirms that this is not a direct quotation from the Talmud. Instead, it is a conflation of several passages. Among them are: b. B. Metz. 59b: "R. Helbo said: One must always observe the honor due to his wife, because blessings rest on a man's house only on account of his wife"; and b. Ber. 17a: "How do women earn merit? By making their sons go to the synagogue to learn scripture, and their husbands to the study house to learn Mishnah, and by waiting for their husbands until they return from the study house." The text, as Szold quotes it, widely circulated in the late nineteenth century. It may first have appeared in Emanuel Deutsch, "What Is the Talmud," *LQR* 123 (1867); the quotation appears on page 243 in the American edition (New York: Leonard Scott, 1867), 220–44. This essay was translated into multiple languages and frequently reprinted. On Deutsch, see Joseph Jacobs and Goodman Lipkind, "Emanuel Oscar Menahem Deutsch," *JE* (1906), https://tinyurl.com/SBL6007a.

In the end, Szold's vision of women's roles within American Judaism remained that of the "woman of valor" (Prov 31:10–31) honored for her industriousness by her husband and children, even as she advanced an argument, fitting for her day, that Judaism affirmed women's equality, of a kind.

4. Leading American Judaism into the Future

Lazarus and Szold's addresses claim our attention not only for the significance of two women representing Judaism under the auspices of the World's Parliament of Religions but also for their coming to such different conclusions about Judaism's essence. These two women by themselves displayed to this Parliament the tremendous range of late nineteenth-century Judaism. The development of multiple visions of Judaism was, of course, the result of the Jewish collision with modernity. Its concomitant decline of an authoritative Jewish communal leadership had enabled individuals—now, in 1893, including women as well as men—to assert the validity of their own interpretations of Judaism. All modern expressions of Judaism—Reform, Liberal, Conservative, even Orthodox—emerged out of this encounter. That women too would assert the right to fashion Judaism, to reinterpret the tradition, to claim for themselves the authority to explicate the Bible, to read rabbinic texts, and to apply their understanding of this sacred literature to the great questions of their day was surely one of many unanticipated outcomes of Judaism's encounter with the nineteenth century.

It is also possible to draw a straight line from all the Jewish women addressing the Congress of Jewish Women and the World's Parliament of Religions to those who eventually would also use the Bible and Jewish sacred texts to assert other demands, including women's right to study, to learn, to teach, even to become a scholar and a rabbi. In fact, a number of the women appearing in this essay, including Cohen, Frank, and Szold, played significant roles in the debate on the woman rabbi then emerging in American Jewish life. Surely, they already intuited that, in acquiring the knowledge to explicate Jewish texts and in demonstrating their capacity to do so in public at the World's Parliament of Religions, they had put in motion a process that, even though it would take nearly a century to resolve, would end in other startling changes for Judaism—including the woman rabbi.[69]

---

69. For further information, see Pamela S. Nadell, *Women Who Would Be Rabbis: A History of Women's Ordination, 1889–1985* (Boston: Beacon, 1998).

Bibliography

American, Sadie. "Organization." Pages 218–62 in *Papers of the Jewish Women's Congress (1893)*. Philadelphia: Jewish Publication Society of America, 1894.

Baskin, Judith R. *Midrashic Women: Formations of the Feminine in Rabbinic Literature*. BSJW. Hanover, NH: University Press of New England, 2002.

Cohen, Mary M. "The Influence of the Jewish Religion in the Home." Pages 115–21 in *Papers of the Jewish Women's Congress (1893)*. Philadelphia: Jewish Publication Society of America, 1894.

Deutsch, Emanuel. "What Is the Talmud." *LQR* 123 (1867): 220–44 (American edition).

Diamant, Anita. *The Red Tent*. New York: St. Martin's, 1997.

Frank, Ray. "Women in the Synagogue." Pages 52–65 in *Papers of the Jewish Women's Congress (1893)*. Philadelphia: Jewish Publication Society of America, 1894.

Ilan, Tal. *Mine and Yours Are Hers: Retrieving Women's History from Rabbinic Literature*. AGAJU 41. Leiden: Brill, 1997.

Jacobs, Joseph, and Goodman Lipkind. "Emanuel Oscar Menahem Deutsch." *JE* (1906). https://tinyurl.com/SBL6007a.

Lazarus, Emma. "The New Colossus." 1883. Jewish Women's Archive. http://jwa.org/media/new-colossus-from-emma-lazarus-copy-book.

Lazarus, Josephine. "The Outlook of Judaism." Pages 295–304 in *Judaism at the World's Parliament of Religions*. Cincinnati: Union of American Hebrew Congregations, 1893.

Lichtenstein, Diane. *Writing Their Nations: The Tradition of Nineteenth-Century American Jewish Women Writers*. Bloomington: Indiana University Press, 1992.

Mannheimer, Louise. "Jewish Women of Biblical and Medieval Times." Pages 15–25 in *Papers of the Jewish Women's Congress (1893)*. Philadelphia: Jewish Publication Society of America, 1894.

Nadell, Pamela S. *Women Who Would Be Rabbis: A History of Women's Ordination, 1889–1985*. Boston: Beacon, 1998.

Remy, Nahida. *Nahida Remy's The Jewish Woman*. Translated by Louise Mannheimer. Cincinnati: Krehbiel & Co., 1895.

Richman, Julia. "Women as Wage-Workers." Pages 91–114 in *Papers of the Jewish Women's Congress (1893)*. Philadelphia: Jewish Publication Society of America, 1894.

Rosenberg, Pauline. "Influence of the Discovery of America on the Jews." Pages 66–73 in *Papers of the Jewish Women's Congress (1893)*. Philadelphia: Jewish Publication Society of America, 1894.

Solomon, Hannah G. "Address." Pages 10–12 in *Papers of the Jewish Women's Congress (1893)*. Philadelphia: Jewish Publication Society of America, 1894.

———. "Address." Pages 166–67 in *Papers of the Jewish Women's Congress (1893)*. Philadelphia: Jewish Publication Society of America, 1894.

Szold, Henrietta. "What Has Judaism Done for Woman?" Pages 304–310 in *Judaism at the World's Parliament of Religions*. Cincinnati: Union of American Hebrew Congregations, 1893.

Weil, Helen Kahn. "Jewish Women of Modern Days." Pages 26–42 in *Papers of the Jewish Women's Congress (1893)*. Philadelphia: Jewish Publication Society of America, 1894.

Weissler, Chava. *Voices of the Matriarchs: Listening to the Prayers of Early Modern Jewish Women*. Boston: Beacon, 1998.

The Bible in the Evangelizing Activity of the Biblewomen

Marina Cacchi

Then afterward I will pour out my Spirit on all flesh; your sons and your daughters shall prophesy.... Even on the male and female slaves, in those days, I will pour out my Spirit.
— Joel 2:28–29 NRSV

Nelle nostre Valli non si conosce altro libro che la Bibbia e nel nostro campo di evangelizzazione non abbiamo portato altro libro che questo.
— P. Lantaret, Moderator of the Tavola Valdese, Florence, 1872

The scope of the present research is limited to a specific aspect of the literary work of the "Biblewomen," or, as they defined themselves less emphatically, biblical lectors-visitors. Its task is to study the role of sacred Scripture in their periodic service reports to the Evangelization Committee. In particular, this paper focuses on the emphasis given to the biblical text by a sample of Waldensian female preachers during their evangelizing activity between the first decade of the twelfth century and the end of the eighteenth century. It also concentrates on the role played by the Bible in the formation of these preachers as women, believers, and teachers, as this can be observed by studying their reports to the committee.

The present analysis does not aim to discuss the widest theme of Waldensian female preaching tout court, something that has been thoroughly examined by numerous scholars in other publications.[1] Rather,

---

Translated from the Italian by Michele Alessandro Lucchesi. I wish to thank especially Professor Adriana Valerio, my Tutor in the Master's Program in Women's Studies at the Centro Adelaide Pignatelli of the Università Suor Orsola Benincasa in Naples, and Gabriella Ballesio, who is responsible for the Archive of the Tavola Valdese in Torre Pellice for their support and interesting interpretative keys.

1. One can refer to the studies on the preaching of "mulieres Valdenses" during

within so general a topic, my research tries to isolate the "sense of the Bible" in a limited number of women who preached systematically for some years or for the greater part of their lives.

1. Who Were the Biblewomen?

Part of the correspondence of five women to the members or the president of the Evangelization Committee is preserved in series 9 of the Archive of the Tavola Valdese in Torre Pellice (*Operai della Chiesa*), subseries 3 (*Lettrici Bibliche*), bundle 439.[2] The documents cover the whole period when they conducted their evangelizing activity, or to put it in their own words, their "piccola opera" as biblical visitors.[3]

These are the women and writings in question: Eugenia Arzani Poggi, two letters from 1879 to 1880 (folder 1); Annina Celli, seven service reports from 1893 to 1896 (folder 2); Emma Celli, three letters of 1904 (folder 3); Adelina Malanot, one letter dated 1897 (folder 4); and Demetra Poli, several service reports of 1882 (folder 5). These five women represent the tip of the iceberg of a much larger world of women and men who contributed to the work of the Evangelization Committee

---

the first years of the movement and in the Late Middle Ages by Giovanni Gonnet, "La Donna Presso i Movimenti Pauperistico-Evangelici," in *Movimento Religioso Femminile e Francescanesimo nel Secolo XIII* (Assisi: Società Internazionale di Studi francescani, 1980), 103–29. See also Giovanni Grado Merlo, *Identità Valdesi nella Storia e nella Storiografia II*, SStor (Turin: Claudiana, 1991), 93–112; and Peter Biller, "What Did Happen to the Waldensian Sisters? The Strasbourg Testimony," in *Studi in Onore del Prof. Jean Gonnet (1909–1997)*, Pro 54 (1999): 222–33. For a brief, yet rigorous examination of early female Waldensian preaching and the numerous inquisitorial depositions in the fourteenth and fifteenth centuries, see Marina Benedetti, "La Predicazione delle Donne Valdesi," in *Donne Cristiane e Sacerdozio: Dalle Origini all'Età Contemporanea*, ed. Dinora Corsi, LV 41 (Rome: Viella, 2004), 135–58.

2. Series 9 of the archive is formed by nine subseries. The first one includes the personal files created at the time of the reorganization in the fifties as much as the correspondence and, in many cases, the service reports of pastors, evangelists, masters, and door-to-door salesmen from 1860 to the present day. Subseries 2 is devoted to teachers. Subseries 3 concerns female Biblereaders, or Biblewomen. The fourth subseries focuses on door-to-door salesmen. Subseries 5 gathers the correspondence between lay members of administrations. Subseries 6, finally, is devoted to widows.

3. With these words, Annina Celli defined her service activity at the beginning of the letter dated August 6, 1896 and addressed to Pastor Pons, in ATV, series 9, subseries 3, bundle 439, folder 2, letter n. 7.

as biblical readers.⁴ Their service reports are kept in the first subseries of the Archive, devoted to the collection of the (particularly rich) correspondence of evangelists, teachers (very often female teachers), and door-to-door salesmen. One should notice that it is difficult—if not misleading—to distinguish between preachers and teachers, since often both women and men had the double responsibility of teaching and evangelizing. An emblematic example is that of Giuseppina Pusterla, whose letters are kept in subseries 1 of the Archive.⁵ She was a teacher for more than forty years—though with some breaks due to her precarious health and a temporary removal in 1870—and Biblewoman beginning in 1878.⁶

1.1. Working Conditions and Salary

Some interesting details emerge by crosschecking the service reports and the coeval minutes of the committee. We find confirmation that the activity as Biblereader was not a spontaneous endeavor that became institutionalized in the course of the years. Rather, it was a formal appointment, deliberated upon in specific meetings of the committee and witnessed by minutes. The appointment determined the city of destination and the eventual mentor, who provided financial backing and the funds for his or her salary. In this regard, the minutes of the sessions in which Pusterla's appointment and her salary were decided are significant. In the assembly of September 21, 1878, one can read under article 5: "Milan—we announce that Ms. Ranyard (London) generously offered to pay a sum of twelve lire, so that we can try out a Biblewoman,

---

4. Their exact number has not been determined yet; one should consult systematically the reports of the Evangelization Committee from the beginning of its activities (1861) to its closure (1915), isolating the tasks formally assigned to Biblereaders and Biblewomen.

5. On the evangelizing and teaching activity of Giuseppina Pusterla and for a partial reconstruction of her biography, see my "Giuseppina Pusterla e l'Evangelizzazione Valdese di Fine Ottocento," in *Archivio per la Storia delle Donne II*, ed. Adriana Valerio (Naples: D'Auria, 2005), 102–25.

6. Although from the meeting minutes of the Evangelization Committee it emerges that Pusterla's official appointment can be dated back to September 21, 1878, already the correspondence of the end of 1877 reveals increasingly more extensive references to the preaching activity to families, and the letters progressively display the traits of "service reports."

Ms. Pusterla. The committee gratefully accepts the offer. Ms. Pusterla will receive a monthly subsidy of fifty lire."[7]

The following year, during the meeting of May 8, 1879, it became known that the foreign benefactor who had promoted Giuseppina Pusterla's employment as biblical reader died. Nonetheless, the committee decided to confirm Pusterla in her role, hoping for contributions from her brothers and sympathizers: "General questions, point E—The Bible-woman from Milan (Ms. Pusterla) continues very satisfactorily her work, and the committee hopes that, despite Ms. Ranyard's death, other friends will show an active interest in this activity."[8]

Other minutes of the committee, which refer to meetings of 1883, prove that the duty to evangelize was assigned to both women and men without any distinction of remuneration, something that confirms how the activity of the committee was characterized by an egalitarian spirit.[9] By examining the minutes of the following years, one can notice that the salary was commensurate with the type of service, but it was never related to the number of families visited. In case of double appointment, the salary was doubled, too; it also increased in the course of the years, probably following the increase of the cost of living.[10] This can be inferred from

---

7. *Milano—Si partecipa che la Signora Ranyard (London) si è generosamente profferta a corrispondere una somma di Lire st. dodici, perché si tenti la prova di una Bible-woman, in persona della Signora Pusterla. Il Comitato gradisce l'offerta, con riconoscenza. La Signora Pusterla avrà un sussidio mensile di lit. cinquanta.*

8. *Questioni generali, punto e—La Bible-woman di Milano (Signora Pusterla) prosegue l'opera sua in modo molto soddisfacente, ed il Comitato nutre speranza che, malgrado la morte della Signora Ranyard, altri amici dimostreranno verso quest'opera il loro attivo interessamento.*

9. Meetings of September 10, 11, and 12, 1883, article 15: *Milano—Sulla raccomandazione del signor Turino* [the pastor Jean David Turin], *il Comitato gli concede di prendere sotto la sua direzione in qualità di Bible-reader il Signor Zuliani, portiere della Chiesa di S. Giovanni in Conca e gli assegna L. 50 mensili a partire dal mese di novembre 1883* ("Milan—About the recommendation of Mr. Turino, the committee allows him to take under his direction Mr. Zuliani, porter of the Church Saint Giovanni in Conca, as Bible-reader, an grants him L. 50 every month, starting from November 1883"), in ATV, series 4, "*Tavola, Comitato di Evangelizzazione, Corpo pastorale,*" subseries 1.

10. Meetings of July 10 and 11, 1885, article 17: *Roma—Il Comitato decide di prendere definitivamente a suo servizio il Sig. Gherardo Benincasa in qualità di Maestro di scuola serale e Lettore della Bibbia. Stipendio L. 100 mensili* ("Rome—The committee decides to employ permanently Mr. Gherardo Benincasa as teacher at the evening school and Biblereader. Salary: L. 100 per month"), in ATV, series 4, "*Tavola, Comitato*

the fact that in the autumn of 1885, the committee granted a Biblereader who worked in Rome a salary of eighty lire per month as against fifty lire granted to a reader in Milan two years earlier. It is also noteworthy that evangelizers enjoyed some vacation time, which was paid, since, in the minutes of the committee, there was no mention that during the holidays the salary was reduced. In the letter of pastor Bartolomeo Revel to the pastor of Milan Longo, in which there is a reference to Pusterla's "usual" vacation time, one can find proof of the right to time off: "My dear brother, … first and foremost I have no difficulty allowing Ms. Giuseppina Pusterla to take her holiday during the month of August just as in the past years."[11]

1.2. The Bible as the Beginning of Their Work

As Gian Paolo Romagnani has correctly noted, with the birth of the committee, the Waldensians entered a new phase of their history. After the "emancipation," they started the era of the evangelization of the reign of Italy, that is, a politically and culturally heterogeneous community that, nonetheless, was religiously homogeneous. The preaching activity was the result of "the patient and stubborn work of dozens of evangelizers and itinerant preachers" (*paziente e testarda (opera) di decine di evangelizzatori e di predicatori itinerant*) who tried to spread a new way of living the Christian faith, which was fundamentally based on the direct reading of the Bible and on the direct relationship of each believer with God.[12] The Waldensian male and female preachers (at least, in the intentions of the committee leaders) wished to counter the "church of dogma," accustomed to a hierarchic system that gave great importance to the function of sacerdotal mediation, with a "church of the Bible" and pure preaching.[13] They

---

di Evangelizzazione, Corpo pastorale," subseries 1. Double appointments (teaching and preaching), however, were not episodic, and Pusterla's case is paradigmatic. Besides, this corresponded to a specific model of evangelization, which the committee tried to develop outside the areas of historical settlement. The construction of schools was promoted next to cult places, that is, the temples.

11. *Caro fratello, … anzitutto non ho difficoltà alcuna ad autorizzare che la signora Giuseppina Pusterla abbia la sua vacanza durante il mese di Agosto, come gli anni decorsi*; Bartolomeo Revel to the Pastor of Milan, July 20, 1899, doc. 363.

12. Gian Paolo Romagnani, "I Valdesi nel 1848: Dall'Emancipazione alla Scelta Italiana," in *Dalle valli all'Italia: I Valdesi nel Risorgimento (1848–1998)*, ed. Bruno Bellion et al., CSSV 16 (Turin: Claudiana, 1998), 96.

13. Mario Cignoni, "I Valdesi in Italia (1848–1870)," in *Dalle Valli all'Italia: I*

thought of a sober and industrious community, which considered reading the Bible individually and methodically (very often in the Italian translation by Diodati) the mark that distinguished Waldensians from Catholics.[14] In the same years, a Protestant periodical exhorted Evangelical people to preach militantly so as to "Agitate the masses, shake the asleep ... to throw the word of the gospel to twenty-six million Italians."[15] It is no chance that in the service reports of female readers, the theme of the gift of the Bible or the gospel recurs as a refrain, as the first step toward a potential conversion. All six Biblewomen whose letters I have consulted partly or entirely frequently invite their interlocutors to follow them in reading biblical passages and encourage their families to buy a Bible in order to read it assiduously every day. In this regard, particularly significant are Poggi's words to a Catholic family, the Sasso, which she went to visit. They showed her a book about St. Joseph, which the local parish priest had given them. After leafing through it, Poggi said: "See, my dear friends, if you had knowledge of the true Christian doctrine, which is the gospel of Jesus Christ, you would understand that what is written in this book is false, and they replied 'Unfortunately, it is true that we do not understand anything, for us religion is mystery and blind obedience.'"[16] Poggi often

---

Valdesi nel Risorgimento (1848–1998), ed. Bruno Bellion et al., CSSV 16 (Turin: Claudiana, 1998), 103–30.

14. The Italian translation by Diodati was published by the *Società Biblica e Forestiera* of London and was secretly distributed in Italy through the alpine crossings or Malta.

15. *Agitare le masse, scuotere i dormienti ... a gittare la parola del Vangelo in mezzo a ventisei milioni di italiani*; *Il Rinascimento: Giornale dell'Evangelizzazione Italiana*, November 25, 1865. This was a bimonthly magazine published in Milan between 1865 and 1885 and connected with Free Church (Chiesa Libera).

16. *Vedete miei cari, se voi aveste la conoscenza della vera dottrina cristiana, che è il Vangelo di Gesù Cristo, voi comprendereste che ciò che è scritto in questo libro è falso ed essi mi dissero "Purtroppo è vero che non comprendiamo nulla, per noi la religione non è che mistero e cieca obbedienza"*; Poggi, service report of December 1879, Naples, in ATV, series 9 *"Operai della Chiesa"* ("Church Workers"), subseries 3, bundle 439, folder 1. Annina Celli does the same thing during her first visit to Mrs. Rigo, a sincere Catholic woman, intelligent and interested in God's matters: *In principio misi poco del mio, ma subito le imprestai la Bibbia tradotta dal Martini, segnata in certi passi* ("At the beginning, I was little involved, but soon I lent her the Bible translated by Martini with some passages marked"); service report of March 1893, Turin, in ATV, series 9, subseries 3, bundle 439, folder 2.

returns to the idea that one cannot be called Christian unless she or he follows Christ's footsteps, and one cannot follow what is not known:

> And then I said: "So answer me: by defining yourself as Catholic, I believe you mean that you are Christian, isn't it?" "Certainly," he replied. "Then, by calling yourself Christian, you say you are a follower of Christ. How can you call yourself Christian, if you do not know the foundations of Christ? What would you say about someone who were to be proud, for instance, to be Mazzinian, and, being asked what are the principles and the doctrines of the man he calls Master, were to reply that he ignores them?" I do not want to judge anyone, but this is the sad position of Roman Catholics: they call themselves Christians, but they have not the faintest idea of this fine name, and go and buy from men what God gives for free."[17]

Poggi has a direct and vigorous style; she often quotes the Scripture and almost never recites it by heart. Rather, having a profound knowledge of the biblical text, she paraphrases its concepts with the aim of making sacred Scripture more intelligible for her interlocutors. For instance, while talking with Ms. Liberti, Poggi explains that the cult of saints is useless and "true Christians" ought to turn to Christ directly, as he is the only mediator between God and humans and the only source of comfort. In order to strengthen these concepts, she quotes Matt 11:28: "God does not want us to turn to creatures like ourselves to be consoled; rather, he wants us to go to him directly, and Jesus says to us: 'Come to me, all you who labor and are overburdened, and I will give you rest.' Can one find more affectionate and confidence-inspiring words than these? Surely not."[18]

---

17. *Ed io gli dissi: "Ebbene mi risponda, lei nel dirsi cattolico io credo voglia sottendere di essere cristiano, non è vero?" "Certamente," mi rispose. "Or bene dicendosi cristiano si dice seguace di Cristo. Come lei può dirsi cristiano non conoscendo gli statuti di Cristo? Che direbbe lei di un individuo che si gloriasse per esempio di essere Mazziniano, e domandato di spiegare quali siano i principi e le dottrine di quello che lui chiama Maestro rispondesse che le ignora? Io non voglio qualificare nessuno ma questa è la triste posizione dei cattolici romani: essi si chiamano cristiani mentre non conoscono neppure per ombra il significato di questo bel nome, e vanno a comprare dagli uomini ciò che Iddio dà gratuitamente"*; Poggi, service report of January 1880, Naples, in ATV, series 9, subseries 3, bundle 439, folder 1.

18. *Il Signore non vuole che andiamo a ricorrere a creature come noi per essere consolati; ma vuole andiamo direttamente a Lui, e Gesù Cristo ci dice: "venite a me voi tutti che siete travagliati e aggravati ed io vi solleverò." Si possono trovare parole più affettuose*

By consulting other service reports (especially that of Poli, a biblical visitor in Naples), we can find confirmation that the references to the gospel constitute an established custom and a fundamental point of evangelization. In the report of June 1, 1882, Poli narrates one of her visits: "I read her a chapter of the gospel, as usual" (*Come il solito le feci la lettura di un capitolo dell'Evangelo*). She writes to the "most distinguished Mr. Pons" (*pregiatissimo Signor Pons*), a pastor. Reading Jesus's miracles—among which one can mention the resurrection of Jairus's daughter and the healing of the woman suffering for twelve years—strikes the interlocutor, who objects that "today" people do not engage in spiritual matters, and she would not have time for it, even wanting it, since she has to look after many young kids. Poli tries to avoid the obstacle, showing some sympathy, but does not give up: "I understand it, but it is our duty to read a little of the Word of the Lord so as to learn to walk in his paths. Who is truly Christian feels the need to listen to evangelization in order to be edified and to know fully God's will."[19]

The promotion of the knowledge of the gospel and the desire for such a knowledge not to be limited to reading superficially sacred Scripture but, conversely, to become a daily habit, do not diminish in the course of time. In the letter of December 2, 1903, which includes the service report of November, the Biblewoman Emma Celli[20] writes: "I conducted a small worship and prayer in ten houses. In some of the families 'considered' Evan-

---

e che ispirano più confidenze di queste? Certo che no; Poggi, service report of December 1879, Naples, in ATV, series 9, subseries 3, bundle 439, folder 1.

19. *Capisco, ma è nostro dovere di leggere un poco la Parola di Dio, per imparare a camminare nelle Sue vie e chi è veramente Cristiano [majuscule in the original] sente il bisogno di ascoltare la Evangelizzazione per essere edificati e conoscere appieno il volere di Dio*; Poli, service report of June 1882, Naples, in ATV, series 9, subseries 3, bundle 439, folder 5.

20. This is her first monthly report to pastor Longo. Emma Celli, who works as a Biblewoman in Turin, writes at the beginning of the first letter: "Dear Mr. Longo, I frankly tell you that I accepted with great trepidation the job of Biblewoman, which you kindly offered me, considering my reticence and my inability to conduct so great an activity. Nevertheless, since I have the burning desire to be a little less useless in this world, I accepted the job having hope in God's help with all my heart" (*Egregio Sig. Longo, francamente le dico, che fu con grande trepidanza che accettai l'opera da lei gentilmente offertami come "Donna Biblica" viste le mie reticenze e la mia incapacità a compiere una tanta opera. Essendo però vivo in me il desiderio d'essere un po' meno inutile a questo mondo, accettai fidando di tutto cuore nell'aiuto di Dio*).

gelical, unfortunately I found profound moral gaps. As you said well in one of your discourses, I also noticed widespread ignorance about the gospel."[21] Thus, a direct, personal, and profound knowledge of the Scriptures is not an abstract Christian ideal which should be proclaimed during the evangelizing activity. Rather, it is a categorical imperative to which Evangelicals themselves should live up. If this does not happen, Biblewomen are called to encourage, correct, and, if necessary, even reproach their brothers and sisters in the faith who have abandoned the sound biblical principles and the "way of Truth" because of persecution or spiritual weakness.

In this regard, Annina Celli's harsh rebuke to her brother Rigo is particularly significant; he was "guilty" of betraying his Evangelical faith to please his relatives, especially his old mother. In fact, Celli fears that behind his decision are economic reasons, and she is furious. After speaking with his wife, she goes to her brother's workplace. She screams from the pages of the service report of November 1894:

> I immediately went to see her husband at his office in the Guardhouse. As he saw me, he was very disconcerted and tried to take the matter lightly, as he had his mother to please.... After all, his heart would not change anything he would do externally.... "Oh, if you," I said, "feel ashamed of the Lord Jesus, he will be ashamed of you before his Father ... but do you not know that you are about to commit a sin that will never be forgiven.... You commit a sin against the Holy Spirit! Indeed, you do this out of self-interest.... It cannot be otherwise. Do they pay your debts for you?"[22]

In these sentences, one can clearly recognize the echo of Jesus's words recorded by Mark the Evangelist, even if they are not explicitly men-

---

21. *Ho fatto un piccolo culto e una preghiera in dieci case. Nelle famiglie "considerate" evangeliche* [one should note the word "considerate" (considered) in the text] *purtroppo, in alcune ho trovato profonde lacune morali; e, come ben disse Lei in un suo discorso, constatai io pure non poca ignoranza riguardo all'Evangelo*; Celli, service report of December 2, 1903, Turin, in ATV, series 9, subseries 3, bundle 439, folder 3.

22. *Mi recai subito dal marito nel suo ufficio al corpo di Guardia, vedendomi rimase non poco sconcertato, si provò a prendere la cosa alla leggera, aveva la madre da contentare ... del resto il suo cuore non avrebbe cambiato qualunque cosa avesse fatto esternamente....* "*Oh! Se lei,*" *gli dissi,* "*ha vergogna del Signore Gesù, Questi avrà vergogna di Lei davanti al Padre suo ... ma non sa che lei si prepara a commettere il peccato che non sarà mai più perdonato ... va a commettere peccato contro lo Spirito Santo! Certo lei lo fa per interesse. Non può essere diversamente, le pagano i debiti?*"

tioned: "Truly I tell you, people will be forgiven for their sins and whatever blasphemies they utter; but whoever blasphemes against the Holy Spirit can never have forgiveness, but is guilty of an eternal sin" (Mark 3:28–29 NRSV).

2. Giuseppina Pusterla, from Master to Preacher

Pusterla's letters cover a long time span, from 1865 to 1907, and deeply change at the time of her appointment as a Biblewoman. In fact, between the appointment (which can be dated back to September 1878 thanks to the committee minutes) and the content of the letters, there is a difference of six months. In the letter dated December 29, 1877, which concerns the service report of the same month, Pusterla already refers to the evangelizing activity:

> Reverend Mr. Pastor Longo, I thank you immensely, because for the love of God's work, which had already begun thanks to our dearest Mrs. Turino [the wife of pastor Jean David Turin], you requested to receive the means to continue the work from the "Reverendissima Commissione."[23] Resuming, therefore, my old visits, the Lord made me find three new families, as I mentioned. It is not difficult to find the way to speak, but then difficulties arise when speaking and opening the Scripture, which says "The Lord your God is the one to whom you must do homage, him alone you must serve. God is Spirit, and those who worship must worship in Spirit and Truth." Then the question becomes serious, as one needs to abandon old habits such as the worship of saints and madonnas, the mass, and the confession to a priest.[24]

---

23. By "Reverendissima Commissione" Pusterla means the Evangelization Committee (*Commission* in French). The adjective "Reverendissima" was typical as much as the use of the adjective "Venerabile" (revered) for the Tavola Valdese.

24. *Reverendo Signor Pastore Longo, infinitamente ringrazio la S.V. che per amore dell'opera del Signore già stata incominciata per mezzo della carissima Signora Turino, la spinse a fare istanza alla Reverendissima Commissione, onde ottenere mezzi per continuare detta opera. Riprendendo dunque le mie vecchie visite, altre tre nuove famiglie il Signore mi fece trovare come ne dissi già parola: già trovar di parlare non è tanto difficile, ma le difficoltà nascono poi in seguito allorquando discorrendo ed aprendo la S. Scrittura che dice "Adora un Dio solo e servi a Lui solo. Dio è Spirito, perciò conviene che coloro che l'adorano l'adorino in Spirito e Verità e non in materia." Oh allora la questione la si fa seria dovendo lasciar le vecchie abitudini come l'adorazione di santi e madonne,*

Pusterla refers to old visits in the letter, making us think that she had already preached, though not officially. As one may suppose, these might have been occasional visits to the families of the children who attended the Evangelical school. Under the date of the letter, one can find the caption "Biblewoman-report" (*Biblewoman-rapporto*), which confirms that this document was considered in all respects a "service report" since its writing. Doubtless, the handwriting is not of Pusterla. Everything makes one believe that this is a note added by Longo for quick archiving. One thing is certain: starting with this one, Pusterla's letters assume the character of periodic reports or—to put it better—of service reports, which treat in greater detail the doctrinal topics discussed during the visits. There are numerous references to the passages of sacred Scripture read together with her Catholic and Evangelical interlocutors. When she visits her brothers and sisters in the faith, she mostly reads chapters from the Psalms and passages from the Old Testament—especially from the prophet Isaiah—and ends the meeting with a common prayer. When she visits Catholic families or nonbelievers, she quotes or reads more often the New Testament, in particular the gospels and the letters that the Apostle of the Nations, originally known as Saul of Tarsus, addresses to the Romans and the Hebrews. Doubtless, the letters with a richer theological meaning are those of the age of maturity, especially those of the period 1894–1899, addressed to the three pastors: Matteo Prochet, Paolo Longo, and Bartolomeo Revel.

2.1. Evangelizing through the Bible

In the letter-report of November 1, 1894, Pusterla writes that she visits the house of the Catholic woman Ms. Carolina Gianotti, where there is also a neighbor, Ms. Moneta. Pusterla presents the figure of Christ, whom she defines as "the only purification for our sins" (*solo purgamento dei nostri peccati*), and his role as the only mediator between God and men. She tries to undermine her interlocutors' faith in the Catholic purgatory and to show that prayers and other practices aiming to "earn" (*guadagnare*) or "build" (*costruirsi*) salvation are useless. In a caustic tone, which is rather unusual for her, she affirms: "One does not go out of there [from Purgatory] unless

---

messa e confessione al prete; Pusterla, service report, December 29, 1877, Milan, in ATV, series 9, subseries 1, folder 36.

he or she pays the priest.... Read God's commandments: you will not find anything about the many doctrines invented by the church."[25]

In the service report of December 1894, addressed to the President of the Evangelization Committee, Prochet, Pusterla—despite acknowledging that "conversion belongs to the Lord" (*il convertire appartiene al Signore*)—reiterates her firm intention to offer her contribution: "Reverend Mr. Prochet, by the grace of God this year too I begin my visits. If only the Lord wished to increase them and to make me find souls thirsty for justice! Indeed, I will be happy to lead them to him, alone I can do really nothing!"[26] Immediately after the incipit, she starts the account of the families visited. The first one is a Catholic family, whose head is described as a sympathizer, curious to learn the truths of the gospel (we will find traces of her in numerous later reports):

> I am always happy to visit Mrs. Rosa Molina, Catholic, because this woman is thirsty to learn. She sits next to my knees, leaves aside all her occupations, and listens with hunger to the word of the Lord just as Mary. This good woman prays her husband to spark the fire to warm me up, since I was shivering with cold. As we were concentrated on reading chapter 13 of the Gospel of Luke and on making religious conversation, our attention focused more on the parable of the fig tree. Molina listened to everything carefully, stared at my face, and approved with head signs what I was saying. The wife was totally happy to see her husband attentive to the word of the Lord.[27]

---

25. *Di là* [from purgatory] *non si esce se non pagando il prete.... Leggete i comandamenti di Dio e voi non troverete nulla delle tante dottrine inventate dalla Chiesa*; Pusterla to Pastor Prochet, service report, November 1, 1894, Milan, in ATV, series 9, subseries 1, folder 36c.

26. *Reverendo Signor Prochet, per grazia di Dio anche in quest'anno incomincio le mie visite, volesse Iddio aumentarle e farmi trovare delle anime assetate di giustizia! E sì, io sarò felice di guidarle a Lui, ma da me stessa non posso proprio nulla!*; Pusterla, service report, January 1, 1895, Milan, in ATV, series 9, subseries 1, folder 36. One can notice that Pusterla writes "souls thirsty for justice" rather than people thirsty for the truth. Probably, in her view, being Evangelical—or better, Christian—meant primarily to desire and long for justice.

27. *Sono sempre felice di visitare la sig.ra Molina Rosa, cattolica, perché questa donna ha sete d'imparare, essa si siede vicino alle mie ginocchia e pone da un lato tutte le sue occupazioni e ascolta con fame la Parola di Dio come Maria. La buona donna prega il suo marito di far del fuoco per riscaldarmi, perché io tremavo dal freddo e più presi a far lettura del cap. 13 di s. Luca e conversazione religiosa, la nostra attenzione si fermò molto più sulla parabola del fico. Il Molina* [this is not clear] *ascoltò tutto attentamente e*

While presenting her "sheep," Pusterla clearly mentions Martha's sister, who in the account of Luke the Evangelist postpones the domestic activities in order to listen to Jesus's words. By paraphrasing the Messiah's words, Pusterla seems to say that Mrs. Rosa, just as Mary, "has chosen the better part, which will not be taken from her" (Luke 10:42 NRSV).

2.2. "Reading Little and Thinking a Lot"

Slightly later in the same report, Pusterla narrates her visit to two Catholic women, one of whom was a widow:

> I talked about the gospel and the New Testament, and then Mrs. Moneta said to me: "How much I like listening to someone talking about the Scripture! I knew many things, because I had a book, which contained many facts about the gospel and the New Testament." I replied: "Not only does one enjoy listening to someone talking about the Scripture in order to know God's will and the way how to reach Jesus in order to be saved, but Jesus is also among those who reflect on him." Mrs. Giannotti: "Is this true, Giuseppina? Is he, then, here among us, while we talk about Jesus?" "Sure." [I read] the Gospel according to John, chapter 24, and discussed about the section from verse 13 to the end.[28]

Ten readings of biblical texts out of a total number of thirty-five families visited are mentioned in the letter. In the periodic report of May 1899, the ratio of biblical passages read to families visited is almost the same: ten references to reading biblical passages out of a total number of thirty-two families contacted. This last monthly report, dated June 1, 1899, is certainly one of the most interesting from a theological and doctrinal perspective, since such themes such as salvation, redemption from sins, or

---

mi fissava gli occhi in faccia, e con segni del capo approvava quanto io dicevo. La moglie era tutta felice di vedere suo marito attento alla Parola di Dio; Pusterla, service report, January 1, 1895, Milan, in ATV, series 9, subseries 1, folder 36.

28. *Parlai del Vangelo e del N.T., e poi la Signora Moneta mi disse: "Come fa piacere sentire parlare della s. Scrittura, tante cose conoscevo anch'io perché avevo un libro il quale conteneva tanti fatti del V. e N.T." Io le risposi: "Non solo fa piacere di sentir parlare delle s. Scritture per conoscere la volontà di Dio e la via per andare a Gesù onde essere salvati, ma Gesù si trova in mezzo di coloro che ragionano di Lui." La Sig.ra Giannotti: "Davvero Giuseppina? Si trova dunque qui in mezzo di noi ora che parliamo di Gesù?" "Sicuramente." [Lessi] l'Evangelo di s. Giov. cap. 24, e raccontai del ver. 13 fino alla fine*; Pusterla, service report, January 1, 1895, Milan, in ATV, series 9, subseries 1, folder 36.

ecumenism are treated here, and reveals Pusterla's preaching style, which is simple, direct, effective, and very close to her interlocutors' daily lives. The examples employed by Pusterla are taken from the surrounding social environment and, despite their evident simplification, aim to make profound doctrinal concepts immediately intelligible. Even if she prefers female interlocutors, probably for reasons of social convenience, Pusterla also tries wherever possible to involve the male members of the family in reading the Bible and having theological conversations. An emblematic example of this style can be found in the description of the visit to Mrs. Letizia Pesini, who was Catholic. On that occasion, the lady of the house hosts her sister, with whom Pusterla has had the chance to talk about religious matters in the past:

> I started to talk again about religion.... Then I had in my pocket a copy of the Gospel of Luke. I offered it to the lady and she said: "And how about giving it back? I will leave for Milan in a few days." "It does not matter: keep it. You can give it back, if you wish, and, if you want, you can keep it." "But I will read it fast. Between today and tomorrow I will read your book and then I will leave it to my sister." "Do as you prefer. Mind you, though, this book should not be read in the same way as other profane books. When reading the gospel, God speaks to us; thus, one should read little and think a lot."[29]

Reading little and thinking a lot: Pusterla recommends this method to the neophyte, who for the first time approaches the pages of the Bible. These pages, she stresses, have nothing to do with those of other secular books.

Talking with a lady, to whom she goes regularly, and her neighbor, Pusterla affirms:

> Our people, my dear, is so uneducated as regards religion, the system of the Roman Church is too materialistic and teaches to hate who does not think as she does. God's commandment, conversely, says: "Love the Lord

---

29. *Cominciai a discorrere di nuovo di religione ... Poi io avevo in tasca un vangelo di s. Luca l'offersi alla sig.ra ed essa disse: "Ma e restituirlo? Io parto da Milano fra qualche giorno." "Non importa, lo tenga, se crede restituirlo me lo dia con suo comodo e se vuole tenerlo lo tenga." "Ma io farò presto a leggerlo, tra oggi e domani lo leggo e poi lo lascerò alla mia sorella il suo libro." "Faccia come crede guardi solamente che questo libro non va letto come altri libri profani, leggendo il Vangelo Iddio parla a noi, quindi si deve leggere poco e pensare molto"*; Pusterla, service report, June 1, 1899, Milan, in ATV, series 9, subseries 1, folder 36.

your God with all your heart and love your neighbor as yourself."... Were these commandments put into practice, how beautiful would it be to live among Christians. The church, however, invented other commandments such as the confession to the priest, salvation through works, and so forth. Yet, conversely, our Lord Jesus says: "My blood cleanses you from all sins." The Lord alone sees your condition of condition of sin, while the priest hears, but does not sees deep into your heart. The priest, moreover, is a sinner himself; therefore, he cannot forgive your sins. Let us go, then, to the Lord, who can and wants to forgive us, if we go to him with all our hearts.[30]

These words condense some key elements of Reformed thought: the need for an individual knowledge of sacred Scripture; open-mindedness about and dialogue with other faiths; nonmediated relationship between believers and God; and salvation by faith alone. The language is certainly simple, but the message is clear and perfectly in line with the Reformed mainstream. A few pages later, in the same report, Pusterla returns to the theme of salvation and reaffirms that it only depends on the expiatory sacrifice of Christ:

> Do you want to read chapter 9 from the Gospel of Luke, "The Transfiguration of Jesus"?—her interlocutor asks. Indeed. I start to read and discuss from the beginning, and we stopped to debate verse 35, "And a voice came from heaven etc...." The Father loved us so much that he gave his divine Son for our salvation, he talks to us from the cloud: "This is my Son, my Chosen One; listen to him!" Doubtless, the Father solemnly declared [Jesus] his Son on the Tabor, just as he had done at the Jordan. Let us listen to him, then, the most trustworthy preacher among preachers, and let us not listen to the voices of the world, who talk to us about everything else than the voice from heaven. Jesus offered himself

---

30. *Il nostro popolo care mie è sì mal educato in materia di religione, il sistema della chiesa romana è troppo materiale e poi insegna a odiare chi non la pensa come lei. Invece il comandamento di Dio dice: "Ama il Signore con tutto il tuo cuore, e ama il tuo prossimo come te stesso."... Se si mettessero in pratica questi comandamenti come bello sarebbe il vivere tra cristiani. Ma la chiesa ha inventati altri comandamenti, la confessione al prete, la salute per le opere ecc. Ma al contrario il Signore Gesù ci dice: "Il mio sangue vi purga da ogni peccato." Il Signore solo vede lo stato vostro di peccato, ma il prete sente ma non vede nel fondo del vostro cuore, poi il prete è un peccatore anch'egli quindi non può perdonare i nostri peccati. Andiamo dunque al Signore che può e vuole perdonare se di tutto cuore andremo a Lui*; Pusterla, service report, June 1, 1899, Milan, in ATV, series 9, subseries 1, folder 36.

for us; his sheep know his voice and follow him. We will not follow the foreigner, who leads to other ways. A few evenings ago, a foreigner preached and said: "Who among yourselves will be able not to come close to a Protestant heretic will obtain thirty days of indulgence. Who will be able to convert him to the Catholic faith will obtain a hundred years of indulgence." Let us not listen to these voices, but let us listen to the voice of the word of God.[31]

This is an appeal that does not leave doubts: salvation is due only to the expiatory sacrifice of Christ, which is a free and undeserved act in favor of humanity. It is useless to search for salvation elsewhere and to pretend that it derives from individual works or, worse, from buying indulgences from some preacher, while we can have access to the "Preacher of preachers."[32]

3. Annina Celli, from Catholic Woman to Little Evangelical "Worker"

"By a person I revere very much, I was offered to describe some fact or episode, which happened to me during my work as a biblical reader here in Turin. I promised and I try to do it, though with great hesitancy, knowing how badly it can turn out. One would need more intelligence and education than … my poor pen! Thus I will be very happy if I will be at least

---

31. *Ha intenzione di leggere il cap. 9 del vangelo di s. Luca "La trasfigurazione di Gesù"?—domanda la sua interlocutrice—Appunto. Comincio da principio a leggere e conversare e più ci siamo fermati a conversare sopra il verso 35 "E una voce venne dal cielo ecc…". Il Padre ci ha tanto amati da dare il Suo Divin Figliolo per la nostra salute, Egli ci parla dalla nuvola: "Questi è il mio diletto Figliolo ascoltatelo." Indubbiamente e solennemente il Padre sul Tabor, come già al Giordano, lo ha dichiarato il Suo Figliolo. Ascoltiamo questo, dunque, il predicatore più degno dei predicatori e non ascoltiamo le voci del mondo che ci parlano ben tutt'altro che della voce del cielo. Gesù ha dato sé stesso per noi e le sue pecore conoscono la Sua voce e lo seguono. Non seguiremo lo straniero che conduce per altre vie. Uno straniero poche sere fa predicava e disse: "Chi di voi sarà capace di non avvicinarsi ad un eretico protestante acquisterà 30 giorni di indulgenza, e chi sarà capace di convertirlo alla fede cattolica guadagnerà 100 anni di indulgenza." Queste voci non ascoltiamo, ma ascoltiamo la voce della Parola di Dio*; Pusterla, service report, June 1, 1899, Milan, in ATV, series 9, subseries 1, folder 36.

32. About the question of salvation, the message of the Biblewomen is essentially in line with Reformed orthodoxy as regards the salvation *sola fide* and predestination. God created the world and men *ad majorem Dei gloriam*, and from the beginning predestined some of them to salvation, others to eternal damnation. Men cannot change in any way this unchangeable judgement: no sacrament, no ceremony, no vision can help them anticipate or alter the divine plans.

understood and indulged"[33]: these are the first words of Annina Celli as newly appointed biblical reader in Turin in March 1893.

After only one year and a half after this timid beginning, in a letter dated December 2, 1894, Celli writes: "I thank S. L. for giving me the job of biblical reader. I will do my best to make myself useful in spreading sacred Scripture, making many hearts know the infinite love of God manifested by Jesus Christ. I attach my report and others will follow at the end of each month, as requested by the President Cavaliere Mr. Matteo Prochet. I will try to make these reports short in order not to bore whoever will have to read them."[34]

3.1. Fascinated by Sacred Scripture and Converted

It is clear that, although quite a few months have passed between the first report and this one, Celli has changed a lot. She no longer limits herself to being "understood and indulged" (*capita e compatita*); now she knows well that she carries with herself not only a high-ranking, centuries-old culture but also the "inestimable and sublime treasure" (*tesoro incalcolabile e sublime*) of sacred Scripture. She wants to be useful in promoting its knowledge among the families of the territory that has been attributed to her—and she is aware that she can do it. She will do this with zeal, determination, and method. Her service reports are punctual, as she always writes on the second or the third day of the following month of that to which she refers. Rarely are her accounts synthetic: in this respect, she does not maintain the promise of "making them short" (*renderli brevi*). Surely, they are accurate—she even mentions the names and the addresses of the absent families, probably at the explicit request of the committee—and can offer an overall picture of the families that she visits, giving information not only about their religious confession but also about the social, cultural,

---

33. A. Celli, service report of March 1893, Turin, in ATV, series 9, subseries 3, bundle 439, folder 2.

34. *Ringrazio S.L. d'avermi dato ancora l'impegno di lettrice biblica: farò il mio possibile onde rendermi utile alla diffusione delle Sacre Scritture, facendo conoscere a tanti cuori l'infinito amore di Dio, manifestato in Cristo Gesù. Unisco il mio rapporto che farò seguire da altri alla fine di ogni mese, come m'espresse desiderare il Presidente Cav.re Sig. Matteo Prochet. In questi mi studierò di renderli brevi per non troppo tediare chi dovrà leggerli*: Celli, service report of November 1894, Turin, in ATV, series 9, subseries 3, bundle 439, folder 2.

and health conditions of their various members. Celli shows a good ability to reconstruct the psychology of her interlocutors and demonstrates deep empathy. Her empathy partly depends on the fact that she and her family come from the Catholic world. Celli does not belong to a Waldensian family of ancient lineage; she is a convert, a former Catholic who groped in spiritual darkness, just as those whom she visits. This aspect of her biography is particularly interesting because it illustrates that the Evangelization Committee did not attribute any special value to origin family or parental ties when "recruiting" its workers. The fact that in her letters our biblical reader explicitly talks about having been a Catholic proves that this did not pose a problem for her. In fact, she instrumentally uses this biographical element to convince her interlocutors that there is nothing wrong in converting to a new faith. Indeed, there is nothing to lose; in fact, if anything, a lot to gain:

> Being born a Roman Catholic, it was extremely useful to me the fact that I could say to some devout soul "I, too, was like you; since I was a young girl, I, too, had immense religious needs. How great a penance did I do, how many signs of the cross, how many rosaries badly repeated, how many kisses to crucifixes and images of saints and Virgin Maries, how many other Catholic practices did I obey!" How many times did people exclaimed with surprise to my statements "And could you leave everything to become a Protestant?"[35]

In the service report of August 6, 1896, Celli mentions an episode that happened during her visit to Mrs. Muris, a Catholic woman married to a Waldensian man, "who unfortunately does not appear to be among the most fervent ones" (*che purtroppo non mi pare dei più ferventi*), as Celli

---

35. *Nata cattolica romana mi fu di grande aiuto il poter dire a qualche anima devota "anch'io ero come Lei; fin da bambina ebbi io pure degli immensi bisogni religiosi: quanta penitenza feci, quanti segni di croce, quanti rosari malamente ripetuti, quanti baci a crocefissi ed immagini di santi e madonne, a quante altre pratiche cattoliche ubbidii!" A questa mia dichiarazioni quante volte mi fu esclamato con stupore "ed ha potuto lasciar tutto per farsi protestante?"*; Celli, service report, March 3, 1893, in ATV, series 9, subseries 3, bundle 439, folder 2. In the service report of November 1894, too, Celli describes the emotive reaction of a woman, regularly visited by her, when she knows about her conversion: "You left our Saint Mother the Church. Ah! Return, return as you were before. I love you very much, but I would love you more if you were to return to your first beliefs" (*Lei ha lasciata la nostra Santa madre Chiesa. Ah! Ritorni, ritorni com'era prima! L'amo tanto ma l'amerei di più se ritornasse alle sue primiere credenze*).

caustically notes.³⁶ In his wife's presence, Mr. Muris says to Celli that he would prefer his wife to remain Catholic: "Everyone as he or she is born" (*Ognuno come siamo nati*), he exclaims. Celli is irritated and inflamed, and cannot believe that a brother in the faith has thought and said what she has just heard. She replies on the spot: "I was a Catholic too, and I changed without having any remourse ever; on the contrary, how many consolations did I have and my family with me just as well."³⁷ Subsequently, her empathic ability emerges again and, probably remembering her own fear or reluctance when she changed faith, she reassures him that "Indeed, we should not force anyone … after all, the diversity of the two religions is not huge: we have the same Father, Son, and Holy Spirit. The same Savior … for the Evangelicals, religion is simply purer: it is the same as our Lord Jesus and his disciples gave it to us."³⁸

3.2. The Gospels Are Useful to the Indifferent

Celli proves to have great consideration for the people who have faith, even if their faith is different from hers. She does not tolerate, conversely, apathy and a state of indifference or tepid unresponsiveness (Rev 3:15–16), nor does she accept whoever considers himself superior to the message of the gospel, being "excessively learned in secular science" (*troppo istruito in scienza del secolo*). In the same service report, she mentions the visit to Ms. Merini. Just as on other occasions, Celli records a great religious coldness and adds: "I believe that there only one thought able to shake her up a little: the fear that her usual apathy may be broken up."³⁹ The same annoyance shines through a few pages later, where she describes her visit to Ms.

---

36. Celli, service report, August 6, 1896, in ATV, series 9, subseries 3, bundle 439, folder 2.

37. *Anch'io ero Cattolica ed ho cambiato senza che me ne sia mai pentita, al contrario … quante consolazioni ne ebbi e con me tutta la mia famiglia*; Celli, service report, August 6, 1896, in ATV, series 9, subseries 3, bundle 439, folder 2.

38. *Certo che non bisogna sforzare nessuno … del resto la diversità delle due religioni non è grandissima: abbiamo lo stesso Dio Padre, Figliolo e Spirito Santo. Lo stesso Salvatore … solo per gli evangelici la religione è più pura: è tal quale ce l'ha data il nostro Signore Gesù ed i suoi apostoli*; Celli, service report, August 6, 1896, in ATV, series 9, subseries 3, bundle 439, folder 2.

39. *Credo che sia uno solo il pensiero capace di scuoterla alquanto; il timore che venga turbata quella sua consueta apatia*; Celli, service report, August 6, 1896, in ATV, series 9, subseries 3, bundle 439, folder 2.

Olivero, about whom she affirms that "I cannot call her a Catholic" (*non posso chiamarla Cattolica*): "Being very learned in secular science, she does not want to submit herself to the simplicity of the gospels.... She does not want to believe in the miracles of our Lord Jesus, in his Passion, Resurrection, and Ascension: her mind, with her high studies, cannot explain these things."[40] She appears to be even more disheartened after visiting widow Bruno; in the service report of June 1895, she writes that she finds widow Bruno apathetic and indifferent. What she finds most painful is to see widow Bruno in that state despite the fact that she has owned a Bible for many years and that she has even educated her daughter in the Evangelical faith. Celli cries out: "It was really pitiful to see the mother being outside everything, neither Evangelical nor Catholic."[41] On the other hand, she admires devout Catholics, people who believe sincerely despite being in error: "I visited Ms. Perotti at the Cottolengo hospital. She is still a sincere and religious Catholic."[42] During her visits to both Catholic and Evangelical families, Celli often reads entire chapters of the gospels, passages of the New Testament, and Psalms, especially the chapters 16, 34, and 51, which constitute a source of encouragement for the brothers and the sisters in the faith who are in hardship.[43] She also reads passages of the Old Testament, especially extracts from the book of Jeremiah and the book of Exodus. On one occasion, in order to outline the reasons for the Protestant aversion to sacred images, Celli mentions chapter 20 of Exodus, especially the

---

40. *Essendo molto istruita in scienza del secolo non vuole sottomettersi alla semplicità dei Vangeli ... non vuole credere nei miracoli del Signore Gesù, nella sua passione, risurrezione, ed ascensione: quelle cose la sua mente, con i suoi alti studi, non se le può spiegare*; Celli, service report, August 6, 1896, in ATV, series 9, subseries 3, bundle 439, folder 2.

41. *Vedere la madre all'infuori di tutto, né evangelica, né cattolica, mi faceva proprio pena*; Celli, service report of June 1895, in ATV, series 9, subseries 3, bundle 439, folder 2.

42. *Visitai la Signora Perotti all'Ospedale Cottolengo. È ancora cattolica, sincera e religiosa*; Celli, undated service report, in ATV, series 9, subseries 3, bundle 439, folder 2.

43. One can see, for instance, the service report of November 8, 1894. During her visit to the "sister in the faith" Carolina Ferrari, who was ill, Celli reads the whole Psalm 34. In the same service report, she narrates her visit to Ms. Lora, a Catholic woman. Since Ms. Lora cannot read but listens to the good news with interest and pleasure, Celli entrusts Ms. Lora's elder son with reading out the Psalm to her mother that very evening.

second commandment: "I took the Bible, read out the commandments in Exodus to her, and said: 'Can you see why Protestants do not [approve] sculptures nor images, as with this commandment of the Lord we can still adapt things according to our limited intelligence?'"[44] Sometimes, she lends or gives away copies of the Bible (that of Martini's version), of the gospels (Diodati's version), or unspecified Evangelical books (*libri evangelici*) under the pretext of coming back in future to read some passages together. Celli feels the need to read biblical verses often during her evangelizing activity (just as the committee seems to urge) and has no qualms about saying it explicitly: "I wish I could read more frequently the Bible with the families I visit. I often suffer from this shortcoming; yet from time to time, I also have the chance to do it. May the Lord make it easier for me to fulfill this duty."[45]

Yet there is no shortage of exhortations to read. During a visit to Ms. Scala, a former Catholic disheartened and disappointed for living "bad moments of real incredulity" (*momenti brutti di vera incredulità*), Celli encourages her not to stop praying and, at the same time, nurturing and strengthening her weak faith by reading regularly and every day sacred Scripture. On the occasion of a visit to sister Barbero, "guilty" of being responsive to Sabbatarian preaching, Celli exhorts her not to separate from the doctrines of the Bible, which "should be our only rule of faith" (*devono*

---

44. *Presi la Bibbia, le lessi i comandamenti nell'Esodo, e dissi: "Vede perché i protestanti non [approvano] sculture né immagini, con questo comandamento del Signore possiamo ancora adattarci le cose secondo la nostra limitata intelligenza?"*; Celli, service report, March 2, 1895, Turin, in ATV, series 9, subseries 3, bundle 439, folder 2, mentioning Exod 20:3–5. A few pages later, in the same report, Celli refers to the commandments that God gave to Moses on Mount Sinai, quoting the same chapter from the book of Exodus: "Do you see the second commandment? What a prohibition! Only for this should the Roman Church close her temples, which are all full of images" (*Ha visto il secondo comandamento? Qual proibizione! Solo per questo la Chiesa romana dovrebbe chiudere i suoi Templi tutti pieni di immagini*).

45. *Vorrei poter leggere più sovente la Bibbia nelle famiglie che visito, di questa mancanza ben sovente ne soffro, ma pure di rado mi si offre l'opportunità di farlo: il Signore mi faciliti l'adempimento di questo mio dovere*; Celli, service report, March 2, 1895, Turin, in ATV, series 9, subseries 3, bundle 439, folder 2. In the service report of November 1894, Annina Celli complains that in Turin there are no places where to buy freely the Bible: "How great would it be if here in Turin Bibles, New Testaments, and religious essays were on display to sell!" (*Quanto sarebbe buono che qui in Torino fossero esposte in vendita Bibbie, nuovi Testamenti e trattati religiosi!*).

essere la nostra sola regola di fede), not even for a moment.[46] Besides, as she explains in the same report, the Bible is certainly not a book that is difficult to understand or obscure. The example of sister Gillone's father, a humble and uneducated man ("an ordinary farmer with very little education" [*semplice contadino con pochissima istruzione*], as Annina Celli defines him), gives her the opportunity to reiterate this point, which is central in the teaching of the Reformation. Formerly, Mr. Gillone was a fervent Catholic, who read almost entirely the Bible at his son-in-law's insistence, approaching Evangelicalism later in life. As Celli affirms, her teaching method consists of avoiding attaching the theories of the Roman Church when the knowledge of the gospel is still unstable in the people's hearts: "I find it necessary to have sympathy for those hearts in the dark and then to erase gently and gracefully their tragic mistakes, and even earlier to add the reward … the great reward, the promises of the Lord through His forgiveness, consolation … his peace!"[47] This strategy is better shown a few pages later in the same report: "In some cases and for some time, I believe it is better not to say that we are Protestants; let us make people appreciate the great gifts of the gospel and the joy that it has brought to our hearts … and the Catholics, before being scared by superstitions and prejudices about our position, will have seen the light that surrounds us, and it will be easier to attract them to the only and true God and His law."[48]

4. Conclusion: A Particular Attention to the Condition of Women

The meticulous service reports of the Biblewomen—the "workers of the church" (*operaie della Chiesa*), whom I prefer to call "Ladies of the Bible,"

---

46. Annina Celli, service report, March 2, 1895, Turin, in ATV, series 9, subseries 3, bundle 439, folder 2.

47. *Trovo necessario compatire quei cuori ottenebrati, togliervi quindi, con delicatezza e garbo, i loro funesti errori, e prima ancora mettervi il compenso … il grande compenso, le promesse del Signore col suo perdono, le sue consolazioni … la sua pace!*; Celli, service report of March 1893, Turin, in ATV, series 9, subseries 3, bundle 439, folder 2.

48. *In certi casi, e per qualche tempo credo sia bene non dire che siamo protestanti, facciamo prima apprezzare i grandi doni del Vangelo, e la gioia che ha recato ai nostri cuori … ed i cattolici prima d'essere spaventati da superstizioni e pregiudizi aderenti alla nostra posizione, avranno visto la luce che ci circonda e sarà più facile attrarli al solo e vero Dio e alla sua Legge*; Celli, service report of March 1893, Turin, in ATV, series 9, subseries 3, bundle 439, folder 2.

attract, move, and astonish at the same time. This happens not so much (or, to put it better, not only) because of the candour with which the Biblewomen try to deal with complex theological themes—for example, the transubstantiation,[49] the expiatory sacrifice of Christ and his second coming (*parousia*), the cult of saints, the meaning of the Last Supper, the resurrection, the sense of evil and sufferings, the role of Mary and right form of respect that "true Christians" should pay her—without having a real curriculum of academic studies, but also because of the generous passion with which they take note of the face-to-face conversations with various interlocutors during their daily preaching activity. Such a zeal shines through each line and page, and while the empathy for the people, known through the house-to-house work, is natural, in any case it appears to be even admirable. As we have seen, the Biblereaders' interlocutors are not only committed atheists or, on the contrary, fervent Catholics, but also apathetic (*né caldi né freddi*) individuals or brothers and sisters who have lost their zeal in the course of time. Our protagonists do not seem to wish to neglect any vice or virtue of the poor devils whom they visit. They list weaknesses, spiritual improvements, sudden steps back, hesitancies, acts of unexpected courage, misfortunes, diseases, and, indeed, the passages of the Bible read and discussed together.

Overall, however, the theological importance of the letters is secondary to their sociological relevance. They reveal a picture of Italian society at the end of the nineteenth century, with a special attention for the condition of women, namely because women are the main interlocutors. Only as a secondary level do they offer a credible account of the religious beliefs and knowledge of the working and lower middle class of that time.

4.1. Monitoring the Quality of Their Service

Little emerges about the Biblewomen's theological formation and knowledge of the Scripture as regards exegesis and personal habits of biblical study. Many questions remain unanswered. What was the weight attrib-

---

49. Transubstantiation is defined by Celli as "a horrible and wretched doctrine … with pretensions to making us believe that all the greatness of that God is in that small piece of miserable meal … feeble substance" (*dottrina orribile e meschina … con la pretesa di farci credere che tutta la grandezza di quel Dio si trovi in quel pezzetto di misero pasto … inconcludente materia*); Celli, service report, March 2, 1895, Turin, in ATV, series 9, subseries 3, bundle 439, folder 2.

uted to their role, which, as we saw, was institutional, by the historical authorities of the church, that is, the Tavola and the Synod? What was the real contribution (both in quantitative and qualitative terms) of Biblewomen to the diffusion of the Evangelical creed? Which forms of implicit and explicit control over their activity were exerted by the Evangelizing Committee? It is impossible to answer exhaustively some of these questions; others can only receive a partial response.[50] As far as the numerical contribution is concerned, it is impossible to reconstruct the percentage of Catholic or atheist families, visited by the Biblewomen, which converted to Evangelism and remained in that condition until their deaths. Surely, from the letters we have evidence that a certain number of people took full part in the Reformed world, although we cannot produce an accurate statistical representation of the phenomenon. As regards the qualitative contribution, we can certainly assert that the Biblewomen's effort was constant and enduring. Considering the average level of religious (especially biblical) culture of the whole population, we can safely say that their ministry contributed to increasing it significantly. We have partly written about the control exercised by the committee and its members; indeed, it depended on the personality of the president in office, but, doubtless there was a direct and evident checking (one may think about the analytical service reports requested).[51] Similarly, there was also a constant monitoring of the quality of the Biblewomen's service. Besides, I do not think that this could be different. It would have been at least risky (and, realistically, even dangerous) to leave "on the field" workers (evangelizers or door-to-door salesmen) in complete freedom.

The most intimate aspects of the Biblewomen's private lives, such as their familiar and sentimental relationships, friendships, love affairs, or their lonely nights, remain obscure, too. We are merely informed about some relative's illness, a son's hospital stay, or minor ailments becoming chronic in the course of the years, and little more. It is clear that the technical format of service reports is not ideal to uncover the Biblewomen's

---

50. In order to understand how significant the Waldensian Synod and Tavola considered the Biblewomen's activity, one should analytically consult the minutes of the meetings of the years when the Biblewomen provided their ministry, that is, from 1865 to circa 1915. These minutes are kept at the ATV, series 4, subseries 1.

51. By conducting empirical research, it emerges that the more limited the role of a Biblewoman within the organization, the lower her cultural level, and the more recent her appointment, the greater was the frequency of the reports.

private spheres, personal dissatisfactions, or professional and sentimental disappointments. The scant information that we have seems to emerge by chance from their writings, either when they justify themselves to the President for reports that are not as accurate as the previous ones or when they request to receive in advance an allowance, or simply by distraction or tiredness. Pusterla mentions her increasing economic difficulties, which have become harsher after her husband's illness and subsequent suspension from the activity of door-to-door salesman.[52] Celli suffers from unclear "neuralgia" and apologizes to the members of the committee for the disappointing service report of December 1895:

> When I gave Mr. Tron my service report of November, I said that I wished to do more in that of December. Unfortunately, it did not happen. My poor health conditions prevented me from devoting all my days to the Lord. I have great faith, however, that in future I will be able to fulfil better my duty. May God wish so! My neuralgia at the head will make this report be among the least satisfactory, and for this I beg your pardon in advance.[53]

4.2. Self-Awareness of Being an Instrument of God

Our protagonists are not used to the religious practice of confession. Their letters reveal their strict adherence to the principles of Reformed faith, especially because they perceive themselves as instruments of the divine will. They constantly repeat that they manage to preach the gospel and to contribute in this way to the conversion of some people not because of their intelligence or rhetoric but because "the Lord opens our mouth and puts in it expressions depending on the needs" (*il Signore apre la nostra bocca*

---

52. For instance, in a letter of 1894 addressed to Prochet, in a post scriptum, Pusterla asks the members of the committee to receive her trimonthly pay a few days earlier since the contributions of the last months have been rather modest, and "they would do me a great favor, as I find myself in need, being my husband ill" (*farebbero un grande favore trovandomi proprio nel bisogno avendo ammalato mio marito*); letter of November 1, 1894, page 20 in ATV, series 9, subseries 1, folder 36.

53. *Quando consegnai al Sig. Tron il mio rapporto di novembre dissi che speravo fare un po' di più nel dicembre, ma purtroppo non fu così; la poca salute m'impedì di consacrare al Signore tutte le mie giornate: ho però molta fiducia che in avanti potrò disimpegnare meglio il mio compito. Lo voglia Iddio! La mia nevralgia al capo farà pure che questo mio rapporto riesca dei meno soddisfacenti, di cui chiedo anticipate scuse*; Celli, service report, January 3, 1895, Turin, in ATV, series 9, subseries 3, bundle 439, folder 2.

e vi mette le espressioni a seconda dei bisogni).[54] They are not asked to do a "loud and ostentatious activity, but a simple and hidden, constant and sincere work" (*opera chiassosa e appariscente, ma un lavoro semplice e nascosto, costante e sincere*).[55] Besides, the Biblewomen are fully aware that thanks to their activity, they simply contribute to fulfilling the biblical prophecy concerning the fact that "the gospel has to be preached everywhere before the second coming [*parousìa*] of our Lord Jesus" (*il Vangelo dev'essere predicato in tutti i luoghi avanti la seconda venuta del Signore Gesù*) (cf. Matt 24:14).[56] A common element in their preaching activity, if we want to find one, is that Biblewomen essentially viewed themselves as instruments for spreading the gospel in manners and times fixed *ex-ante* by the divine will. Their successes—the conversions, or the fact that a sympathizer started to participate in the meetings at the temple or began biblical studies, eventually being accepted as an effective member of the community by taking part in the Lord's Supper—are never interpreted as personal successes. They are, rather, the outcome of a superior design produced at the right time.

Doubtless, from a certain viewpoint Biblewomen can be defined as prophetesses, and we can refer to them using the same words that the last Jewish prophet John the Baptist said about himself: "I am a voice of one crying out in the wilderness" (John 1:23 NRSV). In fact, none of them ever claimed to be an exceptional woman or a heroine, although somehow each one of them was a prophetess and a heroine, if we give these terms a very sober meaning.[57]

In no respect, however, were their "discreet lives" ever "common lives."[58] As witnessed by the correspondence examined, the Biblewomen's passion for the Truth, personal sacrifice, indisputable organizational skills, and ability to maintain long-term relationships both with the members of the community and external people have made it possible that these women

---

54. Celli, service report of June 1895, Turin, in ATV, series 9, subseries 3, bundle 439, folder 2.

55. Celli, service report of March 1893, Turin, in ATV, series 9, subseries 3, bundle 439, folder 2.

56. Celli, service report of March 1893, Turin, in ATV, series 9, subseries 3, bundle 439, folder 2.

57. As Max Weber said, whoever tries to carry out a difficult, if not impossible, task can be defined a "hero," in the secular meaning of this term; cf. Weber, *Il Lavoro Intellettuale come Professione* (Turin: Einaudi, 1948), 120–21.

58. This definition has been used by Bruna Peyrot and Graziella Bonansea, *Vite Discrete: Corpi e Immagini di Donne Valdesi*, SD 22 (Turin: Rosenberg & Sellier, 1993).

have not been forgotten. At the same time, the example of the Biblewomen reminds us that women's charisma can have a great value in every type of organization, indeed in the religious ones too.

Bibliography

Benedetti, Marina. "La Predicazione delle Donne Valdesi." Pages 135–58 in *Donne Cristiane e Sacerdozio: Dalle Origini all'Età Contemporanea*. Edited by Dinora Corsi. LV 41. Rome: Viella, 2004.

Biller, Peter. "What Did Happen to the Waldensian Sisters? The Strasbourg Testimony." Pages 222–33 in *Studi in Onore del Prof. Jean Gonnet (1909–1997)*. Pro 54 (1999).

Cacchi, Marina. "Giuseppina Pusterla e l'Evangelizzazione Valdese di Fine Ottocento." Pages 102–25 in *Archivio per la Storia delle Donne II*. Edited by Adriana Valerio. Naples: D'Auria, 2005.

Cignoni, Mario. "I Valdesi in Italia (1848–1870)." Pages 103–30 in *Dalle Valli all'Italia: I Valdesi nel Risorgimento (1848–1998)*. Edited by Bruno Bellion et al. CSSV 16. Turin: Claudiana, 1998.

Gonnet, Giovanni. "La Donna Presso i Movimenti Pauperistico-Evangelici." Pages 103–29 in *Movimento Religioso Femminile e Francescanesimo nel Secolo XIII*. Assisi: Società Internazionale di Studi francescani, 1980.

Il Rinascimento: Giornale dell'Evangelizzazione Italiana. November 25, 1865.

Merlo, Grado Giovanni. *Identità Valdesi nella Storia e nella Storiografia II*. SStor. Turin: Claudiana, 1991.

Peyrot, Bruna, and Graziella Bonansea. *Vite Discrete: Corpi e Immagini di Donne Valdesi*. SD 22. Turin: Rosenberg & Sellier, 1993.

Romagnani, Gian Paolo. "I Valdesi nel 1848: Dall'Emancipazione alla Scelta Italiana." Pages 71–101 in *Dalle valli all'Italia: I Valdesi nel Risorgimento (1848–1998)*. Edited by Bruno Bellion et al. CSSV 16. Turin: Claudiana, 1998.

Weber, Max. *Il Lavoro Intellettuale come Professione*. Turin: Einaudi, 1948.

Biblical Inspiration in the Transformations of Women's Religious Communities in Nineteenth-Century Italy

Adriana Valerio

Introduction: The Bible: A Dangerous Reading

In 1550, the *Index librorum prohibitorum* established that "vulgar works by the female sex are universally prohibited, including those by female monastics."[1] Women and their readings represented the main preoccupation of the Catholic hierarchy, which sought to counteract the Protestant crisis that was tearing Christian Europe apart. This strategy was due to the fact that the primary readers of biblical translations, which were available in great number since the end of 1400, were women. For this reason, women tried not to remain passive before the prohibitions against reading and studying the sacred texts enforced after the Council of Trent. In particular, *women* did not hesitate to send protests, requests for exemption, or pleas. Female monastic communities were treated especially harshly, as strip searches were conducted in order to take Bibles away from the nuns who showed some familiarity with the sacred texts. The decision to tighten up the state of perpetual enclosure imposed by the conciliar fathers on nuns interrupted the positive exchange between religious communities and lay circles, which during the time of humanism found in sacred Scripture an important point of common reflection and debate.

These measures ended up breaking the reading habits that were becoming established, though hesitantly, in the modern age in both the female lay and religious worlds. Direct knowledge of Scripture was judged dangerous by the ecclesiastic authority, which found it necessary to forbid and

---

This chapter has been translated by Michele Lucchesi.
1. "Biblia vulgari idiomata aedita universo foemineo sexui prohibita sunt, etiam monialibus in monasteriis inclusis."

discourage "autonomous reading" by any means. The biblical text, therefore, was subordinated to catechesis with the clear pedagogical intention of nourishing the faithful with a few simple notions, thus avoiding any direct contact with the sacred text. This led to many grave consequences. In particular, biblical studies remained underdeveloped in the Catholic world, since it was discredited and considered unseemly, especially for women. The results of this ecclesiastical policy, together with nonexistent or inadequate state structures, can be clearly seen from the 1861 census data, which showed that in Catholic Europe 78 percent of the population was illiterate.[2]

1. Nuns in Nineteenth-Century Italy

The underdevelopment of biblical studies in the Catholic world, which continued until the nineteenth century, was not balanced by pastoral care. Thus the faithful were driven to show devotion rather than to develop consciousness and were encouraged to adopt a fideistic attitude rather than to adhere to beliefs validated by the Bible.[3]

To the Jansenists, in whose view the neglect of sacred Scripture was a sign of the church's religious and cultural decay, Pope Pius VI answered with the bull *Auctorem fidei* in 1794, in which some of the eighty-five propositions condemned related to the reading of the Bible. The ecclesiastical opposition against the French Enlightenment, German rationalism, or any other ideological position that tried to demolish the foundations of revelation ended up excluding Italy from the lively and rich cultural exchange that animated Europe. This hindered the formation of an Italian school of biblical studies in favor of a scholastic and apologetic model.[4]

On three occasions—in 1816, 1844, and 1846—Pius VII, Gregory XVI, and Pius X, worried about the dangers of the autonomous reading of sacred texts as much as the advance of secular aspirations and condemned

---

2. Gigliola Fragnito, *La Bibbia al Rogo: La Censura Ecclesiastica e i Volgarizzamenti della Scrittura (1471-1605)* (Bologna: Il Mulino, 1997); Fragnito, *Proibito Capire: La Chiesa e il Volgare nella Prima Età Moderna* (Bologna: Il Mulino, 2005).

3. Michela De Giorgio, "Il Modello Cattolico," in *L'Ottocento*, vol. 4 of *Storia delle donne*, ed. Geneviève Fraisse and Micelle Pierrot (Rome: Laterza, 1991), 155-91; Simonetta Soldani, ed., *L'Educazione delle Donne: Scuole e Modelli di Vita Femminile nell'Italia dell'Ottocento*, SRS (Milan: Angeli, 1991).

4. Cf. Yves-Claude Gélébart, "La Bible dans l'*Aufklärung* Catholique," in *Le Siècle des Lumières et la Bible*, vol. 7 of *Bible de Tous les Temps*, eds. Yvon Belaval and Dominique Bourel (Paris: Bauchesne, 1986), 563-77.

the translation of the Bible into national languages. Severe limitations on the education of girls (reading and writing) were imposed on women's religious communities; the wounds of Christ were considered sufficient to fill the gap with any type of knowledge.[5]

As a result of the laws of suppression passed between 1808 and 1866, Italian women's religious congregations were seriously harmed and forced to go through deep transformations, especially through a complex and contradictory modernization process. In order to survive as nuns, women had to find different forms of communal identity, becoming less concentrated on an exclusively contemplative lifestyle and more driven to taking action in social fields such as education and social work. These choices played an important role in making women's congregations change their structures and adapt to a continuously transforming society. New congregations founded from the middle of nineteenth century onward implemented a series of initiatives that let them acquire an unusual dynamism that de facto went beyond the confines imposed by the post-Tridentine church.

We can see, therefore, that Catholic women assumed new leading roles in society, although this attitude was marked by contradictions. On the one hand, women's activity was characterized by traditional faith and conservative politics. On the other hand, in their renewed apostolic commitment, women held modern values such as freedom of movement, personal autonomy, social visibility, and the right to freedom of speech and expression and to decision making. In particular, founders of religions congregations carried out what has been defined as "antimodern modernization," changing considerably the traditional forms of religious life.[6]

In this process of redefining religious identity and vocation, for some founders biblical inspiration started to become, albeit slowly, a new resource for religious life as much as the foundation of new vocational relationships. The use of the Bible, however, remained controversial and antinomic. While there were new possibilities of reflection on sacred

---

5. Giancarlo Rocca, *Donne Religiose: Contributi ad una Storia della Condizione Femminile in Italia nei Secoli XIX–XX* (Rome: Paoline, 1992); Luciano Pazzaglia, ed., *Chiesa e Prospettive Educative in Italia tra Restaurazione e Unificazione*, Paed. (Brescia: La Scuola, 1994).

6. Marina Caffiero, *Religione e Modernità in Italia (Secoli XVII–XIX)*, Stor 2 (Pisa: Istituto Poligrafico, 2000); Giuliana Boccadamo, "Modernità e Antimodernità: Fondatrici e Rivoluzioni," in *Scritture Femminili e Storia*, ed. Laura Guidi (Naples: Clio, 2004), 307–19.

Scripture, its presence in the language of the founders was not very significant. The Bible was still not at the heart of religious life. This absence was based, on the one hand, on the principle of expiation—which nuns had to embody so as to redeem a world marked by secularist revolutions. On the other hand, the absence was based on undertaking an active life in order to care for and educate the young so that they could return to Catholic faith. In this regard, we can discuss some examples.

1.1. Maria De Mattias (1805–1866)

Maria De Mattias[7] founded the congregation of the Adorers of the Blood of Christ (*Congregazione delle Suore Adoratrici del Sangue di Cristo*) in Acuto, a territory belonging to the Papal States (1834).[8] We know that, when De Mattias was a young girl, her father, Giovanni De Mattias, used to read her passages from the Bible. Her brothers also hung on the walls of their room some pieces of paper with sentences from the Bible. Such a familiarity with the Bible, which De Mattias acknowledged having learned at a young age, is not present in her vocabulary, which is unadorned and essential. In her letters there is no explicit reference to sacred Scripture, nor was it used as a repertory of exempla.

In her works there is a brief mention of the image of the "useless servant" (Luke 17:7–10) that focuses on the merits of the crucified and indicates, perhaps, the evangelical inspiration and motivation for her pastoral commitment. Yet De Mattias started to preach as a laywoman not only in the enclosed space of houses or schools but also in squares and open areas. Furthermore, she did not address her preaching only to a female audience but also to men and to women of different social conditions: widows, wives, unmarried women, parents, ministers, and children. We know little about the content of her preaching, but her oratory probably did

---

7. Cf. Maria Paniccia, *La Spiritualità e l'Opera di Maria de Mattias* (Rome: Università Gregoriana, 1983). On this figure, see the careful and extensive bibliographic review in Angela Di Spirito and Luciana Coluzzi, eds., *Santa Maria De Mattias: Lettere* (Rome: CIS, 2005), 1:41–59; and Adriana Valerio, "L'Originalità di Maria de Mattias, Santa della Restaurazione," *AISP* 18 (2005): 199–215.

8. Rita Fresu, "'Si è Avvicinata l'Ora di Fare l'Istruzione': Santa Maria De Mattias, le Congregazioni Religiose e l'Acculturazione Femminile nel XIX Secolo," in *Come un Filo d'Erba: Quattro Sguardi Contemporanei sull'Epistolario di Santa Maria de Mattias* (Rome: Adoratrici del Sangue di Cristo, 2007), 59–91.

not contain abundant biblical references. Certainly De Mattias promoted traditional teaching and education, that is, a formative itinerary modeled on the Ignatian spiritual exercises and enriched by the in-depth analysis of the foundation of faith. This process of examination was designed to prepare one for sacraments and liturgical prayer as much as for increasing the spread of devotional practices. The itinerary was characterized by spiritual teachings, which aimed to instill solid piety and a fervent apostolic spirit in women. The love of Christ and his redeeming passion, the Virgin Mary's sufferings, huamn sin, and the Catholic doctrine (perhaps illustrated by simple passages from sacred Scripture) were the most common subjects to induce the audience to go to Confession and Holy Communion.

1.2. Gaetana Sterni (1827–1889)

Similarly, in a different cultural and geographic context (northern Italy), in 1873 Gaetana Sterni founded with a few companions the congregation of the Daughters of Divine Mercy (*Figlie della Divina Misericordia*) in Bassano del Grappa (Vicenza).[9] The spirituality of Sterni is based on two biblical references that indicate the close connection between obedience and love: the annunciation (Luke 1:38) and judgment day (Matt 25:31–46). In the Virgin Mary's *Fiat*, Sterni underlined not only the attitude that she and her sisters needed to assume to do God's will, even when this went against the ordinary direction of their lives, but also the necessity of becoming flexible, that is, open to changes, unforeseen events, and the unusual choices that God might suggest.

Through the image of the judgment day, Sterni hoped to lead nuns to acknowledge the central roles of practicing charity in finding salvation and exercising Christian discipleship. In this case, too, in the few remaining texts she does not show any familiarity with sacred Scripture beyond some passages or images learned through catechism or liturgy.

1.3. Maria Mazzarello (1837–1881)

The same lack of biblical perspective can be found in Maria Mazzarello, who in 1872 founded together with Giovanni Bosco the Congregation of the Daughters of Mary Help of Christians (*Congregazione delle Figlie*

---

9. Adriana Valerio, "I Conflitti dell'Anima: Gaetana Sterni (1827–1889)," *Bail* 14 (1993): 92–103.

di Maria Ausiliatrice), whose main goal was to educate the young.[10] Of humble origins, Mazzarello does not appear to have been very knowledgeable. Furthermore, having devoted all of her short life to the education of (often illiterate) young girls, she could not concentrate on sacred Scripture.

2. Leopoldina Naudet and Maria Carmela Ascione

In a context of what might be characterized as "biblical anorexia," Leopoldina Naudet (1773–1834) and Maria Carmela Ascione (1799–1875) are two exceptions, for, although in different areas (one in Verona, one in Bourbon Naples), they showed new interests and offered new interpretations of Scripture.

2.1. Leopoldina Naudet (1773–1834)

Born in Florence to a French father and a German mother, Naudet was in contact with three different linguistic and cultural areas and received an unusually European training thanks to her father, who wanted a "perfect education" for his daughter.[11] Naudet was in France from 1783 to 1789 at the Congregation of the Dames of Our Lady of Soisson (*Congregazione delle Dame di Nostra Signora di Soisson*); in Florence, as instructor of the children of the Grand Duke Leopold (1789); in Vienna (1790), following Maria Luisa, the wife of Leopold, who had in the meantime become emperor; and, finally, in Prague (1792), as maid of honor of the archduchess Maria Anna, abbess of the city's canonesses.

Naudet took part in many of the great events that occurred in Europe. Her way of thinking and her activities were influenced not only by the revolutionary uprisings but also by an acrimonious dispute with Jansenism and the still-burning question about the suppression of the Society of Jesus (1773). Naudet invested considerable effort, on the one hand, trying

---

10. Maria Pia Giudici and Mara Borsi, *Maria Domenica Mazzarello* (Turin: Elledici, 2008).

11. Adriana Valerio, "Da Donna a Donne: Leopoldina Naudet e l'Educazione Femminile agli Anni dell'800," in *Santi, Culti, Simboli nell'Età della Secolarizzazione (1815–1915)*, ed. Emma Fattorini, S/S 11 (Turin: Rosemberg & Sellier, 1997), 515–28; Valerio, "Leopoldina Naudet, l'Amicizia Cristiana e la Bibbia: L'influenza dei gesuiti nell'apostolato del libro," *AHSI* 167 (2015): 79–109; Rino Cona, *Leopoldina Naudet (1773–1834)*, 2 vol. (S. Pietro in Cariano, Verona: Gabrielli, 2016).

to protect those French exiled because of the revolution and, on the other hand, supporting the Jesuits. During these years she pursued her vocation as a foundress. This would acquire a stronger and clearer connotation later, after meeting the Fathers of the Sacred Heart, who not only tried to train people apt to reestablish the Society of Jesus but also thought it opportune to create a women's congregation for the education of the young following Ignatian spirituality. After finding a suitable place in Verona in 1807, Naudet could establish the Sisters of the Holy Family (*Sorelle della Sacra Famiglia*) (1833), a community of Jesuit inspiration devoted to training teachers and educating girls of the upper-middle class.

Naudet's personality was characterized by a great passion for studying, something on which she based her large project for the education of women. An avid reader, she left a library of almost two thousand books that cover three main subjects: the Bible and homiletics, devotion and hagiography, and apologetics. With regard to the first subject, her attention to sacred Scripture was certainly uncommon. We find the *Historia del Testamento Vecchio e Nuovo*[12] with comments from the church fathers, some editions of the gospels based on their concordances,[13] an ancient testament translated by Antonio Martini,[14] translations of the Acts of the Apostles by Cavalca,[15] popular (at that time) parenetic expositions of sacred Scripture,[16] and liturgical com-

---

12. *Historia del Testamento Vecchio e Nuovo Rappresentata con Figure in Rame, Intagliate da Domenico Rossetti e con Esplicazioni Estratte da' Santi Padri* (Venice: Girolamo Albrizzi, 1708); *Storia del Testamento Vecchio e Nuovo con Spiegazioni Estratte da' Santi Padri* (Venice: Andrea Santini, 1801).

13. *Il Vangelo secondo la Concordanza dei Quattro Evangelisti in Meditazioni e Distribuito per Tutti i Giorni dell'Anno*, trans. a priest from Turin (Florence: Francesco Alessandri, 1790); *Il Vangelo secondo la Concordanza dei Quattro Evangelisti Esposto in Meditazioni e Distribuito per Tutti i Giorni dell'Anno*, trans. a priest from Turin (Milan: Maspero e Buocher successori De' Galeazzi, 1814).

14. Antonio Martini, *Del Vecchio Testamento Tradotto in Lingua Volgare, con Annotazioni Illustrato* (Venice: Giuseppe Rossi, Qu. Bortolo, 1786).

15. Domenico Cavalca, *Volgarizzamento degli Atti degli Apostoli* (Milan: Tipografia Manini e Rivolta, 1726).

16. Paolo Medici, *Dialogo Sacro sopra i Vangeli e il Nuovo Testamento*, 17 vols. (Venice: Angiolo Geremia, 1733); Medici, *Dialogo Sacro sopra l'Antico Testamento*, 31 vols. (Venice: Angiolo Geremia, 1737); *Storia del Vecchio e Nuovo Testamento ad Uso delle Scuole Elementari delle Province Venete* (Venice: Francesco Andreola e Gio B. Missiaglia, 1823); Agostino Tialmet, *La Scoria dell'Antico e Nuovo Testamento*, 2 vols. (Venice: Niccolo Pezzana, 1725); Ferdinando Zucconi, *Lezioni Sacre sopra la Divina Scrittura*, 5 vols. (Venice: Stamperia Baglioni, 1791); Andrea Micheli, *Istoria*

ments.[17] In addition to handbooks for a first introduction to the Bible, we find the works of great orators such as Francesco Panigarola, Paolo Segneri, Louis Bourdaloue, and Jean-Baptist Massillon.[18] Other texts known and annotated by Naudet herself are Jesuit-style *exhortationes domesticae*, which continued the traditional *collatio*; the *Sermoni familiari fatti alle monache dette Angeliche* of Carlo Borromeo; the *Entretiens Spirituels* of Francis de Sales to the Visitandines; and the *Spiritual Conferences* by Saint Vincent de Paul.

All these works prove Naudet's predilection for a type of rhetoric that aimed to edify the religious community. Her pastoral method was inspired especially by the biblical lectures of the erudite Antonio Cesari (1760–1828) on Jeremiah, Joseph, Moses and Joshua, Daniel, the Maccabees, Abraham and Tobias, and Jesus and the apostles.[19] Cesari used the Jesuit model of the Scriptural Lectures, which constituted a real innovation adopted often in eighteenth-century Italian oratory. By reviving the reading of the Bible through the liturgical cycles, the Lectures recalled historical-literal interpretation so as to emphasize its moral application.

Cesari's placement of the Bible at the heart of his preaching cycles with an attention to actualization certainly constituted a model for Naudet. She, too, convened regular meetings in the community that focused on the

---

dell'Antico Testamento: Divisa per le Vite dei Santi e Personaggi Illustri Che in Esso Florirono (Milan: Tipografia Pogliani, 1828).

17. Giovanni Crasset, *Considerazioni Cristiane per Tutti i Giorni dell'Anno cogli Evangelj di Tutte le Domeniche* (Venice: Stamperia Baglioni, 1771); *Epistole ed Evangelj, Che si Leggono Tutto l'Anno alle Messe, secondo l'Uso della Santa Romana Chiesa, e l'Ordine del Messale Romano*, trans. Remigio Fiorentino (Venice: Giambattista Negri, 1800); Giuseppe Morani, *Sermoni per Tutte le Domeniche e Feste dell'Anno*, 4 vols. (Turin: Librai in Dora Grossa- Brado e Destefani, 1790).

18. Francesco Panigarola, *Dichiarazione dei Salmi di David* (Venice: Fabio e Agostino Zoppini, 1586); Paolo Segneri, *Esercizi Spirituali, Esposti da Antonio Ludovico Muratori* (Venice: Gio' Recurti, 1723); Segneri, *La Manna dell'Anima* (Venice: Bortoli, 1728); Segneri, *Panegirici Sacri* (Venice: Biambattista Novelli, 1757); Louis Bourdaloue, *Sermons pour le Carême* (Lion: Les Frères Bruyset, 1708); Bourdaloue, *Sermoni per le Domeniche dell'Anno* (Venice: Francesco Andreola, 1801); Bourdaloue, *Prediche Quaresimali* (Venice: Stamperia Baglioni, 1802); Jean-Baptist Massillon, *Quaresimale* (Venice: Simone Occhi, 1803); Massillon, *Prediche* (Venice: Simome Occhi, 1803).

19. These are biblical homilies that were collected into the *Lezioni storico morali sopra la Sacra Scrittura* (1815–1817), *La vita di Gesù* (1817–1821), and *I fatti degli Apostoli* (1821). Cf. Cesare Bissoli, "La Bibbia nella Chiesa e tra i Cristiani," in *La Bibbia nell'Epoca Moderna e Contemporanea*, ed. Rinaldo Fabris, CBS 17 (Bologna: EDB, 1992), 171–72.

saints of the day (e.g., Francis Assisi, Francis Xavier, Teresa of Ávila, Jane Frances de Chantal, Ignatius of Loyola, Mary Magdalene of Pazzi) and spiritual subjects such as simplicity, mortification, poverty, perseverance, or patience. These conferences were true lessons with moral ends so as to exhort, correct, and animate the community.[20] One should note, however, that biblical references to the gospels and Paul's letters, despite their presence, do not constitute the structure of Naudet's discourse nor represent the basis for her reflection. Rather, these allusions and quotations appear to derive from the passages of pastoral liturgy.

In Naudet, one notices a renewed attention to sacred Scripture, which, nonetheless, was still directed toward the formation of Christians and the spiritual direction of sisters. The pastoral and parenetic intent was superior to any critical approach to the sacred text. The Bible was a prelude to both contemplation and ethical practice.

2.2. Sister Maria Luisa di Gesù, Originally Known as Maria Carmela Ascione (1799–1875)

Born in Naples in 1799 into a family that had a strong attachment to the Third Dominican Order, Ascione received the basics of faith from her father, who read meditations on the gospels to her every night.[21] At the age of seventeen, she entered the Benedictine monastery of Donnaromita. In 1825, she became oblate in the Ritiro dell'Addolorata all'Olivella, taking the name of Maria Luisa di Gesù. In 1840, Ascione opened a school for poor girls and founded the Institute of Our Lady of Sorrows and Saint Philomena (*Istituto di Maria Santissima Addolorata e di Santa Filomena*), joining the Servants of Mary.[22]

In 1835, she met the priest Luigi Navarro, who became her spiritual director as well as a significant advisor and supporter of her activity.[23]

---

20. Adriana Valerio, *Leopoldina Naudet: Conferenze spirituali* (Verona: Gabrielli, 2014).

21. Giuseppe M. Besutti, "Ascione M. Luisa," in *Dizionario degli Istituti di Perfezione*, eds. Guerrino Pelliccia and Giancarlo Rocca (Rome: Dizionario degli Istituti di Perfezione, 1974), 1:cols. 926–31.

22. See Giuliana Boccadamo, "Maria Luisa Ascione e le Illustrazioni della Bibbia," in *La Bibbia nell'Interpretazione delle Donne*, ed. Claudio Leonardi, Francesco Santi, and Adriana Valerio (Florence: Il Galluzzo, 2002), 147–67.

23. Father Luigi Navarro was born in Gaeta on the tenth of July 1803. After being ordained, he became court chaplain. Navarro met Ascione in 1835, when she was

Indeed, Navarro favored the circulations of Ascione's texts, centered on her personal commentary on the whole Bible, an uncommonly ambitious work for a woman of that time.

On February 26, 1836, after receiving the Eucharist, Jesus ordered Ascione to devote herself to writing about the sacred text; he gave her as a gift a *capellatura d'oro*, that is, shining hair, which symbolized the ability to understand sacred Scripture. In obedience to her spiritual director and in a unique and extraordinary way, Ascione started a systematic commentary on biblical texts. Her first commentary, written in 1836, focused on the Apocalypse; one on the Song of Songs followed after it.

In a letter written in 1871, she remembered the difficulties in beginning what she considered a work that was beyond her human possibilities:

> I remember that, when I received the order to write about the Apocalypse, I said to the Lord: "Lord, why do you want me to write about this book, which seems to me to be so difficult? Order me to write about some easier book." I heard him answer: "By assigning the Apocalypse to you, I gave you the key to sacred Scripture. For this reason, I want you to write this book first." I understood then that I had to write about the entire Scripture, and this appeared to be something difficult to achieve. Subsequently, I said: "Lord, there are many educated people, yet you give this order to me, a person barely able to read?" The Lord answered: "Among the apostles, Peter was the most ordinary and ignorant, yet I chose him as head of the church, so that people would be aware that it was not Peter who was governing the church; rather, God was governing and carrying it. The same goes with you: everyone knows that it is me, not you, who has written."[24]

---

mother superior of the Ritiro dell'Addolorata all'Olivella, where he went driven by the desire to know her. He died in 1863.

24. "Mi ricordo che quando io ricevetti l'ordine di scrivere sull'Apocalisse, dissi al Signore dopo la santa comunione: 'Signore, perché volete che io scriva su questo libro che a me sembra tanto difficile? Datemi l'ordine di scrivere su qualche altro libro più facile.' Sentì che rispose: 'Nel darti l'Apocalisse ti ho dato la chiave della Scrittura; per questo io voglio che tu scriva prima questo libro.' Allora capii che avrei dovevo scrivere sull'intera Scrittura e mi sembrò una cosa molto difficile da attuare. Allora dissi: 'Signore, ci sono tante persone istruite e a me, che so leggere appena, date questo comando?' Il Signore rispose: 'Tra gli apostoli Pietro era il più semplice e ignorante, e io lo elessi a capo della Chiesa, affinché gli uomini avessero coscienza che non era Pietro a governare la Chiesa, bensì Dio che la governava e la reggeva. Lo stesso vale per te: tutti vedono che sono io e non sei tu ad aver scritto'" (ASMSA, Letter 10/3,

The publication of the two commentaries on the Apocalypse and the Song of Songs raised doubts among the Neapolitan ecclesiastical auditors, who refused to grant the *nihil obstat quominus imprimatur* to the commentaries on the book of Joshua and on the letter of Paul to the Romans. However, in 1839 these works were published in first edition in Imola thanks to Canon Giuseppe Stella, who was secretary of Bishop Giovanni Maria Mastai Ferretti, later Pope Pius IX. Beginning in 1843, the Neapolitan publisher Andrea Festa overcame local censorship and published the other works of Ascione with the title *Illustrazioni sulla Sacra Scrittura*, printing the texts as fortnightly issues of sixty-four pages each.

2.2.1. Commentaries on the Bible Attributed to Sister Maria Luisa di Gesù

In twenty-five years, Ascione wrote forty-five commentaries or *Illustrazioni* of the Bible,[25] an activity to which she would devote her entire life, until she died at the age of seventy-six.

1837–1839	The Apocalypse
1837–1839	Song of Songs
1837–1839	Joshua
1837–1839	Letter to the Romans
1843–1844	Psalms (2 vols.)
1844	Gospels (2 vols.)
1845	Book of Isaiah
1845	Jeremiah and Baruch
1845	Ezekiel
1846	Judges and Ruth
1846	Exodus and Leviticus
1846	Genesis
1846	Daniel
1846	Numbers and Deuteronomy
1847	Chronicles (1 and 2 of Paralipomena)
1847	Ezra, Tobit, Judith, and Esther
1847	Job
1847	1 and 2 Kings

September 15, 1872). I wish to thank Mother Elisabetta Torres for letting me consult the archive and see these letters, which she catalogued and transcribed.

25. These books can be found at ASMSA in Naples.

1847	3 and 4 Kings
1847	1 and 2 Maccabees
1848	Wisdom of Solomon and Sirach
1848	The Gospels of Matthew and Mark
1848	The Gospels of Luke and John
1848	Proverbs and Ecclesiastes
1849	Twelve Minor Prophets
1849	The Acts of the Apostles
1849	Letters of Saint Paul: Corinthians, Galatians, Ephesians, Philippians, and Colossians
1849	Song of Songs (second edition)
1850	Letters of Saint Paul: Thessalonians, Timothy, Titus, Philemon, and Hebrews; Letters of James, Peter, John, and Jude
1858	Gospels of Luke and John (second edition)
1859	Psalms vol. 1 (second edition)
1860	Psalms vol. 1 (second edition)
1865	Song of Songs (third edition)

We know that Ascione used the *Bible De Port-Royal*, a French translation of the Bible edited by Lemaistre De Sacy with the Latin text. This could lead one to believe that she was not as illiterate as it seemed and as she presented herself, following the stereotype of the uneducated mystic who receives everything from God. We know nothing, however, about the origin of each commentary—what text she had at her disposal or if she could consult other commentaries—for we do not have Ascione's autograph manuscripts except for a considerable number of handwritten notes.

Nevertheless, the editorial format of the work reveals her great care in approaching the biblical text. Her comments are preceded by the Latin text and, in parallel, the historical version of the Vulgate by Antonio Martini of 1778.[26] Furthermore, she added an accurate description to each excerpt, which is discussed and annotated in every aspect: the so-called *Illustrazione*. For instance, while writing her commentary for John 20:1-18, Ascione added to the traditional interpretation some remarks about Mary Magdalene, the beloved disciple, the apostle of apostles, whom she

---

26. See Pietro Stella, "Produzione libraria religiosa e versioni della Bibbia in Italia tra età dei lumi e crisi modernista," in *Cattolicesimo e Lumi nel Settecento Italiano*, ed. Mario Rosa, IS 33 (Rome: Herder, 1981), 99–125.

contrasted with both the other disciples who left Jesus alone for fear of the Jews and Eve, the "ambassador" of death, for with her love, Mary Magdalene overcame the "weakness" of her gender and, being present at the tomb as a witness of the Master's resurrection, became the "ambassador" of life and faith.[27]

2.2.2. The Spiritual Direction of Father Luigi Navarro

It is not clear how Ascione was able to write so ponderous a work. Her education was mediocre, and her writing was full of spelling and syntactic mistakes, since it was heavily influenced by Neapolitan. Indeed, as she dealt with the text of the Apocalypse, Ascione affirmed: "Opening the Apocalypse, I did not understand anything."[28]

We know that the spiritual director Navarro used to give Ascione a biblical text to meditate on every evening after finishing her work, when she remained alone. Navarro then checked the pages for misspellings and corrected the literary form, presenting the text to her again for the final approval. Thus under Navarro's guidance, Ascione spent most of her time commenting on sacred Scripture. From the correspondence with her spiritual director, it emerges that almost all the letters sent to him concerned the commentaries.[29]

It is difficult to understand the authorship and the originality of Ascione's *Illustrations*, as she was not always aware of the meaning that she attributed to the various biblical passages: "I felt out of myself, while I was inside myself, something that astonished me, as I did not understand what was happening."[30] The *Illustrazioni sulla Sacra Scrittura*, therefore, did not owe their origin to acquired science but to direct inner illumination.

---

27. See *Illustrazioni su i Vangeli di San Luca e San Giovanni*, vol, 2 (Naples: Stamperia Reale, 1858), 474–80.

28. "Aprendo l'Apocalisse non capivo niente": Alberto Radente, ed., *Vita ed Intelligenze Spirituali della Serva di Dio Suor Maria Luisa di Gesù, Scritte dalla Medesima* (Naples: Stabilimento Tipografico dell'Ancora, 1878), 170.

29. Only fourteen letters (from November 1, 1836 to February 1844) survive. Yet the explanation for so modest a number lies in the fact that after the foundation of the new Institute, Father Navarro, being the superior, lived in an annex of the monastery. In these letters, one can find frequent biblical allusions, which entered her vocabulary and became part of her typical Neapolitan speech.

30. "Mi sentivo fuori di me, mentre stavo in me: cosa che a me stessa faceva meraviglia, non capendo cosa accadesse" (*Vita*, 197).

Ascione put on paper what she received in her heart (*deposita sulla carta ciò che ha ricevuto nel cuore*) and wrote in obedience to an order given by God, not by humans.[31] She only wanted to carry out the command received by God and hoped that her works would be useful to herself and possible readers, so that they could "profit from his Word, because it is a fire that illuminates and purifies and a hammer that breaks the stones, even the hardest ones."[32] She was only an instrument (*istrumento*): it was the Lord who "pierced the veil that covered sacred Scripture" and "provided the key to Scripture."[33]

2.2.3. The Intervention of the Dominican Alberto Radente

After Navarro died in 1863, the Dominican Alberto Radente replaced him as spiritual director, soon showing diffidence toward the work of Ascione.[34] In fact, he invited her to write something new on sacred Scripture in order to verify whether all the publications really should be attributed to her or rather to the previous spiritual director. Having put her to the test, Radente acknowledged her gift. However, unlike Navarro, who had simply corrected spelling mistakes, he seems to have made more marked interventions in her texts.

Under his direction, the third edition of the commentary on the Song of Songs was published in 1865 and the commentary on the Apocalypse was reprinted twice.[35] Ascione also wrote a new commentary to the Apocalypse. To what extent should this work be attributed to her? What is the influence of the revisions made by her spiritual directors? As an example

---

31. See Letter 12/3; 12/4.
32. "Ricavare profitto dalla sua Parola, perché essa è un fuoco che illumina e purifica ed un martello che spezza le pietre benché le più dure."
33. *Vita*, 169: "il velo che copriva la Sacra Scrittura" and "chiave della Scrittura."
34. In 1856, the Dominican Radente (1817–1885) (originally known as Michele) was elected prior of S. Domenico Maggiore in Naples. Being the confessor of Bartolo Longo, he was responsible for the Third Order. After becoming Ascione's spiritual director, he edited her autobiography, which was published posthumously. See L. G. Esposito, "Alberto Radente O.P. (1817–1885): Cenni Bibliografici," *AFP* 55 (1985): 389–447.
35. The commentary to the Apocalypse had a wide circulation, as is proven by the fact that there is even a French translation of it.

in this regard, we can compare a comment of Ascione to the Song of Songs taken from a manuscript to the print edition approved by Radente.[36]

Ascione's Manuscript	Radente's Print Edition
Le porte sempre aperte sono figura della Chiesa sempre aperta a ricevere chiunque voglia entrare, ma anche aperta a quanti ne vogliano uscire, come gli eretici e gli increduli, che escono dalla Chiesa e si gettano nell'errore. La Chiesa non lo impedisce, così come non forza alcuno ad accostarsi ad essa	Le porte della Chiesa poi sono sempre aperte, non solo per ricevere chiunque vuole in essa entrare, ma eziandio per farne liberamente uscire, o cacciarne meritatamente, chi vuole da essa allontanarsi, a lei ribellarsi e tramare insidie, come fanno gli eretici e i miscredenti, che escono del Santo Tempio della Chiesa per gettarsi negli errori, e ne sono per questo scomunicati
The always-open doors represent the Church, which is always open to receive whoever wants to enter but is also open for those who want to exit such as heretics and skeptics who leave the Church and fall into error. The Church does not prevent them from doing so as much as it does not force anyone to come closer.	The doors of the Church are always open not only to receive whoever wants to enter but also to make one exit freely or to expel deservedly who wants to leave, rebel, or plot schemes, just like heretics and disbelievers who exit the sacred temple of the Church to rush into errors, being excommunicated for this.

It seems evident how the language of the spiritual director was more markedly juridical, something that made him push the interpretation of Ascione's words too far, while she offered an image of the church more tolerant than that of Radente. This example clearly demonstrates that the question of the authorship of Ascione's works is still open, yet one cannot deny her exceptional ability to give new importance to sacred Scripture in her commentaries through numerous images and allusions.

Even if she lived in a time characterized by profound ignorance of the Bible, Ascione found in the word of God a great source for her extraordinary spirituality. Despite being presented as parenetic literature, for the first time the Bible in its entirety appears to have provided the basis for the

---

36. This example is presented by Boccadamo, "Maria Luisa Ascione," 165; Cf. Adriana Valerio, "Differenziate Strategie Comunicative tra una Mistica e il suo Padre Spirituale: Il Caso delle Illustrazioni della Bibbia di Maria Luisa Ascione (1799–1875)," in *Lingue e Testi delle Riforme Cattoliche in Europa e nelle Americhe (secc. XVI–XXI)*, ed. Rita Librandi, QR 78 (Florence: Cesati, 2012), 473–90.

growth of a believer and a foundress. This opened a new path that, after a few years, gave birth to Catholic feminism in Italy, which was deeply indebted to Elisa Salerno (1873–1937) and her *Commenti Critici alle Note Bibliche Antifemministe*.[37] With this figure, however, we are in a lay field and at the beginning of modernism.

Bibliography

Besutti, Giuseppe M. "Ascione M. Luisa." Cols. 926–31 in vol. 1 of *Dizionario degli Istituti di Perfezione*. Edited by Guerrino Pelliccia and Giancarlo Rocca. Rome: Dizionario degli Istituti di Perfezione, 1974.

Bissoli, Cesare. "La Bibbia nella Chiesa e tra i Cristiani." Pages 171–72 in *La Bibbia nell'Epoca Moderna e Contemporanea*. Edited by Rinaldo Fabris. CBS 17. Bologna: EDB, 1992.

Boccadamo, Giuliana. "Modernità e Antimodernità: Fondatrici e Rivoluzioni." Pages 307–19 in *Scritture Femminili e Storia*. Edited by Laura Guidi. Naples: Clio, 2004.

———. "Maria Luisa Ascione e le Illustrazioni sulla Bibbia." Pages 147–67 in *La Bibbia nell'Interpretazione delle Donne*. Edited by Claudio Leonardi, Francesco Santi, and Adriana Valerio. Florence: Il Galluzzo, 2002.

Bourdaloue, Louis. *Prediche Quaresimali*. Venice: Stamperia Baglioni, 1802.

———. *Sermoni per le Domeniche dell'Anno*. Venice: Francesco Andreola, 1801.

———. *Sermons pour le Carême*. Lion: Les Frères Bruyset, 1708.

Caffiero, Marina. *Religione e Modernità in Italia (Secoli XVII–XIX)*. Stor 2. Pisa: Istituto Poligrafico, 2000.

Cavalca, Domenico. *Volgarizzamento degli Atti degli Apostoli*. Milan: Tipografia Manini e Rivolta, 1726.

Cona, Rino. *Leopoldina Naudet (1773–1834)*. 2 vols. S. Pietro in Cariano, Verona: Gabrielli, 2016.

---

37. Elisa Salerno, a self-educated and passionate scholar, devoted herself to the defence of women's dignity in family, work, social, and ecclesiastical contexts. Among her biblical works, one can remember Salerno, *Commenti Critici alle Note Bibliche Antifemministe*, 2 vols. (Vicenza: Arti Grafiche Vicentine G. Rossi e C., 1926). Cf. Elisa Vicentini, *Una Chiesa per le Donne: Elisa Salerno e il Femminismo Cristiano*, Dracma 5 (Naples: D'Auria, 1995).

Crasset, Giovanni. *Considerazioni Cristiane per Tutti i Giorni dell'Anno cogli Evangelj di Tutte le Domeniche*. Venice: Stamperia Baglioni, 1771.
De Giorgio, Michela. "Il Modello Cattolico." Pages 155–91 in *L'Ottocento*. Vol. 4 of *Storia delle Donne*. Edited by Geneviève Fraisse and Micelle Pierrot. Rome: Laterza, 1991.
Di Spirito, Angela, and Luciana Coluzzi, eds. *Santa Maria De Mattias: Lettere*. Vol. 1. Rome: CIS, 2005.
Epistole ed Evangelj, Che si Leggono Tutto l'Anno alle Messe, secondo l'Uso della Santa Romana Chiesa, e l'Ordine del Messale Romano. Translated by Remigio Fiorentino. Venice: Giambattista Negri, 1800.
Esposito, L. G. "Alberto Radente O. P. (1817–1885): Cenni Bibliografici." *AFP* 55 (1985): 389–447.
Fragnito, Gigliola. *La Bibbia al Rogo: La Censura Ecclesiastica e i Volgarizzamenti della Scrittura (1471–1605)*. Bologna: Il Mulino, 1997.
———. *Proibito capire: La Chiesa e il Volgare nella Prima Età Moderna*. Bologna: Il Mulino, 2005.
Fresu, Rita. " 'Si è Avvicinata l'Ora di Fare l'Istruzione': Santa Maria De Mattias, le Congregazioni Religiose e l'Acculturazione Femminile nel XIX Secolo." Pages 59–91 in *Come un Filo d'Erba: Quattro Sguardi Contemporanei sull'Epistolario di Santa Maria de Mattias*. Rome: Adoratrici del Sangue di Cristo, 2007.
Gélébart, Yves-Claude. "La Bible dans l'*Aufklärung* Catholique." Pages 563–77 in *Le siècle des Lumières et la Bible*. Vol. 7 of *Bible de Tous les Temps*. Edited by Yvon Belaval and Dominique Bourel. Paris: Beauchesne, 1986.
Giudici, Maria Pia, and Mara Borsi. *Maria Domenica Mazzarello*. Turin: Elledici, 2008.
Historia del Testamento Vecchio e Nuovo Rappresentata con Figure in Rame, Intagliate da Domenico Rossetti e con Esplicazioni Estratte da' Santi Padri. Venice: Girolamo Albrizzi, 1708.
Illustrazioni su i Vangeli di San Luca e San Giovanni. Vol. 2. Naples: Stamperia Reale, 1858.
Martini, Antonio. *Del Vecchio Testamento Tradotto in Lingua Volgare, con Annotazioni Illustrato*. Venice: Giuseppe Rossi, Qu. Bortolo, 1786.
Massillon, Jean-Baptist. *Prediche*. Venice: Simome Occhi, 1803.
———. *Quaresimale*. Venice: Simone Occhi, 1803.
Medici, Paolo. *Dialogo Sacro sopra l'Antico Testamento*. 31 vols. Venice: Angiolo Geremia, 1737.

———. *Dialogo Sacro sopra i Vangeli e il Nuovo Testamento*. 17 vols. Venice: Angiolo Geremia, 1733.

Micheli, Andrea. *Istoria dell'Antico Testamento: Divisa per le Vite dei Santi e Personaggi Illustri Che in Esso Florirono*. Milan: Tipografia Pogliani, 1828.

Morani, Giuseppe. *Sermoni per Tutte le Domeniche e Feste dell'Anno*. 4 vols. Turin: Librai in Dora Grossa- Brado e Destefani, 1790.

Paniccia, Maria. *La Spiritualità e l'Opera di Maria de Mattias*. Rome: Università Gregoriana, 1983.

Panigarola, Francesco. *Dichiarazione dei Salmi di David*. Venice: Fabio e Agostino Zoppini, 1586.

Pazzaglia, Luciano, ed. *Chiesa e Prospettive Educative in Italia tra Restaurazione e Unificazione*. Paed. Brescia: La Scuola, 1994.

Radente, Alberto, ed. *Vita ed Intelligenze Spirituali della Serva di Dio Suor Maria Luisa di Gesù, Scritte dalla Medesima*. Naples: Stabilimento Tipografico dell'Ancora, 1878.

Rocca, Giancarlo. *Donne Religiose: Contributi ad una Storia della Condizione Femminile in Italia nei Secoli XIX-XX*. Rome: Paoline, 1992.

Salerno, Elisa. *Commenti Critici alle Note Bibliche Antifemministe*. 2 vols. Vicenza: Arti Grafiche Vicentine G. Rossi e C., 1926.

Segneri, Paolo. *Esercizi Spirituali, Esposti da Antonio Ludovico Muratori*. Venice: Gio' Recurti, 1723.

———. *La Manna dell'Anima*. Venice: Bortoli, 1728.

———. *Panegirici Sacri*. Venice: Biambattista Novelli, 1757.

Soldani, Simonetta, ed. *L'educazione delle Donne: Scuole e Modelli di Vita Femminile nell'Italia dell'Ottocento*. SRS. Milan: Angeli, 1991.

Stella, Pietro. "Produzione Libraria Religiosa e Versioni della Bibbia in Italia tra Età dei Lumi e Crisi Modernista." Pages 99-125 in *Cattolicesimo e lumi nel Settecento italiano*. Edited by Mario Rosa. IS 33. Rome: Herder, 1981.

Storia del Testamento Vecchio e Nuovo con Spiegazioni Estratte da' Santi Padri. Venice: Andrea Santini, 1801.

Storia del Vecchio e Nuovo Testamento ad Uso delle Scuole Elementari delle Province Venete. Venice: Francesco Andreola e Gio B. Missiaglia, 1823.

Tialmet, Agostino. *La Scoria dell'Antico e Nuovo Testamento*, 2 vols. Venice: Niccolo Pezzana, 1725.

Valerio, Adriana. "I Conflitti dell'Anima: Gaetana Sterni (1827-1889)." *Bail* 14 (1993): 92-103.

———. "Differenziate Strategie Comunicative tra una Mistica e il Suo Padre Spirituale: Il Caso delle Illustrazioni della Bibbia di Maria Luisa Ascione (1799–1875)." Pages 473–90 in *Lingue e Testi delle Riforme Cattoliche in Europa e nelle Americhe (secc. XVI–XXI)*. Edited by Rita Librandi. QR 78. Florence: Cesati, 2012.

———. "Da Donna a Donne: Leopoldina Naudet e l'Educazione Femminile agli Anni dell'800." Pages 515–28 in *Santi, Culti, Simboli nell'Età della Secolarizzazione (1815–1915)*. Edited by Emma Fattorini. S/S 11. Turin: Rosemberg & Sellier, 1997.

———. *Leopoldina Naudet: Conferenze spirituali*. Verona: Gabrielli, 2014.

———. "Leopoldina Naudet, l'Amicizia Cristiana e la Bibbia: L'influenza dei gesuiti nell'apostolato del libro." *AHSI* 167 (2015): 79–109.

———. "L'Originalità di Maria de Mattias, Santa della Restaurazione." *AISP* 18 (2005): 199–215.

Il Vangelo secondo la Concordanza dei Quattro Evangelisti Esposto in Meditazioni e Distribuito per Tutti i Giorni dell'Anno. Translation by a priest from Turin. Milan: Maspero e Buocher successori De' Galeazzi, 1814.

Il Vangelo secondo la Concordanza dei Quattro Evangelisti in Meditazioni e Distribuito per Tutti i Giorni dell'Anno. Translation by a priest from Turin. Florence: Francesco Alessandri, 1790.

Vicentini, Elisa. *Una Chiesa per le Donne: Elisa Salerno e il Femminismo Cristiano*. Dracma 5. Naples: D'Auria, 1995.

Zucconi, Ferdinando. *Lezioni Sacre sopra la Divina Scrittura*. 5 vols. Venice: Stamperia Baglioni, 1791.

Conservative Feminism in Catholic Spain in the Nineteenth Century: Gimeno de Flaquer's "Evangelios de la Mujer"

Inmaculada Blasco Herranz

In 1900, Spain was a land marked almost exclusively by Catholicism. On the basis of the prevailing constitution of 1876, it was a confessional Catholic state, although other worship services in private spaces were tolerated. Critical voices, however, that spoke against the preponderant role of Catholicism in political and social life and that demanded a more modern orientation of conventional Catholic faith and practice had been raised already for decades. This questioning of a long, monolithic, and domineering Catholic tradition, although expressed by only a very few, had a far-reaching influence upon the entire work of the author, essayist, and journalist María de la Concepción Gimeno de Flaquer (1850–1919), who described herself as a conservative feminist.[1]

1. Concepción Gimeno de Flaquer

Born in Alcáñiz in the Aragonese province of Teruel, Gimeno de Flaquer went to Madrid at the age of twenty, where she wrote articles for various periodicals and moved in literary circles that were frequented by such renowned authors as Carolina Coronado (1820–1911) and Juan Valera (1824–1905). In 1872, she founded the magazine *La Ilustración de la Mujer* in Barcelona, the declared purpose of which was "the defense of

---

1. A list of her works is found in María del Carmen Simón Palmer, *Escritoras españolas del siglo XIX: Manual bio-bibliográfico*, NBEC 3 (Madrid: Castalia, 1991), 363–74; See also "María de la Concepción Jimeno de Flaquer," escritoras.com, April 6, 2003, https://tinyurl.com/SBL6007c.

her sex." In this period, her essays *La Mujer Española* (1877) and *La Mujer Juzgada por una Mujer* (1880) also were published. In addition, Gimeno de Flaquer wrote her first novels in this period: *Victorina o Heroísmo del Corazón* (1873) and *El Doctor Alemán* (1880). In the year 1879, she married the journalist Francisco de Paula Flaquer, the editor of the magazine *El Álbum Ibero-Americano*. This marriage meant for her both the beginning of her work for this periodical as well as also the start of a series of fruitful stays in France, Portugal, and Mexico. In Mexico, where she lived for seven years, she founded and led the magazine *El Álbum de la Mujer* and emerged as an ambassador of Spanish culture. She returned to Spain in 1890 and campaigned there for the cultural exchange with Mexico by making that country's history and literature more well-known. She also took over the direction of *Álbum Ibero-Americano*, continued to take part in literary gatherings (*tertulias*), wrote essays such as *Evangelios de la Mujer* (1901), and delivered lectures on the question of feminism (*El Problema Feminista* [1903]) at the academic literary association Ateneo Científico y Literario de Madrid, the forum for the progressive forces in Spain. In 1917, she undertook a journey through Latin America. She died two years later in Madrid.

The essay *Evangelios de la Mujer* (Women's Gospels) is one of Gimeno de Flaquer's most representative works since it shows most clearly how her Catholicism served in underpinning the validity and legitimacy of her feminist demands. This is true for the biblical citations as well as for the voices of ecclesiastical authorities that she puts forward. At the same time, her writings also represented a challenge to the prevailing Catholic hermeneutic insofar as her interpretation of the history of Catholicism and her interpretation of the biblical texts were guided by the conviction that women and men are intellectual equals and that women had had a significant role in the history of humanity in general and in church history in particular. Such a constant, if also not so systematic, reference to the Bible and church history is probably not to be found in any other conservative feminist, including the confessional feminists (to which Gimeno de Flaquer did not belong). This would suggest a knowledge of the subject matter that was not often to be met with at that time.

2. Gimeno de Flaquer and Conservative Feminism

In the texts written by Gimeno de Flaquer between 1869 and 1908, she resolutely defended the intellectual and moral capacity of women and, on this basis, demanded improved education for the female sex. She was a contemporary of the writers Concepción Arenal (1820-1893) and Emilia Pardo Bazán (1851-1921), both renowned advocates of access to education for women. Her work is representative of "conservative feminism," to which she herself gave the name. By means of this designation, Gimeno de Flaquer wanted to distance herself from the other feminist views of her time. These currents were connected with anarchism and socialism, two ideologies that found greater and greater dissemination in Spain toward the end of the nineteenth century. She considered both as too extreme because they, in her opinion, furthered the antagonism between women and men. She herself, on the other hand, advocated a feminism that mediated between the sexes and that respected marriage but still demanded that "in the moral, legal, and economic sense, the same laws" had to apply "for both sexes." With the realization of these ideas, the woman no longer would "have a status lower than that of a man and morally [would] no longer be a slave."[2] Gimeno de Flaquer shared the understanding of gender prevalent in the nineteenth century, according to which two irreducible, complementary human natures existed. Women and men possessed different moral and psychic qualities that enabled each to fulfill different tasks.

On the basis of this understanding, Gimeno de Flaquer developed her critique of those who were of the opinion that women are morally and intellectually inferior to men. Against them, she formulated her defense of the intellectual and moral capacity of women and her demand for the necessary education of the female sex. Her insistence upon acknowledgement of the intellectual equality of women did not necessarily mean, however, that they had to fulfill the same social responsibilities as men. In fact, Gimeno de Flaquer justified her demand precisely with the different, though upgraded, role of women as wives and mothers. Important for her was the fact that incumbent upon women were such important responsibilities as caring for the moral education of the children and taking part in the life of their men as alert companions.

Gimeno de Flaquer's work has been interpreted in very different, and even contradictory, ways. For some female authors, Gimeno de Flaquer takes up a liberal position insofar as she shares liberalism's view of women

---

2. María de la Concepción Gimeno de Flaquer, *Evangelios de la Mujer* (Madrid: Librería de Fernando Fé, 1900), 108.

as a perfectible subject. Seen from this position, she becomes a tireless defender of women's rights.[3] By others, though, her work is classed as reactionary on the basis of its conservative Catholic aspect, and her analysis of the causes for the social and legal discrimination of Spanish women is seen "as a reflection of the limits of a reformism impregnated with Catholic dogmas."[4] A third approach sees in Gimeno de Flaquer's work a mixture of two worlds, a product of the transition from the old to the new, or the result of the contradiction present in the period at the turn of the century.[5]

---

3. Maria José Lacalzada Mateo, "Las mujeres en la 'cuestión social' de la Restauración: Liberales y católicas (1875–1921)," *HC* 29 (2004): 702. "Concepción Gimeno de Flaquer developed an intensive journalistic activity that was congruent with the possibilities which existed at that time for the realization of liberal ideas in society." On the basis of this standpoint, she considered women as independent persons and spoke up for their self-determination.

4. See Solange Hibbs-Lissorgues, "Tous les chemins mènent à Dieu: l'Église et les femmes dans la deuxième moitié du XIX siècle," *Femmes et démocratie: Les Espagnoles dans l'espace public (1868–1978)*, ed. Marie-Aline Barrachina et al. (Nantes: Temps, 2007), 43–59. From this, Hibbs-Lissorgues concludes that Gimeno de Flaquer's defense of a moralizing feminism conveys a notion to what extent the Catholic culture of nineteenth century Spain represented an obstacle to a real emancipation of women. Outside of the academic framework, Gimeno de Flaquer is interpreted along these same lines also by the journalist Lola Campos in her article in the daily newspaper *Heraldo de Aragón*. She advocates the opinion that Gimeno de Flaquer's writing, such as *Victorina o Heroísmo del Corazón* (*Victorina; or, Heroism of the Heart*), for example, "suggests her partiality for Romanticism and for a conservatism that often stands in opposition to the open-minded spirit found in her journalistic writings." This is true also for her second novel, *El Doctor Alemán* (*The German Doctor*), in which she "once again persistently assigned women a self-sacrificial and patiently tolerant role." In her Mexican novels, too, "she held fast stubbornly to stale Romanticism. It is sufficient to call to mind the title of one of these novels, *Suplicio de una Coqueta* [*Anguish of a Coquette*], to be able to get an idea of her views. Or the title of her last novel, published in 1890, *Culpa o Expiación?* [*Guilt or Expiation?*], in which the heroine pays for her manner of conduct in regard to men with her death." Campos, "Concepción Gimeno Gil," *Heraldo de Aragón*, May 3, 1998.

5. According to Diego Chozas, "the tensions and conflicts at that time between progressive feminist ideas and traditional tendencies are reflected in the *Álbum Ibero-Americano* and in the so characteristically contradictory mentality of Gimeno de Flaquer herself" (Chozas, "La mujer según el *Álbum Ibero-Americano* [1890–1891] de Concepción Gimeno de Flaquer," *Espéculo: Revista de Estudios Literarios*, https://tinyurl.com/SBL6007d). The same view is articulated also by Maryellen Bieder, "Feminine Discourse/Feminist Discourse: Concepción Gimeno de Flaquer," *RQ* 37] (1990): 459–77; see also María de los Ángeles Aylala Aracil, "La Mujer Española de

This would explain the tensions and ambivalences that are to be detected in her journalistic work as well as in her essays. The major tension is said to exist in reconciling a conservative way of thinking with feminist demands. This way of thinking, which goes back to positions held by the so-called women writers of domesticity during the reign of Isabella II (1843–1868), is claimed to belong within the framework of the bourgeois model of domesticity of the nineteenth century. The feminist demands, however, were rooted in an enlightened liberal thought that took a critical view of the aforementioned model.

The first two interpretations, which place Gimeno de Flaquer at the apparently opposite poles of liberalism and Catholicism, as well as also the third interpretation, which sees her work as the contradictory product of a time in the midst of change, suffer from the fact that they are too much rooted in the present: that is, they apply present-day feminist concepts to the past. They also do not provide an exact analysis of how Gimeno de Flaquer's feminism articulated itself in the light of a particular reading of Catholicism, both in view of the tradition as well as the Bible. Instead of labeling her thought as backward or progressive, which occasionally occurs only implicitly, the task ought to be to find out how she arrived at her concept of feminism, which she herself called conservative in order to distance herself from the feminist orientations of socialism or anarchism.

My suggested interpretation aims at the possibility of seeing Gimeno de Flaquer as a representative of a symbiosis of two worldviews, a symbiosis that is difficult to unravel. She may not necessarily have experienced this symbiosis as a tension or contradiction, and it is not to be interpreted as such. It is the symbiosis including a worldview that is close to that of liberalism—the ideal image of the human being and women stemming from the Enlightenment are always present in her work—and a second one that is thoroughly influenced by a Catholicism that is not always in complete conformity to traditional church doctrine. Gimeno de Flaquer's education and training already bound both traditions with each other. Thus, for example, she tells in her book *La Mujer Española* that she received her training as a teacher in a secular institution, while in her family, which belonged to the local aristocracy, she enjoyed a deeply religious education.

Concepción Gimeno de Flaquer," Biblioteca Virtual Miguel de Cervantes, https://tinyurl.com/SBL6007b.

The interpretation that I suggest requires an exact analysis of the hermeneutic that Gimeno de Flaquer applied to the biblical texts and to the Catholic tradition. It must pursue the question of which role these texts played in the formulation of her feminism and of the concept of a woman as its central subject. This aspect hardly has been researched until now, neither in Gimeno de Flaquer's work in particular nor in regard to so-called conservative feminism in general, which was designated as such at that time. This aspect, though, is of central significance for understanding conservative feminism. In this sense, it can be shown that in the liberal feminist initiatives of the nineteenth and the first third of the twentieth centuries, Catholicism carried great weight.[6] Initiatives such as those by Celsia Regis, in 1925 one of the first female city councilors in Madrid, together with Asociación Nacional de Mujeres Españolas, probably the most important feminist women's organization during its period of activity from 1918 to 1936, were not of a confessional nature, to be sure, but had an unquestionable Catholic foundation.

My essay investigates the question of what Catholicism formed the foundation of Gimeno de Flaquer's feminism and her conception of women. In this way, a more complex and a historically rooted view of her work is to be offered. In the thought process that led Gimeno de Flaquer to her definition of women and of feminism, and in which Catholicism was an integral component, she worked out a critique of the prevailing interpretation of Catholicism and so contributed to the transformation of the orthodox view of Catholicism in Spain. She herself preferred the term Christianity. Within this framework, the issue is thus the question of Gimeno de Flaquer's reading of the biblical texts, that is, which passages she preferred to select, how she interpreted these, and for what purpose she did so. The same question can be asked also in regard to

---

6. On the commonalities shared by Gimeno de Flaquer's work and the so-called female writers of domesticity, or "female writers of virtue," in the Isabelline era, see Íñigo Sánchez Llama, *Galería de Escritoras Isabelinas: La Prensa Periódica entre 1833 y 1895*, Femin 61 (Madrid: Cátedra, 2000); Sánchez Llama, *Antología de la Prensa Periódica Femenina Escrita por Mujeres (1843–1894)*, TEM 2/2 (Cádiz: Universidad de Cádiz, 2001); Alda Blanco, *Escritoras Virtuosas: Narradoras de la Domesticidad en la España Isabelina*, Fem 8 (Granada: Universidad de Granada, 2001); and Rebeca Arce Pinedo, *Dios, Patria y Hogar: La Construcción Social de la Mujer Española por el Catolicismo y las Derechas en el Primer Tercio del Siglo XX* (Santander: Universidad de Cantabria, 2008), 49–50.

other components of the Catholic tradition, as well as in view of the statements of certain ecclesiastical authorities.

3. Religion and Feminism in the Work of Gimeno de Flaquer

If we expect that *Evangelios de la Mujer* is similar to Elizabeth Cady Stanton's *The Woman's Bible*, then we will be disappointed.[7] Gimeno de Flaquer does not undertake a reinterpretation of biblical texts from the feminist perspective of her time. Her book is, rather, a wide-ranging and not very systematic treatment of the themes of women and feminism. What do the gospels and, in a broader sense, the Christian religion, have to do with her essay in defense of feminism? *Evangelios de la Mujer* presents a conservative feminist program and image of women; both are indebted above all to the historical justification of the Catholic tradition and the Holy Scriptures. Gimeno de Flaquer works out for herself her own concept of the gospels in order to be able to speak about feminism, for, in her view, both concepts contain a promise of redemption that, for her, can be recognized in Scripture as well as in feminist thought. As shown in the following, this is a very concrete feminist thought that she calls conservative. In Gimeno de Flaquer's understanding, the Gospels contained a promise of redemption for humanity, and, accordingly, feminism also meant a promise of redemption for women.

This reference to Holy Scripture in the title of a text about feminism, though, also reveals how much Gimeno de Flaquer's view of women and feminism were influenced by a religious conception in the process of change. An attentive reading of the text shows clearly how her formulation of feminism was born by a certain religious view of the world. Of course, to be more precise, one must say that this was a vision of the world that underwent a redefinition through the influence of the thought of enlightened liberalism and of Krausism.[8] Gimeno de Flaquer can be placed

---

7. Elizabeth Cady Stanton, ed., *The Woman's Bible*, 2 vols. (New York: European, 1895–1898).

8. Krausism refers to the doctrinal system of the Heidelberg university lecturer Karl Christian Friedrich Krause (1781–1832) that was based on German idealism. From the middle of the nineteenth century, it won lasting influence through its bourgeois liberal reform ideas in the humanities and legal and political sciences in Spain. The Madrid professor for the history of philosophy Julián Sanz del Rio (1814–1869) contributed to the popularization of this school of thought with his translation of

within this reformulated interpretation of the world that was critical of the Catholicism understood and practiced by the majority in Spain but at the same time attempted to reconcile religion and science as well as Catholicism and liberalism.

This referral to the Christian religion as support for her feminist demands and as defense of her feminism is not found only in the *Evangelios de la Mujer* but also quite generally in her essays and also in her lectures. Gimeno de Flaquer had a quite concrete notion of Catholicism, and thereby she distanced herself to a certain extent from the Catholic orthodoxy of her time. For this reason, she preferred to speak of Christianity, for this allowed her to adopt a more comprehensive and less dogmatic understanding of faith. Thus, she insisted repeatedly that feminism and Christianity are compatible and did not represent contrary positions—certainly, in order to counter those voices that claimed just this. This compatibility made Christianity the point of reference and the model for feminism, for both philosophies had for Gimeno de Flaquer two characteristics in common.

First of all, both could be understood as doctrines of salvation. Just as Christianity was seen as a religion of the weak, the oppressed, and the unfortunate, it was also true for feminism that it possessed the aspect of protection and the raising of morality in regard to women. Thus, Gimeno de Flaquer emphasized how much feminism helped to create institutions for harboring socially rejected women and neglected children as well as to support the demand for legislation protecting working women and children. In the face of the lust for domination on the part of the powerful, the feminist way of thinking was characterized as "the apostolate of morality" and as a "mediatrix between the exploiters and the exploited."[9] It was on the basis of this moralizing character of feminism—so Gimeno de Flaquer claimed—that the clergy took a position in favor of it. In *Evangelios de la Mujer*, she cites several examples of an open-minded attitude in the Catholic hierarchy toward feminism. Thus, she reports about Herbert Cardinal Vaughn (1832–1903), the Archbishop of Westminster, and about Monsignor John Ireland (1838–1918), the bishop of Saint Paul, Minnesota, both

---

Krause's work. The term "Krausism" was used as "a collective expression for a movement that was really heterogeneous" and was coined in the second half of the nineteenth century as "a term for the enemy by the neo-Catholic press hostile to reform." Hans Ulrich Gumbrecht, "Krausismo," *HWP* 4 (1976): 1190.

9. Gimeno de Flaquer, *Evangelios*, 132.

of whom took part in the International Women's Congress in London in 1899. An American feminist is said by Gimeno de Flaquer to have spoken with Mariano Cardinal Rampolla del Tindaro (1843–1913), who, in the name of Pope Leo XIII, held out the prospect of the latter's support of the education and training of women and his mediating role regarding the social question. The Archbishop of Canterbury, finally, spoke out in favor of women's right to vote because he was of the opinion that the influence of women was useful for society and legislation.[10]

Another commonality between feminism and Christianity, in Gimeno de Flaquer's view, rested upon the fact that both thought systems started with the idea of the equality of both sexes. As she emphasizes in *Evangelios de la Mujer*, Jesus Christ was, in fact, the first advocate of feminism: "To those who cross themselves in defense against feminism, may it be said that Jesus Christ was the pioneer of feminism. The apostles of this gospel advanced the equality of man and woman, which the Crucified had proclaimed so eloquently with his teaching."[11] The accord between feminism and Christianity concerning the equality of the sexes was useful to her in defining her feminism as conservative. For, in contrast to the feminist schools of thought in socialism and anarchism, which were identified with the idea of the rivalry between the sexes, Gimeno de Flaquer did not want "to cause antagonism between women and men" but rather to break away from the submissive status of women in the relationship between the sexes and to place the woman at the man's side as his companion. In this connection, she believed that if there was a party or an ideology to which feminism could attach itself, then this was Christianity. In her essay *El Problema Feminista*, she says:

> Many people in Spain imagine that feminism is a doctrine that wants to make opponents out of men and women, a struggle not for the rights of women, but rather against their duties. Others again consider feminism to be the product of socialism or anarchism and in the process overlook the fact that it declares its solidarity with no political party, that Jesus Christ was its pioneer when he proclaimed the equality of the sexes. The sacramental marriage formula "a companion I give to you, not a maidservant" contains the feminist program.[12]

---

10. Gimeno de Flaquer, *Evangelios*, 128.
11. Gimeno de Flaquer, *Evangelios*, 108.
12. Gimeno de Flaquer, *El Problema Feminista: Conferencia en el Ateneo de Madrid* (Madrid: Asilo de Huérfanos del S. C. de Jesús, 1903), 6.

According to Gimeno de Flaquer, the equality of the sexes was codified in the Catholic marriage formula, which cited Gen 2:18 in defining the status of the wife as a companion: "A companion I give to you, not a maidservant.... This marriage formula contains the highest aspirations of feminism."[13] In contrast to the emphasis laid by other Catholic thinkers or the church hierarchy upon the subordinate position of the woman in marriage, a bourgeois notion of marriage that was advocated also by the so-called female writers of virtue, or female writers of domesticity, seems to have found expression in Gimeno de Flaquer's work. According to this notion, women were freed by the bond of marriage from their existence as slaves handed over to the concupiscence of men by becoming lifelong companions of only one man.[14] Gimeno de Flaquer's reading of Holy Scripture was determined by this notion, and so the "companion" in the wedding formula was understood by her in the sense of the enlightened bourgeois ideal of marriage, according to which "the unification of thought, the consonance of the souls" was "inevitable." "If there is no intellectual melding of the married couple, then life becomes a hell."[15] In this marital union, which was oriented toward harmony, the women were considered to be a complement to, and a support of, the men; she was to accompany him on his way to the improvement of his nature, to help him, and to understand him. This idea of Christian marriage and Christian faith received its meaning and legitimacy through the fact that it fit

---

13. Gimeno de Flaquer, *Evangelios*, 129.

14. Toward the end of the nineteenth century, the family was understood in Catholic circles as the fundamental nucleus of social organization, as the "fundamental basis of civil society," as the "indispensable organism in the middle" between the state and the individual, the principle of which was the insoluble canonical marriage. In this domestic society, as Pope Leo XIII called marriage in his encyclical *Arcanum*, the man was the superior of the family and the head of the woman, who stood in a hierarchical relationship to him that was based upon submission and obedience. The discourse about domesticity, to which Catholicism in Spain undoubtedly contributed its part, normally was supplemented by the additional idea that "the submission and obedience in no way degrade the woman in marriage," for the sacrament of marriage as well as the institution of the family contributed toward elevating the woman. See Antonio Antonio Oms, "Discurso del M. I. Sr. D. Antonio Oms, Penitenciario de la Catedral de Gerona," *Crónica del Cuarto Congreso Católico Español: Discursos Pronunciados en las Sesiones Publicas, Reseña de las Memorias y Trabajos Presentados en las Secciones y Demás Documentos Referentes a Dicha Asamblea, Celebrada en Tarragona en Octubre de 1894* (Tarragona: Establecimiento Tipográfico de F. Arís é Hijo, 1894), 369.

15. Gimeno de Flaquer, *El Problema Feminista*, 27.

seamlessly into a discourse that was widespread in conservative Catholic circles and also was soon to be present in Catholic feminism. According to this, Christianity had freed women from the slavery under which they had been subjected in the societies of antiquity.[16]

Gimeno de Flaquer looked at the past through the lens of a Christian discourse according to which women had been slaves in pagan societies based upon the strength of the man and the inferiority and submission of women. These slaves, however, were freed by Christianity, namely, by the introduction of canonical marriage as an indissoluble bond. In the pre-Christian societies of antiquity, according to Gimeno de Flaquer, women had experienced a treatment that corresponded to their position as passive and inferior creatures whose task it was to ensure the continued existence of the human race. The women themselves, according to this view, were convinced of their inferiority and had submitted to the commands of their male masters in a referential framework in which strength ruled over reason. This general notion of the inferior importance of women in pre-Christian societies served as a contrastive background for the portrayal of Christianity as that religion from which the woman received her dignity. "Notwithstanding the fact of the actual laws and customs, the mythical woman was portrayed in all her dignity in the religion and poesy of the heathen world; the real, concrete woman, though, attained all her privileges in Christianity. So it is only natural that she, with great enthusiasm, became a zealous propagator of this religion."[17] According to Gimeno de Flaquer, women had experienced the same accordance of dignity in the period of the Crusades:

> The period of the Crusades, which assume such a significant position in the annals of religion, was also a great period in women's history.... The period of the Crusades was very favorable for women: Religion always had given our sex protection, elevated it, and given it dignity. With the rise of Christianity, it was saved; it was freed from its degradation; and, since that time, it stands under the protection of the church.[18]

---

16. Inmaculada Blasco Herranz, *Paradojas de la Ortodoxia: Politica de Masas y Militancia Católica Femenina en España*, Sag 3 (Zaragoza: Prensas Universitarias de Zaragoza, 2003).

17. Gimeno de Flaquer, *Evangelios*, 17–18.

18. Gimeno de Flaquer, *Evangelios*, 23–24.

The basic idea upon which Gimeno de Flaquer's concept of marriage was based was a conception of the woman as a partner to the man who was equal to him in her intellectual abilities; the relationship between husband and wife rested upon their equality with each other. In the context of the intransigent Catholicism prevailing in Spain, Gimeno de Flaquer advocated a concept of equality that originated in enlightened liberal thought and, against the misogynist Catholic tradition of female inferiority, referred to the existence of two genders which by nature were equal to each other. Women and men, so it said, were different and complemented each other but yet were equal to each other in regard to their intellect and ability to think in a rational way. The woman "is endowed with natural abilities; she stands neither below nor over him; she is different than he, but it is a difference in which equality is found."[19]

On the basis of this equality in regard to intellectual abilities, and on the basis of the necessity of attaining balance and harmony in marriage and in domestic life, Gimeno de Flaquer arrived at her demand for the education of the female sex:

> If the man continues to develop and woman remains the way she is, how, do you think, should there be any peace in the house? You make two adversaries out of two creatures who should harmonize with each other.... The woman must be joined together with her life companion by as many bonds as possible, and the understanding is not the weakest of these bonds. She must share the plans and aspirations of her husband in order to create an activity for herself that connects with his and thus fulfills her own life.[20]

Gimeno de Flaquer appears here to follow an enlightened course within the Catholic tradition, in which she, with her defense of the intellectual equality of women and with her demand for education, took up a line of argument that was established by the learned Benedictine monk and pioneer of the Enlightenment in Spain Benito Feijoo (1676–1764).[21] Such an understanding of the Enlightenment within the Catholic tradition is shown clearly in Gimeno de Flaquer's reference to ecclesiastical authorities

---

19. Gimeno de Flaquer, *Evangelios*, 17.
20. Gimeno de Flaquer, *Evangelios*, 37–38.
21. Benito Feijoo, *Defensa de la Mujer: Discurso XVI del Teatro Crítico* (Barcelona: Icaria, 1997). The first volume of his *Teatro Crítico Universal* was published the first time in 1726.

who can be seen to be less orthodox, whether because of their relationship to the Enlightenment and to liberalism, or because they advocated open and modern standpoints in regard to the social value of women and their education and training. In this sense, Gimeno de Flaquer, in regard to individual aspects but also in a constant way, ascribed great authority to certain Catholic voices that were subjects of controversial discussion: Bishop Félix Dupanloup (1802–1878) of Orleans, Pope Benedict XIV, Archbishop François Fénelon (1651–1715) of Cambrai, as well as Fray Martín Sarmiento (1695–1772) and Archbishop Louis-François Sueur (1841–1914) of Avignon, for example.[22] Dupanloup attempted to prevent Pope Pius IX from condemning the errors current in the nineteenth century, and he pleaded for a more generous interpretation of the encyclical *Quanta Cura* and of the *Syllabus*. He also showed himself to be critical of the definition of papal infallibility. In addition, he furthered the discussion about the question of women and about feminism within French Catholicism. Gimeno de Flaquer opened the first part of the *Evangelios*, under the title "Igualdad Moral e Intellectual de los Dos Sexos," with a quotation from Dupanloup, in which she found her argument that women and men are intellectually equal confirmed, since the woman as well as the man was created in the image of God and was furnished with the same rational abilities: "God does not give useless gifts; there is a purpose to all of his works. If the man's companion is a rational creature; if she, like the man, was created in God's image and, like him, has been given understanding by the Creator, then for the purpose of using it."[23] Gimeno de Flaquer's dependence upon Dupanloup becomes apparent when, at another place in the *Evangelios*, she paraphrases him as follows: "Before God, both sexes are equal, for he has provided both with understanding. For this reason, both assume the same responsibility before God; but, for this purpose, both must receive the same education."[24] She makes reference once again to Dupanloup in denouncing the social pressure that was applied to those women who showed academic inclinations. In order to defend her standpoint that intellectual activity on the part of women not only was legitimate but also necessary, she writes: "Much has been said about the shallowness

---

22. Gimeno de Flaquer, *Evangelios*, 132. Fénelon came into conflict with the Holy See at the end of the seventeenth century. Sarmiento was a friend and collaborator of Feijoo, whose enlightened way of thinking he shared.
23. Gimeno de Flaquer, *Evangelios*, 9.
24. Gimeno de Flaquer, *Evangelios*, 113.

of women. But, if they have academic inclinations, are they not then forced to apologize for them, or to hide them as though they were a sin?"[25]

As far as Benedict XIV (1740–1758) was concerned, he was known for his enlightened and open-minded spirit; he also maintained contacts with Voltaire. Gimeno de Flaquer emphasized those gestures of the Pope which she interpreted as support for the intellectual activity of women, such as his support for the work of the mathematician Maria Gaetana Agnesi (1718–1799) from Milan, for example. She cited the following quotation by Benedict: "Women have as much intellectual worth as men when they devote themselves with diligence to their studies."[26]

But, authorities within the church who were more orthodox or who could be classed as hostile to women also have their say in Gimeno de Flaquer's work, but only when their sentiments prove to be useful in the defense of women. Thus, she opened the second part of the *Evangelios*, under the title "El Feminismo y sus Conquistas," with the citation of the Pauline verse (Gal 3:28) about the equality of all human beings in Christianity: "In Christ, there is no difference, neither in nationality nor in social standing nor among the sexes."[27]

Along with the reference to churchmen who inclined openly to the idea of the intellectual equality of women and men, Gimeno de Flaquer worked out her own quite personal interpretation of the Catholic tradition as a defense of her standpoint that both sexes were of equal value and worthy of the same treatment by society. She declared this tradition to be a collection of generally accepted opinions and of narratives which corroborated and reproduced the attitudes in society that were hostile to women. Gimeno de Flaquer explained the fact that Spanish women lacked the initiative to emancipate themselves by pointing out that they "have submitted themselves to the notion of their insignificant worth, a notion forced upon them by men and which was accepted devotedly by the women."[28] This devoted acceptance was nurtured especially, according to Gimeno de Flaquer, by one of those stories handed down by the religious tradition and applied to all women: the narrative about Eve's inclination to sin. Gimeno de Flaquer rejected this view as untenable: "The feminine sex is still burdened with the vulgar tradition of Eve's

---

25. Gimeno de Flaquer, *Evangelios*, 132.
26. Gimeno de Flaquer, *Evangelios*, 132.
27. Gimeno de Flaquer, *Evangelios*, 105.
28. Gimeno de Flaquer, *El Problema Feminista*, 10.

guilt, and in our country more than is the case elsewhere. Insofar as this tradition might withstand analysis, or might be worth a refutation, we could say: If the children inherit the sins of the parents, then it cannot be the case that only one sex can be tarnished and the other remains unsullied."[29]

Gimeno de Flaquer's interpretation of the figure of Mary Magdalene also defied conventional exegesis for several reasons: first, because she was characterized in this portrayal more by her penitence than by her sinful life; but then also because her repentance was presented as a result of her gift of imagination, that is, a quality in women that was socially less appropriate, indeed even dangerous. Finally, Gimeno de Flaquer emphasized how Mary Magdalene became the herald and apostle of Jesus's teaching among the prostitutes:

> The sinner from Magdala is an interesting figure: She was a great beauty, gifted with an ebullient fantasy and had a fiery temperament. She was notorious for her life of dissipation, but the notoriety of her repentance eclipsed the notoriety of her sins. After she had heard about Jesus, about his virtues and his extraordinary perfection, she wanted to get to know him, for what was extraordinary gave wings to her fantasy. When she heard the sublime morality of his teaching, she felt within herself the desire for the renewal of her life, the desire to follow the Blameless One. But, Mary Magdalene did more than to free herself from her sins: She moved innumerable women who, like herself, had led a life of dissipation, to repentance. She filled them with enthusiasm for her faith, and with them she followed Jesus on the path from Gethsemane to Golgatha.[30]

To prove that her defense of the intellectual and creative abilities of women of her time was justified, Gimeno de Flaquer put together an extensive historical catalogue of famous women who were academically or artistically active. This list of historical feminine figures represents one of the outstanding and typical characteristic features of her work. Gimeno de Flaquer thus stands in a tradition that dedicated itself to the reinstatement of women in their rightful position in history—a tradition, thus, which

---

29. Gimeno de Flaquer, *El Problema Feminista*, 10.
30. Gimeno de Flaquer, "Jesucristo y las Mujeres," *AIA* 18 (1900): 146–48. The same text is found already in Gimeno de Flaquer, "Fidelidad de las Mujeres a Jesús," *AIA* 9 (1891): 122–23.

put in its place the androcentric design of history that prevailed in religious as well as in secular historiography.

It should also be mentioned that Gimeno de Flaquer also included secular historical narratives in her work. This shows that she held an open mind in regard to other traditions, while conventional authors of both sexes not only disregarded these traditions but also rejected them. At the same time, the fact that she repeatedly made reference to biblical narratives and the Christian tradition makes clear what significance this tradition had in her understanding of the world and, consequently, in the formulation of her concept of feminism.

Gimeno de Flaquer presented a list of feminine saints and nuns who had been active intellectually or artistically. This was neither chronologically nor thematically arranged but had rather a demonstrative purpose: if all these women—the number of which makes clear that they could not be merely individual exceptions—could boast of such great intellectual gifts and had contributed to knowledge and understanding, then how could someone still make the argument that women had no aptitude for study and for intellectual activity in all its facets?

> Saint Jerome contributed to the transformation of the Roman woman. Fifty of his hundred theological letters were addressed to women. His students, St. Paula and St. Marcella, exercised influence upon the renewal of Roman society. St. Theresa was a learned theologian. St. Catherine of Alexandria excelled in philosophy and rhetoric; St. Hildegard did so in the natural sciences, and St. Thecla again in philosophy. The saints Catherine of Siena, Valeria, Perpetua, Gertrude, and Elizabeth of Hungary were versed in various sciences. His Holiness Benedict XIV congratulated the Milanese scholar Maria Agnesi for her mathematical works and presented her with a wreath of gemstones as a gift. Madeleine-Gabrielle de Rochechouart-Mortemart, abbess and general director of the religious order of Fontevrault, was a brilliant Hellenist, Latinist, and philosopher. Ménage mentions her in his work *Historia mulierum philosopharum*. Mother Stervart founded the Christian temperance society. The Florentine nun Sor Dea de Bardi cultivated the sciences in the convent. Sor Juana Inés de la Cruz wrote her best poems in the convent. The Portugeuese Franciscan Sor Magdalena Eufemia Gloria and the Seville nun Sor Francisca Gregoria de Santa Teresa were inspired poets, just as Sor Elena de Silveira, who predicted the day of misfortune in San Sebastián. The abbess of the convent Nossa Senhora da Esperança in Lisbon, Sor Maria de Ceu, wrote dramatic poetry under a pseudonym. Herrad of Landsberg, abbess of the convent Hohenburg on the Odilienberg in

Alsace, was a learned scholar as well as an artist. In the library in Strassburg, there is a manuscript written by her and, in explanation of the text, decorated with precious miniatures from her own hand.[31]

Along with women's intellectual and artistic abilities, Gimeno de Flaquer also emphasized their significant contribution to the triumph and consolidation of Christianity. Here, it was important to her not only to show the leading role assumed by women but, more than this, to provide evidence that "there was no traitor Judas among those of the female sex, no Peter who denied Jesus, and no Pilate who spoke judgment upon him. While all of his male disciples, except for John, left him, the women followed him everywhere and accepted his teaching; they are to be found at the foot of the Cross and afterwards at the grave."[32]

In this sense, Gimeno de Flaquer picked out not only biblical episodes in which women succored Jesus on his path to the cross but precisely those passages in which "it must make the woman proud to have been distinguished by the savior":

> The Samaritan woman quenched his thirst, Veronica wiped the sweat from his brow, Mary Magdalene anointed his feet with sweet-smelling oil.... For the pious Veronica, he left behind the imprint of his face upon the towel; for Martha, he woke her brother Lazarus from the dead. He healed the daughter of the Canaanite woman, he forgave the woman caught in adultery, and he gave Mary Magdalene her dignity back after the people mocked her. Mary Magdalene is to be seen at the foot of the Cross, crying bitter tears, and at the holy sepulcher, turning herself toward hope.[33]

In her further comments, Gimeno de Flaquer points out how women, in their capacity as mothers and wives, had helped to achieve the final triumph of Christianity: the "God-fearing Helena" and the mother of the Emperor Constantine, for example, or Flacilla, who "sowed the seed of faith in the heart of her husband, the great Theodosius." Saint Basil was "converted by his mother, Saint John Chrysostom by his mother, and the same was true of the sainted Augustine."[34]

---

31. Gimeno de Flaquer, *Evangelios*, 129–31.
32. Gimeno de Flaquer, *Evangelios*, 18.
33. Gimeno de Flaquer, *Evangelios*, 18.
34. Gimeno de Flaquer, *Evangelios*, 20.

In Gimeno de Flaquer's interpretation of the beginnings of church history, neither the disciples, nor the apostles, nor the first church fathers made an appearance, but rather simple women who "endowed ... with a finer sensibility than the men, were the first who accepted that religion that places the beggars on an equal plane with the princes, comforts the sad, stands by the old, watches over the defenseless, defends the weak, and pours the balm of charity and love into human hearts."[35] But, Gimeno de Flaquer also emphasizes that these women exercised special functions in early Christianity that later were assigned to men:

> Mary, the Elect of the Lord, liberated her humiliated sex from slavery, and the other Mary, from Judea, can be numbered among the prophets. The women prophesied and baptized, took part in the assemblies and in the instruction about the sacrifice, and belonged to the clergy. There were women priests in Christianity who were ordained in a way similar to that of the deacons, since the days of the early church. The apostles were accompanied by a group of deaconesses; they are mentioned in Paul's letter to the Romans [cf. Rom 16:1]. The deaconesses were called widows, a designation that derived from their status as widows. The widows were the ones, namely, who carried out the bishop's instructions in everything having to do with women. They decorated the church, comforted the female prisoners, took care of the sick women, and since they, as former mothers with a family, possessed life experience, their counsel was seen as reasonable and wise. The deaconesses had the same significance that the father confessor later was to achieve.[36]

4. Summary

This essay presented an interpretation of the work of Gimeno de Flaquer in which the analysis of the religious elements in the development of her feminist thought and, more concretely, in support of her demand for the recognition of the equality of women and men stands in the foreground. In doing this, her *Evangelios de la Mujer* especially, but also her essays *La Mujer Española* and *El Problema Feminista* were cited. A Catholic disposition can be recognized clearly in Gimeno de Flaquer's work, but it would be wrong to conclude from this that she was a reactionary writer or that her Catholicism put limits on her feminist thought. But, it would be just

---

35. Gimeno de Flaquer, "Jesuchristo y las Mujeres," 148.
36. Gimeno de Flaquer, "Jesuchristo y las Mujeres," 147.

as false to assume that her enlightened liberal approach had detached her concept of feminism from a religious foundation.

It was shown that Gimeno de Flaquer's Catholicism followed an enlightened liberal line that, in the Spain of her time, set itself apart from the Catholic orthodoxy that was dominated by traditionalism and clericalism. Gimeno de Flaquer considered Catholicism to be egalitarian and a form of Christianity compatible with feminism. In order to legitimate her demand for the recognition of the value of women and for their intellectual and moral equation with men, she referred to ecclesiastical authorities who were open-minded in regard to the new ideas of the time related to the theme of gender relationships. She applied an interpretation of biblical texts and church history that not only departed from the dominant androcentric hermeneutic but also took a critical view of its most widespread assumptions, such as the myth of Eve as the epitome of the sinner. What stands out in this interpretation is, above all, Gimeno de Flaquer's tenacity with which she made visible the leading role which a large number of women played in history and the abilities which these women displayed in various political, social, and especially intellectual activities. In the concrete case of the history of Christianity, Gimeno de Flaquer's approach led to a new view of church history brought about by the appearance of new historical figures, namely women. Their presence had been reduced in the traditional transmission of history to the status of an exception—and often not even that.

Bibliography

Arce Pinedo, Rebeca. *Dios, Patria y Hogar: La Construcción Social de la Mujer Española por el Catolicismo y las Derechas en el Primer Tercio del Siglo XX*. Santander: Universidad de Cantabria, 2008.

Ayala Aracil, María de los Ángeles. "La mujer Española de Concepción Gimeno de Flaquer." Biblioteca Virtual Miguel de Cervantes. https://tinyurl.com/SBL6007b.

Bieder, Maryellen. "Feminine Discourse/Feminist Discourse: Concepción Gimeno de Flaquer." *RQ* 37 (1990): 459–77.

Blanco, Alda. *Escritoras Virtuosas: Narradoras de la Domesticidad en la España Isabelina*. Fem 8. Granada: Universidad de Granada, 2001.

Blasco Herranz, Inmaculada. *Paradojas de la Ortodoxia: Politica de Masas y Militancia Católica Femenina en España*. Sag 3. Zaragoza: Prensas Universitarias de Zaragoza, 2003.

Campos, Lola. "Concepción Gimeno Gil." *Heraldo de Aragón*, May 3, 1998.
Chozas, Diego. "La mujer según el *Álbum Ibero-Americano* (1890–1891) de Concepción Gimeno de Flaquer." *Espéculo: Revista de Estudios Literarios*. https://tinyurl.com/SBL6007d.
Feijoo, Benito. *Defensa de la Mujer: Discurso XVI del Teatro Crítico*. Barcelona: Icaria, 1997.
Gimeno de Flaquer, María de la Concepción. *El Problema Feminista: Conferencia en el Ateneo de Madrid*. Madrid: Asilo de Huérfanos del S. C. de Jesús, 1903.
———. *Evangelios de la Mujer*. Madrid: Librería de Fernando Fé, 1900.
———. "Fidelidad de las Mujeres a Jesús." *AIA* 9 (1891): 122–23.
———. "Jesucristo y las Mujeres." *AIA* 18 (1900): 146–48.
Gumbrecht, Hans Ulrich. "Krausismo." *HWP* 4 (1976): 1190–93.
Hibbs-Lissorgues, Solange. "Tous les chemins mènent à Dieu: l'Église et les femmes dans la deuxième moitié du XIX siècle." Pages 43–59 in *Femmes et démocratie: Les Espagnoles dans l'espace public (1868–1978)*. Edited by Marie-Aline Barrachina et al. Nantes: Temps, 2007.
Lacalzada Mateo, Maria José. "Las mujeres en la 'cuestión social' de la Restauración: Liberales y católicas (1875–1921)." *HC* 29 (2004): 691–717.
"María de la Concepción Jimeno de Flaquer." Escritoras.com. April 6, 2003. https://tinyurl.com/SBL6007c.
Oms, Antonio. "Discurso del M. I. Sr. D. Antonio Oms, Penitenciario de la Catedral de Gerona." Pages 365–75 in *Crónica del Cuarto Congreso Católico Español: Discursos Pronunciados en las Sesiones Publicas, Reseña de las Memorias y Trabajos Presentados en las Secciones y Demás Documentos Referentes a Dicha Asamblea, Celebrada en Tarragona en Octubre de 1894*. Tarragona: Establecimiento Tipográfico de F. Arís é Hijo, 1894.
Sánchez Llama, Íñigo. *Antología de la Prensa Periódica Femenina Escrita por Mujeres (1843–1894)*. TEM 2/2. Cádiz: Universidad de Cádiz, 2001.
———. *Galería de Escritoras Isabelinas: La Prensa Periódica entre 1833 y 1895*. Femin 61. Madrid: Cátedra, 2000.
Simón Palmer, María del Carmen. *Escritoras españolas del siglo XIX: Manual bio-bibliográfico*. NBEC 3. Madrid: Castalia, 1991.
Stanton, Elizabeth Cady, ed. *The Woman's Bible*. 2 vols. New York: European, 1895–1898.

Orthodox Women and the Bible in Nineteenth-Century Russia

Alexej Klutschewsky and Eva Maria Synek

Preliminary Remarks

This essay will focus in section 1 on women's access to the Bible and in section 2 on the significance of Holy Scriptures for the spirituality of religious women. Then in the final section (3) we will consider examples of contemporary women's contributions to exegesis.[1]

1. Women's Access to the Bible

Although female participation in religious activities cannot be limited to one or another class, the question of social background cannot be left aside when discussing women's direct access to the Bible. According to the census of 1897, no more than 21 percent of the population of the Russian Empire was literate.[2] Female literacy among the rural population should be estimated even lower than the average despite considerable efforts to improve the situation by the establishment of communal and monastic schools for girls in the preceding years. By contrast, monastic records show a rather different situation. For example, according to the archives of Tvorožkovo monastery, 89 percent of women of peasant origin were able

---

1. An expanded version of this paper with more exentisve bibliography will appear in the Romanian journal *inter*. Russian names have been transliterated according to the scientific transliteration (ISO 9 transliteration standard) except in quotations, in references, and for commonly accepted notations.

2. For more detailed information, see Jeffrey Brooks, *When Russia Learned to Read: Literacy and Popular Literetature, 1861–1917* (Princeton: Princeton University Press, 1988).

to read, and at least 35 percent could also write.[3] Likewise Old Ritualists/ Old Believers, who preserved traditions of the old Muscovite Pre-Nikonian and Pre-Petrian literacy, achieved an above average rate of literacy. Their subcultural tradition contained, among other things, the idea of labor agreeable to God, the veneration of old (pre-Nikonian) books, and an esteem of ecclesiastical literacy. It was founded on the reading of pre-Nikonian Church Slavonic books and included Half-Ustav (Poluustav) Cyrillic book handwriting.[4]

This seems to indicate that, although in principle upper- and middle-class women were much more likely to have direct access to the Bible, women from the lower classes were not per se excluded.[5] Villagers organized their own readers services when they were unable to join regular liturgy in the parish church, which often was far away and difficult to reach, in particular for the old and the sick but also for younger women who were expected to cook and to manage the household.[6] Devoted upper-class women such as the founder of the Borodino-community Margarita Mihailovna Tučkova (Mother Marija after tonsuring, 1781–1851) read from Holy Scripture and patristic texts to the women gathered around her.[7] But also so-called *obetnye devy*, *černicki*, *keleinicy*, or *spasennicy*—unmarried peasant women who lived a religious life without entering a

---

3. See Brenda Meehan, "To Save Oneself: Russian Peasant Women and the Development of Women's Religious Communities in Pre-revolutionary Russia," in *Russian Peasant Women*, ed. Beatrice Farnsworth and Viola Lynne (New York: Oxford University Press, 1992), 128–29.

4. See Валерий В. Тимофеев [Valerij V. Timofeev], "Старообрядческое просветительство: Взаимовлияние предпринимательства и образования" [Old Ritualists enlightenment: reciprocal influences of entrepreneurship and education], Вестник ЧГПУ им. И. Я. Яковлева [*Vestnik ČGPU im. I. Ja. Jakovleva*] 23.4 (2001): 105–13.

5. On women's education and access to books in general, see, e.g., Natal'ia L. Pushkareva, "Russian Noblewomen's Education in the Home as Revealed in Late 18th- and Early 19th-Century Memoirs," in *Women and Gender in Eighteenth-Century Russia*, ed. Wendy Rosslyn (Aldershot: Ashgate, 2003), 111–28; Olga E. Glagoleva, "Imaginary World: Reading in the Lives of Russian Provincial Noblewomen (1750-1825)," in Rosslyn, *Women and Gender*, 129–46.

6. See Vera Shevzov, "Chapels and the Ecclesiastical World of Prerevolutionary Russian Peasants," *Slavic Review* 55 (1996): 585–613.

7. See Brenda Meehan, *Holy Women of Russia: The Lives of Five Orthodox Women Offer Spiritual Guidance for Today* (San Francisco: Harper, 1993), 17–40.

monastery[8]—were expected to take over the teaching of girls and the reading of the Psalter. It seems that they were in general literate. Anastasiia Logačeva (1809–1875),[9] for example, who lived a devoted life in the village before becoming a famous hermit and ending up as the abbess, is said to have learned to read on a pilgrimage.

When there was a school in a village or a nearby monastery, it was likely that peasant girls were taught the Bible together with reading and writing skills. One can easily imagine that it was not literacy as such but rather this biblical-linked literacy that inspired young women to aspire to a devoted life that would transgress the regular pattern for women: getting married, having children, caring for the well-being of one's own family, and so on. There is some evidence that parents sometimes refused to send their girls to school not only because they were unable or unwilling to do without their labor for the moment but because they were afraid of losing their daughter to a religious life in the future. However, just as literacy certainly did not necessarily inspire an ascetic lifestyle, being illiterate did not prevent women from realizing their desired vocation. Many devoted women of low origin learned to read only in an advanced age in order to be able to read the Psalter and/or to participate in a monastic choir, and some had to rely on their fellow sisters' reading skills until the end of their lives.

Literacy, however, was only part of the problem. With respect to the possibility of having direct access to Holy Scripture, the gap between the language of the Bible (Church Slavonic) and the regularly spoken language in the context of the loss of competence in Church Slavonic and the cultural changes after the Petrinian reforms must be taken in account as well. The modern Russian variant of Church Slavonic emerged in the second half of the seventeenth century after the Reform (*knižnaja sprava*) of Patriarch Nikon, when in the Moscow state (Russian Czardom) Holy Scriptures and liturgical books were revised on the basis of contemporary Greek and South West Russian (Kievan) Church Slavonic texts.[10] Until the

---

8. Many of them belonged to Old Ritualist/Old Believer communities.

9. See Alexandr Priklonskii, *Blessed Athanasia and the Desert Ideal*, Modern Matericon 1 (Platina, CA: St. Herman of Alaska Brotherhood, 1990); and Meehan, *Holy Women of Russia*, 41–60.

10. See Борис А. Успенский [Boris A. Uspenskij], *История русского литературного языка (XI–XVIIвв)* [The history of the Russian literary language (eleventh–seventeenth centuries)] (Moscow: Аспект, 2002).

seventeenth–eighteenth centuries Church Slavonic had been used in Muscovite Russia as a literary language in several domains of communication alongside the language of the state chancelleries, based on spoken dialects, but it was not regularly spoken. The Church Slavonic language and the new Russian literary language together formed the written literary part of nineteenth-century Russian culture. For educated pious persons, Church Slavonic remained the language of Holy Scripture and church literature. But with increasing Westernization and secularization, competence and common interest in Church Slavonic declined. For members of the uneducated social strata and for those with a more Western education, Church Slavonic texts became less comprehensible even before Soviet policy caused the ultimate end of a widespread literacy in Church Slavonic.

Beginning in 1816 the Russian Bible Society supported the preparation of a complete Russian translation of Holy Scripture and translations into other languages of the Russian Empire.[11] Already in 1815 Czar Alexander I, who himself used a French Bible, ordered the Chief Procurator of the Most Holy Governing Synod "to propound the M. H. Synod the sincere and exact wish of His Majesty to deliver the Russians with a means to read God's Word in their natural Russian language [because it would be] more understandable for them than the Slavonic dialect in which the books of Holy Scripture are published in our [country]."[12] However, in 1826 the Bible Society was dissolved and the publication of the portions of Scripture that had already been translated was canceled due to fears that a Russian Bible might undermine Orthodoxy[13] and encourage the spread of Protestantism in Russia.[14] Only after the death of Czar Nicolas I could the project be taken up again. The complete translation of Holy Scripture under the auspices of the Most Holy Governing Synod (the so-called Synodal Translation) was not finished until 1876.

---

11. See Boris A. Tichomirov, "Geschichte der russischen Bibelübersetzung," *Stimme der Orthodoxie* 2004.1 (2004): 37–44; 2004.2 (2004): 18–27.

12. Trans. Alexej Klutschewsky. See Значение переводов РБО в создании Синодального перевода [The importance of the translations of the Russian Bible Society for the formation of the synodal translation]. http://www.sbible.ru/qb012.htm.

13. One problem, among others, was the discrepancy between the LXX-based wording of the Slavonic versions of the Old Testament and new scholarly translations from Hebrew, which seemed to alter the meaning of the text.

14. Obviously, the Pietist movement of the eighteenth and nineteenth centuries and the British Bible Society, among others, encouraged interest in the Bible in the Russian Empire and made considerable efforts in promoting Scripture reading.

2. The Significance of Holy Scriptures for the Spirituality of Religious Women

The autobiography of Marija Solopova (Arkadija and later on Taisija by monastic name) (1840–1915) can serve as an example of the impact of the (Slavonic) Bible on a (literate) woman's monastic aspirations, although her narrative in many other points seems to witness quite personal religious experiences that certainly cannot be generalized.[15] Marija/Taisija, a great-grandniece of Alexander Puškin, received her first biblical lessons from her mother. In her fifties, then serving as an abbess to the women's community of Leušino, which, under her leadership had become a flourishing new convent, establishing the pattern for female monasticism in the North of Russia,[16] she remembered: "At the age of four I could already read without having to spell the words out, although not quickly, and I knew all the events in Sacred History which concerned the earthly life of our Saviour (except His teachings and parables). Having a good memory, which has remained with me even until today, I remembered everything that was told to me."[17]

In her teens the gifted child was admitted to the Pavlovsk Institute in Petrograd, one of the rare contemporary institutions offering higher education for girls. Particularly intelligent but also rather sensitive, she was much more interested in religious life than her classmates. On her own initiative she learned the gospel "by heart, word for word, the Slavonic text of all the Gospel events and teachings by those evangelists who gave a

---

15. English quotations here and in the following are taken from Abbess Thaisia [Taisija], *An Autobiography*, Modern Matericon 3 (Platina, CA: St. Herman of Alaska Brotherhood, 1989). The writing was encouraged by Taisijas's spiritual fathers; Taisija finished the text in the 1890s, and it was first printed 1916 in Petrograd. See this work for details about her life, among those an obituary and funeral orations. A recent summary is provided by Meehan, *Holy Women of Russia*, 95–141.

16. Although it was unavailable to us when preparing this paper, see now Scott M. Kenworthy, "Abbess Taisiia of Leushino and the Reform of Women's Monasticism in Early Twentieth Century Russia," in *Culture and Identity in Eastern Christian History: Papers from the First Biennial Conference of the Association for the Study of Eastern Christian History and Culture*, ed. Russell E. Martin and Jennifer B. Spock, Ohio Slavic Papers 9 (Columbus: Ohio State University, Department of Slavic and East European Languages and Literatures, 2009), 83–102.

17. Thaisia, *Autobiography*, 33.

more detailed version of them."[18] When for the final exams the Rector of the Theological Academy turned up at the institute,[19] Marija was brought forward by the headmistress. In her autobiography she relates how she was first asked to recite from Jesus's parting words according to the Gospel of John by the bishop and then, being interrupted in order to explain why she had learned the gospel by heart, answered him: "Every word of the Gospel is so sweet and comforting to the soul that I want to have them always with me, but it is not convenient to have always a book in one's hand. Therefore I resolved to learn it all by heart, so that it could always be present in my mind."[20]

The text proceeds with an account of the further examination: Marija/Taisija was asked about the "young man seeking eternal life." When the bishop interrupted her recitation of Math 19:16–27 with a provocative question, she gave the common explanation of the text: "I explained as well as I could that this commandment [go and sell what thou hast and give to the poor…] is not compulsory for everyone, but only for those who resolve to lead a more perfect way of life, different from the usual way of life in the world—poverty for the sake of Christ, etc."[21]

As distinct from Anastasija Logačeva (Mother Afanasija after tonsuring) and many others who also felt a calling at an early age but were prevented from following it due to family commitments, the well-educated Marija/Taisija succeeded in entering monastic life soon after leaving school. Already at her first monastery she was soon entrusted with the teaching of girls. After being appointed head of the Leušino community for women, she made this a famous center of learning, providing classes for girls as well as a teachers seminary.

It seems significant that Marija/Taisija and her fellow nuns encountered the Word of God not only within the liturgical services, nor was further reading left solely to private initiative. As Marija/Taisija makes clear in her memories of conversations with Ioann Sergiev, better known as Father John of Kronstadt,[22] the nuns enjoyed biblical readings together

---

18. Thaisia, *Autobiography*, 49.
19. At that time Ioannikij (Rudnev), the future Metropolitan of Moscow and Kiev.
20. Thaisia, *Autobiography*, 50.
21. Thaisia, *Autobiography*, 51.
22. According to her own words, Marija/Taisija, beginning in 1891, wrote down these conversations immediately after they took place in the evenings but gave her notes to Father John during his last year of life. "He found them accurate, made several

with readings from devotional literature and some catechesis also in more organized forms.[23]

However, it must be stressed that such Scripture-oriented piety, which recalls contemporaneous Pietist forms of Bible reading, usually remained strongly embedded in the living tradition of the Church: the representation of biblical figures and narratives in contemporary iconography, the liturgical use of Holy Scripture, including the exegesis provided by liturgical chants, the traditional monastic reception of the gospel teaching by ascetic role models, represented by contemporary elders, venerated saints, and/or devotional literature: Thus Marija/Taisija confesses to Father John (and readers of their conversations): "I find my main support in frequent Communion, and in reading the Gospel, which at times really answers my thoughts and gives me enlightenment. I also refer frequently to your 'Diary'. What holy, wonderful thoughts are there!"[24]

Firsthand knowledge of Scripture might have played a more important role in the spirituality of women such as Marija/Taisija or the above-mentioned founder and first abbess of Borodino monastery, Margarita/Marija Tučkova, than in that of less-educated women. However, there is strong evidence that, in spite of the emerging language barrier discussed above, even "barely literate women in particular show an astonishing familiarity with" the Bible.[25] Letters "freely cite phrases from the Psalms, the Gospels,

---

corrections, where with his own hands he inserted additions" (Thaisia, *Autobiography*, 247). The text was published for the first time only after John of Kronstadt's death. For Marija/Taisija's relationship with the reputed priest see also their epistolary dialogue, which, just as the conversations and Marija/Taisija's autobiography, was obviously meant for wider distribution. See Nadieszda Kizenko, *A Prodigal Saint: Father John of Kronstadt and the Russian People* (University Park: Pennsylvania State University Press, 2000), 134.

23. Similar practices are testified for other religious communities as well, e.g., Spaso-Borodino Community.

24. Thaisia, *Autobiography*, 264. In her "Letters to a Beginner" (first published 1900) she bases her own instruction "on the Holy Scripture and the instruction of the Holy Fathers, and on examples from those who have toiled in this work and have pleased God" (quotation from the English translation of letter 7: *Letters to a Beginner: On Giving One's Life to God*, Modern Matericon 4 [Wildwood, CA: St. Xenia Skete, 1993], 57).

25. Nadieszda Kizenko, "Written Confessions and the Construction of Sacred Narrative," in *Sacred Stories: Religion and Spirituality in Modern Russia*, ed. Mark D. Steinberg and Heather J. Coleman (Bloomington: Indiana University Press, 2007), 107.

the lives of saints, and the rituals of the Orthodox Church."²⁶ Anastasija/ Afanasija Logačeva, who enjoyed no formal schooling at all, is reported to have spent whole nights "in prayer or in the reading of the Gospels. Like her model, Saint Serafim of Sarov, she reads one gospel in its entirety every day, repeating the sequence over and over again" during the eremitic period of her life.²⁷ As for Marija/Taisija, this points to a deep scriptural rooting of her spirituality.

The practice of regular Bible reading is in line with early Russian monasticism as well as with contemporary trends in Western Christianity.²⁸ But in contrast to the Pietistic approach to the Bible, there is no idea of any sort of *sola scriptura* principle for Anastasija/Afanasija, Marija/Taisija, or the other pious Russian Orthodox women whose lives were recently investigated by Brenda Meehan.²⁹ As far as we can see, these women all considered Holy Scripture a particularly important part of Christian tradition with which they were more or less directly acquainted. Although the Psalter and the Gospels were more widely known than some other parts of the Bible and the Gospels enjoyed particularly high veneration, this does not suggest that other parts were not read or received. The fact that Marija/Taisija was familiar with the whole Bible can be seen easily by the abundant quotations and references in her own writings. Likewise, Margarita/Marija Tučkova is reported to have uttered a verse from Isaiah (8:18) at her son's burial.³⁰ Later in her life, when living in community with other women in Borodino where her husband had died, she had her favorite lines from the New Testament epistles inscribed over the door of the dining hall (1 Cor 13:3; 1 Pet 1:22).³¹ But there was no tendency to single out the Bible as having any sense of precedence over tradition. Thus intensive gospel reading and recitation of the Psalter is only part of the religious practices

---

26. Kizenko, "Confessions," 107,
27. See Meehan, *Holy Women of Russia*, 47.
28. For genuine Russian roots of a biblical-oriented spirituality, see Robert A. Klostermann, *Probleme der Ostkirche: Untersuchungen zum Wesen und zur Geschichte der griechisch-orthodoxen Kirche* (Göteborg: Elanders Boktryckeri Aktiebolag, 1955), 361– 416.
29. See Martin Brecht, "Die Bedeutung der Bibel im deutschen Pietismus," in *Glaubenswelt und Lebenswelten*, ed. Hartmut Lehmann, Geschichte des Pietismus 4 (Göttingen: Vandenhoeck & Ruprecht, 2004), 102–20; Kurt Aland, *Pietismus und Bibel*, Arbeiten zur Geschichte des Pietismus 9 (Witten: Luther Verlag, 1970), 89–147.
30. Cf. Meehan, *Holy Women of Russia*, 23.
31. Cf. Meehan, *Holy Women of Russia*, 37s.

testified for Anastasija/Afanasija's time as a hermit. She remained linked to liturgical tradition by saying parts of the Divine Office while living in solitude. She is also ascribed the reading of akafisty,[32] the constant repetition of the Jesus prayer and, following the advice of Seraphim of Sarov,[33] the wearing of chains (as did already some of the early ascetics from the Syrian Desert). As for Marija/Taisija, in contrast to Anastasiia/Afanasija, she was explicitly advised to abstain from any rigid asceticism by the spiritual counselor of her youth (and in later times, to some extent, dared to question traditional ascetic mortification at all). At first glance, the ascetic careers of these women seem as different as the social strata of their origin. Nevertheless they do have quite a lot in common despite both women's high veneration for the gospel and ending up as abbesses: going on pilgrimages, seeking the advice of elders and adhering to it, intimacy with liturgical texts, the Jesus prayer, the love for akafisty, and so on. During her stay in Zverin-Protection Convent in Novgorod, Marija/Taisija even wrote an akafist of her own: a hymn in praise of Saint Simeon the God-Receiver (cf. Luke 2:25–36), which after some rearrangements by Bishop Seraphim received formal approval by the Holy Synod.[34] Both women also have in common that they enjoyed particular religious, mystical experiences, although only the educated one was able to make a book of it. The visions

---

32. A hymn to be read while "not sitting." A quite similar practice of prayer, including reading the Psalter, akafisty, and reciting the Jesus prayer, is reported for Matrona Popova; see her portrait in Meehan, *Holy Women of Russia*, 61–94.

33. For Seraphim of Sarov's influence on women in general, see Ольга Викторовна Букова [Olga Viktorovna Bukova], *Женские обители преподобного Серафима Саровского: История десяти нижегородских женских монастырей* [The venerable Seraphim of Sarov's women's cloisters: the history of ten Nižnij Novgorod women's monasteries] (Nižnij Novgorod: Книги, 2003).

34. Таисия [Taisija], *Акафист святому преподобному Симеону Богоприимцу. Творение игум. Таисии Леушинской* [Akathistos for the Holy Venerable Simeon God-Receiver. A creation of Abbess Taisija of Leušino] (Saint Petersburg: Леушинское издательство, 2002). http://kazan.eparhia.ru/bogoslugenie/akafisti/pravednum/simeonbogoes/; for the story of the text, see Marija/Taisija's own account in her *Autobiography*, 161–66. Like several Russian lay women, she also wrote poems. For religious motives in the poems of lay female authors, see Frank Göpfert. "Observations on the Life and Work of Elizaveta Kheraskova (1737–1809)," in Rosslyn, *Women and Gender*, 164–86; and Wendy Rosslyn, *The Prince, the Fool and the Nunnery: The Religious Theme in the Early Poetry of Anna Akhmatova* (Averbury: Amersham, 1984). Some decades later Elizaveta/Marija Pilenko/Skobtsova (Skobcova) (1891–1945) followed up Marija/Taisija by writing a greater number of explicitly religious poetical texts.

and dreams Marija/Taisija enjoyed already in her teens, suggest that—as also for less-educated or even illiterate women—liturgical experiences, iconography, saints' lives, and personal guidance provided by a spiritual father or mother strongly interacted with the wording of the Bible in forming her spirituality. In what Marija/Taisija considered her vocational vision, for example, she saw herself at the feet of Jesus not allowing her to touch his feet—a scene revoking the usual representation of Mary Magdalene's encounter with the risen Lord according to the Gospel of John in Easter iconography.[35] Saint Matthew appeared in this vision just as did the Archangel Michael (together with a copy of his icon!), the Mother of God, or Saint Nicholas in later ones. Like other women of her time, "Taisiia found encouragement and inspiration in a rich reservoir of saints and holy exemplars,"[36] including biblical ones, but not being restricted to them.

> Her lexicon of inspiring figures was broad.... it was without boundaries of gender, place or time. The desert fathers and mothers; various apostles; Saint John the Baptist, Nicholas, Paraskeva, and Anthony of Kiev; the archangel Michael; and of course, the Mother of God all presented themselves as supporters and exemplars with whom she could identify and on whom she could model herself. They were also powerful intercessors in the heavenly realm, whose prayers could bring grace on her and her community.[37]

As Brenda Meehan states in the final chapter of her study on saintly women of nineteenth-century Russia, "it is difficult for many feminists to believe that patriarchal religious traditions can empower women. And it is difficult for modern readers, in general, to accept that tradition can be a path of creativity and a source of liberation." Yet the experience of those women investigated by her show "that the established disciplines of monastic tradition—routines of prayer, meditation, contemplative silence, fasting, and mortification—can be powerful tools for breaking through human mire and suffering to a transcendent freedom. Because holiness goes beyond false attachments and splintered selves to the inner core of being, it allows both women and men to be dully whole and powerful, radiating a life force and fresh energy stunning to its observers."[38]

---

35. See Marija/Taisija, *Autobiography*, 39–44.
36. Meehan, *Holy Women of Russia*, 137.
37. Meehan, *Holy Women of Russia*, 137.
38. Meehan, *Holy Women of Russia*, 151.

3. Women's Contributions to Exegesis

This leads us to the question of how women themselves contributed to the exegesis their day. Of course, the same class distinction observed with regard to women having direct access to Scripture prevailed on this level: women of noble birth were more likely to contribute to written theology[39] than others, while the class gap vanishes with regard to "lived theology." This is seen, for example, in the lives of Matrona Naumova Popova (1769–1851), the founder of the Wayfarer's Home closely connected with the grave of Saint Tichon of Zadonsk, whose life Meehan characterized as "service made flesh,"[40] or Anastasija/Afanasija, mentioned above a number of times. The latter longed to become a hermit already in her teens but following the advice of Seraphim of Sarov continued to serve her family before she was finally able to withdraw to a life of prayer at the age of forty-one. Even then she had again to resign her wish for solitude in order to offer spiritual guidance and eventually even to become the head of a monastery in her old age.

When one tries to single out any common point in these manifold lives, one ends up with Marija/Taisija's advice to aspirants for a monastic life: *"Begin with love; it is higher than all."*[41] As it seems, a significant number of pious Russian Orthodox women of the nineteenth century came to understand their Christian calling as a calling to love Christ in one's neighbor, as Elizaveta (Marija with monastic name) Pilenko (Skobtsova/Skobcova after her second marriage), better known as Mother Mari[j]a of Paris (1891–1945), martyred by the Nazis for rescuing Jews, did some decades later.[42] She is quoted as saying, "At the Last Judgment

---

39. In some way also texts such as the memoir and diary of the lay woman Anna Labzina might be analyzed from a theological perspective. See Gary Marker, "Reflections on Lay Female Spirituality in Late Eighteenth- and Early Nineteenth-Century Russia," in *Orthodox Russia: Belief and Practice under the Tsars*, ed. Valerie A. Kivelson and Robert H. Greene (University Park: Pennsylvania State University Press, 2003), 193–209.

40. See Meehan, *Holy Women of Russia*, 61–94.

41. *Letters to a Beginner,* 26 (*facit* of letter 1).

42. See, e.g., Прот. Сергий Гаккель [Sergij Gakkel'/Serge Hackel], *Мать Мария* [Mother Marija] (Moscow: Издательский отдел Всецерковного Православного Молодежного Движения, 1993); Serge Hackel, *Pearl of Great Price. The Life of Mother Maria Skobtsova 1891–1945* (Yonkers, NY: St. Vladimir's Seminary Press, 1981); Antonia Himmel-Agisburg, "Auf dem Weg göttlich zu werden: Die Spiritualität orthodoxer

I will not be asked whether I satisfactorily practised asceticism, nor how many bows I have made before the divine altar. I will be asked whether I fed the hungry, clothed the naked, visited the sick, and the prisoner in his jail. That is all I will be asked."[43] As Mother Marija found her "neighbors" in refugees and beggars on the streets of Paris as well as Jews persecuted by the Nazis, her nineteenth-century forerunners could see them as well in beggars and pilgrims, in battered women and orphans, in prisoners, sick persons and dying soldiers, in old relatives and troublesome cellmates, sometimes also in a nobleman belonging to the "wrong" confession or anyone seeking spiritual advice, thus interrupting one's own prayer and intimacy with God. According to the memories of the lay woman Anna Jakovleva/Labzina, her mother taught her in short: "If you ever are in a position to do good deeds for the poor and unfortunate, you shall be carrying out God's law, and peace will reign in your heart.... Always remember that they are as close to you as brothers, and for them you shall be rewarded by the Heavenly King."[44]

Thus many nineteenth-century women incorporated the message of Matt 25 and 1 Cor 13 in their lives. Quite a number of women were rather successful in teaching this message also to others by their deeds as well as their words: Anna recalls the good example of her mother together with her words in her memoir written down in the early nineteenth century. As mentioned above, Margarita/Marija Tučkova had 1 Cor 13:3[45] and 1

Frauen am Beispiel Xenias von St. Petersburg und Maria Skobtsovas," in *Theologische Frauenforschung in Mittel- und Osteuropa*, ed. Elżbieta Adamiak et al., Yearbook of the European Society of Women in Theological Research 11 (Leuven: Peeters, 2003), 129–142; Himmel-Agisburg, "Mutter Maria Skobtsova—Diakonia in und für die Welt," in *Diakonat und Diakonie in frühchristlicher und ostkirchlicher Tradition*, ed. Anne Jensen and Grigorios Larentzakis, Grazer theologische Studien 23 (Graz: Institut für Ökumenische Theologie, Ostkirchliche Orthodoxie und Patrologie, 2008), 190–201; see especially Mother Marija's own writings: http://mere-marie.com/bibliography/all/.

43. Quoted in Bonnie A. Michal, "Mother Maria Skobtsova—A Saint of Our Day," *St. Nina Quarterly* 2.2 (1998), https://tinyurl.com/SBLPress6007m.

44. English translation of the memoir by Gary Marker and Rachel May in *Days of a Russian Noblewoman: The Memories of Anna Labzina* (DeKalb: Northern Illinois University Press, 2001), 9.

45. Also Mariia Solopova/Abbess Taisija quotes 1 Cor 13:3,2 as a most basic rule for monastic life in her *Letters to a Beginner*, 26. See also her reference to 1 Cor 13:5, 7–8 in letter 5 (p. 48). According to her conversations with Father John of Kronstadt, 1 Cor 13:4–5 was the point Father John made to her during confession (*Autobiography*, 271; text revised by Alexej Klutschewsky according to the Russian edition of 2007,

Pet 1:22 programmatically written over the entrance of the dining hall of Spaso-Borodino Community.[46] A small number of women were even able to make from it written theology that could reach a greater audience of women and men. Besides Elizabeta/Marija Skobtsova/Skobcova, the first Russian woman admitted to formal theological studies in Saint Petersburg shortly before the 1917 revolution, Marija/Taisija Solopova was certainly the most successful, with her writings being transmitted by the Holy Synod and republished and translated in our day.

Marija/Taisija's friendship with Father John of Kronstadt and her success as a writer show clearly that women's interpretation of Christianity met trends in contemporary male theology, although it seems that women were more ready to dedicate themselves to works of mercy and communal forms of monastic life than men of that time.[47] As far as we can see, on the one hand, the Russian hierarchy of that day was ready to accept women's contribution to theology; on the other hand, it seems that Russian Orthodox women of the nineteenth century were unlikely to articulate any specific pain about "the dominantly male symbols of Godhead, sainthood, and priesthood"[48] as some of their Western sisters did. Nuns were quite aware that "women reached a like degree of asceticism with"[49] men in the past and thus could link what they felt their own vocation with Gal 3:28.[50] There were attempts by bishops as well as by committed women themselves for the restitution of the female deaconate.[51] There were occasional appeals

---

228): "Remember: ... *charity thinketh no evil* (1 Cor. 13:4,5), even when there is evil [literally: the good eye does not see evil]. Cover everything with love; don't dwell on earthly filth; reach for perfection in Christ's love. However, even *Jesus did not commit himself unto them, because he knew all men* (John 2:24)."

46. See Meehan, *Holy Women of Russia*, 37–38.

47. "Commitment to service and charity" as a "gender-specific" feature of female spirituality in Orthodox Russia already in earlier times was recently stressed by Isolde Thyrêt, "Women and the Orthodox Faith in Muscovite Russia: Spiritual Experience and Practice," in Kivelson and Greene, *Orthodox Russia*, 166. However, as far as we see, one should be rather cautious to single out women when discussing concern with good work within Russian spirituality. Well-known male representatives of Russian spirituality such as Seraphim of Sarov or John of Kronstadt were quite concerned with service to the needy as well.

48. Meehan, *Holy Women of Russia*, 140.

49. Marija Solopova/Abbess Taisija, *Letters to a Beginner*, 30.

50. See Marija Solopova/Abbess Taisija, *Letters to a Beginner*, 31.

51. See, e.g., the founder of the Lesna Convent, Евгения Ефимовская/Игуменья Екатерина [Evgenija Efimovskaja/Abbess Ekaterina], "О диакониссах (По поводу

to Christ as an "early feminist" who would have "posited the principle of the liberation of women" as well as "a radical liberationist who 'destroyed all differences of existence between people that divided them into men and women, rich and poor, and strong and weak.'"[52] But there was no project of a "Woman's Bible," although one can observe traces of a remarkable inclusive image of God. In her memoir, Anna Jakovleva/Labzina has her seriously ill mother say to her, "Do you not place your hope in the One who created you and has protected you to this day? He is your father, mother, protector, and friend."[53] Marija/Taisija as well depicted God as mother in the introduction to her autobiography:

> Truthful is the word which says: God's grace and *strength is made perfect in weakness* (2 Cor. 12:9) even *where sin abounded* (Rom. 5:20). *For God desireth not the death of a sinner, but that he should turn again and live* (Cf. Ezek. 33:11). Likewise, all my life the Lord has been seeking me, the sinner, and has guided me by His right hand, like a mother guides her unreasonable child, to prevent it, unable to walk along slippery paths, from falling and injuring itself.[54]

Nadieszda Kizenko recently found the same inclusive imagery in an unpublished diary notice of Ioann Sergiev/John of Kronstadt: "A small child is not as consoled in its mothers's arms after it tears as those who

---

статьи свящ. В. Успенскаго)" ["On Deaconess (concerning the article of Priest V. Uspenskij)"], *Церковныя ведомости* 15/16 (1908): 728–29; *Журналы и протоколы заседаний Высочайше учрежденнаго Предсоборного Присутствия* [Journals and protocols of the sessions of the Most Highly Established Preconciliar Commission], vol. 4. (Saint Petersburg: Печ. по определению Святейшего Синода, 1907), 83–86; *Материалы к житию преподобномученицы великой княгини Елизаветы. Письма, дневники, воспоминания, документы* [Materials to the vita of the Saint Martyr Grand Duchess Elizaveta Feodorovna. letters, diaries, memories, documents] (Moscow: Отчий дом, 1996), 50–58. For the less well known petition of Ljudmila Gerasimova, "a journalist and self-professed specialist in agriculture," see William G. Wagner. "'Orthodox Domesticity': Creating a Social Role for Women," in Steinberg and Coleman, *Sacred Stories*, 119. See also Елена В. Белякова and Надежда А. Белякова [Elena V. Beljakova and Nadežda A. Beljakova], "Обсуждение вопроса о диакониссах на Поместном Соборе 1917-1918 гг" ["The discussion of the question of deaconess on the local council of 1917–1918"], *Церковно.исторический вестник* 8 (2001): 139–61.

    52. E. Ljuleva, quoted in Wagner, "Orthodox Domesticity," 137.
    53. Anna Yakovleva/Labzina, *The Memoir*, 18.
    54. Marija Solopova/Abbess Taisija, *Autobiography*, 26.

are worthy of your love are consoled by it. Your love is soothing, peaceful, full of inexpressible joy which is holy and sublime."[55] In the edited version of conversations between the abbess and her spiritual father we can find a quotation of the biblical reference text: being asked to remember his spiritual daughter and to keep in touch with her by writing, the canonized priest is said to have answered as follows: "This is what I say to you in response—the Lord said through the Prophet: *Can a woman forget her suckling child? ... yet will I not forget thee* (Is. 49:15). And I, according to my strength, will remember you and your sisters."[56]

Thus one might wonder if Marija/Taisija was inspired by her spiritual counselor or if both came to see God as father and mother independently. In any case, both, Mother Taisija and Father John of Kronstadt witness that inclusive speech is neither the invention of heretic Westerners nor a questionable modernism as often suspected in our days; it is rooted in Eastern Orthodox tradition as it is in Western tradition, as both are rooted in the same biblical heritage and the same Judeo-Christian experiences of God as compassionate *love* (1 John 4:16b).[57]

---

55. Ioann Sergiev/John of Kronstadt, diary (1856). Unpublished text from the State Archive of the Russian Federation, f. 1067, op. 1, d. 1,1. 65ob., English trans. by Kizenko, *A Prodigal Saint*, 19.

56. John of Kronstadt, according to Marija Solopova/Abbess Taisija, *Autobiography*, 268. See also Моя жизнь во Христе, или Минуты духовного трезвления и созерцания, благоговейного чувства, душевного исправления и покоя в Боге [My life in Christ, or moments of spiritual serenity and contemplation, of reverent feeling, of earnest self-amendment, and of peace in God] (Moscow: Сретенский монастырь, 2005), 495: "What is surprising in the Lord's offering you His body and blood as your food and drink? ... Just as previously as an infant you were fed by your mother and lives through her, through her milk, so now, having grown up and become a sinful person, you are fed by the blood of your Life-giver in order that you live and grow spiritually into a man of God, a holy man; more briefly: just as then you were your mother's son, so now you are the child of God, educated and nourished by His flesh and blood, and all the more by His Spirit (for His Flesh and blood are spirit and life)" (English trans. by Kizenko, *A Prodigal Saint*, 48; for a full translation of the so-called diary, see John of Kronstadt, *My Life in Christ, or Moments of Spiritual Serenity and Contemplation, of Reverent Feeling, of Earnest Self-Amendment, and of Peace in God*, available online at: http://www.ccel.org/ccel/kronstadt/christlife.html.

57. For the role the theology of 1 John plays in the spiritual writings of Marija Solopova/Abbess Taisija, see *Letters to a Beginner*, 47.

Bibliography

Primary Sources

1. Евгения Борисовна Ефимовская /Игумения [Evgenija Efimovskaja/Abbess Ekaterina]
   "О диакониссах (По поводу статьи свящ. В. Успенскаго)" [On deaconess (concerning the article of Priest V. Uspenskij)]. *Церковныя ведомости* 15/16, Supplement (1908): 728–29.

2. Мария Солопова / Игумения Таисия [Marija Solopova/Abbess Taisija]
   Сочинения игумении Таисии (Солоповой) [Works of Abbess Taisija (Solopova)]. Moscow: Вентана–Граф, 2006.

   Autobiography
   Записки игумении Таисии. настоятельницы первоклассного Леушинского женского монастыря (Автобиография). Petrograd: издание Леушинского монастыря [Memoirs of Abbess Taisija, Mother Mother Superior of the Leušino First Class Monastery (autobiography)]. 1916. https://tinyurl.com/y5n6nmf3; Записки игумении Таисии, настоятельницы первоклассного Леушинского женского монастыря. Автобиография. Moscow: Русскій Хронографъ, 1994.
   An Autobiography. Modern Matericon 3. Platina, CA: St. Herman of Alaska Brotherhood, 1989.

   Conversations with Father John of Kronstadt
   Беседы о. Протоиерея Иоанна с настоятельницею Иоанно-Предтеченского Леушинского первоклассного монастыря Игумениею Таисиею. С присовокуплением описания некоторых особенных событий из жизни игумении Таисии [Conversations of Father Archpriest John with the Mother Superior of the John the Forerunner Leušino First Class Monastery Abbess Taisija]. Saint Petersburg: Синодальная Типография, 1909. https://tinyurl.com/y4ctp3g8.
   Игумения Таисия. Записки. Беседы с отцом Иоанном Кронштадтским [Abbess Taisija. Memoirs. Conversations with Father John of Kronstadt]. Moscow: Отчий Дом, 2006.

"Conversations of St. John of Kronstadt and Abbess Thaisia." Pages 245–95 in *An Autobiography* (postscripts: 297–306).

Letters to a Beginner

Письма к новоначальной инокине о главнейшихъ обязанностях иноческой жизни [Letters to a beginning nun about the main duties of the monastic life]. Saint Petersburg: Печатня С. Яковлева. 1900.

Письма к новоначальной инокине [Letters to a beginning nun]. Saint Petersburg: Леушинское издательство, 2007.

Letters to a Beginner: On Giving One's Life to God. Modern Matericon 4. Wildwood, CA: St. Xenia Skete Press, 1993.

Liturgical Texts and Poems

Акафист святому преподобному Симеону Богоприимцу. Творение игум. Таисии Леушинской [Akathistos for the Holy Venerable Simeon God-Receiver. A creation of Abbess Taisija of Leušino]. Saint Petersburg: Леушинское издательство, 2002. http://kazan.eparhia.ru/bogoslugenie/akafisti/pravednum/simeonbogoes/.

Духовные стихотворения игумении Таисии, настоятельницы Леушинского Иоанно-Предтеченского монастыря [Spiritual Poems by Abbess Taisija, Mother Superior of the Leušino John the Forerunner Monastery]. Saint Petersburg: Синодальная Типография, 1903. https://tinyurl.com/yyg776n5.

Канон на Благовещение Пресвятыя Богородицы. Переложение в стихах игумении Таисии, настоятельницы первоклассного Леушинского Иоанно-Предтеченского монастыря Череповец. уезда Новгородской губернии [Canon of the Annunciation of the Most Holy Theotokos. versification by Abbess Taisija, Mother Superior of the First Class Leušino Monastery in the Čerepoveck uyezd/district of the Novgorod Governorate]. Saint Petersburg: Синодальная типография, 1904.

Полное собрание духовных стихотворений [Complete collection of spiritual poems]. Saint Petersburg: Леушинское издательство, 2002.

3. Елизавета Юрьевна Кузьмина-Караваева/Мария (Скобцова) [Elizaveta Ju. Kuz'mina-Karaveva/Marija Skobcova/Mother Marija]

   Равнина русская: Стихотворения и поэмы. Пьесы-мистерии. Художественная и автобиографическая проза. Письма [The Russian plain: verses and poems. mystery plays. belletristic and autobiographic prose. letters]. Saint Petersburg: Искусство-СПб, 2001.

   Типы религиозной жизни/Предисловие прот [Types of the religious life]. Moscow: Свято-Филаретовская московская высшая православно-христианская школа, 2002.

   Красота спасающая: живопись, графика, вышивка [The saving beauty: painting, graphic arts, embroidery]. Saint Petersburg: Искусство-СПб, 2004.

   Essential Writings. Edited by Helene Klepinin Arjakovsky. Translated by Richard Pevear and Larissa Volokhonsky. Maryknoll, NY: Orbis, 2003.

4. Иван Ильич Сéргиев/о. Иоанн Кроншадтский [Ioan I. Sergiev/Father John of Kronstadt]

   Моя жизнь во Христе, или Минуты духовного трезвления и созерцания, благоговейного чувства, душевного исправления и покоя в Боге [My life in Christ, or moments of spiritual serenity and contemplation, of reverent feeling, of earnest self-amendment, and of peace in God]. Moscow: Сретенский монастырь, 2005. English: http://www.ccel.org/ccel/kronstadt/christlife.html.

   Письма о. протоиерея Иоанна к настоятельнице Иоанно-Предтеченского Леушинского первоклассного монастыря игумении Таисии [Letters of Father Archpriest John to the Abbess Taisija of the Leušino First-Class Monastery]. Saint Petersburg: Синодальная Типография, 1909.

5. Анна Яковлева/Лабзина [Anna Yakovleva/Labzina]

   Воспоминания Анны Евдокимовны Лабзиной. 1758–1828 [Memories of Anna Evdokimovna Labzina, 1758–1828]. Saint Petersburg: Огни, 1914. English: *Days of A Russian Noblewoman: The Memories of Anna Labzina*. Translated and edited by Gary Marker and Rachel May. DeKalb: Northern Illinois University Press, 2001.

6. Additional Sources

Журналы и протоколы заседаний Высочайше учрежденнаго Предсоборного Присутствия [Journals and protocols of the sessions of the Most Highly Established Preconciliar Commission]. Vol. 4. Saint Petersburg: Печ. по определению Святейшего Синода, 1907.

Материалы к житию преподобномученицы великой княгини Елизаветы. Письма, дневники, воспоминания, документы [Materials to the vita of the Saint Martyr Grand Duchess Elizaveta Feodorovna. letters, diaries, memories, documents]. Moscow: Отчий дом, 1996.

Secondary Sources

Aland, Kurt. *Pietismus und Bibel.* Arbeiten zur Geschichte des Pietismus 9. Witten: Luther Verlag, 1970.

Белякова, Елена В., and Надежда А. Белякова [Elena V. Beljakova and Nadežda A. Beljakova]. "Обсуждение вопроса о диакониссах на Поместном Соборе 1917–1918 гг" [The discussion of the question of deaconess on the local council of 1917–1918]. *Церковно-исторический вестник* 8 (2001): 139–61.

Brecht, Martin. "Die Bedeutung der Bibel im deutschen Pietismus." Pages 102–20 in *Glaubenswelt und Lebenswelten.* Edited by Hartmut Lehmann. Geschichte des Pietismus 4. Göttingen: Vandenhoeck & Ruprecht, 2004.

Brooks, Jeffrey. *When Russia Learned to Read: Literacy and Popular Literature, 1861–1917.* Princeton: Princeton University Press, 1988.

Букова, Ольга Викторовна [Olga Viktorovna Bukova]. *Женские обители преподобного Серафима Саровского. История десяти нижегородских женских монастырей* [The venerable Seraphim of Sarov's women's cloisters: the history of ten Nižnij Novgorod women's monasteries]. Nižnij Novgorod: Книги, 2003.

Glagoleva, Olga E. "Imaginary World: Reading in the Lives of Russian Provincial Noblewomen (1750–1825)." Pages 129–46 in *Women and Gender in Eighteenth-Century Russia.* Edited by Wendy Rosslyn. Aldershot: Ashgate, 2003..

Göpfert, Frank. "Observations on the Life and Work of Elizaveta Kheraskova (1737–1809)." Pages 164–86 in *Women and Gender in Eighteenth-Century Russia.* Edited by Wendy Rosslyn. Aldershot: Ashgate, 2003.

Гаккель, Прот. Сергий [Sergij Gakkel'/Serge Hackel]. *Мать Мария* [Mother Marija]. Moscow: Издательский отдел Всецерковного Православного Молодежного Движения, 1993.

Hackel, Serge. *Pearl of Great Price: The Life of Mother Maria Skobtsova 1891–1945.* Yonkers, NY: St. Vladimir's Seminary Press, 1981.

Himmel-Agisburg, Antonia. "Auf dem Weg göttlich zu werden: Die Spiritualität orthodoxer Frauen am Beispiel Xenias von St. Petersburg und Maria Skobtsovas." Pages 129–42 in *Theologische Frauenforschung in Mittel- und Osteuropa.* Edited by Elżbieta Adamiak et al. Yearbook of the European Society of Women in Theological Research 11. Leuven: Peeters, 2003.

———. "Mutter Maria Skobtsova—Diakonia in und für die Welt." Pages 190–201 in *Diakonat und Diakonie in frühchristlicher und ostkirchlicher Tradition.* Edited by Anne Jensen and Grigorios Larentzakis. Grazer theologische Studien 23. Graz: Institut für Ökumenische Theologie, Ostkirchliche Orthodoxie und Patrologie, 2008.

Kenworthy, Scott M. "Abbess Taisiia of Leushino and the Reform of Women's Monasticism in Early Twentieth Century Russia." Pages 83–102 in *Culture and Identity in Eastern Christian History: Papers from the First Biennial Conference of the Association for the Study of Eastern Christian History and Culture.* Edited by Russell E. Martin and Jennifer B. Spock. Ohio Slavic Papers 9. Columbus: Ohio State University, Department of Slavic and East European Languages and Literatures, 2009.

Kizenko, Nadieszda. *A Prodigal Saint: Father John of Kronstadt and the Russian People.* University Park: Pennsylvania State University Press, 2000.

———. "Written Confessions and the Construction of Sacred Narrative" Pages 93–118 in *Sacred Stories: Religion and Spirituality in Modern Russia.* Edited by Mark D. Steinberg and Heather J. Coleman. Bloomington: Indiana University Press, 2007.

Klostermann, Robert A. *Probleme der Ostkirche: Untersuchungen zum Wesen und zur Geschichte der griechisch-orthodoxen Kirche.* Göteborg: Elanders Boktryckeri Aktiebolag, 1955.

Marker, Gary. "Reflections on Lay Female Spirituality in Late Eighteenth- and Early Nineteenth-Century Russia." Pages 193–209 in *Orthodox Russia: Belief and Practice under the Tsars.* Edited by Valerie A. Kivelson and Robert H. Greene. University Park: Pennsylvania State University Press, 2003.

Meehan, Brenda. *Holy Women of Russia: The Lives of Five Orthodox Women Offer Spiritual Guidance for Today.* San Francisco: Harper, 1993.

———. "To Save Oneself: Russian Peasant Women and the Development of Women's Religious Communities in Pre-revolutionary Russia." Pages 121–33 in *Russian Peasant Women.* Edited by Beatrice Farnsworth and Viola Lynne. New York: Oxford University Press, 1992.

Michal, Bonnie A. "Mother Maria Skobtsova—A Saint of Our Day." *St. Nina Quarterly* 2.2 (1998). https://tinyurl.com/SBLPress6007m.

Priklonskii, Alexandr. *Blessed Athanasia and the Desert Ideal.* Modern Matericon 1. Platina, CA: St. Herman of Alaska Brotherhood, 1990.

Pushkareva, Natal'ia L. "Russian Noblewomen's Education in the Home as Revealed in Late 18th- and Early 19th-Century Memoirs." Pages 111–28 in *Women and Gender in Eighteenth-Century Russia.* Edited by Wendy Rosslyn. Aldershot: Ashgate, 2003.

Rosslyn, Wendy. *The Prince, the Fool and the Nunnery: The Religious Theme in the Early Poetry of Anna Akhmatova.* Averbury: Amersham, 1984.

Shevzov, Vera. "Chapels and the Ecclesiastical World of Prerevolutionary Russian Peasants." *Slavic Review* 55 (1996): 585–613.

Tichomirov, Boris A. "Geschichte der russischen Bibelübersetzung." *Stimme der Orthodoxie* 2004.1 (2004): 37–44; 2004.2 (2004): 18–27.

Тимофеев, Валерий В. [Valerij V. Timofeev]. "Старообрядческое просветительство: взаимовлияние предпринимательства и образования" [Old Ritualists' enlightenment: reciprocal influences of entrepreneurship and education]. *Вестник ЧГПУ им. И. Я. Яковлева* 23.4 (2001): 105–13.

Thyrêt, Isolde. "Women and the Orthodox Faith in Muscovite Russia: Spiritual Experience and Practice." Pages 159–75 in *Orthodox Russia: Belief and Practice under the Tsars.* Edited by Valerie A. Kivelson and Robert H. Greene. University Park: Pennsylvania State University Press, 2003.

Успенский, Борис А. [Boris A. Uspenskij]. *История русского литературного языка (XI–XVIIвв.)* [The history of the Russian literary language (eleventh–seventeenth centuries)]. Moscow: Аспект, 2002.

Wagner, William G. "'Orthodox Domesticity': Creating a Social Role for Women." Pages 119–45 in *Sacred Stories Religion and Spirituality in Modern Russia.* Edited by Mark D. Steinberg and Heather J. Coleman. Bloomington: Indiana University Press, 2007.

The Bible in Liturgy and Spirituality: The Example of the *Kreuzeskränzchen* in Bonn

Angela Berlis

Throughout church history, worship and church interiors certainly have been the most important places for people to get to know the Bible, to deal with its contents, and to take this experience into their own daily lives. The cultural formative power of the Bible remains incomprehensible if this factor of encounter with the Bible in daily ecclesiastical and liturgical practice is ignored.[1] How formative is it, for example, when people sit in churches whose glass windows tell and interpret the stories of believing men and women of the Bible, and when statues of the saints stand in churches as examples of lived discipleship, or perhaps are lacking there? What influence do psalms and readings from the Bible have that are prayed or sung during the service or are read and learned by heart at home? How formative for one's own faith experience and to practice is the instruction given in catechism classes and the sermon held by office holders, and what role does the Bible play here? For centuries, there was a gender-specific division of labor and space in worship; women were not visible as actors in the central events that took place there, while they at the same time formed a considerable, if not even the larger part of the worshipping community. A seating arrangement that separated the sexes was usual until far into the twentieth century.[2] What role does gender play in the mediation and reception of biblical texts and of interpretations that take place in the

---

I am indebted to Teresa Berger, Yale University, for her commentary on an earlier version of this essay.

1. For the cultural impact of the Bible, see John F. A. Sawyer, ed., *The Blackwell Companion to the Bible and Culture*, BCR (Malden, MA: Blackwell, 2006).

2. See Margaret Aston, "Segregation in Church," in *Women in the Church: Papers Read at the 1989 Summer Meeting and the 1990 Winter Meeting of the Ecclesiastical*

realm of the church?³ In what way do women and men appropriate the Bible and actively interpret its statements and narratives for their own lives and actions—will they be led toward an emancipatory awakening or to the maintenance of the inherited?⁴

1. Religious Spaces and Their Attraction for Women in the Nineteenth Century

In research literature, a decline in church attendance among men has been observed for the nineteenth century, while women continued to remain faithful church-goers. This finding is interpreted as a sign of an increasing secularization. Religious-sociological studies see secularization as a consequence of industrialization. Some years ago, though, Linda Woodhead and Callum Brown have pleaded for a "gendering" of the secularization thesis by pointing out that industrialization had very different consequences for the lives and working worlds of men and women: while the men worked in the public realm, factory, or office, the women did work that—even if it was paid—was a part of the domestic-private sphere (housework, education, instruction, personal care, etc.). In short, while men saw their lives and work as determined by an "iron cage" (Max Weber) or by a "crumbling cage" (Karl Marx) of paid labor, the women, rather, were imprisoned in the "gentle cage of domesticity."⁵ Weber's

---

History Society, ed. William J. Sheils and Diana Wood, SCH 27 (Oxford: Blackwell, 1990), 237-94.

3. Teresa Berger identifies four different levels here: the Bible as an androcentric document; androcentric translations; the order of readings in the lectionary that shortens, ignores, or overlooks stories about women; and a proclamation of the word through men alone. See Berger, "'I Love Latin Mass': Sonntagsgottesdienst und Frauenleben, " *ET-S* 1 (2010): 273.

4. *Appropriation* is understood here in the sense of an active, interpretative reception of the past. Cf. Willem Frijhoff, "Toeëigening: Van bezitsdrang naar betekenisgeving," *Tra* 6 (1997): 99-118.

5. Linda Woodhead, "Gender Differences in Religious Practice and Significance," *The Sage Handbook of the Sociology of Religion*, ed. James Beckford and N. Jay Demerath III (Los Angeles: Sage, 2007), 550-70. Quoted from online publication: http://eprints.lancs.ac.uk/793/1/Gender_Differences_in_Religious_Practice_and_Significance-revised10th_June.doc, 29. See Woodhead, "Gendering Secularization Theory," *Kvinder, Kønog Forskning* 1 (2005): 24-35. Online: http://eprints.lancs.ac.uk/797/1/copenhagen2.doc.

disenchantment of the world does not apply to men and women in the nineteenth century in the same way. If the relationship between religion and the modern society is described as changing in the nineteenth century, and if this is illustrated by, among other things, the decline of church attendance and the dwindling numbers of church members,[6] then this statement must be considered in a different way for men than for women. It was, above all, men who left the church. Women continued to nurture traditional religious behavior by maintaining and continuing to practice rituals and customs, but also material cultures. This different development among men and women has been noticed in the last several years and discussed under the thesis of the "feminization of religion" in the nineteenth century.[7] Why did women persist in traditional religious practice? This is explained, on the one hand, by referring to the domesticity of women and, on the other, by pointing out the parallels between contemporary role expectations of women (subordination, humility, devotion, the capacity to love) and the Christian life ideal, advocated by the church, with its "feminine" characteristics (charity, devotion).

Of course, one should guard against positing the stereotypical contrast between "feminine piety" and "masculine lack of faith."[8] For there were always examples of pious men and unchurchly women critical of religion, as shown by the example of the women in the so-called Germano-Catholicism

---

6. See Owen Chadwick, *The Secularization of the European Mind in the Nineteenth Century* (Cambridge: Cambridge University Press, 1975), 264. Jürgen Osterhammel distinguishes six fields of secularization, of which personal faith and "participation in religious practices" are two. Cf. Jürgen Osterhammel, *Die Verwandlung der Welt: Eine Geschichte des 19. Jahrhunderts*, 2nd ed., HBGHS (Munich: Beck, 2009), 1248-49. This was translated into English: Osterhammel, *The Transformation of the World: A Global History of the Nineteenth Century*, trans. Patrick Camiller, AW (Princeton: Princeton University Press, 2014).

7. See Barbara Welter, "The Feminization of American Religion: 1800-1860," in *Clio's Consciousness Raised*, ed. Mary Hartman and Lois W. Banner (New York: Harper & Row, 1974), 137-57. See also the critical reception by Bernhard Schneider, "Feminisierung der Religion im 19. Jahrhundert: Perspektiven einer These im Kontext des deutschen Katholizismus," *TTZ* 111 (2002): 123-47; see also the essay by Bernhard Schneider in this volume.

8. See McLeod, "Weibliche Frömmigkeit—männlicher Unglaube? Religion und Kirchen im bürgerlichen 19. Jahrhundert," in *Bürgerinnen und Bürger: Geschlechterverhältnisse im 19. Jahrhundert*, ed. Ute Frevert, KSG 77 (Göttingen: Vandenhoeck & Ruprecht, 1988), 134-56.

(*Deutschkatholizismus*) in the nineteenth century.[9] In addition, certainly not all men in the nineteenth century were in the same situation; thus, for example, the life and work world of scholars and officeholders in the church differed considerably from the world of workers or from members of the lower middle-class (the same is true mutatis mutandis for women). It should be mentioned further that there were also efforts made in opposition to an all-too-pervasive feminization of the church, such as the promotion among men of a "muscular Christianity" in England. Detailed case studies are necessary here in order to avoid a too-hasty constraint of the diversity in lived piety. One that lends itself to this purpose is the investigation of the various ways in which Mary could be interpreted and made accessible for "masculine" or "feminine" spirituality.[10]

What is certain is that various factors in the nineteenth century produced a strong, lasting, and reawakened attraction to religious spaces among women. The church space had a family-tinged atmosphere and thus was easily accessible for women. The same is true—though in a specific way in each case—for linguistic-religious forms of expression in Roman Catholicism[11] and in the *praxis pietatis* in Protestantism.[12] Possibilities arise "to

---

9. The *Deutschkatholizismus* (Germano-Catholicism) arose out of the critical reaction to the Holy Robe pilgrimage in Trier in 1844 and quickly merged with free-thinking religious currents. The equality of the sexes was upheld—not least of all under the influence of the democratic concerns behind the revolution of 1848. See Sylvia Paletschek, *Frauen und Dissens: Frauen im Deutschkatholizismus und in den freien Gemeinden: 1841–1852*, KSG 89 (Göttingen: Vandenhoeck & Ruprecht, 1990), 146–52; Paletschek, "Frauen und Säkularisierung Mitte des 19. Jahrhunderts: Das Beispiel der religiösen Oppositionsbewegung des Deutschkatholizismus und der freien Gemeinden," in *Religion und Gesellschaft im 19. Jahrhundert*, ed. Wolfgang Schieder, IW 54 (Stuttgart: Klett-Cotta, 1993), 302.

10. See, for example, Carol Engelhardt Herringer, *Victorians and the Virgin Mary: Religion and Gender in England: 1830–1885*, GH (Manchester: Manchester University Press, 2008), 144–81; Engelhardt Herringer, "The Virgin Mary and Victorian Masculinity," in *Masculinity and Spirituality in Victorian Culture*, ed. Andrew Bradstock et al. (London: Macmillan, 2000), 44–57.

11. See Irmtraud Götz von Olenhusen, ed., *Wunderbare Erscheinungen: Frauen und katholische Frömmigkeit im 19. und 20. Jahrhundert* (Paderborn: Schöningh, 1995).

12. See Ute Gause, "Frauen und Frömmigkeit im 19. Jahrhundert: Der Aufbruch in die Öffentlichkeit," *PN* 24 (1998): 309–27; slightly changed reprint in Gause, *Kirchengeschichte und Genderforschung: Eine Einführung in protestantischer Perspektive*, UTB 2806 (Stuttgart: Mohr Siebeck, 2006), 157–81.

help in promoting over the long term an emancipation of Christian women, which, however, are in no way connected with secularization."[13]

2. Bible—Women—Liturgy

This essay treats the theme of the relationship between the Bible and women in the nineteenth century under the aspect of liturgy.[14] The view is directed especially to the manner in which women read the Bible in this century, interpreted it for their lives, and integrated it into their religious practice. The focus here is upon young Catholic women who belonged to a spiritual circle in Bonn; the majority were unmarried. Sources used in this contribution are their unpublished letters to the celibate clerical members of their circle as well as a litany written by these women. The letters and the litany are evidence of the appropriation of the Bible and tradition by these women, and at the same time they eloquently witness the vivid richness of the spiritual and liturgical tradition.

As far as the relationship between women and liturgy is concerned, women generally are invisible where only authoritative, official liturgical texts are consulted. Exceptions are women who, as authors or translators of hymns, made a perceptible contribution to the official liturgical and ritual repertoire and wrote memorable texts and catchy formulations.[15] But, otherwise, women were rarely (mentioned as) framers of liturgical texts in

---

13. So the conclusion by Ute Gause, which she bases upon the Protestant women investigated by her, but which, in my opinion, is also applicable to women of other denominations (Gause, "Frauen und Frömmigkeit," 327).

14. For studies about other centuries, I cite the following: Teresa Berger, "Women in Worship," in *The Oxford History of Christian Worship*, ed. Geoffrey Wainwright and Karen B. Westerfield Tucker (New York: Oxford University Press, 2005), 755–68. See in addition Berger, *Women's Ways of Worship: Gender Analysis and Liturgical History* (Collegeville, MN: Liturgical Press, 1999); Berger, *Sei gesegnet, meine Schwester: Frauen feiern Liturgie; Geschichtliche Rückfragen, praktische Impulse, theologische Vergewisserungen* (Würzburg: Echter, 1999); Berger, *Liturgie und Frauenseele: Die Liturgische Bewegung aus der Sicht der Frauenforschung*, PTH 10 (Stuttgart: Kohlhammer, 1993); and Gisela Muschiol, *Famula Dei: Zur Liturgie in merowingischen Frauenklöstern*, BGAMB 41 (Münster: Aschendorff, 1994).

15. See on this Geoffrey Wainwright, "Catherine Winkworth: 'Königin der Übersetzerinnen' deutscher Kirchenlieder," in *Liturgie und Frauenfrage: Ein Beitrag zur Frauenforschungaus liturgiewissenschaftlicher Sicht*, ed. Teresa Berger and Albert Gerhards, PL 7 (Saint Ottilien: Eos, 1990), 289–305. Winkworth translated almost four hundred German hymns into English.

the nineteenth century, above all when attention is directed to the official, ecclesiastically approved liturgy. More exact studies are appropriate here in which liturgical and ritual forms other than those prescribed by the church ought to be investigated. One of the hurdles for this research is the source situation: where texts were written for a certain situation and for a certain audience, they often are transmitted only in handwritten form and are hard to find. Also, the role of the women as laywomen and not official office-holders, the denominational affiliation, and the dominant understanding of the liturgy in a certain religious denomination or church have an influence upon the circumstance that certain texts are not understood as "liturgical texts." One of the few examples known to me of a nineteenth century text written by Catholic women and used in the framework of a ritual is to be discussed below.

Along with the shaping of spoken and sung texts for the liturgy, women also participated in other ways; first, by the fact of being present in the worship service and helping to shape it by being a corporeal part of the celebration. This "corporeality" expressed itself in presence, in praying, breathing, kneeling, and more. Second, women took part as attentive hearers who often recorded their personal experiences in diaries.[16] They therewith documented at the same time their high degree of learning, such as, for example, their knowledge of Latin. Such ego-documents are important sources for contemporary worship practice and for the manner in which women appropriated this practice for their own personal piety. Along with the diary, the letter is also an important medium of self-reflection. In addition, it often serves in the interactive clarification of liturgical questions as well as of questions of sacramental theology, which arise, for example, in the case of a conversion or during the visit to another religious denomination.[17] Third, women played a role as mediators: sermons, thus, were recorded during their delivery and then handed around in the circle of friends. This is true for the sermons of the Bonn professor Bernhard Joseph Hilgers (1803–1874), which he delivered in the chapel of Saint John's Hospital there. The sermons were recorded by a woman who

---

16. See Friedrich Lurz, *Erlebte Liturgie: Autobiografische Schriften als liturgiewissenschaftliche Quellen*, ATL 28 (Münster: LIT, 2003).

17. See, for example, Susan J. White, *A History of Women in Christian Worship* (London: SPCK, 2003), 145. Questions about the sacraments (baptism, eucharist) are often asked. Cf. Paletschek, *Frauen und Dissens*, 146–52, for the perception expressed by a woman who did not belong to the religious denomination in question.

wanted to remain anonymous.[18] The unknown recorder was possibly the Bonn teacher Wilhelmine Ritter (1834-1870).[19] Fourth, women could appear as propagandists. Thereby, their pleas for liturgical renewal[20] and for the reading of the Bible[21] went hand in hand, as the example of the Bonn Old Catholic Therese von Miltitz (1827-1912) shows.

3. The Bonn *Kreuzeskränzchen* and Its Litany

3.1. The *Kreuzeskränzchen* as Part of the Günther Circle in Bonn

The previously mentioned Ritter played a decisive role in a group of Catholic women in Bonn who belonged to the circle of friends gathered around the philosopher Anton Günther (1783-1863), who lived

---

18. See Bernard Joseph Hilgers, *Homilien gehalten in der Kapelle des St. Johanneshospitals zu Bonn: Nach dem Tode des Verfassers herausgegeben*, 2nd ed. (Bonn: Karl Drobnig, 1896). The popularity of Hilgers's sermons is shown also by the reprint of a Pentecost sermon in the *AF* 18 (1889): 131.

19. See Wilhelmine Ritter to Wilhelm Reinkens, January 14, 1854, in which she summarizes Hilgers's train of thought in his sermon on the wedding feast at Cana (John 2:1-11). This sermon, incidentally, is not identical with the one held on the second Sunday after Epiphany that is printed in Hilgers, *Homilien*, 28-30. Also, on October 23, 1864, Ritter reports about a sermon delivered by Hilgers in the hospital chapel. The letters are found in the archives of the German Province of the Jesuits, Munich (DPJA), Nachlass W. Reinkens, Abt. 47, Nr. 566.

20. An example of this is Therese von Miltitz and other Old Catholic women who, from 1855, published an *Altkatholisches Frauenblatt*. At the end of the third year of publication, it was stated in no uncertain terms: "Further, the *Frauenblatt* endeavored in its pages to contribute toward providing Thürlings's prayer book and hymnal with entry into the families and, from there, into the congregations by seeking to make the details known to individuals. For this purpose, it published gradually, in issues 7 to 10, a selection of those hymns which share the melody with a larger number of other hymns. Thereby, it provided proof that, in learning these twelve hymns, interested persons immediately would be able to sing a further forty other hymns from the hymnal" ("Die Bestrebungen des altkath. Frauenblattes," *AF* 12 (1887): 76-78, here 78.

21. In the early years of German Old Catholicism, the reading of the Bible was encouraged repeatedly. See "Ueber Bibellesen," *DM* 4 (1873): 59-60. This encouragement was repeated also by the first bishop, Joseph Hubert Reinkens, who delivered a programmatic speech on the subject in 1873. See "Vom Constanzer Congreß," *DM* 4 (1873): 297-99. How the Old Catholic women themselves also became active, in 1889, is described in greater detail below.

and taught in Vienna.[22] The focal point of the Bonn circle of Günther's adherents was Wilhelm Reinkens (1811-1899), pastor at Saint Remigius, who since the 1840s had gathered young theological students, among them his younger brother Joseph Hubert, and the young people who benefitted from his Christian religious instruction. The theological students spread out to other lands after their training; the members of a group of girls that emerged in 1850 as a result of his catechetical instruction, with subsequent first communion and confirmation, remained to a great extent in Bonn. From 1855, they called themselves the *Kreuzeskränzchen* ("wreath of the Cross" or "circle of the Cross").[23] Several members of this women's circle founded a private girls' school in 1858 in Bonn that existed into the 1890s. Reform impulses emanated from the Bonn Günther circle in two directions: in the reestablishment of the Benedictines in Germany (from 1863)[24] and in the formation of the Old Catholic movement (after 1870).

Günther's works were condemned by Rome in 1857. Similar to the works of the dogmatic theologian Georg Hermes (1775-1831), who had taught in Bonn and whose books Rome had forbidden after his death,[25] Günther's works in the Roman perspective also were concerned much too much with an accommodation between faith and modernity. From the 1860s on, the rift in theology and the practice of piety between ecclesiastically strict, ultramontane Catholics and those Catholic men and women who were influenced by the thought of the Catholic Enlightenment and were open to the modern spirit of the time became more and more evident. As a result of Vatican I (1869-1870), the ultramontane faction won more influence and for a long time was dominant. The circle of friends in Bonn and other representatives of a liberal Catholicism were pushed to

---

22. See Paul Wenzel, *Der Freundeskreis um Anton Günther und die Gründung Beurons: Ein Beitrag zur Geschichte des deutschen Katholizismus im 19. Jahrhundert* (Essen: Ludgerus, 1965).

23. For a detailed description of this group, its members, and its concerns, see Angela Berlis, *Frauen im Prozess der Kirchwerdung: Eine Studie zur Anfangsphase des deutschen Altkatholizismus (1850-1890)*, BKK 6 (Frankfurt: Lang, 1998), 371-623.

24. See Johanna Buschmann, *Beuroner Mönchtum: Studien zu Spiritualität, Verfassung und Lebensformen der Beuroner Benediktinerkongregation von 1863 bis 1914*, BGAMB 43 (Münster: Aschendorff, 1994). Cf. Herman A. J. Wegman, *Liturgie in der Geschichte des Christentums* (Regensburg: Pustet, 1994), 353, who does not mention this relationship—it is probably unknown to him.

25. Hilgers, mentioned above, is considered to be a Hermesian theologian.

the margin as a result of the ultramontanization of Catholicism, which increased noticeably since the 1850s.[26]

Using letters from the *Kreuzeskränzchen* and a text written by its members, the value of the Bible and its appropriation for the prayer life of the female members of this circle of friends is to be illustrated by the following. This group is not representative in its time for the mainstream of contemporary Catholicism, which is to be designated as ultramontanism. Nevertheless, the texts stand within the broad current of Catholic tradition. At the same time, they have their very own character, which—as will be shown—is distinguished very strongly by a reading of the Bible, its exegesis by the church fathers, and by the reception of the *Heliand*. This latter work, an early medieval, Old Saxon harmony of the gospels and a retelling of the life of Christ, had been translated into German by the scholar of German literature Karl Simrock, who was the father of two members of the *Kreuzeskränzchen*. The texts to be treated form a witness for how the ecclesiastical tradition was appropriated and carried on further by this Catholic group. They show, in addition, what space women could enter as the creators of liturgy and what significance and interpretation they lent to their own liturgical activity. One can only agree with Teresa Berger when she points out that the significance of a worship service "is not anchored and laid down primarily in liturgical texts, but rather is also created by people and their life contexts *in actu*."[27]

3.2. The Litany of the *Kreuzeskränzchen*

Litanies (from λιτή, meaning "supplication") have a long religious tradition. They are sung antiphonally by a precentor and the people present and are often combined with a procession. The Western church took over the form of the litany from the Eastern church from the fifth century onwards. Many litanies arose in the course of the history of the church;

---

26. Various of these nonultramontane Hermesians and Güntherians took an active part after 1870 in the movement in opposition to the dogmas of Vatican I and became members in parishes of the diocese for Old Catholics in the German Empire, which was formed in 1873. For a short overview of the concerns of Old Catholicism, see Wegman, *Liturgie*, 37–39, in the chapters on "Die Kirche in Utrecht, im Jahr 1720" and "Die Kirche in Bonn, im Jahr 1880."

27. Berger, "I Love Latin Mass," 278. This idea corresponds to how the Dutch historian Frijhoff uses the term *appropriation*. See Frijhoff, "Toeëigening."

these were reduced in number in 1601 by Pope Clement VIII to the *All Saints' Litany* and the *Lauretanian Litany* in the official liturgy.[28] In the course of the Catholic Enlightenment, such litanies appeared less often in hymnals and prayer books. Yet, the people in the church continued to pray their litanies and still others that were not officially authorized. Often, the saint(s) of the day were commemorated. The popularity of the *Lauretanian Litany* is shown by the following description by Pauline von Mallinckrodt (1817–1881), the founder of the Congregation of the Sisters of Christian Love: "Every evening after supper, we have May devotions. Candles burn before the image of the dear Mother of God. All the residents of the house gather in the little chapel; we pray the Lauretanian Litany and read a contemplation from the book for the month of May. A Marian hymn ... concludes the celebration."[29]

In the night of Maundy Thursday into the morning of Good Friday, 1855, the members of the *Kränzchen* composed a litany that they then prayed on the second day of Easter on the Kreuzberg (the "hill of the Cross"), a place of pilgrimage near Bonn.[30] A letter from two members, Agnes Simrock (1835–1904) and her cousin Odilia Fabricius (1833–1894) provides more information about it. They sent the sixteen pages of the handwritten litany to the Benedictine Dom Anselmo Nickes in Rome, a longtime member of the Günther circle in Bonn, and added this explanation: "We send to you (the best communication of the thoughts of our hearts) a litany, in which we in the previous Maundy Thursday night gathered all our prayers in order to pray them aloud, to the joy of all the children of the *Kränzchen* on the second day of Easter on the Kreuzberg, whence we wander every year with the disciples to Emmaus."[31] The cita-

---

28. The Roman Catholic Church today officially approves four other litanies.

29. Quoted from Kurt Küppers, *Marienfrömmigkeit zwischen Barock und Industriezeitalter: Untersuchungen zur Geschichte und Feier der Maiandacht in Deutschland und dem deutschen Sprachgebiet* (St. Ottilien: Eos, 1986), 167.

30. For a detailed discussion of the litany, see Berlis, *Frauen*, 453–63. The quotations are documented there, or are to be found in Wenzel, *Freundeskreis*, 80–89. Erentrud Kraft (1934–2015) has submitted this litany to an extensive analysis. She kindly made her manuscript available to me.

31. Agnes Simrock and Odilia Fabricius to Dom Anselmo Nickes, Christmas, 1855, SPR, Dom Anselmo Nickes Papers. Nickes did not reply. The two letter writers reminded him of this in their next letter in December 1856. The litany is printed by Wenzel, *Freundeskreis*, 80–89; seven petitions are lacking here, though. For corrections, see Berlis, *Frauen*, 454–58.

tions show that the fact that the Bonn women's circle, which called itself a *"Kreuzeskränzchen"* only after the litany came into being, prayed a litany was nothing special. At the most, it verifies the popularity of litanies, but also that the praying of them obviously occurred in all currents of Catholicism, independently of whether the praying person was the ultramontane Mallinckrodt or belonged to the Günther circle, like the two cousins Simrock and Fabricius. Wherein, then, does the significance of the litany by the *Kreuzeskränzchen* lie? The *Litanei aus weitem Herzen*[32] has the structure of an All Saints' litany, but, with its approximately three-hundred-fifty invocations, it is much more extensive; in addition, it brings different emphases to the fore than do the conventional litanies. It has three parts: invocations to each of the three persons of the trinity, then to Mary and the saints, and finally supplications for specific concerns. The trinitarian introduction that is usual in every All Saints' litany is expanded considerably in this litany: seven petitions are directed to God the Father, the creator, and the God of loyalty to the covenant; one hundred are directed to the Son; twenty to the Holy Spirit. The sequence follows a salvation-historical scheme. The preponderance of invocations to the Son makes the litany Christocentric. In the second part, thirty-six invocations to Mary follow, then invocations to the angels and to all the "great figures of the Old Covenant," then to holy men and women of the Bible, among them all "you holy women who followed him" and "you, our cherished Lydia, the first confessor of Christianity in Europe."[33] Lydia—the sign of the conversion to Christianity (Acts 16:14–22)—was revered highly by Günther and in the Günther circle.[34] Also mentioned is Mary Magdalene, "who filled the world with the fragrance of nard."[35] Oil of nard is mentioned

---

32. "Litany from a Wide Heart." Erentrud Kraft proposed calling it by this name.

33. For a critical discussion from the present-day view of Lydia as the first European female Christian, see Luise Schottroff, *Lydia's Impatient Sisters: A Feminist Social History of Early Christianity* (Louisville: Westminster John Knox, 1995).

34. Together with Johann Emanuel Veith, Anton Günther published *Lydia, Philosophisches Jahrbuch* in five volumes from 1849 to 1854.

35. The authors apparently consider Mary of Bethany, who anoints Jesus's feet with precious oil of nard (John 12:1–8), to be Mary Magdalene. This interpretation, usual in the Western church since Pope Gregory the Great and found in the Roman Catholic liturgy until after the Second Vatican Council, is exegetically wrong; these are two different women. Nevertheless, it is also clear that the authors of the litany know the Bible and Tradition well and do not class Mary Magdalene as a sinful woman (the woman mentioned in Luke 7:36–50 who anoints Jesus with oil—not with nard

once again later in the litany where the desire is expressed that the praying women "might become a fragrance of Christ" through their discipleship. Two further allusions to Mary Magdalene and her close proximity to Christ are found in the last part of the litany. The approximately twenty-five saints that are mentioned in the second part are all from the ancient church, among them Agnes, Lucia, Caecilia, Paula of Rome, Eustochium, Monica, or the patron saints of the members of the *Kreuzeskränzchen*, such as Hedwig of Silesia, Elisabeth of Thuringia, Hildegard of Bingen, Teresa of Avila, Catherine of Siena, or founders of religious orders such as Benedict and Scholastica, as well as Carlo Borromeo and Vincent de Paul, the "guardians of the sisters of mercy."[36] The history of these saints is part of the history of piety in the church. At the same time, it is obvious that the members of the *Kreuzeskränzchen* see them as models for their own faith and their lives of faith. In the third part of the litany, various concerns are formulated, lifetime wishes of those praying that refer primarily to their discipleship of Christ and to the "partnership in life with the Savior and with each other" in continuity with the discipleship of the first Christians.[37]

A few expressions are typical for the Bonn Günther circle, such as the designation of Christ as "child of God's peace," a reference to the *Heliand*. The ideal of the original times, whether it be the period of the early church or the period of the Christianization of Germany in the early Middle Ages, serves as orientation for the spiritual and intellectual renewal of Germany, now considered as necessary, but also for the renewal of personal faith. The missionary consciousness of a renewal of Christianity is crystallized in the

---

oil!—and who is forgiven many sins by Jesus also was identified since Gregory the Great with Mary Magdalene). Instead, they qualify her as first disciple of Christ. Mary Magdalene is mentioned in the litany already in the petitions to the Son, who appears before her as the resurrected Christ. To what extent the authors also think about the anointing of Jesus's head by an anonymous woman (Matt 26:6–13 and Mark 14:3–9) cannot be answered. On the history of the interpretation of Mary Magdalene in various epochs of church history, see Berlis, "Het ware verhaal van Maria Magdalena…? Over de toe-eigening van een bijbels personage," *Verhaal als identiteits-Code: Opstellen aangeboden aan Gert van Oyen bij zijn afscheid van de Universiteit Utrecht op 1 september 2008*, ed. Bob Becking and Annette Merz, UTR 60 (Utrecht: Universiteit Utrecht, 2008), 60–72.

36. Agnes, Lucia, and Caecilia were three of the seven women mentioned by name in the Canon Romanus. See Berger, "I Love Latin Mass," 272.

37. While in the first part of the litany the answer is "have mercy on us" and in the second part "pray for us," the appeal in the third part is "hear us, we pray."

desire "for a spiritual springtime for the beloved land of the *Heliand*." The reference to current events also is not lacking; it is found in the mention of the trial in Rome against Günther's works, which was still going on in 1855, and of Güntherian concerns, in the invocation, for example, "that you might let scholarship blossom once again, so that it may meet always the needs of the times."

After this short survey of the entire content of the litany, several textual passages are to be examined more closely. Because of the length of the litany, a selection is appropriate. In the following, the invocations directed to Mary are dealt with in more detail. The justification for this selection is the fact that the total of thirty-six invocations, which represent approximately a tenth of the entire litany, together form a thematic unity. They reveal how the authors receive the Bible and tradition and how they position themselves theologically and spiritually with respect to Mary and Marian issues—issues which were omnipresent within nineteenth-century Catholicism.

The invocations are:[38]
1. Holy Mary, pray for us,
2. You, the second Eve,
3. You, Mother of God,
4. Mother of the human race,
5. Mother of the living,
6. Virgin, who has trod on the head of the serpent,
7. You, upon whom God's good will has rested since eternity,
8. You, who has been taken up in the plan of our redemption,
9. You, dawn of eternal day,
10. You, intermediary of our salvation,
11. You, the most delicate, the holiest flower of the people of Israel,
12. You, who has born all the promises in your heart,
13. Whose yearning drew the Savior to earth,
14. You who has entered into the decision of redemption,
15. You humble maid of the Lord,
16. You whose eye resting in eternity was not blinded by the radiance of the angels,

---

38. According to my transcription, SPR, Dom Anselmo Nickes Papers. After each invocation, all respond with "pray for us." My transcription of the litany differs from Wenzel's transcription in Wenzel, *Freundeskreis*, 80–89 in a few places; in this section on Mary, Wenzel reads invocation thirty-four as, "You jewel of the whole church."

17. You who hastened over the mountains of Juda to the holy Elizabeth,
18. You, the one praised as blessed by Elizabeth,
19. You, who has made the dignity of your election to be the praise of the Lord,
20. You bride of the holy Joseph,
21. You, who bore the Savior in the stable,
22. You guardian of the eternal Word,
23. You witness of His deepest humiliation,
24. You who bore all of His words in your heart,
25. You Aeolic harp beneath the Cross,
26. You virgin rich in sorrows,
27. You strong, noble woman who stood under the Cross,
28. You mother comforted from the Cross,
29. You mother of the saved.
30. You who first looked upon the Resurrected One,
31. You comforter of the holy John,
32. You, in whose composure Saint John's enthusiasm found the right balance,
33. You mother loved by the holy John with the devotion of a son,
34. You jewel of the young church,
35. Holy Virgin, whose body saw no decay,
36. You Queen of all the saints.

In the invocations, Mary's role in the incarnation, her status as witness at the foot of the cross (23), as well as in her exemplary significance for the church, stand at the focal point. How is Mary described in particular in the litany?[39] The "second Eve" (2) appears already in the works of the church fathers, who applied Gen 3:15 typologically to Mary and her son. The intercession "Virgin, who has trod on the head of the serpent" (6) likewise takes up this Bible verse. "Mother of God" (3) is a title that harkens back to the ecumenical councils of Ephesus (431 CE) and Chalcedon (451 CE). The first invocations in the litany designate Mary's role in the events of salvation and her creaturely collaboration. "God's good will has rested" upon her "since Eternity" (7) and she has "been taken up in the plan of our redemption" (8). Mary is called "Mother" three times at the beginning

---

39. In the following, I thankfully make use of Erentrud Kraft's exact analysis of the invocations addressed to Mary. I have taken over her comparisons with the *Lauretanian Litany*. The numbers in parentheses refer to the invocations of the litany.

of the litany (from a total of six times): she is the "Mother of God" (3), mother of the human race (4), and—in the succession of Eve—"Mother of the living" (5). The designation "mother of the human race" is not found in other litanies.[40]

In contrast to the *Lauretanian Litany*, where Mary's being a virgin is mentioned seven times and is connected with such adjectives as "pure," "chaste," "undiminished," "immaculate," and "kind," in this litany Mary is called a virgin only three times (6, 26, and 35). The Virgin treads upon the head of the serpent, sees her son die, and her body does not decay after her death—a sign of her saintliness and particularity. The virginal conception as such is not mentioned in this litany.[41] In the invocations, we meet an active Mary: she, "the most delicate, holiest flower of the people of Israel" (11), who has "born all the promises in her heart" (12), with her "yearning drew the Savoir to earth" (13). She "entered" into "the decision of redemption" (14). The "humble maid of the Lord" (15; cf. Luke 1:48) is to be interpreted in connection with the portrayal of Mary as a self-assured woman.

The other invocations describe the events told of in the Bible and draw primarily upon the gospel of Luke: the annunciation by the angel, by whose radiance Mary was not blinded—in contrast to Zacharias, who becomes

---

40. The idea of Mary's representation of all of humanity runs through scholasticism and mysticism. Elisabeth Gössmann counts these ideas among the positive elements of tradition in the teaching about Mary. The idea implies that men, too, can be represented by a woman. See Gössmann, "Mariologische Entwicklungen im Mittelalter: Frauenfreundliche und frauenfeindliche Aspekte," in *Maria für alle Frauen oder über allen Frauen?*, ed. Elisabeth Gössmann and Dieter R. Bauer, RF (Freiburg im Breisgau: Herder, 1989), 69. The formulation in number five in the litany should be seen in relationship to number twenty-nine.

41. This possibly can be understood as evidence of a constraint approaching prudery in regard to physiological processes. In contrast to the hymns of a Hildegard of Bingen or of Mechthild of Magdeburg, the litany of the *Kreuzeskränzchen* does not really describe conception, birth, and education in detail (cf. 21 and 22 in the litany). See, on the other hand, the small selection of Hildegard's invocations to Mary: "*Calor solis in te sudavit, Verbo Dei infusa, Dei Genitrix, Mater integra* [You, in whom the fire of the sun glowed; You, infused with the divine Word; You, who gave birth to God; You unimpaired Mother]." Quoted by Margot Schmidt, "'Maria, Spiegel der Schönheit': Zum Marienbild bei Hildegard von Bingen und Mechthild von Magdeburg," in *Maria für alle Frauen oder über allen Frauen?*, ed. Elisabeth Gössmann and Dieter R. Bauer, RF (Freiburg im Breisgau: Herder, 1989), 86–115. On Hildegard's invocations to Mary, see 112–14.

speechless before the angel (Luke 1:20)—the visit to Elizabeth, the Magnificat, her engagement to Joseph, the birth in the stable. The interest of the members of the *Kreuzeskränzchen* in the entire litany is not concerned with the story of Jesus's childhood. Mary's role is defined concisely as "guardian of the eternal Word" (22), an allusion to the contemporary role of women as guardians and educators, which, however, is placed in a quite different framework through the reference to the eternal Logos.[42] What follows are several invocations that unfold the memory of Mary under the cross (according to the Gospel of John), who bore the words of her Son in her heart (Luke 2:51).[43] Mary is the "Aeolic harp beneath the Cross" (25)— an unusual image that is not easy to interpret. The Aeolic harp, also called a wind harp or weather harp, is an instrument from which a movement of air coaxed various tones from its tuned strings.[44] It appears a number of times in romantic poetry (Eduard Mörike, but also Johann Wolfgang von Goethe). Mary, the Aeolic harp beneath the cross, resonates in soft tones with the suffering of her child. She is at the same time a "virgin rich in sorrows" (26), a "strong, noble woman" (27), and a mother comforted from the cross (28), who becomes the comforter of her adopted child John (31, 32, and 33; cf. John 19:26–27). She is now the mother of the beloved disciple John and, at the same time, mother of all those who have a part in her son's work of redemption (29). Old traditions report that Mary was the first to see her resurrected son—the members of the *Kreuzeskränzchen* share this view (30).[45] In the last invocations, the esteem for Mary and her significance already found in the early church is expressed. She is the

---

42. The mystic Mechthild of Magdeburg takes up the notion of "*Maria lactans*" and recognizes Mary as the "dispenser of the divine Word." See Schmidt, "Maria," 105.

43. There is a connection between numbers twelve and twenty-four of the litany: Mary is the woman who has carried and kept the promises to Israel and the words of her son "in her heart." As to invocation twenty-four: from the statement that Mary after the first word of Jesus kept all words in her heart (Luke 2:51), the members of the *Kreuzeskränzchen* concluded that Mary *from then onwards* bore all words of Jesus in her heart.

44. Hildegard of Bingen represents the divine-human union of God and human being with the help of music: "The Holy Spirit makes music in the tabernacle of virginity." Quoted in Schmidt, "Maria," 98. In the litany, Mary herself is seen as a musical instrument that is made to sound through the wind of the Spirit. Interesting is the fact that, in the litany, this occurs at the foot of the cross.

45. For example, mentioned by Saint Ambrose in his *Liber de Virginitate*. In the Church of the Holy Sepulchre, there is a chapel of the apparition of the risen Christ ded-

"jewel of the young church" (34). The next to last invocation takes up ideas that deal with the unimpaired preservation of Mary's dead body—this, too, is a notion that already appears early in tradition. At the end of this section, and as a transition to the following section, Mary is designed as "Queen of all saints," that is, she is the leader and the first among the saints. Here, too, a difference to the *Lauretanian Litany* can be discerned. In the latter, Mary is addressed repeatedly as a queen.

On the whole, the many biblical references in the petitions, as well as the knowledge of narratives from the early church and of medieval Marian piety, is striking. The section's structure follows the scheme of the history of salvation. It begins with the story of the Jewish woman Mary, continues with her acceptance of the prophesies and with the most important stations in the life of her son (incarnation, crucifixion, resurrection), and ends with her significance for the church as community of saints. References to Jesus's activity and to the supportive and pleading role of his mother (at the wedding feast at Cana [John 2:1–12], for example) are lacking. Remarkable is the fact that the dogma of the immaculate conception, proclaimed by Pope Pius IX on December 8, 1854, half a year before the emergence of the litany, finds no echo in the litany.[46] Holding fast to the

---

icated to Mary; it can be found next to the Magdalene altar and the angel's crypt. With thanks to Erentrud Kraft for the information about the Church of the Holy Sepulchre.

46. Some notions in the litany may remind today's readers of the rhetoric in the papal bull *Ineffabilis Deus* from December 8, 1854, with which Pope Pius IX elevated the immaculate conception of Mary to the level of dogma. The idea that God's good will had rested upon Mary from eternity (7 in the litany), for example, is similar to the statement in the bull that God had chosen Mary "from the beginning and before the ages." See Heinrich Denzinger and Peter Hünermann et al., eds., *Compendium of Creeds, Definitions, and Declarations on Matters of Faith and Morals*, 43rd ed. (San Francisco: Ignatius, 2012), 2800. On this, two things are to be said: (1) Similar ideas are not found first in the bull of 1854, but already much earlier (for example, in the medieval tradition). They are an expression of pious speculation about Mary's importance in the history of salvation. (2) In the rhetoric of the bull *Ineffabilis Deus*, such statements (among others, too, the reference to Mary who has trod upon the head of the serpent; cf. litany 6) serve to prove that Mary was "always and absolutely free" (Denzinger and Hünermann, *Compendium*, 2800) from "the stain of original sin" (Denzinger and Hünermann, *Compendium*, 2801) and that she "would possess such a plenitude of innocence and sanctity … none greater could be known" (Denzinger and Hünermann, *Compendium*, 2800). Such an intention behind the statements is not found in the litany at all. The same is true of the concept of "intermediary of our salvation" (litany 10; in German: "*Vermittlerin*," not "*Mittlerin*"), which may not be

established ancient tradition of the church, this litany concentrates on a Mary who cannot be revered without her son.[47] It differs from the ultramontane piety in the nineteenth century, in which Mary more and more appears alone, without her son—as in Lourdes or in Marpingen.[48] Thus, the Mother Superior of Saint John's Hospital in Bonn, Sister Augustine (Amalie von Lasaulx), tells, for example, of how the French Mother Superior General of the Sisters of Mercy was quite enthused by a statue of Mary without a child.[49]

3.3. Mary in the Letters from Members of the *Kreuzeskränzchen*

In what way does Mary become the theme in letters from the *Kreuzeskränzchen*? In Ritter's letters to Wilhelm Reinkens, Mary does not play a prominent role at all.[50] Ritter often writes her letters to him on the evening before Sundays and feast days; these reflect the times of the liturgical year

---

understood simply in the sense of a "corredemptrix." It is rather a reference to Mary's *fiat* and collaboration in the divine plan of salvation, in which she becomes the bearer of the promise and the Word. As Schmidt shows, it was precisely the Middle Ages that was familiar with many invocations of Mary that were creative and saturated with images—not least of all through the stimulation of the originally Eastern *Hymnus Akathistos*, which was translated into Latin around the year 800. Cf., for example, Schmidt, "Maria," 95. These, however, are not dogmatic statements, but rather the expression of an—occasionally excessive—Marian piety. The litany of the *Kreuzeskränzchen* is, in comparison, restrained and relies strongly on biblical statements.

47. Mary's motherhood, which in the litany applies primarily to her son, but in a figurative sense also to John and then to the entire human race, plays a large role in the invocations (six mentions, in comparison to three mentions of Mary as a virgin).

48. For a sketch of ultramontane Marian piety, see Michael Pammer, ed., *Handbuch der Religionsgeschichte im deutschsprachigen Raum: 1750–1900* (Paderborn: Schöningh, 2007), 5:271–75 and 546. On nonultramontane Marian piety, see Berlis, "Maria in altkatholischer Sicht," *IKZ* 99 (2009): 33–66.

49. The Mother Superior General was of the following opinion: "The child in her arms is so sensual!" Quoted by Reinkens, *Amalie von Lasaulx: Eine Bekennerin* (Bonn: Neusser, 1878), 107. For Sister Augustine, this view was not only a curtailment of traditional faith, but it also derogated from the orientation on Jesus Christ, an orientation that was so characteristic of her own spirituality.

50. On the relationship between the two, see Berlis, "Gotteskindschaft im 19. Jahrhundert: Geistliche Zwiegespräche zwischen Wilhelmine Ritter und Wilhelm Reinkens," in *Kinder haben, Kind sein, Geboren werden: Philosophische und theologische Beiträge zu Kindheit und Geburt*, ed. Annette Esser et al. (Königstein: Helmer, 2008), 87–105.

and frequently point to biblical texts.[51] In her letter of January 14, 1854, she summarizes the sermon delivered by Hilgers on the wedding feast at Cana (John 2:1–12). The preacher and she along with him assess Mary's conduct as positive. The fact that Mary turns to Jesus "in an insignificant need" should teach us not to be ashamed to turn to our redeemer even in the small concerns of daily life.[52]

On August 22, 1855, Ritter deals with the Magnificat and with the Pentecost hymn sung during the confirmation service. Some of the themes addressed in the letter remind one of the statements in the litany:

> And the *Magnificat* was inexpressibly beautiful; that was really worthy praise of our noble Lady and Patroness that may hasten past her to her divine Son, to Him whose mercy passes from generation to generation; you thought that you could hear her singing it herself, the noble empress in the Heavens, with all the rejoicing of her so highly endowed, noble heart, and yet still as the humble maid of the Lord, in whom it has become truer than in all the saints that "to serve God is to rule."[53] It is really quite unique and wonderful in these old, holy hymns: this grandeur and power paired with this *Kindlichkeit* [being a child] and humility; they really give one a presentiment of the new hymn in the eternal Jerusalem.[54]

Mary indeed occupies a firm place in Ritter's spirituality, but at the same time one that is christologically defined and limited.[55] Ritter sees the Magnificat less as a hymn by Mary than as liturgical praise by those who celebrate liturgy, a praise that in the end hastens "past her to her divine Son."[56] Thus, for example, she writes on August 15, 1867—the high feast of

---

51. See Ritter to Reinkens, June 10, 1865, DPJA.

52. Ritter to Reinkens, January 14, 1854, DPJA.

53. This is a citation from a postcommunion prayer in the post-Tridentine Missale Romanum (Missa Pro Pace): "*cui servire regnare est*." Thanks to Roberto H. Bernet, Madrid, for this information. In the contemporary Roman Catholic Missal, it is part of a collect prayer (feast of Saint Casimir or mass in times of war). Thanks to Berger, Yale.

54. Ritter to Reinkens, August 22, 1855, DPJA. "*Kindlichkeit*" (being a child) has a special meaning in the Bonn Günter circle, which refers to the idea of the human being a child of God. See also note 50 above.

55. On the other hand, it is quite different in the case of the convert Luise Hensel, who had visited the *Kreuzeskränzchen* once in Bonn. In Hensel's piety, Mary plays a central role. See Barbara Stambolis, *Luise Hensel (1798–1876): Frauenleben in historischen Umbruchszeiten*, PBG 8 (Cologne: SH-Verlag, 1999), 84–85.

56. Ritter to Reinkens, August 22, 1855, DPJA.

the dormition of Mary—from Saint Valéry in France, where she was taking a cure, that she must write to Reinkens today "because of the composition." Her remarks about Mary's beauty, however, remain quite general.[57] A few years earlier, on March 25, 1863, Ritter had reacted to Reinkens's sermon on the occasion of the feast of the annunciation of Mary with the remark: "We miss the ordering hand of a mother in our circle."[58] On March 19, 1866, the feast of Saint Joseph, she mentions that Christ had accepted the services of Joseph and Mary.[59]

As a conclusion of this short investigation, it can be stated that the Marian piety in the *Kreuzeskränzchen* oriented itself above all on the biblical Mary and on her commemoration during the liturgical year.[60] Interpretations of Mary by the church fathers are seen here as an exegesis of the biblical message. Interesting, in addition, is the significance accruing to the *Heliand* epic. An excessive Marian piety is alien to the circle. In this sense, the following note from Reinkens that he sent in a letter to his cousin Nickes in Rome dated "Octave Day, Immaculate Conception, 1856" may be understood as a critical remark. In Rome, apparently a statue "in honor of the Queen of Heaven" had been unveiled. Reinkens remarked: "And I am thinking of the Child of God's peace so close to Christmas who gave the world the pure 'muoter unde maget' [Mother and Maid]."[61] Mary was

---

57. Ritter to Reinkens, Saint Valéry, August 15, 1867, DPJA.

58. Ritter to Reinkens, March 25, 1863, DPJA. She writes again on December 27, 1861 about John and Mary.

59. Ritter to Reinkens, March 19, 1863, DPJA. The feast of Saint Joseph became established as an independent feast only in the modern period. Pope Pius IX named Joseph as a patron of the Roman Catholic Church in 1870. Ritter mentions Joseph on his feast day together with Mary. It is not to be forgotten that Joseph was the patron saint of Wilhelm Reinkens's younger brother Joseph Hubert.

60. This orientation on the liturgical church year is found also in another letter from the *Kreuzeskränzchen*. At the end of it, the writer of the letter (Fabricius) mentions the "wonderful" celebration of the "Mother of God devotion [herrliche(n) Mutter Gottes Andacht]" shortly before. Fabricius and Simrock to Nickes, August 21, 1857, SPR. Another letter from the two women is accompanied by a poem about Mary written by the deceased Katharina Reinkens (died 1846) or Mrs. Schütter. The title of the poem is *Maria ist mein Trost alleine* (*Mary Is Alone My Comfort*). Fabricius and Simrock to Nickes, April 9, 1859, SPR.

61. Reinkens to Nickes, Octave Day, Immaculate Conception, 1856, SPR. The "muoter unde maget" is a quote from the *Heliand*. A similar view of Mary is found also among later Old Catholics. The writer Antoinette Schweling, for example, who was educated for a time in a convent, was of this opinion (32). For her, Mary is a

not Ritter's preferred biblical role model; it was, rather, Paul, the apostle to the world. On June 7, 1855, she writes to Nickes in Rome: "How wide must your heart become at the sepulcher of the world's apostle, who carried the whole world in his great heart." Later on in this letter, she writes: "Paul is, of course, also our favorite apostle, because of his wide heart."[62] While the "wide heart" is a reference to the importance of "being open wide" in the Reinkens circle, what is remarkable about this passage is the fact that only Paul is mentioned, and Peter is lacking.[63] In many texts and travel reports by (ultramontane) Roman Catholic Christians in the nineteenth century, Rome becomes more and more the place for Peter and his "successor."[64]

Ritter had a special interest in the contemporaries of Jesus and in the holy women and men of the first centuries. In them, she saw models for her own life, which she originally wanted to realize as a religious sister: "the desire in me to proclaim the praise of the Lord, which He in His great mercy put in my heart so early, to many others in order to help them to join in the praise of our Only Lord burns ever higher."[65] Ritter had to give up her original plan to enter the convent because of health reasons. She took another path and, together with three friends from the *Kreuzeskränzchen*, founded a private school for girls in Bonn. Although Ritter and Wilhelm Reinkens lived only a few hundred meters from each other, they

---

"holy prophetess" (33). In her text, she warns against an exaggeration of the "as such so charming Marian cult" (33). The exaggerated contemporary reverence for Mary (in Lourdes or in Marpingen) and the "mania for miracles" accompanying it (34) displeases her. See Schweling, *Rechte und Pflichten der Frauen und Jungfrauen in der Gegenwart* (Heidelberg: Georg Mohr, 1883). The numbers in parentheses indicate the page numbers in this text.

62. Ritter to Nickes, June 7, 1855, SPR. This reference to Paul appears often in her correspondence. Cf. Ritter to Nickes, February 8, 1862, and January 18, 1864. On February 8, 1862, she writes that John was "too noble and holy" for her.

63. The wideness of the heart is found in Paul in 2 Cor 6:11 and also in the church fathers, for example in Cyprian as "pectus capax." In the Reinkens circle, it served as a greeting ("Marhaba"—wideness) and, at the same time, as an imperative: Be opened wide! By means of this wideness, "all spiritual and academic narrowness is to be overcome" (Wenzel, *Freundeskreis*, 11–13, here 11).

64. There is, of course, a special relationship to Paul through the connection of the Reinkens circle with the Benedictines in Rome, whose monastery is at Paul's sepulcher. Still, it is striking that, where Peter appears in the letters, he is mentioned together with Paul and not just alone, while in more ultramontane texts Peter becomes more and more an independent figure.

65. Ritter to Nickes, October 21, 1855, SPR.

preferred to conduct a personal exchange with each other in letter form. Only Ritter's letters have survived. They are very informative about her view of the Bible. The "yearning for the food of the deeper word of God" was the basis of her community that had formed around Reinkens:

> and it is exactly St. Paula and Eustochium, especially in their relationship to St. Jerome, who have become our dearest models. The Holy Scripture, yes, it also has become the most precious treasure of our hearts since it is no longer a sealed book, thanks to the deep, uniquely beautiful and sensuous explanations and exegeses by our pastor, but rather a deep blue heaven, in which innumerable gleaming stars shine in our blessed eyes, and in which, the longer and deeper we look into it, more and more new stars appear before us, since we foresee more and more new and even more beautiful ones behind the last, the most distant.[66]

The reference to Paula, Eustochium, and Jerome, the translator of the Bible, introduces the theme that preoccupies Ritter. She wants to read the Bible so that it is no longer a sealed book but rather surrenders its treasures. In her letter, she reports that Wilhelm Reinkens had delivered lectures about the Old Testament since the winter of 1856. Ritter begins to learn Latin in order "to be able to understand and to appreciate better the incomparably beautiful prayers and hymns in the original language."[67] She asks the Old Testament scholar Nickes to report on the results of his scriptural studies: "I would really like to have an explanation from you of something from the Psalms, which have become my most favorite prayers, or from the Prophets, especially from Isaiah."[68] But, Ritter is not one to accept simply everything that she hears from her correspondent. Two years later, she discusses her differing exegesis of Ps 133:2, "our favorite Psalm" prayed during the confirmation rite, with Nickes.[69] She finds Nickes's exegesis to be interesting, "but I would not like to accept it as the only possible and correct explanation."[70] For his exegesis "does not edify me or instruct me, and doesn't touch me."[71] In other letters, too, the biblically well-grounded Ritter discusses matters with the biblical scholar. The latter apparently had

---

66. Ritter to Nickes, October 29, 1856, SPR.
67. Ritter to Nickes, October 29, 1856, SPR.
68. Ritter to Nickes, October 29, 1856, SPR.
69. Ritter to Nickes, December 30, 1858, SPR.
70. Ritter to Nickes, December 30, 1858, SPR.
71. Ritter to Nickes, December 30, 1858, SPR.

spoken in a fairly depressed manner after the death of one of his fellow brothers and painted a "gloomy picture" for her. "They were really terribly dark times then (the Migration Period [*Völkerwanderung*], in the eleventh century, etc.) but the fears of the Christians at the time that the end had come always have proven to be immature, and to be opinions not supported by thorough study of the Scriptures."[72] Ritter quotes Acts 1:7, Rom 11:15, and Rom 11:25–26 and comes to the conclusion: "No, Christianity has not yet developed All its Grandeur, and the beneficial consequences of redemption must make themselves felt in the human race in a still different way before the end comes."[73]

The quotations cited above show Ritter to be an active Bible reader, hearer, and interpreter. For her, the worship, because of the sermon but also through use of the psalms, is an important place of encounter with the Bible and with learning about the Bible. This is supplemented by conversations with Reinkens and through lectures that he delivered in the girls' school.[74] The girls' school founded by Ritter and her three friends thus became a community of learning. After Ritter's death in October 1870, the school was continued by two of the previous directors, Marie Simrock (1831–1924) and Wilhelmine Dietzer (1835–1914). Both women entered their names in the list of members of the Old Catholic congregation in Bonn in 1873. The Bonn Günther circle, and more particularly the *Kreuzeskränzchen* and the private girls' school, thus represent important connecting links to Old Catholicism and to the role that was assigned to the Bible there. What was true for Wilhelm Reinkens was advocated also in regard to Old Catholic priests: the priest should be "a man who knows his Bible."[75]

4. Outlook: The Bible and Old Catholic Women

At the third Old Catholics' Congress in Constance in 1873, which was held in the Council Hall (of the Council of Constance, 1414–1418), Joseph

---

72. Ritter to Nickes, August 23, 1859, SPR.
73. Ritter to Nickes, August 23, 1859, SPR.
74. Ritter to Nickes, December 16, 1862, SPR. In this letter, Reinkens describes how he recently (with the aid of the Hebrew text) had studied the Psalms thoroughly and explained about a third of them little by little in the girls' school and in his catechesis (*Christenlehre*). His resumé: "They are all delighted with it. How could it be otherwise?"
75. See the poem by Robert Waldmüller, "Echter Priesterberuf," *AF* 15 (1888): 108.

Hubert Reinkens (1821–1896), the younger brother of Wilhelm Reinkens and, at that time, the newly-consecrated bishop of the German Old Catholics, dealt in a speech with Bible reading.[76] He pointed out: "In the first flowering of early Christianity, during the entire period that we call that of the 'Fathers,' all the theologians were biblical theologians. There was no other theology in the first six centuries of the Church, and still longer, than biblical theology."[77] In the Middle Ages, according to Reinkens, the study of the Bible declined. He continued with this theme by mentioning the Council of Constance, which had ended with a defeat. For men such as Jean Charlier Gerson (1363–1429) and others with him went down to defeat because they believed the falsifications and fabrications: "those men who met in this hall succumbed because they were not filled by the spirit of the Holy Scriptures."[78]

It is clear that, for Reinkens, reading and understanding the Bible was a matter of the greatest explosiveness in church policy that was also a protection against mistakes. Thus, it is no wonder that Reinkens states that Pope Pius IX understood neither Greek nor Hebrew.[79] This was not merely a reference to a harmless educational failing, nor to the education of theologians in Italy, but rather a fundamental assessment of this particular pope and of the (mistaken) dogmatic decisions made by him.

For Old Catholics, male and female, according to Reinkens, "who entrust themselves to my episcopal leadership, there exists no prohibition on reading the Bible."[80] In allusion to Mary of Bethany, he encourages the believers to "read again and again in the holy book, sitting at the feet of the Lord in humility and joy; for, 'He alone has the words of eternal life.'"[81] The journal *Altkatholisches Frauenblatt* was to refer eleven years later to Reinkens's appeal in pleading for the introduction of an Old Catholic family Bible. Preceding this was the discovery that translations of the Bible had appeared in revised form since 1870. In the *Altkatholisches Frauenblatt*, it was reported:

---

76. A few months before, in February 1873, an article by an unnamed author with the title "Ueber Bibellesen" (On Bible Reading) had appeared in the *DM* 4 (1873): 59–60.

77. Quoted from "Vom Constanzer Congreß," *DM* 4 (1873): 297.

78. Quoted from "Vom Constanzer Congreß," *DM* 4 (1873): 297.

79. Quoted from "Vom Constanzer Congreß," *DM* 4 (1873): 298.

80. Quoted from "Vom Constanzer Congreß," *DM* 4 (1873): 298.

81. Quoted from "Vom Constanzer Congreß," *DM* 4 (1873): 298.

that thereby the object is all too clearly pursued of reshaping the church constitution and of supporting dogmatically the new dogmas and worship services. In the form of questions, interpolations, and comments, the Papacy—the priestly station devoted over all human beings, even the angels—the excessive veneration of Mary, and the holiness of works, etc. are all moved to the foreground to such an extent that one is diverted entirely from the edifying basic ideas of the piece.[82]

In the next two issues of the *Altkatholisches Frauenblatt*, an *Immediate Appeal by Old Catholic Women to a High Synodical Council for the Production of an Old Catholic Family Bible* was published containing the signatures of Old Catholic women.[83] In their appeal, the women reminded readers that it "is a holy duty to approach the source of revelation by reading the Holy Scriptures, and through this, to deepen our Christian and Old Catholic standpoint even more, and to defend it against Roman attacks. The fact that this long-neglected right is granted to us fully and completely fills us with gratitude and joy."[84]

As a summary of this short outlook, it can be stated that the concern for the biblical foundation of contemporary religious practice is a desideratum of the *Altkatholisches Frauenblatt*.[85] But, the campaign led by Old Catholic women for the introduction of a family Bible also shows how the Bible stood between the two camps in the confrontation. In addition, when women demanded the reading of the Bible as their genuine right, then this did not mean that all (male and female) Old Catholics had uniform ideas on the status of women. In the *Altkatholisches Frauenblatt*, emancipatory opinions as well as those stressing the conventional role of women were expressed,

---

82. Sarah, "Eine altkatholische Familienbibel," *AF* 17 (1889): 119. The contributions made by the female authors in the *AF* are signed as a rule with a biblical pseudonym.

83. "Immediatgesuch altkatholischer Frauen an eine hohe Synodal-Repräsentanz um Herstellung einer altkatholischen Familienbibel," *AF* 18 (1889): 126–27; Rhode, "Eine altkatholische Familienbibel," *AF* 19 (1889): 134–35. The signatories included, among others, Therese von Miltitz, editor of the *Frauenblatt*, and Clara Stens, Mother Superior of the Old Catholic Sisterhood in Essen.

84. *AF* 18 (1889): 126.

85. See, for example, "Erbauliches und Beschauliches: 1. Die Krankensalbung," *AF* 15 (1888): 107–8. This article about the anointing of the sick begins with a quotation from Jas 5:14–15. With reference to the First Bonn Union Conference in 1874, the author emphasizes that the number of the sacraments had been fixed at seven since the twelfth century as a result of theological speculation.

both supported by the Bible.[86] It was to be until well into the twentieth century before women were able to realize their active participation in the liturgy also in the form of liturgical collaboration: as laywomen, as readers/lectors commissioned by ecclesiastical authorities, as leaders of Sunday prayer services without Eucharist, or, since the 1960s, as active creators of women's liturgies;[87] and as ordained women, since the mid-1980s as deacons and since the mid-1990s as priests.[88]

This article has used an example to show how a certain group of women in the nineteenth century read, heard, and interpreted the Bible. The encounter with the biblical texts took place in the context of catechesis, the liturgy, and the (communal) reading of the church fathers, but also in the direct confrontation with the biblical text itself through reflection and discussion. Thereby, a connection was made to personal life. The group described is an example of the "plurality of the life lived by women" in the (Roman and Old) Catholic Church of the nineteenth century.[89] The considerations presented here show not only the importance of the appropriation of the Holy Scriptures in the private sphere and for private use but also how the Bible was seen as an instrument in scholarship and education in early Old Catholicism. This instrument was employed in building up the congregations, but also as a demarcation from ultramontanism.

Bibliography

Aston, Margaret. "Segregation in Church." Pages 237–94 in *Women in the Church: Papers Read at the 1989 Summer Meeting and the 1990 Winter*

---

86. See, for example, the statement by vicar Franz Bergmann that, according to the Bible, the calling of the woman consists "in humble, devoted love for the man" (Franz Bergmann, "Mono: Das Leben des Weibes, part II.," *AF* 16 [1888]: 110–12, here 110).

87. See Berlis, "Laienfrauen und Liturgie: Acht Jahrzehnte 'Frauensonntag' in der altkatholischen Kirche in Deutschland," in *Women, Ritual, and Liturgy/Ritual und Liturgie von Frauen/Femmes, la liturgie et le rituel*, ed. Susan K. Roll et al., YESWTR 9 (Leuven: Peeters, 2001), 215–39.

88. See Berlis, "Women's Ordination in the Old Catholic Churches of the Union of Utrecht," in *Women and Ordination in the Christian Churches: International Perspectives*, ed. Ian Jones et al. (New York: T&T Clark, 2008), 144–54.

89. Berger, "I Love Latin Mass," 267. Berger documents this plurality for the latter part of the twentieth century.

Meeting of the Ecclesiastical History Society. Edited by William J. Sheils and Diana Wood. SCH 27. Oxford: Blackwell, 1990.

Berger, Teresa. "'I Love Latin Mass': Sonntagsgottesdienst und Frauenleben." *ET-S* 1 (2010): 265–81.

———. *Liturgie und Frauenseele: Die Liturgische Bewegung aus der Sicht der Frauenforschung*. PTH 10. Stuttgart: Kohlhammer, 1993.

———. *Sei gesegnet, meine Schwester: Frauen feiern Liturgie; Geschichtliche Rückfragen, praktische Impulse, theologische Vergewisserungen*. Würzburg: Echter, 1999.

———. "Women in Worship." Pages 755–68 in *The Oxford History of Christian Worship*. Edited by Geoffrey Wainwright and Karen B. Westerfield Tucker. New York: Oxford University Press, 2005.

———. *Women's Ways of Worship: Gender Analysis and Liturgical History*. Collegeville, MN: Liturgical Press, 1999.

Bergmann, Franz. "Mono: Das Leben des Weibes, part II." *AF* 16 (1888): 110–12

Berlis, Angela. *Frauen im Prozess der Kirchwerdung: Eine Studie zur Anfangsphase des deutschen Altkatholizismus (1850–1890)*. BKK 6. Frankfurt: Lang, 1998.

———. "Gotteskindschaft im 19. Jahrhundert: Geistliche Zwiegespräche zwischen Wilhelmine Ritter und Wilhelm Reinkens." Pages 87–105 in *Kinder haben, Kind sein, Geboren werden: Philosophische und theologische Beiträge zu Kindheit und Geburt*. Edited by Annette Esser et al. Königstein: Helmer, 2008.

———. "Het ware verhaal van Maria Magdalena…? Over de toe-eigening van een bijbels personage." Pages 60–72 in *Verhaal als identiteitscode: Opstellen aangeboden aan Gert van Oyen bij zijn afscheid van de Universiteit Utrecht op 1 september 2008*. Edited by Bob Becking and Annette Merz. UTR 60. Utrecht: Universiteit Utrecht, 2008.

———. "Laienfrauen und Liturgie: Acht Jahrzehnte 'Frauensonntag' in der altkatholischen Kirche in Deutschland." Pages 215–39 in *Women, Ritual, and Liturgy/Ritual und Liturgie von Frauen/Femmes, la liturgie et le rituel*. Edited by Susan K. Roll, Annette Esser, Brigitte Enzner-Probst, Charlotte Methuen, and Angela Berlis. YESWTR 9. Leuven: Peeters, 2001.

———. "Maria in altkatholischer Sicht." *IKZ* 99 (2009): 33–66.

———. "Women's Ordination in the Old Catholic Churches of the Union of Utrecht." Pages 144–54 in *Women and Ordination in the Christian*

Churches: International Perspectives. Edited by Ian Jones, Janet Wootton, and Kirsty Thorpe. New York: T&T Clark, 2008.

Buschmann, Johanna. *Beuroner Mönchtum: Studien zu Spiritualität, Verfassung und Lebensformen der Beuroner Benediktinerkongregation von 1863 bis 1914.* BGAMB 43. Münster: Aschendorff, 1994.

Chadwick, Owen. *The Secularization of the European Mind in the Nineteenth Century.* Cambridge: Cambridge University Press, 1975.

Denzinger, Heinrich, and Peter Hünermann, ed. *Compendium of Creeds, Definitions, and Declarations on Matters of Faith and Morals.* In collaboration with Helmuth Hoping, Robert Fastiggi, and Anne Englund Nash. 43rd ed. San Francisco: Ignatius, 2012.

Engelhardt Herringer, Carol. *Victorians and the Virgin Mary: Religion and Gender in England, 1830–1885.* GH. Manchester: Manchester University Press, 2008.

———. "The Virgin Mary and Victorian Masculinity." Pages 44–57 in *Masculinity and Spirituality in Victorian Culture.* Edited by Andrew Bradstock, Sean Gill, Anne Hogan, and Sue Morgan. London: Macmillan, 2000.

Frijhoff, Willem. "Toeëigening: Van bezitsdrang naar betekenisgeving." *Tra* 6 (1997): 99–118.

Gause, Ute. "Frauen und Frömmigkeit im 19. Jahrhundert: Der Aufbruch in die Öffentlichkeit." *PN* 24 (1998): 309–27.

———. *Kirchengeschichte und Genderforschung: Eine Einführung in protestantischer Perspektive.* UTB 2806. Tübingen: Mohr Siebeck, 2006.

Gössmann, Elisabeth. "Mariologische Entwicklungen im Mittelalter: Frauenfreundliche und frauenfeindliche Aspekte." Pages 63–85 in *Maria für alle Frauen oder über allen Frauen?* Edited by Elisabeth Gössmann and Dieter R. Bauer. RF. Freiburg im Breisgau: Herder, 1989.

Götz von Olenhusen, Irmtraud, ed. *Wunderbare Erscheinungen: Frauen und katholische Frömmigkeit im 19. und 20. Jahrhundert.* Paderborn: Schöningh, 1995.

Günther, Anton, and Johann Emanuel Veith, eds. *Lydia, Philosophisches Jahrbuch.* 5 vols. Wien: Braumüller, 1849–1854.

Hilgers, Bernard Joseph. *Homilien gehalten in der Kapelle des St. Johanneshospitals zu Bonn: Nach dem Tode des Verfassers herausgegeben.* 2nd ed. Bonn: Karl Drobnig, 1896.

Küppers, Kurt. *Marienfrömmigkeit zwischen Barock und Industriezeitalter: Untersuchungen zur Geschichte und Feier der Maiandacht in Deutschland und im deutschen Sprachgebiet.* Saint Ottilien: Eos, 1986.

Lurz, Friedrich. *Erlebte Liturgie: Autobiografische Schriften als liturgiewissenschaftliche Quellen.* ATL 28. Münster: LIT, 2003.

McLeod, Hugh. "Weibliche Frömmigkeit—männlicher Unglaube? Religion und Kirchen im bürgerlichen 19. Jahrhundert." Pages 134–56 in *Bürgerinnen und Bürger: Geschlechterverhältnisse im 19. Jahrhundert.* Edited by Ute Frevert. KSG 77. Göttingen: Vandenhoeck & Ruprecht, 1988.

Muschiol, Gisela. *Famula Dei: Zur Liturgie in merowingischen Frauenklöstern.* BGAMB 41. Münster: Aschendorff, 1994.

Osterhammel, Jürgen. *Die Verwandlung der Welt: Eine Geschichte des 19. Jahrhunderts.* 2nd ed. HBGHS. Munich: Beck, 2009.

———. *The Transformation of the World. A Global History of the Nineteenth Century.* Translated by Patrick Camiller. AW. Princeton: Princeton University Press, 2014.

Paletschek, Sylvia. *Frauen und Dissens: Frauen im Deutschkatholizismus und in den freien Gemeinden, 1841–1852.* KSG 89. Göttingen: Vandenhoeck & Ruprecht, 1990.

———. "Frauen und Säkularisierung Mitte des 19. Jahrhunderts: Das Beispiel der religiösen Oppositionsbewegung des Deutschkatholizismus und der freien Gemeinden." Pages 300–17 in *Religion und Gesellschaft im 19. Jahrhundert.* Edited by Wolfgang Schieder. IW 54. Stuttgart: Klett-Cotta, 1993.

Pammer, Michael, ed. *Handbuch der Religionsgeschichte im deutschsprachigen Raum: 1750–1900.* Vol. 5. Paderborn: Schöningh, 2007. 271–275.

Reinkens, Joseph Hubert. *Amalie von Lasaulx: Eine Bekennerin.* Bonn: Neusser, 1878.

Sarah. "Eine altkatholische Familienbibel." *AF* 17 (1889): 118–20.

Sawyer, John F. A., ed. *The Blackwell Companion to the Bible and Culture.* BCR. Malden, MA: Blackwell, 2006.

Schmidt, Margot. "'Maria, Spiegel der Schönheit': Zum Marienbild bei Hildegard von Bingen und Mechthild von Magdeburg." Pages 86–115 in *Maria für alle Frauen oder über allen Frauen?* Edited by Elisabeth Gössmann and Dieter R. Bauer. RF. Freiburg im Breisgau: Herder, 1989.

Schneider, Bernhard. "Feminisierung der Religion im 19. Jahrhundert: Perspektiven einer These im Kontext des deutschen Katholizismus." *TTZ* 111 (2002): 123–47.

Schottroff, Luise. *Lydia's Impatient Sisters: A Feminist Social History of Early Christianity*. Louisville: Westminster John Knox, 1995.

Schweling, [Antoinette]. *Rechte und Pflichten der Frauen und Jungfrauen in der Gegenwart*. Heidelberg: Georg Mohr, 1883.

Stambolis, Barbara. *Luise Hensel (1798–1876): Frauenleben in historischen Umbruchszeiten*. PBG 8. Cologne: SH-Verlag, 1999.

"Ueber Bibellesen." *DM* 4 (1873): 59–60.

Wainwright, Geoffrey. "Catherine Winkworth: 'Königin der Übersetzerinnen' deutscher Kirchenlieder." Pages 289–305 in *Liturgie und Frauenfrage: Ein Beitrag zur Frauenforschungaus liturgiewissenschaftlicher Sicht*. Edited by Teresa Berger and Albert Gerhards. PL 7. St. Ottilien: Eos, 1990.

Waldmüller, Robert. "Echter Priesterberuf." *AF* 15 (1888): 108.

Wegman, Herman A. J. *Liturgie in der Geschichte des Christentums*. Regensburg: Pustet, 1994.

Welter, Barbara. "The Feminization of American Religion, 1800–1860." Pages 137–57 in *Clio's Consciousness Raised*. Edited by Mary Hartman and Lois W. Banner. New York: Harper & Row, 1974.

Wenzel, Paul. *Der Freundeskreis um Anton Günther und die Gründung Beurons: Ein Beitrag zur Geschichte des deutschen Katholizismus im 19. Jahrhundert*. Essen: Ludgerus, 1965.

White, Susan J. *A History of Women in Christian Worship*. London: SPCK, 2003.

Woodhead, Linda. "Gender Differences in Religious Practice and Significance." Online: http://eprints.lancs.ac.uk/793/1/Gender_Differences_in_Religious_Practice_and_Significance-revised10th_June.doc.

———. "Gendering Secularization Theory." *KKF* 1 (2005): 24–35. Online: http://eprints.lancs.ac.uk/797/1/copenhagen2.doc.

Let the Woman Keep Silent? Protestant Controversies about Female Preachers and Evangelists

Ruth Albrecht

A Russian countess and a female German tutor are talking about the Bible, which is read in the countess' house in the manner of revivalist piety. The young German woman, who only very recently has come into contact with this kind of Christian life, asks her mistress: "So, when I am convinced that much is not scriptural in my church, may I then not raise my voice against this and bear witness as my heart leads me?" The countess, familiar with this understanding of piety, reacts to this question with the following instruction: "No, my dear, least of all you ... for it is written that the woman should keep silence in the congregation! And history also does not exactly teach us that reformations arise through women."[1] In this short dialogue between the two women, what is expressed clearly is the field of tension attached to the involvement of women in the new piety movements of the nineteenth century. The author describes in an exemplary way how women should conduct themselves according to the view of the broad conservative wing of these groups. Ernst Schrill, the author of this novelistic scene, was one of the first male evangelists who gave up his profession as a pastor in order to be able to devote himself to freer forms of his work.[2]

Among the biblical texts that, in the Christian context, served to circumscribe a woman's place are the famous dicta in 1 Cor 14:34–35 and 1 Tim

---

1. Ernst Schrill, *Jadwiga (Die Natschalniza): Roman aus dem russischen Leben der Gegenwart* (Leipzig: Ungleich, 1897), 53–54.

2. Samuel Keller, who himself grew up in Russia and can be considered as one of the most successful pious writers at the turn of the century, chose the pseudonym Ernst Schrill for his literary works. For his biography, see Ernst Bunke, *Samuel Keller— Gottes Werk und Werkzeug*, ZGG 5 (Gießen: Brunnen, 1961).

2:11–12. Both texts traditionally were explained in the Christian churches in such a way that women were not allowed to proclaim the gospel either orally or in written form. When the social and religious gender models changed in the midst of social upheaval, these texts became the focus of, in part, very vehement confrontations. The history of the Protestant churches in the nineteenth century is characterized by, among other aspects, the fact that numerous free churches, groups, and movements—such as the Salvation Army, the Methodists, the Baptists, the Fellowship Movement,[3] the Holiness Movement, and the Pentecostal Movement—began or spread throughout many areas in Europe. In spite of the differences among them, the concern of the men and women involved in these groups was to intensify, upon an evangelical basis, the daily Christian lives of their members. The orientation upon the Bible and missionary proclamation formed two of the most important elements of the Protestant renewal movements. The great significance ascribed to the biblical texts is expressed, for example, in adult Bible studies. The method of exchanging thoughts and ideas in group discussions about the word of God and its effect upon one's own experiences was a legacy of the Pietism of the late seventeenth century.[4]

Women played a major role in the development and expansion of most of the free churches and groups because the involvement of laypeople of both sexes was one of the characteristics of this Christian milieu. But, exactly here, two lines of tradition collided and led to distinctly different solutions. For if on the one side the unconditional validity of the Bible as God's word was emphasized in the reform groups—against the results provided by exegetical scholarly research, which put into question the truth and revelatory claims of the traditional biblical texts—then there resulted on the other side a tension called forth in the involvement of women active as missionaries, evangelists, and preachers precisely within the framework of these groups. This is shown, for example, in the question of the leadership of Bible study groups, devotions, and missionary meetings; while some women put on events only for their fellow female members, others rejected every form of public or semipublic proclama-

---

3. This typical German movement wanted to bring about reforms in the state churches. It pursued this goal above all through evangelism and the formation of small fellowships which would meet in addition to the worship services.

4. Martin Brecht, "Die Bedeutung der Bibel im deutschen Pietismus," in *Glaubenswelt und Lebenswelten*, ed. Hartmut Lehmann, GP 4 (Göttingen: Vandenhoeck & Ruprecht, 2004), 102–20.

tion as unbiblical. Only a relatively small number of women led meetings for both sexes and also explicitly defended their right to do so. Josephine Butler (1828-1906), the English champion for the rights of prostitutes, reports that, in 1890, she was requested to say a few words in a free church in Geneva. In view of the struggle that she led in common with men and women against the sexual exploitation of women, she complied with this request to speak in the worship service. "All the misgivings against public speaking by women in the church vanished like a light summer cloud in the mid-day sun ... since faith, courage, and patience on the part of women and men alike were necessary."[5] In the case of men who also did not have a theological education, there were hardly any similar debates. Evangelists such as Elias Schrenk, Samuel Keller, and Ernst Modersohn were ordained pastors and had served in a church before they became independent preachers. Male laypeople, such as General Georg von Viebahn, Count Andreas von Bernstorff, Jasper von Oertzen, Jacob Vetter, and Fritz Binde, on the other hand, had been active professionally in the trades, the military, or the administration.[6] They, too, were exposed to, in part, a harsh criticism, although this was sparked more by the content of their statements and not primarily by the fact that, as laypeople, they made the proclamation of the Christian message the content of their lives. The discussions and solutions to the problem of gender as it was focused upon women took very different forms in the evangelical groups. In the following remarks, some of the patterns of theological argument are presented as examples. The diversity in the spectrum of positions and opinions is portrayed by examining five female protagonists. The selection is concentrated upon examples from Germany.

---

5. Letter from Butler on March 25, 1890, cited by George W. Johnson and Lucy A. Johnson, *Von Frauennot und Frauenhilfe: Josephine Butler's Leben nach ihren eigenen Schriften, Aufzeichnungen, Briefen* (Munich: Kaiser, 1928), 203.

6. Jörg Ohlemacher, *Das Reich Gottes in Deutschland bauen: Ein Beitrag zur Vorgeschichte und Theologie der deutschen Gemeinschaftsbewegung*, AGP 23 (Göttingen: Vandenhoeck & Ruprecht, 1986), 48-59; Stephan Holthaus, *Heil, Heilung, Heiligung: Die Geschichte der deutschen Heiligungs- und Evangelisationsbewegung, 1874-1909*, KM 14 (Gießen: Brunnen, 2005), 199-203, 206-12, 393; Ruth Albrecht, "Laientätigkeit als Profession: Profile adliger Männer aus der deutschen Erweckungs- und Gemeinschaftsbewegung," in *Laien gestalten Kirche: Diskurse—Entwicklungen— Profile; Festgabe für Maximilian Liebmann zum 75. Geburtstag*, ed. Michaela Sohn-Kronthaler and Rudolf K. Höfer, TKD 18 (Innsbruck: Tyrolia, 2009), 205-20.

1. On the Diversity of the Activities of Women in the Renewal Movements

1.1. Female Evangelists, Workers in the Kingdom of God, and Biblewomen

Missionaries, deaconesses, Sunday school teachers, and writers—these are descriptions and professions for women that are often met with in the context of the Protestant renewal movements. On the other hand, female preachers, evangelists, or the so-called Biblewomen are spoken of much less frequently. Along with these, there are further descriptions of female activity that did not achieve more than regional currency. A short brochure, for example, speaks of Eva von Tiele-Winckler so: "She was not only the founder and director of a mother house and the other works associated with it, but she was in fact a leader empowered by God of the whole believing community, and the more time goes by the more she also will be recognized as such."[7] This emphatic description, however, was not shared generally; Tiele-Winckler is still seen primarily as the founder of a deaconess community and not as a Christian leadership figure with a far-reaching influence. This example, however, demonstrates the range in the patterns of the perception of active women for whom no concrete models existed. This proved to be both an opportunity and a limitation at the same time. In most cases, no clearly defined job descriptions grew out of the women's involvement. Most were dependent upon either the financial support of their families or earning their own livelihood through their own efforts.

While in the Anglo-American free churches and evangelical movements in the nineteenth century female evangelists were an aspect of many of these communities, there was a markedly strong restraint in Germany in regard to this designation and the phenomenon underlying it. As a rule, there were warnings given about women doing evangelistic work or about female evangelists who occasionally appeared in local contexts. Only a distinctly few women made the claim that their work was comparable to that of the male evangelists and that, for this reason, they could be considered as female evangelists. Stephan Holthaus, in his extensive

---

7. Der Friedenshort, *Unsere Mutter* (Dinglingen: St. Johannes, n. d.), 21. This obituary appeared first in the journal *Die Diakonisse*, which was published by the Association of Mother Houses in Kaiserswerth. On Eva von Tiele-Winckler, see also the article by Ute Gause in this volume.

study on the situation in Germany, summarizes as follows: "Women as full-time evangelists did not exist at all in Germany."[8]

The term *Biblewomen* can be verified only marginally in the German-speaking sphere in the nineteenth century. As a rule, its appearance indicates the direct influence of English models. The German Bible societies, which were founded in close cooperation with the London society beginning in 1806, also partially adopted its methods for disseminating the Holy Scriptures.[9] In 1904, the year of the hundredth anniversary of the British and Foreign Bible Society, there were about eight hundred fifty men worldwide, the so-called colporteurs or Bible messengers, whose task it was to distribute Bibles. In a publication on the occasion of the anniversary of the Bible Society, it says: "The Bible women form a kind of counterpart to the Bible colporteurs."[10] These were sent first of all to oriental countries in order to be able to distribute Bibles to women, since the contact with the opposite sex was denied in general to western men. If it was in any way possible, the Biblewomen attempted to read and to explain sections of the Bible to the women they visited. As theological justification for the attention paid to the Muslim women living in relative isolation, a Pauline text was cited: "In Christ there is neither man nor woman (Gal 3:28). There is no difference. Both are called to the same salvation and can participate in it in the same way."[11] The British Bible Society began in 1884 to employ Biblewomen; by 1904, approximately six hundred fifty were in service. This number makes clear that this model proved to be successful:

> Such work is organized also in the poor quarters of London and other great cities, where the female sex often lives in similar submergence and male evangelists can find no way to them. So, the Bible women join with the Bible messengers and work in their own way on the same task of

---

8. Holthaus, *Heil*, 502.

9. Emil Schultze, *Die Bibel in der weiten Welt: Eine Denkschrift zum 100jährigen Bestehen der Britischen u. Ausländischen Bibelgesellschaft* (Basel: Kober C. F. Spittlers Nachfolger, 1904), 47–51.

10. Schultze, *Bibel*, 97. The *Jahresbericht der Britischen Bibelgesellschaft* in 1880 speaks of sixty colporteurs. The Biblewomen were not mentioned here. See *Auszüge aus dem Jahresbericht der Britischen und Ausländischen Bibelgesellschaft* (London: Bibelhaus, 1854–1887), 16.

11. Schultze, *Bibel*, 101.

paving the way everywhere for the Holy Scriptures and thereby for Him who wants to be the Savior of the entire world.[12]

To the present, the presence of Biblewomen on German soil can be documented only for Berlin. Further research should be devoted to the question of whether there might be indications of this type of evangelical women's work in other large cities with comparable social problems, such as Frankfurt am Main or Hamburg.

This model, of course, was not unknown in Germany, even if only a few examples can be cited. The collection of poems by the Barmen pastor Gustav Adolf Weller contains a contribution dealing with the Christmas celebration held by a young women's association; it has the title *The Bible Cart*. In a kind of prelude, a Spanish Biblewoman with a Bible cart enters the hall where the celebration is taking place and engages in conversation with one of the young women present. The evangelical Spanish woman describes how she travels throughout the country with her cart and, for example, brings a Bible to a shepherd pursuing his work on a faraway hill.[13] The Biblewoman finds fault with the fact that the Holy Scriptures are read so little in Germany. At the end, she presents each woman with a Bible, a bookmark, and a table of Bible readings.

> So, dear daughters, accept gladly,
> What the Spanish Bible woman can give you,
> And may to every one of you in your ranks,
> The Book of Books be a blessing!
> As staff and support, as bread and star,
> May the Word of our God lead you all to the Lord.[14]

This poem illustrates the fact that Biblewomen from the Protestant missionary societies were employed not only in the large cities but also in

---

12. Schultze, *Bibel*, 101.

13. In one passage, she refers to Fritz Fliedner (1845–1901), who looked after evangelical Christians in Spain. He was the son of Theodor Fliedner (1800–1864), who provided the decisive impulse in the origins of the deaconess mother houses in Germany. See Norbert Friedrich, *Der Kaiserswerther: Wie Theodor Fliedner den Frauen einen Beruf gab* (Berlin: Wichern, 2010).

14. Gustav Adolf Weller, *Rosen und Dornen: Dichtungen für die Freuden- und Trauertage des christlichen Hauses* (Barmen: Biermann, 1904), 96. I thank Mr. Günter Balders for making this text available to me.

European countries, such as Spain and Italy, where the majority Catholic populations had little access to the Bible.[15]

The designation *Reichsgottesarbeiterin* (female workers in the kingdom of God) does not go back to English influence but rather reflects much more the fact that the idea of working together on the extension of the kingdom of God lay at the basis of all the social and missionary initiatives undertaken by the female and male representatives of the Protestant revival movements.[16] For this reason, all who moved within this context were considered to be workers in the kingdom of God—all women and men saw themselves committed to the task of proclaiming the gospel as a medium of the divine kingdom. A periodical appeared beginning in 1903 with the title *Der Reichsgottesarbeiter*.[17] This title underlines the fact that women, to be sure, played an important role, but that decisive areas, such as public relations, were characterized by a masculine perspective even in these movements. While men could pursue their activity on behalf of the kingdom of God also within the framework of their professional work as pastors, missionaries, or deacons, this was much more rarely the case among the women. In the context of the holiness and missionary movement, women formed in part their own gatherings in order to think about their specific work profile.[18] Ada von Krusenstjerna, who is dealt with in more detail later in this article, recalled many gatherings in which the committed pious women exchanged views. Among these, especially, were meetings in Berlin: "where deaconesses and women Kingdom of God workers from every part of Germany came together, driven by the fervent desire to sanctify and to cleanse themselves ever more deeply, so that Christ might save unchecked the unfortunate, to whom they have dedicated their lives."[19]

---

15. See, on this, the article by Marina Cacchi in this volume.

16. See Hedwig von Redern, *Andreas Graf von Bernstorff: ein Lebensbild nach seinen Briefen und persönlichen Aufzeichnungen* (Schwerin: Bahn, 1909), 59, 207; Ohlemacher, *Reich Gottes*.

17. Holthaus, *Heil*, 413.

18. See Holthaus, *Heil*, 467–515.

19. Ada von Krusenstjerna, *Im Kreuz hoffe und siege ich: Lebenserinnerungen* (Gießen: Brunnen, 1949), 227.

1.2. Theological Controversies

In the following, only one Bible text is used as an example in order to demonstrate what lines of discussion emerged around the turn of the century in the interpretation of passages that were of decisive significance for women. According to the current widely read Luther translation, based on the revision of 1984, Ps 68:12 reads: "The Lord gives the Word—the women who proclaim good tidings are a great throng" (LB). Martin Luther himself speaks of the "great throng of evangelists."[20] The German Luther Bibles in the nineteenth century follow the reformer so that the Protestant faithful familiar with the Bible knew the term *Evangelist*, but not the word *Evangelistin* (female evangelist).[21] Johann Hinrich Wichern (1808–1881), who provided the impulse for the emergence of the Inner Mission, is a good example of how Luther's translation made its mark on the nineteenth century, so much that it was a matter of course that female evangelists to a great extent became invisible. Wichern referred in his lectures to Luther's translation from the sixteenth century when he demanded that throngs of evangelists (not female evangelists) must arise so that the missionizing of the masses alienated from the church might be a success.[22]

The translation known as the Elberfeld or Brockhaus Bible arose within the ranks of the evangelical revival movements discussed here. It was the declared goal of this translation to reproduce the original text in its most literal form.[23] In accordance with this maxim, the feminine found in the Hebrew text of Ps 68:12 was made recognizable for the first time. In 1871, the formulation of the text was "the women who bring the message are a great army" (EBT). In 1907, the translation became "the women proclaiming the victory are a great throng" (EBT). The text apparatus explains

---

20. Martin Luther, *Die Bibel nach der Übersetzung Martin Luthers* (Stuttgart: Deutsche Bibelgesellschaft Stuttgart, 1985). As a commentary on this translation, reference is made to Luther.

21. Luther, *Die Bibel oder die ganze Heilige Schrift des Alten und Neuen Testaments nach der deutschen Übersetzung D. Martin Luthers*. Im Auftrage der Deutschen Evangelischen Kirchenkonferenz (Halle: Von Cansteinsche Bibelanstalt, 1899).

22. Johann Hinrich Wichern, *Sämmtliche Werke*, ed. Peter Meinhold (Hamburg: Lutherisches Verlagshaus, 1962), 1:94.

23. Albrecht Beutel, "Bibelübersetzungen II.1," *RGG* 1 (1998), 1501; Holthaus, *Heil*, 317–22. The first edition appeared in 1855; John Nelson Darby (1800–1882) and Carl Brockhaus (1822–1899) were the driving forces behind the publication.

that these were "women proclaiming a joyous message."[24] This version of the Bible played an important role in the ranks of the circle of persons investigated in this article.[25]

The Countess Adeline Schimmelmann, as one of the few female evangelists active in Germany, in 1910 used Ps 68:12, among other texts, in her argument in her article "Zum Frauenreden [On Women's Speaking]" in the periodical *Leuchtfeuer*. She maintained that there is a biblical foundation for the evangelical activity carried out by women. The translation used by her probably was inspired by the Elberfeld Bible or by Anglo-American Bible versions. She applies the right granted to women in the Lutheran churches to carry out an emergency baptism to the proclamation of the gospel: "Why ought it not be allowed to them to preach where there is a need for the Gospel? We believe that the powers of darkness would like to delay the hour about which is promised to us that 'throngs of female evangelists [will] preach the joyous message.'"[26] With the aid of this interpretation, the countess saw her own work as confirmed by the Bible. Her adopted son Paul Friedrich Schimmelmann, who supported her missionary and evangelistic work, advocated a similar view in a tract. Here, he considered this psalm as a reference to the "last times" that now have begun. In this eschatological phase, the pronouncement that "the Lord gave the Word through great throngs of women evangelists" will be fulfilled.[27] A further champion of such a translation, who clearly saw that women were meant in Ps 68, was the Swedish-American evangelist Fredrik Franson (1852–1908). Since he at various times was travelling in several European countries, traces of his work became evident in many places, so also in the employment of female evangelists.[28]

---

24. *Die Heilige Schrift aus dem Urtext übersetzt* (Elberfeld: Langewiesche, 1871; repr., Elberfeld: Brockhaus, 1914). The numbering of the verses differs from that in the Luther Bible and counts this verse as Ps 68:11.

25. *Die Bibel in gerechter Sprache*, ed. Ulrike Bail et al. (Gütersloh: Gütersloher, 2006) also uses the formulation "women proclaiming a joyous message."

26. Adeline Gräfin Schimmelmann, "Zum Frauenreden," *Leu* 8 (1910): 26.

27. Paul Friedrich Schimmelmann, *Das Weib schweige?* (Berlin: Adeline Gräfin Schimmelmanns Internationale Mission, n. d.), 4.

28. Edvard P. Torjesen, *Fredrik Franson: A Model for Worldwide Evangelism* (Pasadena, CA: Carey, 1983), 17, 19, 62–63.

The Protestant theologian Gertrud Wasserzug-Traeder (1894–1992) published a study of the missionary work done by women, in which she dealt first of all with questions about the biblical foundation of such work.[29]

> The biblical justification for women's missionary work occupied Bible-believing Christians in Germany very much since the beginning of their work, without a clear and satisfying solution in general having permeated our times. It is without doubt clear that in this question, too, the lines of the Scripture are authoritative for every believing Christian—but it is not so easy really to understand these guidelines given through the Spirit in the Word of God spiritually, and to apply them to life.[30]

Among the arguments cited by Wasserzug-Traeder in her effort to prove that women's right to evangelistic activity is biblically justified is a compilation of Old and New Testament proof texts made by Heinrich Coerper (1863–1936).[31] He cited, among other passages, Ps 68:12 in the following translation: "The women evangelists are a great army."[32] Although Coerper was criticized vehemently in his own ranks for his clear position, Wasserzug-Traeder still adduced him as an "experienced man of God."[33] For both, it was important to get a discussion going in the pious milieu to which they both belonged on the knowledge of the Bible as the divine word. According to this intellectual approach, if women evangelists appeared in the biblical texts, then they had to be considered to be legitimate in the nineteenth and twentieth centuries, too.

2. Reception of the Bible by Selected Women

In the following, a few female protagonists, for whom the Bible was of central significance, will be presented in chronological order. They justified their activities with biblical texts, but in the process developed in

---

29. Gertrud Wasserzug-Traeder, *Deutsche Evangelische Frauenmissionsarbeit: Ein Blick in ihr Werden und Wirken* (Munich: Kaiser, 1927). She taught at the Women's Bible School Malche in Bad Freienwalde. See Holthaus, *Heil*, 497–99, 501–2. The study by Wasserzug-Traeder deals with the development before 1914, that is, above all with the late nineteenth century.

30. Wasserzug-Traeder, *Frauenmissionsarbeit*, 6.

31. Holthaus, *Heil*, 245–48.

32. Wasserzug-Traeder, *Frauenmissionsarbeit*, 9.

33. Wasserzug-Traeder, *Frauenmissionsarbeit*, 9.

quite different ways. Their ways of reading the Bible exhibit many commonalities, which rest upon the premise that the Scriptures of the Old and New Testaments are the revelation of God that speaks directly to individual readers. In the memory of the movements on which these women oriented themselves, they play a subordinate role.

2.1. Marie Palmer Davies (born 1843)

In 1863, the daughter of the Nassau politician Emil Freiherr von Dungern (1802–1862) married the English theologian George Palmer Davies (1826–1881), who had been active in Germany on behalf of the British Bible Society since 1858.[34] As director of the work in Germany and Switzerland, he was ordered to Berlin in 1869,[35] where Marie Palmer Davies continued the involvement that she already had begun in Frankfurt am Main with Sunday school work.[36] At first, she limited herself to typically feminine forms of work in that she primarily turned her attention toward women and children. Beyond this, she was also active as a writer and composed, among other items, an obituary of Butler, whom she had gotten to know personally.[37] According to her, she found in Berlin the model of Biblewomen that had been inspired by two Scottish theologians. The deacons trained by Johann Hinrich Wichern in the *Rauhes Haus* had supported the use of Biblewomen but had withdrawn from the work by the end of the 1860s. Sophie Loesche (née Hahn), the wife of a Berlin banker,

---

34. *Erinnerungsblätter von Freundeshand: George Palmer Davies* (Berlin: Verlag der deutschen Evangelischen Buch- und Tractat-Gesellschaft, 1881), 12. The Society was founded in 1804 in London. See Schultze, *Bibel*; and Holthaus, *Heil*, 65.

35. The depot of the Bible Society was in the Wilhelmstraße 33 and thus in the center of Berlin. The married couple also lived here. In the Berlin address book from 1870, Davies is listed as a preacher: *Allgemeiner Wohnungs-Anzeiger nebst Adreß- und Geschäftshandbuch für Berlin, dessen Umgebung und Charlottenburg auf das Jahr 1870*, 127. In 1880, he is seen as an English preacher and director of the Bible Society: *Berliner Adreß-Buch für das Jahr 1880* (Berlin: Loewenthal, 1880), 132. After his death, his widow moved to the Potsdamer Straße 82c: *Berliner Adreß-Buch für das Jahr 1882* (Berlin: Loewenthal, 1882), 158.

36. Marie Palmer Davies, *Unter Droschkenkutschern: Schlichte Wahrheiten aus dem Berliner Volksleben: Aufzeichnungen*. With a Foreword by Emil Frommel (Schwerin: Bahn, 1903), 5–6.

37. Palmer Davies, *Unvergeßliches aus dem Leben einer gottgeweihten Frau* (Berlin: Trowitzsch, 1907).

continued the work with two Biblewomen and, above all, looked after the families of the cab men. Horse-drawn carriages were the most important means of transportation in the big cities around 1900. Loesche turns up in various contexts of Christian charity work in Berlin.[38]

Palmer Davies took over responsibility for one of the remaining Biblewomen and revived this model that was so little known in Germany. She made reference here to the English woman Ellen Henrietta Ranyard (1810–1879), from whom the suggestions for the employment of Biblewomen had come. Her book, *The Missing Link*, went through numerous editions in England but was not translated into German.[39] Ranyard advocated the idea that, instead of city missionaries, evangelists, or deacons, women from the working class were the most suited for acquainting the impoverished classes of the population with the Bible. She developed clear structures for this work, which were used in Berlin.[40] The Biblewoman employed by Palmer Davies was responsible for about one hundred families and reported to Palmer Davies about her experiences every week. Palmer Davies expanded the work to such an extent that six Biblewomen eventually shared the work. In her experience, "women from the people," from the ranks of minor civil servants, or childless widows were best suited for this work.[41] The Biblewomen were supported by a deaconess, who ministered to the sick.

The network within which Palmer Davies located her work points to the setting of awakened Christians in Berlin, especially to the Fellowship Movement.[42] Thus, there arose a close contact with the Elisabeth

---

38. Thus she took part in Sunday associations as well as in the founding of a children's home. Together with her husband, she gave the Berlin Association for the Care of Feminine Youth a plot of land, upon which a home for young working women was erected in 1892. See Bettina Hitzer, *Im Netz der Liebe: Die protestantische Kirche und ihre Zuwanderer in der Metropole Berlin (1849–1914)*, IW 70 (Cologne: Böhlau, 2006), 193.

39. Ellen Henrietta Ranyard, *The Missing Link; or, Bible-Women in the Homes of the London Poor* (London: Nisbet, 1859). The book was printed in a twenty-sixth edition already in 1861.

40. For Ranyard's biography, see Frank K. Prochaska, *Women and Philanthropy in Nineteenth-Century England* (Oxford: Oxford University Press, 1980), 126–29; and Lori Williamson, "Ranyard, Ellen Henrietta (1810–1879)," *ODNB* 46 (2004), 60–61.

41. Palmer Davies, *Droschkenkutscher*, 12.

42. Palmer Davies was a member of a prayer circle that met at the house of Count Bernstorff. Redern, *Bernstorff*, 207.

church congregation in the Invalidenstraße, as well as with the Moravian Church.[43] Palmer Davies restrained herself from holding public addresses; at the celebrations, to which men were invited, it was, as a rule, male theologians who delivered short talks with biblical exegeses. She also severely limited her contact with the husbands of the women cared for by the Biblewomen. Behind this stood her idea of a classic conservative separation of the genders; the women took care of the daily problems and presented a living example of faith practices that could be followed easily. Palmer Davies instructed the Biblewomen so that they read the Bible, sang, and prayed together with the women and children of the families under their care. In addition, the families were encouraged to have their children baptized. The wives of the cab men were invited to attend a Bible study hour once a week. Palmer Davies led these meetings and delivered talks about biblical texts. Her husband at first took over responsibility for the devotional services. He advised her, though, that she "should begin the evening with a discussion of a Bible text; the women would ask and answer questions uninhibitedly if I myself would take charge of this."[44] There appears not to have been Biblewomen like those Palmer Davies employed in other congregations and associations in the capital city, even though the model of a home visit with Bible reading and prayer definitely was widespread. According to the sources that have become known to the present, the use of Biblewomen in Berlin reached its end with the death of Palmer Davies.

In the German Empire, and especially in the large cities, attention paid to specific groups of persons began to emerge at various places.[45] To this extent, Palmer Davies's activity stood within the context of similar means of procedure. Her Berlin cab men mission found recognition in pious circles. Women, above all, made reference to Palmer Davies; Krusenstjerna, for example, wrote: "She had six Bible women on the English pattern who cared for the families and, once a week, made a report to their director."[46] Countess Marie Esther Waldersee (1837–1914), who was one

---

43. The major celebrations with the cab men's families and the Biblewomen took place in the Moravian Church hall, which was located in the immediate vicinity of the Palmer Davies' residence. Palmer Davies, *Droschkenkutscher*, 13, 26–30.

44. Palmer Davies, *Droschkenkutscher*, 12–13.

45. Holthaus, *Heil*, 225–27.

46. Krusenstjerna, *Kreuz*, 130–31.

of the influential pious benefactors in the empire, characterized Palmer Davies as one of her models.[47]

2.2. Ada von Krusenstjerna (1854–1942)

This noblewoman with Scottish, Swedish, and German antecedents, several generations of which lived at times in the Baltic region and in close connection with the Russian court of the Czar, spent her childhood in Saint Petersburg. The family belonged to the Lutheran Church. Ada Barclay de Tolly-Weymarn married a Baltic nobleman in 1883.[48] Toward the end of the 1870s, she came into contact with noble circles who were influenced by Granville Waldegrave Lord Radstock (1833–1913) and Dwight Lyman Moody (1837–1899), and therewith by the Anglo-American Holiness Movement.[49] In 1888, Krusenstjerna began a sort of Sunday school on her family's estate. "On Sundays … Finnish and Estonian peasants gathered in the great parlor, where I told them about the Savior."[50] She had no second thoughts about whether she, as a woman, might proclaim the gospel to men. The notion of class, which was especially pronounced in the czarist empire, did not permit the male estate dependents and the peasants to appear under the category of men. These, rather, formed a portion of the extensive house and estate community, in relation to which the nobles of both sexes were placed on a higher level.

On her Swedish estate near Kalmar, Krusenstjerna took up forms of work that were widespread in the renewal movements: "I introduced children's worship services, founded a small singing association for youth, conducted Bible study sessions for the parents."[51] About her own Bible reading in this period, she writes: "I learned to read my Bible in a more thorough and systematic way; I realized its magnificence more and more. I was astonished at the consistency and wisdom, which also gave me the

---

47. Elisabeth Gräfin Waldersee, *Von Klarheit zu Klarheit! Gräfin Marie Esther von Waldersee gewesene Fürstin von Noer, geb. den 3. Okt. 1837, gest. den 4. Juli 1914; Ein Lebensbild* (Stuttgart: Deutscher Philadelphia-Verein, 1919), 261. Waldersee, Palmer Davies, and Krusenstjerna met together in the 1880s in Berlin (Waldersee, *Von Klarheit zu Klarheit!*, 271).

48. Krusenstjerna, *Kreuz*, 9–114.

49. Krusenstjerna, *Kreuz*, 80–81, 85; cf. Holthaus, *Heil*, 27–28, 50, 427.

50. Krusenstjerna, *Kreuz*, 133.

51. Krusenstjerna, *Kreuz*, 147.

right solution for earthly life. But I also understood that it must remain a closed book for those who love the darkness more than the light [cf. John 3:19]."[52] This way of interpreting the biblical text clearly shows the influence of those persons and groups on which Krusenstjerna oriented herself and about which she made notes in her autobiography. In Stockholm, she got to know the Salvation Army, which she at first considered with some reservation. The knowledge "that the Gospel and social aid should never be separated" became important for her.[53] The Salvation Army was exemplary in putting this program into action. As long as she lived in the Swedish capital, Krusenstjerna took part in already existing Bible study groups in the women's prison; these were led by "earnest Christians" both female and male.[54] An account in her autobiography shows how she imagined the effect of Bible reading. A female prisoner had to spend several days in solitary confinement as punishment. "There lay a New Testament. She opened it and read the fourteenth chapter of John. Suddenly, she was so overwhelmed that it seemed as though Christ himself spoke with her. She went down on her knees and implored him to save her."[55]

In Germany, Krusenstjerna often took part in the meetings of the Blankenburg Alliance beginning in 1880. Anna Thekla von Weling (1837–1900) had come into contact in England with the Evangelical Alliance, a movement influenced above all by Anglo-Saxon evangelicals. She created the German center of this interdenominational movement in Bad Blankenburg in Thuringia.[56] Here, it was exclusively men who explained the Bible. Through her contacts with the Salvation Army, Krusenstjerna was strengthened in her opinion that biblical texts such as Isa 58:8–9 and Mark 16:17–18, which speak of healings as signs of divine grace, also had to be valid in her time. She herself did not suffer from illness, but she had experienced healings in her environment that were caused by prayer.[57] With this conviction, too, she moved within the range of views and practices that were widespread in the evangelical revival movements of the late

---

52. Krusenstjerna, *Kreuz*, 151.
53. Krusenstjerna, *Kreuz*, 158.
54. Krusenstjerna, *Kreuz*, 171–73.
55. Krusenstjerna, *Kreuz*, 172. By the reference to John 14, she probably means the verse in which Jesus designates himself as the way to the Father (John 14:6, 9).
56. Krusenstjerna, *Kreuz*, 135–38, 188; Holthaus, *Heil*, 177–82.
57. Krusenstjerna, *Kreuz*, 181–83.

nineteenth century.⁵⁸ In Leipzig, Krusenstjerna and her family moved into a house in whose vicinity many cab men lived. On the "model of Mrs. Davies," she began to turn her attention to them with missionary intent. "As soon as we were established, we invited some of them for a cup of tea. From this arose weekly Bible study meetings; our dining room sometimes was so full that some had to sit in the anteroom."⁵⁹

Krusenstjerna was of the opinion that "the Bible must not only be read, but rather also lived."⁶⁰ According to this maxim, exegetical questions were not of any interest at all. The only important thing was to gain practical instruction for one's own life from reading the Bible. When she and her husband had to sell the estate in Sweden, she held a farewell meeting for the estate dependents and the local villagers. She based her remarks on this occasion on John 10:28, according to which no one can snatch the believers out of the hand of Christ:

> This word filled me so much, and I attempted to let it penetrate their hearts, too, as a divine reality. Most of them, of course, were of good will. At the end, all of us knelt down together.... Standing at the doorway, I took leave of them and gave each person a New Testament along with a letter, in which I had described the path to Jesus in the simplest words possible.⁶¹

A passage from Krusenstjerna's notes illustrates what different concepts of gender and piety could collide with each other in the Protestant milieu. The noblewoman Krusenstjerna lived since 1897 in Dresden and sought out those of like mind there:

> I asked a relative whether there was not a small circle in Dresden where one could read the Bible together. "My dear, what you want is, of course, to instruct and covet everyone; it's a dreadful haughtiness; we have everything we need, wonderful worship services. Please, be a little less pious, but have more love." Oh, these dear "devout and reputable women," as Acts 13:50 calls them; how they at all times together with their "superiors," to whom they are blindly subjected, have obstructed the Kingdom of God!⁶²

---

58. Holthaus, *Heil*, 363–94.
59. Holthaus, *Heil*, 138.
60. Krusenstjerna, *Kreuz*, 161–62.
61. Krusenstjerna, *Kreuz*, 166–67.
62. Krusenstjerna, *Kreuz*, 187.

The background of Acts 13:50 was formed by the presence of Paul and Barnabas in Antioch in Pisidia, where they aroused great interest among the Jews as well as among the Greeks; there were numerous conversions. There is evidence that wealthy women were supporters of many synagogues. However, they kept a certain distance in regard to the Jewish faith. Krusenstjerna transfers this negative characterization directly to a supposedly Lutheran Christian woman of the imperial era. As this quotation shows further, Krusenstjerna used a contemporary Luther translation of the Bible. After she had gotten to know several churches in Dresden, she expressed vehement criticism of the preaching in them and of the limitations imposed on the range of women's functions connected with it. The priesthood of all believers, so she said, had been forgotten. In her estimate, the church did nothing against "the degradation of the woman."[63] Krusenstjerna moved within the circles of the evangelical renewal movements, which, more strongly than the Lutheran churches, emphasized the inspired nature of the divine word and, at the same time, proceeded in social matters in a decidedly progressive way. In Dresden she helped to found a congregation as part of the Fellowship Movement, where, "fashionable ladies, workmen's wives, and servant girls [shook] hands" with each other while singing together.[64]

Krusenstjerna's children grew up in the pious world of their mother. "The Bible was the most interesting book for them. The infant Samuel, David, Daniel were their friends, whose experiences and example influenced their lives as children."[65] Their devotions, which they held above all for other children, were published by their mother in 1903 under the title *Unsern Kindern (To Our Children)*.[66] In regard to the origin of the book, she wrote: "It soon became the greatest joy for me to immerse myself in the Bible, to become a child myself and, with a simple heart, let the divine Word work upon me as though I had heard it for the first time."[67] Not only her children, but she herself, too, lived with the figures of the Old Testament: "The widow from Sarepta is my special friend. She was weak and anxious like me, but she listened to God's voice, so that He could give her

---

63. Krusenstjerna, *Kreuz*, 189.
64. Krusenstjerna, *Kreuz*, 195.
65. Krusenstjerna, *Kreuz*, 198.
66. Krusenstjerna, *Kreuz*, 199.
67. Krusenstjerna, *Kreuz*, 198.

commissions and she could recognize the connection between internal and external occurrences [cf. 1 Kgs 17:9; 24]."[68]

2.3. Countess Adeline Schimmelmann (1854–1913)

Born in Ahrensburg, near Hamburg, the countess was one of those women who appeared beginning in the middle of the nineteenth century first in England and then later also in Germany and, like the laymen, made evangelization and mission the chief purpose of their lives. From the end of the 1880s, she involved herself in social-charitable work and then gradually shifted the focus of her activities to addresses and evangelizing lectures. In the 1890s, she began, in addition, to publish her own texts. Her most well-known work is her autobiography, which appeared in 1896/1898.[69] Shortly after the turn of the century, she founded a publishing house in Berlin, in which her monthly journal *Leuchtfeuer* also appeared. After her death, her coworkers and friends were not successful in continuing the work begun by her.[70]

Schimmelmann's parents belonged to the Lutheran Church and let their children be educated at home. The catechism and the Bible formed important elements of this instruction. The countess discusses her love for a Bible edition that was widespread in the nineteenth century: "My most favorite plaything was the large Schnorr Picture Bible. I could lay for hours on the floor looking at the wonderful pictures that were spread out around me, and I lived completely in the scenes that they portrayed. The noble lines of Schnorr's figures made a deep and lasting impression on my child's mind."[71]

Although it can be recognized clearly here that the piety advocated by Schimmelmann reflects the characteristics of the Fellowship and Holiness

---

68. Krusenstjerna, *Kreuz*, 226.

69. Schimmelmann, *Streiflichter aus meinem Leben am deutschen Hofe, unter baltischen Fischern und Berliner Socialisten und im Gefängnis, einschließlich "Ein Daheim in der Fremde" von Otto Funke*, 1898, repr. ed. Jörg Ohlemacher (Leipzig: Evangelische Verlagsanstalt, 2008). The work appeared in 1896 in English; the German edition from 1898 is a translation from English. The reprint used here reproduces the first German edition.

70. Ruth Albrecht et al., *Adeline Gräfin von Schimmelmann: Adlig, Fromm, Exzentrisch* (Neumünster: Wachholtz, 2011), http://www.adelineschimmelmann.de.

71. Schimmelmann, *Streiflichter*, 23. See, in addition, the article by Elfriede Wiltschnigg in this volume.

Movement, she took pains to describe her path as unaffected by outside influences. She attributes her conversion exclusively to her prayers and the reading of the Bible: "My cold heart now began to burn, not because of my love for Christ, but rather because of His love for me. Now I was His and His alone. I felt that I could live only for Him. But, how should I do this? I took my Bible in hand and found to my astonishment that the way was described clearly and distinctly there."[72] After this passage, she cites Luke 14:12–14 in order to emphasize that faith must find expression in charity toward the needy. Already in her time as lady-in-waiting to the German empress Augusta (1811–1890), Schimmelmann began her work in founding a fisherman's home on the Baltic Sea island of Rügen, which provided social support to fishermen threatened with poverty. The home program offered group singing as well as devotional services, which the countess herself conducted for the men.

In her missionary-social work as well as in her evangelistic lectures, the Bible played a significant role. Besides tracts, she also distributed Bible editions to the fishermen and seamen.[73] The way she dealt with the Bible can be termed as nonreflective and naïve. She shows a similar attitude in her theological positions and in her opinions about denominational differences. She characterized her standpoint with the following words: "I am a member of the Lutheran Church, but my position in regard to the Christians of all denominations is simply put by Paul: 'Grace be with all those who love our Lord Jesus Christ with a love incorruptible.'"[74] Her addresses during her evangelistic campaigns had a characteristic feature. One can confirm that, to be sure, she chose Bible passages as her motto and gladly inserted biblical verses in the course of her remarks, but she really did not exegete these. She connected texts in an associative manner with her own experiences, which formed the chief content of her speeches. She quite often encouraged her hearers or readers to take the Bible in their own hands in order to be able to comprehend the faith experiences described by her.

In 1901, the countess gave evangelistic lectures on several evenings in Stuttgart. The second lecture took up several verses from 1 Cor 13. Among the many other Bible passages that the speaker wove into her remarks was Isa 58: "I ask all of you who have a Bible—(I hope that all the listeners have one, and that those who do not will get one)—to read the fifty-eighth

---

72. Schimmelmann, *Streiflichter*, 34.
73. Schimmelmann, *Streiflichter*, 42.
74. Schimmelmann, *Streiflichter*, 119. Cf. Eph 6:24.

chapter of Isaiah carefully and to see in it what simple, clear, and apparently small commands the Lord gives, and what immensely great promises he connects with them." After a few citations from this chapter, the evangelist concludes this passage with the sentence "each promise is more beautiful than the others, and the Lord keeps them all."[75] Schimmelmann then gives an example from her evangelistic work in England and connects several instructions to her Stuttgart audience with it. She had given a New Testament to a longshoreman by the name of Jack and had urged him to read in it and to turn to Christ in prayer. After a time, the man came back and remarked to her: "What kind of book is this that you have given to me? Everything in it is about Jack!" The listeners then are spoken to directly:

> Why don't you just once take up the Bible so scorned by you? Pick out what the Savior himself said, and then you will see: The whole book speaks about Jack; it speaks personally about you, whoever you are, and here are the treasures of the truth; here is the Kingdom of Heaven that soon will show you that you are not such a fine a human being as you think, but rather that you are a poor sinner who has the Savior who pays the penalty for your guilt.[76]

Schimmelmann's biblical explanations make use of the patterns that were widespread in the revival and holiness movements. An application as direct as possible to one's own personal life was one of the interpretive patterns of these groups.

2.4. Cäcilie Petersen (1860–1935)

In 1904, Cäcilie Petersen founded the Deaconess Mother House Salem in Berlin-Lichtenrade, which was moved to Bad Gandersheim in 1960 and continues to exist today as a retirement home.[77] She moved within circles in northern Germany and Berlin that can be ascribed to the Fellowship

---

75. Schimmelmann, *Sechs Vorträge*. Printed as a manuscript (Barmen: the author, 1901), 18.

76. Schimmelmann, *Vorträge*, 50.

77. Johannes Weber, *Die dem Himmelreich Gewalt antun: Die Kraft des Glaubens und des Gebetes im Leben der Diakonissen-Oberin Cäcilie Petersen* (Neumünster: Christophorus, 1936), 65–69. www.dmh-salem.de; https://www.lichtenrade-berlin.de/historisch-diakonissenhaus-salem.

and Holiness Movement.[78] Before the founding of her own fellowship, Petersen moved with a small group of sisters temporarily to Silesia and took up residence in the castle belonging to Count Eduard von Pückler (1853–1924), one of the founders of the Fellowship Movement and an important mentor of the Young Men's Christian Association (YMCA).[79]

Petersen makes the count responsible for the fact that she did not adhere literally to the command of the Bible as a woman to keep silent. She describes the situation in the count's castle so:

> Since service to human souls was the highest and most important to him, he asked me whether I would not be willing to lead devotions. I could not respond to this request immediately because I kept to the word: the woman may keep silence in the congregation, and here I looked at myself. But, since I saw that it did not please the Count that I did not agree, I went to my room and spoke with God.[80]

From a chest of quotations, a collection of Bible verses, she drew a card after a prayer and saw God's answer to the question she directly asked him in prayer. The Bible verse was from Jer 1:7; "Everywhere I send you, you shall go, and all that I command you, you shall speak" (NASB). From this, she drew the conclusion:

> I followed such a divine commission gladly and hurried to the Count to tell him that I was willing to speak. Meetings were appointed straightaway for that very evening and a time of rich blessing began. The gospel of the Savior of all sinners was accepted with great joy and there arose a yearning for forgiveness of sins, and hundreds found their peace.[81]

Here, one Bible verse is trumped by another. With the help of the construct that God intervenes, so to say in direct conversation through prayer and the chance selection of the card, the deaconess who, according to her own understanding of the Bible, is not permitted to speak can accept the divine commission. It is not the request of the like-minded count which

---

78. Holthaus, *Heil*, 433–34, 502–3; Wilhelm Schneider, *Sie hat Gott vertraut: Cäcilie Petersen; Ein Beitrag zur Geschichte der Erweckungsbewegung* (Metzingen: Brunnquell, 1974).
79. Ohlemacher, *Reich Gottes*, 43–48.
80. Schneider, *Petersen*, 21; cf. Weber, *Himmelreich*, 37.
81. Schneider, *Petersen*, 21.

is the legitimation but rather the *vox ipsissima*, God's direct sign. It is not important here to qualify 1 Cor 14:34 with exegetical arguments or to suspend it temporarily, but rather the prohibition remains fundamentally valid. The author of the Bible, God himself, goes beyond his own text. The violation of the biblical instruction is legitimated above and beyond this also through the fact that many came "to the living faith," as it is called in this terminology, through the evangelistic meetings at which Petersen speaks.[82] Hundreds of saved human beings who accept this form of Christian belief represent something of greater value than an unconditional adherence to the literal text as it is laid down in the Letter to the Corinthians. One of Petersen's biographers characterizes her evangelistic lectures so: "The Mother Superior's manner of evangelizing was her very own. The exegesis of a biblical text that she had chosen and that she had read aloud was not her strong suit. Her proclamation had more of the character of witnessing."[83]

In 1905, Petersen took part, at the invitation of Pastor Modersohn, in evangelistic campaigns near Mülheim/Ruhr and delivered sermons and held lectures.[84]

> When, a short time afterward in a circle of leading men and women in the Fellowship Movement, the pros and cons of women speaking in public meetings was discussed, Pastor Modersohn remarked that the great revival in Mülheim/Ruhr and environs was initiated by a woman, and Count Pückler emphasized in opposition to those who were against women speaking that Cäcilie Petersen represented an exception.[85]

Neither Count Pückler nor Modersohn advocated a theological debate about the further validity of 1 Cor 14:34. They also are not generally seen as advocates of female preachers or female evangelists. The fact that revivals were caused by the involvement of women counted for more than the literal adherence to Pauline instruction. Characteristic for the argumentative confrontation, or nonconfrontation, with this question is

---

82. Weber, *Himmelreich*, 37.
83. Weber, *Himmelreich*, 39; on her evangelistic journeys, see 38–39.
84. On Ernst Modersohn, see Holthaus, *Heil*, 567–69. In his autobiography, Modersohn discusses this revival in detail, but does not mention a participation by women as speakers. See Modersohn, *Er führet mich auf rechter Straße* (Stuttgart: Oncken, 1948), 158–69.
85. Schneider, *Petersen*, 28.

the fact that the discussion about it was conducted in small circles in order not to let misunderstandings arise about the validity of the Bible. Only a few male theologians in this milieu clearly took a position in favor of the justification of female preaching and missionary addresses. All practical work, or female support of the men who preached and missionized, did not present any difficulties at all.

According to the recollections of the sisters in her fellowship of deaconesses, the Bible occupied a secure place in Petersen's life: "Our Mother was a Bible reader. I saw her again and again with her dear Bible book.... How often did she caress with a loving hand the open pages of this book, and was glad when God spoke to her so personally, or when He had given a word as confirmation of an answer?"[86] This description makes clear how Bible reading formed a connection with the piety that was nurtured in the Fellowship and Holiness Movement.

2.5. Minna Popken (1866–1939)

While the women presented in this article are in general not really adequately researched, this is true especially for Minna Popken.[87] Interesting is the fact that the Swiss community Oberägeri, where she lived for more than twenty years, devotes a portrait to her on its internet site. Here, it is emphasized that she founded "a rigorously Protestant-oriented spa with a fundamentalist character" in a poor Catholic area.[88] Born in Bremen, Popken began a search without any support from her parents for a religious orientation, which she found only after years of looking.[89]

Popken's biography shows similarities in many passages with those women who took an active part in the women's rights and women's education movements, since she was one of the first to complete her degree in

---

86. Weber, *Himmelreich*, 73.

87. She wrote an autobiographical account, which appeared in two volumes: Minna Popken, *Im Kampf um die Welt des Lichts: Lebenserinnerungen und Bekenntnisse* (Hamburg: Severus, 2010); Popken, *Unter dem siegenden Licht: Lebenserinnerungen und Zeugnisse* (Berlin: Furche, 1940). The biography by Hans Bruns presents excerpts from her autobiographical works. See Bruns, *Minna Popken: Eine Ärztin unter Christus*, ZGG 55–56 (Gießen: Brunnen, 1967). Entries about her in theological lexica do not exist.

88. See http://www.oberaegeri.ch/de; cf. also https://www.zentrum-laendli.ch/geschichte-zentrum-laendli.

89. Popken, *Kampf*, 4–22.

the study of medicine.⁹⁰ She, to be sure, decided to give up her license to practice as a doctor, but she still found use for her medical knowledge. The methods of treatment used in the institutions led by her followed, at that time, the current health concepts.⁹¹ As one of the very few from the sphere of the Fellowship and Holiness Movement, Popken had a positive opinion of Sigmund Freud's psychoanalysis and worked for years with analytical forms of therapy.⁹² Her piety oriented on mysticism stood in tension to these traits of Popken's personality. From time to time, she withdrew for several weeks into seclusion in order to pray.⁹³

After a failed marriage and the death of her child, Popken settled south of Zürich in the canton of Zug in Switzerland. First, she founded a small Christian spa under the name *Rothaus* in the village of Oberägeri; in 1911, she took over a larger building called *Ländli* in the same place.⁹⁴ When she withdrew in 1925, deaconesses with a similar point of view carried on her work further. Decisive impulses for Popken's life orientation came from Samuel Zeller (1834–1912) from Männedorf in Switzerland, Otto Stockmeyer (1838–1917) from Hauptwil, also in Switzerland, as well as from Johannes Seitz (1839–1922) from Teichwolframsdorf in Thuringia. All these men led Christian sanitoria in the spirit of the Holiness Movement.⁹⁵

Popken's autobiographical remarks reflect her intensive occupation with the Bible; literal quotations and associations characterize her writing style. About her work she writes: "The medical art in combination with service to the Gospel formed my chief concern."⁹⁶ According to Popken's recollections, the words of a clergyman from Zürich were the impetus for her to begin to conduct morning devotions. In conversation with him, she referred to 1 Cor 14:34 and explained that the proclamation of the word

---

90. Popken, *Kampf*, 149.
91. Popken, *Kampf*, 38–102, 150–51, 178.
92. Popken, *Kampf*, 129; Popken, *Licht*, 78–128.
93. Popken, *Kampf*, 47–52, 54–59. In these phases, she occupied herself intensively with the works of the French mystic Jeanne-Marie Guyon (1648–1717); see Popken, *Kampf*, 47–48.
94. Popken, *Kampf*, 141–202. In both institutions, only women were admitted to treatment; men could take part in the life of the house community as guests. See especially Popken, *Kampf*, 167.
95. Popken, *Kampf*, 175–76; cf. Holthaus, *Heil*, 336–41, 368–71. Stockmeyer also played a role for Krusenstjerna; see Krusenstjerna, *Kreuz*, 188.
96. Popken, *Licht*, 17.

"was, of course, a matter for the man."[97] His reply was: "A bright woman like you, who already has done so much intellectual work, should not succeed in creating a simple morning devotional service?... Well now, you studied medicine without hesitation, and now you want to draw such a tight circle around yourself?"[98] In the following years, she led a Bible study hour every morning in rotation with two female coworkers "for the deepening of the inner life." "There we were allowed to say something about eternal things, something neither fictitious nor acquired, but rather what was given to us by God. Then there worked among us the life itself that once came from Heaven in order to bring the eternal light to the world and to build God's Kingdom on this dark earth."[99] Medical treatment receded more and more into the background; Popken conceded the greater importance to the proclamation of the word of God.[100] She accounted her institutions among the "houses of faith in which proclamation of the Word is the chief task."[101] Popken considered daily Bible reading with explanation as an element in her holistic approach to healing: "God's Word formed a healthy counterbalance to the strictly-regimented spa life and to our guests' occupation with their physical condition."[102]

Reading the New Testament account of the Eucharist in Mark 14:22–24 sparked the desire in Popken to celebrate the rite with her house community. "We didn't do it, because I didn't have the courage to remove myself so far from the ecclesiastical order. It also would have seemed to me to be presumptuous to do something like that as a woman."[103] Only when an elder of the Methodist Church in Zürich moved to Aegeri and declared himself ready, in agreement with his congregation, to lead these celebrations did eucharistic worship services take place among a small circle of the institution's workers. Popken was open to the exchange between the established churches and Free Church communities; she explicitly included Methodists and the Salvation Army here. She herself conducted Bible study hours for several communities that, for her, belonged to the

---

97. Popken, *Kampf*, 171.
98. Popken, *Kampf*, 171.
99. Popken, *Licht*, 19.
100. Popken, *Licht*, 24–25, 42.
101. Popken, *Licht*, 129.
102. Popken, *Licht*, 42.
103. Popken, *Licht*, 63.

invisible church.[104] She apparently had no reservations about speaking before an assembly composed of both women and men. On the occasion of one of her stays in Teichwolframsdorf, she led two Bible studies, one about Cain and Abel (Gen 4:1–16) and the other about the sinful woman in Luke 7:36–50. Popken had drawn a connection between the Luke pericope and Matt 3:5–6 and John 1:34–36 and concluded that the nameless woman who anointed Jesus had heard John the Baptist's penitential preaching. "Was that woman perhaps also not there, too?"[105] Seitz, however, reprimanded her:

> Where is that described then which you said there about the previous history of this striking action on the part of the woman?... you have fantasized! And women like to do that so much. My wife did the same at the beginning and still was a blessed evangelist! But, I did not let her overlook anything. There were often tears, until she learned to hold strictly to the text of the Bible.[106]

Popken submits to the gender hierarchy advocated by Seitz, a hierarchy that she unquestionably acknowledges. The theologian so highly esteemed by her associates female Bible exegesis with fantasy; for himself, he claims to hold to the wording of the Bible. At the same time, he characterizes his wife Luise Seitz (née Soht) (1863–1919) as a "blessed evangelist"— high praise in the framework of these movements. Historical-exegetical findings do not represent for Seitz and Popken standards against which they measure themselves. What was important was alone the explanation of the biblical text; that this explanation can be ambiguous, and for this reason requires interpretation, is something that does not appear in the thought-context of these two representatives of the Holiness Movement. In preparing her devotional services and Bible studies, Popken, as she herself expressly emphasizes, did not use any exegetical commentaries—she only occasionally drew on the Berleburg Bible. This Bible edition from the early eighteenth century points out the rootedness of the several movements in early modern Pietism.[107] The supposedly exclusive orientation on the Bible is explained by Popken so:

---

104. Popken, *Licht*, 67.
105. Popken, *Licht*, 73.
106. Popken, *Licht*, 73–74.
107. On the Berleburg Bible, see Ruth Albrecht, "'We Kiss Our Dearest Redeemer through Inward Prayer': Mystical Traditions in Pietism," in *The Wiley-Blackwell Com-

I read theological works only rarely; I did not have the time and energy for this. Also, I had little occasion to hear Protestant sermons and lectures, since we lived in a Catholic area. So, the Bible alone remained as my master teacher. Through it, I gained a basic knowledge of the human soul, and of that great, all-encompassing view of the world that delights everyone who has accepted it.[108]

Popken's integration into the context of the international Holiness Movement and its gender concept becomes clear in a scene that she records in her autobiography. In her presence, two men discuss the theme of "women speaking in the congregation." The missionary, who Popken characterizes as a believing man, ends the conversation with the following sentence: "I am against women speaking; I am also against men speaking. But, I am in favor of the Holy Spirit speaking."[109] This commentary indicates the overcoming of the gender limitations that were connected with Gal 3:28 in the Christian tradition.

3. Summary: And the Woman Speaks After All!

Under this title, Countess Schimmelmann invited hearers to a lecture in Rostock in the fall of 1896. Her first series of evangelistic meetings in the Hanseatic city were accompanied by vehement controversies centered around one of the Lutheran pastors there. Ludwig Heinrich Hunzinger (1842–1900) presented her with the classic ensemble of conservative exegetical and theological arguments for why a woman was not authorized to speak in public about the Bible—neither in a church nor in a public inn. The clergyman denied the evangelist the right to continue to call herself a Lutheran Christian since she openly deviated from the confessional foundation of this church.[110] The fact that Schimmelmann did not let herself be deterred by this is shown by the provocative title she gave to her address.

Only a few women around 1900 who took an active part in the new piety movements so openly took the position, as did the countess, that not only men were called to proclamation of the gospel, but rather both

---

panion to Christian Mysticism, ed. Julia A. Lamm, BCR (Malden, MA: Blackwell, 2013), 484. Works by the previously mentioned Guyon entered into the commentary of this Bible edition.

108. Popken, *Licht*, 86.
109. Popken, *Kampf*, 172.
110. Albrecht et al., *Schimmelmann*, 204–6, 325–30.

sexes equally. The female representatives of these groups portrayed here, as well as also the many not named (and still not researched) who were active in a similar way, contributed to a change in biblical interpretation. Even when they persisted in obeying the divine word and in not deviating in the least from its eternally valid instructions, they still participated in the gender paradigms that were modern in their time, without wanting to do so or even perceiving that they did so. While women and male laypersons could involve themselves only to a much smaller extent in the churches of the Reformation tradition because of the relatively rigid official structures, new gender models could be seen to be emerging above all in the movements that originated under Anglo-American influence. These movements influenced the exegesis of the biblical texts using many different approaches.

Bibliography

Albrecht, Ruth. "Laientätigkeit als Profession: Profile adliger Männer aus der deutschen Erweckungs und Gemeinschaftsbewegung." Pages 205–20 in *Laien gestalten Kirche: Diskurse—Entwicklungen—Profile; Festgabe für Maximilian Liebmann zum 75. Geburtstag.* Edited by Michaela Sohn-Kronthaler and Rudolf K. Höfer. TKD 18. Innsbruck: Tyrolia, 2009.

———. "'We Kiss Our Dearest Redeemer through Inward Prayer': Mystical Traditions in Pietism." Pages 473–88 in *The Wiley-Blackwell Companion to Christian Mysticism.* Edited by Julia A. Lamm. BCR. Malden, MA: Blackwell, 2013.

Albrecht, Ruth, Martin Rosenkranz, and Kristina Russeau. *Adeline Gräfin von Schimmelmann: Adlig, Fromm, Exzentrisch.* Neumünster: Wachholtz, 2011. http://www.adelineschimmelmann.de.

Allgemeiner Wohnungs-Anzeiger nebst Adreß- und Geschäftshandbuch für Berlin, dessen Umgebung und Charlottenburg auf das Jahr 1870. Berlin: Hayn, 1870.

Auszüge aus dem Jahresbericht der Britischen und Ausländischen Bibelgesellschaft. London: Bibelhaus, 1854–1887.

Berliner Adreß-Buch für das Jahr 1880. Berlin: Loewenthal, 1880.

Berliner Adreß-Buch für das Jahr 1882. Berlin: Loewenthal, 1882.

Beutel, Albrecht. "Bibelübersetzungen II.1." *RGG* 1 (1998): 1498–1503.

Brecht, Martin. "Die Bedeutung der Bibel im deutschen Pietismus." Pages 102–20 in *Glaubenswelt und Lebenswelten*. Edited by Hartmut Lehmann. GP 4. Göttingen: Vandenhoeck & Ruprecht, 2004.

Bruns, Hans. *Minna Popken: Eine Ärztin unter Christus*. ZGG 55–56. Gießen: Brunnen, 1967.

Bunke, Ernst. *Samuel Keller: Gottes Werk und Werkzeug*. ZGG 5. Gießen: Brunnen, 1961.

Der Friedenshort. *Unsere Mutter*. Dinglingen: St. Johannes, n.d.

Die Bibel in gerechter Sprache. Edited by Ulrike Bail et al. Gütersloh: Gütersloher, 2006.

Die Heilige Schrift aus dem Urtext übersetzt. Elberfeld: Langewiesche, 1871. Repr., Elberfeld: Brockhaus, 1914.

Erinnerungsblätter von Freundeshand: George Palmer Davies. Berlin: Verlag der deutschen Evangelischen Buch- und Tractat-Gesellschaft, 1881.

Friedrich, Norbert. *Der Kaiserswerther: Wie Theodor Fliedner den Frauen einen Beruf gab*. Berlin: Wichern, 2010.

Hitzer, Bettina. *Im Netz der Liebe: Die protestantische Kirche und ihre Zuwanderer in der Metropole Berlin (1849–1914)*. IW 70. Cologne: Böhlau, 2006.

Holthaus, Stephan. *Heil, Heilung, Heiligung: Die Geschichte der deutschen Heiligungs und Evangelisationsbewegung, 1874–1909*. KM 14. Gießen: Brunnen, 2005.

Johnson, George W., and Lucy A. Johnson. *Von Frauennot und Frauenhilfe: Josephine Butler's Leben nach ihren eigenen Schriften, Aufzeichnungen, Briefen*. Munich: Kaiser, 1928.

Krusenstjerna, Ada von. *Im Kreuz hoffe und siege ich: Lebenserinnerungen*. Gießen: Brunnen, 1949.

Luther, Martin. *Die Bibel nach der Übersetzung Martin Luthers*. Stuttgart: Deutsche Bibelgesellschaft Stuttgart, 1985.

———. *Die Bibel oder die ganze Heilige Schrift des Alten und Neuen Testaments: nach der deutschen Übersetzung D. Martin Luthers*. Im Auftrage der Deutschen Evangelischen Kirchenkonferenz. Halle: Von Cansteinsche Bibelanstalt, 1899.

Modersohn, Ernst. *Er führt mich auf rechter Straße*. Stuttgart: Oncken, 1948.

Ohlemacher, Jörg. *Das Reich Gottes in Deutschland bauen: Ein Beitrag zur Vorgeschichte und Theologie der deutschen Gemeinschaftsbewegung*. AGP 23. Göttingen: Vandenhoeck & Ruprecht, 1986.

Palmer Davies, Marie. *Unter Droschkenkutschern: Schlichte Wahrheiten aus dem Berliner Volksleben; Aufzeichnungen*. With a Foreword by Emil Frommel. Schwerin: Bahn, 1903.

———. *Unvergeßliches aus dem Leben einer gottgeweihten Frau*. Berlin: Trowitzsch, 1907.

Popken, Minna. *Im Kampf um die Welt des Lichts: Lebenserinnerungen und Bekenntnisse*. Hamburg: Severus, 2010.

———. *Unter dem siegenden Licht: Lebenserinnerungen und Zeugnisse*. Berlin: Furche, 1940.

Prochaska, Frank K. *Women and Philanthropy in Nineteenth-Century England*. Oxford: Oxford University Press, 1980.

Ranyard, Ellen Henrietta. *The Missing Link; or, Bible-Women in the Homes of the London Poor*. London: Nisbet, 1859.

Redern, Hedwig von. *Andreas Graf von Bernstorff: Ein Lebensbild nach seinen Briefen und persönlichen Aufzeichnungen*. Schwerin: Bahn, 1909.

Schimmelmann, Adeline Gräfin. *Sechs Vorträge*. Barmen: Printed as a manuscript by the author, 1901.

———. *Streiflichter aus meinem Leben am deutschen Hofe, unter baltischen Fischern und Berliner Socialisten und im Gefängnis, einschließlich "Ein Daheim in der Fremde" von Otto Funke*. 1898. Repr. edited by Jörg Ohlemacher. Leipzig: Evangelische Verlagsanstalt, 2008.

———. "Zum Frauenreden." *Leu* 8 (1910): 25–26.

Schimmelmann, Paul Friedrich. *Das Weib schweige?* Berlin: Adeline Gräfin Schimmelmanns Internationale Mission, n.d.

Schneider, Wilhelm. *Sie hat Gott vertraut: Cäcilie Petersen; Ein Beitrag zur Geschichte der Erweckungsbewegung*. Metzingen: Brunnquell, 1974.

Schrill, Ernst. *Jadwiga (Die Natschalniza): Roman aus dem russischen Leben der Gegenwart*. Leipzig: Ungleich, 1897.

Schultze, Emil. *Die Bibel in der weiten Welt: Eine Denkschrift zum 100jährigen Bestehen der Britischen u. Ausländischen Bibelgesellschaft*. Basel: Kober C. F. Spittlers Nachfolger, 1904.

Torjesen, Edvard P. *Fredrik Franson: A Model for Worldwide Evangelism*. Pasadena, CA: Carey, 1983.

Waldersee, Elisabeth Gräfin. *Von Klarheit zu Klarheit! Gräfin Marie Esther von Waldersee gewesene Fürstin von Noer, geb. den 3. Okt. 1837, gest. den 4. Juli 1914; Ein Lebensbild*. Stuttgart: Deutscher Philadelphia-Verein, 1919.

Wasserzug-Traeder, Gertrud. *Deutsche Evangelische Frauenmissionsarbeit: Ein Blick in ihr Werden und Wirken*. Munich: Kaiser, 1927.

Weber, Johannes. *Die dem Himmelreich Gewalt antun: Die Kraft des Glaubens und des Gebetes im Leben der Diakonissen-Oberin Cäcilie Petersen*. Neumünster: Christophorus, 1936.

Weller, Gustav Adolf. *Rosen und Dornen: Dichtungen für die Freuden- und Trauertage des christlichen Hauses*. Barmen: Biermann, 1904.

Wichern, Johann Hinrich. *Sämmtliche Werke*. Vol. 1. Edited by Peter Meinhold. Hamburg: Lutherisches Verlagshaus, 1962.

Williamson, Lori. "Ranyard, Ellen Henrietta (1810–1879)." *ODNB* 46 (2004): 60–61.

A Swiss Champion of Women's Rights: The Reception of the Bible by Helene von Mülinen

Doris Brodbeck

The Bible was important in two ways for the daughter of a Berne patrician family, Helene von Mülinen (1850–1924). It lent her a language—for lamenting the ecclesiastical and social traditions, as well as for formulating new visions. Using biblical texts, she expressed her doubts about interpretations of the Bible that, for her, were hostile to life. But, in the Bible she also found impulse for the strengthening of the emancipation of women and of social policy, which she pursued as president of the Alliance of Swiss Women's Associations (BSF).[1] One, thus, would be able to designate her today as a liberation theologian. The present article intends to show how she arrived at this way of reading the Bible.[2]

To refer to the Bible was usual in Protestant circles, not only among theologians but also in daily use, as descriptions from Mülinen's correspondence prove. She told, for example, of conversations with female friends who remonstrated with her that she should bear her fate with more humility and who used biblical citations in doing so. Thus it is no wonder that in

---

1. The Bund Schweizerischer Frauenvereine (BSF) was founded in 1900 by Helene von Mülinen, the first president. Today it is called alliance F. She remained on its board and in its commissions until 1920. The goal of the BSF was furthering the political sensibility of the women's associations and the exercise of influence upon Swiss legislation. At times, women workers' associations and Catholic women's associations took part. See Silke Redolfi, *Frauen bauen Staat: 100 Bund Schweizerischer Frauenorganisationen* (Zürich: NZZ, 2000).

2. See on this the published dissertation by Doris Brodbeck, *Hunger nach Gerechtigkeit: Helene von Mülinen (1850–1924); Eine Wegbereiterin der Frauenemancipation* (Zürich: Chronos, 2000).

her own way she herself also drew on the Bible. Remarkable, though, is the fact that she consistently seized on the Bible in an emancipatory manner.

On the other hand, it is absolutely not a matter of course that many of her public speeches appeared in printed form and are to be found in the archives of the Gosteli Foundation in Worblaufen near Berne, in the Swiss Archives Zürich, and in the Swiss National Library in Berne. Even her private letters are available in original in the Burgerbibliothek Berne in the Mülinen family archives and form a valuable addition to the printed texts.[3]

The interest on the part of several coworkers in the BSF was necessary so that the private letters were collected and entrusted to the family archives nearly thirty years later. In the course of the new women's movement, the Swiss historian Susanna Woodtli discovered the letters as a historical source and used them for her work *Gleichberechtigung*, which appeared originally in 1974.[4] The biblical references in them, however, were never investigated in detail.

1. Lamenting and Doubting with the Bible

For a long time, lamentation and religious doubt were a top priority for Mülinen. As a patrician's daughter, she was forced into professional idleness and was permitted to attend theological lectures at the University of Berne only as an auditor. To be sure, her mother had encouraged the schooling of her daughter—her private tutor was a theology student who read the Letter to the Romans with the young girl—but she considered professional work or the university study permitted for women in Berne as not befitting the social status of her daughter. Because of the lack of a perspective for her life, the intellectually highly gifted Mülinen fell into deep emotional distress accompanied by a severe health crisis at the age of forty. In order to express what happened to her, she drew on biblical forms of speech.

Mülinen's letters in the years of her illness were directed to the theologian Adolf Schlatter (1852–1938) and his wife Susanna Schlatter-Schoop (1860–1907).[5] She had become friends with the young university lecturer

---

3. See www.gosteli-foundation.ch; www.sozialarchiv.ch; www.snl.ch; and www.burgerbib.ch.

4. Susanna Woodtli, *Gleichberechtigung: Der Kampf um die politischen Rechte der Frau in der Schweiz* (Zürich: Huber, 1983).

5. See Werner Neuer, *Adolf Schlatter: Ein Leben für Theologie und Kirche* (Stuttgart: Calwer, 1996).

in Berne and then maintained a correspondence with him when he moved to Germany with his family in 1888 to teach, first in Greifswald, then in Berlin, and finally in Tübingen.

Mülinen complained to him that she was going mad in God. Her language is marked by biblical notions, although she does not cite the Bible explicitly:

> What is to become of this broken life further I cannot say. Why it was created is still more obscure, still more incomprehensible to me. I wanted what was true and right; I sought God, but I have found only one thing: that He is a hidden God [cf. Isa 45:15]. All striving, struggling, searching, and yearning was for nothing, nothing, and day and night I hear one word in myself incessantly: Tekel, tekel [cf. Dan 5:27].[6]

Mülinen certainly did not consciously seek fitting biblical citations. Rather, she appears to have been so familiar with the Bible that biblical notions forced themselves upon her in her struggle to find a language. In a letter she wrote to Schlatter-Schoop, it becomes clear that her relationship to God shattered on the prevailing notions of social roles. The pious explanations offered by her environment were of no further help to her. She would gladly turn away from God, she said, if this was possible for her.

> I have come to grief in my intellectual yearning. I was supposed to be a quite normal woman, and I couldn't do it. One could deprive me of the means I required for my development, one could cripple me, burden me with all the demands that can be made of a female being, an older sister, and member of a large family, but one could not extirpate in me the desire for a spiritual life and one could not make me into a useful potherb. What purposes God had in giving me this spiritual soul, and yet in imprisoning me in the prejudices at home, I will, of course, never understand, and believing that it was something good is one of the hardest things in life. Is annihilation something good? If consciousness may be annihilated, then, of course, I could be happy about the future. The idea that it is supposed to be easier to accept affliction from the hand of a kind Father rather than from the hand of chance is for me one of the absolute conundrums. If the pious speak as though they would not understand how one could bear the sufferings of these times, death, and the grave without faith in God, then that sounds incomprehensible to me. That is, of course, hard when one is supposed to believe that suffer-

---

6. Mülinen to Schlatter, September 12, 1888, BBB, Ms. Mül 644, 2, folio.

ing is joy, dying is life, death is resurrection. How can they make such a fuss, in spite of all the evidence to the contrary, that it "is good" to hold fast to faith?[7]

To her rebellion against the conventional role of women was joined severe chronic pain that tormented her so much that she saw herself reminded of the crucifixion pericopes. But the consolation sought in a hope in the hereafter did not appear. The Bible, however, turned her back to life on this earth:

> How fully, deeply, and personally do the Gospels set forth the suffering and painful tone in Jesus's words, how His fear grasps His heart—and afterwards—after the Resurrection, how hazy, unclear, impalpable is His figure—not one single clear jubilant brightening, no sound of personal joy in resurrection, no word to which one could hold that might show that He enjoyed life, the new life, that He jubilantly enjoyed it. All is solemn, blurred, and I constantly hear in me: the sounds of pain are the only truth, in life here, in life there.[8]

The acknowledgement of an abdominal tumor, which gave her a justification for being sick, provided her with relief. In addition, she came into the enjoyment of the kind care of the Berne deaconesses. Thus, she understood her surgical emergency as an intervention on the part of God that reconciled her with him. Her acquaintances, though, who now would have conceded her every justification for complaint, did not understand this. So, what helped her was the reflection upon Elijah and Job, both of whom, under the impression of a remoteness of God, recognized that God had showed himself to them in a completely new way:

> Dear Professor, you know without me having to write in so many words about it, that your last letter has been a great comfort for me. While all the others at that time were of the opinion that now would be the time for whining and complaining—but not before—you had understood that I had seen the dawn, that it had become quiet after the storm, for the Lord finally spoke [cf. 1 Kgs 19:11–13]. What difference did it make after all the bitterness of being abandoned by Him, that He spoke through the weather? [cf. Job 38:1]. Was it not completely sufficient that He again lifted His countenance upon me [cf. Num 6:26] and remembered me?

---

7. Mülinen to Schlatter-Schoop, August 12, 1888, BBB, 1–2, folio.
8. Mülinen to Schlatter, January 5/7, 1889, BBB, 2, folio.

And it was not a hard, damning judgment that He made, but He came with justification and compassion. With justification—for it proved to be the case that the physical disorder was of such a kind that it had of necessity to result in a direct psychic disorder. With compassion—for the pressure, bitterness, and hate that I experienced for years was now suddenly taken from me and, instead, God's goodness shone in me. So grandly and mercifully did He stand there that even all of my sin disappeared. How could it even be seen wherever He was? He had been right in the end, but not like the other people said, and thereby tormented me to madness with what they said, but rather so that I could trust Him, so that the relationship to Him could become bright.[9]

This turning point let Mülinen return to faith. She was now ready to expect something new from faith and consequently was receptive to the encounter with the international, Christian-influenced women's movement, about which her friend Emma Pieczýnska-Reichenbach (1854–1927) told her. This future physician had gotten to know a women's movement in Geneva and Boston that was Christian-motivated and oriented toward social reform and also had warmed to a mystical understanding of faith. Mülinen now had her own impetus to unite Christian belief with her own interest in social reforms and in the emancipatory ideas she had found in the work of the liberal English thinker John Stuart Mill (1806–1873).

This step away from her suffering at the hands of society toward a commitment on behalf of women's emancipation was something that the married Schlatter couple could not understand. As a result, Mülinen avoided this topic when corresponding with them. When, however, in 1898, she sent to both the brochure containing her first public lecture, which spoke out in favor of professional training for women and their employment in government offices, she once again encountered a lack of understanding. She replied to this with a letter to Schlatter-Schoop containing a fundamental critique of theology and church:

> Looking at his [Schlatter's] example, I, deeply shaken, recognize why the church has gone wrong and has not been able to understand how to bring the Savior to the world. It has indulged in high, majestic speculations, has drawn wisdom and understanding from God's well [cf. John 4:5–14], has spoken marvelous words about faith and grace—but the

---

9. Mülinen to Schlatter, September 24, 1890, BBB.

scream of distress and despair of those who die, the hungry cry for the bread of righteousness [cf. Matt 5:6] for all, it has not heard, has ignored, and has passed it by [cf. Luke 10:31–32]. That's why it has not completed its task, and why it will be brushed aside. Yes, your letter has shocked me deeply, shaken me in my innermost parts, and because I love you both I cannot keep it a secret, whatever the cost may be to me.[10]

After her image of God, her image of theology and the church now also broke apart. The lecturer in theology had meant much to her: he was able, in her eyes, to provide the living water of which Jesus had spoken to the Samaritan woman at the well. Now, she realized that he lacked sensibility for the difficult situation of women, although Schlatter, by all means, did what he could socially. She played upon the Beatitudes when she spoke of the unheard-of cry of hunger for the bread of righteousness and upon the priest and the Levite in the parable of the Good Samaritan, both of whom carelessly passed by the needy victim. Mülinen had in mind the situation of the working women who suffered under the alcoholism of their husbands and under general social distress, and who could not defend themselves. The theologian, however, considered the situation of women under ideal conditions and did not recognize the obvious injustice. He also did not contradict the theologian Martin von Nathusius (1843–1906), who, at the Ecclesiastical-Social Conference in Berlin in 1900, dismissed women's emancipation as mere rebelliousness, which deeply hurt Mülinen. Although Schlatter was her teacher in Bible and theology, she still approached the Bible now in the light of other prerequisites based upon her experiences of social discrimination.

2. Interpreting Women's Emancipation from the Point of View of the Bible

With the introduction of democracy in Switzerland—a new federal constitution was adopted in 1848—a new ruling class came to power. It was supposed to solve the economic and social problems of industrialization and the growing urban population and to create a new body of law for all of Switzerland. The previous elite class had lost influence, which also affected Mülinen's father, who, to be sure, as a democratically minded man

---

10. Mülinen to Schlatter-Schoop, March 18, 1898, BBB, 2, folio.

had sympathized with left-liberal farmers but in the end had to return to his historical studies.

Although the democratic movement at first also encompassed women's rights, what triumphed in the end in Switzerland was a democratic model that, to be sure, conceded to the (male) population a large say in matters but gave women a part in it only in the form of social work in local associations. Mülinen gathered these socially committed women in the BSF in order, together with them, to exercise influence upon the newly emerging legislation. The women had determined that the conditions in the socially weaker classes demanded a special attention that was lacking among bourgeois politicians.

She resorted to biblical arguments only in front of a churchly audience, such as the Protestant Women's Association for Raising Morality (today the Protestant Women's Aid) or the Religious Socialists, who, after their foundation in 1907, replaced the Christian Social Society of Berne.[11] Her first public lecture, before the Christian Social Society in the canton of Berne in 1896, on "The Stand Taken by Women on the Social Question," supported the idea of admitting women to professional employment and to elected positions on school boards and municipal councils. Among the examples of leading women that she cited, she also referred to the biblical judge Deborah (Judg 4–5).

> Moreover, I consider the danger that we could deny our nature not to be so great as fearful souls believe, or as individual women who have become revolutionary under the influence of heavy pressure appear to conjure it up as a specter.... When Deborah judged Israel and led the tribes of the people into battle, she did men's work and appeared to give up her female nature. But, when she sang her song, that wonderful triumphal song of the prophetess, there we find her female nature once again in each word. We find it again in the detailed discussion of the conduct of the individual tribes ... in the detailed depiction of the minute features of the picture of battle, and above all in the compassionate remembrance of the mother of Sisera.... Who other than a woman could have such sympathy, could still sympathize painfully in the midst of all her enthusiasm in the triumph.... Only a mother's heart could see the misery of the mother of

---

11. The Religious-Social Movement formed beginning in 1906 around the Protestant Swiss theologians Hermann Kutter (1863–1931) and Leonhard Ragaz (1868–1945). The name was a self-designation so that nonreligious socialists and antisocialist Christians would not feel left out.

the dead enemy. Yet Deborah judged Israel, and the tribes still came up to her seat to receive law and justice from her.[12]

Using the example of Deborah, she could show that even judicial work did not ruin the woman; in spite of professional activity, female qualities remained. In bourgeois circles, though, the fear of female students and militant female activists for women's rights circulated everywhere. For such reasons, she, too, was not permitted to study, for her mother considered it unseemly.

2.1. Unfolding the Image of God

An opportunity for an explicitly biblical lecture offered itself in 1903 in Geneva. Mülinen's address, "The Woman and the Gospel [*La femme et l'Evangile*]," was printed only in French but has been preserved as a manuscript in German.[13] She took up the biblical idea of the human being as the image of God (Gen 1:27), the unfolding of which, according to the understanding of that time, was an important task for theology. Mülinen connected this task with the female sex and, under this form of the question, read the Bible in a new way. "What is this teaching that puts us in a position to fulfil His will, to become the perfect woman, who was created in God's image and grows in the faith in His revelation [?]"[14] The word *perfect* (Matt 5:48) may not be immediately understandable in today's view of matters. Mülinen had in mind here the realization of God's kingdom on this earth, while she related *perfect* to eschatology. In her lecture, she pointed out how Jesus summoned people to service to the kingdom of God and thereby made no difference between the sexes:

> Let us place ourselves with all our powers at God's disposal, in order to become the city on the hill, the salt that enlivens, the light on the lamp-

---

12. Mülinen, *Die Stellung der Frau zur socialen Aufgabe: Vortrag gehalten im Schoße der christlich-socialen Gesellschaft des Kantons Bern* (Bern: Schmid & Francke, 1897), 13–15.

13. Mülinen, *La femme et l'Evangile: Conférence donnée à Genève au Séminaire d'activité; chrétienne le 19 novembre 1903* (Paris: Librairie Robert, 1904); German-language original in *Die Frau und das Evangelium*, typescript, 1903, BBB, Ms. Mül 644a; extracts in Brodbeck, ed., *Unerhörte Worte: Religiöse Gesellschaftskritik von Frauen im 20. Jahrhundert; Ein Reader*, GW 5 (Bern: EFeF, 2003), 23–26.

14. Mülinen, *Die Frau und das Evangelium*, 1.

stand [cf. Matt 5:13–16], so that finally the woman becomes what God wanted her to be and will want her to be, the woman who through her wisdom in the Spirit and the largeness of her soul lets us see what all of our pain, all of our humiliation longs for, what Jesus called the Kingdom of God.[15]

Further, she emphasized Jesus's words that man and woman are of the same flesh (Mark 10:8). She also said that Jesus did not condemn the adulteress any more than he did the adulterer, who was permitted to escape (John 8:1–11). With Jesus, so she says, there are no special rules for the woman as with Paul. Against the background of research into early Christianity conducted by Adolf von Harnack (1851–1930), she knew how to qualify the claim in Paul's saying, "let the woman keep silent in the church" (1 Cor 14:34):

> One of the greatest theologians of the present, Professor Harnack from the University of Berlin, has proposed an hypothesis that at first glance appears odd. In the Review of the New Testament and Primitive Christianity, Harnack seeks to prove that the Letter to the Hebrews was written by Priscilla.... These arguments are, of course, only "probabilities," and one probably never will be able to prove with certainty who wrote the Letter to the Hebrews. But, it is a sign of the times that a theologian and German scholar can "assume" that a woman was the author of one of the canonical texts. One might almost feel tempted to smile when one thinks that the church for 2000 years demanded silence from the woman in the congregation, and during this time was taught by her.[16]

In Mülinen's portrayal of early Christianity, there is reflected an insight that she could find not only in the work of Harnack but also in the work of his pupil Leopold Zscharnack (1877–1955). In almost literal agreement with Zscharnack, she describes how Christianity spread, above all, through the circles of women who had turned to Judaism and how the women only later were pushed into the background by the church hierarchy and monasticism. Women, she said, were for Paul, too, indispensable missionaries because they had access to women's quarters and could make Christian ideas known there.[17] In his foreword, Zscharnack explicitly made

---

15. Mülinen, *Die Frau und das Evangelium*, 15.
16. Mülinen, *Die Frau und das Evangelium*, 9.
17. Mülinen, *Die Frau und das Evangelium*, 7; Zscharnack, *Der Dienst der Frau in*

reference to the current interest in the women's movement. But neither in his work nor in Harnack's can one find a theological interpretation of the position of women in early Christianity like the one Mülinen outlines in her lecture in Geneva. Zscharnack even distances himself explicitly from any dogmatic interest. His portrayal, however, still would like to encourage "considering to what extent the good of the past can be reacquired for the future."[18] Mülinen took up this concern. The look back into early Christianity strengthened her in expecting a more active participation of women in the church in the present, too. Thereby, she cited the proclamation of Jesus, which, like a seed, bore fruit and then was suppressed for many years.

2.2. Church Participation

When the Protestant Church Conference, the loose union of the Protestant churches in Switzerland, placed ecclesiastical voting rights for women on the agenda in 1904, Mülinen submitted a petition in the name of the BSF and demanded the participation of women in ecclesiastical service—without directly asking for the pastoral office for women. The church, though, she said, should grant women the room to develop their abilities: "We do not believe that the God who, through the mouth of His apostle, called Himself a God of liberty [cf. 2 Cor 3:17] foresaw and desired stagnation in the growth of His children."[19]

She became more explicit at the congress of the Religious Socialists in 1910 in Berne, where she was the only woman permitted to speak. She placed herself behind the new image of active women and pleaded for the participation of women in church and society. She interpreted the awakening in the women's movement as a divine work that enabled women to take a more active role in service to the kingdom of God. The church, for this reason, should further the women's movement. This church, she said, developed itself one-sidedly over centuries, but Mülinen counted on the power of God to create something new:

---

den ersten Jahrhunderten der christlichen Kirche (Göttingen: Vandenhoeck & Ruprecht, 1902), 20.

18. Zscharnack, *Der Dienst der Frau in den ersten Jahrhunderten der christlichen Kirche*, 20.

19. "Antrag an die schweizerische reformierte Kirchenkonferenz in Frauenfeld Juni 1904," *EB* 6.9 (1904): 1, signed by Mülinen.

The wheel of history, of course, can never be turned back, and what in the course of centuries was neglected cannot be restored in this form. But, we have, indeed, a Lord who not only yesterday, but also today and tomorrow, creates what is new [cf. Isa 43:19] and knows means and ways.

He now opens up such a way in the desire to mobilize women to be visible more often in His church and to serve more actively than heretofore. And what we now hope and also expect is that the church not only frees the way for us, but also makes a way [cf. Isa 40:3; 43:16; 57:14].[20]

Mülinen attributed the fact that, by far, not all female representatives of the women's movement felt themselves any longer allied with the church and also to their adherence to traditional positions.

2.3. Interpreting Political Involvement Biblically

There is not sufficient space here to provide a comprehensive description of Mülinen's political work. Three examples, though, are intended to illustrate the convergence of biblical reflection and political conviction. The German-Swiss Women's Association for the Raising of Morality demanded that the state actively work against prostitution, while certain cantons wanted to establish state-controlled brothels. Mülinen, before the Neuenburg Collection Association, spoke out against both extremes. She wanted to see the state neither as the protector of morality nor as acting against morality. Along with the International Abolitionist Movement led by Josephine Butler (1828–1906), she considered it sufficient when minors were protected and the traffic in women was curbed. She was of the opinion that if the state would more actively pursue morality, then this would turn out to be a double-edged sword also directed against the dignity of women. In order to reinforce this position, she cited Jesus's saying about the tares in the field that are permitted to grow so that the wheat sowed with them also was not rooted up (Matt 13:24–30).[21]

---

20. Mülinen, *Was die Frauenbewegung vom Christentum erwartet: Ansprache an der religiös-sozialen Konferenz in Bern Oktober 1910* (Bern: n. p., 1910), 5.

21.See Mülinen, *Das zukünftige Schweizerische Strafgesetzbuch: Ansprache bei Gelegenheit der jährlichen Generalversammlung des Kollektenvereins zur Hebung der Sittlichkeit in Neuenburg 11. 6. 1908* (Bern: Büro des Sekretariats der Föderation, 1909), 5.

When the author of the Swiss law code, the jurist Eugen Huber (1849–1923), introduced the biblical concept of the man as the "head of the woman" into the area of jurisprudence, she protested against this.[22]

> There is, however, hardly any other doctrine in which the men so steadfastly believe than the doctrine that they are the head of the woman. One constantly hears men who are quite indifferent toward religion and who are little impressed by whether the Bible or the church teaches or commands something, but who appeal in the tones of the deepest conviction to the word of the Apostle that the man is the head of the woman. So much does it correspond to, and flatter, their masculine pride that they have made it the cornerstone of their family life, their social notions, and their bourgeois feeling … although no legal scholar really is able to define what a juridical head really might be.[23]

She elaborated further that the danger existed even in ecclesiastical circles of overlooking the deeper religious content: "But, a sermon on the devotion to, and the self-sacrifice on the part of the man for, his wife is never bestowed upon us, at the most only that the duty of the family's father to provide for his own—above all in the material aspect—is urged more or less pressingly."[24] The Apostle, however, in making the comparison with Christ, demands "from the man a devotion like that which Christ alone accomplished, even unto death."[25] But, she said, instead of devotion, the man's hubris is encouraged. Also, Mülinen's comrade-in-arms in the cause of women's emancipation—Fritz Barth (1856–1912), the Berne theology professor, synodal councilor, and father of the theologian Karl Barth, who was so influential for the twentieth century—furthered the biblical image of the man as the "head" of the woman in a lecture and emphasized the responsibility of the husband as a Christian achievement.[26] In Mülinen's opinion, however, the dependence of the woman upon the morality of her husband, intended by Barth, was in no way sufficient for the legal sphere,

---

22. See Brodbeck, *Hunger nach Gerechtigkeit*, 94; See also the thirteen letters from Mülinen to Eugen Huber, 1898–1907, Swiss Federal Archives in Bern, Nachlass Eugen Huber J. I. 109.443.

23. Mülinen, "Zur schweizerischen Frauenbewegung: Eine Notwehr," *MCS* 32.8 (1910): 480.

24. Mülinen, "Zur schweizerischen Frauenbewegung," 482.

25. Mülinen, "Zur schweizerischen Frauenbewegung," 482.

26. See the lecture in the Grossratssaal Berne, SA by Fritz Barth, "Die Frauenfrage und das Christentum," *SBWS* 10.8 (1902): 1–10.

and the right of legal action granted to the wife by Huber was of no use to her if she had no financial means, for the head of the family administered both incomes and could decide about the place of residence and the education of the children. She explained how ignoble was when the husband sold his wife as a wet nurse, collected her earnings and spent it on drink, and his wife saw nothing of them and not even could care for herself and her children with those earnings. For this reason, the first female Swiss jurist Emilie Kempin-Spyri (1853–1901) demanded that the wife must be enabled economically to exercise her rights by being given half of the family income.[27]

At her last official appearance, in 1919, Mülinen attempted to win the favor of the BSF assembly for a petition that demanded the incorporation of women's active civil rights in the constitution. She cited two biblical images: without these rights, women could not intervene where the "distress lies along the wayside" (Luke 10:33). All that would remain to them would be the role of the lamenting women who bewailed the sorrow of the city (Luke 23:27–28). She demanded the right to have a say in political matters, "so that we do not, like the lamenting daughters of Jerusalem, only just in mourning look upon where murder dwells [cf. Lam 2:10]."[28] This submission came before the male voters only in 1959 and was rejected. Finally, in 1971, the woman's right to vote was accepted on the national level.

3. Summary

In her letters, lectures, and articles, Mülinen often employed biblical images and expressions without making this explicit. Her hearers or readers who were knowledgeable about the Bible, though, were not likely to have missed these echoes, although she cited rather freely. Before a secular audience, she limited herself in most cases to images from Greek mythology or from politics and history. Only on special occasions did she comment upon and discuss concrete biblical passages, but here, too, with

---

27. Emilie Kempin-Spyri, *Die Ehefrau im künftigen Privatrecht* (Zürich: Müller, 1894), 19–20; Kempin-Spyri, "Protokoll der Jahrestagung des schweizerischen Juristenvereins," ZSR 13 (1894): 713–14.

28. Mülinen, *Die Revision der Bundesverfassung und die Politischen Rechte der Schweizerfrauen: Vortrag an der Delegiertenversammlung des Bundes Schweizerischer Frauenvereine am 22. 1. 1919 in Bern* (Geneva: Richter, 1919), 16.

hardly any precise statements. Her constant concern was the development of the woman and her emancipation—themes that she sought to connect with her biblical faith. The recourse to the Bible took the polemical sting out of the struggle for women's rights. Mülinen avoided such emotive words as "women's right to vote" or "woman's pastorate," but demanded what, in essence, stood behind them: namely, the right and the duty to develop God's gifts in women and the legitimation of their work in helping to build the kingdom of God, to the realization of which she counted solidarity and social justice.

Bibliography

Barth, Fritz. "Die Frauenfrage und das Christentum." *SBWS* 10.8 (1902): 1–10.

Brodbeck, Doris. *Hunger nach Gerechtigkeit: Helene von Mülinen (1850–1924); Eine Wegbereiterin der Frauenemancipation.* Zürich: Chronos, 2000.

———, ed. *Unerhörte Worte: Religiöse Gesellschaftskritik von Frauen im 20. Jahrhundert; Ein Reader.* GW 5. Bern: EFeF, 2003.

Kempin-Spyri, Emilie. *Die Ehefrau im künftigen Privatrecht.* Zürich: Müller, 1894.

———. "Protokoll der Jahrestagung des schweizerischen Juristenvereins." *ZSR* 13 (1894): 713–14.

Mülinen, Helene von. *La femme et l'Evangile: Conférence donnée à Genève au Séminaire d'activité; chrétienne le 19 novembre 1903.* Paris: Librairie Robert, 1904.

———. "Petition to the Swiss Reformed Church Conference in Frauenfeld, June 1904." *EB* 6.9 (1904): 1–2.

———. *Die Revision der Bundesverfassung und die Politischen Rechte der Schweizerfrauen: Vortrag an der Delegiertenversammlung des Bundes Schweizerischer Frauenvereine am 22. Januar 1919 in Bern.* Geneva: Richter, 1919.

———. *Die Stellung der Frau zur socialen Aufgabe: Vortrag gehalten im Schoße der christlich-socialen Gesellschaft des Kantons Bern.* Bern: Schmid & Francke, 1897.

———. *Was die Frauenbewegung vom Christentum erwartet: Ansprache an der religiös-sozialen Konferenz in Bern Oktober 1910.* Bern: n. p., 1910.

———. *Das zukünftige Schweizerische Strafgesetzbuch: Ansprache bei Gelegenheit der jährlichen Generalversammlung des Kollektenvereins zur*

Hebung der Sittlichkeit, Neuenburg 11. Juni 1908. Berne: Büro des Sekretariats der Föderation, 1909.

———. "Zur schweizerischen Frauenbewegung: Eine Notwehr." *MCS* 32.8 (1910): 470–83.

Neuer, Werner. *Adolf Schlatter: Ein Leben für Theologie und Kirche*. Stuttgart: Calwer, 1996.

Redolfi, Silke. *Frauen bauen Staat: 100 Bund Schweizerischer Frauenorganisationen*. Zürich: NZZ, 2000.

Woodtli, Susanna. *Gleichberechtigung: Der Kampf um die politischen Rechte der Frau in der Schweiz*. Frauenfeld: Huber, 1983.

Zscharnack, Leopold. *Der Dienst der Frau in den ersten Jahrhunderten der christlichen Kirche*. Göttingen: Vandenhoeck & Ruprecht, 1902.

In the Discipleship of Jesus: Deaconesses and Biblical Explanation; The Example of Eva von Tiele-Winckler

Ute Gause

The genuinely Protestant women's profession of deaconess was developed beginning in 1833 by Pastor Theodor Fliedner (1800–1864), active in Kaiserswerth in the Rhineland. His idea of a Christian-motivated occupation for women carried out by unmarried or widowed women, who were to take over pastoral as well as nursing work in congregations, hospitals, prisons, and children's homes, achieved an immediate triumphal success.[1]

1. The "Invention of the Deaconess" and the Century of Christian Social Welfare

In 1836, the so-called Deaconess Institution, a hospital in which nurses were to be trained, was opened in Kaiserswerth. By 1842, a hundred women had entered service in the Deaconess Institution. By 1861, 336 nurses were working domestically and abroad.

---

1. See Martin Cordes, *Diakonie und Diakonisse: Beiträge zur Rolle der Frauen in kirchlicher sozialer Arbeit*, QFESH 4 (Hemmingen: Sozialwissenschaftliche Studiengesellschaft, 1995); Adelheid M. Von Hauff, ed., *Frauen gestalten Diakonie 2: Vom 18. bis zum 20. Jahrhundert* (Stuttgart: Kohlhammer, 2006); Jochen-Christoph Kaiser and Rajah Scheepers, eds., *Dienerinnen des Herrn: Beiträge zur weiblichen Diakonie im 19. und 20. Jahrhundert*, HTG 5 (Leipzig: Evangelische, 2010); Silke Köser, *Denn eine Diakonisse darf kein Alltagsmensch sein: Kollektive Identitäten Kaiserswerther Diakonissen, 1836–1914*, HTG 2 (Leipzig: Evangelische, 2006); Ute Gause and Cordula Lissner, eds., *Kosmos Diakonissenmutterhaus: Geschichte und Gedächtnis einer protestantischen Frauengemeinschaft*, HTG 1 (Leipzig: Evangelische, 2005); and Jutta Schmidt, *Beruf: Schwester; Mutterhausdiakonie im 19. Jahrhundert*, GG 24 (Frankfurt: Campus, 1998).

A deaconess lived in a family-like society, that is, in a mother house with a male and a female superintendent as "parents"—Theodor Fliedner and his second wife, Caroline, were addressed by their nurses as "Father" and "Mother." After a probationary period, the deaconesses would be consecrated. The nurses, or sisters, had a clear identity; they were "servants of the Lord Jesus," "servants to the needy for the sake of Jesus," and "servants among each other."

In the nineteenth century, other institutions arose alongside the Kaiserswerth model—such as those by Wilhelm Löhe (1808–1872) in Neuendettelsau (Franconia) and by Friedrich von Bodelschwingh (1831–1910) in Bethel near Bielefeld—but also individual foundations such as that founded by Eva von Tiele-Winckler (1866–1930).

In the Protestant view, the nineteenth century was seen essentially as a century of Christian social welfare. This characterization for the Protestantism of the nineteenth century is appropriate not least of all because in social welfare work, which was designated as "inner mission" by Johann Hinrich Wichern (1808–1881),[2] a piety was also addressed that is typical for this epoch: an experienced-based piety urging practial action became the focus of attention. To this also definitely belong Friedrich Schleiermacher's theology with its reference to religious feeling and especially the ecclesiastical form of the revival movement, Neo-Protestantism, or the confessionalism of Lutheran character.[3]

---

2. The term itself comes from Friedrich Lücke (1791–1855), Wichern's teacher at the University of Göttingen who, in 1842, delivered a lecture on "the two-fold, inner and outer mission of the Protestant church," which then, in 1843 and afterwards, appeared in print in Hamburg. See Otto Ladendorf, "Innere Mission," in *Historisches Schlagwörterbuch* (Strassburg: Trübner, 1906), http://www.textlog.de/schlagworte-innere-mission.html; as well as Volker Herrmann, "Wichern," *TRE* 35 (2003): 733–39.

3. Revival movements are piety movements existing since the early modern period, in which individual faith experience is combined with the effort on behalf of ecclesiastical and social renewal. Revivalist piety is characterized by earnestness in faith, a biblical and Jesus piety, often apocalyptic overtones, but also interdenominational and transnational communication networks; *Neo-Protestantism* designates that liberal Protestantism of the nineteenth century in the German Reich that insisted upon the freedom of the individual and was influenced by Idealism and by the liberal bourgeoisie; Precipitated by the waves of pluralization in the nineteenth century, a strong emphasis upon confessional peculiarities and distinctions arose among the churches. Confessionalism, thus, displaced Irenicism and the first ecumenical reconciliations from around 1800.

Thanks to the revival movement, numerous social initiatives arose on the Protestant side in the nineteenth century. This was due not only to the misery caused by industrialization among the families of factory workers in the big cities such as Hamburg—where Wichern, for example, got to know these living conditions during his visits in the workers' homes—or in the countryside, as in Upper Silesia, where Tiele-Winckler became active. The spirit of a piety that considers active love of neighbor an indispensable part of Christian life prompted Protestant women in the nineteenth century to assume an increasingly larger role in public.[4] A further mental root that provided women with the possibility for articulation was the renewed emphasis stimulated by the revival movement upon the "priesthood of all believers." Laypeople—as already in the Reformation period—were motivated successfully by this principle. The boom in the founding of societies and associations, which promoted lay involvement, likewise offered opportunities for women to become active.

The profession of deaconess was not a modern female profession in the sense that it was connected with an emancipatory claim. On the contrary, Fliedner himself placed great value on humility, obedience, and self-denial as ideal female virtues. It was a matter of course that an exegesis of the Bible was provided for the deaconesses by the respective institutional pastor and superintendent. Neither Fliedner's first or second wife nor any other females in the nineteenth century had the possibility of independent exegesis or preaching within the framework of the existing Protestant regional churches. Thus they had hardly any possibilities to be active themselves in exegesis or even to publish scriptural exegetical work.

For this reason, the present article concentrates upon a deaconess who published numerous biblical explanations and also designed them as texts for her sisters or for the sisterhoods founded by her.

2. Eva von Tiele-Winckler, Founder of the Deaconesses of the Refuge of Peace

Eva von Tiele-Winckler exemplifies a specific diaconal founding personality who unites in herself the interdenominationality and transconfessionalism of the revival movement, the vigor of pastoral care, and her own brand

---

4. See Gause, *Kirchengeschichte und Genderforschung: Eine Einführung in protestantischer Perspektive*, UTB 2806 (Stuttgart: Mohr Siebeck, 2006), 156–81.

of Bible piety.[5] She was born on October 31, 1866, as the daughter of the Catholic noblewoman Valeska von Winckler and the industrialist Herbert von Tiele. She was baptized as a Catholic but was later confirmed in the Lutheran church of Silesia. This is explained by, among other reasons, the religious education provided by her Protestant stepmother. In 1890, Tiele-Winckler founded her first house, Refuge of Peace, in Miechowitz in Silesia as a kind of infirmary. Previously, she had learned the care of the sick in Bethel. Her consecration as house mother was combined with the dedication of the house. In June 1892, Bodelschwingh visited Miechowitz and suggested to Tiele-Winckler that she found her own independent motherhouse. By the beginning of the twentieth century, the number of nurses had increased so much that a motherhouse building had to be erected. This was dedicated on October 1, 1905. The number of nurses increased within twenty-five years from fifty (1905) to seven hundred (1930).

A milestone in the development was the founding of the Home for the Homeless in 1910, which was devoted to working with orphaned and abused children. Beginning in 1912, Tiele-Winckler also sent nurses to the mission in China. She died on June 21, 1930. Nowadays, Tiele-Winckler is almost exclusively known in pious circles. The sisters of the Refuge of Peace still exist today and still feel themselves obligated to the legacy of "Mother Eva."[6]

3. Two Examples of Biblical Explanation

Tiele-Winckler designed her biblical explanation primarily for her nurses and conceivably also for an interested public of laypeople. In each instance, it is always an edifying explanation of Scripture and not an exegesis. The explanations of texts from Isaiah were chosen here because they were understood as a kind of legacy of the late deaconess. Although Tiele-Winckler wrote these actually "only for herself alone in her quiet hours," the sisters of the Refuge of Peace published them posthumously.[7]

---

5. See Paul Toaspern, *Eva von Tiele-Winckler: Mutter Eva—Ein Leben aus der Stille vor Gott* (Neuhausen: Hänssler, 1995).

6. See Gause, "Die Freudenberger Friedenshortdiakonissen," *WestF* 56 (2006): 365–77.

7. Foreword in Eva von Tiele-Winckler, *Siehe dein König kommt zu dir!* (Dinglingen: St. Johannis-Druckerei, 1930), n. p.

3.1. Isaiah

Tiele-Winckler's interpretation of Isaiah remains characterized by a peculiar timelessness. The biblical text is, to be sure, brought up to date and existentialized, but allusions to and examples of historical persons and events are almost totally lacking.

For Tiele-Winckler, Isaiah speaks in the present time, as he did in his own, about the indifference and godlessness of the people, which, in the long run, will lead to ruin:[8]

> But, the call to penitence and grace still sounds! There is still time for repentance—repentance in disposition, in way of life and being, in all of one's own doings. There is a possibility of cleansing! The Blood of the Lamb frees from sin and guilt and cleanses thoroughly. Not only forgiveness, but also power to abandon evil is given to those who are sincere, and the renewed heart engenders only good works of righteousness, love, and mercy.[9]

The echoes of sermons from the revival movement noticeable here are not coincidental and also not singular. Tiele-Winckler is in every respect influenced by them.

The judgment is pronounced first of all upon the leader of the people but also upon the women (cf. Isa 3:16–24). Here the commentary says that this picture "fits well with our women's world today."[10] Isaiah 4:4–6, as an allusion to the millennial kingdom, is also understood chiliastically.[11] The deplorable state of affairs described in Isaiah are clarified and applied to the present: "Egoism and a life of indulgence lead to their own ruin. God pronounces His woe over those who love alcoholic drink, who sit long over wine and listen to the sounds of dance music, but, they do not think upon God's word and God's work, and have no time for it and no interest in it."[12] Here, there exists a clear connection to her own work: The neglected children who were taken in by the Refuge of Peace deaconesses often came from families with alcoholic parents.

---

8. See Tiele-Winckler, *Siehe dein König kommt zu dir!*, 5–6.
9. Tiele-Winckler, *Siehe dein König kommt zu dir!*, 6–7.
10. Tiele-Winckler, *Siehe dein König kommt zu dir!*, 11.
11. Tiele-Winckler, *Siehe dein König kommt zu dir!*, 12.
12. Tiele-Winckler, *Siehe dein König kommt zu dir!*, 14.

Tiele-Winckler does not shy away from drawing a parallel between her own calling and that of Isaiah. She assumes a divine commission for all Christians. "It is also so in our hours of grace and of calling. Only later does the magnitude of God's demand become clear to us. But, by then, one is bound and goes back no longer."[13] Human magnificence must decline so that Christ's message of grace can be accepted. First of all, God judges all people who rebel against him. Only out of this "bankruptcy of all humanity coming from Adam" does the new human being Christ arise.[14] Her interpretation emphasizes that everything depends upon true faith: "Only faith can maintain the field. Only faith breaks through steel and stone and can comprehend Omnipotence. Natural courage and one's own power melt away and vanish in the moments of great decision and danger. Faith rests in God, the Unmovable, Eternal, Almighty."[15] The promise of Immanuel is not only understood as a judgment upon the people of God but is also interpreted in an individual sense. The individual human being, too, at first must get to know poverty and helplessness before he or she seeks a redeemer.[16]

The promises in Isa 9 should be reason for jubilation for all of Christianity, for Christ is promised to all people: "To us, us! To all of humanity, all people and races of this earth is given this God-child, the Father's gift of peace and reconciliation, the herald of eternal truth and love."[17] Waiting until the end of the night is interpreted with the individual in mind: "This is true also in times of inner darkness and external distress and perplexity: waiting, abiding, not giving up hope, not discarding trust. The light finally will shine forth after all; morning will come."[18] The following textual statements are brought up-to-date and applied to mission: "Bring water to the thirsty; offer bread to the refugees. What an admonition! Lord, remind me of this always! We who have water and the bread of life and are people of Zion, we are to come to the thirsty, the despondent, and the wanderers with love, and to lead them home."[19] The time of mercy for the redeemed in Isa 25 is described as a time in which

---

13. Tiele-Winckler, *Siehe dein König kommt zu dir!*, 18.
14. Tiele-Winckler, *Siehe dein König kommt zu dir!*, 19.
15. Tiele-Winckler, *Siehe dein König kommt zu dir!*, 20.
16. See Tiele-Winckler, *Siehe dein König kommt zu dir!*, 21.
17. Tiele-Winckler, *Siehe dein König kommt zu dir!*, 24.
18. Tiele-Winckler, *Siehe dein König kommt zu dir!*, 39.
19. Tiele-Winckler, *Siehe dein König kommt zu dir!*, 39.

all national barriers and all confessional disputes are ended.[20] Perhaps Tiele-Winckler alludes here to the Holy Alliance[21] and its ecumenical goals, or to the Evangelical Alliance,[22] which likewise was born by the Irenicism of the revival movement.

Even if God's judgment always aims at salvation, there is no pardon without judgment and repentance (Isa 26). Isaiah 26:19 is understood as a clear announcement of the resurrection. The dew of lights are the people who arise "at the appearance of the great sun of life, Christ" and will "shine like little lights."[23] The greatness of God as creator of the world in Isa 40 is placed in opposition to the pretension of clever free-thinkers and atheists in the nineteenth century.[24] Isaiah 50 and 51 depict Christ as he is portrayed later in the gospels, and who, in suffering and defeat, still remains the victor and whose obedience is intended to be a model for human beings: "Even in the most severe trials, when we see no light and we must wander through the valley of darkness, it is important to trust in the name of the Lord and to adhere to His God. So does one become the conqueror in the discipleship of the suffering Savior."[25] The christological interpretation of the book of Isaiah finally breaks off with Isa 52. The reason for this lies in the illness and death of Tiele-Winckler.

The difficulty of discipleship is explained fundamentally for her own sisters. Such difficulty can be endured only by means of a firm faith in God and trust in Christ, the conqueror and redeemer.

3.2. The Sermon on the Mount

The author's intensive reference to Christ becomes even more important in her explanation of the Sermon on the Mount. First of all, however, she

---

20. See Tiele-Winckler, *Siehe dein König kommt zu dir!*, 43.

21. In 1815, Kaiser Franz I of Austria, King Friedrich Wilhelm III of Prussia, and Tsar Alexander I bound themselves by treaty to orient their policies in the future on the Christian religion. This agreement reflected the reaction of the old powers to the French Revolution and Napoleon Bonaparte.

22. The Evangelical Alliance was the result of the Irenicism within the revival movement at the beginning of the nineteenth century. It was the union, achieved in London in 1846, of various denominations in a common international umbrella organization. The Evangelical Alliance today still has a conservative-revivalist character.

23. Tiele-Winckler, *Siehe dein König kommt zu dir!*, 45.

24. See Tiele-Winckler, *Siehe dein König kommt zu dir!*, 65.

25. Tiele-Winckler, *Siehe dein König kommt zu dir!*, 92–93.

emphasizes its exclusive application to the disciples: "The Sermon on the Mount is, first of all, not a call made to the world, but is primarily directed only at His Disciples.... To them He directs these words in order to be able to reach the great mass of the people through these disciples. The Lord does it the same way even today!"[26] The disciples are prepared to perform a "service of witness and rescue."[27] The task of Christians, male and female, is to bear witness to Christ and, thereby, to save human beings, whereby the allusion to active so-called rescue work also can be meant here.[28] Such a role was certainly intended also for the Sisters of the Refuge of Peace.

Jesus's separation is understood as a recommendation: The people should turn away from the activities of the world, from stressful work, and should come to God in quietness and seclusion.[29] The Old and the New Covenant are contrasted: while the Old Covenant begins with the thunder of judgment, the New Covenant begins with the word "blessed."[30] The application of this idea, however, is that Jesus's speech is directed to all people as their task:

> If the Lord teaches us, then an inner transformation of our being should be the consequence. We are to be reshaped in accordance with this teaching, be a manifestation of this divine teaching, and a letter from God to the world. We should not only speak the words of the Sermon on the Mount, no—we should live it out; our life itself should be a living portrayal of the Sermon on the Mount.[31]

Tiele-Winckler does not translate the text as "poor in the Spirit" (Matt 5:3), as does Luther, but rather as "beggars in the Spirit"—and refers in this context to the Greek text, which she apparently could read and

---

26. Tiele-Winckler, *Glückselig: Matthäus 5, 1-12* (Dinglingen: St. Johannis-Druckerei, 1935), 7.
27. Tiele-Winckler, *Glückselig*, 8.
28. The idea of rescue work corresponds to the concerns of awakened Christians to lead people to God and, thereby, to save them in several respects from sin: from falling away from God and, thus, damnation, but also from spiritual and social distress. The goal here is not a form of social security but rather an individual change of heart, which is intended to make it possible for the male or female individual to lead his or her life meaningfully, responsibly, and successfully in the future.
29. See Tiele-Winckler, *Glückselig*, 10.
30. See Tiele-Winckler, *Glückselig*, 11.
31. Tiele-Winckler, *Glückselig*, 12–13.

translate.[32] The beggars in the Spirit, then, are those who renounce their own reputation and orient themselves completely on God. They are given faith and prayer as gifts, but this means that they set out upon a difficult path: "But what is important here is to be stripped of all arrogance, all pride of virtue, all beauty of character, and of all good works, of all the good opinions of us held by other people, and of the good opinion we have of ourselves."[33] The promises to those who suffer applies only to the true disciples of Christ, his followers. Fundamental suffering is first of all penitential suffering, the genuine remorse felt about one's own corruption. Once repentance has effected a true change, then next comes the encounter with disciplinary suffering, which can also mean physical suffering: "Every disciplinary suffering accepted willingly will also bring us a corresponding wonderful, sweet, divine comfort, if not immediately, then in God's good time."[34] As a next step, there follows the suffering of purification, and, finally, the suffering to the glorification of God. Every sacrifice and pain for Jesus's sake, but also persecution for his name's sake, belongs to this. The highest level of suffering, though, is the suffering in communion with Jesus, that is, that a human being has "Jesus's suffering in his heart" and, thereby, carries Jesus's wounds on his own body.[35] Here, Tiele-Winckler—certainly consciously—picks up Catholic or mystical ideas. Meekness is discussed as a foremost feminine virtue:

> So as many a daughter in the household already has conquered in a difficult situation through her silent, acquiescent meekness; so as many a wife under difficult conditions has overcome her irascible husband through the inner power of meekness! And in our profession in particular, we will see that the meek sister in her house and sphere of activity has more authority, more influence, more real deep authority of the heart than the wrathful, irritable, domineering sister who contends for herself and her honor.[36]

---

32. See her own reference in the text to the Greek meaning of repentance (Tiele-Winckler, *Glückselig*, 19).
33. Tiele-Winckler, *Glückselig*, 16–17.
34. Tiele-Winckler, *Glückselig*, 22.
35. Tiele-Winckler, *Glückselig*, 27.
36. Tiele-Winckler, *Glückselig*, 30.

It is quite a matter of course that she speaks of the deaconess's profession, which is inseparably connected with a divine calling and a Christian way of life.

The hunger and thirst for righteousness is satisfied first in Christ: "The foundation of all righteousness is the righteousness of the blood of Christ imputed to us."[37] From this, then, there results the pursuit of holiness. Compassion, as a capacity for sympathy and love, is a human precondition for participating in the compassion of Christ, who practiced this many times.[38] A pure heart, finally, can be gained only by those who let Christ rule in themselves: "Christ in us—the King of Peace—ascends the throne of our heart; He takes sovereignty over the life placed at His mercy in all its areas—He Himself, Christ in us, will be our new heart."[39] The charge to practice peace is connected with the sisters especially, since they, of course, use the word peace in the name of their society.[40] That is their charge, so that it is said explicitly: "You sisters of peace, you children of God! Try yourselves and carry your name rightly before God and human beings!"[41] In this passage, it again becomes clear how much Tiele-Winckler intends to have her explanation understood as one that is binding in the present.

Persecution and vilification likewise belong almost necessarily to the Christian life—a reference to church history makes this plausible. The secularized church, she said, frequently persecuted true Christian men and women. Among these, in the Middle Ages, were the "Friends of God," the Waldensians, the Albigensians, Wycliffe, and Hus; in later times, these were the Quakers, the Pietists, and also Gottfried Arnold (1666–1714), from which Tiele-Winckler's knowledge of church history probably came.[42] She also counts Gerhard Tersteegen (1697–1769) and Catherine Booth (1829–1890), the "mother of the Salvation Army," among the true Christians.[43] These affinities confirm Tiele-Winckler's rootedness in the revival movement, which goes back to early Pietism, among other movements.

---

37. Tiele-Winckler, *Glückselig*, 33.
38. See Tiele-Winckler, *Glückselig*, 38–40.
39. Tiele-Winckler, *Glückselig*, 45.
40. See Tiele-Winckler, *Glückselig*, 47.
41. Tiele-Winckler, *Glückselig*, 50.
42. Arnold was a Pietist theologian and historian who became known through his *Unparteyische Kirchen—und Ketzerhistorie* (1699–1700), a pioneering work for modern church historiography; see Tiele-Winckler, *Glückselig*, 54.
43. Gerhard Tersteegen was a Pietist lay theologian and mystic from Mülheim an der Ruhr; see Tiele-Winckler, *Glückselig*, 55–56.

The concluding words of the text dedicate the biblical explanation to her own sisters and describe the Sermon on the Mount as "rules of professional conduct and of life for conquerors."[44] Tiele-Winckler emphasizes the separation of the true believers, their self-denial, and their search for devotion and contemplation, which she describes as a "quiet hour." Because she concedes a high value to this form of the practice of piety, she, in contrast to other founding personalities, allows the sisters to live alone in their own rooms and to use them as a place of retreat.

4. Existential Biblical Explanation as a Stimulus to Diaconal Action

The exemplary analysis of Tiele-Winckler's explanation of Scripture shows her to be a typical representative of the revival movement insofar as the following characteristics are found in her explanations: a theology that, in the words of Erich Beyreuther, is biblicistic and emotionally edifying, leads to a conquest, as Gerhard Ruhbach has described it, of rationalism through a Bible-oriented, lively piety.[45] Combined with this is the pursuit of an interdenominational, worldwide-oriented community of Christians.[46] The strong emphasis upon contemplation and devotion, as well as the working of the Holy Spirit, are forms that have been mentioned rather less frequently as characteristic of the revival movement, although in Tiele-Winckler's work they stand out clearly. One perhaps could describe them, in the words of Walter Wendland, as "devotion to the idea of redemption." Or, as he summarizes: "For this reason, the grace of God stands at the focus of revivalist piety."[47] Influences from the Holiness Movement are likewise not to be excluded.[48]

---

44. See Tiele-Winckler, *Glückselig*, 61.

45. Beyreuther, however, assigns both of these characteristics to different groups. Nevertheless, both apply at the same time to Tiele-Winckler and probably also to many other male and female representatives of the revival movement. See Beyreuther, *Die Erweckungsbewegung*, KIG 4 (Göttingen: Vandenhoeck & Ruprecht, 1963), 29–30.

46. See Ruhbach, "Erweckungsbewegung, " *ELThG* 1 (1992): 531–32.

47. Wendland, "Erweckungsbewegung," *RGG* 2 (1928), 303; cf. Gustav Adolf Benrath, "Die Erweckungsbewegung innerhalb der deutschen Landeskirchen 1815–1888: Ein Überblick," in *Der Pietismus im 19. und 20. Jahrhundert*, ed. Ulrich Gäbler, GP 3 (Göttingen: Vandenhoeck & Ruprecht, 2000), 153.

48. The Holiness Movement is a revivalist movement from the end of the nineteenth and the beginning of the twentieth century that places the accent upon the triad of salvation, healing, and sanctification. At the focus stands the optimistic assump-

Tiele-Winckler ranks as a typical representative of the century of Christian social welfare insofar as her pious impulses always are oriented upon the realization of charity. Even if these Bible explanations do not belong in the context of historical-critical exegesis, they still represent a genuine expression of a piety that characterized the nineteenth century and, above all, the women working in social welfare. For these women who appeared before the public out of this kind of interest in social welfare—as well as for their journalistic success in the devotional explanation of the Bible—is true what Reiner Strunk said in 1971 about the revival theologians in general: they did not want to be systematic theologians, but understood themselves rather as "pure and impartial 'admirers of the Bible'... This had the consequence, of course, that they could take up ideas eclectically from quite different sources and could integrate them in the explanation of the Bible."[49]

Tiele-Winckler's involvement is based upon this lively piety and existentialization of the Bible, which she wants to see realized radically and which she herself also practices. The reference to her female addressees leads here to specific accents in her explanations, for the founder of the Refuge of Peace speaks to her sisterhood, which is obligated to the discipleship of Jesus and is placed in his service. But, what comes first is always the self-assurance of wanting to act in accordance with the will of God, of taking appropriate subjects from the Bible for interpretations for the present, as well as of obtaining standards of conduct.

Bibliography

Arnold, Gottfried. *Unparteyische Kirchen und Ketzerhistorie*. Frankfurt am Main: Fritsch, 1699–1700.

Benrath, Gustav Adolf. "Die Erweckungsbewegung innerhalb der deutschen Landeskirchen 1815–1888: Ein Überblick." Pages 150–271 in *Der Pietismus im 19. und 20. Jahrhundert*. Edited by Ulrich Gäbler. GP 3. Göttingen: Vandenhoeck & Ruprecht, 2000.

---

tion that spiritual and physical health is to be recovered through a lively faith life in a personal relationship with God. See Stephan Holthaus, *Heil, Heilung, Heiligung: Die Geschichte der deutschen Heiligungs—und Evangelisationsbewegung 1874-1909*, KM 14 (Gießen: Brunnen, 2005).

49. Strunk, *Politische Ekklesiologie im Zeitalter der Revolution*, GT 5 (Munich: Kaiser, 1971), 102.

Beyreuther, Erich. *Die Erweckungsbewegung*. KIG 4. Göttingen: Vandenhoeck & Ruprecht, 1963.
Cordes, Martin. *Diakonie und Diakonisse: Beiträge zur Rolle der Frauen in kirchlicher sozialer Arbeit*. QFESH 4. Hemmingen: Sozialwissenschaftliche Studiengesellschaft, 1995.
Gause, Ute. "Die Freudenberger Friedenshortdiakonissen." *WestF* 56 (2006): 365–77.
———. *Kirchengeschichte und Genderforschung: Eine Einführung in protestantischer Perspektive*. UTB 2806. Stuttgart: Mohr Siebeck, 2006.
Gause, Ute, and Cordula Lissner, eds. *Kosmos Diakonissenmutterhaus: Geschichte und Gedächtnis einer protestantischen Frauengemeinschaft*. HTG 1. Leipzig: Evangelische, 2005.
Herrmann, Volker. "Wichern." *TRE* 35 (2003): 733–39.
Holthaus, Stephan. *Heil, Heilung, Heiligung: Die Geschichte der deutschen Heiligungs—und Evangelisationsbewegung, 1874–1909*. KM 14. Gießen: Brunnen, 2005.
Kaiser, Jochen-Christoph, and Rajah Scheepers, eds. *Dienerinnen des Herrn: Beiträge zur weiblichen Diakonie im 19. und 20. Jahrhundert*. HTG 5. Leipzig: Evangelische, 2010.
Köser, Silke. *Denn eine Diakonisse darf kein Alltagsmensch sein: Kollektive Identitäten Kaiserswerther Diakonissen, 1836–1914*. HTG 2. Leipzig: Evangelische, 2006.
Ladendorf, Otto. "Innere Mission." Pages 140–41 in *Historisches Schlagwörterbuch*. Strassburg: Trübner, 1906. http://www.textlog.de/schlagworte-innere-mission.html.
Ruhbach, Gerhard. "Erweckungsbewegung." *ELThG* 1 (1992): 531–36.
Schmidt, Jutta. *Beruf: Schwester; Mutterhausdiakonie im 19. Jahrhundert*. GG 24. Frankfurt: Campus, 1998.
Strunk, Reiner. *Politische Ekklesiologie im Zeitalter der Revolution*. GT 5. Munich: Kaiser, 1971.
Tiele-Winckler, Eva von. *Glückselig: Matthäus 5, 1–12*. Dinglingen: St. Johannis-Druckerei, 1935.
———. *Siehe, dein König kommt zu dir!* Dinglingen: St. Johannis-Druckerei, 1930.
Toaspern, Paul. *Eva von Tiele-Winckler: Mutter Eva—Ein Leben aus der Stille vor Gott*. Neuhausen: Hänssler, 1995.
Von Hauff, Adelheid M., ed. *Frauen gestalten Diakonie 2: Vom 18. bis zum 20. Jahrhundert*. Stuttgart: Kohlhammer, 2006.
Wendland, Walter. "Erweckungsbewegung." *RGG* 2 (1928): 295–304.

Bible Reading as Motivation for Diaconal-Social Initiatives: The Example of Countess Elvine de La Tour (1841–1916)

Michaela Sohn-Kronthaler

In Ezek 47:1–12, the prophet is shown a river of living water that runs from the threshold of the Temple, flows after noon down through the plain in order, in part, to fertilize the arid soil and, in part, to fill the waters of the Dead Sea with renewed power of life. This should be an image that shows us what the Lord desires to accomplish even through our work in a mostly faithless, dead world. If no river of life springs up out of this work, the institutions, etc., then they have no value, then the fertilizing element is lacking which is able to convert the wasteland into a delightful garden. It must be the fervent wish of all our hearts that we experience what Isa 58:11–12 says: "The Lord will continually guide you, and satisfy your soul in the desert, and give strength to your bones; and you will be like a watered garden, and like a spring of water whose waters do not fail. And those from among you will rebuild the ancient ruins, and you will lay down the foundations that remain forever."[1]

With these words from the prophets Ezekiel and Isaiah, Countess Elvine de La Tour (1841–1916) construed the purpose and goal of the social institutions established by her at that time in Friaul and Carinthia. She was, along with the brothers Ernst and Ludwig Schwarz, one of the most important personalities in Protestant social welfare work in Austria in the late nineteenth and early twentieth centuries.[2] She is also one of the

---

1. Elvine de La Tour, *Jahresbericht über die Werke der Inneren Mission im österreichischen Küstenland und in Treffen, Kärnten* 1915, Archiv der Diakonie Kärnten (ADK), AOO5-1, 9–10.

2. On Senior Pastor Ernst Schwarz (1845–1925), the younger brother of Ludwig Schwarz and pastor in Waiern, see Kurt Schaeffer, *Ernst Schwarz, Das Werk der Liebe*

most significant pioneers and representatives of the Inner Mission in the Cisleithanian half of the empire of the Habsburg monarchy. The Carinthian Protestant of Lutheran provenance, and with Italian roots, founded schools, reform schools for girls and boys, houses for the aged and for children, a Christian sanctuary for the homeless, and was a renowned promotor of evangelization. With her social initiatives, the Countess laid the cornerstone for a lasting work that continues to exist in the present in the Foundation de La Tour, a major pillar of Protestant social welfare work in Austria.[3]

1. The Yearly Reports by Elvine de La Tour as a Source for Her Reception of the Bible

Although numerous larger and smaller portrayals of de La Tour already exist, above all biographical treatments, there are nevertheless none that deal in detail with her understanding of the Bible.[4] This is all the more remarkable since the countess can be assigned to the many-faceted revival movements of the nineteenth century that carried on earlier Pietism.

The present essay illustrates the application of the Holy Scripture by de La Tour by using the articles published by her in the *Yearly Report on the Work of the Inner Mission*, which appeared regularly between 1906 and 1917.[5] These yearly reports, which she published herself, document

---

zu Waiern: *Das Verlorene suchen; Das Leben finden* (Feldkirchen: Schaeffer, 1986); On Ludwig Schwarz (1833–1910), the founder of the Gallneukirchen Institutions and one of the founders of the Upper Austrian Association for Inner Mission, today the Diakoniewerk, see Anna Katterfeld, *Die erfüllte Prophezeihung* (Lahr-Dinglingen: St. Johannis-Druckerei C. Schweickhardt, 1959).

3. See www.diakonie-delatour.at.

4. A bibliographical survey of the literature up to the present is presented by the detailed bibliography by Heidrun Szepannek, *Elvine Gräfin de La Tour (1841–1916): Protestantin, Visionärin, Grenzgängerin*, KL 38 (Klagenfurt: Kärntner Landesarchivs, 2011), 247–58. The author deals briefly in her publication with de La Tour's biblical reception in Szepannek, *Elvine Gräfin de La Tour*, 73–77.

5. All the issues of the *Jahresbericht über die Werke der Inneren Mission* are preserved in the ADK in Treffen under the call number A005-1. The yearly reports from 1906 to 1910 and in 1915 were printed by Heinrich Schlick in Saint Veit an der Glan in Carinthia, from 1911 by the L. Herrmannstorfer Press in Trieste, and in 1916 by Chr. Scheufele Printers in Stuttgart. A further issue appeared in 1917 after the death of de La Tour. My thanks are due to Christl Szepannek, who directs the ADK, for permitting inspection of the documents.

not only the development of the institutions she created, but also her internalized and lived Christian faith. At the beginning of every issue of this periodical always stands the "Report of the Countess de La Tour" as the first item. But, there are also in the yearly reports articles by her coworkers, who report about a concrete social work project sponsored by the founder. The many-faceted texts by de La Tour show not only autobiographical characteristics but also let her readers take part in her daily life, in the progress of her foundational activity, and in her Bible piety. The reports of the writer are permeated deeply with a profound knowledge of the Holy Scriptures, to which reference is made either directly by the Countess through exact quotations of textual passages, or also indirectly. One of the editions of the Luther Bible that de La Tour personally possessed and used still is preserved in the Archiv der Diakonie Kärnten (ADK) in Treffen. On the inside of the book cover is the handwritten name "Elvine de La Tour" as well as "Job 28" and "Isaiah 40" noted in pencil.[6] These texts presumably were important and decisive for her personal life interpretation.

With the help of the Bible, which served her as the ethical standard for her treatment of her neighbors and as a devotional book in daily life, the events of the bygone year were subjected to reflection. The reports show a constant pattern: in most cases, they were written at the beginning of the year, opened almost always with a Bible passage, less often with a line from a hymn or a prayer, and then followed with the review of the past year. The text ended with thanks expressed to friends and benefactors, also often with a Bible quotation. The first article providing a report by the countess appeared in 1906. The last one written by her originated in May 1916, only six months before her death, and is much like a review of her life.

---

6. *Die Bibel oder die ganze Heilige Schrift des Alten und Neuen Testaments, nach der deutschen Übersetzung D. Martin Luthers* (Stuttgart: Priviligierte Württembergische Bibelanstalt, 1901), ADK, GO01-1. In this Bible text, there are numerous markings of biblical passages made by the countess herself. In the ADK, there are two further Luther Bibles that de La Tour had presented to young women as gifts on the occasion of their confirmations. The Bibles carry the names of Emilie von Molitor and Christine Hinteregger. The flyleaves of both editions, which differ from each other only in the year of publication (1894 and 1896), contain personal dedications by Elvine de La Tour along with quotations of Bible verses. *Die Bibel oder die ganze Heilige Schrift des Alten und Neuen Testaments, nach der deutschen Übersetzung D. Martin Luthers* (Berlin: Britische und Ausländische Bibelgesellschaft, 1894 and 1896), ADK GO01-2 and GO01-3.

The beginning lines with which the countess opens her very first annual review in the *Yearly Report* of 1906 already show her existential appropriation of the words of the Bible. These few lines make manifest how precisely the writer, on the basis of her revivalist piety, oriented herself on Holy Scripture, how she exegeted her life and work in the light of the Bible, and how she trusted in God's help in all life situations:

> When, in the prayer of Moses, the man of God, it says (Ps 90:10) that, if our life has been blissful, then it has been labor and sorrow, then we also may say in review of the bygone year, which offers us a picture of strenuous labor, that it was a blissful one. Not alone because of the work that we were allowed to carry out for the Lord, but also still more especially in thankful acknowledgement of the mercy of our God that we experienced so many times in adversity and tribulation.[7]

As evidence for the lasting experience of God's help, de La Tour cites the line "In how much distress has not the gracious God spread his wings over you," which comes from the well-known hymn *Lobe den Herren* (1680) by Joachim Neander and which recalls Deut 32:11.[8]

By using the yearly reports published by de La Tour, it is possible to document, in extracts but also in an impressive way, what an immense knowledge of the Bible this Protestant Christian woman possessed on the basis of her regular reading and encounter with Holy Scripture. This was true although she took up neither the profession of deaconess nor did she become a missionary.[9] The Bible played a decisive role in her life and in the interpretation of her life and became the motivation for her social initiatives.

2. The Bible as the Standard for Life Orientation and Social Action

2.1. The Leitmotif for Her Social Welfare Work: John 21:15

De La Tour, born as a Knight of Záhony, came from a well-to-do Lutheran merchant family in Friaul, the ancestral line of which on the paternal side

---

7. *Jahresbericht* 1906, ADK, AOO5-1, 3.
8. *Jahresbericht* 1906, ADK, AOO5-1, 3.
9. Among the written sources that de La Tour left behind are, in addition, her correspondence, several shorter articles in Protestant periodicals, as well as her written recollections from the time of World War I. These are preserved in the ADK.

can be traced back to the lifetime of the German Reformer.[10] She saw the light of the world for the first time there on December 8, 1841. The families of her parents had a large part in the development of the Protestant congregations in Görz and Trieste. Her father, Julius Hektor Knight of Záhony, urged the foundation of an independent congregation in Görz, functioned as congregational custodian there, and supported the building of the Protestant church dedicated in 1864. In her childhood, de La Tour lost her mother and, as a young person, her eldest brother. She received her spiritual formation above all through conversations with her pastor, Ludwig Schwarz, who led the newly founded Protestant congregation in Görz from 1864 to 1871. Through Schwarz, she became acquainted with the ideas of the initiator of the Allgäu revival movement, Martin Boos.[11]

Social inequality, the contrast between the poor and the rich, moved de La Tour already in the years of her youth. She herself noted that she came from "radiant circumstances" but that she was surrounded by destitute people. For this reason, she wanted to choose a life path that had the aim of contributing to "alleviating the distress of my fellow human beings."[12] Thus, the "suffering world of the children" was "to become the mainspring for my later work with the poor children." Especially the meditation upon the Bible verse John 21:15 was decisive for her diaconal-social work, the more so since she "heard Jesus' commission: 'Tend my lambs!' and I thought: 'I, too, love the Savior and would like to tend his lambs.'—I understood these to be the children."[13] Looking back, she described the "rescue mission to children and adults" as "the burning desire of my soul."[14]

After her marriage in 1868 to the Catholic Count Theodor de La Tour (1845–1894), the married couple lived on the wine-growing estate

---

10. Michaela Sohn-Kronthaler, "Ein Leben im Zeichen der Diakonie: Elvine Gräfin de La Tour (1841–1916) und ihre sozial-karitativen Gründungen in Italien und Österreich," in *Frauen gestalten Diakonie 2: Vom 18. bis zum 20. Jahrhundert*, ed. Adelheid M. von Hauff (Stuttgart: Kohlhammer, 2006), 351–67.

11. On Marin Boos (1762–1825), see Georg Schwaiger, "Boos," *LThK* 2 (1994): 590; on the Allgäu revival movement and Boos, see Horst Weigelt, "Die Allgäuer katholische Erweckungsbewegung," in *Der Pietismus im 19. und 20. Jahrhundert*, ed. Ulrich Gäble, GP 3 (Göttingen: Vandenhoeck & Ruprecht, 2000), 88–95.

12. *Jahresbericht* 1916, ADK, AOO5-1, 3.

13. *Jahresbericht* 1916, ADK, AOO5-1, 3; cf. *Christentum der Tat* 1 (1923), Folge 4, 7–8.

14. De La Tour, "Aus Kärnten," *Worte der Wahrheit und Liebe für Österreich und Ungarn* 9 (1913): 190.

of Russiz, which, near the hill country of Görz, belonged to the village of Capriva, near Cormons in Friaul. The count showed himself to be open to the coexistence of the two confessions, which for the time was in no way natural. The region of the Austrian Littoral boasted at this time the considerably high Catholic proportion of 99.9 percent of the population. The count, in addition, supported the social and interdenominational initiatives undertaken by his wife. With the purchase of the manor of Treffen, near Villach in Carinthia, which the couple used as a secondary residence in the summers, de La Tour came to an area in which she encountered an environment that was more strongly Protestant: "In the year 1885, the Lord led me to Carinthia, where my husband and I had acquired possession of the manor Treffen. Thus, I was permitted to enter upon a large field of labor, of which about a tenth was inhabited by Protestant people."[15] There, the countess looked after the children of the very poor in a Sunday school that very quickly enjoyed great popularity. De La Tour inquired about the causes of social inequalities and, through her instruction, gained:

> a first insight into the dreadful misery and the moral degradation of our people here, who had departed so much from any divine order. The many illegitimate children, the disregard for marriage, the prevailing immorality, godlessness, fornication, drunkenness, etc. are witnesses to this. How the poor, neglected children who never had a home strengthened through the word of God did grow up!... Thus, here, too, a work project developed through the gathering and recovery of the lost, endangered, needy little lambs [cf. John 21:15; Luke 15:3-7].[16]

In her second home in Treffen, de La Tour founded a private Protestant school for boys and girls (1891). Over the door to the school, she had placed the inscription "One is our Master: Christ," following Matt 23:8, and next to it the Psalm verse "The fear of the Lord is the beginning of wisdom" (Ps 111:10 LB). She also started a home for babies and infants, a nursing station, the home called Herrnhilf for the aged and boys, as well as Elim for impoverished and destitute children. The name Elim recalls

---

15. *Jahresbericht* 1916, ADK, AOO5-1, 5. In fact, in Carinthia, 94.9 percent of the population was Catholic and 5.1 percent Protestant; in the community of Treffen, the denominational relationship was 61.9 percent Catholics to 37.8 percent Protestants (Szepannek, *Elvine Gräfin de La Tour*, 24–25).

16. *Jahresbericht* 1916, ADK, AOO5-1, 5. On her foundations in Carinthia, see Szepannek, *Elvine Gräfin de La Tour*, 88–94.

the designation mentioned in the Old Testament for the oasis with twelve springs of water (cf. Exod 15:27; Num 33:9).[17] Shortly before the end of her life, de La Tour summarized in May 1916: "The promise that I received shortly after my arrival here in Treffen, Revelation 3:7–8, in which I trusted all these years and never to no avail, was to be fulfilled there, too."[18]

De La Tour, as a woman from the nobility, had at her disposal corresponding material resources that she used for her social projects.[19] She was convinced of her individual calling and thanked God for choosing her to be his coworker, and for his blessing: "For to him, the God who called me to his service and who has blessed my work, is alone due praise and thanks for this."[20] At another place, she shifted her work into the context of Jesus's judgment upon the world (Matt 25:40: "Amen, I say to you: What you have done for one of the least of these, my brothers, you have done it to me") and concluded: "God's reward and blessing will not fail to appear."[21] In the *Yearly Report* of 1911, she interpreted the growth of her institutions, in spite of the hardships and difficulties that she continued to encounter, with the biblical passage from Ps 126:5–6: "Those who sow in tears shall reap with joyful shouting. He who goes to and fro weeping, carrying his bag of seed, shall come again with joy, bringing his sheaves with him."

Even as a seventy-year-old, she expressed her joy over her election by God which, in spite of her advanced age, still remained and over the continued existence of her projects, with biblical echoes:

> It is blissful to be assured of the fact that the Lord has called me to the work in which I am involved. Sometimes, I thought I had to withdraw when I saw how the work continued to gain in extent, continued to develop new branches of activity, and I, in comparison, had to take into account my weakness, my increasing age. But, my second thoughts and my resistance always vanished in face of the already established great grace and promises of our God. I had to obey and to say to the Lord: "If the commission really is meant for me, then I place myself at your disposal, for I know that your power, O Lord, will carry me further, as it has done up to this point." I also never have been ashamed of my trust in this. [cf. Ps 25:20].[22]

---

17. Szepannek, *Elvine Gräfin de La Tour*, 88–94, 102–6.
18. *Jahresbericht* 1916, ADK, AOO5-1, 6.
19. Szepannek, *Elvine Gräfin de La Tour*, 153–63.
20. *Jahresbericht* 1907, ADK, AOO5-1, 3.
21. *Jahresbericht* 1907, ADK, AOO5-1, 11.
22. *Jahresbericht* 1914, ADK, AOO5-1, 3.

2.2. Jer 17:5–7 and 2 Cor 6:14 as Aids in Decision-Making

The significance of the social welfare institutions founded by de La Tour can be assessed correctly only when the social conditions that prevailed in the nineteenth century among the population of the Austrian Littoral and Alps are taken into account.[23] Social institutions and educational institutions, such as kindergarten, schools, hospitals, or homes for the aged, were not at all a matter of course. In addition, the circumstances for denominational charitable initiatives were made more difficult because the two major Christian denominations in Austria in the nineteenth century acted as though they were enemies.

The starting point for de La Tour's oldest institution was, in 1873, the foundation in Görz of a relief association with the goal "of looking after and educating completely destitute or orphaned girls."[24] She herself had been elected superintendent of this—for the time remarkable—interdenominational organization for the care of orphans, although the Protestant Christians were a minority there. The goal of the association was a religious one: "To win the young souls accepted in the name of Jesus for the Savior of the world always appeared to me to be the chief purpose and hoped-for goal of this education of children."[25] Since she soon encountered obstacles "that more and more threatened my freedom of conscience," de La Tour decided to give up her superintendent's position. As she said, she had felt herself obligated "to place this newly originated work on a Protestant basis (Matt 7:24–27). As a result, I encountered many reservations and the resistance of most of the members of the association, who had no understanding for my approach to faith."[26] For "reasons of conscience," she was "forced with a heavy heart … to take another path."[27] Especially the Bible passages Jer 17:5–8 and 2 Cor 6:14 provided her with

---

23. See Lucia Angelmaier, *Wohltätigkeitsvereine in Triest: Private Initiativen gegen die Armut im Zeitalter der österreichisch-ungarischen Monarchie*, BNGO 14 (Frankfurt: Lang, 2000); and Vinzenz Jobst, *Arbeitswelt und Alltag: Ein sozialgeschichtliches Lesebuch; Kärntner Arbeiterleben im 19. und beginnenden 20. Jahrhundert* (Klagenfurt: Kärntner, 1985).

24. The *Bericht der Gräfin de La Tour* from the *Jahresbericht* 1910 has no title page and no pagination. It comprises only the two pages of de La Tour's report. *Jahresbericht* 1910, ADK, AOO5-1, [1]. See also *Jahresbericht* 1909, ADK, AOO5-1, 16.

25. *Jahresbericht* 1910, ADK, AOO5-1, [1].

26. *Jahresbericht* 1916, ADK, AOO5-1, 4.

27. *Jahresbericht* 1916, ADK, AOO5-1, 4.

a source of further action, that is, to terminate her cooperation with the "unbelievers"—meaning the non-Protestant Christians. At another place, too, she wrote that, in her decision-making, the Bible verses from Jer 17 sparked a "vehement inner struggle" in her: "I had to make the choice between what human cleverness prescribed and what I recognized as prescribed. The words of Jer 17:5 and 7 stood compellingly before my soul and sparked within me a vehement inner struggle."[28] In her devotional book, the use of which was usual in the milieu of the awakened, she found—as she established later in retrospect—concrete help in making the correct decision: the saying "One is not strong who is slack in the day of distress" (Prov 24:10).[29]

Because of her withdrawal, the association disbanded. She was allowed to take the children into her own home without receiving any money for doing so. Her husband agreed to the housing of the girls at his estate in Russiz, where the countess began with their instruction. In 1875, she received the official permit for the erection of a reformatory and a school, in which students of both sexes and regardless of denomination could be instructed.[30] A school building was begun and soon also the new construction of a reformatory. The press of applicants was so great that, in spite of repeated enlargements, the space available still proved to be too small, and the construction of an enlarged building had to be considered. The countess used a biblical image in describing the decision:

> that I gladly would expand the space available and roll out my carpets. Isa 54:2. Thus, faith proved to be a major force in my life at that time, and so it has remained to the present day. To him, the Lord, and not to me, is due the honor! I know through how many weaknesses I have gone, since his power and love, which does not extinguish the glowing wick, carried me [cf. Isa 42:7].[31]

---

28. *Jahresbericht* 1910, ADK, AOO5-1, [1].

29. The first devotional book originated in 1731 in the Herrnhut brotherhood.

30. Szepannek, *Elvine Gräfin de La Tour*, 80–86. A vivid report about the more than thirty-year activity of the institution and school is provided by the former superintendent Anna Heber: "Bericht über die Arbeit in der evang[elischen] Mädchen-Erziehungs-Anstalt zu Russiz bei Cormos österr[eichisches] Küstenland" (*Jahresbericht* 1911, ADK, AOO5-1, 14–21).

31. *Jahresbericht* 1910, ADK, AOO5-1, [2]. See also note 24.

The achievement that her two foundations in Russiz still continued to exist after three decades in a primarily Catholic-Italian region was explained by the writer with the passage from Matt 7:24–29: "It is simply not built upon sand, but rather upon the rock that neither falters nor gives way."[32] She interpreted the success of her social-pedagogical initiatives with the aid of Matt 6:13 (LB): "What is divine cannot perish. For this reason, we remain comforted and know that, in gloomy and in bright times, we have only to praise and to thank the One whose kingdom and power and glory is forever."[33] In view of her numerous projects, de La Tour thought of herself as a "rich mother," although she herself had no natural children—she, who "received a great commission from the Lord and upon whom a still greater responsibility is incumbent." These circumstances had to overwhelm her if she had not had the knowledge that the Lord constantly gave her "wisdom, light, and power" and "that he lets the upright succeed! [cf. Prov 2:7]."[34]

The countess saw to the nursing and care of the small children, even of the babies, who came from the families of day laborers and domestics, for instance, and lived in impoverished circumstances and were "endangered in body and soul." She took these into her children's home beginning in 1902 and thereby applied the following biblical image: "'My father and my mother forsake me, but the Lord takes me up.' Ps 27:10 [LB]."[35] About the deaconess who directed the home for the aged and infirm, de La Tour reported that she embraced her charges not only with care but also saw to the salvation of their souls. This sister had "no higher desire than to lead the wards entrusted to her to the Shepherd and Bishop of our souls, the dear Savior. 1 Pet 2:25 [LB]." In this connection, de La Tour used the example in the biblical text Luke 23:43 in describing the fate of a woodcutter who found the way to Christian faith and by whom the countess personally stood when he died a Christian death.[36]

---

32. *Jahresbericht* 1906, ADK, AOO5-1, 9.

33. The last sentence is only in the Luther Bible, but not in the ecumenical translation. *Jahresbericht* 1906, ADK, AOO5-1, 9.

34. *Jahresbericht* 1909, ADK, AOO5-1, 5.

35. *Jahresbericht* 1909, ADK, AOO5-1, 9.

36. *Jahresbericht* 1909, ADK, AOO5-1, 10–12.

3. Evangelization as Her Most Important Concern

Along with her diaconal-social activity, an interest in the missionary evangelization of the people played an important role for de La Tour. The countess is to be assigned to the revival movements influenced by Anglo-American ideas that took hold of some Protestant regional churches in German-speaking areas in the second half of the nineteenth century.[37] At that time, there arose several fellowship circles that developed an autonomous congregational life and addressed themselves especially to those alienated from the church and also to social fringe groups.[38]

De La Tour maintained contacts with the branches that aligned themselves with the Evangelical Alliance and the Holiness Movement. She was part of the international network in obtaining evangelists. On her journeys, she personally visited, among others, the center at Saint Chrischona near Basel,[39] from whence most of her preachers who she employed in Carinthia and Friaul came. Presumably, she also gathered ideas here for her social projects. In addition, she was successful in winning evangelists for missionary activity from Bahnau[40] in East Prussia as well as from the Dea-

---

37. See Gustav Adolf Benrath, "Die Erweckung innerhalb der deutschen Landeskirchen 1815–1888: Ein Überblick," in *Pietismus im 19. und 20. Jahrhundert*, ed. Ulrich Gäbler, GP 3 (Göttingen: Vandenhoek & Ruprecht, 2000), 150–71. Unfortunately, de La Tour is not mentioned in this comprehensive portrayal of Pietism in the nineteenth and twentieth centuries.

38. See Jörg Ohlemacher, "Gemeinschaftschristentum in Deutschland im 19. und 20. Jahrhundert," in *Pietismus im 19. und 20. Jahrhundert*, ed. Ulrich Gäbler, GP 3 (Göttingen: Vandenhoek & Ruprecht, 2000), 393–464.

39. The Pilgrim Mission at Saint Chrischona was erected in 1840 by Christian Friedrich Spittler and had the goal of training people for service in proclamation, pastoral counseling, and mission. Spittler's successor, Carl Heinrich Rappard, developed the training school into the first school for evangelists in the German-speaking sphere. See Edgar Schmid, *Wenn Gottes Liebe Kreise zieht: 150 Jahre Pilgermission St. Chrischona 1840–1990* (Basel: Brunnen, 1990); and Karl Rennstich, "Mission: Geschichte der protestantischen Mission in Deutschland," in *Pietismus im 19. und 20. Jahrhundert*, ed. Ulrich Gäbler, GP 3 (Göttingen: Vandenhoek & Ruprecht, 2000), 308–10. From De La Tour's report emerges the fact that she was there during her journey in the summer of 1910 and presumably appeared there in search of a preacher, since, on December 1, 1910, a Chrischona brother, the preacher Rüdt, came to Villach (*Jahresbericht* 1914, ADK, AOO5-1, 3).

40. A Protestant mission school had been erected there in 1906.

coness Mother House Hensoltshöhe near Gunzenhausen.[41] From Korntal in Württemberg, a center in which the older Pietism had combined with ideas from the Fellowship Movement to form a quite independent life model, she invited the Swabian preacher Eugen Zimmermann to Treffen in May 1911. Previously, Zimmermann had held evangelization meetings in Russiz and in Triest, in the Christian Hospice opened by de La Tour in 1908, as well as in the Protestant church there.[42] She herself sent her favorite grandnephew, Theodor von Gall, to Korntal for training.[43]

The central elements of the revival movements—namely, mission work, the proclamation of the gospel, and the love of neighbor practiced in the form of diaconal-social initiatives—are also reflected in de La Tour's sense of mission.[44] She designated the "Fellowship Movement and evangelization" as the "most important branch of work" in all she did.[45] She began with evangelization in 1893.[46] Thus, she understood Jesus's parable in Matt 13:1–23 in this context: "The seed from God's Word was now sown, and many a seed found good soil in which it could put down roots, flourish, and bring forth fruit."[47] She consistently brought evangelists to Carinthia for the work of spreading the faith.[48] The positive development of the evangelization over the space of a decade in Treffen and environs unfolded in an active life of faith "to the honor of God and the joy of the people." She interpreted this development with the passage in Isa 52:7 (LB): "How lovely on the mountains are the feet of him who announces peace, who says to Zion: Your God is king!"[49]

In her review of the work of the year 1910, de La Tour joyously recorded that smaller fellowship circles had formed at other places in Carinthia, too. The countess assessed the work of evangelization that had been carried out in the winter by three evangelists as very animated. These workers had

---

41. *Jahresbericht* 1913, ADK, AOO5-1, 5.
42. *Jahresbericht* 1912, ADK, AOO5-1, 4.
43. Szepannek, *Elvine Gräfin de La Tour*, 72.
44. Arnd Götzelmann, "Die Soziale Frage," in *Pietismus im 19. und 20. Jahrhundert*, ed. Ulrich Gäbler, GP 3 (Göttingen: Vandenhoek & Ruprecht, 2000), 272–307.
45. *Jahresbericht* 1911, ADK, AOO5-1, 6.
46. *Jahresbericht* 1909, ADK, AOO5-1, 5. The *Jahresbericht* 1916 mentions a "Carinthian trained in St. Chrischona" as a first evangelist in the year 1893. Meant here was Alfred Galsterer (*Jahresbericht* 1916, ADK, AOO5-1, 5).
47. *Jahresbericht* 1916, ADK, AOO5-1, 5.
48. Szepannek, *Elvine Gräfin de La Tour*, 73, 94–96.
49. *Jahresbericht* 1909, ADK, AOO5-1, 5.

not shrunk from the arduous path "of winning human souls for the Savior and his discipleship, of admonishing the unruly, of comforting the fainthearted, of helping the weak. 1 Thess 5:14 [LB]."[50] Men and women, as well as sisters and brothers "from our fellowships," were active in the distribution of the many writings and tracts by the German evangelist and writer Ernst Modersohn (1870–1948) from Blankenburg and by the well-known evangelist Georg von Viebahn (1840–1915).[51]

De La Tour had the fellowship hall in Treffen painted. The walls were decorated with Bible verses, and the hall was provided with a pulpit, pews, an altar, as well as with a portrayal of Christ in the act of blessing, made of bronze and mounted in a frame. On this was seen the Bible verse Matt 11:28 (LB): "Come to me, all who are weary and heavy laden."[52] To the dedication of the hall, she invited Pastor Modersohn, who visited Carinthia for the first time in 1909 and, in 1913, once again attended the annual celebration in Waiern. Modersohn in his autobiography later recalled the "dear Countess La Tour" who "conducted ... a blessed Protestant work of love in a Catholic land."[53]

The deaconesses who de La Tour had requested from the mother house Großheppach in Württemberg, Vandsburg in West Prussia, and Hensoltshöhe in Gunzenhausen (Bavaria) cared for the evangelization of the female sex: "These deaconesses hold meetings—mostly for women and girls— conduct a Sunday school and Bible studies in private homes, and are a blessing in their work in visiting, the care of the sick, etc."[54] The sisters also always visited among the fringe groups of the society: "the sick, needy, and alcoholics, and endeavored to act in accordance with the commission: 'Admonish the unruly, encourage the fainthearted, help the weak, be patient with everyone.'

---

50. *Jahresbericht* 1911, ADK, AOO5-1, 7. Among them was Matthias Dopplinger who, however, moved in the spring of 1910 to Gallneukirchen (Upper Austria). De La Tour separated from the other two because they tended toward the Pentecostal movement and Jonathan Paul's doctrine of sinlessness. Housefather Friedrich Gienger then took over the office of community guardian (*Gemeinschaftspfleger*) in Treffen. In the meantime, the missionary Hauser, from Rottweil, was active in Treffen.

51. *Jahresbericht* 1914, ADK, AOO5-1, 6.

52. *Jahresbericht* 1912, ADK, AOO5-1, 4–5.

53. Ernst Modersohn, *Er führet mich auf rechter Straße* (Stuttgart: Oncken, 1948), 231. See also Holger Böckel, "Modersohn, Ernst," *RGG* 4 (2008): 1389.

54. *Jahresbericht* 1908, ADK, AOO5-1, 5; see also *Jahresbericht* 1914, ADK, AOO5-1, 5.

1 Thess 5:14 [LB]."⁵⁵ De La Tour described the activity of a sister in the home for the aged and the sick with words from Holy Scripture: "Her work had brought forth many a fruit and provided a blessing. This will one day make manifest the great day on which is brought to the light all that is hidden [cf. Dan 2:47; 2 Macc 12:41]."⁵⁶ The success of the evangelization was shown in the fact that the rooms in Treffen had to be enlarged: "The rooms everywhere became too small, and so I had to decide to make many an extension, primarily in Herrnhilf." The founder thus interpreted the enlargement of her social initiatives in Carinthia with Isa 54:2 (LB): "Enlarge the room of your tent and spread out the carpets of your dwelling."⁵⁷

To the joy of the countess, it was possible to send two evangelists and a deaconess to Trieste in the summer of 1913 to carry out evangelization. She attributed this development to divine activity: "The Lord gave me a wonderful blessing and also heard my prayer to show us a hall that was to serve us as a place for proclamation of the Word. Mark 14:15 [LB]."⁵⁸ The Protestant-Lutheran church was placed at her disposal for this purpose, and her experience was that:

> The Lord ... [reveals] his greatness and glory in a different way than the world does. There always stands the word "modest" before the paths that his people follow. But, those who take the same are able to say much about a hidden glory that brings forth a great peace and an indescribable joy. This one day will reach its culmination in which it will then be true that: "That which eye has not seen and ear has not heard and has not entered the heart of a human being, all that God has prepared for those who love him." 1 Cor 2:9 [LB].⁵⁹

After ten years of evangelization, the countess succeeded in obtaining the use of a hall in Trieste for several further months. On the basis of this event, she decided that she could trust in laying her works in the hands of God and summarized her report in the words: "We are comforted that the Lord then will continue to provide. Indeed, we pray for a house of our own and expect that the Lord will hear us, if it be his will."⁶⁰

---

55. *Jahresbericht* 1914, ADK, AOO5-1, 4.
56. *Jahresbericht* 1915, ADK, AOO5-1, 7.
57. *Jahresbericht* 1908, ADK, AOO5-1, 7.
58. *Jahresbericht* 1914, ADK, AOO5-1, 5.
59. *Jahresbericht* 1914, ADK, AOO5-1, 5.
60. *Jahresbericht* 1914, ADK, AOO5-1, 5.

Since the evangelists remained only a few years, de La Tour was constantly in search of new coworkers. She referred literally to the "prayer that the Savior himself puts into our mouth," namely, the Bible passage "Therefore beseech the Lord of the harvest to send out workers into his harvest" (Matt 9:38; Luke 10:2).[61] She repeatedly recorded in her yearly reviews that her prayers found a hearing. Thus, she could report about the visits of Pastor Theophil Krawielitzki (1866–1942), the founder of the Fellowship Social Welfare Association of Vandsburg, who brought with him an evangelistically gifted deaconess by the name of Wilhelmine. Together, they conducted meetings in Russiz, Trieste, Villach, and Treffen. After their departure, they were replaced by the deaconess Marie Kuhl, who worked as a communal nurse in the Treffen center and in the surrounding area. She was supported by a second sister. Along with these two sisters, two further deaconesses from Vandsburg worked in Treffen, one with the sick and aged and the other in the day nursery. Likewise, she mentioned a sister from the mother house in Großheppach responsible for the training of nurses for infant care; a fifth deaconess from Vandsburg worked as an assistant in the girls' reformatory in Russiz.[62] At another place, the countess wrote that two evangelists were drafted into the military because of the outbreak of the First World War, which led to a lack of personnel in the missionary work. Once again, she articulated her request to the Lord to send new workers.[63]

Among the efforts at evangelization undertaken by de La Tour were also the annual celebrations in the month of August, presumably beginning in 1898. Connected with these were conferences lasting several days for the deepening of the life of faith. Her engagement in establishing a Blue Cross Association for Carinthia with its headquarters in Treffen also stands in the context of her missionary work. The Association, dedicated to the care of alcoholics, began its work on March 2, 1913.[64]

De La Tour often reported the difficulties, crises, and hostilities she encountered in the course of evangelization. Thus she wrote in the 1912 *Yearly Report*: "Our work of evangelization, of fellowship, and in the Blue Cross also meets with much protest, even from many who have become

---

61. *Jahresbericht* 1908, ADK, AOO5-1, 4.
62. *Jahresbericht* 1908, ADK, AOO5-1, 5.
63. *Jahresbericht* 1915, ADK, AOO5-1, 6.
64. *Jahresbericht* 1914, ADK, AOO5-1, 3. See also Szepannek, *Elvine Gräfin de La Tour*, 96–97, 107–8.

convinced that we stand grounded in God's Word and that we want to offer this Word alone to those human beings who have fallen away from obedience to the Creator of all things."[65] She encountered resistance not only from the Catholic office-holders, as described in more detail in the next section, but also in part from within her own church, which did not take kindly to many a preacher from the outside and to their way of working. So, there was controversy already in 1910 over two evangelists from Bahnau who displayed fanatical conduct in the congregations. The conflicts led to a pastors' conference in Villach. This assembly deliberated on the fundamental question of the continued existence of the missionary work, and decided finally in favor of the countess, that is, for the continuance of the evangelization in Carinthia, even if some Protestant pastors later still entertained "distrust and resistance" in regard to the evangelists.[66]

Because of a new Bible translation for the Slovenians, two Bible distributors employed expressly for this work had to endure temporary prison sentences. In spite of the hindrances that she experienced in her work, de La Tour was convinced "that the cause in which we stand is the Lord's, who has all power, and who will protect the work and help it to victory. I hold to this faith in unswerving trust, and for this reason I am comforted."[67] The fellowship work founded by de La Tour continues to exist today in the form of the "Christian Missionary Association for Austria" (CMV), a member in the "Evangelical Fellowship Association Gnadau," as well as in the *Diakonisches Werk* in Austria.[68]

4. The Existential Appropriation of Holy Scripture

In the texts written by de La Tour, one can gain an impressive understanding of the existential appropriation of Holy Scripture by the writer. This is typical of members of the revival movements. In the yearly reports, too, the countess's personal experience of God and salvation, the "individualistic motif," is reflected.[69] She felt herself to be addressed directly by God, or by Jesus, her Savior, who had a direct effect upon her in her concrete life situations.

---

65. *Jahresbericht* 1914, ADK, AOO5-1, 5.
66. Szepannek, *Elvine Gräfin de La Tour*, 151–52.
67. *Jahresbericht* 1913, ADK, AOO5-1, 5.
68. See the Christian Missionary Association for Austria at www.cmv.or.at.
69. Götzelmann, "Die Soziale Frage," 274.

The grace and forbearance of God (cf. 1 Cor 15:10) and the hearing of prayer form a central theme of her Bible piety.[70] In writing the report for the year 1910, de La Tour described her awakened faithfulness and attitude of humility with the words that "I am nothing and am able to do nothing, and I have alone the grace of our great God to thank when I am permitted to contribute toward carrying out his intentions of love among our people here, too [cf. Eph 2:8]." She had "sometimes considered with pain and inner submission" that "the Lord [could] have achieved even more through a more complete devotion, through more obedience and faith on my part." For this reason, "the forbearance of my God, which carries us in our weakness and does not let us fall [cf. 2 Cor 12:]," appeared to her to be all the greater.[71] The countess felt her life to be permeated always by grace: "Yes, it is only grace after all that I may praise in looking back over a long series of years in which the divine forbearance has carried me, campaigned for my soul and, after I as a poor, bankrupt sinner had embraced the Savior and given myself over to him, was called and equipped by him to serve him through work with the children."[72] De La Tour was convinced that "no prayer presented in faith can remain unheard!" and that, at all times in her life, she had received what she had asked for from God.[73] She explained the difficulty in life with God's pedagogical intentions: She "[had] also to learn again how the misery, the temptation, and the struggles which never stop in the life of a child of God must serve the purpose of shaking us out of our lethargy and hardness of heart and, in prayer and supplication, of trusting in the one to whom no faith is too weak, no hour is too late, and no distress appears too great."[74] God would wait until human beings choose a path on which he could show "how great his power is and how gladly he helps and hears prayers."[75]

A trusting faith as to the realization of all her social-missionary initiatives ran through her reports like a common thread. Thus she referred confidently to Deut 28:8, John 2:4, and 8:2: "The Lord will give everything and let everything succeed when his hour will have come; of this I am certain!" She closed the *Yearly Report* 1909 with the words: "The Lord

---

70. *Jahresbericht* 1908, ADK, AOO5-1, 8–9.
71. *Jahresbericht* 1911, ADK, AOO5-1, 3.
72. *Jahresbericht* 1912, ADK, AOO5-1, 7.
73. *Jahresbericht* 1912, ADK, AOO5-1, 3.
74. *Jahresbericht* 1912, ADK, AOO5-1, 3.
75. *Jahresbericht* 1912, ADK, AOO5-1, 3.

heard my sighs and let me experience much love through his children and instruments here on earth. But he will repay each and every person—this his servant David believed and experienced since ancient days—according to each's righteousness and faith. 1 Sam 26:23."[76] Using the example of a small group of fellow Protestant brothers and sisters in the faith, she showed how rewarding it could be to trust in God's help. These congregational members, in spite of their meager incomes, had been ready to provide the financial means for support of a deaconess. She applied the Bible verse 1 Sam 14:6 (LB), according to which one may count on the help of the Lord in apparently hopeless situations. "It is not hard for the Lord to help through many or a few [cf. 2 Chr 14:10]."[77] De La Tour concluded her remarks with the wish directed to her readers to yield themselves even more completely to God's possibilities:

> How much could we, too, experience and attain if we would trust our Lord and God more in faith, indeed in everything! We would then continually experience Jesus' word to us: "If you would believe, you should see the glory of God." John 11:40 [LB]. That we do not cause any dishonor to this powerful, wonderful Lord through our lack of faith and our shrinking back, but rather magnify his name where we undertake our work for him is my fervent desire and yearning. In him, we will always have victory! And now may the work in God's Kingdom in our country be commended in further love and intercession to all dear brothers and sisters from near and far who are bound to us as members in the body of Christ. Thanks to all for the love already shown! The Lord will reward them and bless them! [cf. Num 6:24][78]

De La Tour interpreted her own life as a fluctuating series of events. In the first place, she referred indirectly to Rev 5:12, according to which "the songs of rejoicing in the praise and acclamation of the Lamb [shall] never die away" (LB). On the other hand, she reported about the experience of becoming quiet that "under the weight of dark days and long anxious nights, where we can do nothing other than what stands in Jas 5:13 [LB]: 'Is anyone among you suffering? Let him pray,' it is not so easy for the heart to do as in the next sentence: 'Is anyone cheerful? Let him sing praises.'"[79]

---

76. *Jahresbericht* 1909, ADK, AOO5-1, 16.
77. *Jahresbericht* 1908, ADK, AOO5-1, 11.
78. *Jahresbericht* 1908, ADK, AOO5-1, 12.
79. *Jahresbericht* 1908, ADK, AOO5-1, 3–4.

She mentions both experiences also in the 1909 *Yearly Report*: God's continuing help, but also the "hard paths, all the effort, struggle, anxiety, and many a humiliation," that in the past year she "was not spared; but I knew myself to be carried by the strong arms of my God, who causes all things to work together for good to those who love him [cf. Rom 8:28]."[80] Everything, even what was difficult, the affliction, suffering came "from 'above,'" since it was God's "intention in salvation and love" to bind human beings ever closer to himself, so that his name might be glorified (cf. John 12:28).[81] In summary, she came to the knowledge that:

> I am able only to praise and to give thanks—give thanks for all the compassion and loyalty shown by the Lord, for which I, his maid, am too insignificant; give thanks for my God's wonderful mercy, not alone in the major incidents but also in the smallest of them, in the life of the institutions and in regard to other undertakings; and give thanks especially also for the fact that I have been permitted to experience it again and again that the Lord always gives the victory to those who trust in him [cf. 2 Cor 2:14].[82]

De La Tour liked to use the metaphor of the "visible and invisible side" born by her work and referred here to the First Letter to the Corinthians:

> Certainly much has occurred that will prove to be wood, hay, and stubble, 1 Cor 3:12ff, but also precious metal, and this certainly hidden, has been among it all. The day, which one day will come, will make all things visible and clear. Meanwhile, we may give thanks that the Lord is so true and lets so much be destroyed through the fire of tribulation that in his eyes was not suitable and, therefore, useless. But, the divine smelter also will let stand what can be purified, like gold and silver, Mal 3:3, and will accept it in grace as a thank offering presented from a full and loving heart.[83]

The theme of God's hidden ways with human beings is also found in another biblical passage cited by de La Tour. God, to be sure, fulfills his promises, but does this in a way different than human beings can conceive:

---

80. *Jahresbericht* 1909, ADK, AOO5-1, 4.
81. *Jahresbericht* 1913, ADK, AOO5-1, 3.
82. *Jahresbericht* 1909, ADK, AOO5-1, 4.
83. *Jahresbericht* 1913, ADK, AOO5-1, 3.

In Mark 16:20, it says: "But the apostles went out and preached everywhere; and the Lord worked with them and confirmed the word through the accompanying signs" [LB]. Where the one, as a pre-condition, occurs in the proper manner, the second, the consequence of it, also will not fail; for every promise of our God without doubt is fulfilled. Of course, this does not always happen in the way we, in the human perspective, expect. About Stephen, it is said in Acts 6:8: "And Stephen, full of grace and power, was performing great wonders and signs among the people" [LB]. And then, what do we see at the end of this so richly blessed life? A defeat before the eyes of humans, in the discipleship of Jesus, a fate similar to that of our Lamb, which gives us an example of how we, too, can and will overcome. For this reason, we want to be comforted in regard to the future veiled to us. Even in defeat, we will be victorious, for the victory belongs to the Lord under every circumstance, and we have a part in it when we belong to him. These are the hidden ways that lead to glory.[84]

As already indicated, the countess met with vehement attacks and resistance in her sphere of work in Carinthia and Friaul from individual Catholic clergymen. They charged that her institutions were interdenominationally oriented and, for this reason, also accepted non-Protestant children. The *Reichspost*, the daily newspaper of the Christian Social Party in Austria, called her, as de La Tour herself reported, a "Protestant proselytizer" over whose "institutions an invisible, protecting hand [rules]," since even all the edicts and efforts of the school department and ordinariates could do nothing against her.[85] In 1914, she once again had to go through stormy experiences and spoke about "enmity, struggles, distress of every kind," about "accusations and conflicts, under which we had to suffer for months."[86] Meant here was the attempt made by the Catholic Church in the Austrian Littoral, with the help of state agencies, to take the non-Protestant children out of her institutions. She refused "to hand over the lambs" and "wanted to stand as a good shepherd that does not flee when the wolf comes in order to force himself into the herd."[87] In Russiz, women and girls who had gone forth from the reform school placed themselves at the side of their benefactress. At a public rally, they expressed "their pain"

---

84. *Jahresbericht* 1914, ADK, AOO5-1, 6.
85. *Jahresbericht* 1910, ADK, AOO5-1, [2]. See also note 24 above and *Jahresbericht* 1909, ADK, AOO5-1, 16.
86. *Jahresbericht* 1915, ADK, AOO5-1, 3.
87. *Jahresbericht* 1915, ADK, AOO5-1, 4.

over the accusations made against the countess but also "their recognition, love, and thankfulness" of and to the founder.[88] De La Tour found the conflicts which she went through because of her social institutions to be very painful. The texts of the Bible and her orientation on the suffering of Jesus gave her consolation:

> It pained me all the more to experience that my work toward attaining this purpose and goal finds such manifest resistance, and that the greatest tribulations are caused because of it. What I do out of love encounters misinterpretation and hate from many sides, which would not be understandable if the Word of God, our dear Bible, would not have an explanation for it. How many times were people who placed themselves in the service of humanity hated; Scripture declares them to be blessed (Matt 10:22-24; Mark 13:13; Luke 21:17; Luke 6:22). Our Savior did not experience it in any other way here on earth (John 15:18) and could say: "They hate me without cause" (John 15:25). So we must not wonder if we experience a similar fate.[89]

Because of the Italian invasion in the Austrian Littoral during World War I, de La Tour had to leave her home at Russiz in the fall of 1915. Since the return to Treffen at first was refused to her, she stayed until the end of January 1916 in Berne and Stuttgart before she could travel again to Carinthia.[90] Her troubles and the war, as well as also the unexpected death after a short illness of her thirteen-year-old grandnephew von Gall, sapped her vitality. He was "the dearest that we had on earth" for her and his parents. She accepted his sudden passing with the words of Job 1:21 (LB): "The Lord knew why he had to do this; praised be his name in everything!"[91]

The concluding words of the last report that de La Tour wrote in 1916, five months before her death, contain consolation and the hope in eternal life with God:

> I am thinking of the words in 1 Pet 3:13 where it says "And who is there to harm you if you prove zealous for what is good?" [LB] and in 1 Cor 7:23: "You were bought with a price; do not become slaves of men" [LB]. The Lord, before whom I endeavor to walk and who I endeavor to obey, will stand by his Word. About that I may be unconcerned. This is and

---

88. *Jahresbericht* 1915, ADK, AOO5-1, 4.
89. *Jahresbericht* 1916, ADK, AOO5-1, 7.
90. *Jahresbericht* 1916, ADK, AOO5-1, 6.
91. *Jahresbericht* 1916, ADK, AOO5-1, 7.

remains my comfort and my faith in all tribulation, in which I do not stand alone here on earth. But I also hope, along with an unnumbered throng, to stand one day there where the hallelujah of the redeemed, blessed children of God will resound in eternity![92]

5. Summary

On the basis of the yearly reports, written between 1906 and 1916 about the work of the Inner Mission, it is possible to show impressively what existential significance the Bible had for de La Tour and how the Bible piety of the revival movements of the nineteenth century motivated her remarkable social commitment. The Holy Scriptures played a fundamental role in the countess's internalized faith in Christ and in her interpretation of her life. There, she found orientation, help in making decisions, and support in daily life. She also interpreted the development of her foundations in the social area and in evangelization in the light of the Bible. Interdependence existed between her diaconal-social initiatives and her missionary evangelization among the people.[93] De La Tour encouraged evangelization in Austria; she characterized evangelization as an important area of her responsibility and had at her disposal a network of international contacts for the purpose of winning preachers in her homeland. As a woman of noble background, she disposed of a corresponding material means that she employed to the benefit of her charitable works. With her reform and educational institutions for girls and boys, and with the homes for the aged and children, she created not only institutions in the Protestant church significant for the time in which she lived but therewith also lasting works of Christian social welfare in present-day Austria.

Bibliography

Angelmaier, Lucia. *Wohltätigkeitsvereine in Triest: Private Initiativen gegen die Armut im Zeitalter der österreichisch-ungarischen Monarchie*. BNGO 14. Frankfurt: Lang, 2000.

Benrath, Gustav Adolf. "Die Erweckung innerhalb der deutschen Landeskirchen 1815–1888: Ein Überblick." Pages 150–71 in *Pietismus im*

---

92. *Jahresbericht* 1916, ADK, AOO5-1, 8.
93. See Götzelmann, "Die Soziale Frage," 274.

19. und 20. Jahrhundert. Edited by Ulrich Gäbler. GP 3. Göttingen: Vandenhoek & Ruprecht, 2000.

Böckel, Holger. "Modersohn, Ernst." *RGG* 4 (2008): 1389.

Die Bibel oder die ganze Heilige Schrift des Alten und Neuen Testaments, nach der deutschen Übersetzung D. Martin Luthers. Berlin: Britische und Ausländische Bibelgesellschaft, 1894, 1896. ADK GOO1-2 and GOO1-3. Repr., Stuttgart: Priviligierte Württembergische Bibelanstalt, 1901. ADK, GOO1-1.

Götzelmann, Arnd. "Die Soziale Frage." Pages 272–307 in *Pietismus im 19. und 20. Jahrhundert.* Edited by Ulrich Gäbler. GP 3. Göttingen: Vandenhoeck & Ruprecht, 2000.

Jobst, Vinzenz. *Arbeitswelt und Alltag: Ein sozialgeschichtliches Lesebuch; Kärntner Arbeiterleben im 19. und beginnenden 20. Jahrhundert.* Klagenfurt: Kärntner, 1985.

Katterfeld, Anna. *Die erfüllte Prophezeihung.* Lahr-Dinglingen: St. Johannis-Druckerei C. Schweickhardt, 1959.

La Tour, Elvine de. "Aus Kärnten." *Worte der Wahrheit und Liebe für Österreich und Ungarn* 9 (1913): 190.

———. *Jahresbericht über die Werke der Inneren Mission im österreichischen Küstenland und in Treffen, Kärnten.* St. Veit an der Glan: Heinrich Schlick 1906–1910, 1915; Trieste: L. Herrmannstorfer Press, 1911; Stuttgart: Chr. Scheufele Printers, 1916. Archiv der Diakonie Kärnten (ADK), AOO5-1.

Modersohn, Ernst. *Er führet mich auf rechter Straße.* Stuttgart: Oncken, 1948.

Ohlemacher, Jörg. "Gemeinschaftschristentum in Deutschland im 19. und 20. Jahrhundert." Pages 394–464 in *Pietismus im 19. und 20. Jahrhundert.* Edited by Ulrich Gäbler. GP 3. Göttingen: Vandenhoek & Ruprecht, 2000.

Rennstich, Karl. "Mission: Geschichte der protestantischen Mission in Deutschland." Pages 308–29 in *Pietismus im 19. und 20. Jahrhundert.* Edited by Ulrich Gäbler. GP 3. Göttingen: Vandenhoek & Ruprecht, 2000.

Schaeffer, Kurt. *Ernst Schwarz, Das Werk der Liebe zu Waiern: Das Verlorene suchen; Das Leben finden.* Feldkirchen: Schaeffer, 1986.

Schmid, Edgar. *Wenn Gottes Liebe Kreise zieht: 150 Jahre Pilgermission St. Chrischona (1840–1990).* Basel: Brunnen, 1990.

Schwaiger, Georg. "Boos." *LThK* 2 (1994): 590.

Sohn-Kronthaler, Michaela. "Ein Leben im Zeichen der Diakonie: Elvine Gräfin de La Tour (1841–1916) und ihre sozial-karitativen Gründungen in Italien und Österreich." Pages 351–67 in *Frauen gestalten Diakonie 2: Vom 18. bis zum 20. Jahrhundert*. Edited by Adelheid M. von Hauff. Stuttgart: Kohlhammer, 2006.

Szepannek, Heidrun. *Elvine Gräfin de La Tour (1841–1916): Protestantin, Visionärin, Grenzgängerin*. KL 38. Klagenfurt: Kärntner Landesarchiv, 2011.

Weigelt, Horst. "Die Allgäuer katholische Erweckungsbewegung." Pages 87–111 in *Pietismus im 19. und 20. Jahrhundert*. Edited by Ulrich Gäble. GP 3. Göttingen: Vandenhoeck & Ruprecht, 2000.

Reading among German-Speaking Catholic Women and the Significance of the Bible between 1850 and 1914

Bernhard Schneider

Gender as a relational category also interacts with religion.[1] For this reason, connections between gender constructions and the religious reading done by women exist; the following article pursues these connections in two respects. It discusses first of all whether gender-specific statements were available in the Catholic discourses about reading during the period researched. In this context, the article will deal in particular with the question whether the reading of the Bible appears in this connection and what role possibly was assigned to Bible reading among women. Finally, on the basis of a series of works from the devotional and edificatory literature that was written for women, it will be explained whether and in what way the Bible plays a role in this kind of literature. To be explained is also whether and how constructions of the images of women are connected with the Bible and biblical designs of womanhood. A treatment of the biblical images of women is, accordingly, not intended.

1. Catholicism and Gender in the Nineteenth Century

Historical research has discussed the connection between religion and gender first of all by using the thesis of a "feminization of religion" in the nineteenth century. Many contemporary statements and further observations gave rise to this. This thesis originated in Anglo-American women's

---

1. See Claudia Opitz-Belakhal, *Geschlechtergeschichte*, HE 8 (Frankfurt: Campus, 2010), 34–38; and Jürgen Martschukat and Olaf Stieglitz, "Es ist ein Junge," in *Einführung in die Geschichte der Männlichkeiten in der Neuzeit*, HE 11 (Tübingen: Edition Diskord, 2005), 55.

and gender history in the 1970s and 1980s.[2] It was taken up intensively in German research in the 1990s.[3] The formula "feminization of religion" in research literature describes various aspects and processes: the code conversion of religion as feminine; an independent interpretation of faith by women; a process of withdrawal by men from the ecclesiastical-religious area; and a greater-than-average presence of women in ecclesiastical-religious life. The fields in which these tendencies toward a feminization were said to be shown were named in research literature as personnel, piety, organization, and representation. In the meantime, the criticism of a too-simplified manner of speaking has grown, although the designation "feminization of religion" continues to be used merrily.[4]

In regard to the Catholicism in the German-speaking region, the findings provide a somewhat more discriminating picture.[5] In the area of "ecclesiastical personnel," the feminine gender gained appreciably in relevance. This was owing to the many new women's orders or women's congregations, which gave a feminine countenance to ecclesiastical charity in particular.[6] In the narrower area of piety, numerous contemporary

---

2. See Barbara Welter, "'Frauenwille ist Gotteswille': Die Feminisierung der Religion in Amerika, 1800–1860," in *Listen der Ohnmacht: Zur Sozialgeschichte weiblicher Widerstandsformen*, ed. Claudia Honegger and Bettina Heintz (Frankfurt: Europäische, 1981), 326–28.

3. See Irmtraud Götz von Olenhusen, ed., *Frauen unter dem Patriarchat der Kirchen: Katholikinnen und Protestantinnen im 19. und 20. Jahrhundert*, KG 7 (Stuttgart: Kohlhammer, 1995); and Götz von Olenhusen, ed., *Wunderbare Erscheinungen: Frauen und katholische Frömmigkeit im 19. und 20. Jahrhundert* (Paderborn: Schöningh, 1995).

4. See Bernhard Schneider, "Feminisierung der Religion im 19. Jahrhundert: Perspektiven einer These im Kontext des deutschen Katholizismus," *TTZ* 111 (2002): 123–47. From the Protestant perspective, see Ute Gause, "Frauen und Frömmigkeit im 19. Jahrhundert: Der Aufbruch in die Öffentlichkeit," *PN* 24 (1998): 309–27. Most recently see Tine van Osselaer and Thomas Buerman, "Feminization Thesis: A Survey of International Historiography and a Probing of Belgian Grounds," *RHE* 103 (2008): 497–544; and Patrick Pasture, "Gendering the History of Christianity in the Nineteenth and Twentieth Centuries," in *Gender and Christianity in Modern Europe: Beyond the Feminization Thesis*, ed. Jan Art Pasture and Thomas Buerman, KADOC 10 (Leuven: Leuven University Press, 2012), 7–33.

5. On the following, see Schneider, "Feminisierung," 123–47.

6. See Schneider, "The Catholic Poor Relief Discourse and the Feminization of the Caritas in Early Nineteenth Century Germany," in Pasture and Buerman, *Gender and Christianity in Modern Europe*, 34–55.

reports indicate that women took part more frequently in worship services and partook of the sacraments more regularly.[7] The disproportionally strong participation of women in many pilgrimages and in many religious associations can be shown statistically.[8] One can hardly speak, however, of a comprehensive distancing of the men from pilgrimages, as is shown by special men's or workers' pilgrimages.[9] In the associations outside the purely "pious" ones, the men were decidedly dominant. In view of the strong position of priests as leaders of most of the pious associations, these were hardly places of feminine self-determination, in spite of the dominance of their feminine members.[10] On the other hand, this was the case in the Catholic German Women's Association, founded in 1903.[11] The "feminization of pious literature" postulated by some parts of research has not yet found an empirically secure confirmation.[12] On the whole, the proportion of devotional literature specifically addressed to a particular gender is comparatively small.[13] We will come back to this topic presently.

Against this background, the "feminization thesis," at least in regard to German Catholicism, must be distinctly modified. One cannot speak of a general masculine unbelief or of a strong disposition toward withdrawal

---

7. See Schneider, "Feminisierung," 130–37; Rudolf Schlögl, *Glaube und Religion in der Säkularisierung: Die katholische Stadt; Köln, Aachen, Münster, 1700–1840*, AR 38 (Munich: Oldenbourg, 1995), 316–26.

8. See Schneider, "Feminisierung," 134–41; Andreas Kotulla, "Nach Lourdes!," in *Der französische Marienwallfahrtsort und die Katholiken im Deutschen Kaiserreich, 1871–1914* (Munich: Meidenbauer, 2006), 252, 305–6; Volker Speth, *Katholische Aufklärung, Volksfrömmigkeit und "Religionspolicey": Das rheinische Wallfahrtswesen von 1816 bis 1826 und die Entstehungsgeschichte des Wallfahrtverbots von 1826; Ein Beitrag zur aufklärerischen Volksfrömmigkeit*, EW 5 (Frankfurt: Lang, 2008), 244–46.

9. See Hans-Jürgen Brandt and Karl Hengst, *Das Bistum Paderborn im Industriezeitalter: 1821–1930*, vol. 3 of *Geschichte des Erzbistums Paderborn*, VGMK 14 (Paderborn: Bonifatius, 1997), 494–95.

10. See Joachim Oepen, "Bruderschaften im 19. Jahrhundert," *RQCAK* 99 (2004): 205.

11. See Michaela Sohn-Kronthaler and Andreas Sohn, *Frauen im kirchlichen Leben vom 19. Jahrhundert bis heute* (Kevelaer: Topos, 2008), 24–25; Gisela Breuer, *Frauenbewegung im Katholizismus: Der Katholische Frauenbund, 1903–1918* (Frankfurt: Campus, 1998).

12. Rudolf Schlögl, "Sünderin, Heilige oder Hausfrau? Katholische Kirche und weibliche Frömmigkeit um 1800," in *Wunderbare Erscheinungen*, ed. Götz von Olenhusen (Paderborn: Schöningh, 1995), 37–38.

13. See Schneider, "Feminisierung," 137–39.

among Catholic men. Nevertheless, men caused increasing concern to pastoral theology, particularly in the last third of the nineteenth century. A Catholic discourse on masculinity attempted to put a stop to the tendency present in society to assign religiousness alone or primarily to women. The church, as well as religion, was to be demonstrated as masculine.[14] The combination of faith and action affected through the aggressive representation in public of the church and its faith was considered the ideal posture of the Catholic man. Through a calculated rhetoric and symbolism, the attempt was made at the same time to shape pious practices (especially the veneration of the Sacred Heart) in a more masculine manner and to create special men's associations or to organize men's pilgrimages.[15] The concern on the whole was less a re-Christianization of an unbelieving masculine world than a desire to bind this world to an ultramontane model of strict churchliness and submission to the clergy.[16]

2. Reading Women in Catholicism

The Catholic milieu prevailing in the period of our investigation in German-speaking countries (at least in the area of present-day Germany and Switzerland) is understood in recent research on Catholicism increasingly as a network held together by common values, interpretations of the world, and meaningful convictions.[17] Accordingly, it could not at all be a matter

---

14. See Schneider, "Masculinity, Religiousness and the Domestic Sphere in the German-Speaking World around 1900," in *Christian Homes: Religion, Family, and Domesticity in the Nineteenth and Twentieth Centuries*, ed. Tine van Osselaer and Patrick Pasture, KADOC 14 (Leuven: Leuven University Press, 2014), 27–51.

15. See Brandt and Hengst, *Paderborn*, 496; Norbert Busch, *Katholische Frömmigkeit und Moderne: Die Sozial- und Mentalitätsgeschichte des Herz-Jesu-Kultes in Deutschland zwischen Kulturkampf und Erstem Weltkrieg*, RKM 6 (Gütersloh: Kaiser, 1997), 267–78; Olaf Blaschke, "The Unrecognised Piety of Men: Strategies and Success of the Re-Masculinisation Campaign around 1900," in *Christian Masculinity: Men and Religion in Northern Europe in the Nineteenth and Twentieth Centuries*, ed. Yvonne Maria Werner, KADOC 8 (Leuven: Leuven University Press, 2011), 21–45.

16. See van Osselaer and Buerman, "Feminization Thesis," 534–38.

17. See as an interim review Johannes Horstmann and Antonius Liedhegener, eds., *Konfession, Milieu, Moderne: Konzeptionelle Positionen und Kontroversen zur Geschichte von Katholizismus und Kirche im 19. und 20. Jahrhundert*, AV 47 (Schwerte: Katholische Akademie, 2001). Some open questions are discussed by Andreas Henkelmann, *Caritasgeschichte zwischen katholischem Milieu und Wohlfahrtsstaat: Das Seraphische Liebeswerk, 1889–1971*, VKZ 113 (Paderborn: Schöningh, 2008), 18–24, 465–

of indifference in regard to who read what literature. A battle about good
and bad literature, about the craze for reading and its alleged terrible consequences, raged for many decades. The *Index of Forbidden Books* is only
one aspect of this, for, in the Catholic press or at the annual meetings of the
Catholic associations (the so-called Catholic congresses), the complaints
died away just as little as did the number of perpetually new initiatives
for steering reading habits in the desired direction.[18] One can also cite
the Borromean Association, steeped in tradition and still existing today,
which, since 1844, dedicated itself to building Catholic libraries and to the
promotion of the "good book" in the "intellectual struggle."[19] Catholic periodicals, works such as *1000 Good Books*, or Heinrich Keiter's (1853–1898)
Catholic Literary Calendar also served in steering reading.[20] The world of
reading material obviously was considered eminently important especially

---

69; and Winfried Becker, "Katholisches Milieu: Theorien und empirische Befunde," in *Grenzen des katholischen Milieus: Stabilität und Gefährdung katholischer Milieus in der Endphase der Weimarer Republik und in der NS-Zeit*, ed. Joachim Kuropka (Münster: Aschendorff, 2012), 23–62.

18. With a view to the genre of the press, Michael Schmolke, *Die schlechte Presse: Katholiken und Publizistik zwischen "Katholik" und "Publik," 1821–1968* (Münster: Regensberg, 1971); Dominik Burkard, "Presse und Medien," in *Laien in der Kirche*, ed. Erwin Gatz, GKL 8 (Freiberg im Breisgau: Herder, 2008), 559–602. On Catholic liter-ary criticism, see especially Jutta Osinski, *Katholizismus und deutsche Literatur im 19. Jahrhundert* (Paderborn: Schöningh, 1993), 253–402; Susanna Schmidt, "Handlanger der Vergänglichkeit," in *Zur Literatur des katholischen Milieus, 1800–1950* (Paderborn: Schöningh, 1994), 131–35.

19. See Osinski, *Katholizismus*, 272–77 (for the middle of the nineteenth century); as well as especially Steffi Hummel, *Der Borromäusverein, 1845–1920: Katholische Volksbildung und Büchereiarbeit zwischen Anpassung und Bewahrung*, VHKT 18 (Cologne: Böhlau, 2005).

20. For Catholic periodicals, see, for example, the *Literarischer Handweiser (für das katholische Deutschland)* [from 1890 "first of all for all Catholics of German tongue"] (Freiberg im Breisgau: from 1861 until 1930). On the publisher Franz Hüls-kamp (1833–1911), see Georg Schreiber, "Westfälische Wissenschaft, Politik, Publizis-tik im 19./20. Jahrhundert: Franz Hülskamp und sein Kreis," *WestF* 8 (1955): 74–94. For *1000 Good Books*, see Hülskamp, *1000 gute Bücher, den Katholiken deutscher Zunge zu Festgeschenken empfohlen* (Münster: Theissing, 1882); Franz Xaver Wetzel, *Die Lek-türe: Ein Führer beim Lesen* (Ravensburg: Dorn, 1897). For Heinrich Keiter, see Hein-rich Keiter, ed., *Katholischer Literaturkalender* (Freiburg im Breisgau: 1891–1897). Also continued after Keiter's death up to 1914 by Karl Menne, ed., *Keiters Katholischer Literaturkalender* (Freiberg im Breisgau: 1898–1914). See also Heinrich Keiter, *Die Kunst, Bücher zu lesen* (Essen: Fredebeul & Koenen, 1901).

in those circles, such as priests or bishops, who saw themselves as responsible for leading the believers to their salvation. At the same time, though, priests as well as bishops in the late nineteenth century were confronted with wishes coming from the ranks of the believers. These aimed at widening the narrow world of strictly Catholic-oriented, primarily devotional literature and at gaining permission to read other material.[21]

2.1. Reading and the Female Sex

From the gender-specific perspective, there emerges a double tendency since the late eighteenth century. On the one hand, the reading done by girls and women expanded quite fundamentally, and reading took on a new form. The form of extensive reading, at least in certain classes, replaced the older form of reading in which a small number of works were read intensively and repeatedly. On the other hand, as a reaction to these new reading habits, distinct attempts were made to condemn sharply what was called "book learning" as well as the flight into the imaginary world of the novel. In this discourse about the "reading craze," or "reading mania," girls and women especially were considered to be endangered, and, correspondingly, the attempt to regulate their reading habits was especially energetic. Herein was reflected a piece of reality because women did become a new class of readers and because women of the upper bourgeoisie even formed the most important group of readers of *belles lettres*, especially of novels. But, the solidifying polar constructions of gender in this discourse, whereby the extensive and false reading done by women was presented as a danger to the social order, became palpable at the same time.[22] Accordingly, the range of problems connected with reading played

---

21. See on this Jeffrey T. Zalar, "The Process of Confessional Inculturation: Catholic Reading in the 'Long Nineteenth Century,'" in *Protestants, Catholics and Jews in Germany, 1800–1914*, ed. Helmut Walser Smith (Oxford: Berg, 2001), 121–52.

22. On feminine reading in general: Martyn Lyons, "Die neuen Leser im 19. Jahrhundert: Frauen, Kinder, Arbeiter," in *Die Welt des Lesens: Von der Schriftrolle bis zum Bildschirm*, ed. Roger Chartier and Guglielmo Cavallo (Frankfurt: Campus, 1999), 455–97. On Germany, see Marie-Claire Hoock-Demarle, "Lesen und Schreiben in Deutschland," in *19. Jahrhundert*, vol. 4 of *Geschichte der Frauen*, ed. Geneviève Fraisse and Michelle Perrot (Frankfurt: Campus, 1994), 165–86. See further Günter Häntzschel, *Bildung und Kultur bürgerlicher Frauen, 1850–1918: Eine Quellendokumentation aus Anstandshilfen und Lebenshilfen für Mädchen und Frauen als Beitrag zur weiblichen literarischen Sozialisation* (Tübingen, Niemeyer, 1986); Alfred Messerli,

a considerable role also in the diverse books of manners and the guides for bourgeois girls and women, in which a canon of recommended books often was contained along with general judgments about the purpose of and proper form of reading. Reading thereby seems to a great extent to be assigned to a different department than religion in general and the Bible in particular. Bible reading is spoken of only very occasionally and is not mentioned specifically in the canon of literature.[23]

2.1.1. Bad Reading Matter

In the Catholicism of the nineteenth century, discussion about women who read was not lacking.[24] In the aforementioned general Catholic literary guides by Franz Hülskamp, Keiter, or Franz Xaver Wetzel, a gender-specific differentiation is, however, hardly to be recognized. Only Wetzel's book *Lektüre* offers several indications. His very critical remarks about the prevailing "reading craze" at first appear, however, to be gender-neutral, with the exception of the examples he cites: The "victims" of the reading craze are all men.[25] In the chapter about the "Consequences of Bad Reading Matter" then, however, the "Christian mother with a novel in her hand" becomes the terrible vision and the greatest conceivable scandal, against which "our fantasy and our understanding" bristles.[26] She neglects her household and children and endangers her chastity: "A chaste woman

---

"Gebildet, nicht gelehrt: Weibliche Schreib- und Lesepraktiken in den Diskursen vom 18. zum 19. Jahrhundert," in *Die lesende Frau*, ed. Gabriela Signori, WF 121 (Wiesbaden: Harrassowitz, 2009), 295–320. On denominational discourses about education for girls (and its limits) see Maria-Anna Zumholz, *"Das Weib soll nicht gelehrt seyn": Konfessionell geprägte Frauenbilder, Frauenbildung und weibliche Lebensentwürfe von der Reformation bis zum frühen 20. Jahrhundert eine Fallanalyse am regionalen Beispiel der Grafschaft Oldenburg und des Niederstifts Münster, seit 1744/1803 Herzogtum Oldenburg* (Münster: Aschendorff, 2016).

23. Daily reading in the Bible, among those works documented by Häntzschel, is required only by Caroline Milde and is declared by her to be her "dearest desire." Her book was published in 1871 and went through fourteen editions up until the First World War. See Häntzschel, *Bildung*, 377–449, esp. 405, 494.

24. For an introduction, see Michela De Giorgio, "Das katholische Modell," in Fraisse and Perrot, *19. Jahrhundert*, 201–6 (very few references to the German-speaking sphere).

25. See Wetzel, *Lektüre*, 11–33.

26. Wetzel, *Lektüre*, 264, 266.

never reads novels."[27] A comparable passage in regard to the reading man and father is, by the way, lacking.

The twenty Catholic, German-language devotional, edificatory, and guide books for women from the second half of the nineteenth century examined by me share the reservations against the novel, although this type of reading matter does not become a prominent theme here.[28] In view of the further developed range of reading matter, several authors saw themselves prompted also to include newspapers, especially the feature pages, in their warnings. Wetzel's book, *Die Frau* (the woman) makes this clear: "protect yourselves especially against the reading of newspapers and novels."[29]

---

27. Wetzel, *Lektüre*, 264. Wetzel cites here Rousseau's *Emile*. On Rousseau's position, see Margit Hauser, *Gesellschaftsbild und Frauenrolle in der Aufklärung: Zur Herausbildung des egalitären und komplementären Geschlechtsrollenkonzepts bei Pollain de la Barre und Rousseau* (Vienna: Passagen, 1992).

28. Examined were the following: Matthias von Bremscheid, *Die wichtige Stellung der christlichen Frauen* (Dülmen: Laumann, 1889); Clara Britz, *Gedanken und Ratschläge zur Beherzigung für die weibliche Jugend* (Mainz: Haas, 1883); Paul Combes, *Das Buch der Frau: Ein Handbuch für christliche Frauen in ihrer Stellung als Gattin, Hausfrau, Mutter und Erzieherin*, rev. P. Weber (Saarlouis: Hansen, 1912); Wilhelm Cramer, *Die christliche Mutter in der Erziehung und ihrem Gebete* (Dülmen: Laumann, 1903); Arsenius Dotzler, *Myrtenkranz! Ein geistlicher Brautführer und Andachtsbuch für die christliche Frau* (Kevelaer: Butzon & Bercker, 1900); Félix Dupanloup, *Die großen Pflichten der christlichen Frau: Conferenzreden* (Mainz: Kirchheim, 1881); Augustin Egger, *Die christliche Mutter: Erbauungsund Gebetbuch* (Einsiedeln: Benziger, 1914); Adele Gräfin von Hoffelize, *Kurze Unterweisungen im christlichen Leben für Frauen und Jungfrauen* (Mainz: Kirchheim, 1880); Jean Baptiste François Landriot, *Die fromme Frau: Conferenzen für Frauen, die in der Weltleben* (Mainz: Kirchheim, 1889); Anna von Liebenau, *An's Frauenherz: Worte der Liebe und Freundschaft für die katholische Frau* (Dülmen: Laumann, 1903); Victor Marchal, *Das Bild der christlichen Frau* (Regensburg: Pustet, 1899); Gaspar Mermillod, *Die christliche Frau in unserer Zeit: Vorträge* (Neisse: Huch, 1875); Heinrich Müller, *Himmelsweg: Ein katholisches Gebet und Lehrbuch für Jungfrauen mit bischöflicher Approbation* (Cologne: St. Josephs-Verein, 1913); Anton Passy, *Lese und Gebetbuch für katholische weibliche und geistliche Jungfrauen* (Regenburg: Manz, 1850); Anton Raffenberg, *Die betende Mutter: Vereins-Gebetbuch für die Mitglieder der Erzbruderschaft der christlichen Mütter* (Dulmen: Laumann, 1929); Michael Sintzel, *Das christliche Frauengeschlecht in seinem Wandel und Gebete: Ein Lehr und Gebetbuch*, 2 vols. (Augsburg: Kollmann, 1856); Theodor Temming, *Die christliche Frau: Gebet und Unterweisungen; zugleich Andachtsbuch für die Mitglieder des Vereins christlicher Mütter* (Kevelaer: Butzon & Bercker, 1912); and Wetzel, *Die Frau: Ein Büchlein für die Frauen* (Ravenburg: Dorn, 1896).

29. Wetzel, *Frau*, 104. See also Dupanloup, *Frau*, 270: "In general, novels with very few exceptions are bad." "I have spoken only about novels; but, there are also

The negative consequences of bad literature are painted in somber colors—as already a hundred years before—by, for example, Gaspar Mermillod (1824–1892), bishop in Freiburg in Switzerland.[30] He detects an "incessant diet" of self-delusion and a lack of religious orientation in modern reading matter, so that the woman afflicted by the addiction to reading "[becomes the source of] unrest in her family, the distress of her doctor, the anguish of her unhappy father confessor. Thus arises an over-excited mind, a disorderly power of imagination, and you become unfit for the noble work of life."[31] The idea that women through such reading fled their daily life and produced imaginative ideas that evaded the control of the masculine authorities of father, husband, or priest stands unmistakably behind these warnings. Augustine Egger (1833–1900), prominent writer of devotional literature and bishop of Saint Gallen in Switzerland,[32] saw therein among the "people of the better classes" a specific form of feminine weakness, namely, the inclination toward "sentimentality and nervousness."[33] Thereby we encounter, as with Mermillod, the key words of a psycho-medicinal discourse that was typical for the fin de siècle.[34] Added to this, in addition, were anxieties in regard to faith and church morality, so that many a Catholic author could seriously call for book burning.[35] Finally, concrete apprehen-

---

journals with their feature pages that penetrate everywhere; one pays no attention to them, and believes they have no significance" (Dupanloup, *Frau*, 271). See, in a similar vein, Müller, *Himmelsweg*, 395–96: "The reading of novels is almost always harmful; for even the best of them, with few exceptions, aren't much good."

30. For an introduction to the determinedly ultramontan Cardinal Mermillod, see Franz Xaver Bischof, "Mermillod, Gaspar," *BBKL* 5 (1993), 1325–28.

31. Mermillod, *Frau*, 28. See Müller, *Himmelsweg*, 395: "Seldom does a novel reader preserve the purity of the heart; gradually does sensuality begin to stir; gradually do evil thoughts, notions, and appetites begin to arise." See also Combes, *Frau*, 235: "the clarity of thought, the consistency, uprightness, and stability of action, the purity of the heart, the integrity of fantasy, the noble harmony of all the powers of the soul are at stake."

32. On him, see Cornel Dora, *Augustinus Egger von St. Gallen, 1833–1900: Ein Bischof zwischen Kulturkampf, sozialer Frage und Modernismusstreit*, St.GKG 23 (Saint Gallen: Staatsarchiv, 1994).

33. Egger, *Mutter*, 71.

34. See only Joachim Radkau, *Das Zeitalter der Nervosität: Deutschland zwischen Bismarck und Hitler* (Munich: Hauser, 1998). On several aspects also Yvonne Knibiehler, "Leib und Seele," in Fraisse and Perrot, *19. Jahrhundert*, 373–415.

35. "So, for this reason avoid like poison such books, writings, and newspapers, which endanger religion and morals.... So, away with all the books or writings that

sions also were heard that the social order and, thereby, also the conduct of the sexes and their relation to each other might be affected negatively.[36] We encountered this idea above already in the citation from Wetzel about the novel-reading mother who neglects her children and household. One of the authors speaks of this openly in his devotional book for the women in the Catholic Mothers' Association: "A woman should not understand novels, the theater, and dancing better than she does the cooking pot."[37] In view of a middle-class public and a clear ordering of the living spaces according to gender, newlywed women without children or with a nanny were thought to be at special risk of succumbing to excessive, unregulated reading without positive profit.[38] The fact that, apart from masculine fears and persisting apprehensions, tendencies toward a trivial literature with escapist tendencies definitely did exist in the reading public can be considered as sure.[39]

2.1.2. Proper Reading and Recommended Reading Material

Even Catholic authors, of course, did not envision a general prohibition on reading for women. The well-known bishop of Orléans and writer of spiritual books Félix Antoine Philibert Dupanloup (1802–1878), whose speeches held before women's groups also appeared in German translation, even defended women against "foolish judgments." [40] Women who devoted themselves "unwaveringly for several hours of their day to the nurture of their spirit," he said, were exposed to such judgments.[41] The goal was "to accommodate the healthy desire for reading material and to keep away from what is harmful."[42] Accordingly, along with their warnings

---

straight away or indirectly undermine your faith, and can rob you of your purity and shame! Away with them into the fire!" (Müller, *Himmelsweg*, 395). See also Dupanloup, *Frau*, 272, who, in referring to Acts 19:9 (burning of the books of sorcery), rejects bad literature.

36. On this background, already recognizable in the discourse about the "reading craze" in the late eighteenth century, see Messerli, "Schreib- und Lesepraktiken," 307–15.

37. Temming, *Frau*, 61.

38. See Dupanloup, *Frau*, 273.

39. See Zalar, "Process of Confessional Inculturation," 130–31.

40. On this leader of French Catholicism, see Christiane Marcilhacy, *Le Diocèse d'Orléans sous l'épiscopat de Mgr. Dupanloup (1849–1878): Sociologie religieuse et mentalités collectives* (Paris: Plon, 1962).

41. Dupanloup, *Frau*, 59.

42. Combes, *Frau*, 235.

about bad literature, authors also offered advice for orderly, proper reading according to content and form. Reading thus was definitely allowed to women for "recreation" and for the "formation of the spirit and the heart," when it took place only "occasionally" and when it concerned a "good book, especially about child-rearing or the life of pious and holy women." But, the clear admonition was not absent: "But never make reading the most important thing."[43] In Wetzel's parallel work about the man, such a warning, remarkably, is lacking.

Concrete reading recommendations by the authors sometimes encompass suggestions for establishing a "small home library." In this case, religious literature stood at the top. Wetzel gives a list of works in his book for men but not in his parallel work for women. The Catechism, Leonhard Goffiné's (1648–1719) devotional book with the texts of the readings and gospels read in the Mass, and a volume of saints' lives were for Wetzel the foundation of a "small home library." To be added to this were "then several good prayer books, a Catholic calendar, and a Catholic newspaper."[44]

Hülskamp offers a more detailed plan for a small home library, which a "better-situated family" could establish and later expand. According to this, the following volumes were to be acquired one by one:

1. a sufficient number of prayer and devotional books;
2. a Catechism or other textbook of religion;
3. a biblical history;
4. a life of Jesus and Mary;
5. a devotional handbook with the readings in the Mass;
6. a shorter and a detailed volume of the lives of the saints;
7. a larger world history;
8. a good geographical handbook with corresponding atlas;
9. a good encyclopedia;
10. uplifting biographies of great persons;
11. popular descriptions of nature;
12. individual volumes on general geography and ethnology;
13. the best volumes on local history and culture;
14. poetical anthologies;

---

43. Wetzel, *Frau*, 104. According to Dupanloup, *Frau*, 59, reading could come into its own for the woman in her free time after all the "duties in the household and in child-rearing and in piety."

44. Wetzel, *Der Mann: Ein Büchlein für die Männer* (Ravensburg: Dorn, 1900), 79.

15. a careful selection of the most distinguished "classics";
16. the best Catholic poetry;
17. illustrated and artistic works of impeccable orientation;
18. particular favorites.[45]

The preeminent position of devotional and edificatory literature is directly visible. On the other hand, belles lettres and even Catholic poetry are accorded only a secondary importance. Devotional literature generally was considered in the Catholic "reading discourse" as an antidote to all the widespread bad literature.[46] With this priority of religious literature, the reading paradigm of the premodern era is, on the one hand, continued.[47] On the other hand, though, this paradigm goes through an extension in the sense of a bourgeois education of the nineteenth century through the addition of history and science. One can term this as a compromise for accommodating the growing wishes within the Catholic population for a greater participation in contemporary educational culture. At the same time, such a literary program was the expression of a certain posture in the circle of "reading experts" from the clerical estate. They held fast to the primary position of what was religious, of course, but they did not close themselves off to a limited and managed opening to secular education and did this in order to counter the charge of backwardness.[48]

An interesting finding emerges from these reading recommendations by Wetzel and Hülskamp for the question of the relationship of the sexes to religion. Both quite clearly intend that religious literature be read, also by the men; indeed, they shift this literature into the foreground. According to their intentions, it thus in no way could suffice if only the women educated and edified themselves through religious literature. An exclusive assignment of what was religious to the female sphere was incompatible with their concept of reading.

---

45. Hülskamp, *1000 gute Bücher*, 8.
46. See Zalar, "Process of Confessional Inculturation," 124.
47. See, on this, the references given by Edith Saurer, "'Bewahrerinnen der Zucht und Sittlichkeit': Gebetbücher für Frauen; Frauen in Gebetbüchern," *HZFG* 1 (1990): 37–58; as well as the classic volume by Rudolf Schenda, *Volk ohne Buch: Studien zur Sozialgeschichte der populären Lesestoffe, 1770–1910* (Frankfurt: Klostermann, 1970).
48. See also Zalar, "Process of Confessional Inculturation," 127–33. On the discussion about an alleged Catholic inferiority, see Martin Baumeister, *Parität und katholische Inferiorität: Untersuchungen zur Stellung des Katholizismus im deutschen Kaiserreich*, PKV 3 (Paderborn: Schöningh, 1987).

2.2. Devotional Literature and the Question of Its Gender-Specific Orientation

If small home libraries with an emphasis on religious literature already were outlined by Catholic authors, then one ought to be able to assume that spiritual reading matter also played a role in devotional and edificatory literature.

This is unmistakably the case in Egger's book for the *Christian Mother*. The frontispiece already directs the reader's glance to this aspect, for it shows Mary, together with her mother Anna, reading in a book. The pictorial motif is quite well-known from medieval art and presents Mary as the model of the reading woman.[49] The caption under the picture makes clear what a woman who follows in Mary's footsteps had to read: "Have God in your heart all the days of your life (Tob 4:6 [today Tob 4:5])." In fact, we encounter the reading, even the reading in common, of edificatory literature in Egger's advice and prayer book.[50] "To read in a spiritual book" daily for a quarter or a half of an hour is the advice given by several authors.[51] The purpose of reading was not entertainment but rather instruction and/or edification and, in the end—in the words of Mermillod—deepening the "insight into the teachings of the church."[52] Therefore, the attitude in reading also had to be different: Only little was to be read, but this intensively, attentively, and, if necessary, even repeatedly. This, so to say, meditative manner of reading put back into force the old mode prevailing before the "reading revolution" since the late eighteenth century and, to be sure, not only for religious literature. This is shown by Wetzel's detailed directions for correct reading.[53] At the same time, a tendency toward the complete rational organization of the whole daily routine makes itself felt, in which reading was given only a limited space.[54]

At least Dupanloup was conscious of the problem of boring and less useful devotional books for the reading of spiritual literature, which was

---

49. See Klaus Schreiner, *Maria: Jungfrau, Mutter, Herrscherin* (Munich: Hanser, 1994), 116–48.

50. See Egger, *Mutter*, 135, 190, 268.

51. See Hoffelize, *Unterweisungen*, 114–15; Sintzel, *Frauengeschlecht*, 1:194–96.

52. Mermillod, *Frau*, 113.

53. See Wetzel, *Lektüre*, 49–67. "Read little, read well" was the characterization also by De Giorgio of the recommended type of reading (De Giorgio, "Modell," 201).

54. See also De Giorgio, "Modell," 214–15.

seen by him, too, as a part of the order of daily living. He eloquently complains about this and, thereby, makes the interesting side remark that it was precisely fathers and their sons who really were put off by the "ridiculous little devotional books" with which the market is "flooded" because of all their "pious inanities." From this, he derives the following demand for his female hearers and readers: "Never read such books that constrain the spirit and deprive religion of its reputation. Such always will be only pathetic nourishment for your faith and for your piety. Do we not also have serious, dignified books, which are able to offer powerful nourishment to the intelligence? Those are the books that you must read!"[55] But, did this flood of devotional books actually exist, and were they really addressed primarily to a female public and its tastes? In the discussion about a possible "feminization" or a "(re)masculinization of religion," heed is to be taken of religious literature, which to the present has not happened sufficiently. In regard to the German-speaking sphere, Rudolf Schlögl several years ago postulated not only a change in the content but also a clear increase in the amount of devotional and edificatory literature especially for women in the course of the first half of the nineteenth century. This literature is said to have corresponded to the changed discourse that classified religion as a matter for women.[56] Exact figures for this claim are lacking in Schlögl's work, as well as in the work of Edith Saurer, who likewise assumes that, at the end of the eighteenth century, a new type of special women's prayer books had come on the market.[57] In my own critical treatment of the "feminization thesis," I have already drawn attention to the fact that an absolute increase in this kind of literature alone does not mean much. In point of fact, these decades at the end of the eighteenth century and the beginning of the nineteenth are on the whole marked by a rapidly growing book market.[58]

The only tenable methodology is a direct comparison of the figures for devotional literature with a gender-specific orientation (against the total figures for this literary genre), which, of course, represents an enormous practical research challenge. Some time ago, I undertook a first attempt at doing this. The *Literarischer Handweiser* mentioned above lists 605 Catholic theological titles for the year 1862. Of these, 186 were academic works, 131

---

55. Dupanloup, *Frau*, 208–9.
56. See Schlögl, "Sünderin, Heilige oder Hausfrau?," 37–38.
57. See Saurer, "Bewahrerinnen," 47.
58. See Schneider, "Feminisierung," 137–38.

were practical-theological works, and 208 were ascetic texts, that is, devotional and edificatory literature. In the catalogue of recommended books issued yearly by the Borromaus Association, there was a category "Prayer Books," under which no less than 1,229 items are listed for the sample year of 1890.[59] Even if every number does not represent a book—different editions of a single work each are listed with their own numbers—one still with justification can speak of an abundance of devotional literature. At the same time, a type of book arose in the German-speaking sphere from the middle of the nineteenth century that attained all the dimensions of a real bestseller: the diocesan song and prayer book.[60] Jeffrey T. Zalar is undoubtedly right when he characterizes the Catholic women of the nineteenth century as enthusiastic readers of religious literature.[61]

The minority of these books were intended as gender-specific; the diocesan song and prayer books were fundamentally not gender-specific. Among the other books belonging to the examined body of works from 1862, merely 5 of the 208 devotional works, according to title and subtitle, were addressed especially to a female reading public; four, on the other hand, were especially meant for a masculine public. In the following four years, nine titles for women stood over against three for men, which, in view of the more than two hundred new works of Catholic theological literature published yearly, is a very modest proportion. In a review of the publications listed by the *Literarischer Handweiser* from the years 1862 to 1872 and 1882 to 1887, twenty-one prayer, devotional, and edificatory books could be identified as for men and young men and, on the other hand, forty-six for women and girls. However, if one includes the numerous titles of spiritual literature especially for Catholic priests, as well as the numerous published works for ministrants (adolescent males), completely ignored in research, then the findings shift quite fundamentally. In the

---

59. Verein vom Heil, *Verzeichniß der von dem Verein vom heil. Karl Borromäus empfohlenen Bücher für das Jahr 1890* (Bonn: Verein vom Heiligen Karl Borromäus, 1890), 191–219.

60. See Schneider, "Das Diözesangesangbuch: Eine Klammer für die Bistümer im 19. Jahrhundert," *RQCAK* 99 (2004): 210–28; and Andreas Scheidgen, "Diözesangesangbücher und Kirchenliedrestauration im 19. und 20. Jahrhundert," in *Geschichte des katholischen Gesangbuchs*, ed. Dominik Fugger and Scheidgen, MHS 21 (Tübingen: Francke, 2008), 35–48. The Paderborn *Sursum corda*, for example, was published no less than a hundred times between 1874 and 1897. See Brandt and Hengst, *Paderborn*, 383–84.

61. Zalar, "Process of Confessional Inculturation," 125.

catalogue of books issued by the Borromaus Association, the devotional literature without consignment to a specific gender likewise dominated by far. Among the relatively few titles that, in fact, were directed to men and youths, or to women and young women, the prayer books for the female sex clearly predominated: twenty out of twenty-seven books.

On the whole, this analysis does indeed prove a strong consideration of women in Catholic literature. But it also, on the other hand, shows the overriding desire, in principle, to reach all people and the entire family.

3. Bible Reading between Recommendation and Caution

At the beginning of the nineteenth century, there was something like a Catholic Bible movement in Germany that even nurtured contacts with the Protestant Bible societies.[62] Then, in the provocative confessional climate beginning in the 1820s and 1830s, the tendency to emphasize pointedly the respective confessional character also flourished. Now, Bible reading increasingly was once again one of the themes of confessional controversy.

Statements by popes or Catholic bishops against the Bible societies stood over against Protestant polemics against Catholic ignorance of the Bible. A consequence of this was also the publication of several polemical theological texts on this topic.[63] The details are not to be treated here. Merely the question of gender-specific statements on Bible reading is to be examined in the following. The unambiguous as well as concise finding in three Catholic texts examined by me is: There are no specific statements on Bible reading by women or men. It is spoken quite generally of the fact that knowledge of the Bible is extant among Catholics, too, through ecclesiastical instruction and the liturgy. It is said that—as the Council of Trent teaches—it is, however, unnecessary for Catholics to read the Bible, since the church offers them everything needed for their salvation.

---

62. See Johannes Altenberend, *Leander van Eß (1772–1847): Bibelübersetzer und Bibelverbreiter zwischen Aufklärung und evangelischer Erweckungsbewegung*, SQWG 41 (Paderborn: Bonifatius, 2001); and Peter Scheuchenpflug, *Die Katholische Bibelbewegung im frühen 19. Jahrhundert*, STPS 27 (Würzburg: Echter, 1997).

63. See Jean-Baptiste Malou, *Das Bibellesen in der Volkssprache: Beurtheilt nach der heil. Schrift, der Tradition und der gesunden Vernunft; Eine Streitschrift*, 2 vols. (Schaffhausen: Hurter, 1849); H. von Noit [= Johann Baptist Helten], *Ueber Bibelkenntnis und Bibellesen in älterer und neuerer Zeit: Wittenberg und Rom; Christ oder Antichrist* (Berlin: Germania, 1896); Josef Rebbert, *Das Bibellesen auf eigene Hand*, BonB 18 (Paderborn: Bonifatius, 1887).

In addition, the authors make reference to the preconditions lacking in the broad, simple public for a profitable reading of the Bible not detrimental to salvation. It is not gender but rather piety and education that function as boundary marks between allowed and prohibited reading of the Bible.[64] The question of Bible reading was not especially prominent in the late nineteenth century, as a look into the catalogues of the *Literarischer Handweiser* shows. A review of the issues from 1884 to 1896, as an example, revealed only a single title of a controversial theological nature about Bible reading from among several thousand listed texts. This was a work by Josef Rebbert (1837–1897). In addition, there is an introduction to biblical history by Magnus Jocham (1808–1893).[65] Of course, special exegetical studies are not lacking. In regard to our special theme, Bible reading by women, the investigation—as expected—produced no result. There also was no reference to this question under the rubric "survey of periodicals" in the *Literarischer Handweiser*, in which the most important Catholic periodicals regularly were presented along with their content.

The information in the literary guides by Hülskamp and Wetzel are to be appreciated against this rather sobering background. In Hülskamp's *Home Library*, the Bible was assigned an important place after prayer and devotional books, as well as was the Catechism. In regard to Bible reading, however, it must be apparent how clearly Hülskamp's home library omits full native-language editions of the Bible, while the biblical content definitely is present in the books of the home library conceived by him to be ideal. This content, though, appears in a form prepared especially for laypeople: "biblical history" and the "devotional handbook," as well as the pious retelling of the lives of Jesus and his mother Mary. Hülskamp cites examples of such books at another place in his book.[66] Behind this stood the fear—unarticulated here—that not all the content of the Bible was appropriate reading for all Christians.[67] In addition, as was known, there were official ecclesiastical regulations in existence since the sixteenth century, which regulated Bible reading. Hülskamp reminded his readers of these in a chapter about works of "popular or lay theology." According

---

64. Especially concise is Malou, *Bibellesen*, 81–84, 318–20, 337–38.

65. Magnus Jocham, *Anleitung zum Gebrauch der Biblischen Geschichte* (Munich: Zentral-Schulbücher, 1884).

66. See Hülskamp, *1000 gute Bücher*, 77–80, 88–89.

67. Explicit warnings about a "complete Bible" for school children are found in Noit, *Bibelkenntnis*, 106.

to him, only "a text accompanied by explanations, and these with ecclesiastical approbation, [may] come into the hands of laypeople."[68] After this preliminary remark, Hülskamp then also presented full Bible editions, whereby, he said, the most popular of the various editions was the Vulgate translation by Joseph Franz Allioli.[69] Hülskamp's other references have to do with explanations of the entire Bible and with popularized scholarly presentations of individual aspects.[70]

In the work of Wetzel, Bible reading at first enjoyed the greatest esteem. The Bible, for him, is a letter come "from heaven," the reading of which develops "miraculous power," as long as it is read "with understanding."[71] He lets a woman sing the praise of the Bible poetically, namely, the poetess Luise Hensel (1798–1876).[72]

> Jesus in the Holy Scriptures
>
> Always must I read again
> In the old, holy book,
> How the Lord was so good,
> Without guile and deception.
>
> How He called the children to Him,
> Lovingly he looked upon them,
> And took them in His arms,
> And pressed them to His heart.
>
> How He helping mercy
> Gladly showed to all the sick,
> And the lowly and the poor
> He called His dear brethren.
>
> Always must I read again,
> Read and not cry enough,
> How the Lord was so true,
> How He loved us.
>
> Had gently led the flock
> That His Father gave Him;
> Had spread out His arms,
> To draw all to His heart.
>
> Let me kneel at His feet,
> Lord, the love breaks my heart!
> Let me dissolve in tears,
> Vanish in bliss and pain.

---

68. Hülskamp, *1000 gute Bücher*, 30.

69. See Hülskamp, *1000 gute Bücher*, 30. On Joseph Franz Allioli and his translation, see Wilhelm Baumgärtner, *Joseph Franz Allioli (1793–1873): Leben und Werk* (Amberg: Buch & Kinstverlag Oberpfalz, 1993).

70. See Hülskamp, *1000 gute Bücher*, 31.

71. Wetzel, *Lektüre*, 163.

72. Wetzel, *Lektüre*, 163. Hensel came from a Lutheran pastor's family, in which Pietist influences played a role. In 1817, the poetess, who was close to the circle of romantics gathered around Clemens Brentano, converted to Catholicism. See Oskar Köhler, *Müde bin ich geh' zur Ruh': Die hell-dunkle Lebensgeschichte Luise Hensels* (Paderborn: Schöningh, 1991).

How He refused no sinner,
Who came to Him with remorse,
How He graciously instructed him.
And took death from his heart.

Bible reading appears here as a sentimental visualization of a gentle, comforting Jesus, but Wetzel, in reference to the biography of the church father Augustine, also assigns to it an appellative, proselytizing effect.[73] Only now, after a double "proof" was provided for the high esteem accorded the Bible, also in the Catholic church, does the allusion to the well-known restrictions upon Bible reading by laypeople follow. In justification of this, Wetzel cites the "peculiar oriental manner of presentation" in the Bible and its "deep content," which presented "innumerable difficulties for the understanding."[74] After the Protestant critique of the restrictive Catholic position thus appears to be rebutted, Wetzel concludes his reflections on Bible reading with an attack on the principle of "free biblical research," which is documented also in the polemical theological texts on Bible reading cited above. This, he said, had led to the fact that already 270 Protestant sects had arisen within a century. The missionary efforts of the Protestant Bible societies are not only rejected by Wetzel, but also become the object of satire.[75] Thus, here, too, fear and caution dominate, on the one hand: "Thus, may only those called to do so draw from that divine well and may they direct the water full of blessing into other hearts, too, through word and text!"[76] On the other hand, there follows the recourse to a "Bible light" in the form of those devotional books and life of Jesus portrayals mentioned above. Wetzel's suggestion, stylized as an ideal, that the biblical texts and the printed explanations of them from a devotional book be read on Saturday, or be read aloud by the father of the house, so that the sermon on Sunday could be understood better, fits in with this scheme.[77]

This last suggestion is instructive in several respects for the concept of Bible reading in German-speaking Catholicism around 1900. First of all, Wetzel makes reference to a deeply traditional motif ("housefather"), to which Catholic authors held fast even in those times in which the order of

---

73. See Wetzel, *Lektüre*, 165. He alludes here to the *Confessions*.
74. Wetzel, *Lektüre*, 166.
75. Wetzel, *Lektüre*, 186.
76. Wetzel, *Lektüre*, 166.
77. See Wetzel, *Daheim: Ein Büchlein für's Volk* (Ravensburg: Dorn, 1900), 54.

the so-called whole house already to a great extent had become questionable. His remark likewise shows the intention to hold fast to the father as religious teacher and guardian of religious convictions. Contrary to the thesis of a "feminization of religion," religion here is not assigned to the feminine sphere, and religious education and responsibility are not conferred upon the mother alone. Finally, this passage also shows the *Sitz im Leben* to which Bible reading is assigned. In this case, it was communal domestic devotions and not simply individual reading. In addition, it had a clear goal: the proclamation of the word of God in the liturgy. In this concept, communal Bible reading combined the "house church" (family) with the official established church and the worship service prescribed by it. A strict separation of private religion from public religion was in this way avoided.[78]

4. Importance and Application of the Bible in Pious Catholic Women's Literature

The twenty works of religious literature already treated above, which in the second half of the nineteenth century were written especially for the instruction and/or the devotions and edification of women, also offer various insights into the position of the Bible and Bible reading in Catholic piety.

First of all, a finding is apparent that, to a large extent, is rather sobering. Only in one of these books is the reading of the Bible considered in more detail; in a few others, it is mentioned more or less in passing. In the majority, however, it is not discussed at all. Egger calls the neglect in reading the Catechism and biblical stories the main shortcoming of his time and emphatically recommends both to the Christian mother as reading matter in her task of bringing up her children. From the Bible, he says, "an abundance of encouraging and deterrent examples" can be gained, which a mother can hold out to her children.[79] Bible reading is here a pedagogical instrument in that it provides examples for what is good and bad. The knowledge of the Bible thus acquired becomes at the same time oral paraenesis. Egger, thus, like his countryman Wetzel, also does not recommend reading the complete text of the Bible.

---

78. On this entire section, see Schneider, "Masculinity."
79. See Egger, *Mutter*, 268–69.

A different *Sitz im Leben* emerges where the reading of the Bible is conceived as a part of the private spiritual ordering of life. This is the case with Adele Countess von Hoffelize, who, for the daily half-hour of spiritual reading to be done by her female readers, suggests that "one can take several verses from the Gospel as objects of contemplation. One single verse is sometimes sufficient. If it is a narrative, then one can read somewhat more. There is almost always a teaching, an instruction, contained in it."[80] Thereby, she explicitly ranks the biblical texts above the devotional books, which, to be sure, are also useful, "but one never finds in them the nourishment and power that every line, every word of the Holy Book offers us." The books of wisdom, the letters of Paul, and, among the gospels, that of John, appear to her to be "beneficial for us."[81] Michael Sintzel (1804–1889) also recommends the Bible to women before all other spiritual books.[82] In both cases, it remains unclear in which form the biblical texts are to be read, whether in complete Bibles or rather in collections of biblical stories.

Only Bishop Dupanloup, in his speeches for women, treats Bible reading in more detail and offers a closer justification for it. In the case of this leading representative of the Catholic Church in France, the Bible served as the point of departure for his lectures and formed a constant reference point.[83] In contrast to many false notions held by his contemporaries who wanted to allocate Bible reading to priests and members of the religious orders, Dupanloup, in fact, makes the reading of Holy Scripture a veritable duty of a Catholic woman and mother.[84] On the model of the circle of women around Saint Jerome, she should read the Bible herself and then also teach this to her own daughters.[85] "They should insist that

---

80. Hoffelize, *Unterweisungen*, 141.
81. Hoffelize, *Unterweisungen*, 152.
82. Sintzel, *Frauengeschlecht*, 1:196.
83. According to the preface by the French publisher, Bishop Dupanloup in these conference addresses for women "almost always" drew upon "the Holy Scriptures; one time he simply read out the biblical passage without giving hardly any explanation of it; the next time he explored it to its very foundations and there shot forth lightning bolts of a completely unexpected, and all the more gripping, eloquence; then he once again resumed the calm pace of his usual manner of speaking" (Dupanloup, *Frau*, ix).
84. Dupanloup, *Frau*, 3.
85. On the women's circle gathered around Jerome and on his image of women, see Christine Steiniger, *Die ideale christliche Frau: virgo, vidua, nupta; Eine Studie zum Bild der idealen christlichen Frau bei Hieronymus und Pelagius* (Saint Ottilien: Eos, 1997). On the reading of the Bible within the framework of Christian training for girls,

their daughters, once they have grown to adolescence, be able to recite to them every day some of the most beautiful passages of Holy Scripture, which they were to have chosen as appropriate for their understanding."[86] He, too, of course, cannot avoid mentioning regulatory ecclesiastical instructions. But, he imparts them in such a way that the reading of the Bible is not to be taken away even from the simple believers.[87] For him, the problem is not too much Bible reading but rather too little.[88] He treats the manner of Bible reading only briefly. He mentions explicitly the integral reading of the entire biblical books, but counsels, in this case, the use of a commentary as an indispensable aid. This, of course, assumes a corresponding educational level among his listeners, as well as the financial means, which reveals something about the social position of the female listeners the Bishop had in view.[89] Along with this manner of reading the Bible, he also recommends the biblical texts in the breviary—the textbook for the celebration of the liturgy of the hours, especially by the priests and members of the religious orders—as a "splendid way and manner of reading Holy Scripture."[90] Note that he recommends the breviary to normal women, not nuns or sisters. He himself, by the way, drew his biblical inspirations for his women's lectures precisely from this book and recited them using the biblical readings or other biblical elements of the liturgy of the hours (responsories, antiphons). Whether Dupanloup thereby actually thought of the regular breviary, intended for the priests and written in Latin, or of a native-language translation, or of a kind of lay breviary, is not recorded. In the German-speaking sphere, both of the last two variants mentioned did, in fact, exist.[91]

If, on the basis of previous statements, one should have gained the impression that the Bible was of small relevance in the women's books

---

see especially 102–3. Further, see Christa Krumeich, *Hieronymus und die christlichen feminae clarissimae* (Bonn: Habbelt, 1993). On the Bible in the context of the education of girls, here see 219–27.

86. Dupanloup, *Frau*, 6.
87. See Dupanloup, *Frau*, 7–8.
88. See Dupanloup, *Frau*, 5–6, 19.
89. See Dupanloup, *Frau*, 8.
90. Dupanloup, *Frau*, 8.
91. So, for example, the editions prepared by Markus Adam Nickel. See Günter Duffrer, *Auf dem Weg zu liturgischer Frömmigkeit: Das Werk des Markus Adam Nickel (1800–1869) als Höhepunkt pastoralliturgischer Bestrebungen im Mainz des 19. Jahrhunderts*, QAMK 6 (Speyer: Jaeger, 1962).

investigated, then this would be a false conclusion. In fact, the devotional and edificatory books investigated are, with few exceptions, thoroughly "impregnated" with the Bible. The extent of this is, of course, quite variable. One half of the books shows only a few biblical references scattered throughout the whole book,[92] while others refer quite frequently to the Bible.[93] In this respect, too, the book by Bishop Dupanloup proves to be especially biblically oriented since he deals with Holy Scripture on at least every third page of the text. Whether one of the investigated works was written by a man or a woman had no effect upon whether the Bible was treated intensively or less intensively. The example of Clara Britz (born 1848) shows that female authors, too, possessed such a great knowledge of the Bible that they, like the authors from the clergy, could cite the relevant biblical passages in diverse contexts.[94]

The manner in which the Bible is treated is varied, even if several clear patterns emerge. A popular method is to place a biblical citation before a chapter as a program. For example, in Arsenius Dotzler's *Bride's Guide*, the verse "let each of you lead the life that the Lord has assigned, to which God called you" (1 Cor 7:17 NRSV) is found as a programmatic introduction to the chapter "The Peace of a Good Choice of Estate."[95] In Sintzel, again, the chapter about true humility is opened with a citation from the Letter of James (Jas 4:6 NRSV: "God opposes the proud, but gives grace to the humble").[96] Seldom, on the other hand, does a chapter lead to a, so to say, summary biblical citation. This is the case, however, in Matthias von Bremscheid's (1846–1911) book for women when he ends the chapter on the "Influence of Women upon Religious Life" with Prov

---

92. See Combes, *Frau*: on approximately fourteen of three hundred pages; Hoffelize, *Unterweisungen*: approximately thirty references on nearly seven hundred pages; Raffenberg, *Mutter*: three of 758 pages.

93. See Britz, *Gedanken*: eighty pages with biblical references among 246 pages; Dotzler, *Brautführer*: forty-three of 633; Landriot, *Frau*: seventy-four pages from 308; Sintzel, *Frauengeschlecht*, 1: forty-two of 336 pages (on the other hand, vol. 2: twelve of 364 pages).

94. Little is known about this female writer. Some information is given by Sophie Pataky, *Lexikon deutscher Frauen der Feder: Eine Zusammenstellung der seit dem Jahre 1840 erschienenen Werke weiblicher Autoren, nebst Biographien der lebenden und einem Verzeichnis der Pseudonyme*, repr. (Berne: Lang, 1971), 105.

95. Dotzler, *Brautführer*, 28.

96. See Sintzel, *Frauengeschlecht*, 1:129.

18:22: "He who finds a wife finds a good thing, and obtains favor from the Lord"[97] (NRSV).

The mass of the biblical citations serves the clarification of a factual connection and, as it were, as authoritative proof for the remarks of the author, both male and female. Thus, statements about cheerfulness as a gift from heaven are underlined and confirmed by fitting biblical passages (Sir 30:23; Prov 15:13; Phil 4:4; 2 Cor 9:7),[98] or the aspiration to perfection explicitly recommended by the author is legitimated and supported by reference to relevant biblical texts (Matt 24:13; 1 Cor 9:24).[99] The Bible then can appear along with "the infallible teaching office of the Cath[olic] Church" in order, so in Britz, to furnish "innumerable proofs for the freedom of the human being" "through the clearest remarks."[100] Of course, the citation can be embedded in the continuous text so that, in reading, the statements of the author and Scripture really flow into each other, even when the citations are marked as such and are substantiated by means of footnotes. This method is particularly pronounced in Anton Passy's (1788–1847) *Reading and Prayer Book*.[101]

Holy Scripture is made use of quite deliberately in every possible context in order to describe individual ways of conduct or virtues or to emphasize their value. The special responsibility of women for the care of the poor is shown by Bremscheid, in a chapter about the social life, by citing Vulgate Sir 36:27 ("Where no woman can be found, there does the poor man sigh"),[102] and Sintzel demonstrates the duty to work with 2 Thess 3:10 ("If anyone will not work, neither let him eat") or the virtue of discretion with several Old Testament proof texts from wisdom literature.[103] Thereby, a quite free, associative bridge between the Bible and the desired mode of conduct also sometimes can be built. Wetzel connects Jesus's command, in the context of the so-called miraculous multiplication of the loaves, to "gather up the fragments left over, so that nothing may be

---

97. Bremscheid, *Frauen*, 35.
98. See Dotzler, *Brautführer*, 106.
99. See Passy, *Lese und Gebetbuch*, 280.
100. Britz, *Gedanken*, 11 (cf. Deut 30:19).
101. See Passy, *Lese und Gebetbuch*, 33–35, where, in regard to the theme of the proper use of time, Rom 6:22, Eph 5:16, 1 Cor 7:29, and John 12:35 are integrated.
102. See Bremscheid, *Frauen*, 48.
103. See Sintzel, *Frauengeschlecht*, 1:140, 259.

lost" (John 6:12 NRSV), with the woman's frugal and careful housekeeping—of this, the Bible certainly does not speak.[104]

Finally, recourse also is made to the Bible where the devotional and edificatory books do not employ a paraenetic style but rather intend to lead their female readers to prayer and the liturgy. Within the range of books with devotions for the Mass, biblical texts are cited that, however, are not geared to the concrete liturgical order of readings, as in the later popular books for the Mass. In his "first Mass devotions," Anton Raffenberg offers a reading from the book of Judith, and Theodor Temming readings from Ps 50 and 1 Cor 3.[105] With Sintzel, his entire Mass devotional book is permeated with biblical citations.[106] The connection of liturgy and the Bible is different with Dupanloup. As mentioned, the breviary serves him as a way to access the Bible, and in the breviary, he also finds a concentration of biblical motifs on the subject of women:

> When I dealt with the famous image of the strong woman before you, it undoubtedly was my task to erect for you a perfect model for your veneration and imitation. But, how many features are there still in the Old and New Testament, which can complete this image, stirring and shining features that are found scattered here and there in the holy books, and which the church has collected in this part of its liturgy [Commune Sanctorum, i.e., texts in the liturgy of hours for the feasts of the saints], the explanation of which I have undertaken today before you.[107]

5. Biblical Images of Women and Female Figures in the Bible

In the passage from Dupanloup's book just cited, there are echoes of another aspect: The devotional literature for women makes reference to feminine figures from the Bible and, by means of them, explains several contemporary images of women. Before, however, individual instances of these images of women or these feminine figures are treated, some basic tendencies in the examined material should be underlined first in the following.

---

104. See Wetzel, *Frau*, 25.
105. See Raffenberg, *Mutter*, 88–89; Temming, *Frau*, 200–1.
106. See Sintzel, *Frauengeschlecht*, 2:60–66.
107. Dupanloup, *Frau*, 126.

5.1. The Reference to Female Figures from the Bible: General Tendencies

It must be said quite bluntly: the reference to female figures from the Bible, or developed images of women, is easily identifiable in the devotional and edificatory books; however, it lags purely quantitatively far behind the selective reference to individual verses, as explained in the previous section, which were used as an illustration or legitimation of individual virtues or patterns of conduct.

A further general finding consists in the fact that the Old Testament, with its women and images of women, is much more frequently present than the New Testament. In about twice as many cases, the authors refer to the detailed passages on women and feminine figures in the Old Testament, which, of course, also has comparably many more and, on the whole, also the more impressive passages to offer than does the New Testament. Among the Old Testament books, the wisdom literature—apart from a completely selective citation, to be sure—is the only type more frequently cited. Within this group, the book of Proverbs is taken note of most often, followed by Jesus Sirach. On the other hand, Wisdom of Solomon plays a role, to be sure, for the virtue of wisdom, but otherwise not. The other parts of the Old Testament are employed only weakly: the Torah, with the story of creation, is a point of reference only in two books; among the historical books, the book of Judith, the books of the Maccabees, and the book of Tobit are cited only a few times; the prophetic books, finally, are present only quite peripherally. But, here, the reference to Isa 66:12–13 deserves special interest insofar as it is used to emphasize the motherliness of God, which in turn is intended to prove the outstanding dignity of the mother's role.[108] The body of especially relevant texts, thus, is relatively small.

5.2. Judith

Female biblical figures in the real sense, in accord with this finding, appear seldom: Judith, the mother of the Maccabees, Sarah, Hannah, and Eve are named and discussed in concrete contexts. Most prominent among them is certainly Judith. This fits with the popularity of Judith in the second half of the nineteenth century.[109] She appears as an ideal image of the Christian

---

108. See Dupanloup, *Frau*, 91–92.
109. See Daniela Hammer-Tugendhat, "Judith und ihre Schwestern: Konstanz

woman. Her virtue is publicly known, just as her honor is intact, because her fear of God ensures that nothing evil can be said of her.[110] In addition, she is also present as a strong woman whose praise rings out because she had "acted like a man," was "keenly courageous," and also because she proved her love of chastity.[111] In Dupanloup's view, Judith's action is measured, so to say, against the masculine model and, at the same time, is given a fine feminine point. First of all, he laments the lack of bravery, courage, and masculinity in his times. These, he says, can no longer be found very often, "not even among the men."[112] This sentence is to be placed in the discourse about a "crisis of masculinity," and especially of masculine religiousness, mentioned in the first section of my essay. Dupanloup's text, of course, also plays with the contemporary manner of speaking about the "weak sex." But, with the cited biblical ideal of Judith, he also aims precisely at the strength of the woman, too: "Oh, Christian women, much is said about your weakness, but not enough about your strength."[113] He indubitably wants strong women. Their strength, however, shows itself precisely in their renunciation of so-called specifically female weaknesses: vanity, haughtiness, the tendency toward external pomp, too careless talk, and negative remarks.[114] Judith is cited by Dupanloup at another place, and rather *en passant*, in order to illustrate divine compassion.[115] Where this strong biblical figure of a woman is mentioned sporadically by other authors, a very isolated, selected reference always dominates. In this, the motif of Judith's proven chastity after the death of her husband stands in the foreground.[116] The figure of Judith is, in this way, desexualized, so to speak, and she does not go through that ambivalent stylization into the men-threatening "femme fatale," which was to be observed otherwise in the late nineteenth century.[117] On the whole, it hardly will be possible to

---

und Veränderung von Weiblichkeitsbildern," in *Geschlecht und Moral*, ed. Annette Kämmerer and Agnes Speck (Heidelberg: Das Wunderhorn, 1999), 124–80.

110. Jdt 8:8; Jdt 15:9 (Vulg. 15:10); cf. Dupanloup, *Frau*, 202, 227. Similar is Marchal, *Frau*, 196.

111. Jdt 15:10 (Vulg. 15:11): here is also the basis for speaking of masculine action and of high courage; cf. Dupanloup, *Frau*, 203–4.

112. Dupanloup, *Frau*, 204.

113. Dupanloup, *Frau*, 204.

114. See Dupanloup, *Frau*, 204–8.

115. See Dupanloup, *Frau*, 224–25, with reference to Jdt 13:14 (Vulg. 13:18).

116. See Dotzler, *Brautführer*, 120; Passy, *Lese und Gebetbuch*, 457.

117. See Hammer-Tugendhat, "Judith," 126–31.

claim that the moralizing statements based on female gender stereotypes in Catholic devotional literature had understood completely the biblical dimensions of the Judith who saved her people.

5.3. Sirach

Sirach 26:1–27 is the most frequently received Old Testament women's text after Prov 31. This passage is presented in part in long literal citations in the introductory section of a chapter on the "good wife," in order to establish it as an ideal. Thereby, the effect of such a passage can be properly sanctified: It has become a "holy profession."[118] Egger likewise sees in it the image of an ideal but does not apply it formally to the "good wife," but rather cites the passage in detail in order to demonstrate fundamentally the positive, ideal view of the woman in the Holy Scriptures, to which, for him, of course, a quite negative perspective corresponds. "Standing over against these sentences overflowing with praise are other remarks that describe the inscrutable evil of the woman in the shrillest tones.… But, both descriptions are true, because there were, and still are, women of both kinds, women of admirable virtue and sanctity, and true monsters of depravity and evil."[119] He unfolds the negative dimension, too, in another chapter, likewise referring to Jesus Sirach, here 25:13–17.[120] Apart from this, Dupanloup deals in several passages selectively with the pericope Sir 26, in order, for example, to praise a discreet, a wise, or a God-fearing woman.[121] He, too, uses Sir 25:15–16 to pronounce the verdict against a woman "who does not comprehend her duties, who does not possess the qualities and virtues that ought to be her inherited traits."[122]

5.4. Proverbs 31, or the Strong Woman and Her Limits

Even more broadly received than Sir 26 is Prov 31:10–31, the praise of the "industrious" woman.[123] Especially in the book by Bishop Dupanloup, this pericope assumes a paradigmatic position. For this reason, it

---

118. Temming, *Frau*, 51–52; cf. also Dotzler, *Brautführer*, 216–18.
119. Egger, *Mutter*, 41–42.
120. See Egger, *Mutter*, 41–42, 74–75.
121. See Dupanloup, *Frau*, 194, 212–14.
122. Dupanloup, *Frau*, 2.
123. On this passage, its exegetical problems, and its interpretation, see Irmtraud

was also recited by him in his lectures, or printed in his book, to the full extent, and the author constantly makes reference to it.[124] The "strong woman" presented in this passage is for Dupanloup a "perfect image ... for admiration and imitation" by his female Christian hearers.[125] Apart from Dupanloup, his Swiss counterpart Egger also deals more intensively with this text.[126] For both, the idea of the "strong woman" is the leading motif in their exegesis. The translation of the Hebrew concept in Prov 31:10 is the term as given here.[127] Egger contrasts the "strong woman" of Prov 31 with the "natural" weaknesses of women, to which he devotes a complete chapter.[128] "In the way one speaks of a weak sex, so can one also speak of a strong woman. By nature, all are weak; the inequality begins with the fact that some submissively abandon themselves to their natural weaknesses, while others find the means, and use them, in order to make strong what in them is weak."[129] It is exactly this that he sees embodied in the ideal image of the "strong woman" in Prov 31, who unites "power and grace and all the virtues of her sex in the most beautiful harmony."[130] But the means for achieving this strength and for reaching the goal of that feminine heroism, which are found in the mother of the Maccabees (2 Macc 7:20–41) and the early Christian female martyrs and ascetics, are faith and God's grace.[131] It is clearly perceptible here how the contemporary naturalistic gender types are taken up by Egger and, at the same time, are specifically sharpened.[132] In view of the experiences in the *Kulturkampf* (culture war)

Fischer, *Gotteslehrerinnen: Weise Frauen und Frau Weisheit im Alten Testament* (Stuttgart: Kohlhammer, 2006), 146–72.

124. See Dupanloup, *Frau*, 12.

125. Dupanloup, *Frau*, 126, similarly 13. Cf. Hoffelize, *Unterweisungen*, 50: "The Holy Scripture presents us the Christian woman in the image of the strong woman, the most beautiful model that it can give us."

126. See Egger, *Mutter*, 76–83.

127. On the translation problems, see Fischer, *Gotteslehrerinnen*, 152–56. In other devotional books (as in the Ecumenical Translation, for example) stands "industrious housewife" (Combes, *Frau*, 46) or "keenly courageous woman" (Dotzler, *Brautführer*, 252).

128. Egger, *Mutter*, 67–86: "The Weak Sex."

129. Egger, *Mutter*, 83.

130. Egger, *Mutter*, 76.

131. See Egger, *Mutter*, 77–78, 91.

132. On the "naturalization" of the so-called gender characters in the nineteenth century, see Ute Frevert, *"Mann und Weib, und Weib und Mann": Geschlechter-Differenzen in der Moderne*, BR 1100 (Munich: Beck, 1995), 18–60.

and of the phenomenon of secularization in Swiss society, this means for Egger not least of all the mobilization of women strong in the faith and loyally bound to the church.

Dupanloup, too, builds upon the contrast between the "weak sex" and a "strong woman," but he explicitly considers the speech about the "weak sex" to be only a specific characteristic of those who "know [their] nature only superficially."[133] He holds out to them their own experience with "strong women" who mastered situations in which men were broken (such as experiences of bereavement, for example). More than this, the strength of women qualifies them, for Dupanloup, for their first commission from the time of creation, namely, according to Gen 2:18, to be the "helpmeet of the man," his supporter and helper.[134] Here the concept of the complementarity of the sexes comes into effect, which indeed grants women a considerable significance. It is, nevertheless—as was commonly the case—by Dupanloup, too, consistently unfolded in a patriarchal sense. The "strong woman" is to be the advisor and helper, full of devoted care, and she is to be this in "meekness and tenderness" but should never reverse the roles. As Dupanloup says, "Do not usurp anything to yourself. Do not forget that it is not you who is the head of the family, but that the man is such; you must obey."[135]

In accord with this, Bishop Dupanloup certainly perceived the tension, emphasized by Veronika Jüttemann, in the concept of head and female helper and sought to mitigate it in accordance with his ideal of the "strong woman" developed from Prov 31.[136] The discourse about gender in this passage clearly becomes one about power. In the framework of the hierarchical order of the sexes, however, Dupanloup stands by his high valuation of the woman and her role. He characterizes her as a "representative of what is good" in the family. Therewith, the woman's preferred radius of activity is at the same time assigned to her. Such an idealizing characterization, however, also could overwhelm the individual concrete woman considerably.[137] In addition, Prov 31 also is applied by Dupanloup quite concretely to the woman's activity in the household. In this case, he

---

133. Dupanloup, *Frau*, 14.

134. Dupanloup deals with this text passage in more detail later, too. See Dupanloup, *Frau*, 80–89.

135. Dupanloup, *Frau*, 15.

136. See Veronika Jüttemann, *Im Glauben vereint: Männer und Frauen im protestantischen Milieu Ostwestfalens, 1845–1918* (Cologne: Böhlau, 2008), 262–63.

137. Dupanloup, *Frau*, 16.

makes recourse to the Old Testament and outlines the ideal of the tirelessly working, diligent housewife. In contrast to her, he places the image of the idle lady of the nobility or bourgeoisie, who only kills time. His lecture aims therefore to construct an ideal family, a goal that contrast with the reality in particular among the poorer levels of the French society in the nineteenth century.[138]

While the text of Prov 31:10–31 is dealt with by Dupanloup from multiple perspectives, the other authors apply it directly to the motif of the "industrious housewife" or "housekeeper." Appropriately, in Dotzler's guide for brides, it stands at the beginning of the chapter about the housewife, combined with the following exhortation to the young female reader (and future spouse and housewife): "If you want to have an effect so pleasant and full of blessings in your new estate, too, then you must already have acquired the necessary knowledge and abilities in your parents' home or in an institution."[139] Diligence, household skills, thriftiness, but also the ability to maintain an overview in the house and over housekeeping, form that knowledge and those abilities that are listed immediately following the citation from Prov 31. The concept of separate gender spheres, as well as of the "bourgeois heaven of values," in which the sphere of house and family is assigned to the woman, is given in this way, so to say, a biblical prefiguration and, therewith, its legitimation.[140]

---

138. See Dupanloup, *Frau*, 30–38. On the development of gender-specific areas of work in the context of the history of the family, see Andreas Gestrich, "Neuzeit," in *Geschichte der Familie*, ed. Gestrich, Jens-Uwe Krause, and Michael Mitterauer, EK 1 (Stuttgart: Kröner, 2003), 525–34; Saurer, *Liebe und Arbeit: Geschlechterbeziehungen im 19. und 20. Jahrhundert* (Wien: Böhlau, 2014), 75–113. More specifically on the French development, see Michelle Perrot, "Rollen und Charaktere," in *Von der Revolution zum Großen Krieg*, vol. 4 of *Geschichte des privaten Lebens*, ed. Perrot (Frankfurt: Fischer, 1992), 145–53; and Rachel G. Fuchs, *Contested Paternity: Constructing Families in Modern France* (Baltimore: John Hopkins University Press, 2008).

139. Dotzler, *Brautführer*, 251–53. See also Combes, *Frau*, 46: citation from Prov 31:11 for the purpose of illustrating the important role of the woman as a "good housekeeper."

140. On this concept in the relationship of the sexes developed at first mainly in bourgeois circles since the late eighteenth century, and on the historiographical debates on the "separate spheres," see Opitz-Belakhal, *Geschlechtergeschichte*, 98–116; and van Osselaer, "Religion, Family, and Domesticity in the Nineteenth and Twentieth Centuries: An Introduction," in van Osselaer and Pasture, *Christian Homes*, 7–25. On the "bourgeois heaven of values," see Manfred Hettling and Stefan-Ludwig Hoffmann, eds., *Der bürgerliche Wertehimmel: Innenansichten des 19. Jahrhunderts* (Göttingen:

The texts investigated provide evidence for the interdenominational effectiveness and importance of these concepts. Dotzler's use of Prov 31 as a kind of "brides' instruction," by the way, corresponds to a possible exegetical determination of the *Sitz im Leben*.[141]

5.5. New Testament Women's Texts and Female Figures

Against the background of this, in part, intensive preoccupation with Old Testament women's texts, it is striking that no New Testament texts are treated in the investigated works in a comparatively detailed manner. Of course, complete series of New Testament verses can be compiled without any difficulty, verses which are recited literally or indirectly to illustrate or to legitimate any sort of circumstance. The New Testament is, thus, definitely present. What is lacking to the greatest extent is only the feminine figures in the New Testament.[142] If one asks about women in the Pauline letters or in Acts, then it can only be said: no chance. In regard to the women around Jesus, the picture is not much better. It can occur that Elizabeth and her husband Zechariah are touched upon as an example for a peaceable marriage,[143] or Mary Magdalene and the Samaritan woman are mentioned in a passage in order to show Jesus's compassion and love (John 4) and to stimulate the female readers to do the same as these two women and to direct their hope toward the Lord.[144] The Canaanite woman, on the other hand, is held up to the female readers as a model for a woman who prays a persevering and humble prayer of supplication (Matt 15:21–28), while the widow from Nain (Luke 7:11–17) is presented as an example of a grieving mother who has lost her son and experiences salvation from Jesus.[145] More than these citations of New Testament women from among the hundreds of biblical passages is not to be found.

Vandenhoeck & Ruprecht, 2000); Gunilla Budde, *Blütezeit des Bürgertums: Bürgerlichkeit im 19. Jahrhundert* (Darmstadt: Wissenschaftliche Buchgesellschaft, 2009).

141. See Fischer, *Gotteslehrerinnen*, 149.

142. For an introductory overview, see Ross Saunders, *Frauen im Neuen Testament: Zwischen Glaube und Auflehnung* (Darmstadt: Wissenschaftliche Buchgesellschaft, 1999).

143. See Marchal, *Frau*, 54.

144. See Marchal, *Frau*, 19.

145. See Dupanloup, *Frau*, 171, 176–78.

Only Mary, the mother of Jesus, forms an exception. Complete chapters are devoted to her in individual books, which, of course, were published amid the so-called Marian century.[146] However, she is in no way prominently featured generally as "the model" for woman in all the investigated women's books. Bishop Dupanloup speaks of her in only two passages with biblical references—out of over three hundred pages—and presents her as a model in suffering and in her willingness to sacrifice.[147] In Britz's advice book, a single Marian-oriented biblical passage, an extract from the *Magnificat*, is cited alone in the context of remarks about humility.[148] Only very seldom is the Eve-Mary typology developed.[149] On the basis of this line of interpretation, the unique role of Mary in salvation becomes for Victor Marchal the proof generally that in Christianity the dignity of the woman, which was lost after the fall, has been restored. "One sees her [the woman] appearing in the scenes of the gospels, honored by the Apostles, protected by the church, which in a quite special way pays her respect, gives her education and charity."[150]

More important than the concrete feminine figures in the New Testament for central questions concerning the relationship of the sexes are several paradigmatic texts. These are especially—less surprisingly—individual Pauline letters (Corinthians, Ephesians), 1 Timothy, attributed to Paul, and 1 Peter, all of which were received accordingly. The reception is concentrated in each case upon those few passages that, in content, stood closest to the object of the devotional books—instruction about the female sex and advice for women. Chapter seven from 1 Cor is accordingly discussed especially frequently. It is considered to be an orientation for the so-called choice of status, that is, the decision whether one ought to seek a marriage or to live as a virgin. The question, of course, is given special attention in the books that are aimed at young women, such as Dotzler's *Bride's Guide*. Thereby, the Catholic authors, against a certain social disdain of unmarried women, hold fast to the excellence of this status, assess it tra-

---

146. So Marchal, *Frau*, 293–318; Passy, *Lese und Gebetbuch*, 362–408; and Sintzel, *Frauengeschlecht*, 1:247–55. On this concept and the popularity of Mary in the nineteenth century, see Anton Ziegenaus, ed., *Das marianische Zeitalter: Entstehung, Gehalt, bleibende Bedeutung*, MS 14 (Regensburg: Pustet, 2002).
147. See Dupanloup, *Frau*, 94, 96.
148. See Britz, *Gedanken*, 152–53.
149. See Combes, *Frau*, 165; Dupanloup, *Frau*, 94.
150. Marchal, *Frau*, 8.

ditionally as superior to the married state, and relate the text, in part also directly, to the monastic form of life for women.[151] The authors certainly had the flowering of women's congregations beginning in the middle of the nineteenth century in view but nevertheless do not deal with this circumstance further because of the intended reading public.[152] Nowhere does one find a denigration of marriage posed against the background of the ideal of virginity; it is much rather the case that the authors, in referring to 1 Cor 7, give to understand that one ought to live in the estate into which God has called one and that therefore marriage, too, may be chosen after a thorough review.[153] Other sections of this letter are quoted more seldom; even the well-known remarks in 1 Cor 11 about the conduct of women in the worship service are taken up only seldom and then explained in the sense of the submission of women under men. Bishop Dupanloup, of course, expends a great amount of rhetorical and argumentative effort to keep this submission free from every streak of masculine tyranny and, on the contrary, to bring out clearly the obligation of the men to have an appreciative love for their wives.[154] Above and beyond this, he takes up the statements in this chapter about marriage between Christians and pagans and transfers them into his own present time. From this, he derives the high responsibility of mothers to care for a good Christian marriage in the case of the pending marriages of their daughters.[155]

The theme of Christian marriage is developed by individual authors on the basis of Eph 5:21–33.[156] Its sacramentality is emphasized as an upgrading of marriage and as a restoration of this institution, which had been dysfunctional since the fall.[157] Its value is appraised, by Bishop Dupan-

---

151. See Dotzler, *Brautführer*, 31; Dupanloup, *Frau*, 191; Passy, *Lese und Gebetbuch*, 409–30. Britz, *Gedanken*, does not discuss the subject, although she writes for young females. Marchal, *Frau*, 205–30, treats formally of the women of the religious orders as "brides of Christ" and defends this form of life. On the Catholic ideal of virginity, see De Giorgio, "Modell," 208–11. On single women in the bourgeoisie, see Bärbel Kuhn, *Familienstand: Ledig; Ehelose Frauen und Männer im Bürgertum, 1850–1914*, HS 5 (Cologne: Böhlau, 2000).

152. See especially Relinde Meiwes, *"Arbeiterinnen des Herrn": Katholische Frauenkongregationen im 19. Jahrhundert*, GG 30 (Frankfurt: Campus, 2000).

153. See Dotzler, *Brautführer*, 30; Passy, *Lese und Gebetbuch*, 478.

154. See Combes, *Frau*, 44; Dupanloup, *Frau*, 80–88, 219–23.

155. See Dupanloup, *Frau*, 289–90.

156. See Dotzler, *Brautführer*, 142–63; Dupanloup, *Frau*, 127–28, 181–91.

157. See Dotzler, *Brautführer*, 144–45; Dupanloup, *Frau*, 185–86.

loup, for example, as very high and this, to be sure, under the double perspective of the marital communion and the participation in God's work of creation through the conception of offspring.[158] He then refers anew to Eph 5:21-33 in connection with his remarks about mutual "sanctification in marriage," that is, about the reciprocal support on the path to eternal salvation.[159] It is precisely this sanctification that he sees at the center of this biblical passage and as the essential purpose of marriage.

From 1 Timothy, the section 2:8-10 is most cited. These verses deal with the adornment of women and the good works of piety, which the woman should wear as adornment instead of the pearls, gold, costly garments, or a magnificent hairstyle. On the other hand, the authors completely ignore the following verses 10 and 11, which are especially controversial today, about the silence of women and the prohibition of teaching by women.[160] The subject of adornment and extravagant clothing in contrast to true piety also is treated using 1 Pet 3:3-4.[161] Finally, 1 Pet 3:1-2 is taken up repeatedly in combination with other biblical passages in order to legitimate the submission of women to men authoritatively.[162]

6. Seldom Read, Yet Familiar: Catholic Women, the Bible, and the Role of Women

At the end, the result for me is a quite clear tendency: the Bible did not stand at the center of the spiritual life and spiritual reading of women in Catholic Germany in the nineteenth century. It was a point of reference for the authors of devotional and edificatory literature for women, but only one among many. Little speaks in favor of seeing this finding as gender-specific. On the basis of the general instruction on reading and on the home libraries, as well as on the basis of individual remarks in guidebooks for men, the Holy Scripture apparently was not of greater significance as pious "reading material" for the Catholic man, either.[163] Must one then speak, in

---

158. See Dupanloup, *Frau*, 183-85.
159. See Dupanloup, *Frau*, 285.
160. See Combes, *Frau*, 44; Egger, *Mutter*, 94-95, 101 (a chapter devoted to the subject of "The Beautiful Sex"); Marchal, *Frau*, 148, 196 (An entire chapter deals with the subject of "Women and Fashion."); Wetzel, *Frau*, 31.
161. See Egger, *Mutter*, 60, 101.
162. See Dupanloup, *Frau*, 214-15; Egger, *Mutter*, 201.
163. See Tilman Pesch, *Das religiöse Leben: Ein Begleitbüchlein mit Rathschlä-*

view of our theme, of a nonbiblical women's piety? What is important is, in fact, to differentiate the raw findings a bit more. A close connection of the Bible and liturgy can be reconstructed for Catholic piety and for that of women, too. In apologetic literature, this becomes the central argument against the Protestant charges of not reading the Bible and, consequently, not knowing it. The argument runs so: The Bible was proclaimed from the very beginning by the church in the liturgical context. The Bible's *Sitz im Leben* is there in the readings and in the gospel readings, and this since the time of the early church. The people, too, hear the biblical message in the liturgy in this way, and the Catholic faithful also ritually display the reverence for the Bible in the liturgy by means of an appropriate posture and gestures.[164]

In connection with this, the knowledge of the Bible among Catholic women can be understood as a result of oral culture; biblical history and stories were told in the family, in the liturgy, in catechesis, as well as in school. The direct and private reading of the Bible then appears to be less necessary. Jean-Baptiste Malou characterizes the Catholic access to the Bible exactly in this way:

> Catholic people, too, possess a knowledge of the Bible, but to a lesser extent, of course [than the educated class]. From their earliest days on, the children of Catholic families hear the chief episodes of the Old and New Testaments told to them. It is one of the chief joys for them to look into the books where these episodes are presented in pictures. The story of Creation, of the first Fall, of the promises of the Savior,… all of that takes hold of their youthful faculty of imagination and draws their attention to the facts that form the foundation of religion. The history of the Old Testament is followed by the narrative of the life of the Savior and by the instruction about His teaching, using the simple and popular parables of the gospel, which instill in youth the love for truth and virtue. The children then learn to fear the punishments for those who are evil and to hope for the rewards for those who are just. Thus do the truths of the Holy Scripture penetrate into their spirit and enlighten them with divine light precisely at the time when their reason begins to develop.[165]

---

gen und Gebeten zunächst für die gebildete Männerwelt (Freiburg im Breisgau: Herder, 1878), 228–29. Pesch does not recommend the Bible at all to men but rather a handbook on biblical history, an exegesis of the gospels, and the life of Jesus by the Capuchin Martin von Cochem (1634–1712), a work from the Baroque period.

164. To the point is Rebbert, *Bibellesen*, 69–71.
165. Malou, *Bibellesen*, 81.

The Bible is, after all, doctrine; accordingly, it was used as a collection of dogmas and drawn upon as an authority along with the Catechism, in order to confirm and to legitimate the authors' dogmas. It is encountered in the same way, too, in catechesis and proclamation. In this function, the biblical text appears in the devotional literature in most cases in the reduced form of brief or briefest citations. The concepts of femininity in the investigated works use the Bible in the latter sense. For them, the concrete feminine figures of the Bible are of comparably little relevance. The authors, with the possible exception of Dupanloup, do not develop an image of the woman on the basis of the Bible but rather substantiate their already-existing images of women through the Bible and project the desired conduct back upon the biblical figures. In the same way, they illustrate false conduct with the corresponding biblical examples. If Jüttemann could say that a handful of biblical citations from the creation story and the letters of the apostle Paul were sufficient in combination with Luther's catechism to structure and to legitimate the "gender-oriented milieu standards" in the Protestantism of eastern Westphalia, then this is also true as a tendency for German-speaking Catholicism.[166] For it, however, as shown by the investigated women's literature, two further paradigmatic texts (Sir 26 and Prov 31) were joined to the creation story. The authors see their ambivalent image of women and the structural asymmetry in the relationship of the sexes as anticipated in the Bible, and they interpret the Bible accordingly.

Bibliography

Altenberend, Johannes. *Leander van Eß (1772–1847): Bibelübersetzer und Bibelverbreiter zwischen Aufklärung und evangelischer Erweckungsbewegung*. SQWG 41. Paderborn: Bonifatius, 2001.

Baumeister, Martin. *Parität und katholische Inferiorität: Untersuchungen zur Stellung des Katholizismus im deutschen Kaiserreich*. PKV 3. Paderborn: Schöningh, 1987.

Baumgärtner, Wilhelm. *Joseph Franz Allioli (1793–1873): Leben und Werk*. Amberg: Buch & Kunstverlag Oberpfalz, 1993.

Becker, Winfried. "Katholisches Milieu: Theorien und empirische Befunde." Pages 23–62 in *Grenzen des katholischen Milieus: Stabilität*

---

166. Jüttemann, *Im Glauben vereint*, 262.

und Gefährdung katholischer Milieus in der Endphase der Weimarer Republik und in der NS-Zeit. Edited by Joachim Kuropka. Münster: Aschendorff, 2012.

Bischof, Franz Xaver. "Mermillod, Gaspar." *BBKL* 5 (1993): 1325–28.

Blaschke, Olaf. "The Unrecognised Piety of Men: Strategies and Success of the Re-Masculinisation Campaign around 1900." Pages 21–45 in *Christian Masculinity: Men and Religion in Northern Europe in the Nineteenth and Twentieth Centuries*. Edited by Yvonne Maria Werner. KADOC 8. Leuven: Leuven University Press, 2011.

Brandt, Hans-Jürgen, and Karl Hengst. *Das Bistum Paderborn im Industriezeitalter: 1821–1930*. Vol. 3 of *Geschichte des Erzbistums Paderborn*. VGMK 14. Paderborn: Bonifatius, 1997.

Bremscheid, Matthias von. *Die wichtige Stellung der christlichen Frauen*. Dülmen: Laumann, 1889.

Breuer, Gisela. *Frauenbewegung im Katholizismus: Der Katholische Frauenbund, 1903–1918*. Frankfurt: Campus, 1998.

Britz, Clara. *Gedanken und Ratschläge zur Beherzigung für die weibliche Jugend*. Mainz: Haas, 1883.

Budde, Gunilla. *Blütezeit des Bürgertums: Bürgerlichkeit im 19. Jahrhundert*. Darmstadt: Wissenschaftliche Buchgesellschaft, 2009.

Burkard, Dominik. "Presse und Medien." Pages 559–602 in *Laien in der Kirche*. Edited by Erwin Gatz. GKL 8. Freiberg im Breisgau: Herder, 2008.

Busch, Norbert. *Katholische Frömmigkeit und Moderne: Die Sozial- und Mentalitätsgeschichte des Herz-Jesu-Kultes in Deutschland zwischen Kulturkampf und Erstem Weltkrieg*. RKM 6. Gütersloh: Kaiser, 1997.

Combes, Paul. *Das Buch der Frau: Ein Handbuch für christliche Frauen in ihrer Stellung als Gattin, Hausfrau, Mutter und Erzieherin*. Revised by P. Weber. Saarlouis: Hausen, 1912.

Cramer, Wilhelm. *Die christliche Mutter in der Erziehung und ihrem Gebete*. Dülmen: Laumann, 1903.

De Giorgio, Michela. "Das katholische Modell." Pages 187–220 in *19. Jahrhundert*. Vol. 4 of *Geschichte der Frauen*. Edited by Geneviève Fraisse and Michelle Perrot. Frankfurt: Campus, 1994.

Dora, Cornel. *Augustinus Egger von St. Gallen, 1833–1900: Ein Bischof zwischen Kulturkampf, sozialer Frage und Modernismusstreit*. St.GKG 23. Saint Gallen: Staatsarchiv, 1994.

Dotzler, Arsenius. *Myrtenkranz! Ein geistlicher Brautführer und Andachtsbuch für die christliche Frau*. Kevelaer: Butzon & Bercker, 1900.

Duffrer, Günter. *Auf dem Weg zu liturgischer Frömmigkeit: Das Werk des Markus Adam Nickel (1800–1869) als Höhepunkt pastoralliturgischer Bestrebungen im Mainz des 19. Jahrhunderts*. QAMK 6. Speyer: Jaeger, 1962.
Dupanloup, Félix. *Die großen Pflichten der christlichen Frau: Conferenzreden*. Mainz: Kirchheim, 1881.
Egger, Augustin. *Die christliche Mutter: Erbauungs und Gebetbuch*. Einsiedeln: Benziger, 1914.
Fischer, Irmtraud. *Gotteslehrerinnen: Weise Frauen und Frau Weisheit im Alten Testament*. Stuttgart: Kohlhammer, 2006.
Frevert, Ute. *"Mann und Weib, und Weib und Mann": Geschlechter-Differenzen in der Moderne*. BR 1100. Munich: Beck, 1995.
Fuchs, Rachel G. *Contested Paternity: Constructing Families in Modern France*. Baltimore: John Hopkins University Press, 2008.
Gause, Ute. "Frauen und Frömmigkeit im 19. Jahrhundert: Der Aufbruch in die Öffentlichkeit." *PN* 24 (1998): 309–27.
Gestrich, Andreas. "Neuzeit." Pages 364–652 in *Geschichte der Familie*. Edited by Andreas Gestrich, Jens-Uwe Krause, and Michael Mitterauer. EK 1. Stuttgart: Kröner, 2003.
Götz von Olenhusen, Irmtraud, ed. *Frauen unter dem Patriarchat der Kirchen: Katholikinnen und Protestantinnen im 19. und 20. Jahrhundert*. KG 7. Stuttgart: Kohlhammer, 1995.
———, ed. *Wunderbare Erscheinungen: Frauen und katholische Frömmigkeit im 19. und 20. Jahrhundert*. Paderborn: Schöningh, 1995.
Hammer-Tugendhat, Daniela. "Judith und ihre Schwestern: Konstanz und Veränderung von Weiblichkeitsbildern." Pages 124–80 in *Geschlecht und Moral*. Edited by Annette Kämmerer and Agnes Speck. Heidelberg: Das Wunderhorn, 1999.
Häntzschel, Günter. *Bildung und Kultur bürgerlicher Frauen, 1850–1918: Eine Quellendokumentation aus Anstandshilfen und Lebenshilfen für Mädchen und Frauen als Beitrag zur weiblichen literarischen Sozialisation*. Tübingen: Niemeyer, 1986.
Hauser, Margit. *Gesellschaftsbild und Frauenrolle in der Aufklärung: Zur Herausbildung des egalitären und komplementären Geschlechtsrollenkonzepts bei Pollain de la Barre und Rousseau*. Vienna: Passagen, 1992.
Heil, Verein vom. *Verzeichniß der von dem Verein vom heil. Karl Borromäus empfohlenen Bücher für das Jahr 1890*. Bonn: Verein vom Heiligen Karl Borromäus, 1890.

Henkelmann, Andreas. *Caritasgeschichte zwischen katholischem Milieu und Wohlfahrtsstaat: Das Seraphische Liebeswerk, 1889–1971.* VKZ 113. Paderborn: Schöningh, 2008.

Hettling, Manfred, and Stefan-Ludwig Hoffmann, eds. *Der bürgerliche Wertehimmel: Innenansichten des 19. Jahrhunderts.* Göttingen: Vandenhoeck & Ruprecht, 2000.

Hoffelize, Adele Gräfin von. *Kurze Unterweisungen im christlichen Leben für Frauen und Jungfrauen.* Mainz: Kirchheim, 1880.

Hoock-Demarle, Marie-Claire. "Lesen und Schreiben in Deutschland." Pages 165–86 in *19. Jahrhundert.* Vol. 4 of *Geschichte der Frauen.* Edited by Geneviève Fraisse and Michelle Perrot. Frankfurt: Campus, 1994.

Horstmann, Johannes, and Antonius Liedhegener, eds. *Konfession, Milieu, Moderne: Konzeptionelle Positionen und Kontroversen zur Geschichte von Katholizismus und Kirche im 19. und 20. Jahrhundert.* AV 47. Schwerte: Katholische Akademie, 2001.

Hülskamp, Franz. *1000 gute Bücher, den Katholiken deutscher Zunge zu Festgeschenken empfohlen.* Münster: Theissing, 1882.

Hummel, Steffi. *Der Borromäusverein, 1845–1920: Katholische Volksbildung und Büchereiarbeit zwischen Anpassung und Bewahrung.* VHKT 18. Cologne: Böhlau, 2005.

Jocham, Magnus. *Anleitung zum Gebrauch der Biblischen Geschichte.* Munich: Zentral-Schulbücher, 1884.

Jüttemann, Veronika. *Im Glauben vereint: Männer und Frauen im protestantischen Milieu Ostwestfalens, 1845–1918.* HS 16. Cologne: Böhlau, 2008.

Keiter, Heinrich, ed. *Katholischer Literaturkalender.* Freiburg im Breisgau: Herder, 1891–1897.

———. *Die Kunst: Bücher zu lesen.* Essen: Fredebeul & Koenen, 1901.

Knibiehler, Yvonne. "Leib und Seele." Pages 373–415 in *19. Jahrhundert.* Vol. 4 of *Geschichte der Frauen.* Edited by Geneviève Fraisse and Michelle Perrot. Frankfurt: Campus, 1994.

Köhler, Oskar. *Müde bin ich geh' zur Ruh': Die hell-dunkle Lebensgeschichte Luise Hensels.* Paderborn: Schöningh, 1991.

Kotulla, Andreas. "Nach Lourdes!" Pages 252–305 in *Der französische Marienwallfahrtsort und die Katholiken im Deutschen Kaiserreich, 1871–1914.* Munich: Meidenbauer, 2006.

Krumeich, Christa. *Hieronymus und die christlichen feminae clarissimae.* Bonn: Habbelt, 1993.

Kuhn, Bärbel. *Familienstand: Ledig; Ehelose Frauen und Männer im Bürgertum, 1850–1914*. HS 5. Cologne: Böhlau, 2000.
Landriot, Jean Baptiste François. *Die fromme Frau: Conferenzen für Frauen, die in der Weltleben*. Mainz: Kirchheim, 1889.
Liebenau, Anna von. *An's Frauenherz: Worte der Liebe und Freundschaft für die katholische Frau*. Dülmen: Laumann, 1903.
Lyons, Martyn. "Die neuen Leser im 19. Jahrhundert: Frauen, Kinder, Arbeiter." Pages 455–97 in *Die Welt des Lesens: Von der Schriftrolle bis zum Bildschirm*. Edited by Roger Chartier and Guglielmo Cavallo. Frankfurt: Campus, 1999.
Malou, Jean-Baptiste. *Das Bibellesen in der Volkssprache: Beurtheilt nach der heil. Schrift, der Tradition und der gesunden Vernunft; Eine Streitschrift*. 2 vols. Schaffhausen: Hurter, 1849.
Martschukat, Jürgen, and Olaf Stieglitz. "Es ist ein Junge." Page 55 in *Einführung in die Geschichte der Männlichkeiten in der Neuzeit*. HE 11. Tübingen: Edition Diskord, 2005.
Marchal, Victor. *Das Bild der christlichen Frau*. Regensburg: Pustet, 1899.
Marcilhacy, Christiane. *Le Diocèse d'Orléans sous l'épiscopat de Mgr. Dupanloup (1849–1878): Sociologie religieuse et mentalités collectives*. Paris: Plon, 1962.
Meiwes, Relinde. *"Arbeiterinnen des Herrn": Katholische Frauenkongregationen im 19. Jahrhundert*. GG 30. Frankfurt: Campus, 2000.
Menne, Karl, ed. *Keiters Katholischer Literaturkalender*. Freiburg im Breisgau: Herder: 1898–1914.
Mermillod, Gaspar. *Die christliche Frau in unserer Zeit: Vorträge*. Neisse: Huch, 1875.
Messerli, Alfred. "Gebildet, nicht gelehrt: Weibliche Schreib- und Lesepraktiken in den Diskursen vom 18. zum 19. Jahrhundert." Pages 295–320 in *Die lesende Frau*. Edited by Gabriela Signori. WF 121. Wiesbaden: Harrassowitz, 2009.
Müller, Heinrich. *Himmelsweg: Ein katholisches Gebet und Lehrbuch für Jungfrauen mit bischöflicher Approbation*. Cologne: St. Josephs-Verein, 1913.
Noit, H. von. *Ueber Bibelkenntnis und Bibellesen in älterer und neuerer Zeit: Wittenberg und Rom; Christ oder Antichrist*. Berlin: Germania, 1896.
Oepen, Joachim. "Bruderschaften im 19. Jahrhundert." *RQCAK* 99 (2004): 180–209.
Opitz-Belakhal, Claudia. *Geschlechtergeschichte*. HE 8. Frankfurt: Campus, 2010.

Osinski, Jutta. *Katholizismus und deutsche Literatur im 19. Jahrhundert.* Paderborn: Schöningh, 1993.

Osselaer, Tine van. "Religion, Family, and Domesticity in the Nineteenth and Twentieth Centuries: An Introduction." Pages 7–25 in *Christian Homes: Religion, Family, and Domesticity in the Nineteenth and Twentieth Centuries.* Edited by Tine van Osselaer and Patrick Pasture. KADOC 14. Leuven: Leuven University Press, 2014.

Osselaer, Tine van, and Thomas Buerman. "Feminization Thesis: A Survey of International Historiography and a Probing of Belgian Grounds." *RHE* 103 (2008): 497–544.

Passy, Anton. *Lese und Gebetbuch für katholische weibliche und geistliche Jungfrauen.* Regenburg: Manz, 1850.

Pasture, Patrick. "Gendering the History of Christianity in the Nineteenth and Twentieth Centuries." Pages 7–33 in *Gender and Christianity in Modern Europe: Beyond the Feminization Thesis.* Edited by Patrick Pasture, Jan Art, and Thomas Buerman. KADOC 10. Leuven: Leuven University Press, 2012.

Pataky, Sophie. *Lexikon deutscher Frauen der Feder: Eine Zusammenstellung der seit dem Jahre 1840 erschienenen Werke weiblicher Autoren, nebst Biographien der lebenden und einem Verzeichnis der Pseudonyme.* Reprint. Berne: Lang, 1971.

Perrot, Michelle. "Rollen und Charaktere." Pages 127–93 in *Von der Revolution zum Großen Krieg.* Vol. 4 of *Geschichte des privaten Lebens.* Edited by Michele Perrot. Frankfurt: Fischer, 1992.

Pesch, Tilman. *Das religiöse Leben: Ein Begleitbüchlein mit Rathschlägen und Gebeten zunächst für die gebildete Männerwelt.* Freiburg im Breisgau: Herder, 1878.

Radkau, Joachim. *Das Zeitalter der Nervosität: Deutschland zwischen Bismarck und Hitler.* Munich: Hauser, 1998.

Raffenberg, Anton. *Die betende Mutter: Vereins-Gebetbuch für die Mitglieder der Erzbruderschaft der christlichen Mütter.* Dulmen: Laumann, 1929.

Rebbert, Josef. *Das Bibellesen auf eigene Hand.* BonB 18. Paderborn: Bonifatius, 1887.

Saunders, Ross. *Frauen im Neuen Testament: Zwischen Glaube und Auflehnung.* Darmstadt: Wissenschaftliche Buchgesellschaft, 1999.

Saurer, Edith. "'Bewahrerinnen der Zucht und Sittlichkeit': Gebetbücher für Frauen; Frauen in Gebetbüchern." *HZFG* 1 (1990): 37–58.

———. *Liebe und Arbeit: Geschlechterbeziehungen im 19. und 20. Jahrhundert.* Wien: Böhlau, 2014.

Scheidgen, Andreas. "Diözesangesangbücher und Kirchenliedrestauration im 19. und 20. Jahrhundert." Pages 35–48 in *Geschichte des katholischen Gesangbuchs*. Edited by Dominik Fugger and Andreas Scheidgen. MHS 21. Tübingen: Francke, 2008.

Schenda, Rudolf. *Volk ohne Buch: Studien zur Sozialgeschichte der populären Lesestoffe, 1770–1910*. Frankfurt: Klostermann, 1970.

Scheuchenpflug, Peter. *Die Katholische Bibelbewegung im frühen 19. Jahrhundert*. STPS 27. Würzburg: Echter, 1997.

Schlögl, Rudolf. *Glaube und Religion in der Säkularisierung: Die katholische Stadt; Köln, Aachen, Münster, 1700–1840*. AR 38. Munich: Oldenbourg, 1995.

———. "Sünderin, Heilige oder Hausfrau? Katholische Kirche und weibliche Frömmigkeit um 1800." Pages 13–50 in *Wunderbare Erscheinungen*. Edited by Irmtraud Götz von Olenhusen. Paderborn: Schöningh, 1995.

Schmidt, Susanna. "Handlanger der Vergänglichkeit." Pages 131–35 in *Zur Literatur des katholischen Milieus, 1800–1950*. Paderborn: Schöningh, 1994.

Schmolke, Michael. *Die schlechte Presse: Katholiken und Publizistik zwischen "Katholik" und "Publik," 1821–1968*. Münster: Regensberg, 1971.

Schneider, Bernhard. "The Catholic Poor Relief Discourse and the Feminization of the Caritas in Early Nineteenth Century Germany." Pages 34–55 in *Gender and Christianity in Modern Europe: Beyond the Feminization Thesis*. Edited by Patrick Pasture, Jan Art, and Thomas Buerman. KADOC 10. Leuven: Leuven University Press, 2012.

———. "Das Diözesangesangbuch: Eine Klammer für die Bistümer im 19. Jahrhundert." *RQCAK* 99 (2004): 210–28.

———. "Feminisierung der Religion im 19. Jahrhundert: Perspektiven einer These im Kontext des deutschen Katholizismus." *TTZ* 111 (2002): 123–47.

———. "Masculinity, Religiousness and the Domestic Sphere in the German-Speaking World around 1900." Pages 27–51 in *Christian Homes: Religion, Family, and Domesticity in the Nineteenth and Twentieth Centuries*. Edited by Tine van Osselaer and Patrick Pasture. KADOC 14. Leuven: Leuven University Press, 2014.

Schreiber, Georg. "Westfälische Wissenschaft, Politik, Publizistik im 19./20. Jahrhundert: Franz Hülskamp und sein Kreis." *WestF* 8 (1955): 74–94.

Schreiner, Klaus. *Maria: Jungfrau, Mutter, Herrscherin*. Munich: Hanser, 1994.

Sintzel, Michael. *Das christliche Frauengeschlecht in seinem Wandel und Gebete: Ein Lehr und Gebetbuch*. 2 vols. Augsburg: Kollmann, 1856.

Sohn-Kronthaler, Michaela, and Andreas Sohn. *Frauen im kirchlichen Leben vom 19. Jahrhundert bis heute*. Kevelaer: Topos, 2008.

Speth, Volker. *Katholische Aufklärung, Volksfrömmigkeit und "Religionspolicey": Das rheinische Wallfahrtswesen von 1816 bis 1826 und die Entstehungsgeschichte des Wallfahrtverbots von 1826; Ein Beitrag zur aufklärerischen Volksfrömmigkeit*. EW 5. Frankfurt: Lang, 2008.

Steiniger, Christine. *Die ideale christliche Frau: virgo, vidua, nupta; Eine Studie zum Bild der idealen christlichen Frau bei Hieronymus und Pelagius*. Saint Ottilien: Eos, 1997.

Temming, Theodor. *Die christliche Frau: Gebet und Unterweisungen; zugleich Andachtsbuch für die Mitglieder des Vereins christlicher Mütter*. Kevelaer: Butzon & Bercker, 1912.

Welter, Barbara. "'Frauenwille ist Gotteswille': Die Feminisierung der Religion in Amerika, 1800–1860." Pages 326–55 in *Listen der Ohnmacht: Zur Sozialgeschichte weiblicher Widerstandsformen*. Edited by Claudia Honegger and Bettina Heintz. Frankfurt: Europäische, 1981.

Wetzel, Franz Xaver. *Daheim: Ein Büchlein für's Volk*. Ravensburg: Dorn, 1900.

———. *Die Frau: Ein Büchlein für die Frauen*. Ravensburg: Dorn, 1896.

———. *Die Lektüre: Ein Führer beim Lesen*. Ravensburg: Dorn, 1897.

———. *Der Mann: Ein Büchlein für die Männer*. Ravensburg: Dorn, 190Zalar, Jeffrey T. "The Process of Confessional Inculturation: Catholic Reading in the 'Long Nineteenth Century.'" Pages 121–52 in *Protestants, Catholics and Jews in Germany, 1800–1914*. Edited by Helmut Walser Smith. Oxford: Berg, 2001.

Ziegenaus, Anton, ed. *Das marianische Zeitalter: Entstehung, Gehalt, bleibende Bedeutung*. MS 14. Regensburg: Pustet, 2002.

Zumholz, Maria-Anna. *"Das Weib soll nicht gelehrt seyn": Konfessionell geprägte Frauenbilder, Frauenbildung und weibliche Lebensentwürfe von der Reformation bis zum frühen 20. Jahrhundert; Eine Fallanalyse am regionalen Beispiel der Grafschaft Oldenburg und des Niederstifts Münster, seit 1744/1803 Herzogtum Oldenburg*. Münster: Aschendorff, 2016.

Between Service and Rebellion: German-Speaking Women Authors and Their Relationship to the Bible

Magda Motté

The adaptation of biblical material according to gender-specific aspects is a peripheral matter in literature and art in the nineteenth century and, on the whole, follows the traditional interpretations of the original texts. The noted German-speaking representatives of the major cultural-historical and literary currents kept their distance to the firmly-established structures and doctrines of the churches, that is, also to the Bible. With few exceptions, they took their material from Greek mythology (e.g., Johann Wolfgang Goethe, Franz Grillparzer, Johann Gottfried Herder, and Heinrich von Kleist), European history (e.g., Christian Dietrich Grabbe, Grillparzer, Heinrich von Kleist, and Friedrich Schiller), or from the realism of current daily events (e.g., Georg Büchner, Heinrich Heine, and Theodor Fontane). With his text *Die jüdischen Dichtungen und Fabeln* (1781), as well as with the uncompleted manuscript *Vom Geist der Ebräischen Poesie* (1782), Herder, to be sure, provided the impulse for appreciating the Bible as world literature and won over Goethe, Heine, and others as admirers, but this had little effect on creative literary work. This applies, with few exceptions, for those men who wrote as well as for the women, too. In this article, after a short overview of the general situation of women authors, two prominent examples concerning Lilith and Judith will be dealt with, both of which illustrate the tenor of the gender problems in the nineteenth century.

1. The Search for Evidence: Women Authors and the Bible—A Meager Result

After a search of numerous works by more than sixty well-known women authors from the nineteenth century, it must be said fundamentally: for those women writers striving for freedom during the Enlightenment, the classical period, and the Romantic age, such as Bettina von Arnim, Karoline von Günderode, Meta Klopstock, Sophie La Roche, Sophie Mereau, Caroline Schlegel, or Dorothee Schlegel, the Bible and religion were of little or no interest as sources of material for literary production. In these works, hardly any religious references are to be found and no involvement of any kind with biblical texts or biblical women in regard to the problem of gender, since ecclesiastical interests stood diametrically opposed to their own interests.

The same is true for female writers from the middle of the century, such as Louise Aston, Marie von Ebner-Eschenbach, Ida Hahn-Hahn, Marie Janitschek, Berta Lask, Fanny Lewald, Luise Mühlbach, Louise Otto-Peters, and Kathinka Zitz-Halein. In their commitment to social justice,[1] they, too, could hardly have resorted to ecclesiastical support, for the Protestant and Catholic churches, apart from socially committed congregations and associations, were to a great extent in agreement with the nobility and the upper bourgeois classes that the God-given class barriers were to be maintained.

For this reason, Mühlbach, for example, in her novels *Des Lebens Heiland* (1840), *Gisela* (1845), and *Aphra Behn* (1849), among others, posed with special urgency questions for herself dealing with phenomena such as intrigues, false piety, hypocrisy, and discrimination against Jews and women, and categorically rejected ecclesiastical authorities and their institutions, of course without concrete resort to definite biblical models.[2] Some women authors, such as von Günderode, Lewald, Grete Meisel-Hess, and Clara Müller-Jahnke, of course, cite the outcast, disenfranchised, lonely Hagar as an image for the situation of many women,

---

[1]. See especially Gabriele Schneider, "Arbeiten und nicht müde werden: Ein Leben durch und für die Arbeit; Fanny Lewald (1811–1889)," in *Beruf: Schriftstellerin; Schreibende Frauen im 18. und 19. Jahrhundert*, ed. Karen Tebben (Göttingen: Vandenhoeck & Ruprecht, 1998), 188–214.

[2]. See Cornelia Tönnesen, "Überhaupt hat sie eine kecke, ungezügelte Phantasie: Luise Mühlbach (1814–1873)," in Tebben, *Beruf: Schriftstellerin*, 215–43.

but they do not develop the material further. It is surprising that none of the female authors refers to strong women such as Tamar, Deborah, Miriam, Esther, Judith, Hannah, or Vashti. This possibly also has to do with a lack of biblical knowledge.[3] Even among the strongly Christian women writers, such as Luise Hensel, Annette von Droste-Hülshoff, von Ebner-Eschenbach, and others, no work upon a biblical basis is found that might have a landmark character for the treatment of the problem of gender.

2. Voice of the Voiceless—Biblical Models as Aids in Argumentation

In spite of this, in general, meager result, it is still possible, upon closer inspection, to uncover remarkable aspects on the subject of the Bible and Women in several nonfictional works.

The already-mentioned aspirations for freedom and the critical distance maintained in regard to ecclesiastical practice are found in von Arnim's (1785–1859) pamphlet *Dies Buch gehört dem König*. In a dialogue between a pastor and the councilor's (Goethe's) wife about God and the devil, authority and the law, the Bible and the commandments, especially in regard to women, the councilor's wife bluntly expresses her vehement criticism of the phrases and unrealistic maxims of the preachers and presents the Bible as the great book of freedom.

> Mister Pastor, I would already for a long time have been wasted away on the digestion of the Christian faith if I had not gotten out of it any better nourishment than that offered us by its priests. Sometimes I myself am petrified by you phrasemongers. In all the experiences of life, in all the books that blind chance puts into my hands, I see clearly written on every page: freedom of the spirit!, and so also in the book about the Inquisition, and so also in the Bible,—everywhere the same striking truth: The spirit must enjoy freedom, but not stone![4]

---

3. Presumably, a complete Bible in Luther's translation was available in most Protestant households among the nobility and bourgeoisie. Most Catholic women, however, were less well-versed in the Bible. They knew individual Old Testament passages as exemplary stories from catechetical instruction or from pictures, and New Testament passages from the Mass and preaching. Because of limited space, we must do without individual investigations here.

4. Bettina von Arnim, "Dies Buch gehört dem König" (1843), in von Arnim, *Werke und Briefe*, ed. Gustav Konrad, vol. 3 (Frechen: Bartmann, 1959), 72.

Von Arnim, in the role of the councilor's wife, complains about the "phrasemongers" that misuse the Bible for their own purposes and also proclaim dubious laws to be biblically-founded morality. They keep secret the exhilarating message of Jesus to join him in freedom. Thus, this citation says a great deal about ecclesiastical practice current at that time and also explains the distance maintained by a whole generation to the church and to faith. Only whoever was in possession of a Bible, and was able to read it, could realize all the power of its liberating message. There were only few of these.

The author Otto-Peters (1819–1895), today little known but in her time influential, was a passionate champion of the rights of women and the socially disadvantaged and also lent her voice to those without rights and without a voice of their own. In a lecture before the Democratic Women's Association (1849), she employed a reference to Jesus's authority and his conduct toward women to substantiate her demands for admitting girls and women to education and university study:

> As Jesus preferably did with the poor and those despised by their cocky, high-ranking fellow citizens, in that he proclaimed the gospel of love for all people and of freedom and equality …, so he also took the women to himself and did not disdain to instruct them and to lead them on the right path, just as he did the men, for he indeed had come to redeem all of humanity.[5]

Otto-Peters then touchingly describes the scene of Jesus's visit to the sisters Mary and Martha in Bethany, and concludes:

> "Mary has chosen the better part—that shall not be taken away from her" (Luke 10:42). We adhere to this word of our Master: that shall not be taken away from her! Thereby, it is pronounced for all time and established as a Christian principle: the woman should strive for what is higher, open her soul to the teachings of superior people, and nourish

---

5. Louise Otto-Peters, "Vortrag, gehalten im demokratischen Frauen-Verein zu Oederan, im Januar 1849. Fortsetzung: Aufsätze aus der Frauen-Zeitung," in *Frauenleben im Deutschen Reich* (Leipzig: Schäfer, 1876), 106–8, quoted in Mark Lehmstedt, ed., *Deutsche Literatur von Frauen: Von Catharina von Greifenberg bis Franziska von Reventlow*, Digitale Bibliothek 45 (Berlin: Directmedia, 2000), 58010. Subsequent citations are to Lehmstedt's edition.

her spirit with spiritual food—that is her better part that shall not be taken away from her!⁶

Since Otto-Peters knows that women hungry for education were not only mocked by men as being "bluestockings," but also were rebuked by their feminine equals for neglecting their household duties, she also refers indirectly to Jesus's word to the "Marthas":

> My sisters, let us answer with these words all the Marthas that we meet in our circles and who inundate us with their reproaches because, along with our peculiar feminine duties, we also subscribe to still higher endeavors, which they do not want to allow; these higher endeavors are precisely that better part, of which our Master said: that shall not be taken away from her. But if we know that we act in his spirit, how then can the judgments of the world bother us?⁷

In the further course of the text, the author also cites, among other instances, Jesus's conversation with the woman at Jacob's well (John 4:1–26) as justification for the assertion that women are capable of disputing about theological and moral questions.

On the whole, the Bible is drawn upon in this lecture in a striking way as an aid in argumentation in order to lend force to the demands of women. This is shown in the author's summary:

> Just how can one call oneself Christian and yet shove women from the position to which Christ Himself assigned them? The women, by following Jesus and serving Him, served the cause of freedom—the love for all human beings, for Jesus was the first hero and proclaimer of it—so then: Thus do we, too, in this way prove that we are genuine Christian women!⁸

Also in her poem "Für alle," Otto-Peters seeks a biblical basis in the widest sense for her call for equal rights:

> For all! do we hear the words resound,
> Our heart suddenly becomes big and wide!
> …

---

6. Otto-Peters, "Vortrag," 58011.
7. Otto-Peters, "Vortrag," 58011.
8. Otto, "Vortrag," 58012.

> For no holy work can be crowned any other way
> And struggle and strife can never be ended,
> Than when a salvation that has come into the world
> Like the sun begins to glow for all alike.[9]

In the individual verses, the author takes up the fundamental promise of salvation in Christian proclamation: God has become a human being "for all," as the angels sang in the fields around Bethlehem (second verse); the cup of redemption serves "for all" (third verse); Jesus is the liberator "for all"; freedom applies "for all" (fourth and fifth verses), and so on.

3. Mary Magdalene: A Sinful Woman?—Misuse of a Biblical Figure

One theme governed women especially in their poems and novels throughout the whole century until well into the time after 1900: the relationship between the sexes in general, as well as marital and free love. Ecclesiastical commandments from both confessions and the social order fixed and sanctioned by men produced, in their one-sided application to women, lasting feelings of guilt among the latter. Numerous novels and poems tell of their conflicts and moral dilemmas. Thereby, as a rule, reference is made to the questionable image of Mary Magdalene as a sinner, penitent, and blessed woman in the centuries-old traditions of popular piety and pastoral theology.[10] Such references were made, for example, by Hedwig Dohm, von Droste-Hülshoff, von Ebner-Eschenbach, Hahn-Hahn, Hensel, Agnes Miegel, Lily Braun, Therese Huber, Janitschek, La Roche, Lewald, Otto-Peters, Franziska Countess zu Reventlow, and others. No other saint is so often cited or invoked—ca. forty times only in literature by women!—as is Mary Magdalene, although never as *apostola apostolorum*, but rather exclusively in the above mentioned manner, as in the poem "St. Magdalena. Am Morgen der ersten Beichte," by Hensel (1798–1876):

> Beseech love and tears for me
> You stern penitent,

---

9. Louise Otto-Peters, *Mein Lebensgesang: Gedichte aus fünf Jahrzenten* (Leipzig: Schäfer, 1893), 262–64, quoted in Lehmstedt, *Deutsche Literatur von Frauen*, 56551.

10. See on this, among others, Magda Motté, *Esthers Tränen, Judiths Tapferkeit: Biblische Frauen in der Literatur des 20. Jahrhunderts* (Darmstadt: WBG, 2003), 230–70, and the literature listed there.

So that I with pure longing
Strive toward Jesus![11]

In the style of pious utilitarian literature, the lyrical I petitions for the intercession of the holy Magdalene. The word field of contrite repentance, "tears," "longing," "dissolving," "vanishing," and others, characterizes the prayer and testifies to an attitude of prayer that is pure feeling. For this, the biblical figure is used as a model.

If the poem by Hensel can be read as gender-neutral, then Miegel's (1879–1964) text "Magdalena" (1901) makes the gender problems massively clear. With indescribable *Kitsch*, she disfigures the image of the biblical woman:

> From the rosy toes
> Slip off the golden rings,
> Your purple sandals
> Throw into the stony brook.
> Repent, repent,
> Golden-haired sinful woman!
> Your cosseted feet
> Stride through thorns and thistles.[12]

With a ballad-like tone and in opulent images, the author builds up a scene of sin and repentance over the span of six stanzas. An unidentifiable lyrical I—masculine in style and self-consciousness—addresses a woman who is equipped with all the attributes of Baroque visual artistic decoration: golden hair, precious jewelry, delicate limbs, beautiful clothes and robes, the aura of aromatic nard, and a soft bed. In every stanza, the speaker presents the penitent woman—the saint? a sinful woman? a prostitute?—with a different attribute of seduction and contrasts this with the urgent call for total repentance.

---

11. Luise Hensel, *Lieder* (Paderborn: Schöningh, 1879), 250; see also therein "Aschermittwoch" (117), "Die Gesunden bedürfen des Arztes nicht, sondern die Kranken" (211), "Ostermorgen 1818" (79). Here, to be sure, the female bearer of ointment is spoken of, but the lyrical I experiences itself in prayer as a repentant sinner and Mary as the blessed one.

12. Agnes Miegel, "Magdalena" (1901), in Miegel, *Wie Bernstein leuchtend auf der Lebenswaage: Gesammelte Balladen*, ed. Ulf Diederichs (Munich: Diederichs, 1988), 16–17.

> Your streaming hair
> Wherein the feverish craving raged,
> Tear this out, until the morning
> Cools your burning temples.
> Weep, weep,
> The day arises out of the east's door,
> Victor in the glow of the flames
> Rises above your penance.[13]

What remains unanswered is with which authority the lyrical I speaks to the Magdalene—as a father confessor?—and who possibly is meant concretely by name. The entreaties "repent, repent" (first stanza), "beat, beat / ... yourself raw" (third stanza), "weep, weep" (fourth stanza), "lower, lower / Your forehead" (fifth stanza) leave no room for doubt. The penitential exercises point more to late medieval sadistic penitential rites and punishments than to spiritual discussion. Only the line "There had a god mercy upon you" (fifth stanza) puts an end to this almost sensual torment. The last two stanzas describe the period of repentance and renunciation by this woman in the desert, where she "waits" in a "shielding grotto" upon "refreshment" from the "rock" (seventh stanza). Here, the legendary traits of the penitent Mary of Egypt and of the Magdalene in the cave in southern France are mixed with each other. What might have moved Miegel, a recognized writer of ballads, to write these verses? Yet, this text reflects many of the social problems involved in determining how women in such situations—men are not accused of being a "sinner" (!) in this way—were to be treated.

Several legend novels written by women on the theme of Mary Magdalene, for example by Clara Commer, Dora Duncker, Catharina Gondlach, and Anna Baroness of Krane, appear within the framework of the renaissance of biblical material in the arts and literature at the turn of the century. Like the novel from Baroness Krane, these works were read widely, but they offer no gender-specific treatment. Mary Magdalene is firmly connected with the pattern "sinful woman—penitent woman" until well into the twentieth century, as is shown clearly by the titles of novels by Ebner-Eschenbach (*Unsühnbar*, "Unatoneable") or Baroness Krane (*Magna peccatrix*), and Lilian Fischinger (*Magdalena Sünderin*). The

---

13. Miegel, "Magdalena," 16.

bearer of ointment, the *apostola apostolorum*, hardly ever appears.[14] As far as the literary quality of the named works is concerned, most of them are rightly forgotten today and are still of interest at most in a literary-historical or sociological sense in regard to the gender question.

4. The Bible as a Refuge in Spiritual Distress

Most of the female authors mentioned to this point are known today to only a few. One female writer, however, remains in the consciousness of many readers both male and female: von Droste-Hülshoff (1797–1848). A daughter of a noble Westphalian family centered on Munster and a recipient of a strict Catholic education, she could be the source for filling in the blank spaces that have emerged to this point. Linguistically gifted, she recorded all her experiences poetically, beginning at a young age. Her cycle of poems *Das geistliche Jahr*, a poetic *confessio* on the basis of the Sunday and feast day gospels throughout the church year, is considered to be a unique document of religious poetry in the nineteenth century. In addition, there are further *Geistliche Gedichte*, in which she deals with her life of faith. With her *Geistliches Jahr*, the author continues a more than three-hundred-year-old tradition. The poems, in spite of their traditional forms, are an important religious document of the subjective and existentialist management of life in the nineteenth century through the Bible. In its skepticism and questioning attitude, it was ahead of its time.[15]

In regard to the theme the Bible and Women, however, it is to be stated that there is no reference to the Old Testament in von Droste-Hülshoff's complete works; the New Testament forms the basis of the cycle already mentioned and of several spiritual poems. Apart from Mary, the transfigured and pure woman (see the poems "Maria Lichtmeß," "Mariä Verkündigung"), only the sinful and penitent woman Mary Magdalene ("Christi Himmelfahrt"), the young daughter of Jairus ("Am. 25. So. nach Pfingsten"), and the Canaanite woman ("Am 2. So. in der Fasten") also are named here. Otherwise no other biblical woman! Among the numerous books that the author names in letters are works by Thomas á Kempis,

---

14. For examples of well-known authors who deal with this motif up until the middle of the twentieth century, see Motté, *Esthers Tränen*, 230–70.

15. See Annette von Droste-Hülshoff, *Des Grauens Süße: Ein Lesebuch*, ed. Dieter Borchmeyer (Munich: Hanser, 1997), 76–95.

Johannes David, Guido Görres, Friedrich von Spee, and the religious poetry of the seventeenth and eighteenth centuries, but not the Bible.[16]

Nevertheless, the poems of the *Geistliches Jahr* show the writer's quite independent treatment of the Sunday and feast day gospels in the celebration of the Mass. A direct reference to the biblical pericope is hardly ever made. The pericope serves exclusively as an object of meditation in the manner of an allegorical interpretation, that is, as a spark for free lines of thought by a lyrical I on the theme of faith. This thought was burdened with doubt about tradition and about the role imposed on her as a woman. Von Droste-Hülshoff could, but did not want to, believe all of what was demanded of her in Scripture and the sermon. To be sure, she placed the heart above reason, but the latter led her along paths that got her into difficulty. She lived in the dichotomy of the incontestable Catholic faith tradition on the one side and subjective free thought as a woman on the other. For this reason, she again and again lets the lyrical I articulate feelings of guilt.

A special place in von Droste-Hülshoff's thought is occupied by the Canaanite woman. The biblical pericope according to Matthew (Matt 15:21–28; Mark 7:24–30) tells of the tremendous courage of a heathen woman from Canaan who overcomes every barrier of foreignness, gender, and antagonism in order to come to Jesus and to obtain from him a promise of healing for her daughter. Von Droste-Hülshoff chose this Bible text twice as the basis for a personal treatment: in the cycle the poem "Am Zweiten Sonntag in der Fastenzeit" (1820) and for a single spiritual poem (1818). This speaks in favor of the idea that she felt herself spoken to by the humility of this woman as well as by her courage. Nevertheless, she treats the text in a highly selective way. In the cyclical poem, she mentions neither the story nor the woman, but rather transfers only the woman's metaphor of the dog that lives from the crumbs from the table of the rich to the situation of the lyrical I.

> Like a little dog I want to feel
> For the crumbs of your favor
> …

---

16. See Herbert Kraft, *Annette von Droste-Hülshoff*, Rowohlts Monografien 50517 (Reinbek bei Hamburg: Rowohlt, 1997), esp. 21–22; Walter Gödden, *Tag für Tag im Leben der Annette von Droste-Hülshoff: Daten—Texte—Dokumente* (Paderborn: Schöningh, 1996).

> I am only like a little dog,
> And so I also do not want to yield,
> Firmly in the footsteps of your children,
> And hope they will give me a bite to eat.[17]

Here speaks the Canaanite woman. She knows that she has no right to Jesus's attention; she is a foreigner and, in addition, a woman who makes a request for her daughter. But if Jesus does not take notice of her, then perhaps his children, his followers, will do so. Her firm will is not to leave Jesus's side.

In the single poem, "Als der Herr in Sidons Land gekommen," the poetess sketches out the biblical situation in the first two stanzas and repeatedly emphasizes the woman's humility and the desire of the lyrical I to do as she does:

> But, she gazes into the glory of his eyes,
> And her loyal heart remains not frightened.
> She wants to see herself as like a little dog,
> That licks the crumbs from the earth,
> Her humility has broken through.[18]

Then, the lyrical I transfers the situation to its own:

> Can only humility bring us blessing,
> And do I, despicable mortal worm,
> Still think that I must be successful,
> Since I am still so far away from humility?[19]

In the struggle in regard to submission, the lyrical I places its hope in grace:

> Yes, I want to build upon Jesus's words,
> Even if I don't see him at once, but only the night,

---

17. Annette von Droste-Hülshoff, "Am Zweiten Sonntag in der Fastenzeit" (1820), in von Droste-Hülshoff, *Das Geistliche Jahr—Gestliche Lieder* (Leipzig: Hesse, 1904); Droste-Hülshoff, *Sämtliche Werke in zwei Bänden, nach dem Text der Originaldrucke und der Handschriften*, ed. Günter Weydt and Winfried Woesler (Munich: Winkler, 1973), 591.

18. Droste-Hülshoff, "Als der Herr in Sidons Land gekommen," in von Droste-Hülshoff, *Gesammelte Werke*, vol. 1 (Weimar: Lichtenstein, 1923), 714.

19. Droste-Hülshoff, "Als der Herr in Sidons Land gekommen," 714.

Only firm, firm in humility and trust,
My soul, with your entire might![20]

The fact that von Droste-Hülshoff herself is concealed behind the lyrical I is not difficult to infer from biographical details. Her confrontation with faith questions, her doubt, her defiance, and the fear resulting from it, arise, to be sure, from traditional Catholic-Christian moral teaching and its overemphasis placed upon the consciousness of sin. But, the freedom-craving poetess, who repeatedly wished that she was a man,[21] finds relief from her spiritual distress in reflection upon the gospels. Of course, though, one seeks in vain in her work for open resistance by using biblical models against religious constraints.

5. Lilith—God's Plan?

Women authors who, in dramas, stories, or novels, took up biblical material concerning women especially, and who shaped this material in regard to gender problems, are rare in the German-speaking realm. Janitschek's (pseudonym: Marius Stein) titles *Königin Judith* (1895), *Ninive* (1896), *Die neue Eva* (1902), or Clara Viebig's novel *Kinder der Eifel* (1897), arouse attention, of course, but all of these are merely contemporary novels with general allusions to biblical figures. Individual works written by women, such as Gondlach's story "Judith" (1918), Marie Itzerott's drama *Delila* (1899), and Anna Sartory's drama *Judith, die Heldin von Bethulia* (1907) reproduce traditional interpretations and show no gender-specific treatment. All the more remarkable is the epic by Isolde Kurz, *Die Kinder der Lilith* (1908), which contributes a new interpretation to the gender problem.

When, in the eighteenth and nineteenth centuries, as a result of the Enlightenment, a new interpretation of the Fall was discussed, the artistic interest among well-known writers and painters in the Lilith myth as a model of the psychological and cultural-historical meaning of the relationship between men and women also was awakened. Since then, Lilith has

---

20. Droste-Hülshoff, "Als der Herr in Sidons Land gekommen," 716.

21. See Droste-Hülshoff, *Sämtliche Werke in zwei Bänden, nach dem Text der Originaldrucke und der Handschriften*, ed. Günter Weydt and Winfried Woesler, vol. 1 (Munich: Winkler, 1973): "Am Turme" (68); "Der zu früh geborene Dichter" (106–7); see also Kraft, *Annette von Droste-Hülshoff*, 46ff.

received not only more attention in European literature,[22] but she also step by step has been rehabilitated. The only woman who dared to deal with the material was the emancipated, eccentric writer Kurz (1853–1914): she published her sweeping epic in 1908 and thereby interpreted the material in a highly unconventional manner.

Lilith, a figure from Babylonian-Assyrian mythology, is mentioned by name only in Isa 34:14 as a night-spirit that, through God's judgment upon the heathen, is banished to a fixed location. Otherwise, Lilith does not appear in the canonic Bible but is definitely in the Talmud. According to it, she is, like Adam, created by God from the earth; that is, she is not flesh of his flesh, is equal to him, and is not willing to submit to him sexually. When he attempts to force her, she leaves him. Yet, God sends three of his angels to bring her back. Since she refuses, she is punished by God with the loss of her children, and she is condemned to fly about through the air as a ghostly spirit. In revenge, she threatens to kill newborn children if these do not wear an amulet with the names of the three angels. Another source says that she seduces the old Adam and, as a consequence, gives birth to demons and spirits. In her independence, Lilith is seen as a strong woman and, for this reason, as a seductive beauty—snake-like body with flowing hair—and as a female devil. She becomes the mythical figure of a men-corrupting female demon, a vamp, a siren, a Lorelei.[23]

In Kurz's work,[24] however, she is no winged demon who leaves Adam, but rather a kind of angel with deeper insights. God gives the fairy-like, winsome Lilith to the "clod of earth" Adam as a companion. Both, so thinks God, would bring life, playfulness, and wit into creation. In the first part, the Creator declares to the Elohim/Cherubim and to Sammael/Lucifer what he has in mind with Lilith:

---

22. Examples: Johann Wolfgang von Goethe in *Faust* ("Walpurgisnacht"), Paul Heyse in *Lilith* (1903), Victor Hugo in *Remy de Gourmont*, Gabriel Rossetti in *Eden Bower*, Anatole France in *La Fille de Lilith*, George Macdonald in *Lilith*. See on this: Herbert Haag et al., *Große Frauen der Bibel in Bild und Text* (Freiburg: Herder, 1993); Marianne Wallach-Faller, "Für eine Versöhnung mit Lilith," in *Unerhörte Worte: Religiöse Gesellschaftskritik von Frauen im 20. Jahrhundert*, ed. Doris Brodbeck, Gender Wissen 5 (Berne: eFeF, 2003), 253–56.

23. See, among others, Haag, *Große Frauen der Bibel*, 19–31; Vera Zingsem, *Lilith: Adams erste Frau* (Leipzig: Reclam, 2000), 81–117.

24. Isolde Kurz, "Die Kinder der Lilith" (1908), in Kurz, *Gesammelte Werke*, vol. 1 (Munich: Müller, 1925), quoted by Zingsem, *Lilith*, 81–114. Subsequent citations to Zingsem's edition.

> From Adam, the poor clod of earth,
> I build through Lilith a ladder
> to the highest seat of Heaven.
> For this I paired the woman friend with him,
> Half of his and half of your kind,
> That she with thorns of love
> May awake him, steel him, spur him on,
> He too bulky and she too fine,
> Incapable each for themselves alone.
> I gave her no earthly weapons,
> She is intended to inspire; he is to create
> From him comes the might that splits the rock,
> Who orderly governs the firm mind;
> From her the flame always moving,
> The unrest that moves the clock's works.
> ...
> Where she appears must everything bloom,
> And Lilith's mouth can never lie,
> Wherever she roams on flights of fantasy,
> The sluggish giant must follow her![25]

Here, the image of a woman is outlined who, equipped with angel-like properties, is intended to move the sluggish Adam toward something higher. Yet, only the two together are capable of creating something new. All of this displeases the archangel Sammael, the lord of the morning star, who fears for his autocratic rule. He intends to lead Adam to lethargy through coarse sensuality. For this, he creates Eve from Adam's rib, a creature in bondage to Adam and concerned only with sensuality. Adam is torn between the two women, but finally tends toward Eve, who warns him about Lilith's superiority. This grieves Lilith severely; she flees. What follows is the story of the Fall and the expulsion from Paradise.

In the last part of the epic, Kurz provides a bold interpretation of the origin of the Messiah: The child that was born of the bond between Lilith and Adam is brought up by the archangels in the heavenly regions as the Messiah and is intended someday to redeem the human beings born of the bond between Adam and Eve, in order to restore the original plan of God. This good news is delivered by the angel Gabriel to Adam, who expects the worst because of his disobedience:

---

25. Kurz, "Die Kinder der Lilith," 86–87.

Adam:
You come to extinguish my race
Execute your office; God is just.
Gabriel:
You are wrong. He did not send me in wrath,
I bring you comfort from His spring of love.
Do you see the arch of peace there created,
Transfiguring over all your land?
Why do you not ask about Lilith?
Adam, you are silent and do you cast down your countenance?
…
Hear: Her loins were blessed,
From them wrestled free a fair little boy.
Adam, your genuinely-born child,
To whose will the angels of the Lord submit.[26]

In the following, Gabriel outlines the future of the Messiah with all its highs and lows. He will come as a hero and as a savior, and, to be sure, as one—this is emphasized by the messenger Gabriel—who "sprouted from Lilith's blood" and whose spirit (the legacy of his mother) inspires the seers, poets, and musicians in all times:

He comes as a hero when nations bleed,
As a seer when their faith diminished,
With golden images of the poets' dreams
He fills the dark realms of the earth,
Sweeps through the poor suffering world
With flowing melodious sound from the heavenly firmament,
…
Until He appears before the Eternal's throne,
The Consummator of humanity, your glorious son![27]

This is the vision of the creation story by a woman: the old myth of the compulsively sinful woman is finally to be laid aside, and, in Lilith, a spiritually-gifted woman is to be placed at the beginning who, together with the man and not against him or without him, shapes the future. To be sure, all of this is presented like a joke, nimbly and in loosely-rhymed verses, and with a subversive tone. But, it does not conceal from knowing read-

---

26. Kurz, "Die Kinder der Lilith," 112–13.
27. Kurz, "Die Kinder der Lilith," 115.

ers the sober earnestness of a committed woman author who had suffered under the hegemony of the men in the society of her time and who, by means of the figure of Lilith, attempts to establish her dignity as a woman.

6. Biblical Women in the Masculine View

This survey would be incomplete if the biblical adaptations by masculine authors also would not be mentioned shortly. But here, too, the yield of landmark works for the question with which we are concerned is meager. Some authors, such as Franz Held (*Jephtas Tochter*), Friedrich Wilhelm Gotter (*Die stolze Vasthi*), Grillparzer (*Esther. Fragment*), and Levin Schücking (*Hagars Klage in der Wüste*), to be sure, updated the biblical material. Others transformed it into comic material, such as Goethe did with the Esther story in *Das Jahrmarktsfest zu Plundersweilern*, or parodied the material, such as Johann Nepomuk Nestroy in *Judith und Holofernes*. But, none of them, with the exception of Friedrich Hebbel, spark a discussion of the gender question. When, at the turn of the century, tendencies toward a demonization of women as vamps, femme fatales, or men-ruining seductresses began to show themselves, a strong interest in the biblical figures of women also arose in parallel.[28]

Apart from Mary who, in her other-worldliness, is hardly appropriate for a dramatic plot, or the daughter of Jephtah who at all times aroused

---

28. Reference might also be made, in addition, to authors of Jewish faith who, at the beginning of the twentieth century, found themselves in pressing situations, and who were in search of their identity. They placed the fates of biblical women at the focus of their works, but, however, make no gender-specific allusions. See, for example, Else Lasker-Schüler, "Esther" (1913), in Lasker-Schüler, *Gedichte*, vol. 1.1 of *Werke und Briefe: Kritische Ausgabe*, ed. Norbert Oellers et al. (Frankfurt: Jüdischer Verlag, 1996), 159; Franz Werfel, "Esther, Kaiserin von Persien: Dramatisches Gedicht" (1914), in Werfel, *Die Dramen*, vol. 2 of *Gesammelte Werke*, ed. Adolf Klarmann (Frankfurt: Fischer, 1959), 343–78; Max Brod, *Eine Königin Esther: Drama in einem Vorspiel und drei Akten* (Leipzig: Wolff, 1918); Karl Wolfskehl, "Abram: Hagar die Verstoßene vor der Tür" (1935–1938), in Wolfskehl, *Dichtungen*, vol. 1 of *Gesammelte Werke* (Hamburg: Claassen, 1960), 56–64; Fritz Rosenthal (Ben-Chorin), "Hagar" (1934), in Rosenthal, *Die Lieder des ewigen Brunnens* (Leipzig: Löwit, 1934), 5; Else Lasker-Schüler, "Hagar und Ismael" (1919), in Lasker-Schüler, *Gedichte*, 108; Stefan Zweig, "Rahel rechtet mit Gott: Eine Legende," in *Legenden* (Frankfurt: Fischer, 1959), 20; Yvan Goll, "Noemie," in *Dichtungen, Lyrik, Prosa*, ed. Claire Goll (Darmstadt: Luchterhand, 1960), 47–50; Richard Beer-Hofmann, *Der junge David: Sieben Bilder* (Berlin: Fischer, 1933).

the interest of artists because of her terrible fate, or Hagar, the outcast, who is seen as the prototype of many women in a similar situation, the figures chosen are almost exclusively those who present a spectacular life story already in the biblical documents and who, as objects of desire, quicken the fantasies, primarily, of the men. Such female figures are, for example, Lilith, Potiphar's wife (Suleika), Delilah, Bathsheba, Judith, Esther, Salome, and the Magdalene. Women, on the other hand, who make history in the Old and New Testaments and show self-assurance, such as Sarah, Rebekkah, Tamar, Rahab, Ruth, Abigail, Hannah, and Martha, or who are victims, such as Rachel, Dinah, Michal, Vashti, and Job's wife, are not at all or hardly ever considered.[29]

Hebbel (1813–1863) is in this connection not only among the most well-known German authors and not only is his work *Judith. Eine Tragödie*[30] in structure, language, and use of metaphor of recognized quality, but he also, with his interpretation of the biblical original, created a psychological drama and a remarkable example for the portrayal of the gender problem. His tragedy, in addition, became the basis for a number of further adaptations in the early twentieth century that underline more or less clearly the figure of Judith as an independently-acting woman. The contributions made by women to the Judith material are not of much use for the question under discussion here.

Hebbel, of course, follows completely the biblical course of events in his plot but places his own accents upon it. In Judith's first appearance and monologue, he already shows her as a woman who, of course, hopes for God's sign but is uncertain whether she correctly recognizes this sign. The distress of her people arouses not only compassion, but also energy, in her. The latter is ignited above all in conversation with Ephraim,[31] who woos her, but is not a match for her. For, full of fear, although ready to die for her, he rejects her demand to "Go in and kill Holofernes!"[32] Thereby, Judith's hope of gaining Ephraim as a partner equal to her dies. For this reason, she is tempted by the idea of challenging the feared and bold Holofernes

---

29. For tables with names, titles, and dates of publication, as well as interpretations, see Motté, *Esthers Tränen*, 273–320.

30. Friedrich Hebbel, "Judith: Eine Tragödie in fünf Akten" (1841), in Hebbel, *Werke*, ed. Gerhard Fricke et al., vol. 1 (Munich: Hanser, 1963–1967), 7–75.

31. Hebbel introduces further persons for the purpose of dramatic effect, for example, Ephraim, who courts her, and the servant girl Mirza.

32. Hebbel, "Judith," 26.

herself, namely, the man who appears to be a match for her and who corresponds to her idea of the relationship between the sexes, as she admits to her servant girl and confidant Mirza.

> Judith.... Every woman has a right to demand from every man that he be a hero. Is it it not so for you that when you see one, it is though you might see what you would like to be, wanted to be? A man may forgive another man his cowardice, but a woman can never do so. Do you forgive the pillar when it breaks? Can you forgive the fact that you need the pillar?[33]

Therewith, the tenor of this adaptation already is fixed: Hebbel did not choose the material in order to demonstrate God's intervention through Judith's act but rather to illustrate the passionate struggle of the sexes. God is, to be sure, spoken of a great deal in the entire drama but is not really a partner in the action or the inner driver of the actors; these are driven much more by their own instincts and their own personal desires, which Judith also repeatedly admits: "And, yet, I can think of nothing other than myself," or: "nothing drives me but the thought of myself."[34]

According to Hebbel's concept, Holofernes will be successful in making Judith compliant to his will: He will overcome the woman with her own weapon, the art of seduction. But, the proud woman cannot accept this humiliation, to which she had agreed in the intoxication of love, and plans her revenge. For, in Judith, Hebbel confronts the commander with a woman who, to be sure, succumbs to him, but who also sees through him, disdains him, and overpowers him.[35] Thus, his superiority will have a deadly effect for him in the decisive moment: Judith will bring him down, too, with his own weapon, his own sword. Out of Judith's originally altruistic motif of liberation, "I want to avenge the dead and protect the living,"[36] grows a personal act of revenge arisen out of the injured pride of a woman. Judith is a woman in conflict who, on the one hand, claims a great amount of autonomy for herself, but, on the other hand, does not clearly recognize her own drives and lets herself be seduced by the man. In committing a murder out of base motives, she is not only untrue to her mission, but also acts against her nature as a woman. The narrative about her dream, in the

---

33. Hebbel, "Judith," 30.
34. Hebbel, "Judith," 68–69.
35. Hebbel, "Judith," 60.
36. Hebbel, "Judith," 43.

first act, already reveals the state of her soul and contains *in nuce* the whole subsequent drama. This dream is not only the key to Judith's conduct but, above and beyond this, is a classic example of personal psychological analysis like that which, fifty years later, Sigmund Freud undertook upon literary figures in his psychoanalyses. Hebbel's figures, in spite of their stage presence, are not realistic persons, but rather models for a psychological textbook. This is a result not only of the play's action, but also of the theatrical gestures and of the pathetic language of archaic effect, which aroused the interest of several parodists.[37] Hebbel stylizes Judith as a covetable woman seducible by a strong man, as woman who, against the conventions of the time, takes her fate into her own hands, and he makes Holofernes into a tyrannical and wild macho.[38]

Following Hebbel's Judith, Georg Kaiser and Jean Giraudoux[39] continued the actualization of the material. Their interest focusses above all on Judith as a woman who "escapes the conventions, constraints, and expectations of her time"[40] and thereby stands nearer an emancipated woman of the modern age than to the biblical or Hebbel model. For all further adaptations in the twentieth century, the biblical book of Judith is only more material for illustrating the struggle between the sexes, or for co-opting Judith as a resistance fighter; these works no longer have much to do with a treatment in the sense of the question about the relationship of women to the Bible.

The fact that the roles of the sexes frequently were set in opposition to each other with such stridency at the end of the nineteenth and the beginning of the twentieth centuries lies in the circumstance that many women became conscious of their own value and sought to free themselves from their centuries-old submission, while the men feared this emancipation and demonized the desires of the female sex (femme fatale, vamp, etc.).

---

37. See Jürgen Hein, "Aktualisierungen des Judit-Stoffes von Hebbel bis Brecht," in *Hebbel-Jahrbuch 1971/72*, ed. Hebbel-Gesellschaft (Heide: Boyens, 1972), 63–92.

38. See Judith's dream, in Hebbel, "Judith," 13, and her monologue in Hebbel, "Judith," Act 5, 58.

39. See Georg Kaiser, "Die jüdische Witwe: Bühnenspiel in fünf Akten" (1920), in Kaiser, *Stücke: 1895–1917*, vol. 1 of *Werke*, ed. Walter Huder (Frankfurt: Propyläen, 1971), 117–98; Jean Giraudoux, "Judith: Tragödie in drei Akten" (1931), in Giraudoux, *Dramen*, ed. Otto F. Best, vol. 1 (Frankfurt: Fischer, 1961), 181–270.

40. Hein, "Aktualisierungen des Judit-Stoffes," 64.

7. Concluding Remark

In this only roughly-outlined survey—only a few pages for an eventful century—much could merely be traced out. Yet, one thing becomes clear: only a few German-speaking female writers devoted their attention to biblical material and motifs. This may have been the result of ignorance, disinterest, rejection, or a lack of courage. For, the religious education of girls and women and the ecclesiastically-controlled reading of the Bible made interpreting biblical stories in freedom more difficult.

In addition, there was the fear of sin. As can be seen from autobiographical testimonies, many women suffered under the strict moral code of the churches and, when they failed, under their own self-consciousness. Even independent thinking and critical questioning led, for example, with von Droste-Hülshoff, to the self-accusation of a lack of humility. So, it is no wonder that the emancipation of women in the nineteenth century hardly made any progress with the aid of the Bible or the churches, but rather for the most part against them. Women who wrote had first to achieve a standing in the general public before they dared, like their masculine colleagues, for example, Hebbel, to interpret biblical material on their own. Apart from Otto-Peters's lecture and *Die Kinder der Lilith* by Kurz, there are only a few more extensive works that discuss the gender question seriously while using biblical material or motifs.

Bibliography

Arnim, Bettina von. *Werke und Briefe*. Edited by Gustav Konrad. Vol. 3. Frechen: Bartmann, 1959.

Beer-Hofmann, Richard. *Der junge David: Sieben Bilder*. Berlin: Fischer, 1933.

Brod, Max. *Eine Königin Esther: Drama in einem Vorspiel und drei Akten*. Leipzig: Wolff, 1918.

Droste-Hülshoff, Annette von. *Das Geistliche Jahr—Gestliche Lieder*. Leipzig: Hesse, 1904.

———. *Gesammelte Werke*. Vol. 1. Weimar: Lichtenstein, 1923.

———. *Des Grauens Süße: Ein Lesebuch*. Edited by Dieter Borchmeyer. Munich: Hanser, 1997.

———. *Sämtliche Werke in zwei Bänden, nach dem Text der Originaldrucke und der Handschriften*. Edited by Günter Weydt and Winfried Woesler. Munich: Winkler, 1973.

Giraudoux, Jean. *Dramen.* Edited by Otto F. Best. Vol. 1. Frankfurt: Fischer, 1961.
Gödden, Walter. *Tag für Tag im Leben der Annette von Droste-Hülshoff: Daten—Texte—Dokumente.* Paderborn: Schöningh, 1996.
Goll, Yvan. "Noemie." Pages 47–50 in *Dichtungen, Lyrik, Prosa.* Edited by Claire Goll. Darmstadt: Luchterhand, 1960.
Haag, Herbert, et al. *Große Frauen der Bibel in Bild und Text.* Freiburg: Herder, 1993.
Hebbel, Friedrich. *Werke.* Edited by Gerhard Fricke et al. Vol. 1. Munich: Hanser, 1963–1967.
Hensel, Luise. *Lieder.* Paderborn: Ferdinand Schöningh, 1879.
Hein, Jürgen. "Aktualisierungen des Judit-Stoffes von Hebbel bis Brecht." Pages 63–92 in *Hebbel-Jahrbuch 1971/72.* Edited by Hebbel-Gesellschaft. Heide: Boyens, 1972.
Kaiser, Georg. *Stücke: 1895–1917.* Vol. 1 of Werke. Edited by Walter Huder. Frankfurt: Propyläen, 1971.
Kraft, Herbert. *Annette von Droste-Hülshoff.* Rowohlts Monografien 50517. Reinbek bei Hamburg: Rowohlt, 1997.
Kurz, Isolde. *Gesammelte Werke.* Vol. 1. Munich: Müller, 1925.
Lasker-Schüler, Else. *Gedichte.* Vol. 1.1 of *Werke und Briefe: Kritische Ausgabe.* Edited by Norbert Oellers et al. Frankfurt: Jüdischer Verlag, 1996.
Lehmstedt, Mark, ed. "Deutsche Literatur von Frauen: Von Catharina von Greifenberg bis Franziska von Reventlow." *Digitale Bibliothek* 45. Berlin: Directmedia, 2000.
Miegel, Agnes. *Wie Bernstein leuchtend auf der Lebenswaage: Gesammelte Balladen.* Edited by Ulf Diederichs. Munich: Diederichs, 1988.
Motté, Magda. *Esthers Tränen, Judiths Tapferkeit: Biblische Frauen in der Literatur des 20. Jahrhunderts.* Darmstadt: WBG, 2003.
Otto-Peters, Louise. *Mein Lebensgesang: Gedichte aus fünf Jahrzenten.* Leipzig: Schäfer, 1893.
———. "Vortrag, gehalten im demokratischen Frauen-Verein zu Oederan, im Januar 1849. Fortsetzung: Aufsätze aus der Frauen-Zeitung." Pages 106–8 in *Frauenleben im Deutschen Reich.* Leipzig: Schäfer, 1876.
Rosenthal (Ben-Chorin), Fritz. *Die Lieder des ewigen Brunnens.* Leipzig: Löwit, 1934.
Schneider, Gabriele. "Arbeiten und nicht müde werden: Ein Leben durch und für die Arbeit; Fanny Lewald (1811–1889)." Pages 188–214 in

Beruf: Schriftstellerin; Schreibende Frauen im 18. und 19. Jahrhundert. Edited by Karen Tebben. Göttingen: Vandenhoeck & Ruprecht, 1998.

Tönnesen, Cornelia. "Überhaupt hat sie eine kecke, ungezügelte Phantasie: Luise Mühlbach (1814–1873)." Pages 215–43 in *Beruf: Schriftstellerin: Schreibende Frauen im 18. und 19. Jahrhundert.* Edited by Karen Tebben. Göttingen: Vandenhoeck & Ruprecht, 1998.

Wallach-Faller, Marianne. "Für eine Versöhnung mit Lilith." Pages 253–56 in *Unerhörte Worte: Religiöse Gesellschaftskritik von Frauen im 20. Jahrhundert.* Edited by Doris Brodbeck. Gender Wissen 5. Bern: eFeF, 2003.

Werfel, Franz. *Die Dramen.* Vol. 2 of *Gesammelte Werke.* Edited by Adolf Klarmann. Frankfurt: Fischer, 1959.

Wolfskehl, Karl. *Dichtungen.* Vol. 1 of *Gesammelte Werke.* Hamburg: Claassen, 1960.

Zingsem, Vera. *Lilith: Adams erste Frau.* Leipzig: Reclam, 2000.

Zweig, Stefan. "Rahel rechtet mit Gott: Eine Legende." Pages 7–21 in *Legenden.* Frankfurt: Fischer, 1959.

Portraits of Mary and of Biblical Scenes in the Work of Marie Ellenrieder (1791–1863): The Construction of Feminine Religious Spheres of Communication

Katharina Büttner-Kirschner

1. Stages in Life and Work

The portrait and historical painter Marie Ellenrieder was born on March 20, 1791, in the former episcopal seat of Constance on Lake Constance. She was the youngest of four daughters of Maria Anna, née Hermann (1747–1820), from a family of painters, and of the court clockmaker Konrad Ellenrieder (1744–1834) (fig. 1). In the intimate house of her parents in Constance, in which she lived together with her sister Josepha until her death on July 5, 1863, the still-existing wall paintings on the staircase landing with their feminine figures and scenes with children testify today to the combination of the lived-in world and art, which is also characteristic for this female artist.

Ellenrieder received her first systematic instruction in painting, which was concentrated one-sidedly on precision, from the miniaturist Joseph Bernhard Einsle (1774–1829). In 1813, the young woman succeeded, with the help of the enlightened Reform-Catholic Vicar-General of Constance and patron of the arts Ignaz Baron von Wessenberg (1774–1860), in enrolling as the first woman at the Royal Bavarian Academy of Fine Arts in Munich, where she studied under the classicist academy professor Johann Peter von Langer (1756–1824).[1] Ellenrieder's

---

1. The present article is based in part on the following articles: Katharina Büttner, "Vor der Fassade von 'Schutzgeist' und 'Kunstgenius': Ignaz Heinrich von Wessenberg und die Künstlerin Marie Ellenrieder; Essay einer Spurensuche," in *Ignaz Heinrich von Wessenberg, 1774–1860: Kirchenfürst und Kunstfreund; Ausstellungskatalog Wessen-*

Marie Ellenrieder, *Self Portrait*, 1818. Oil on Canvas, 53 x 43.5 cm. Courtesy of the Staatliche Kunsthalle Karlsruhe.

pioneering role in taking the obstacle-strewn path toward the professionalization of feminine artistic work is described by the Weimar court artist and friend of Ellenrieder Louise Seidler (1786–1866) in her still-readable memoirs: "With acceptance of Maria Ellenrieder as a student at the Academy in Munich, by the way, a precedent was established that had good consequences; more than one of my sex trained in the city on the Isar, and, to be sure, neither to the detriment of art, nor to the disadvantage of feminine dignity."[2] Characteristic for the work of the later court painter in Baden are graphic assurance, clear composition, vibrant coloring, a surface silkiness achieved through an enamel-like blending of colors, and the, in part, gold-based spiritual glazing technique as a symptom of the internalization of religious art. Ellenrieder's individual strategies of pictorial invention make an independent contribution to the variants of Romantic-Nazarite currents in art in the first half of the nineteenth century. Her increasing fixation upon religiously idealized motifs, however, threatens here and there to drift off into sentimentality.

As a painter of ecclesiastical subjects, the artist's altarpieces succeeded in penetrating a prestigious and lucrative masculine domain.[3]

---

berg-Galerie Konstanz, ed. Barbara Stark (Konstanz: Wessenberg-Galerie, 2010), 109–18; for further literature on the biography and artistic development of Ellenrieder, see Büttner, "Vor der Fassade von 'Schutzgeist' und 'Kunstgenius,'" 117n1; and Büttner, "Marie Ellenrieder (1791–1863): Bildfindungen einer badischen Nazarenerin," in *Kunst und Architektur in Karlsruhe: Festschrift für Norbert Schneider*, ed. Katharina Büttner and Martin Papenbrock (Karlsruhe: Universitätsverlag, 2006), 45–58.

2. Seidler, *Goethes Malerin: Die Erinnerungen der Louise Seidler*, ed. Sylke Kaufmann (Berlin: Aufbau Taschenbuch, 2003), 131–32.

3. On Ellenrieder's biblical portrayals and portrayals of the saints, which represent a predominant part of her complete works, see the work catalogue compiled by

Ellenrieder's first journey to Italy (1822–1825), with longer stays in Rome and Florence, proved to be of great personal and artistic scope.[4] Especially Papal Rome—with its religious-visual strategies of impressing—the contact with the works of Raffael, and the study of the early Renaissance masters such as Giotto, Fra Giovanni da Fiesole, and Perugino influenced her aesthetic-religious artistic ideal decisively. The programmatic art of the German-Roman group of artists called Nazarenes, centered on the charismatic convert Johann Friedrich Overbeck (1789–1869), encouraged the already religiously socialized young female painter to dedicate herself henceforth more extensively to sacred subjects as a counterpart to profane portraiture. In her turn to Nazarene art, though, Ellenrieder cannot be reduced to the role of a rigid programmatic adept.[5]

The following analysis of selected portraits of Mary and of biblical scenes in Ellenrieder's work concerns itself with unity and difference in the representation of gender. The choice of pictures is oriented hereby especially on the degree of the intensity of communicative impact of each specific constellation of figure and space.[6]

2. Mary—Mediatrix, Muse, Magistra

2.1. Mary Taking the Boy Jesus by the Hand

Among the predominantly New Testament feminine figures in Ellenrieder's artistic work, Mary assumes a prominent position. Traditional Marian types and symbols are here varied according to the Nazarene style and, in part, given a new cast. In an entry in her Roman diary from March

---

Sigrid von Blanckenhagen, in Friedhelm Wilhelm Fischer, *Marie Ellenrieder: Leben und Werk der Konstanzer Malerin; Ein Beitrag zur Künstlergeschichte des neunzehnten Jahrhunderts* (Constance: Thorbeke, 1963), 144–53.

4. See, on Ellenrieder's work in Italy, Katrin Seibert, *Rom besuchen: Italienreisen deutscher Künstlerinnen zwischen 1750 und 1850* (Munich: Meidenbauer, 2009), 1:293–345.

5. On the Nazarenes, see Max Hollein and Christa Steinle, eds., *Religion, Macht, Kunst: Die Nazarener* (Cologne: König, 2005). In the exhibition documented by this volume, the Marian pictures analyzed in the present article also were shown; see 53, 219, 250.

6. On gender studies in art history, see Hildegard Frübis, "Kunstgeschichte," in *Gender-Studien: Eine Einführung*, ed. Christina von Braun and Inge Stephan (Stuttgart: Metzler, 2000), 262–75.

Marie Ellenrieder, *Mary Taking the Boy Jesus by the Hand*, 1824. Oil on canvas, 185 x 123 cm. Courtesy of the Staatliche Kunsthalle Karlsruhe.

1823, the author affords an insight into the often complex and arduous artistic process, accompanied by self-accusations, in the creation of one of her chief large-format works, the *Maria mit dem Jesusknaben an der Hand* (fig. 2):[7] "I could hardly force myself to work diligently at it, and I really most unfavorably indulged myself in my negligence. But, may all that I saw among the German artists encourage me mightily to persevering diligence. May God give me grace that I, in my work, may meet courageously the demands of art!"[8]

The motif of the staged act of climbing stairs reverses in a certain sense the traditional sequence of movement depicted in "Mary's Visit at the Temple."[9] In the particular selection of the mother-child constellation, Ellenrieder employs a strategy of pictorial invention that possibly has an iconographic source in the tradition of the Infantia Christi group.[10] On the basis of apocryphal legends about the youthful years of Christ, there emerges in medieval art an "independence typical of devotional pictures" of single episodes, such as that of Jesus's walk to school hand-in-hand with his mother.[11] The reception-aesthetically motivated moment of movement in the space-consuming simultaneous descent of the stairs undertaken by both figures creates transitions from the spherically designed pictorial space to the concrete space of the observer—and further to the spiritual level of inner devotion, and vice versa. While the golden background, which provides an archaic effect and resembles Byzantine icon painting, negates every kind of spatial illusion and materiality, the stair motif in the picture's foreground increasingly gains in concretion. In spite of Mary's frontal position, the cast-down eyes and the pinion-like positioning of the arm shrouded in antique style produce distancing effects. The impact strategies of approach and distancing also differ here clearly from the model of

---

7. See Jan Lauts and Werner Zimmermann, eds., *Katalog Neuere Meister: 19. und 20. Jahrhundert*, SKK (Karlsruhe: Staatliche Kunsthalle, 1971), 1:59 (Nr. 511); cf. Fischer, *Ellenrieder*, 148 (Nr. 329).

8. See the entry from February/March 1823 in Ellenrieder, *3. Tagebuch, Manuskript vom 7 Oktober 1822 bis 4 August 1823* (Konstanz: Rosgartenmuseum, 1823); provided is a transcription of the original text without editorial corrections.

9. See, for example, Giotto's early and famous fresco cycle on the life of Mary in the Scrovegni Chapel in Padua, which originated at the beginning of the fourteenth century.

10. On the Infantia Christi iconography, see Rainer Haussherr, "Jesuskind," *LCI* 2 (1990): 400–6.

11. Rüdiger Becksmann, ed., *Voraussetzungen, Entwicklungen, Zusammenhänge*, vol. 1 of *Deutsche Glasmalerei des Mittelalters* (Berlin: Kunstwissenschaft, 1995), 111.

Raffael's *Sixtine Madonna*. A particular feature of Ellenrieder's painting of Mary with its transgressive spatial construction is the personal union of the person addressed and the producer of the painting. Even if the work was exhibited repeatedly during Ellenrieder's lifetime, it was still intended exclusively for the artist alone and remained her private property until her death.[12] For the period beyond this, Ellenrieder stipulated in her will that the proceeds from the sale of her picture be used for charitable purposes.

The high personal value that the artist accorded her Madonna painting resulted in the first place from the context of the history of its origins—the sojourn in Italy decisive for her artistic development—and in the second place from the extensive function of the work. For the artist, it assumed the role of a private devotional picture, from which she hoped for divine and artistic succor and which she also implored. This is documented by the prayer that she wrote down in her Roman diary in June 1823, in which elements of contemporary Romantic emphasis also find expression:

> To my picture of the Madonna.
> Holy Mary, mother of our Redeemer!… Descend and come to my aid, and let the blessing of the divine child rest upon my spirit; Send me moments for feeling the infinite divinity of eternal love. Highest Mother, bowed down in the dust I await your protection beseechingly. May a sphere of the nebulous universe surround me, so that no earthly care comes near me, and so I now will begin the daily work assigned to me, in the name of the Father, the Son, and the Holy Spirit. Amen.[13]

The emotionalized devotional space for the feminine communication of the religious through supplication combines here directly with Ellenrieder's artistic-aesthetic reflection and production. Thereby, it is not only Mary as feminine divine principle and representative of the feminine history of salvation, as well as aspects of Marian popular piety,[14] which stand

---

12. See Elisabeth von Gleichenstein, ed., *"… und hat als Weib unglaubliches Talent" (Goethe): Angelika Kauffmann (1741–1807) und Marie Ellenrieder (1791–1863); Malerei und Graphik* (Constance: Rosgartenmuseum, 1992), 204.

13. Ellenrieder, *3. Tagebuch*, entry from June 1823 [transcription without editorial corrections].

14. On the development of conceptions of Mary, see Renate Jost, "Von altorientalischen Göttinnen zu Marienvorstellungen: Eine feministisch-evangelische Perspektive," in *Gender, Religion, Kultur: Biblische, interreligiöse und ethische Aspekte*, ed. Renate Jost and Klaus Raschzok, TA 6 (Stuttgart: Kohlhammer, 2011), 37–54.

at the middle point but rather, in analogy to the masculine-dominated cult of genius, the figure of Mary also fulfills the expanded role of a muse as inspiration for feminine creativity.

2.2. Mary Writes the Magnificat

A further visual documentation of Ellenrieder's inventive creation of a Marian image is represented by the oil painting *Maria schreibt das Magnifikat*, from 1833 (fig. 3).[15] The artist had been appointed court painter in Baden in 1829, and she delivered this painting to the grand ducal house as an obligatory picture for the years 1835 and 1836.[16] Once again, drapery and columns as symbols of dignity form the background for Mary, while the artist integrates a detail from a view of a bluish-green southern Renaissance landscape. A hair ribbon and ornamental carvings provide decorative Biedermeier-like accents. With the bright, gleaming color glazes, the artist creates her own unconventional nuances, which deviate from the Nazarene color aesthetic, and applies them to her intimate subject of an idealized single figure viewed in close-up.[17] The idea of Mary's ability to

Marie Ellenrieder, *Mary Writes the Magnificat*, 1833. Oil on canvas, 64.8 x 46.2 cm. Courtesy of the Staatliche Kunsthalle Karlsruhe.

---

15. See Lauts and Zimmermann, *Katalog Neuere Meister*, 59 (Nr. 514); Fischer, *Ellenrieder*, 147 (Nr. 319); see also Siegmar Holsten, ed., *Kunst in der Residenz: Karlsruhe zwischen Rokoko und Moderne*, SKK (Heidelberg: Edition Brauns, 1990), 115–16.

16. Ellenrieder was obligated to produce and deliver artworks regularly for the Baden court within the framework of her commitments as court artist.

17. See Gleichenstein, ed., *"... und hat als Weib unglaubliches Talent"*, 210. On the cultural-historical context of the medieval and early modern portrayal of Mary's intel-

read and write goes back to the authors of medieval Marian *vitae*, among others. On the basis of given pictorial themes from Sibylline iconography and also on the basis of the image of the female author—as we encounter it in medieval book illumination in the image of Hildegard of Bingen (1098–1179) as writer and in the self-portraits of feminine book makers in initials[18]—the artist transforms the traditional received motif of Mary's reading into the productive portrayal of the Mother of God as *femina docta* as she writes her own song of praise. In the certainty of her role as the bearer of the Messiah, Mary begins to compose this hymn in the house of the pregnant Elizabeth and of her husband Zacharias (Luke 1:46–55). On the writing tablet positioned at an angle to the plane of the picture—not dissimilar to the artist's implement of a sketching tablet—there stands in golden letters the beginning of this key mariological text: "*Magnificat anima mea dominum et exsultavit spiritus in deo salutari.*"[19]

No external sign of inspiration is visible; no child Jesus guides the hand of the Mother of God; no crowning angelic personnel is present, as in Botticelli's tondo *Madonna del Magnificat* from 1485, for example. In Ellenrieder's later work, the motif of the female author culminates in the allegorical figure of the pious female pilgrim who enters her name in the angel's book (fig. 4).[20]

3. The New Testament—Presence and Dominance of Feminine Communication

3.1. Blessing of the Children: "Let the Children Come to Me"

The biblical theme of Jesus's blessing of the children runs continually through Ellenrieder's body of work. The pictorial portrayal of the scene refers to the passage in Matt 19:14, where Jesus elevates the children to the rank of exemplary nearness to God, in contrast to the disdainful and

---

lectuality, see Klaus Schreiner, *Maria: Jungfrau, Mutter, Herrscherin* (Munich: Hanser, 1994), 113–15.

18. See Katrin Graf, *Bildnisse schreibender Frauen im Mittelalter: 9. bis Anfang 13. Jahrhundert* (Basel: Schwabe, 2002).

19. The word "*Meus*" is left out of the text.

20. See Fischer, *Ellenrieder*, 144 (Nr. 290). The painting is today in possession of the Wessenberg-Galerie in Constance; the inscription: *Entscheidung für Gott & seine heiligen Gebote*.

Marie Ellenrieder, *The Female Pilgrim*, 1854. Oil (with gold) on canvas, 112.2 x 89.4 cm. Courtesy of the Städtische Wessenberg-Galerie.

defensive attitude on the part of the disciples. Toward the end of the eighteenth and in the first half of the nineteenth century, male and female artists from various stylistic schools took up the subject: the recognized painter Angelika Kauffmann (1741–1807), the Swiss artist Johann Heinrich Lips, Ellenrieder's teacher Langer in Munich, Overbeck in Rome, and finally, also, Ellenrieder's friend Seidler are to be mentioned here.[21] In contrast to Overbeck and Langer, for example, Ellenrieder abstains from the

---

21. See Bernhard von Waldkirch, "'Bewusste Tätigkeit und bewusstlose Kraft': Zeichnungen und Entwürfe zur Kindersegnung von Marie Ellenrieder," in *"... und hat als Weib unglaubliches Talent" (Goethe): Angelika Kauffmann (1741–1807); Marie Ellenrieder (1791–1863); Malerei und Graphik*, ed. Gleichenstein (Constance: Rosgartenmuseum, 1992), 109–22; for a short comparison of pictures, see, further, Bärbel Kovalevski, *Marie Ellenrieder, 1791–1863* (Berlin: Kovalevski, 2008), 42–46.

reproduction of a pathos-laden masculine authority, monumentality, and a distance maintained by the Jesus figure, as well as from classicistic-construed architectural space. In the diverse versions of the picture, the artist integrates many of her detailed model and individual studies from daily life as she experienced it during her stay in Italy and transfers the scene into the public realm of a southern landscape.

During her second journey to Italy (1838–1840), she created a large-format cartoon (fig. 5) in Rome as a preparatory sketch for the altarpiece in the chapel of Castle Kallenberg near Coburg.[22] Among the many figures of the scene, women and children dominate. Some of the angel-like figures of small children appear to be gender-neutral. Romantic religious conceptions of heart, soul, and innocent purity of the naïve, childlike nature are here imparted as the central categories of perception. The left half of the picture is dominated by the masculine figures of the sitting Jesus and his statuesquely positioned disciples. Hairstyle, beards, body size, the circumference of the heads, and advanced age characterize this masculine block, which is separated spatially from the two women on the right side of the picture by the pyramidal-arranged group of children and young people. The degree of body coverage is portrayed differently depending upon gender and age. It increases with the progressing age of the figures and reaches its maximum on the feminine side with the employment of the veil. The intentions of historicization combine here with traditional Marian iconography and gender-specific moral notions. In the Kallenberg altarpiece, then, Ellenrieder employs a coloristic means of structuring by using shared bright colors as a connecting element between the Jesus figure and the two women on the right. Striking is the affectionate, indeed physical Jesus-child relationship. The motifs of the lap and of caressing show parallels to Ellenrieder's portrayals of mother and child units in her family portraits and genre paintings. In a commentary on Ellenrieder's cartoon, clichés about feminine limitations, emotionality, and superficiality, all typical of the time, are reflected, in spite of words of praise:

> The beautiful, carefully executed drawing reflects a beautiful soul that never leaves the boundaries of femininity. She has devoted herself with excessive zeal not merely in the execution to those objects by which a woman is permitted to linger undisturbed without injury to her in-born

---

22. See Fischer, *Ellenrieder*, 146 (Nr. 307 A); cf. the figures on the walls in the stairwell of the Ellenrieder house in Constance, 146 (Nr. 307 E, F).

Marie Ellenrieder, *Blessing of the Children*, 1839. Cartoon for the altarpiece in the chapel of Castle Callenberg near Coburg. Black chalk over pencil sketch, heightened with white, on prepared paper, 257.5 x 221 cm. Private collection.

mode of sensitivity, but the characters of her artistic creations also show everywhere the same modesty in entering into their depth.[23]

Three figures clearly distinguishable as feminine assume prominent positions at the base and at the center of the picture's central axis stretching off into the ether: contemplation and an attitude of prayer and devotion are manifested here in gesture, facial expression, and posture. To a high degree the picture's feminine personnel thus advance to the special feminine model of the practice of piety.[24]

---

23. Report in *Kunstblatt* 52 (June 30, 1840), 222, quoted in http://digi.ub.uni-heidelberg.de/diglit/kunstblatt21_1840/0238.

24. On the thesis of the feminization of religion from the social-historical perspective, see Hugh McLeod, "Weibliche Frömmigkeit—männlicher Unglaube? Religion und Kirchen im bürgerlichen 19. Jahrhundert," in *Bürgerinnen und Bürger:*

3.2. The Awakening of Tabitha by Peter

The small-format oil painting *Erweckung der Tabita durch Petrus* (fig. 6) was created in 1844, a few years after the *Blessing of the Children*.[25] The portrayal is based on Acts 9:36–43 and shows the moment of gathering in the house of the dead Tabitha before Peter consummates the miracle of her raising. Ellenrieder is likely already to have encountered Masolino's and Masaccio's cycles of Renaissance frescoes on the life of Peter in the Brancacci Chapel of S. Maria del Carmine in Florence. The focus in the fresco there is on the moment of awakening and the astonishment of the onlookers. The city landscape and spatial opening characterize the spatial construction in this picture, while Ellenrieder transfers events into the more intimate situation of an architecturally structured interior. The gender proportions also differ considerably from the constellation of figures in the Renaissance model. The figure of Saint Peter there lingers in the masculine-dominated space of the public *res publica*. The Apostle looks into a room occupied, to be sure, by equal numbers of each sex. The two women in the habit of Carmelite nuns and Tabitha, in the process of sitting up, however, assume positions of subordination in their bowed body positions. Ellenrieder fuses the hierarchical gender compartments by placing the figure of the apostle Peter in the middle of the group of female protagonists. The age, hairstyle, and beard of the apostle show similarities to the masculine attributes of the apostle figures in the scene of the blessing of the children discussed above and deviate from the traditional Petrine iconography (Petrine tonsure, or rather a garland of curls and a forelock).[26] The pilaster placed behind the Apostle's head towering above the others enhances the vertical spatial effect of the Peter figure by increasing its significance. The plasticity of the voluminous fall of the folds of tunic and cloak, as well as the arms folded before the body, lend a statuary coherence to the Peter figure. At the same time, facial expression and gestures evoke concern and reverence. The dead body of Tabitha lies in repose along the horizontal parallel of the picture; a halo around the head on the pillow

---

Geschlechterverhältnisse im 19. Jahrhundert, ed. Ute Frevert, KSG 77 (Göttingen: Vandenhoeck & Ruprecht, 1988), 134–56.

25. See Lauts and Zimmermann, *Katalog Neuere Meister*, 60–61 (Nr. 511); cf. Fischer, *Ellenrieder*, 147 (Nr. 312).

26. On Petrine iconography, see Wolfgang Braunfels, "Petrus, Apostel," *LCI* 8 (1990): 158–74.

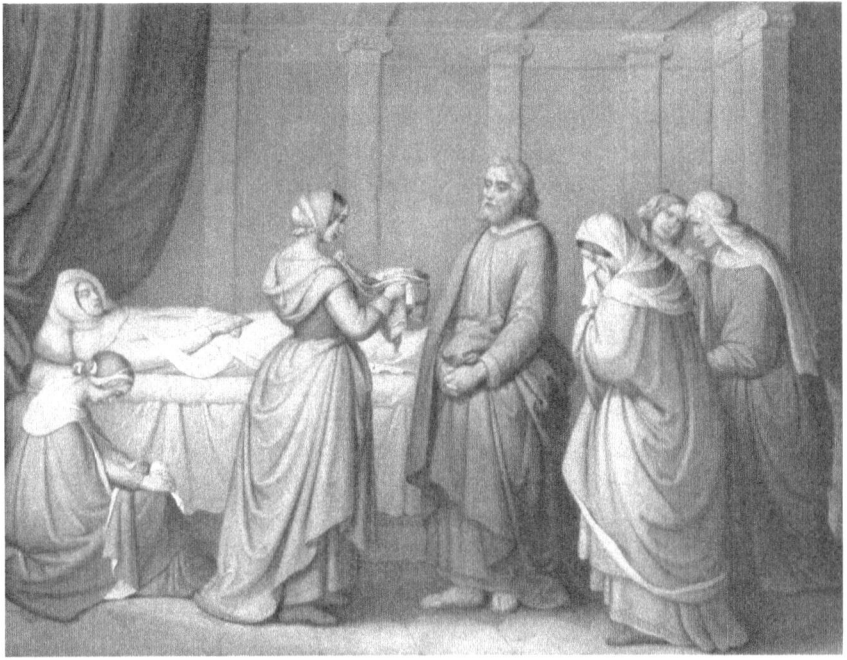

Marie Ellenrieder. *The Awakening of Tabitha by Peter*, 1844. Oil on canvas, 47 x 60 cm. Courtesy of the Staatliche Kunsthalle Karlsruhe.

and the drapery as a symbol of dignity form the background—details that indicate Tabitha's special status as a follower in the discipleship of Christ. The figure of the ecclesiastical patriarch Peter thus receives, so to say, a feminine counterpart.

The visual-spatial presentation of the deceased shows a dependency upon the form of medieval or early modern raised tombs with their three-dimensional lying figures, to which threnodic figures also were added. The crying figure in the right foreground corresponds to such a weeping form of a sepulchral "pleurant." The pair of women communicating with each other extrovertedly in the right background embodies through the gesture of friendly feminine solidarity the idea of different phases of life. The self-absorbed, isolated feminine figure in profile sitting at the deathbed represents the introverted part of the described emotional states in the situation. The only feminine figure that enters into direct interaction with Peter by showing him the garments sewn by Tabitha is the figure of the woman in seemingly Biedermeier-like bodice and lace bonnet. She functions to a certain extent as an identification and appellative figure for the (feminine) public external to the picture.[27]

4. Ellenrieder's Portrayals of Women

Composition, artistic expression, and the function of biblical themes and figures enter together with Ellenrieder's portrait painting, her genre pictures, and her religious allegories into an iconographic, religious-historical, mentality-historical, and gender-historical horizon of meaning.[28] What is striking in the analysis of the pictures presented here is that Ellenrieder's portrayals of women are integrated into a concept of female communicative space. The pictorial theme of feminine reflection upon and communication of the religious is continued consequently and finally achieves a life of its own in 1849 in the oil painting *Drei Jungfrauen im Gespräch*, intended for the court in Baden (fig. 7).[29]

In analogy to the scheme of composition of Bible scenes in close-up used by Venetian early Renaissance painting—by Andrea Mantegna and Giovanni Bellini, for example—Ellenrieder lets three feminine figures act behind a balustrade. The three figures in the triad of red, blue, and green tones are found in a situation of religiously motivated conversation, characterized by rhetorical gestures and signs of friendship. The inscription imprinted on the embossed-like background strengthens the message of the picture: Let us speak of God and his holy commandments. With the low balustrade, the artist again lowers the aesthetic threshold between the close-up section of the pictorial space and the sphere of the beholder. The partial blending of different levels of reality that is hereby produced, as well as the specific picture-word relationship, stimulates the participation

---

27. On the reception-aesthetic approach in the history of art, see Wolfgang Kemp, "Kunstwissenschaft und Rezeptionsästhetik," in *Der Betrachter ist im Bild: Kunstwissenschaft und Rezeptionsästhetik*, ed. Kemp (Berlin: Reimer, 1992), 7–27.

28. See, on the relationship of Catholicism and gender models in the nineteenth century, Michela De Giorgio, "Das katholische Modell," in *19. Jahrhundert*, vol. 4 of *Geschichte der Frauen*, ed. Geneviève Fraisse and Michelle Perrot (Frankfurt: Campus, 1994), 187–220.

29. See Lauts and Zimmermann, *Katalog Neuere Meister*, 61 (Nr. 517); and Fischer, *Ellenrieder*, 160 (Nr. 460); on the communicative aspect of the painting, see also Cordula Grewe, "Objektivierte Subjektivität: Identitätsfindung und religiöse Kommunikation im nazarenischen Kunstwerk," in Hollein and Steinle, *Religion, Macht, Kunst*, 86.

Marie Ellenrieder, *Three Young Women in Conversation*, 1849. Oil on canvas, 85 x 109 cm. Courtesy of the Staatliche Kunsthalle Karlsruhe.

of the observing public in the act of speech and reflection portrayed within the painting.

Bibliography

Becksmann, Rüdiger, ed. *Voraussetzungen, Entwicklungen, Zusammenhänge*. Vol. 1 of *Deutsche Glasmalerei des Mittelalters*. Berlin: Kunstwissenschaft, 1995.

Braunfels, Wolfgang. "Petrus, Apostel." *LCI* 8 (1990): 158–74.

Büttner, Katharina. "Marie Ellenrieder (1791–1863): Bildfindungen einer badischen Nazarenerin." Pages 45–58 in *Kunst und Architektur in Karlsruhe: Festschrift für Norbert Schneider*. Edited by Katharina Büttner and Martin Papenbrock. Karlsruhe: Universitätsverlag, 2006.

———. "Vor der Fassade von 'Schutzgeist' und 'Kunstgenius': Ignaz Heinrich von Wessenberg und die Künstlerin Marie Ellenrieder; Essay einer Spurensuche." Pages 109–18 in *Ignaz Heinrich von Wessenberg, 1774–1860: Kirchenfürst und Kunstfreund; Ausstellungskatalog Wessenberg-Galerie Konstanz*. Edited by Barbara Stark. Konstanz: Wessenberg-Galerie, 2010.

De Giorgio, Michela. "Das katholische Modell." Pages 187–220 in *19. Jahrhundert*. Vol. 4 of *Geschichte der Frauen*. Edited by Geneviève Fraisse and Michelle Perrot. Frankfurt: Campus, 1994.

Ellenrieder, Marie. *3. Tagebuch, Manuskript vom 7 Oktober 1822 bis 4 August 1823*. Konstanz: Rosgartenmuseum, 1823.

Fischer, Friedhelm Wilhelm. *Marie Ellenrieder: Leben und Werk der Konstanzer Malerin; Ein Beitrag zur Künstlergeschichte des neunzehnten Jahrhunderts*. Constance: Thorbeke, 1963.

Frübis, Hildegard. "Kunstgeschichte." Pages 262–75 in *Gender-Studien: Eine Einführung*. Edited by Christina von Braun and Inge Stephan. Stuttgart: Metzler, 2000.

Gleichenstein, Elisabeth von, ed. *"... und hat als Weib unglaubliches Talent" (Goethe): Angelika Kauffmann (1741–1807) und Marie Ellenrieder (1791–1863); Malerei und Graphik*. Constance: Rosgartenmuseum, 1992.

Graf, Katrin. *Bildnisse schreibender Frauen im Mittelalter: 9. bis Anfang 13. Jahrhundert*. Basel: Schwabe, 2002.

Grewe, Cordula. "Objektivierte Subjektivität: Identitätsfindung und religiöse Kommunikation im nazarenischen Kunstwerk." Page 86 in *Religion, Macht, Kunst: Die Nazarener*. Edited by Max Hollein and Christa Steinle. Cologne: König, 2005.

Haussherr, Rainer. "Jesuskind." *LCI* 2 (1990): 400–6.

Hollein, Max, and Christa Steinle, eds. *Religion, Macht, Kunst: Die Nazarener*. Cologne: König, 2005.

Holsten, Siegmar, ed. *Kunst in der Residenz: Karlsruhe zwischen Rokoko und Moderne*. SKK. Heidelberg: Edition Brauns, 1990.

Jost, Renate. "Von altorientalischen Göttinnen zu Marienvorstellungen: Eine feministisch-evangelische Perspektive." Pages 37–54 in *Gender, Religion, Kultur: Biblische, interreligiöse und ethische Aspekte*. Edited by Renate Jost and Klaus Raschzok. TA 6. Stuttgart: Kohlhammer, 2011.

Kemp, Wolfgang. "Kunstwissenschaft und Rezeptionsästhetik." Pages 7–27 in *Der Betrachter ist im Bild: Kunstwissenschaft und Rezeptionsästhetik*. Edited by Wolfgang Kemp. Berlin: Reimer, 1992.

Kovalevski, Bärbel. *Marie Ellenrieder, 1791–1863*. Berlin: Kovalevski, 2008.

Lauts, Jan, and Werner Zimmermann, eds. *Katalog Neuere Meister: 19. und 20. Jahrhundert*. Vol. 1. SKK. Karlsruhe: Staatliche Kunsthalle, 1971.

McLeod, Hugh. "Weibliche Frömmigkeit—männlicher Unglaube? Religion und Kirchen im bürgerlichen 19. Jahrhundert." Pages 134–56 in

Bürgerinnen und Bürger: Geschlechterverhältnisse im 19. Jahrhundert. Edited by Ute Frevert. KSG 77. Göttingen: Vandenhoeck & Ruprecht, 1988.

Schreiner, Klaus. *Maria: Jungfrau, Mutter, Herrscherin*. Munich: Hanser, 1994.

Seibert, Katrin. *Rom besuchen: Italienreisen deutscher Künstlerinnen zwischen 1750 und 1850*. Vol. 1. Munich: Meidenbauer, 2009.

Seidler, Louise. *Goethes Malerin: Die Erinnerungen der Louise Seidler*. Edited by Sylke Kaufmann. Berlin: Aufbau Taschenbuch, 2003.

Waldkirch, Bernhard von. "'Bewusste Tätigkeit und bewusstlose Kraft': Zeichnungen und Entwürfe zur Kindersegnung von Marie Ellenrieder." Pages 109–22 in *"... und hat als Weib unglaubliches Talent" (Goethe): Angelika Kauffmann (1741–1807); Marie Ellenrieder (1791–1863); Malerei und Graphik*. Edited by Elisabeth von Gleichenstein. Constance: Rosgartenmuseum, 1992.

Old Testament Women in Bible Illustrations of the Nineteenth Century in the Works of Julius Schnorr von Carolsfeld and Gustave Doré

Elfriede Wiltschnigg

Biblical scenes represented a substantial portion of artistic production well into the eighteenth century. The feminine figures of the Old and New Testaments, above all, were of interest to artists and their patrons. With the coming of the French Revolution and the secularization connected with it, religious themes receded from this dominant position. From the middle of the nineteenth century, other graphic motifs, such as working people and landscape portrayals, gained in significance. Orientalism furthered the interest of buyers in pictorial themes from faraway lands; this also had an effect on illustrated editions of the Bible.[1]

In the following, the Bible illustrations done by Julius Schnorr von Carolsfeld and Gustave Doré are investigated. The view is directed above all toward the iconographic and interpretative representation of women individually and in mass scenes. Only a few artists, whether male or female, take up biblical themes in the nineteenth century; an exception is the German painter Marie Ellenrieder (1791–1863).[2] In general, women were prohibited from attending the academy and so were excluded from drawing nudes. Since the human body stands at the center

---

Many thanks are due to Professor Irmtraud Fischer for her professional advice.

1. See, for example, Roger Diederen and Davy Depelchind, eds., *Ausstellungskatalog Orientalismus in Europa: Von Delacroix bis Kandinsky*, Musées Royaux des Beaux-Arts de Belgique, Brussels; Kunsthalle der Hypo-Kulturstiftung, Munich; Centre de la Vielle Charité, Marseille (Munich: Hirmer, 2010); and Kristian Davies, *The Orientalists: Western Artists in Arabia, the Sahara, Persia and India* (New York: Laynfaroh, 2005).

2. On Ellenrieder, see the article in this volume by Katharina Büttner-Kirschner.

of Bible illustration—architecture, landscape, plants, and animals are only an embellishing or descriptive accessory—women are as good as unrepresented in this field of art. They did not receive a lucrative major commission such as the illustration of a Bible intended for the book trade.

Since the advent of the printing press made possible the simplified reproduction of texts and pictures, books and therefore also Bibles were within the financial means of wider circles of readers.[3] In the nineteenth century, it was the artists of Romanticism who, born by their enthusiasm for the Renaissance, envisaged the illustration of the Bible under new assumptions. Since all of the techniques arising in this century allowed the use of color, the reproduction of pictures in color emerged beginning about 1850.[4] The illustrative support of the text by means of graphic embellishment was of essential significance for the great success of Protestant editions of the Bible in the nineteenth century. Protestantism encouraged the distribution of Bibles. In contrast to Catholicism, the concern with the biblical text in Protestantism was considered since the Reformation to be an essential part of the maintenance of the faith, in which all were called to participate, explicitly including women also.

Before the illustrated editions of the Bible by Schnorr von Carolsfeld and Doré are presented, it is necessary to investigate the artistic, national, and religious background, and to explain the applied techniques—woodcuts and wood engravings. In addition, the question for what group of buyers the Bibles were intended also poses itself.

1. On the Biographical and Stylistic Positioning of the Two Artists

1.1. Julius Schnorr von Carolsfeld (1794–1872)

In April 1821, the Nazarenes Joseph Anton Koch, Johann Friedrich Overbeck, and Julius Schnorr von Carolsfeld founded an artists' association together with friends in Rome for the purpose of publishing a popular picture Bible jointly. The illustration of the Bible formed a central theme of the Nazarene program, which continued to have influence well into the

---

3. See Hildegard Fuchs, "Bibelillustrationen des 19. Jahrhunderts" (PhD diss., University of Erlangen-Nuremberg, 1986), 1.

4. See Diethelm Lütze, ed., *Ausstellungskatalog: Bibel-Illustrationen; Bücher aus 5 Jahrhunderten, Sammlung Lütze IV* (Stuttgart: Lütze, 1996), 16.

twentieth century.⁵ Overbeck was the first to wear shoulder-length hair. This fashion "*alla nazarena*," which was intended to imitate Jesus of Nazareth and thereby was reminiscent of Raffael's portraits, eventually gave the group of young artists the name "Nazarenes."⁶ In their work, they followed a commonly held orientation informed by their interest in the religious, patriotic, and artistic reform ideas that had gained broad currency, especially in students' circles, through the works of Novalis, Wilhelm Heinrich Wackenroder, and Friedrich Schlegel.⁷

Schnorr von Carolsfeld's work *The Bible in Pictures*, with 240 portrayals and texts from the Luther Bible, became the defining illustrated Bible for generations.⁸ It comprises 160 woodcuts on the Old Testament and eighty on the New. The introduction contains "Reflections on the Profession and the Means of the Fine Arts to Take an Interest in the Training and Education of the Human Being, along with an Explanation of the Manner of Perception and the Manner of Treatment of the Bible in Pictures" from the pen of Schnorr von Carolsfeld, as well as explanations by Heinrich Merz. The latter comments upon the illustrations in the following way:

> Just as the Bible explains itself to the inquiring and praying reader, so must the *Bible in Pictures* also be of itself clear to the one versed in the

---

5. Fuchs, "Bibelillustrationen des 19. Jahrhunderts," 142.

6. See Kristiane Müller and Eberhard Urban, *Die Kunst der Romantik: Beliebte und unbekannte Bilder nebst Zeichnungen und Studien* (Menden: Edition Aktuell, 1987), 121–22.

7. Jutta Assel, "Deutsche Bilderbibeln im 19. Jahrhundert: Insbesondere nazarenische Bilderfolgen zum Alten und/oder Neuen Testament," in *Julius Schnorr von Carolsfeld: Die Bibel in Bildern und andere biblische Bilderfolgen der Nazarener; Catalogue for the Exhibition in Clemens Sels Museum Neuss, 28. 11. 1982–27. 2. 1983* (Neuss: Clemens-Sels-Museum, 1982), 28.

8. Julius Schnorr von Carolsfeld, *Die Bibel in Bildern* (Zurich: Flamberg, 1972), was published on the one-hundreth anniversary of the death of the artist as a reprint of the edition *Die Bibel in Bildern: 240 Darstellungen, erfunden und auf Papier gezeichnet von Julius Schnorr von Carolsfeld* from 1860, published by Georg Wiegand in Leipzig. In 1909, a Catholic edition, approved by the Breslau Cardinal and Prince Bishop Georg Kopp (1837–1914) was published with Schnorr von Carolsfeld's pictures as *Katholische Bilderbibel des Alten und Neuen Testaments*, in which the artist—because he was a Protestant—at first was not named. The texts from Luther were replaced by other translations, obtained "according to new theological findings." In addition, this edition did without illustrations such as *Der Sundenfall*. See Irmgard Feldhaus, "Julius Schnorr von Carolsfeld: Die Bibel in Bildern," in *Julius Schnorr von Carolsfeld*, 20.

> Bible and who has an eye with which to see. Still, the friends of the divine Word have since millennia desired and welcomed what deeper knowledge the divinely-gifted and those taught of God have brought forward from the inscrutable depths, and also in the areas of general knowledge have produced for the illumination of biblical history and doctrine. Nevertheless, guidance and hints in regard to the pictures are desired, pictures in which J. Schnorr, an artist filled with God's Spirit and Word and a true disciple of his Lutheran Church, so comprehensively and so alertly in the Spirit like no other before him has looked upon the great deeds, the holy men, and the whole history of the Kingdom of God according to the Word of Scripture, and has placed it all before our eyes in the vestments of beauty.[9]

Merz's remarks underline the religious intention that led decisively to the publication of the *Bible in Pictures*: The content of the Bible is to be made accessible to the Protestant faithful not only textually but also in a graphic interpretation. The fact that he emphasizes only the "holy men" underscores the negligible significance attached to women in the Bible.

Under every woodcut in the *Bible in Pictures*, there is a textual extract of approximately two lines. The chosen technique of the woodcut was justified by Schnorr von Carolsfeld in a preface:

> There is no doubt that copper-plate or steel engraving permits a more complete forming of the exposition in all its details, and allows a finer shading, a more delicate modelling, etc. than the woodcut. But, I do not believe that this is so especially important in a work like that undertaken by me. Whatever cannot be presented in robust, clean outlines may remain unpresented. The work is intended to be a popular book in the true sense of that word and to hold before the eyes of the people the holy history of the world in robust, clean outlines.[10]

Schnorr von Carolsfeld's project aimed at producing a Bible with educational elements for as large a section of readers as possible; this was also intended to further general education. Its working method can be classed as traditional, stylistically based on the sketches of John Flaxman, more

---

9. Heinrich Merz, "Erklärungen zu der Bibel in Bildern von Julius Schnorr von Carolsfeld," in Schnorr von Carolsfeld, *Die Bibel in Bildern*, 1.

10. Schnorr von Carolsfeld, *Die Bibel in Bildern: 240 Darstellungen erfunden und auf Holz gezeichnet von Julius Schnorr von Carolsfeld: Mit Bibeltexten nach Martin Luthers deutscher Übersetzung* (Munich: Borowsky, 1980), n. p.

narrative than theatrical. This method offered no new interpretation of the figures but rather pointed out the accepted theological interpretation.

Schnorr von Carolsfeld began in 1851 with the realization of this project, which appeared in complete form for the first time at the beginning of 1861, in a people's edition as well as in two deluxe editions. In the latter, the woodcuts were set within borders, for which he himself had made the design.[11] "All the pages, by the way, contain only the title of the picture and the corresponding textual passage from the Bible."[12]

When the *Bible in Pictures* appeared, the reaction was mixed. The copies sent to England brought forth a positive echo. In Germany, though, "the competent Saxon ministry refused in 1855 to recommend the *Picture Bible* for the schools because several portrayals were considered morally objectionable, and, at the same time in Mecklenburg, the acquisition of the book for the schools was prohibited explicitly."[13] Only after 1860 did the work begin its triumphal advance, which continued into the twentieth century. Merz, in his "Explanations," noted in regard to the connection between text and picture:

> The language of the Bible is not understood by the natural human being and by those educated only in worldly subjects; it must first be taught, and fortunate is the one who knows it from childhood from the school of devoted mothers, fathers, and teachers. Art also has received from God a special gift of language so that it may speak to the human being through the eye, and may let that take on shape and life in him, which cannot be said and described with mere words. This language of art, however, is still more foreign and more incomprehensible to today's generations than the language of the Bible.[14]

1.2. Gustave Doré (1832–1883)

His work as a graphic artist and illustrator made Doré famous far beyond the borders of France. He was active also as a painter and sculptor and

---

11. Bernhard Bach, ed., *Das Bild in der Bibel: Bibelillustrationen von der Reformation bis zur Gegenwart aus evangelischen Archiven und Bibliotheken in Bayern* (Munich: Claudius, 1995), 33.
12. Feldhaus, "Julius Schnorr von Carolsfeld," 12.
13. Feldhaus, "Julius Schnorr von Carolsfeld," 15.
14. Merz, "Erklärungen zu der Bibel in Bildern," 1.

exhibited his works in Parisian salons. The probably most versatile, most prolific, and most successful book illustrator of the second half of the nineteenth century was self-taught. In 1861, he began with works on the *Inferno* from Dante's *Divine Comedy* as a first step in creating illustrations within the framework of his monumental project of an illustrated library of the great works of world literature. Doré utilized the technical possibilities of modern book illustration and book production. His plan to produce deluxe works in folio and, at the same time, to offer many people the opportunity to be able to afford them, can be seen as a typical phenomenon of this period.

The first edition of the Doré Bible was published in 1866 and contained, along with the foreword from the editor, the complete text of the Vulgate printed in double columns.[15] The 228 illustrations in wood engraving (118 for the Old and 110 for the New Testament) are found on separate pages. In the same year, the same publisher printed a second edition with 230 engravings (119 for the Old and 111 for the New Testament).[16] For this edition, about forty illustrations from the first edition were revised, left out, or added. Altogether, Doré created 312 drawings or preparatory drawings, of which 306 were engraved. The German edition used the Luther text.[17]

The essential difference in the effect achieved by wood engraving in contrast to the woodcut exists in the circumstance that the engraving, through the possibility of a more refined light and dark shading, is able to produce intensive artistic effects. Doré used this method and developed it together with his engravers to the highest level of mastery. His picture Bible is a component in his undertaking to create a world library and, thus, has a clearly different relative value than does Schnorr von Carolsfeld's Bible: While the latter's creation was intended to become a national work, Doré's interest was geared toward an international audience, which is also clearly evident in his further publications. He illustrated books by Balzac,

---

15. Jean-Jacques Bourassé et al., *La Sainte Bible traduction nouvelle selon la Vulgate* (Tours: Mame, 1866).

16. Gustave Doré, *Doré-Bibel: Auszüge aus dem Alten und Neuen Testament mit 230 Illustrationen von Gustave Doré* (Munich: Parkland, 1995). In 1867 to 1870 there followed German editions on the basis of the Luther translation of the Bible and the Vulgate translation by Joseph Franz Allioli.

17. See Bach, *Das Bild in der Bibel*, 34.

Rabelais, La Fontaine, Perrault, Dante, Milton, and Cervantes. His graphic work comprises more than ten thousand pages.[18]

Doré placed his biblical scenes in an oriental atmosphere and attempted to reproduce landscapes, architecture, and, with few exceptions, also figures from the biblical stories as picturesquely as possible, based upon descriptions, engravings, and drawings from travelers to the Near East. The precursors of these milieu-true scenes are found in the oriental style of painting that flourished especially in France as a consequence of Napoleon's campaigns.[19] Pictorial motifs from Algeria, Morocco, Egypt, and the Ottoman Empire with streets and bazaars, portraits, battle scenes with animals, as well as motifs from the harem, sold extremely well.[20] Doré's reproduction of oriental local color stands in contrast to that of Schnorr von Carolsfeld, whose scenes, with few exceptions, are designed on the classicist or romantic-Italian model. Doré employs light and shadow as a striking structural means. Dramatic effects in the sense of a theatrical conception, just as much as sentimentality, belong to the characteristics of the times in the fine arts. Doré, a passionate lover of the theater, employs them for his purposes in the graphic arts, too, and above all when inner emotional sensibilities or external agitation of the protagonists are to be revealed.[21] Looked upon by his contemporaries as a "genius of the art of drawing," Doré nevertheless at first was forgotten after his death.[22]

1.3. On the Selection of the Pictured Scenes

The Old Testament with its, in part, broad narrative style offers more material on women than does the New Testament.[23] The feminine figures

---

18. See Bach, *Das Bild in der Bibel*, 34.

19. See Gérard-Georges Lemaire, *Orientalismus: Das Bild des Morgenlandes in der Malerei* (Cologne: Könemann, 2000).

20. The work illustrated by Doré includes Benjamin Gastineau, *La France en Afrique et l'Orient à Paris: Voyage, Colonisation, Exposition; Egypte, Inde, Chine, Grêce, Turquie*, illustrated by Gustave Doré (Paris: Barba, 1856).

21. Herwig Guratzsch and Gerd Unverfehrt, eds., *Ausstellungskatalog: Gustave Doré (1832–1883); Illustrator, Maler, Bildhauer; Beiträge zu seinem Werk*, 2 vols., BT 348 (Dortmund: Harenberg, 1982), 45.

22. See Gotthard Brandler, ed., *Gustave Doré*, KK 26 (Berlin: Eulenspiegel, 1988), 101.

23. See Lütze, *Ausstellungskatalog: Bibel-Illustrationen*, 17.

in the New Testament, to be sure, are found, in part, at decisive points of New Testament narratives, but the contexts of their lives are described in less detail than is the case, for example, with Judith or Delilah in the Old Testament. Thus, it is no wonder that the illustrators of the nineteenth century portrayed predominantly the women of the Old Testament in their cycles and that, on the whole, Old Testament pictorial themes predominate because of the abundance of subject matter from the tradition. Schnorr von Carolsfeld and Doré place women especially in scenes with groups of people in the foreground, even when the given text contains no mention of them. On the other hand, women who were effective politically and publicly, such as Miriam (Exod 15), the woman from Tekoa (2 Sam 14), the woman from Abel-Bet-Maacha (2 Sam 20), and Hulda (2 Kgs 22), but also Tamar (2 Sam 13) and Dinah (Gen 34), both of whom were raped, are, significantly, lacking. Doré, however, does devote two pictures to the raped concubine of the Levite in Judg 19, in which the lifeless body of the woman indicates what has happened.[24]

What is of further significance is what textual version is used by the artists or how many scenes of a narrative are portrayed. While Doré chooses only three scenes from the creation texts (*Es werde Licht! Genesis 1, 1–18; Die Erschaffung Evas. Genesis 2, 15–25; Die Vertreibung aus dem Paradies, Genesis 3, 9–24*), Schnorr von Carolsfeld devotes a picture to each of the seven days from Gen 1, leaves out a portrayal of Gen 2, and portrays four scenes from Gen 3, the story of the fall and expulsion. The question whether the selection of pictures reflects a Catholic (Doré) or a Protestant (Schnorr von Carolsfeld) program cannot be pursued in this context. In carrying out such an investigation, it would be necessary to inquire to what extent the Bible text chosen for printing—the Vulgate, on the one hand, and the Luther translation, on the other—indicates a confessional attachment on the part of the artist, or whether sales strategies played a role here.

In the following, a series of selected pictorial themes, which place women as central figures in various scenes, is to be discussed by way of

---

24. Only Doré illustrates the story of the rape of the Levite's concubine and thereby chooses as a first scene that in which the Levite finds the lifeless woman in the morning before the house (*Die Frau des Leviten Efraim* [Judg 19:18–27]). The second portrayal shows the motionless woman bound on the back of an ass before the maltreated body is cut into pieces by her husband (*Efraim führt seine Frau fort* [Judg 19:28–30]). Both artists refrain from portraying excessive violence.

example.²⁵ In addition, attention is directed toward so-called mass scenes since in these, gender stereotypes come to light especially clearly. The portrayals by Schnorr von Carolsfeld and Doré are to be investigated under the aspect of whether and to what extent conclusions can be drawn from them about notions of masculinity and femininity in the nineteenth century.

2. Women in the Bible Illustrations by Doré and Schnorr von Carolsfeld

2.1. The Creation of Man and Woman

Schnorr von Carolsfeld chooses the creation of man and woman as the theme of his sixth woodcut (fig. 1: *Der sechste Schöpfungstag* [Gen 1:26]).²⁶ He refers here to the first report of the creation, which describes the human being as masculine and feminine and as in the image of God. God as an imposing masculine being forms the central figure in the middle of the page. To the left, Adam and Eve stand in an observant attitude; to the right, the land animals created on the same day, among them a bull, a lion, an elephant, a horse, and a snake, epitomize symbolically the world, which God gives to human beings as a place in which to live. The man and woman are naked; Adam's loins are covered with leaves, those of Eve by her long hair. While Eve holds her hands crossed before her breasts, without being able to conceal them completely, Adam is pictured as observant and with hands folded in devotion. The man is brought into connection with piety; the woman with chastity. With his right hand, God emphasizes the commission made to humanity to subdue the earth; his left hand, though, points to the animals, which are not shown in precise perspective, but rather in an irritating staggered arrangement from the bottom to the top. The portrayal reminds one of Raffael's *Creation of the Animals*, above all in the figure of God. Schnorr von Carolsfeld lets man and woman stand peaceably next to one another without giving any indication of a gender hierarchy. The assignment of gender characters such as pious for the first man, on the one hand, and as chaste for the first woman, on the other,

---

25. The sequence of the pictures presented here follows the arrangement in both Bible editions.

26. Original picture titles come from the edition Schnorr von Carolsfeld, *Die Bibel in Bildern*; captions accompanying the illustrations have been translated into English. *Die Bibel in Bildern* can be viewed online at https://archive.org/details/diebibelinbilder00schn.

Top: Fig. 1. Schnorr von Carolsfeld, *The Sixth Day of Creation*. Bottom: Fig. 2. Doré, *The Creation of Eve*.

must not necessarily be conceived as a relationship of super- or subordination. To be noted, however, is the fact that this is a picture of paradisiacal conditions before the fall.

Doré does not picture the creation of the human being from Gen 1 but rather remarkably the creation story from Gen 2 (*Die Erschaffung Evas* [Gen 2:15–25]).[27] According to the textual record, Eve was created by God from Adam's side. The woman endowed with voluptuous feminine contours stands erect and inclined slightly to the side (fig. 2). While the loins of the first human pair are suggested by clumps of leaves, their bodies are well-formed nude figures discernible plastically, modeled through the use of light and shadow, and consciously presented to observers. Adam, in the foreground, is portrayed as a young, energetic bacchant who appears to be exhausted and sunken in sleep and who, thereby, fully relaxed, stretches out his limbs. In the figure of Eve, Doré is likely to have made reference to the motif of *Galatea* by Raffael. She is characterized by him as a soft, feminine being with long, undone hair and does not appear conscious of her beauty and eroticism, but rather casts a searching glance upon the naked man, her future husband, at her feet.

The scenes that show Adam and Eve in paradise belong among those few opportunities in Bible illustration for portraying the naked human body. These were, in spite of somatophobic tendencies on the part of the churches, a fixed component of the pictorial motifs, even if the body parts that according to the standards of the time were considered as indecent were covered as far as possible through the aid of hands, leaves, and hair. The figure of God the creator in the background, whose head is enwreathed in a transparent aureole, was pictured by Doré with a raised right hand in order thereby to indicate his power, which has found expression through the creation of the woman. Neither of the two genders symbolized by Adam and Eve is endowed with specific distinguishing features, as with Schnorr von Carolsfeld. Both are beautiful, young, naked human beings.

2.2. Fall and Expulsion from Paradise

Schnorr von Carolsfeld created four pictures in all on this theme. On the leaf with the title *Der Sundenfall* (Gen 3:6), Eve is portrayed as standing upright

---

27. Original picture titles come from the edition Doré, *Doré-Bibel*; captions accompanying the illustrations have been translated into English.

and offering an apple to Adam, who sits against the tree trunk (fig. 3). The artist emphasizes the active part played by the woman in the fatal event by showing her in a striding position. Adam, who sits with crossed legs at the foot of the tree, obviously is not conscious of the danger emanating from the serpent. Seemingly unwittingly, he reaches for the tempting fruit offered him. Although they are naked, the erotic magnetism of their bodies does not form the subject of the image; the greatest seduction is suggested by Eve's arms, the left resting on the tree (cf. Gen 3:3) and the right passing on the plucked fruit. Only Eve's knowing look at the apple gives an indication of the conscious action of the woman driven to her act by the serpent: she is the one who seduces the unsuspecting man to commit sin. He does not see the serpent that winds its way up the tree between him and the woman and stretches its head toward Eve while flicking out his tongue in the direction of the one who, according to the Bible text, is not only more active than Adam, but who is interpreted as curious, inquisitive, and attentive.

The only pictorial theme from this narrative of prehistory chosen by Doré is *Die Vertreibung aus dem Paradies* (Gen 3:9–24). The pair of human beings is, to be sure, moved to the foreground, but the predominant figure in the composition is the angel in the background (fig. 4). Dazzling rays of light fall upon him; everything else is immersed in a threatening darkness. The wings emphasize the tall, slender form wrapped in a flowing robe. The raised hand and the sword underline his regal attitude. The man and woman have submitted to this sovereign command; they leave the brightly illuminated garden in the background and stride into wild, dark nature. The Adam leaving paradise, and who looks back once again, offers his protection to Eve, who is searching for help and cowering against his shoulder. In spite of his stride, he seems bowed down and anxious. In view of the violence that emanates from the angel and from nature, the human beings become submissive creatures who are dependent upon each other. In spite of the difference in their bodily postures, man and woman are united in the fact that both have to bear the same fate: they must obey the divine command. Eve's role in the work of both artists changes from a self-assured beauty into a woman in need of support and who obviously has accepted the dominating and protecting function of the man (see Gen 3:16).

2.3. The Mothers of Israel: Rachel and Leah

Schnorr von Carolsfeld as well as Doré portray Rachel's encounter with Jacob at the well. In Doré's *Jakob bei Laban* (Gen 29:4–19), Rachel with a jug

Top: Fig. 3. Schnorr von Carolsfeld, *The Fall*. Bottom: Fig. 4. Doré, *The Expulsion from Paradise*

on her shoulder alone at the well is the dominant figure in the foreground (fig. 5). Her herd of sheep already has gathered around Jacob sitting in the background. Both appear to be far away from one another: His eyes are turned toward her, but she stands very erect and seems to be withdrawn into herself, as though the man in the background does not exist. Here, the encounter between the two is not presented but rather a moment of hesitation. According to the Genesis text, Jacob helps the woman to water her sheep. Doré uses this narrative to place an oriental beauty predominantly in the foreground. What binds the portrayed man and the woman in the foreground remains an open question.

Fig. 5. Doré, *Jacob with Laban*.

Schnorr von Carolsfeld makes his subject the rivalry between the two sisters Leah and Rachel. Already in the scene at the well (*Jacob und Rahel am Brunnen* [Gen 29:10–12]), in which Rachel in the foreground is embraced passionately by Jacob, the sinister figure of the sister gazing at the pair stands in the background. In the courtship scene, *Jakob wirbt um Rahel* (Gen 29:18–19), both sisters, not only the desired bride Rachel, are pictured along with the two bargaining men, Jacob and Laban. Also, in the two mass scenes in which Schnorr von Carolsfeld summarizes Gen 33, both women appear as a pair. In the flight scene, *Jakobs Flucht* (Gen 31:17–18), both ride on the same camel—their small children pressed against the breast—while their female slaves walk alongside. In the reconciliation scene, *Esau versöhnet sich mit Jakob* (Gen 33:3–4), the two maids prostrate themselves with their children in the first row, while Leah and Rachel stand behind them. Doré pictures only the second of these events, whereby in his picture all the women with their children gather around the embracing pair of brothers: *Jakobs Versöhnung mit Esau* (Gen 33:1–14). These mass scenes stereotype women with their children as mothers in need of protection but also as caring mothers.

2.4. Joseph and Potiphar's Wife

The scene *Josephs Keuschheit und der Potiphar Untreue* (Gen 39:9) is found only in the work of Schnorr von Carolsfeld. In an Egyptianized ambience with column capitals and palm trees, the artist develops a dramatically animated seduction scene. Thus, the woman rises from her bed along the ascending diagonal; her naked arms grasp for the fleeing youth. Her back is uncovered; a loose sheet covers the feminine body. She attempts to grab onto the young man by his tunic. Joseph flees with his arms raised to fend off the woman and, with an energetic stride, plunges toward an opening through which he can leave the room. His face is turned toward the opening; temptation in the form of the woman is not able to hold him back. Joseph's face lies in shadow; hers is accentuated with light. The body of the woman represents the epitome of lust; the man appears not to let the woman appeal to him in any way. In accordance with the text, the married woman attempts to seduce the young man. Joseph, the Hebrew servant in the house of the high Egyptian official, judges loyalty toward his Lord as higher than a sexual contact to which he is at first invited but then pressured. It is not the woman who serves as the symbol of chastity but rather the man.

2.5. The Finding of Moses

This scene is portrayed by both illustrators. Schnorr von Carolsfeld's *Die Findung Mosis* (Exod 2:5–6) is positioned in the reed beds of the Nile (fig. 6). A group of musicians accompanies the daughter of Pharaoh; she stands in the center of the picture and is inclined slightly toward the water. Behind her, a servant girl holds a fan in the form of a papyrus bloom as a symbol of her power, while in the foreground a kneeling woman holds out to her the baby boy in a reed basket. In the background, in the shade of a palm tree, stands Moses's sister as an observer. In accordance with the biblical text, Schnorr von Carolsfeld shows a group of women in which all the motherly empathy is directed toward the masculine child. The attempt to produce an Egyptian flair is only moderately successful; only the headdresses and necklaces, as well as the papyrus and palm motifs, give an indication of the location of the action.

Top: Fig. 6. Schnorr von Carolsfeld, *The Finding of Moses*. Bottom: Fig. 7. Doré, *Moses's Miraculous Salvation*.

Doré presents Moses in a rush basket two times: the first as a small baby floating in an artfully contoured gondola between swaying reeds on the Nile bathed in moonlight, protected by four guardian angels (*Moses auf dem Nil* [Exod 1:8-22; 2:1-3]). He lets the women mentioned in the Bible text appear only in the second portrayal: *Moses' wunderbare Errettung* (fig. 7; Exod 2:4-9). In this picture the daughter of Pharaoh is shown as a dignified princess flanked by two female servants with ostrich feather fans. While he lets the background swim in a southern light, the princess and her entourage are sharply outlined. This leaf is a particularly good example for the enthusiasm for the Orient in the nineteenth century that found a stylistic highpoint in a mania for things Egyptian. Doré's preoccupation with the cultures of the Mediterranean area becomes clear, for example, in the reproduction of the robes and in elements of decorative headdress. The basket rocks leisurely upon the waves with the chubby baby; a female servant brings it to the shore at the behest of the princess. Both portrayals make use of classical clichés, which to a great extent reflect the reality of gender roles in the nineteenth century: women are responsible for the care and upbringing of the children. Consequently, in many areas men do not appear at all.

2.6. Deborah

Schnorr von Carolsfeld does not take up the theme of the great prophetess and judge.[28] His selection shows that independent women in political leadership positions obviously were not representable for him since they contradicted the image of the woman that was to be conveyed by his work. In the nineteenth century, there were several women in political leadership roles, but these, of course, represented only a minority. European queens and empresses—apart from only a few exceptions—did not act independently in a manner analogous to that attributed to Deborah. They were much rather integrated into structured power frameworks that set limits to their action. There existed no counterpart to the variety of offices carried out by Deborah; in the major churches, women could not assume any position of leadership. Schnorr von Carolsfeld is not likely to have had available to him a model of the combination of religious and political authority embodied in a feminine leadership figure, so it was possibly for

---

28. See on this the article by Christiana de Groot in this volume.

this reason that he did not draw upon such a significant figure like Deborah for his Bible illustration.

Fig. 8. Doré, *Deborah's Song of Victory*.

The case is different with Doré and his *Deboras Siegeslied* (fig. 8; Judg 5:1–13). On the steps of an imposing building, Deborah is moved to the center of his picture. With almost ecstatic gesticulation, she has risen from the steps and appears to be in the act of communicating the news of the victory in verse. She dominates the page and also the persons arranged around her. Surrounded to the right and the left by dark masculine figures at a proper distance, she sings—her left hand laid upon her breast, the right hand pointing upward—her song of victory. The one lighter figure among the men and who stands upon the same step as she is evidently Barak. He is robbed of every form of activity through the dramatic action of the feminine figure. With one hand on the step and the other supported on his hip, he appears to be listening to the song of the prophetess. Doré emphasizes the right hand stretched high and thereby exaggerated the figure of Deborah. She stands there as a prophetic herald, whom all hear.

2.7. Jephthah's Daughter

Jephthah's daughter becomes a theme in Schnorr von Carolsfeld's work through the return home by her father: *Jephthah und seine Tochter* (Judg 11:35). The picture is in two parts. In the center and foreground of the picture is the armor-clad Jephthah on his horse, around him the victorious warriors. The left-hand part of the picture belongs to the civilian population: old men and women with babies and small children come out of the city, above all the daughter of Jephthah standing on the highest step of a flight of stairs in the foreground. She beats upon a taboret as a greeting to the glorious army and appears in turn in a dance. Dismayed, Jephthah turns his shadowed face away and holds up his hand in defense against the roundelay sung by his daughter. He had vowed, in the case of a victory, to sacrifice the first person who came toward him out of the city. With dismay, he must observe that this person is his own daughter. The young woman, garlanded with flowers, beams with naïve joy in the direction of her father and does not suspect that her fate already has been sealed.

Doré creates a scene marked by an energetic femininity and a joyous expectation in *Jiftachs Tochter geht ihrem Vater entgegen* (fig. 9; Judg 11:29–36). Jephthah's daughter, who dances toward her father, appears at the point of the crossing diagonals in the center of the leaf. In the background, five women play upon various musical instruments. The postures of the young women remind one of oriental dance poses: their robes fall loosely around their bodies; their naked feet appear hardly to touch the ground. Their arms are raised in joy. Doré concen-

Fig. 9. Doré, *Jephthah's Daughter Approaches Her Father*.

trates upon the reception of the victorious army by the women of its own people. These women represent the public opinion by singing praises to the returning warriors and, thus, to the divinity who granted the victory. The female and male observers find themselves in the position of the men of the army, toward whom the women rush.

Doré's second picture on this complex of themes, *Jiftachs Tochter mit ihren Freundinnen* (Judg 11:37–40), shows the young woman with seven companions sitting in grief on a hilltop. They bewail the imminent death of their friend who must lose her life because of her father's vow. Both leaves deal with intensive feelings from overwhelming joy to devastating pain. The man responsible for the joy as well as the catastrophe remains outside the picture. Jephthah's daughter is not the only example of the child sacrifice theme made in the Old Testament. In the case of Abraham, though, an angel sent by God intervenes and prevents the killing of Isaac precisely in the moment when Abraham intends to sacrifice his son (Gen 22).

2.8. Samson and Delilah

Among the episodes of the Old Testament most frequently interpreted by artists are those with Samson and Delilah (Judg 16:4–22). The big, strong hero who is duped and made prisoner through the cunning and guile of a beautiful woman has always given wings to the fantasies of painters both male and female. Schnorr von Carolsfeld does not show the moment of erotic temptation but rather, in his leaf *Simsons Fall* (fig. 10; Judg 16:21), the temptress already has cut off Samson's hair, robbed him of his power, and castrated him, as it were. The figure of the woman is portrayed as triumphant with a raised hand that holds scissors and locks of hair, with half her breast exposed and with the other hand pulling back the bed curtain. The hero, dragged out of bed, is shown in a skirmish with his conquerors. His legs and head already are caught in the cords of the Philistines. But, four more men are necessary to detain the man who has lost his power through deception. In the background, two men, one with chains and the other with a dagger, wait to ensure the capture. The understanding of the gender relationship expressed here is revealing. The power and strength of a man is not invulnerable; it can be broken when he naively falls victim to sexual temptation. Delilah could carry out her cunning plan because she employed typically feminine means but combined these with other intentions that were not discernible for the man.

Old Testament Women in Bible Illustrations 445

Top: Fig. 10. Schnorr von Carolsfeld, *Samson's Fall*. Bottom: Fig. 11. Doré, *Samson and Delilah*.

Doré takes up the theme quite differently in his *Simson und Delila* (fig. 11; Judg 16:4–5, 15–22). Naïve and apparently honored by her attention, Samson, who considers himself to be invincible, divulges the secret of his strength to Delilah, listening spellbound to him. In the richly decorated, palace-like room, the magnificently clothed Delilah, with pouting lips and cast down eyes that betray nothing about her true thoughts, attempts to dupe Samson. His eyes look with desire upon the woman's breasts wrapped in precious robes. His glance is given greater intensity by the ray of light streaming through the window into the room. A strong woman who pretends to be weak is placed over against the man bursting with power but suspecting nothing. The resonating gender stereotypes reverse themselves: the bodily strength of the man offers no protection when he falls victim to sexual temptation through a willfully deceitful woman. The intelligently employed physical charms of the woman reach their goal. In this case, they receive a positive assessment since they serve the higher goal, the victory of the people of Israel over its enemies.

2.9. King Saul and the Spiritist Woman

Although there are ordinances for the Israelites, against mediums and those conjuring up the dead (e.g., Lev 19:31; 20:6; Deut 18:11), it is reported that King Saul violated this commandment. Saul became frightened in view of the imminent attack by the Philistines, no longer sure of his victory. In this situation, he availed himself of a means that he himself had forbidden for his people (1 Sam 28:3, 9): consulatation of the dead. Samuel, the great prophet and judge who had given the Israelites ordinances in the name of God, had died. When Saul was unsuccessful in eliciting a reaction from God in response to his prayer for victory over the Philistines, he hoped to receive the necessary aid from Samuel. The role of mediator here can be assumed only by the spiritist woman; the ruler fearing for his position made use of a woman with supernatural abilities that were unavailable to him in spite of his abundance of power.

In Schnorr von Carolsfeld's *Saul bei der Wahrsagerin zu Endor* (fig. 12; 1 Sam 28:16–17), the conjuring of Samuel already has taken place. Enveloped in fire, Samuel's spirit with raised right hand in the lefthand part of the picture appears to confirm Saul's downfall. The latter lies in the foreground with his head thrown back and, deeply wounded by Samuel's words, moves his right hand in the direction of his heart. Behind him, with consternation in her features and turned toward the right, the woman of

Top: Fig. 12. Schnorr von Carolsfeld, *Saul with the Soothsayer from Endor*. Bottom: Fig. 13. *Saul and the Spiritist Woman*.

Endor, who has conducted the conjuring, is seen. Her long, undone hair is covered by a cloth; her facial features have a masculine, severe look, just as do her muscular arms. On the wall, as a symbol, one might say, for her magical arts, there leans a skeleton from whose ribcage a snake emerges and wends its way in Samuel's direction.

Doré realized this text in a still more dramatic fashion in his wood engraving *Saul und die Totenbeschwörerin* (fig. 13; 1 Sam 28:9-20). In the open air before a threatening sky, which only in the upper right corner is brightened, stand Samuel and the woman from Endor upon a low elevation in the left half of the picture, while on the right Saul and his men wait. Doré, too, lets the king sink to the earth, although he is supported by his companions so that he is to be seen in a semiprone position. Samuel, to the far left, appears as a robed figure, as well as does the woman from Endor, who points to Samuel with her left hand. She is portrayed as a figure with her back turned to the viewer; her long flowing robe falls in large folds to the earth. Her—compared with the size of her body—rather small head with knotted hair is turned toward Saul. In contrast to Schnorr von Carolsfeld, who shows his woman from Endor, with her striking facial features, as more or less in the tradition of a witch, the figure by Doré seems to be a youthful person who appears as an upright figure. Doré provides a hint of the conjuring that has just taken place: below the elevation upon which the woman stands is a kettle next to which two snakes coil.

2.10. The Queen of Sheba

Schnorr von Carolsfeld as well as Doré take up the portrayal of the Queen of Sheba. Schnorr von Carolsfeld places Solomon's lion throne in the center of his picture *Die Königin aus Arabien huldiget Salomo* (1 Kgs 10:6-7, 10). Before this throne, to his left, the queen from Arabia sits with outspread arms that point out the precious objects that her female and male servants bring. Gold, precious jewels, and the most precious spices do not interest the king at all; his attention is directed entirely to the beautiful young woman.

The picture *Salomon empfängt die Königin von Saba* is one of the most elaborately designed leaves of the Doré Bible (fig. 14; 1 Kgs 10:1-9). The queen approaches Solomon on the stairs; the servants following her bear the gifts. The room in which the meeting takes place is decorated magnificently; animal and plant motifs alternate with various types of ornaments. Although Solomon looks down upon the queen from an

Fig. 14. Doré, *Solomon Receives the Queen of Sheba*.

elevated position, her dignified attitude and her noble figure dominate the leaf. While Schnorr von Carolsfeld captures a private encounter, in which servants are not relevant, Doré lets the meeting take place before a large number of people. They form the background for the dialogue between two people who claim the same dignity. Solomon, though, is the one who is portrayed head-on and who remains standing above on an upper step. The Queen of Sheba, on the other hand, whose face cannot be seen, appears to be in the process of climbing upward toward him.

2.11. Judith and Holofernes

The beautiful and rich widow Judith sets out to save her people while the men of her village lose heart before the threat posed by the approaching enemy, the Assyrian commander Holofernes and his army. In his Bible edition, Schnorr von Carolsfeld records the moment just after the killing of Holofernes by Judith: *Judith enthauptet den Holofernes* (fig. 15; Jdt 13:9–10). The young woman looks with disgust back upon the headless corpse; she grasps her prize firmly by a shock of hair. The successful united action by the two women, mistress and her servant, is made clear in Schnorr von Carolsfeld's second Judith leaf: *Judith kehrt unversehrt zu ihrem Volk zurück. Judith* (Jdt 13:11–12). The women—the one with the raised sword in her hand, the other carrying the head of Holofernes in a sack, whereby the facial features of the man show through the thin material—return to Betulia, where they are received by the men entrenched cravenly behind the wall. Schnorr von Carolsfeld is said to have used the photograph of a female opera singer as a model for the figure of Judith.[29] He thus demonstrates that, above and beyond all his admiration for Raffael and Michelangelo, he knew how to make use of the technical possibilities of his time in that he did not work with living models but rather employed the new medium of photography.

In Doré's *Judit und Holofernes* (Jdt 13:2–10), the killing also has been carried out. With her eyes raised toward heaven, which reminds one of the portrayals by Guido Reni, the victorious Judith grasps the head of Holofernes. In contrast to Schnorr von Carolsfeld's interpretation, she alone dominates the scene; no female servant as her helper has been added. The latter appears only on Doré's second leaf on the Judith narrative: *Judit zeigt das Haupt des Holofernes* (fig. 16; Jdt 13:2–10). Here a second feminine figure crouches unassumingly on the ground next to the triumphant heroine. Doré shows Judith in an almost dance-like pose; she obviously has changed her clothes, and her seductive costume moves her iconographically in the vicinity of Salome. Thereby, she shows the head of Holofernes as a trophy to a group of men moved to the background.

2.12. Susannah

Like Bathsheba (2 Sam 11:2), Susannah (Dan 13) embodies the type of the secretly observed beauty who is innocently maligned by two old

---

29. See Fuchs, "Bibelillustrationen des 19. Jahrhunderts," 196.

Old Testament Women in Bible Illustrations 451

Fig. 15. Top: Schnorr von Carolsfeld, *Judith Beheads Holofernes*. Bottom: Fig. 16. *Judith Shows the Head of Holofernes*.

men. Schnorr von Carolsfeld sketches the scene in a traditional manner (*Susanna und die zween Aeltesten*): The two lecherous old men approaching the young, surprised woman, who has just dipped her left foot cautiously in the water, are the symbol for a misguided desire typical of old age, characterized by the artist through the men's facial expressions. On his leaf *Susanna im Bade* (fig. 17; Dan 13:7-27), Doré moves the figure of the observed woman into the foreground, pictured with an innocent expression on her face and effectively wrapped in her sheet, which she gathers around her naked body. The two old men are in the background in a diffuse light; the two figures appear unclear and threatening.

The second scene that Schnorr von Carolsfeld chooses from the Susannah story shows her salvation from death: *Daniel errettet Susanna*

Fig. 17. Doré, *Susannah Bathing*.

vom Tod. While Daniel announces his decision, the men are seized and led to their punishment. Susannah looks in devotion upward to heaven with her hands folded in prayer. Under the title *Die Rechtfertigung der Susanna*, Doré shapes the scene in which Daniel pronounces judgment like a scene upon a large stage. The slanderous old men are seized and led away. Susannah stands there with her hands folded across her breast, in the interpretation of the figure much like that of the portrayal by Schnorr von Carolsfeld.

3. Concluding Remarks

The Bible illustrations by Schnorr von Carolsfeld and Doré aroused great interest in the nineteenth century for two reasons above all. First, it was the large number of the portrayals, and second, the—to be sure individually different—mastery on the part of both artists in capturing the biblical scenes in their essence and in realizing them graphically, which captivated many people. The long-lasting reception of their works, which stretched into the twentieth century, illustrates the special status that these illustrated Bible editions were able to acquire on the book market. Schnorr von Carolsfeld's feminine biblical figures show themselves, in their simplicity, as obliged to Nazarene ideas and ideal of beauty. His goal existed in "taking an interest in the education and training of the human being."[30] Doré, on the other hand, makes use of the entire range of late Romantic and historicist pictorial motifs available to him for the graphic conversion of the biblical texts. Dramatic effects of light and shadow, facial expressions, effective gestures and poses, and not least of all unusual pictorial motifs produce a work that, in its emotionality, appeals less to the contemplative soul than to observers, both male and female, who find pleasure in extravagantly designed scenes and erotic showpieces. His work is directed rather toward educated readers who already know the corresponding motifs from the great works of art history.

The image of women that these artists convey corresponds to the times in which the picture cycles originated as well as to the standards of traditional interpretation upon which they could draw. Thereby, the artistic environment must be taken into consideration. Schnorr von Carolsfeld in Germany had different sources of inspiration than did Doré, who lived and

---

30. Schnorr von Carolsfeld, *Die Bibel in Bildern*, 7.

worked in Paris in the center of modern art. In regard to the question of biblical interpretation in the nineteenth century, the following conclusions can be drawn from these illustrations: The biblical texts, above all those of the Old Testament, offered such different artists as Doré and Schnorr von Carolsfeld stimulating material with which they could concern themselves graphically. Thereby, two tendencies can be discerned that derive from the image analyses of the individual woodcuts and wood engravings. First of all, the gender model reflected within their graphic interpretations was determinant in social as well as cultural concerns in the nineteenth century. Second, the traditional inventory also required them to move closer to alien types of conduct among women and men from long-past times. The artistic creative work of both suggests that the relationship of the sexes to each other was traditional; it reflects, however, only to a small extent the actual world of the life of women that, at the time of the printing of the two works, especially in France, already was marked by the first successes of the women's movement.

Bibliography

Assel, Jutta. "Deutsche Bilderbibeln im 19. Jahrhundert: Insbesondere nazarenische Bilderfolgen zum Alten und/oder Neuen Testament." Pages 25–42 in *Julius Schnorr von Carolsfeld: Die Bibel in Bildern und andere biblische Bilderfolgen der Nazarener; Catalogue for the Exhibition in Clemens Sels Museum Neuss, 28. 11. 1982–27. 2. 1983*. Neuss: Clemens-Sels-Museum, 1982.

Bach, Bernhard, ed. *Das Bild in der Bibel: Bibelillustrationen von der Reformation bis zur Gegenwart aus evangelischen Archiven und Bibliotheken in Bayern*. Munich: Claudius, 1995.

Bourassé, Jean-Jacques, Pierre Janvier, Gustave Doré, and Hector Giacomelli. *La Sainte Bible traduction nouvelle selon la Vulgate*. Tours: Mame, 1866.

Brandler, Gotthard, ed. *Gustave Doré*. KK 26. Berlin: Eulenspiegel, 1988.

Davies, Kristian. *The Orientalists: Western Artists in Arabia, the Sahara, Persia and India*. New York: Laynfaroh, 2005.

Diederen, Roger, and Davy Depelchind, eds. *Ausstellungskatalog Orientalismus in Europa: Von Delacroix bis Kandinsky*. Musées Royaux des Beaux-Arts de Belgique, Brussels; Kunsthalle der Hypo-Kulturstiftung, Munich; Centre de la Vielle Charité, Marseille. Munich: Hirmer, 2010.

Doré, Gustave. *Doré-Bibel: Auszüge aus dem Alten und Neuen Testament mit 230 Illustrationen von Gustave Doré*. Munich: Parkland, 1995.

Feldhaus, Irmgard. "Julius Schnorr von Carolsfeld: Die Bibel in Bildern." Pages 6–23 in *Julius Schnorr von Carolsfeld: Die Bibel in Bildern und andere biblische Bilderfolgen der Nazarener; Catalogue for the Exhibition in Clemens Sels Museum Neuss, 28. 11. 1982–27. 2. 1983*. Neuss: Clemens-Sels-Museum, 1982.

Fuchs, Hildegard. "Bibelillustrationen des 19. Jahrhunderts." PhD diss., University of Erlangen-Nuremberg, 1986.

Gastineau, Benjamin. *La France en Afrique et l'Orient à Paris: Voyage, Colonisation, Exposition; Egypte, Inde, Chine, Grêce, Turquie*. Illustrated by Gustave Doré. Paris: Barba, 1856.

Guratzsch, Herwig, and Gerd Unverfehrt, eds. *Ausstellungskatalog: Gustave Doré (1832–1883); Illustrator, Maler, Bildhauer; Beiträge zu seinem Werk*. 2 vols. BT 348. Dortmund: Harenberg, 1982.

Lemaire, Gérard-Georges. *Orientalismus: Das Bild des Morgenlandes in der Malerei*. Cologne: Könemann, 2000.

Lütze, Diethelm, ed. *Ausstellungskatalog: Bibel-Illustrationen; Bücher aus 5 Jahrhunderten, Sammlung Lütze IV*. Stuttgart: Lütze, 1996.

Müller, Kristiane, and Eberhard Urban. *Die Kunst der Romantik: Beliebte und unbekannte Bilder nebst Zeichnungen und Studien*. Menden: Edition Aktuell, 1987.

Schnorr von Carolsfeld, Julius. *Die Bibel in Bildern*. Zurich: Flamberg, 1972.

———. *Die Bibel in Bildern: 240 Darstellungen erfunden und auf Holz gezeichnet von Julius Schnorr von Carolsfeld; Mit Bibeltexten nach Martin Luthers deutscher Übersetzung*. Munich: Borowsky, 1980.

Contributors

Ruth Albrecht, Professor at the Institute for Church History and the History of Dogma at the Department of Protestant Theology, University of Hamburg (Germany).

Angela Berlis, Professor of History of Old Catholicism and Church History, Department of Old Catholic Theology, and codirector at the Competence Centre for Liturgy at the University of Bern (Switzerland).

Inmaculada Blasco Herranz, Assistant Professor at the Faculty of History at the University of La Laguna (Spain).

Doris Brodbeck, head of communication and humanitarian affairs at the Reformed Church in canton Schaffhausen (Switzerland).

Katharina Büttner-Kirschner, freelance art historian and historian in Lindau (Germany).

Marina Cacchi, researcher and lecturer on the Faculty of Political Science "Roberto Ruffilli," Campus di Forlì at the University of Bologna (Italy).

Paul W. Chilcote, Professor of Theology, Asbury Theological Seminary, Orlando, Florida (USA).

Elizabeth M. Davis, leader of the Congregation of the Sisters of Mercy of Newfoundland and part-time faculty member at Saint Augustine's Seminary at the Toronto School of Theology, Ontario (Canada).

Ute Gause, Professor of Church History on the Faculty of Protestant Theology at the Ruhr University Bochum (Germany).

Christiana de Groot, Professor Emerita of Religion at Calvin College, Grand Rapids, Michigan (USA).

Alexej Klutschewsky, linguist and social scientist, nonstaff researcher at the Department of Legal Philosophy at the Faculty of Law, University of Vienna (Austria).

Magda Motté, Professor Emerita at the Institute of German Language and Literature, University of Dortmund (Germany).

Pamela S. Nadell, Professor of History, chair in Women's and Gender History, and director of the Jewish Studies Program at the American University in Washington, DC (USA).

Bernhard Schneider, Professor of Church History of the Middle Ages and the Modern Times at the Faculty of Theology, University of Trier (Germany).

Michaela Sohn-Kronthaler, Professor of Church History and chair of the Department of Church History and Contemporary Church History at the Faculty of Catholic Theology, University of Graz (Austria).

Eva Maria Synek, Associate Professor at the Law Faculty (Institute for Legal Philosophy) at the University of Vienna (Austria).

Marion Ann Taylor, Professor of Old Testament at Wycliff College at the University of Toronto (Canada).

Adriana Valerio, Professor of Christianity and Church History at the Department of Humanistic Studies of the University of Naples Frederico II (Italy).

Elfriede Wiltschnigg, lecturer in Art History at University of Graz (Austria).

Ancient Sources Index

Hebrew Bible/Old Testament

Genesis 3, 11, 32, 37, 42–43, 45, 49, 58, 60, 66, 173, 438

1	45, 48, 432, 435
1:1–18	432
1:3	23
1:26	433
1:27	129, 294
2	48, 432, 435
2:15–25	432, 435
2:18	192, 370
2:18	69
2:20	69
3	48, 432
3:3	436
3:6	435
3:9–24	432, 436
3:15	238
3:16	436
4:1–16	280
7:2	38
18	108
20	33
21	33
21:12	129
22	444
28:1	130
29:4–19	436
29:10–12	438
29:18–19	438
31:17–18	438
33	438
33:1–14	439
33:3–4	438
34	432
39:9	439
49:19	24

Exodus	42–43, 58, 154–55, 173
1:8–22	441
2:1–3	441
2:4–9	441
2:5–6	439
7:19	43
7:22	42
15	432
15:20	121–22
15:21	121
15:27	323
19:6	123
20	154
20:3–5	155
21:7	79
25:40	107

Leviticus	173
11	38
19:31	446
20:6	446
22:2	24

Numbers	173
6:24	334
6:26	290
12:1	121
12:15	122
27:4	123
27:7	123
32:12	119

Numbers (cont.)		17	46
33:9	323	26:23	334
		28:3	446
Deuteronomy	49, 51, 173	28:9	446
18:11	446	28:9–20	448
21:10–14	79	28:16–17	446
21:18–19	130		
26:11	120	2 Samuel	
28:8	333	11:2	450
30:19	364	13	432
32:11	320	14	432
		20	432
Joshua	37, 58, 64, 170, 173		
		1 Kings (LXX 3 Kings)	173–74
Judges	5, 63–65, 88–89, 91–96, 173	10:1–9	448
1	91	10:6–7	448
2	96	10:10	448
4–5	64, 66, 93, 293	17:9	272
4:4	70	17:24	272
5	79	19:11–13	290
5:1	122		
5:1–13	442	2 Kings (LXX 4 Kings)	173–74
5:6–7	67	4:8	108
5:7	120	13:28	103
5:9a	67	22	432
5:12	83	22:14	122
6	93		
11:29–36	443	1 Chronicles	173
11:35	443	4:10	25
11:37–40	444		
16:4–5	446	2 Chronicles	173
16:4–22	444	14:10	334
16:15–22	446		
16:21	444	Ezra	37, 58, 173
19	432		
19–21	32, 60	Nehemiah	37, 58
19:18–27	432		
19:28–30	432	Esther	173
Ruth	173	Job	51, 173
		1:21	337
1 Samuel		28	319
1:24	120	38:1	290
14:6	334		
16:21	46		

Ancient Sources Index 461

Psalms	32, 60, 75, 145, 154, 173–74, 209, 247	Isaiah	40–41, 49, 51, 145, 173, 306–9, 317
11:6	24	3:16–24	307
16	154	8:18	210
23:1	23	9	308
25:20	323	25	308
27:10	326	26	309
34	154	26:19	309
37:16	24	33:14	24
40:17	24	34:14	397
46:1	19	40	309, 319
50	365	40:3	297
51	154	40:11	20
68	263	40:15	23
68:11	263	40:31	21
68:12	262–64	41:10	19
73:25	24	42:7	325
90:10	320	43:16	297
94:1	103	43:19	297
111:10	322	45:15	289
117:24	109	49:3–4	40
118:28	24	49:15	103, 217
126:5–6	323	50–51	309
133:2	246	50:4	v, 99, 111
		52	309
Proverbs	174, 366	52:7	328
2:7	326	54:2	325, 330
15:13	364	55:8	102
18:22	364	57:14	297
21:28	102	58	273–74
23:26	108	58:8–9	269
24:10	325	58:11–12	317
31	35, 368–72, 377	66:12–13	366
31:10	369		
31:10–31	120, 132	Jeremiah	154, 170, 173
31:11	371	1:7	275
31:13	120	17	325
31:16	120	17:5	325
		17:5–7	324
Ecclesiastes	174	17:5–8	324
7:12	43	17:7	23, 325
		18:6	21–22
Song of Songs	34, 172–74, 176–77		
		Lamentations	
		2:10	299

Ancient Sources Index

Ezekiel	173, 317	36:27	364
33:11	216		
47:1–12	317	Baruch	173
Daniel	34, 38, 47, 51, 170, 173	Daniel	
2:47	330	13	450
5:27	289	13:7–27	452
Hosea		1–2 Maccabees	170, 174, 366
14:5	22		
		2 Maccabees	
Joel		7:20–41	369
2:28–29	135	12:41	330
Micah		**New Testament**	
6:4	122		
		Matthew	174
Malachi		3:5–6	280
2:7	24	3:11	24
2:14	131	5:3	310
3:3	335	5:4	52–53
		5:6	292
Deuterocanonical Books		5:11	109
		5:13–16	295
Tobit	173, 366	5:16	104
4:5	353	5:48	294
4:6	353	6:12	109
		6:13	326
Judith	173, 365–67, 403	7:7	21
8:8	367	7:24–27	324
13:2–10	450	7:24–29	326
13:9–10	450	9:38	331
13:11–12	450	10:22–24	337
13:14	367	11:28	19, 104, 109, 141, 329
15:9	367	11:29	107
15:10	367	11:30	103
		13:1–23	328
Wisdom of Solomon	174, 366	13:24–30	297
		15:16	24
Sirach	55, 174, 366, 368	15:21–28	372, 394
25:13–17	368	18:5	106
25:15–16	368	19:14	414
26	368, 377	19:16–27	208
26:1–27	368	22:12	20
30:23	364	23:1–12	106

Ancient Sources Index 463

23:8	322	10:33	299
24:13	364	10:38	108
24:14	160	10:38–42	104
25	20, 214	10:41	24
25:31–46	110, 167	10:42	147, 388
25:40	106, 323	12:49	106
26:6–13	236	13:5	24
26:41	21	14:12–14	273
26:42	22	15:3–7	322
		15:7	109
Mark	174	17:7–10	166
3:28–29	144	19:5	108
7:24–30	394	21:17	337
10:5	50	22:33	19
10:8	295	23:27–28	299
10:15	23	23:43	326
13:13	337		
14:3–9	236	John	24, 174, 208, 212, 240, 361
14:15	330	1:23	160
14:22–24	279	1:34–36	280
16:15	109	2:1–11	231
16:17–18	269	2:1–12	241, 243
16:20	336	2:4	333
		2:24	215
Luke	148, 174, 239	3:5	107
1:20	240	3:19	269
1:38	167	4	372
1:46–55	107, 414	4:1–26	389
1:48	239	4:5–14	291
1:48–49	105	4:14	23
1:68–79	107	6:12	365
2:25–36	211	8:1–11	295
2:29	109	8:2	333
2:29–32	107	10:28	270
2:51	240	10:28–29	20
6:22	337	11:40	334
6:27–28	109	12:1–8	235
7:11–17	372	12:28	335
7:36–50	235, 280	12:35	364
9	149	13:8	103
9:23	21	14	269
9:35	149	14:6	269
10:2	331	14:9	269
10:25	81	14:15	20
10:31–32	292	14:27	109

John (cont.)
- 15:18 — 337
- 15:25 — 337
- 17:24 — 110
- 19:26–27 — 240
- 20:1–18 — 174
- 20:22–23 — 105
- 21 — 52
- 21:15 — 320–22
- 21:17 — 20
- 24 — 147

Acts — 174, 372
- 1:7 — 247
- 6:8 — 336
- 9:36–43 — 418
- 13:50 — 270–71
- 16:14–22 — 235
- 27:29 — 26

Romans — 145, 173, 288
- 3:10 — 24
- 3:24 — 20
- 5:5 — 19
- 5:20 — 216
- 6:22 — 24, 364
- 7:24 — 24
- 8:14 — 102
- 8:15 — 24
- 8:17 — 21
- 8:28 — 21, 335
- 8:39 — 20
- 11:15 — 247
- 11:25–26 — 247
- 12:6 — 15
- 12:14 — 24
- 15:13 — 23
- 16:1 — 200

1 Corinthians — 174, 276, 373
- 2:9 — 330
- 3 — 365
- 3:12 — 335
- 6:13 — 22
- 6:15 — 22
- 7 — 374
- 7:17 — 363
- 7:23 — 337
- 7:29 — 364
- 9:24 — 364
- 11 — 16–17, 374
- 13 — 214, 273
- 13:1 — 26
- 13:3 — 210, 214
- 13:4–5 — 214–15
- 13:5 — 214
- 14 — 16–17
- 14:34 — 276, 278, 295
- 14:34–35 — 255
- 15:10 — 333
- 15:55 — 102

2 Corinthians — 174, 373
- 1:20 — 18–19
- 2:14 — 335
- 3:17 — 296
- 6:11 — 245
- 6:14 — 324
- 9:7 — 364
- 12 — 333
- 12:9 — 216

Galatians — 174
- 3:28 — 196, 215, 259, 281
- 4:6 — 102
- 5:6 — 20, 25

Ephesians — 174, 373
- 2:8 — 333
- 3:19 — 25
- 5:16 — 364
- 5:21–33 — 374–75

Philippians — 174
- 2:5 — 107
- 3:20 — 103
- 4:4 — 364
- 4:13 — 21

Colossians — 174

1 Thessalonians	174	Jude	174
5:14	329–30		
5:22	21	Revelation	42, 64, 172–73, 175–76
		2:10	102
2 Thessalonians	174	3:7–8	323
3:10	364	3:15–16	153
		3:20	108
1 Timothy	174, 373	5:12	334
2:8–10	375		
2:10–11	375	Rabbinic Works	
2:11–12	255–56		
2:13	66	b. B. Metz. 59b	131
2 Timothy	174	b. Ber. 17a	131
Titus	174	Midrash Haggadah	114
Philemon	174		
Hebrews	145, 174, 295		
7:18–19	50		
7:25	21		
James	174		
4:6	363		
5:13	334		
5:14–15	249		
1 Peter	174, 373		
1:5	24		
1:22	210, 214–15		
2:25	326		
3:1–2	375		
3:3–4	375		
3:13	337		
2 Peter	174		
1 John	217		
2:15	24		
3:18	106		
3:21	103		
4:16b	217		
4:18	24		

Modern Authors Index

Aguilar, Grace 64–65, 72–77, 79–80, 87, 88–91, 93–95
Aland, Kurt 210, 221
Albrecht, Ruth 257, 272, 280–82
Altenberend, Johannes 356, 377
American, Sadie 116–18, 133
Angelmaier, Lucia 338
Anthony, Susan B. 78, 88, 96
Arce Pinedo, Rebeca 188, 201
Arnim, Bettina von 386–88, 404
Arnold, Gottfried 312, 314
Assel, Jutta 427, 454
Aston, Margaret 225, 250
Ayala Aracil, María de los Ángeles 201
Bach, Bernhard 429431, 454
Bacon, Nathaniel 108, 111
Bail, Ulrike 263, 283
Balfour, Clara Lucas 64–65, 69–72, 85, 87, 89–90, 93–95
Barth, Fritz 298, 300
Barton, John 100, 111
Baskin, Judith R. 114, 131, 133
Baubérot, Jean 3, 10
Baumeister, Martin 352, 377
Baumgärtner, Wilhelm 358, 377
Baxter, Elizabeth 64–69, 75–76, 89, 91, 94, 97
Beaumont, Joseph 24–25, 27
Becker, Winfried 345, 377
Becksmann, Rüdiger 411, 421
Beer-Hofmann, Richard 400, 404
Beljakova, Elena V. 216, 221
Beljakova, Nadežda A. 216, 221
Benckhuysen, Amanda W. 42, 44, 57
Benedetti, Marina 136, 161
Benrath, Gustav Adolf 313–14, 327, 338
Berger, Teresa 225–26, 229, 233, 236, 243, 250–51, 254
Bergmann, Franz 250–51
Berlis, Angela 232, 234, 236, 242, 250–51
Besutti, Giuseppe M. 171, 178
Beutel, Albrecht 262, 282
Beyreuther, Erich 313, 315
Bieder, Maryellen 186, 201
Biller, Peter 136, 161
Bischof, Franz Xaver 349, 378
Bissoli, Cesare 170, 178
Blanco, Alda 188, 201
Blaschke, Olaf 344, 378
Blasco Herranz, Inmaculada 193, 201
Boccadamo, Giuliana 165, 171, 177–78
Böckel, Holger 329, 339
Bolster, Mary Angela 102, 111
Bonansea, Graziella 160–61
Bonomi, Joseph 36, 57
Borsi, Mara 168, 179
Bourassé, Jean-Jacques 430, 454
Bourdaloue, Louis 170, 178
Boydston, Jeanne 78, 81, 94
Brandler, Gotthard 431, 454
Brandt, Hans-Jürgen 343–44, 355, 378
Braunfels, Wolfgang 418, 421
Bray, Gerald 100, 111
Brecht, Martin 210, 221, 256, 283
Bremscheid, Matthias von 348, 363–64, 378
Breuer, Gisela 343, 378
Britz, Clara 348, 363–64, 373–74, 378

Brod, Max 400, 404
Brodbeck, Doris 287, 294, 298, 300, 397, 406
Brooks, Jeffrey 203, 221
Bruns, Hans 277, 283
Budde, Gunilla 372, 378
Buerman, Thomas 342, 344, 382–83
Bukova, Olga Viktorovna 211, 221
Bunke, Ernst 255, 283
Burder, Samuel 35, 57
Burkard, Dominik 345, 378
Burstyn, Joan N. 30, 57
Busch, Norbert 344, 378
Buschmann, Johanna 232, 252
Büttner, Katharina 407–8, 421
Caffiero, Marina 165, 178
Cacchi, Marina 137, 161
Calvert-Koyzis, Nancy 3, 10, 31, 60, 79, 95
Campbell, John 36, 57
Campos, Lola 186, 202
Carroll, Mary Austin 101, 111
Carus-Wilson, Mary 49–51, 56–57
Cavalca, Domenico 169, 178
Chadwick, Owen 227, 252
Charles, Elizabeth Rundle 5, 51–54, 56–57, 60
Chilcote, Paul W. 13, 15, 26–28
Choi, Agnes 3, 11
Chozas, Diego 186, 202
Cignoni, Mario 139, 161
Clarke, Adam 21, 23, 27
Cohen, Mary M. 118, 120, 124, 132–33
Colenso, John William 37, 58
Coluzzi, Luciana 166, 179
Combes, Paul 348–50, 363, 369, 371, 373–75, 378
Cona, Rino 168, 178
Corbaux, Fanny 35–36, 56, 58
Cordes, Martin 303, 315
Cornwallis, Mary 34–35, 56, 58, 60
Cramer, Wilhelm 348, 378
Crasset, Giovanni 170, 179
Crosby, Sarah 17, 19, 21, 27
D'Amico, Diane 42–43, 58

Davies, Kristian 425, 454
De Giorgio, Michela 3, 10, 164, 179, 347, 353, 374, 378, 420, 422
Degnan, Mary Bertrand 101, 103, 111–12
Delitzsch, Franz 36–37, 58
Denzinger, Heinrich 241, 252
Depelchind, Davy 425, 454
Der Friedenshort 258, 283
Deutsch, Emanuel 131, 133
Di Spirito, Angela 166, 179
Diamant, Anita 113, 133
Dibdin, Emily 92, 95
Diederen, Roger 425, 454
Doern, Kristin G. 69, 95
Dora, Cornel 349, 378
Doré, Gustave vii, 10, 425–26, 429–38, 440–46, 448–50, 452–55
Dorland, William A. Newman 83, 95
Dotzler, Arsenius 348, 363–64, 367–69, 371–74, 378
Doyle, Mary Ann 99, 111
Driver, Samuel R. 41, 44, 48, 58
Droste-Hülshoff, Annette von 387, 390, 393–96, 404–5
Duffrer, Günter 362, 379
Dulles, Avery Robert 100–101, 111
Dupanloup, Félix 195, 348–51, 353–54, 361–63, 365–75, 377, 379, 381
Efimovskaja, Evgenija (Ekaterina, Abbess) 215, 218
Egger, Augustin 348–49, 379
Ekaterina, Abbess. *See* Efimovskaja, Evgenija
Ellenrieder, Marie vii, 10, 407–23, 425
Ellis, Sarah Stickney 73, 77, 95
Engelhardt Herringer, Carol 228, 252
Entwisle, Mary 19, 27
Esposito, L. G. 176, 179
Ewald, Heinrich 40, 58
Feijoo, Benito 194–95, 202
Feldhaus, Irmgard 427, 429, 455
Feuerbach, Ludwig 36, 58
Fischer, Friedhelm Wilhelm 409, 411, 413–14, 416, 418, 420, 422

Fischer, Irmtraud 369, 372, 379
Fletcher, Mary 14, 21–22, 25–27
Fowler, Lois 84, 95
Fragnito, Gigliola 164, 179
Fraisse, Geneviève 2–3, 10–11, 164, 179, 346–47, 349, 378, 380, 420, 422
Frank, Ray 118, 120–24, 132, 133
Fresu, Rita 166, 179
Frevert, Ute 227, 253, 369, 379, 418, 423
Friedrich, Norbert 260, 283
Frijhoff, Willem 226, 233, 252
Frübis, Hildegard 409, 422
Fuchs, Hildegard 426–27, 450, 455
Fuchs, Rachel G. 371, 379
Fuller, Reginald H. 40, 58
Gage, Matilda J. 88, 90, 96
Gakkel', Sergij (Hackel, Serge) 213, 222
Galchinsky, Michael 73, 77, 95
Gastineau, Benjamin 431, 455
Gause, Ute 228–29, 252, 303, 305–6, 315, 342, 379
Gélébart, Yves-Claude 164, 179
Gestrich, Andreas 371, 379
Giacomelli, Hector 454
Gimeno de Flaquer, María de la Concepción vi, 7, 183–202
Giraudoux, Jean 403, 405
Giudici, Maria Pia 168, 179
Glagoleva, Olga E. 204, 221
Gleichenstein, Elisabeth von 412–13, 415, 422–23
Gödden, Walter 394, 405
Goll, Yvan 400, 405
Gonnet, Giovanni 136, 161
Goodwin, C. W. 37, 60
Göpfert, Frank 211, 221
Gössmann, Elisabeth 239, 252–53
Götz von Olenhusen, Irmtraud 228, 252, 342–43, 379, 383
Götzelmann, Arnd 328, 332, 338–39
Graf, Katrin 414, 422
Green, Nancy 3, 11
Greswell, Julia 31, 58
Grewe, Cordula 420, 422

Groot, Christiana de 3, 11, 33–34, 42, 51, 57, 60–61, 63, 79, 95, 97
Gumbrecht, Hans Ulrich 190, 202
Gunn, David M. 93, 95
Günther, Anton 231–37, 247, 252, 254
Guratzsch, Herwig 431, 455
Haag, Herbert 397, 405
Hackel, Serge. *See* Gakkel', Sergij
Hammer-Tugendhat, Daniela 366–67, 379
Häntzschel, Günter 346–47, 379
Harnett, Mary Vincent 109, 111
Harper, Steve 14, 15, 28
Hauser, Margit 348, 379
Haussherr, Rainer 411, 422
Hebbel, Friedrich 400–405
Heil, Verein vom 355, 379
Hein, Jürgen 403, 405
Henell, Charles Christian 36, 58
Hengst, Karl 343–44, 355, 378
Henkelmann, Andreas 344, 380
Hensel, Luise 243, 254, 358, 380, 387, 390–91, 405
Herder, Johann Gottfried 79, 82, 95, 385
Herrmann, Volker 304, 315
Hettling, Manfred 371, 380
Hibbs-Lissorgues, Solange 186, 202
Hilgers, Bernard Joseph 230–32, 243, 252
Himmel-Agisburg, Antonia 213–14, 222
Hitzer, Bettina 266, 283
Hoffelize, Adele Gräfin von 348, 353, 361, 363, 369, 380
Hollein, Max 409, 420, 422
Holsten, Siegmar 413, 422
Holthaus, Stephan 257–59, 261–62, 264–65, 267–70, 275–76, 278, 283, 314–15
Hoock-Demarle, Marie-Claire 346, 380
Horstmann, Johannes 344, 380
Hülskamp, Franz 345, 347, 351–52, 357–58, 380, 383
Hummel, Steffi 345, 380
Hünermann, Peter 241, 252
Ilan, Tal 114, 133

Modern Authors Index

Jacobs, Joseph 131, 133
Janvier, Pierre 454
Jay, Elizabeth 31, 58
Jobst, Vinzenz 324, 339
Jocham, Magnus 357, 380
Johnson, George W. 257, 283
Johnson, Lucy A. 257, 283
Jost, Renate 412, 422
Jowett, Benjamin 37–40, 60
Jüttemann, Veronika 370, 377, 380
Kaiser, Georg 403, 405
Kaiser, Jochen-Christoph 303, 315
Katterfeld, Anna 318, 339
Keil, Carl Friedrich 36–37, 58
Keiter, Heinrich 345, 347, 380
Keller, Rosemary Skinner 2, 11
Kelley, Mary 78, 81, 94
Kemp, Wolfgang 420, 422
Kempin-Spyri, Emilie 299–300
Kempis, Thomas à. 108, 111, 393
Kent, David A. 42–43, 58
Kenworthy, Scott M. 207, 222
Kern, Kathi 90, 92, 95
Kizenko, Nadieszda 209–10, 216–17, 222
Klostermann, Robert A. 210, 222
Köhler, Oskar 358, 380
Köser, Silke 303, 315
Kotulla, Andreas 343, 380
Kovalevski, Bärbel 415, 422
Kraft, Herbert 394, 396, 405
Kraus, Hans-Joachim 29, 59
Kronstadt, Father John of. *See* Sergiev, Ioan I.
Krumeich, Christa 362, 380
Krusenstjerna, Ada von 261, 267–72, 278, 283
Kuhn, Bärbel 374, 381
Küppers, Kurt 234, 253
Kurz, Isolde 396–99, 404–5
Kuz'mina-Karaveva, Elizaveta Ju. (Skobcova, Marija; Marija, Mother) 204, 211, 213–15, 220, 222
La Tour, Elvine de vi, 9, 317–40
Labzina. *See* Yakovleva, Anna

Lacalzada Mateo, Maria José 186, 202
Ladendorf, Otto 304, 315
Landriot, Jean Baptiste François 348, 363, 381
Larsen, Timothy 44, 59
Lasker-Schüler, Else 400, 405
Lazarus, Emma 126, 133
Lazarus, Josephine 6, 125–28, 130, 132–33
Lehmstedt, Mark 388, 390, 405
Lemaire, Gérard-Georges 431, 455
Lichtenstein, Diane 119, 133
Liebenau, Anna von 348, 381
Liedhegener, Antonius 344, 380
Lipkind, Goodman 131, 133
Lissner, Cordula 303, 315
Loads, Anne 3, 11
Lurz, Friedrich 230, 253
Luther, Martin 2, 262, 283, 310, 377, 387, 427
Lütze, Diethelm 426, 431, 455
Lyons, Martyn 346, 381
MacHaffie, Barbara J. 39, 41, 59
Malou, Jean-Baptiste 356–57, 376, 381
Mannheimer, Louise 117–24, 133
Marchal, Victor 348, 367, 372–75, 381
Marcilhacy, Christiane 350, 381
Margolis, Anne 78, 81–82, 94
Marija, Mother. *See* Kuz'mina-Karaveva, Elizaveta Ju.
Marker, Gary 213–14, 220, 222
Marmion, John P. 109, 111
Martini, Antonio 140, 155, 169, 174, 179
Martschukat, Jürgen 341, 381
Martyn, Sarah Towne 64, 95
Massillon, Jean-Baptist 170, 179
McAuley, Catherine v, 5, 6, 99–112
McDonald, Lynn 38–40, 59
McLeod, Hugh 227, 253, 417, 422
Medici, Paolo 169, 179
Meehan, Brenda 204–5, 207, 210–13, 215, 223
Meiwes, Relinde 374, 381
Melnyk, Julie 30, 59
Menne, Karl 345, 381

_# Modern Authors Index

Mercier, Anne   30–31, 44–50, 59
Merlo, Grado Giovanni   136, 161
Mermillod, Gaspar   348–49, 353, 378, 381
Messerli, Alfred   346, 350, 381
Michal, Bonnie A.   214, 223
Micheli, Andrea   169, 180
Miegel, Agnes   390–92, 405
Mill, Harriet Taylor   78, 95–96
Mill, John Stuart   78, 82, 85–86, 95–96, 291
Modersohn, Ernst   257, 276, 283, 329, 339
Moore, Mary Clare   103, 106–9, 112
Morani, Giuseppe   170, 180
Morgan, Lady   64, 93, 96
Morgan, Lewis Henry   89, 96
Motté, Magda   390, 393, 401, 405
Mülinen, Helene von   vi, 8, 287–300
Müller-Kessler, Christa   55, 59
Müller, Heinrich   348–50, 381
Müller, Kristiane   427, 455
Muschiol, Gisela   229, 253
Nadell, Pamela S.   132–33
Neuer, Werner   288, 301
Neyman, Clara   64–65, 88–92, 94, 96
Noit, H. von   356–57, 381
Norval, Leigh   64, 96
Oepen, Joachim   343, 381
Ohlemacher, Jörg   257, 261, 272, 275, 283–84, 327, 339
Oms, Antonio   192, 202
Opitz-Belakhal, Claudia   341, 371, 381
Osinski, Jutta   345, 382
Osselaer, Tine van   342, 344, 371, 382–83
Osterhammel, Jürgen   1, 11, 227, 253
Otto-Peters, Louise   386, 388–90, 404–5
Paletschek, Sylvia   228, 230, 253
Palmer Davies, Marie   265–68, 284
Pammer, Michael   242, 253
Paniccia, Maria   166, 180
Panigarola, Francesco   170, 180
Passy, Anton   348, 364, 367, 373–74, 382
Pasture, Patrick   342, 344, 371, 382–83
Pataky, Sophie   363, 382
Pattison, Mark   37, 60
Pazzaglia, Luciano   165, 180
Perrot, Michelle   2–3, 10–11, 346–47, 349, 371, 378, 380, 382, 420, 422
Pesch, Tilman   375–76, 382
Peyrot, Bruna   160–61
Popken, Minna   277–81, 283–84
Powell, Baden   37, 60
Priklonskii, Alexandr   205, 223
Prochaska, Frank K.   266, 284
Purcell, Mary Teresa   103–4, 106–7, 112
Pushkareva, Natal'ia L.   204, 223
Raffenberg, Anton   348, 363, 365, 382
Radente, Alberto   175–77, 179–80
Radkau, Joachim   349, 382
Ragussis, Michael   73, 96
Ranyard, Ellen Henrietta   266, 284–85
Rebbert, Josef   356–57, 376, 382
Redern, Hedwig von   261, 266, 284
Redolfi, Silke   287, 301
Reinkens, Joseph Hubert   231, 244, 248, 253
Remy, Nahida   118, 133
Rennstich, Karl   327, 339
Richman, Julia   118, 133
Rocca, Giancarlo   165, 171, 178, 180
Rogers, Hester Ann   18–19, 28
Rogers, William   38–39, 59
Rogerson, John   29, 32, 37, 56, 59
Romagnani, Gian Paolo   139, 161
Rosenberg, Pauline   118, 134
Rosenkranz, Martin   282
Rosenthal (Ben-Chorin), Fritz   400, 405
Rossetti, Christina   5, 41–44, 51–52, 54, 57–59
Rosslyn, Wendy   204, 211, 221, 223
Rothschild, Annie Henrietta de   5, 40–41, 59
Rothschild, Constance de   5, 40–41, 59
Rowson, Susanna   93, 96
Ruether, Rosemary Radford   2, 11
Ruhbach, Gerhard   313, 315
Russeau, Kristina   282
Russett, Cynthia Eagle   71, 96_

Salerno, Elisa 178, 180–81
San Cameron, Nigel M. de 44, 59
Sánchez Llama, Íñigo 188, 202
Sandys-Wunsch, John 100, 112
Sarah (pseudonym) 249, 253
Satter, Beryl 90, 96
Saunders, Ross 372, 382
Saurer, Edith 352, 354, 371, 382
Sawyer, John F. A. 225, 253
Schaeffer, Kurt 317, 339
Scheepers, Rajah 303, 315
Scheidgen, Andreas 355, 383
Schenda, Rudolf 352, 383
Scheuchenpflug, Peter 356, 383
Schimmelmann, Adeline Gräfin 8, 263, 272–74, 281–82, 284
Schimmelmann, Paul Friedrich 263, 284
Schlögl, Rudolf 343, 354, 383
Schmid, Edgar 327, 339
Schmidt, Jutta 303, 315
Schmidt, Margot 239–40, 242, 253
Schmidt, Susanna 345, 383
Schmolke, Michael 345, 383
Schneider, Bernhard 227, 254, 342–44, 354–55, 360, 383
Schneider, Gabriele 386, 405
Schneider, Wilhelm 275–76, 284
Schnorr von Carolsfeld, Julius vii, 10, 425–41, 443–55
Schottroff, Luise 29, 61, 235, 254
Schreiber, Georg 345, 383
Schreiner, Klaus 353, 384, 414, 423
Schrill, Ernst 255, 284
Schultze, Emil 259–60, 265, 284
Schwaiger, Georg 321, 339
Schweling, Antoinette 244–45, 254
Segneri, Paolo 170, 180
Seibert, Katrin 409, 423
Seidler, Louise 408, 415, 423
Sergiev, Ioan I. (Kronstadt, Father John of) 208–9, 214–20, 222
Shevzov, Vera 204, 223
Simón Palmer, María del Carmen 183, 202
Sintzel, Michael 348, 353, 361, 363–65, 373, 384
Skobcova, Marija. See Kuz'mina-Karaveva, Elizaveta Ju.
Smend, Rudolf 29, 60
Smith, George Adam 44, 60
Sohn-Kronthaler, Michaela 257, 282, 321, 340, 343, 384
Sohn, Andreas 343, 384
Soldani, Simonetta 164, 180
Solomon, Hannah G. 115–16, 118, 124–25, 134
Solopova, Marija (Taisija, Marija) 207–20
Soskice, Janet 55, 60
Speth, Volker 343, 384
Stambolis, Barbara 243, 254
Stanley, Arthur P. 37, 60
Stanton, Elizabeth Cady 3, 11, 64–65, 78, 88–93, 95–96, 189, 202
Stefan-Ludwig Hoffmann 371, 380
Steiniger, Christine 361, 384
Steinle, Christa 409, 420, 422
Stella, Pietro 174, 180
Stieglitz, Olaf 341, 381
Stowe, Harriet Beecher 64–65, 70, 77–83, 87–88, 96–97
Strauss, David Friedrich 36, 39, 60
Strunk, Reiner 314–15
Sullivan, Mary C. 99, 101–2, 104, 106–9, 111–12
Szepannek, Heidrun 318, 322–23, 325, 328, 331–32, 340
Szold, Henrietta 6, 125, 128–32, 134
Taft, Zechariah 21, 28
Taisija, Marija. See Solopova, Marija
Taylor, J. Glen 31, 60
Taylor, Marion Ann 3, 11, 30, 32–34, 41–42, 51, 57, 60–61, 63, 66, 79, 87, 95, 97
Temming, Theodor 348, 350, 365, 368, 384
Temple, Frederick 37, 60
Thyrêt, Isolde 215, 223
Tialmet, Agostino 169, 180

Tichomirov, Boris A. 206, 223
Tiele-Winckler, Eva von vi, 8–9, 258, 303–15
Timofeev, Valerij V. 204, 223
Toaspern, Paul 306, 315
Tönnesen, Cornelia 386, 406
Torjesen, Edvard P. 263, 284
Tracy, David 105, 112
Trimmer, Sarah 5, 33–35, 61
Unverfehrt, Gerd 431, 455
Urban, Eberhard 427, 455
Uspenskij, Boris A. 205, 223
Valerio, Adriana 137, 161, 166–68, 171, 177–78, 180
Veith, Johann Emanuel 235, 252
Vicentini, Elisa 178, 181
Von Hauff, Adelheid M. 303, 315, 321, 340
Wacker, Marie-Theres 29, 61
Wagner, William G. 216, 223
Wainwright, Geoffrey 229, 251, 254
Waldersee, Elisabeth Gräfin 268, 284
Waldkirch, Bernhard von 415, 423
Waldmüller, Robert 247, 254
Wallach-Faller, Marianne 397, 406
Ward, Mary Augusta 47, 49, 61
Wasserzug-Traeder, Gertrud 264, 285
Weber, Johannes 274–77, 285
Weber, Max 160–61, 226
Wedgwood, Julia 47–51, 56, 61
Wegman, Herman A. J. 232–33, 254
Weigelt, Horst 321, 340
Weil, Helen Kahn 118, 134
Weir, Heather E. 3, 10–11, 30–33, 41, 60–61, 66, 79, 87, 95, 97
Weissler, Chava 114, 134
Weller, Gustav Adolf 260, 285
Welter, Barbara 227, 254, 342, 384
Wendland, Walter 313, 315
Wenzel, Paul 232, 234, 237, 245, 254
Werfel, Franz 400, 406
Wesley, John 13–16, 18, 25–28
Wetzel, Franz Xaver 345, 347–48, 350–53, 357–60, 364–65, 375, 384
White, Barbara A. 78, 82, 97
White, Susan J. 230, 254
Wichern, Johann Hinrich 262, 265, 285, 304–5, 315
Williams, Rowland 37, 60
Williamson, Lori 266, 285
Wilson, Henry Bristow 37, 60
Wilson, Linda 32, 61
Wiseman, Nathaniel 66, 97
Wolff, Robert Lee 47, 61
Wolfskehl, Karl 400, 406
Woodhead, Linda 226, 254
Woodtli, Susanna 288, 301
Wright, Julia McNair 64–65, 83–88, 95, 97
Yakovleva, Anna (Labzina) 213–14, 216, 220
Yarchin, William 100, 112
Yonge, Charlotte 31, 58, 61
Ziegenaus, Anton 373, 384
Zingsem, Vera 397, 406
Zscharnack, Leopold 295–96, 301
Zucconi, Ferdinando 169, 181
Zumholz, Maria-Anna 347, 384
Zweig, Stefan 400, 406

www.ingramcontent.com/pod-product-compliance
Lightning Source LLC
Chambersburg PA
CBHW051202300426
44116CB00006B/408